*PARTY BUILDING IN A NEW NATION*

# PARTY BUILDING IN A NEW NATION

## The Indian National Congress

BY MYRON WEINER

THE ⬦ UNIVERSITY OF CHICAGO PRESS

*Library of Congress Catalog Card Number: 67–12150*
THE UNIVERSITY OF CHICAGO PRESS, CHICAGO & LONDON
The University of Toronto Press, Toronto 5, Canada
© *1967 by The University of Chicago. All rights reserved*
*Published 1967. Printed in the United States of America*

*To Sheila, Beth, and Saul*

# PREFACE

The Indian National Congress has been an extraordinarily successful party in recruiting new members, winning competitive elections, and avoiding fragmentation. This book is an attempt to explain why, and, I hope, will not only throw light on how the Indian political system works but will also illuminate the process of party building in newly independent nations.

To conduct this study I have had to be not just a political scientist but an amateur anthropologist as well. The data I needed were generally to be found, not in the national or state party offices, but in the villages and towns where party workers are actually recruited and election campaigns conducted. In all, I worked in five major areas. I lived in each place for several months, interviewing party workers, administrators, villagers, and townsmen, collecting voting and party membership data, and examining party records. And though this is not an historical study, I have also given some attention in my perusal of old party records and interviews with older Congressmen to how the local party organizations have changed in the past few decades.

I began the field research for this study in mid-1961 and returned to the United States eighteen months later, in early 1963. Although since then I have followed developments in the party, basically this account deals with how the party worked until the end of 1962 — that is, until shortly before Nehru's death. I have, however, tried to take into account recent developments in the party resulting from the elections of 1967 when Congress lost control of half of the state legislatures and its national parliamentary majority was much reduced. In the concluding chapter I discuss some of the problems now facing the party and suggest some of the pos-

sible alternative courses of development for it, but I have tried not to engage in prophecy. It is difficult enough for the social scientist to explain how and why people have behaved and are behaving without having to predict how they will behave under a wide variety of new circumstances.

It is impossible for me to acknowledge individually the hundreds of Congress party leaders and cadres in the national, state, and district organizations to whom I am deeply grateful for the cooperation that made this study possible. I do, however, wish to express my deep appreciation to two Congressmen who died shortly after I left India and to whom I owe perhaps more gratitude than to any others: U. S. Malliah, a member of parliament from Mysore and former general secretary of Congress, and G. Rajagopalan, a member of parliament from Madras and general secretary of the Congress party.

A number of people were kind enough to suggest corrections for or to comment on all or portions of this manuscript: Alan Beals, Cora DuBois, Carolyn Elliot, Howard Erdman, Marcus Franda, Robert Frykenberg, Eugene Irschick, David Mandelbaum, W. H. Morris-Jones, Lucian W. Pye, George Rosen, Susanne and Lloyd Rudolph, Arvind M. Shah, M. N. Srinivas, Bert Stein, and Charles Tilly; and from the areas studied: Robi Chakravorty, Krishna Dhar, Atulya Ghosh, Prafulla Kanti Ghosh, Gulam Jeelani, K. Lakshminarasimhan, G. V. S. Mani, Babubhai J. Patel, and A. K. Sen.

In the preparation of the bibliographies, statistical appendices, and tables, I was greatly aided by my research assistants, William Quandt and Naomi Kies. I have received splendid secretarial and editorial assistance from Eleanor Mamber and Helaine Levi. The maps were prepared by Russell Lens. I prepared the Glossary with the helpful advice of Jean Luc Chambard.

I have benefited greatly from presenting the findings of this study to the Joint M.I.T.-Harvard Seminar on Political Development and to my own graduate seminars at M.I.T.

Finally, this study was made possible through support from the John Simon Guggenheim Memorial Foundation and the Rockefeller Foundation, and from the Center for International Studies of the Massachusetts Institute of Technology from its Carnegie Corporation grant. Needless to say, none of the institutions or people acknowledged here shares responsibility for the results of this study.
Paris, France
June, 1967

# *CONTENTS*

## TABLES

## CHARTS AND MAPS

## ABBREVIATIONS

| | |
|---|---|
| AICC | All India Congress Committee |
| AITUC | All India Trade Union Congress |
| APCC | Andhra Pradesh Congress Committee |
| BDO | Block Development Officer |
| CD | Community Development |
| CMPO | Calcutta Metropolitan Planning Organization |
| CPI | Communist Party of India |
| DCC | District Congress Committee |
| DMK | Dravida Munnetra Kazhagam |
| GPCC | Gujarat Pradesh Congress Committee |
| IAS | Indian Administrative Service |
| ICS | Indian Civil Service |
| INC | Indian National Congress |
| INTUC | Indian National Trade Union Congress |
| KLP | Krishikar Lok Party |
| KMPP | Kisan Mazdoor Praja Party |
| KPCC | Karnataka Pradesh Congress Committee |
| MES | Maharashtra Ekikaran Samiti |
| MLA | Member of the Legislative Assembly |
| MLC | Member of the Legislative Council |
| MP | Member of Parliament |
| NES | National Extension Scheme |
| PCC | Pradesh Congress Committee |
| PSP | Praja Socialist Party |
| RSS | Rashtriya Swayam Sevak Sangh |
| SRC | States Reorganization Commission |

| | |
|---|---|
| TCC | Taluka Congress Committee |
| TNCC | Tamilnad Congress Committee |
| TVS | T. V. Sundaram, Ltd. |
| UCC | United Citizens Council |
| YC | Youth Congress |

*PART I. INTRODUCTION*

# 1. THE PROBLEM

It is surprising that so few Western scholars and government officials have given attention to the problems of party building in new nations. In contrast, enormous attention has been given to the problems of creating effective bureaucracies or building armies or, more recently, establishing new educational institutions. This is especially surprising when one considers the American commitment to the creation of democratic societies and when one recalls that communists in the developing areas have given so much attention to questions of political organization.

It is often presumed that while bureaucracies, armies, and educational systems are created in a conscious, deliberative fashion, parties are the products of historical change, impersonal social forces, or personal ambitions. Scholars generally describe parties as the outgrowth of parliamentary institutions, the result of the establishment of adult suffrage, the product of ideological movements, or the consequence of forces of economic modernization — almost never as the product of a deliberate human act.

But parties are, after all, instruments of collective human action no less than are armies, bureaucracies, and universities. In one sense, of course, parties are an outgrowth of the modernization process, for with modernization individuals begin to participate in public life and the entire pattern of government-citizen relations changes. But parties are also creatures of political elites — either politicians trying to control governments or government elites trying to control the masses. In competitive systems, parties are organized by politicians to win elections; in authoritarian systems, parties are organized to affect the attitudes and behavior of the population. In either instance an organizational structure must be forged, money must be

1

raised, cadres recruited, officers elected or selected, and procedures for internal governing established and agreed upon. In short, party building has a logic of its own.

In this study we have looked at the Indian National Congress as an example of party building. The Congress party of India is surely one of the most successful political parties to be found anywhere in the developing areas. Its success in recruiting political workers, in resolving internal conflict, and, above all, in winning four successive national elections has made it possible for India to sustain stable and relatively effective government at the local, state, and national levels since independence was achieved in 1947.

Moreover, the Indian National Congress is the oldest political party in Asia and one of the oldest and largest non-Communist political parties in the world. It was founded in 1885, only three decades after the founding of the Republican party in the United States and in the same decade in which the British Labour party was organized. Since independence the party membership has averaged several million and the number of party cadres has hovered around seventy-five thousand. Its organization can be found in all sixteen states and in almost every one of the country's nearly four hundred districts, and there are few of the country's half million villages which do not have at least a single member.

Since independence Congress has won every one of the four elections to the national parliament and until the February, 1967, elections almost every election for state legislative assemblies. Though the Congress party has been riddled with factional disputes and there have been a number of important defections, no Congress government in the states (with the exception of Kerala in 1964) or in New Delhi has ever collapsed because the party was unable to command the loyalties of its legislative members. Unlike the Muslim League in neighboring Pakistan and the Anti-Fascist People's Freedom League in Burma, the Congress party has been able to govern the country. Moreover, Congress has governed in a society in which the press is free to criticize, opposition parties to organize, and citizens to choose their local, state, and national governments in free elections.

Few other nationalist movements have been so successfully transformed into political parties. Indeed, creating and sustaining a competitive party system have proved to be an elusive goal in most new nations. Nationalist movements have often fragmented and been replaced by military governments or converted into one-party authorization states. It is a rare new

nation which has succeeded in developing political parties able to provide stable and effective government in a competitive environment.

In most democratic societies we take for granted the fact that human beings may voluntarily organize to achieve some common objectives through political action. In traditional societies few persons have such organizational capabilities; political organization is largely viewed as unnecessary, undesirable, or dangerous. However, modernizing elites in transitional societies sense the need to organize the population — to mobilize it for modernization or for defense, to contain antisocial behavior, to restrain demands which impede efforts to modernize, to integrate the society, or simply to establish popular support against competitors for power. Nearly all modernizing elites in the new nations have felt the need for some kind of mass organization; only a few have been willing to organize their parties in a competitive environment; still fewer have succeeded.

This study has a dual purpose: to explain why the Congress party of India, almost alone among former nationalist movements, has been so successful in winning competitive elections and in providing the country with stable government; and to contribute to the theory of political development by exploring the conditions under which a modern political organization develops.

## Political Organization and Political Development

How important political organization is in the process of political development has been much discussed by scholars of development. Samuel Huntington speaks of the need for a modernizing system to develop the "capacity to assimilate into the system the social forces which result from modernization." [1] Lucian Pye, in a similar vein, notes that "political development is related to an increased ability to organize associations of people and to manage complex structures." [2] Through the writings of many scholars of the development process runs this persistent theme: the need for human organization for the achievement of goals which individuals, by themselves, are unable to achieve.

[1] Samuel P. Huntington, "The Political Modernization of Traditional Monarchies," (Mimeographed), p. 8. Huntington develops the theme of political development as "institutionalization" in his article "Political Development and Political Decay," *World Politics* XVII (April, 1965).

[2] Lucian W. Pye, *Aspects of Political Development* (Boston: Little, Brown, and Company, 1966), p. 100. This theme is also discussed in his *Politics, Personality, and Nation Building* (New Haven: Yale University Press, 1962).

The readiness of individuals to work together in an organized fashion for common purposes and to behave in a fashion conducive to the achievement of these common purposes is an essential behavioral pattern of complex modern societies.[3] Modern societies have all encountered organizational revolutions — in many respects as essential and as revolutionary as the technological revolution which has made the modern world. To send a missile into outer space, to produce millions of automobiles a year, to conduct research and development, to manage complex mass media — all require new organizational skills. One cannot conceive of a modern economy without complex industrial institutions, credit and banking facilities, and an elaborate transportation and communications network — all of which involve new forms of human association. In the realm of politics and government, one cannot conceive of collecting taxes, ensuring order, and providing services without governmental bodies at the local, intermediate, and national levels that carry out multitudinous functions, or without voluntary associations, including trade unions, professional associations, welfare bodies, and political parties, in which individuals come together to satisfy their professional, economic, social, cultural, or political needs.

This is not to suggest that all modern systems contain the same types of organizations or that the citizens of all modern societies have an equal propensity to organize or, for that matter, that the more organized society is the more developed it is. Far from it. If de Tocqueville was right in saying that Americans have a greater tendency to associate together than other peoples, that does not make American society more developed than other societies — although, incidentally, there may be a relationship between American organizational capacities and the high performance of the American economy. There may, however, be a minimum threshold for associating together insofar as political development is concerned that is passed when there are organized structures to which individuals can and do go in order to attempt to deal with shared social problems.

The consequences of an organizational lag as an impediment to development are quite apparent. The inability of many political leaders to maintain internal party and government unity in many new nations has resulted in the collapse of parliamentary government and the establishment of military dictatorships. Further, the much vaunted organizational skill of the military has often failed in many new nations. In Ceylon a planned military coup collapsed when several of the conspirators spoke

---

[3] This discussion draws from my article "Political Integration and Political Development," *The Annals* (March, 1965), 52–64.

of their plans so openly that even a disorganized civilian government had time to take action; in many Latin American countries, as in Vietnam, the military has proved as incapable of maintaining cohesive authority as their civilian predecessors.

The capacity — or lack of capacity — to organize with one's fellows may be a general quality of societies. A society with a high organizational capacity appears to be competent at creating industrial organizations, bureaucracies, political parties, universities, and the like. Germany, Japan, the United States, the Soviet Union, and Great Britain come quickly to mind. In contrast, one is struck by a generalized incompetence in many new nations where organizational breakdowns seem to be greater bottlenecks to economic growth than breakdowns in machinery. In some new countries technological innovations, such as industrial plants, railways, and telegraph and postal systems, have expanded more rapidly than the human capacities to make the technologies work, with the result that mail is lost, the transport system does not function with any regularity, industrial managers cannot implement their decisions, and government administrative regulations impede, rather than facilitate, the management of public sector plants.

Some scholars have suggested that the modernization process itself produces political organizations, that political organization is a consequence of increased occupational differentiation, which in turn results from economic growth and technological change — an assumption, incidentally, that underlies much foreign economic assistance. The difficulty with viewing political change in such a sequential fashion is that however logical it may appear to be, in the history of political change no such sequence can be generally found. Indeed, political organization often precedes, and may be an important factor in whether or not there is, large scale economic change. Moreover, just as the presence of entrepreneurial talents in a traditional society is a key element in whether or not economic growth occurs, so the presence of organizational talents may be an important element in whether or not there emerges a leadership with the capacity to run a political party, an interest association, or a government.

Although modern societies certainly have more individuals with organizational skills than do traditional societies, among traditional societies there is variance in the capacity to produce individuals with organizational skills.[4] But it is far from clear why some societies, whether tra-

---

[4] For an analysis of the attitudes which inhibit organized activity, see Edward Ban-

ditional or modern, produce people with organizational skills and others do not. We do know, of course, that at the most elementary level all societies have the capacity to organize — at least to create some kind of kinship organization so that the society may propagate itself and care for and socialize its young. As other needs and desires arise within a society, some societies quickly produce new organizations capable of carrying out new purposes. Sometimes this capacity to organize is limited to a small elite — those with authority. In such circumstances only the state has the capacity to expand for the carrying out of new functions. In still other societies organizational capacities seem more evenly spread throughout the population, and individuals without coercive authority are willing and able to organize with others for some common purposes. Finally, there are some societies with large numbers of persons capable of associating together but whose organizations prove ineffectual because they can neither maintain sufficient internal cohesion nor gain enough external support to achieve their purposes. Thus, many underdeveloped areas have a large number of ineffectual political organizations that play no role in the decision-making or decision-implementing process and that often produce in their membership a sense of political frustration.

By contemporary American or Western standards, Indians are not especially skillful at organization, though compared to many other developing societies they would probably rank high. India has a substantial number of trade unions, cooperatives, castes, religious and tribal organizations, and literary societies, and a considerable number of political parties.[5] One often gets the impression that while Indians can organize readily, the organizations which they create are torn by internal factional disputes and thus are often unable to carry out the functions for which they were created. Many Indians would be among the first to describe themselves and the organizations which they create as ineffectual.

Despite this general impression, it is fair to say that the Congress party is today perhaps the most successful political party functioning in a competitive political system in the new nations of the underdeveloped world. It certainly succeeds in its primary objectives: to win elections for state and national assemblies, and to form governments. Beyond these it also plays a significant role in Indian political development by contributing,

field, *The Moral Basis of a Backward Society* (Glencoe, Ill.: The Free Press, 1958). Though Banfield's study is confined to a single village in Italy, it raises the general problem of analyzing the capacities of a people to organize for common purposes.

[5] For a description of voluntary associations in India, see my *Politics of Scarcity* (Chicago: University of Chicago Press, 1962).

in ways we shall consider later, to India's national integration, to the legitimacy of the present political system, to the expression of political demands, to the management of social conflict, and — although here the claim is more indirect and thus less apparent — to India's economic development.[6]

But whatever roles the party plays for the society as a whole, it is clear that these roles are possible only if the party is able to perform certain essential roles for itself. We need to be clear, therefore, as to what we mean when we say that Congress is a successful party organization.

A successful party organization operating in an open competitive environment must be able to: (1) recruit and train its personnel, thereby perpetuating itself as an organization; (2) win support (goodwill, money, votes) from the population or substantial parts thereof; and (3) maintain internal cohesion. If the party is unable to recruit personnel, then it has no durability and its life span is no greater than that of its members. If the party is unable to win support from a substantial portion of the population, one would hardly describe it as successful in a competitive system. (What proportion of votes is required for a successful party is academic: Congress has won enough to gain control of the central government and half or more of the state governments in four successive national elections.) And if the party is unable to form a government when it has a majority of seats in a parliamentary body, it would not only be inappropriate to speak of the party as successful but it would also be doubtful as to whether we were speaking of one or of several parties.

## Theoretical Orientations

This study of the Congress party is primarily concerned with describing — and therefore explaining — how the party succeeds. It does not ask how the party became what it is — it is therefore not a history — nor is it an effort to predict the future of the party, though obviously our capacity to predict its future is affected by our knowledge of how it works now.

Nothing is more fundamental or more difficult for social scientists than explaining how something works or, in current social science terminology, describing a process. I have tried to explain how the party works by look-

[6] For a general examination of the role played by parties in the larger processes of political development, see Joseph LaPalombara and Myron Weiner, editors, *Political Parties and Political Development* (Princeton: Princeton University Press, 1966), especially the concluding chapter by the editors, "The Impact of Parties on Political Development."

ing at the party itself, who is in it, and what its cadres and leaders do. I have tried to report to the reader what others have told me, what I have read in party documents, and, above all, what I have seen of how the party workers behave. I attended party meetings, accompanied party workers as they spoke to villagers and to bureaucrats, and spoke to party workers about their activities. This is to say, I have tried to explain how the party works by reporting what I have seen, heard, and read about the way in which party workers behave.

But in order to describe, one must be guided by some theoretical considerations as to what is important. In this study I have had a number of such considerations in mind. First of all, I have assumed that successful organizations are able to maintain themselves precisely because their leaders give a higher priority to maintaining the organization than to any external goals. By looking at the response of party leaders to proposals to change the structure of the organization or to adopt new policies, we can not only see why some proposals are rejected and others accepted but also, and more fundamentally, discover what the party leadership views as essential to the survival of the organization.

Second, I have assumed that a successful organization is able to fit the needs of the individuals who join the organization to the self-maintaining needs of the organization. I have thus been concerned with the kinds of considerations and interests which lead men to join and remain in the Congress party and the kinds of incentives which the Congress organization provides to retain the support and loyalty of its members. How, in short, has the organization made its own goals congruent with the ambitions, motives, and purposes of its membership?

There has been a growth in political participation in India during the past few decades, and this growth has both provided an opportunity and created a need for an institutional structure, such as a political party, which can provide for the articulation or management of new political participants. It is thus necessary that we understand what factors are at work in India that are leading to this rise in political participation and the kind of response that local units of the Congress party make to demands for participation. Throughout the study I have assumed that Congress operates in a dynamic environment in which social groups are constantly making new demands upon the political system. It is for this reason that I have given much attention to Indian social organization — not just to discover how the party responds to its social environment, but, more importantly, to see how Indian social organization is changing (often a

result of how the party and the government behave) and how the party adapts to these changes.[7]

To understand how the party copes with its environment, one must see how the party functions at the local level. The capacity of the state and national party units to work rests ultimately on the performance of the constituent units which actually recruit members and deal with the public in their day-to-day activities. If the local units are unable to raise money, recruit cadres, win electoral support, and, at a minimal level, resolve internal disputes, it hardly seems likely that the state and national organizations can function. In a fundamental sense, therefore, party building involves the creation and successful performance of the party at the constituency level. If the party does not work at the constituency level, can we even speak of a political party? A cabal, a clique, a faction, perhaps, but not a political party in the modern sense, for when we speak of parties today we mean organizations which exist at the local level.

I have therefore chosen to structure my investigation by studying how the party works in five districts in different parts of the country. Later I shall explain why I have chosen the district organization as the unit for study, why these particular districts were selected out of the nearly four hundred units into which India is divided, what the justifications and limitations are of a clinical as opposed to a statistical study of a larger number of units, and, finally, what questions were asked and what kinds of data were collected in each of these districts. I would note here only that I am concerned, not with the performance of local government or the study of community power, but with how the local units of the party recruit and train personnel, win electoral support, resolve internal disputes, and are related to the larger state and national party organizations to which they belong.

I have already noted that a major assumption of this study is that we can best understand how the party functions by observing the behavior of its members. This assumption has led me to observe what party workers do at the local level: how they spend their time, what they fight over,

[7] I must at this point pay my intellectual debt to the many anthropologists who have given attention to the study of Indian social organization and how it is now changing, and in particular to Milton Singer, McKim Marriott, and Bernard Cohn of the Department of Anthropology at the University of Chicago. It is regrettable that so many political scientists have a poor, and in my judgment misguided, impression of the work that many anthropologists are now doing and of the relevance of that work to the study of political change. Fortunately, no such gulf exists between anthropologists and political scientists now studying the relationship between political and social change in India.

how they resolve (or live with) those conflicts, and how they deal with voters, bureaucrats, and one another. In observing their behavior I was guided by two theoretical considerations. One is the assumption that behavior is patterned in some way — that is, that the activities of workers are institutionalized into roles. In other words, there are regular jobs which workers perform according to their own and other's expectations. I have tried to identify these roles and how they are carried out. My second assumption is that in a successful organization the roles which individuals play are not only related to one another but also are essential to the successful functioning of the whole organization.

Although this study focuses on *how* people within the party behave, I have often had to consider *why* people behave as they do. If we are to relate the needs and interests of party leaders and cadres to the maintenance requirements of the party organization, we must consider their beliefs and motives. The difficulty, of course, is that one must not readily accept as reliable the statements politicians make about their own beliefs and motives. In India, as in other societies, there is a gap between the cultural symbols (the language, if you will) through which people express their beliefs and the beliefs themselves. Moreover, few occupations in any culture are as dependent upon the dissimulation of beliefs and motives as is the profession of politics. While a politician may say he believes in human equality, he may be deeply prejudiced and display his prejudice in the way he behaves. A politician may condemn corruption but accept bribes; condemn casteism but recruit members of only his own caste; give "modern" answers to questions but be fundamentally traditional in beliefs and behavior. Where I have described the beliefs and motives of a politician, I have not simply accepted his statements at face value but have evaluated them against my knowledge of how he has actually behaved. In short, I have made inferences from behavior.

Most of the politicians whose beliefs and motives I describe are men I have come to know reasonably well. I interviewed them at length, accompanied them on tours, visited their homes. Like most human beings, they often hold conflicting beliefs and are often unaware of their own motives. In assessing, therefore, why a politician has acted in a particular way, often the best we can do is to say that he has acted *as if* he believes in such and such or that he has acted *as if* he wants such and such. It is obvious that there are difficulties and dangers in making inferences from behavior about beliefs and motives (even when the inferences are used, as in this study, to supplement and evaluate oral statements), but these difficulties are preferable to those that come from accepting oral

statements at face value or from making inferences about behavior from what politicians say about their beliefs and motives — two tendencies which have characterized a substantial amount of writing on the developing areas and which seem to me to account for some of the naïveté in that writing. Too often we make assumptions about the convictions and behavior of politicians because they use words like "socialism," "revolution," "social transformation," "mobilize," and "social justice" without probing into what these words mean to those who use them and how in fact they affect the way they behave.

To sum up — in an effort to examine how the Congress party works I have made the following assumptions: (a) that the party leadership is concerned with organizational maintenance; (b) that the party has fit the interests and ambitions of the individuals who join it to the needs of the organization for its own maintenance; (c) that the party has adapted to new demands, often from new participants in politics; and (d) that any assessment of how the party recruits members, wins elections, and copes with internal conflicts must be based upon an examination of what party workers do and how their jobs are institutionalized into political roles.

Each of these assumptions has affected the kind of data I have provided in this book. The first assumption led me to examine the major decisions the party leadership has made which affect the structure and character of the organization. The second led me to examine the motives, beliefs, and interests of party cadres and leaders, the kinds of incentives provided by the party, and the services which party members must perform to earn these rewards. The third led me to examine how Indian social structure is changing and how these changes are propelling groups to satisfy their interests through political activities. And, finally, the fourth led me to describe how party workers behave.

## The Theme

The party's success has been commonly explained in two ways, and it is necessary to show the inadequacy of both explanations before advancing alternative suggestions. One explanation attributes party success to Nehru, a dynamic, charismatic leader capable of winning popular support and maintaining internal party discipline; the other explanation focuses on the preeminent role Congress played before independence as a nationalist movement.

As for the first explanation, there can be no doubt that Nehru was an important force in the Congress party. His presence in an election campaign stirred party cadres to campaign harder; his intervention in intra-party disputes often saved the party from fragmentation; and the fact that local candidates belonged to "the party of Nehru" meant votes they might otherwise not have received. Yet the Great Man thesis, while a familiar historical explanation, can be neither refuted nor supported. The prime minister's presence in state-wide elections in Kerala did not prevent electoral losses there, but it can be argued that without him Congress might have done much worse. While many other party leaders have been involved in settling intra-party disputes, it can be claimed that Nehru's authority enhanced their authority. To the argument that dissident elements have left the party in some states, it can be answered that fragmentation would have been worse had Nehru not been the party leader. Future events can neither refute nor substantiate these claims. If the party continues to function effectively now that Nehru has left the political scene, will this demonstrate that the party's success was not dependent upon a single figure? Or will it simply prove that Nehru was so effective in his leadership that the party is now capable of carrying on in his absence? If the party should fragment or continue to lose popular support, that might be a strong reason for giving primacy to Nehru's role, but then one could probably point to many intervening factors. Can the electoral defeats suffered by Congress in 1967 be attributed primarily to the absence of a popular leader comparable to Nehru, or to the food shortages, industrial slowdown, increased unemployment, and high prices that occurred before the elections?

One cannot disprove the Great Man thesis; one can only suggest its inadequacy. There are, for example, other new nations whose great leaders at the time of independence — Sukarno in Indonesia, U Nu in Burma, Kotelawala in Ceylon — failed to convert nationalist movements into effective parties. To reply that in each instance the circumstances were different is actually to admit that we need to look beyond the individual leader to the circumstances in which he functioned. Further, and more seriously from a theoretical perspective, all explanations which start, as this one does, by emphasizing what is essentially idiosyncratic are inelegant. To pose the issue in its most extreme form, should we accept chance factors as explanations before other explanations have been put to the test? Only if we turn to the party itself to see how it functions and solves its problems can we see the role of leadership in relation to the environment in which that leadership operates. When, in other words,

we understand all the conditions that the party organization requires for its success, we can understand more precisely what role leadership — whether by one man or by many — actually plays.

The second popular explanation for the success of the Congress party is simply that it brought independence to India and continues to retain much of the following and leadership created before 1947 — in short, that Congress bears the legacy of being one of the most successful nationalist movements in the colonial world. Though this argument has much force, it is not an adequate explanation of the present success of the party. If one wishes to argue comparatively, one can note that many nationalist movements have not been successfully converted into ongoing political parties. The Muslim League in Pakistan, the Anti-Fascist People's Freedom League (AFPFL) in Burma, the Nationalist party (PNI) in Indonesia, the United National party in Ceylon, and, one might add, the Kuomintang in Nationalist China — all failed to maintain popular support and avoid internal disintegration. It is not unusual for nationalist movements to lose their appeal when independence is established, for internal factionalism to fragment the organization, or for corruption to disillusion those who in the past have supported the party.

In fact, the Congress party did lose much popular support immediately after independence. The Congress Socialist party, until 1948 an integral part of Congress, broke away to create its own independent party. With the assassination of Gandhi, the emotional ties which bound some individuals to the party were broken and large-scale defections took place, particularly in 1950 and 1951. Yet, unlike many other nationalist movements, Congress successfully retained popular support and maintained enough cohesion to manage governments. Congress continues to do well in areas of the country in which it was weak at the time of independence. In several former princely states and in some of the princely areas which made up Orissa, Rajasthan, Madhya Pradesh, Mysore, and Kerala, there was no Congress party organization at the time of independence: Congress was first created in these areas *after* 1947. In several of these states Congress did poorly in the first general elections of 1952 but was able to build organizations of such effectiveness that in subsequent elections the party triumphed easily. Moreover, in West Bengal and in the Punjab, Congress was a minority party before independence. The Bengali Congress unit was, in fact, expelled from the parent organization before independence, and a new organization was created by a small minority. The powerful Congress party organization we see today in West Bengal was not firmly built until the early fifties. Similarly, the Congress organiza-

tion in the Punjab is a relatively new organization. The historic legacy thesis certainly does not explain these successes, nor does it recognize that nearly a generation has passed since India became independent. The typical Congressman today is under forty, and a large number of active party cadres are in their twenties and early thirties — young men who were in their teens at the time of independence. For a substantial portion of the party, therefore, the nationalist era is already history not memory.

Nonetheless, the legacy does play a role in the present position of the party. Much of the esteem Congress has among its supporters results from its role in the nationalist struggle. Congress still contains many party workers who joined when it was a nationalist movement and who continue to contribute their skills and reputations to support the party. And among the other legacies the Congress leadership had in 1947, two are of overwhelming importance: Congressmen were given governmental power as the British vacated and Congress, alone among Indian parties, had an organizational network throughout the country.

Nationalist movements have often squandered their legacies. In other countries some movements have been absorbed by, or become the instruments of, governments. Some claim to be concerned with "mobilizing" the population for development activities but are unwilling to take the risk of competing for electoral support against opposition parties. Some, in failing to provide adequate rewards for their supporters, have lost the support which they enjoyed before independence. Still others have failed to find ways of resolving the internal disputes that typically fragment and splinter nationalist movements after independence. In contrast, the Congress party built upon its legacy, extended its organization into portions of the country it had not touched before, and successfully made the adjustment from a nationalist movement concerned with winning independence to a political party concerned with and capable of winning and holding political office.

In the pages that follow, and especially in the concluding chapters, I set forth a number of alternative hypotheses which seem to me to explain, more satisfactorily than either the Great Man or the legacy thesis, why Congress has been such a successful organization. All my hypotheses are related to a single theme: that Congress party leaders, in order to succeed politically, are concerned, first and foremost, with doing whatever is necessary to adapt the party to its environment. This proposition is deceptively simple, but it immediately calls attention to the difference between the Congress party and many other political parties in the developing world. Elsewhere, many governing parties are concerned with

either mobilizing or controlling the population. In contrast, Congress is primarily concerned with recruiting members and winning support. It does not mobilize; it aggregates. It does not seek to innovate; it seeks to adapt. Though a few Congressmen dream of transforming the countryside, in practice most Congressmen are concerned simply with winning elections.

In its effort to win, Congress adapts itself to the local power structures. It recruits from among those who have local power and influence. It trains its cadres to perform political roles similar to those performed in the traditional society before there was party politics. It manipulates factional, caste, and linguistic disputes, and uses its influence within administration to win and maintain electoral and financial support. It utilizes traditional methods of dispute settlement to maintain cohesion within the party.

This process of adaptation — some might say the use of tradition by the party — is made more difficult by the fact that the environment in which the party functions is undergoing great change. Paradoxically, much of this change is brought about by government itself. The result is a political system with considerable tension between a government concerned with modernizing the society and economy and a party seeking to adapt itself to the local environment in order to win elections. Of course, this is an oversimplification. Members of the government are also members of the party, and they are interested both in modernizing policies and in doing what is best for the party. Similarly, party leaders want to win, but many are also concerned with modernizing India. Then too the two concerns are not necessarily incongruent: the expansion of education, for example, is probably essential for modernization, and it is also a political asset.

Nonetheless, there are times when the two aims conflict, for what will accelerate modernization is not necessarily politically popular within the party or the electorate — what is good for India is not necessarily good for the party. However, a party concerned primarily with winning may make as significant a contribution to modernization as a party concerned with transforming. A transforming party may be so concerned with mobilizing the population that it fails to transmit popular discontent to government. Moreover, many so-called mobilist parties in practice neither mobilize nor adapt. As a party primarily concerned with winning and maintaining support, Congress is relatively sensitive to local discontent, which it communicates to government in its effort to reduce discontent and

thereby avoid political defeat. In short, while Congress may limit what government can do, it also cushions the tensions created by the modernization process.

The central aim of this study, therefore, is to examine how the Congress party copes with a changing environment in its effort to win and maintain support.

We turn now to a description of how this study was conducted.

## 2. THE METHOD

The starting point of this study is the exploration of the ways in which the local operating unit of the Congress party carries out the tasks of political recruitment, resolves internal conflicts, and wins competitive elections. I have chosen the district organization as the local unit and selected five districts, each somewhat different from the others, in order to explore how the party leadership adapts to different types of environments. Thus, I have looked at districts which vary in their social configurations and social conflicts, in their market patterns, population densities, occupational patterns, and structures of local government. Despite this diversity there are some general factors at work as a result of actions of the national and state governments which affected all district party organizations. The first part of this chapter deals with why these five district units were chosen; the second, with some of the general factors at work in all the districts.

### The Five Districts

It is not easy to define the local operating unit of Congress. The smallest unit of the party is the mandal committee, which covers an area with about twenty thousand persons. The mandal committees are grouped into taluka committees covering areas with about a hundred thousand persons; the taluka committees are grouped under District Congress Committees (391 in all), each covering an area with about a million and a quarter persons.

The constitution of the party makes no explicit mention of taluka com-

mittees, and it is generally agreed that mandal committees rarely function. Both the national and state party organizations view the District Congress Committees (DCCs) as the basic units of the party organization, and we shall do likewise. Both the state and national organizations communicate almost exclusively with the DCCs. It is rare that the national and state organizations deal directly with the smaller units under the DCCs. It is the DCC which communicates in the local language with the taluka and mandal committees under its jurisdiction. Moreover, none of the smaller local units of the party organization coincides with state assembly or parliamentary constituencies. The DCC — though it too does not coincide with any electoral unit — takes primary responsibility for the organization of all elections within the district. It makes recommendations to the Pradesh Election Committee at the state level and to the Central Election Committee at the national level as to who in the party ought to receive tickets for assembly and parliamentary elections, and it suggests to the state organization the names of candidates for district local board elections. Moreover, auxiliary organizations associated with the Congress party are typically organized at the district level. The Youth Congress, the Mahila (Women's) Congress and the Seva Dal (service society) have units at the district level, and it is not uncommon for the state organization to finance an organizer to work for each of these units at the district level. Membership records are generally kept in the district organization offices rather than with the mandal or taluka committees. Finally, the District Congress Committee office is a meeting place for party workers throughout the district. Offices are rarely maintained by mandal committees, occasionally by taluka committees, but always by District Congress Committees. Any study, therefore, of the local Congress party organization, including mandal and taluka committees, must start at the district level.

In determining which district organizations ought to be studied, it should first be pointed out that no effort was made to sample the nearly four hundred district organizations of the Congress party. During the eighteen months in which the field research was conducted for this study it proved impossible to study more than five district organizations in depth. It was apparent from the very beginning, therefore, that it would be impossible to select statistically "typical" units of the party organization. Moreover, apart from whatever theoretical considerations ought to enter into the selection of the five district organizations, some practical considerations would clearly have to be involved. Unless contacts were available in advance and the party organization were receptive to re-

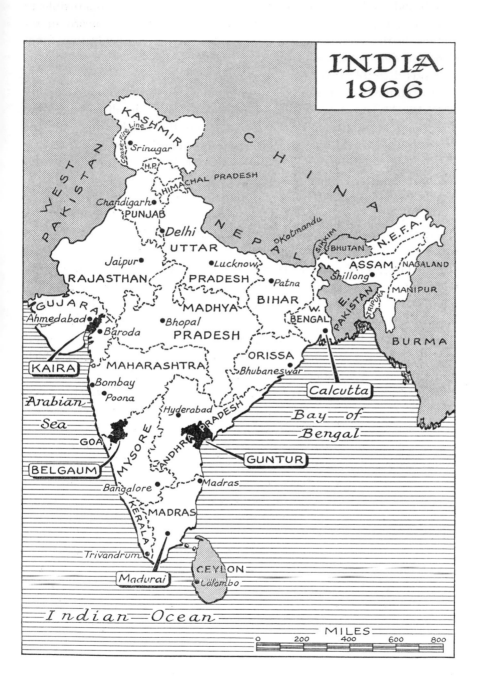

search and willing to open its party records, it would be impossible to work in any particular district organization. The major concern in selecting districts, however, was to see how the party organization functioned in different kinds of economic, social, and political environments.

It was desirable that at least one of the districts be characterized by intense ethnic conflict of a linguistic, religious, or caste nature. Belgaum district in Mysore state seemed eminently qualified. The district is in the northern part of Mysore state bordering on the neighboring state of Maharashtra. A Marathi-speaking linguistic minority has been pressing for the bifurcation of the district so that their portion of the district would be transferred to the state of Maharashtra. The tasks of recruiting, winning elections, and maintaining internal party cohesion have all been complicated by the bitter linguistic conflict in the district.

Far to the north, in the state of Gujarat, I selected Kaira district, a prosperous cash crop area and one of the most developed agricultural regions in the subcontinent. Here was an opportunity to see the ways in which the party was functioning in an area in which large-scale economic development was occurring. Moreover, Kaira has one of the oldest, most active, and best organized Congress party organizations to be found anywhere in India. As a nationalist organization which launched several civil disobedience movements in the pre-independence era, and which produced so many leaders for the nationalist movement, the Kaira Congress had a "classic" quality. During the course of the research, however, a dissident group of castes within Kaira district became increasingly active in the district's political life. In the elections which took place during the field research, the Congress party of Kaira district was badly defeated. The focus of my study shifted, therefore, from the special problems of a party organization in a growing agricultural area to how the party attempted to deal with a participation crisis.

Moving from Gujarat on the Arabian Sea to the Bay of Bengal on the east coast of India, I selected a third rural district — Guntur district in Andhra state. This district is the largest of the rural areas studies and, in fact, with its population of approximately three million, is one of the largest rural districts in the country. It too has had an old and active nationalist movement and is one of the most competitive political districts in the country for the Congress party, since in this area both the Communist party and the conservative Swatantra party have been very active. But the major reason for selecting this district is that it is an area in which panchayati raj has been in effect for several years. Panchayati raj is a new system of rural local government which, in an effort at de-

centralization, was established in 1959 in the states of Rajasthan and Andhra and has since been adopted by other states throughout the country. We shall say more of panchayati raj later, but suffice it to say here that we were concerned with examining the ways in which the Congress party organization adapted itself to the creation of new institutions of local government and to the changing character and functions of existing local bodies.

These three rural districts together — Belgaum, Kaira, and Guntur — contain approximately seven million persons, who are scattered in three different states in three different parts of the subcontinent. Guntur and Kaira are relatively prosperous agricultural regions, while portions of Belgaum are frequently famine-stricken. Language, religion, and faction play important roles in the internal politics of these districts. Though, in the main, each contains old nationalist organizations — and is therefore typical of most of the rural districts of India — two of them also contain areas which were once part of former princely states. Belgaum district contains the small former princely state of Ramdurg and a portion of the larger state of Kholapur. Kaira district borders on the large state of Baroda and also contains within its boundaries the small former princely state of Cambay.

The political competition faced by the Congress party varies considerably among these three districts. In some parts of Belgaum district Congress is unopposed, while in others competition is fierce. The major struggle in Belgaum is, as we have noted, between two major linguistic groups. In Guntur, conflict has primarily been between the Congress and Communist parties. In Kaira, Congress has faced competition from the conservative Swatantra party.

Two urban areas were also selected for investigation. One of these, the city of Madurai in Madras state, was selected because it contains a large industrial constituency. This ancient city of approximately half a million persons contains several large textile mills and is the center of the bus transport industry in south India. Here was an opportunity to see how the party dealt with an industrial work force and its trade unions. Moreover, since Madurai is an ancient city whose political leadership has been deeply involved in the countryside, we can see how the Congress party functions in an environment where the line between urban and rural political life is thin.

Finally I wanted to select one large metropolitan area in order to take a close look at how the Congress party functions in the midst of a middle-class population. I selected Calcutta city and, in particular, the Dis-

trict Congress Committee of north Calcutta, which functions in an old middle-class section of the city. The Congress party controls the parliamentary seat in north Calcutta, although it has lost control of the other three parliamentary constituencies in the city. Here I could see how the Congress party has battled for control — with considerable success — of a portion of the city which contains a restive middle class and a substantial refugee population. Unlike the other areas studied, the four district Congress committees in Calcutta are relatively newly reorganized post-independence organizations. In both Calcutta and Madurai, the Congress party has in the past decade not won as many elections as it has in the rural areas of the country. This calls attention to the fact that in general the Congress party has not performed as well in the urban areas as in the countryside — a phenomenon which I shall attempt to analyze as we look at the party organization in Calcutta and in Madurai.

The special problems encountered by the Congress party in each of these areas are typical of those encountered elsewhere in India and in other developing countries. We are thus able to explore, for example, how, in Kaira, the party copes with the changing relationship of social groups; in Belgaum, the role of a party in the task of integration; and in Guntur, the adaption of the party to new institutions and structures of power at the local level. In both Madurai and Calcutta we can look at the special problems of political organization in heterogeneous urban areas.

One difficulty in analyzing the Congress party is that an analysis is bound to be affected by the special events which occur while the study is being conducted. Indeed, it is difficult to think of any studies of contemporary India which have not in one way or another been profoundly affected by recent events. An account, for example, of Indian politics written during the great linguistic agitations of the mid-1950's is likely to stress the disintegrating elements at work, but a decade later less importance might be assigned to these developments. A study of Indian economic growth written in the early 1960's might pessimistically record the low rate of growth and be concerned primarily with factors impeding modernization. But an economic historian of the future might view the same period as a germinal one in which important structural changes in the economy took place and provided the basis for a later upsurge in economic growth. A study of India's foreign policy in the 1950's might emphasize the effects of a non-alignment policy on increasing India's international stature and her capacity to affect the behavior of other states, including the great powers. But a study written after the Chinese invasion

of late 1962 might be more concerned with India's failure to provide for her own security. Even anthropologists, sociologists, and psychologists, with their concern for the more enduring qualities of human beings and societies, are affected by the special events which occur during the time in which they do their research. One scholar may see personality traits in the light of child-rearing practices reinforced by enduring patterns of social life and religious belief, while another may interpret the same personality traits as the consequence of recent disturbing changes in the social or political environment.

In this study every effort has been made to see the functioning of the Congress party in the perspective of nearly two decades since independence. Nonetheless, the reader should be aware of the special events which took place during the time in which the field investigation for this study was conducted. The field research for this study extended over an eighteen month period in 1961 and 1962; it began before the 1962 elections and continued for some months thereafter. There was an opportunity, therefore, to see the party in the relatively quiet months that follow an electoral campaign. The study was conducted after the great upheaval associated with the linguistic agitations had come to an end and the states had been reorganized. At the very end of the field study, the Chinese invasion of Ladakh and of the North East Frontier Agency took place. The rate of economic growth of the 1950's had slowed down in 1961 and 1962, but there were no visible political effects in the areas studied. Four of the five units selected for investigation were in the midst of a crisis during some portion of the study. One district organization had been suspended by the state party. Another was so torn by factional disputes that different sections of the party supported opposing candidates in the 1962 general elections. In a third district a newly organized opposition party was able to defeat Congress in assembly and parliamentary elections. In the fourth district the organization was engaged in a dispute with a linguistic minority with such intensity that two state governments and the central government were involved.

As a draft of the study was being completed, Prime Minister Nehru died; but the data for the study had already been collected and analyzed, and the field work for this study does not bear the imprint of that important event. No time period selected for a study of the Congress party since independence would be typical. On the other hand, during the eighteen months in which the field research was conducted no events of unusual character appeared to distort the investigation within the district organizations.

*Public Policy and the District Party*

Thus far we have spoken of the differences among the districts selected and have noted the special qualities of each district which warranted its selection as a case study. Let us now turn to some of the general factors at work affecting all the districts under examination.

The local Congress party functions amidst social and economic changes directly or indirectly resulting from governmental action. The party itself can be viewed as a link between the particular social environment in which it operates and a larger governmental arena. Before we explore the peculiarities of each of the districts, let us turn to some of the activities of government which have been important for them.

Five areas of governmental action have been of great importance. The first, and in some respects the most important, has been the establishment of universal adult suffrage by the 1950 constitution. There was remarkably little debate over this issue in the constituent assembly, especially considering its revolutionary potential. Everyone in the assembly assumed that in independent India all individuals, whether or not they were literate, ought to have the right to participate in elections. Elections had taken place on a state and national level earlier, particularly in 1937 and 1946, but not until the general elections of 1951–52 was the entire adult population invited to participate. In the 1951–52 elections Congress therefore had to create for the first time an electoral machinery which would reach all portions of the population. Moreover, the constitution provided for the establishment of separate reserved constituencies for untouchables and depressed tribes (now widely referred to as scheduled castes and scheduled tribes, since these individual castes and tribes are listed on a government schedule). Congress units, most of which were controlled by prosperous agriculturalists and landlords and by members of high castes, now found it essential to appeal to scheduled castes and tribes and to lower castes. Social classes which had not actively participated in politics previously were now encouraged by the Congress party to enter the political arena within Congress. The confrontation which ensued between the district party organization and the new politically active social classes was not always a pleasant one and, as we shall see, produced considerable tension within the party.

An expansion in education as a result of increased national and state investment has been another important governmental action which has affected the environment of the Congress party. An explosion in university education has taken place. While only a quarter of a million

students attended colleges and universities at the time of independence, by the late 1950's well over a million students were enrolled. Twenty-five million children were attending schools of all kinds in the year 1950, but by 1960 more than forty million students were in schools and colleges throughout the country. In the youngest school age group, six to eleven, only 13 per cent were attending school in the year 1950, but in the year 1960 almost 23 per cent were at school. The number of secondary schools had doubled from seven thousand in 1950 to fourteen thousand in 1960, and the number of primary schools had jumped from a little over two hundred thousand to approximately three hundred fifty thousand.

This phenomenal expansion in education has had important political consequences for the Congress party. The desire for increased education has become an important political issue in both urban and rural areas. Individuals in almost all social groups now view education as an important vehicle for social mobility. How much should be spent for education, at what level, and in what location — these have become controversial political issues. In multi-lingual areas there are invariably controversies over what ought to be the language of instruction. Each social group is eager to improve its own educational opportunities in competition with other neighboring groups. Scheduled castes, scheduled tribes, and backward castes (a term used to describe low castes who are not untouchable) are particularly active in trying to obtain special facilities for their own students. There is a growing awareness within each caste and ethnic group that their own status as a community depends upon how many younger members of their community become educated and find jobs in administration and in other white-collar positions. In 1959 there were 715,000 primary school teachers and 470,000 secondary school teachers. Another forty-five thousand teachers were in colleges and universities. In many areas control over appointments and the assignment of teachers is an important element of patronage in the party organization. Finally, a lopsided pattern of education which is often unrelated to the country's manpower needs has created a substantial class of educated unemployed, particularly in the major urban centers. The existence of a substantial number of unemployed university graduates in Calcutta and in other major cities presents a special problem for the governing Congress Party.

A third major area of public policy is in land reform. Every state government has passed land reform legislation. The most inequitable systems of landownership — such as the zamindari, jagirdari, and inamdari sys-

tems — have been abolished. It is no longer possible for one man or one family to control tens of thousands of acres and to have vast numbers of villages under their jurisdiction. Absentee landlordism has diminished. Smaller rent collectors who were primarily engaged in urban occupations are now less likely to earn income from their land as a result of the new legislation. Thus, one important link between the city and the countryside — often an exploitative link — has diminished. As the power of the very large landlords has diminished in the countryside, the power of the smaller peasant proprietors has increased. And though it is difficult to generalize about the countryside in a land as diverse as India, it would be reasonably accurate to say that peasant proprietors with medium-sized holdings, many of whom do not personally cultivate the land but who employ agricultural labor, have become the single most important political group in the countryside and in the rural units of the Congress party.

I have briefly referred to the fourth major area of public policy which has affected the local environment in which the Congress party operates: the establishment of the system of local government known as panchayati raj. This new system of rural government has unsettled the local power structure in some areas. With the establishment of universal adult suffrage in village panchayat (council) elections, numbers have become an important element in political power. Men of high caste and property must now compete with one another to win popular village support. Numerically large low-income, uneducated, low-caste groups now have the opportunity to exercise influence within the village panchayats and even to attempt to control these local government bodies. It is still too early to say that this potential power will be converted into actual power or, if low-status groups gain control of local government bodies, to say what effect this will have on the attitude of the economically powerful high-status persons in the community. It might also be noted that while greater powers have been given to local bodies in the rural areas, no such expansion of municipal government has taken place. While local governments at the village, taluka, and district level have greater financial resources than ever before, no comparable expansion has taken place in the financial resources available to municipal governments in India. This contrast in local government activity has an important bearing on the difference in performance of the urban and rural Congress party organizations.

A fifth and final area of government policy is in the realm of economic and social planning. While it is not quite accurate to say, as some In-

dians do, that the British colonial administration was concerned exclusively with revenue administration and with the maintenance of law and order, it is true that development is of far greater concern to India's administration today than it was before 1947. Government is engaged in exercising control over the private sector, new industries are being established in the public sector, and there has also been heavy public investment in the establishment of multi-purpose dams. In the countryside two major areas of governmental development activities warrant our special attention. The first is the establishment of the community development program. Under this program the countryside has been divided into community development blocks, each of which is run by an appointed block development officer (BDO), assisted by technical advisors and a large number of village-level workers. The community development program is concerned with agricultural development, animal husbandry, child welfare, maternity care, public health, education, and other aspects of development. Until the late 1950's and early 1960's the community development program was run almost exclusively by government officers. The establishment of panchayati raj resulted in the transfer of these development activities to popularly elected bodies.

The government has also created a large number of quasi-governmental administrative bodies for development, the most important of which are the cooperatives. These handle agricultural credit, the purchase and distribution of fertilizers and seeds, and in some instances the storage and marketing of agricultural commodities. The establishment of all these new or enlarged institutions with considerable power and patronage — quasi-governmental cooperatives, the community development program, and the new local government bodies — has been accompanied by increased rural conflict as individuals and groups attempt to gain access to or control over these new institutions. The local Congress party organization has thus been faced with a changing power structure, considerable local conflict, and new patterns of relationships between elected bodies and local administration. These changes in the structures and functions of local administration have been important to the development of the Congress party since independence.

I have tried to suggest briefly how the local social, economic, and administrative environment has been affected by policies pursued by the state and national governments. In the case studies I shall demonstrate how these environmental changes have affected the character and performance of the local Congress party. The adoption of universal adult suffrage, an expansion in education at all levels, changes in land tenure,

the establishment of new patterns of local government, and the expansion of a developmental administration — all have brought about profound changes in the behavior of administration, in the relations between social groups, in the aspirations of individuals, and in the instruments now available to fulfill these aspirations. These changes have created both problems and opportunities for local Congress party organizations.

It would be misleading, however, to explain the character of the local Congress party simply in terms of its adaptation to its environment. The national party leadership has played an important role in converting the nationalist movement into the kind of political party that exists today. In the post-independence period many internal organizational problems arose which had to be resolved if the party was to deal with the many changes taking place. It is these organizational developments to which we now turn.

TABLE 1
POPULATION AND AREA OF FIVE DISTRICTS

| | AREA (Square Miles) | Population (1961 Census) |
|---|---|---|
| Belgaum . . . . . . . . . | 5,163 | 1,983,811 |
| Calcutta (entire city) . . . . | 40 | 2,927,289 |
| Guntur . . . . . . . . . . | 5,802 | 3,009,900 |
| Kaira . . . . . . . . . . | 2,621 | 1,977,540 |
| Madurai town . . . . . . . | 9 | 424,810 |

TABLE 2
CONGRESS PARTY VOTE IN FIVE DISTRICTS

| | 1952 | | | 1957 | | | 1962 | | |
|---|---|---|---|---|---|---|---|---|---|
| | % of Vote | Seats Won | Total Seats | % of Vote | Seats Won | Total Seats | % of Vote | Seats Won | Total Seats |
| Parliamentary Elections | | | | | | | | | |
| Belgaum . . . . . | 55.6 | 2 | 2 | 50.3 | 1 | 2 | 56.7 | 1 | 2 |
| Calcutta (entire city) | 36.8 | 1 | 4 | 40.3 | 1 | 4 | 46.3 | 1 | 4 |
| Guntur . . . . . | 31.6 | 1 | 2 | 56.5 | 3 | 3 | 43.5 | 1 | 3 |
| Kaira . . . . . . | 61.1 | 2 | 2 | 50.6 | 1 | 2 | 45.6 | 0 | 2 |
| Madurai town . . | 52.6 | 2 | 2 | 34.5 | 1 | 1 | 39.6 | 1 | 1 |
| Legislative Assembly Elections | | | | | | | | | |
| Belgaum . . . . . | 54.3 | 12 | 15 | 47.4 | 7 | 17 | 54.1 | 10 | 16 |
| Calcutta (entire city) | 39.7 | 17 | 26 | 42.6 | 8 | 26 | 47.2 | 14 | 26 |
| Guntur . . . . . | 25.2 | 3 | 18 | 39.3 | 16 | 25 | 41.5 | 12 | 25 |
| Kaira . . . . . . | 52.6 | 13 | 13 | 50.0 | 8 | 13 | 43.8 | 4 | 13 |
| Madurai town . . | 38.6 | 1 | 2 | 48.6 | 2 | 2 | 51.0 | 2 | 2 |

## 3. THE DEVELOPMENT OF
## THE CONGRESS ORGANIZATION

Like many other nationalist movements, the Congress began largely as an organization of the country's urban professional and middle classes concerned with obtaining greater privileges from the British colonial government. In the 1870's and early 1880's there were already a number of political associations in Poona, Bombay, Calcutta, and Madras. By the end of the nineteenth century there were some mass rumblings in the nationalist movement, especially in the provinces of Bengal and Maharasthra and in portions of the Punjab, but it was not until after the First World War that the movement took on the characteristics which we now associate with Congress.

### Historic Characteristics

*Its mass character.* Under Gandhi's leadership nationalist workers set out to rally all social classes behind Congress. With great insight Gandhi understood that colonial authority rested not simply on the coercive powers of the imperialist rulers but also upon the passive consent of the governed. The essential need of the nationalist movement, as he saw it, was to destroy the legitimacy of British authority. Thus Gandhi and his supporters sought to persuade millions of Indians to support the nationalist movement and to view going to jail as appropriate behavior. Large-scale civil disobedience movements were organized in the early 1920's and again in the early 1930's to demonstrate popular rejection of British

authority and to increase membership in and loyalty to the nationalist movement. Congress was open to mass membership, and anyone willing to pay the sum of four annas (approximately five cents) could become a primary member of the nationalist movement.

*Its national character.* From an organization primarily active in the coastal states of Bombay, Bengal, and Madras, and in the interior of the Punjab, Congress now reached out to nearly every district of British India. In the princely states which were under indirect British rule, nationalist organizations were established in the 1930's which were closely allied to and later absorbed organizationally by the Congress party. Moreover, national leaders came from all portions of the country. Party presidents elected each year came from many different states, and the Working Committee, the small governing group of the party, tended to be geographically representative.

*Its rural character.* While the movement before the First World War was largely though not exclusively urban, after the war it became well established in the countryside. In the early 1920's Gandhi and his close supporters launched movements against the payment of land taxes, particularly in the rural areas of Bihar, Gujarat, and Uttar Pradesh. The famous Salt March of the early 1930's was essentially a rural movement. In the mid-1930's agitation in favor of various land reform measures took place in many parts of India, particularly in Bihar and Andhra. A majority of the nationalist cadres came from the small towns and rural areas of the country. By the 1930's, perhaps even earlier, a growing number of Congress leaders at the state level were of rural, even peasant, background. Moreover, many of the new national leaders, such as Rajendra Prasad, India's first president, were of rural background.

*Its non-violent character.* Though under Gandhi's leadership civil disobedience was an instrument for destroying the authority of British colonial rule, the movement was committed to pursuing this strategy in a non-violent fashion. For some Congressmen, particularly Gandhi and his supporters, non-violence was a principle of faith; for others, it was a political strategy necessarily pursued because the instruments of violence were not available. It was this willingness of Congressmen to abjure violence which made it possible for the British in India to permit this extra-parliamentary movement to flourish. A few Englishmen were in fact sympathetic to the nationalist cause — it was after all, Allan Octavian Hume, an English member of the Indian Civil Service, who was the organizer and general secretary of the Indian National Congress in 1885. Though the British government in India ruthlessly arrested nationalist leaders

when they threatened to violate the law, no effort was made to crush the movement as such or to force it underground — except for a brief period during the Second World War.

*Its organized character.* In 1908 the present organizational structure of the Congress was established. Scattered units of the nationalist movement were assembled into a three-tiered structure. The basic local units were taluka and District Congress Committees, to coincide with the basic local administrative units of India — the talukas and districts. At the second level was the Pradesh (state) Congress Committee. The Congress constitution of 1920 established twenty-one such provincial organizations to coincide with the country's principal linguistic regions — a major change, incidentally, since previously Congress provincial units coincided with existing non-linguistic provincial boundaries. At the third level was the All-India Congress Committee (AICC), a national "legislative" council consisting of elected representatives from lower units of the party. The AICC elected a party president, who then selected his own "cabinet" or Working Committee which in practice governed the party. But perhaps more important than the establishment of a formal hierarchical organization was the development of a cadre of personnel concerned with the work of the party. In addition to the millions of "primary" members, the movement was to have "active" members. After an appropriate probationary period and after demonstrating that the candidate for active membership had fulfilled certain obligations to the movement, including the spinning of cotton and the carrying out of various social welfare activities prescribed by the party, an individual could become an active member.

*Its aggregative character.* When the Indian National Congress was first organized, its primary concern was to improve conditions for the middle classes within the framework of British rule. As this limited objective became frustrated and as nationalist sentiment grew, the demands of the movement increased and the organization's membership became more diversified. No racial, religious, linguistic, or caste communities were excluded; though the movement did not become representative in any perfect sense, its ethnic and occupational diversity was considerable. (It attracted few Muslims, and there was limited participation from the lower castes.) Factory workers were organized into trade unions, peasant associations were created by rural Congress workers, and special attention was paid to the organization of untouchables. Though many of the larger landowners feared the nationalist movement, there was no such fear among the small landowners and peasant proprietors, who joined the

movement in large numbers. The social and economic diversity of the membership thus laid the foundation for internal organization conflict — between landless laborers and peasant proprietors; tenants and landlords; untouchables and high castes; factory laborers and businessmen; tribesmen and Hindus; hills people and plains people; and between castes and linguistic or religious groups. There was therefore bound to be disagreement over such questions as: (1) the means by which independence was to be achieved — whether through constitutional or non-constitutional methods; (2) the kind of political, economic, and social system which ought to be created once independence was achieved; and (3) the specific interests which were to be served by an independent government and which were to be pressed even before independence. The Indian National Congress was not only a movement which propagated the cause of independence; it was also an organization through which individuals and social groups sought to achieve their own purposes.

*Its diffuse ideological character.* The Congress party contained many ideologies that were not only diverse but often only vaguely defined. Many of the younger members of the movement, especially in the 1930's, saw in socialism, communism, or some religious revivalist notions a scheme for social, economic, and political reorganization, but the leadership of Congress remained skeptical of blueprints. Even the Gandhians saw no direct relationship between their ideological beliefs and public policy. Though a few Congressmen called for the creation of a Gandhian constitution for India and even a Gandhian Congress party organization with constructive work as its sole purpose, these proposals were never seriously entertained by those who held authority in either the government or the party. In any event, most of the Gandhians were more concerned with the qualities of one's inner spirit than in any precise institutional framework or body of laws. Certainly in the pre-independence days the Congress leadership carefully avoided commitment to any precise notions as to the ideological character of an independent India.

This is not the place for a systematic exposition of ideologies within the Congress party; suffice it to say that since independence Congress has dominated the central range of the Indian ideological spectrum. The Hindu communal bodies — the Hindu Mahasabha, Ram Rajya Parishad, and to a lesser extent Jan Sangh — have called for the creation of a vaguely defined Hindu state. The Congress leadership has stood for secularism and social reform while expressing an attachment for and pride in many aspects of India's traditional society. The Communist party and the left wing within Congress have called for a larger public sector and greater

restrictions on private enterprise, while the conservative Swatantra party has criticized the Congress government for what it calls "permit raj" (rule by permit) — referring to the many regulations involved in opening factories, obtaining foreign exchange, and engaging in imports or exports. Time and time again Congress has declared itself in favor of a "socialistic pattern of society," a phrase loosely defined to cover the goals of economic development, state planning, economic and social equality, and a large public sector. Its precise legislative and policy expressions have varied through the years.

*Its social reform character.* Though social reform was not absent from the pre-1914 nationalist movement, it found a central place after the advent of Gandhi. Under Gandhi's leadership efforts were made to eliminate untouchability and other forms of social injustice and to revive village handicrafts, cottage industries, and the rural handloom industries in order to improve rural life. Gandhi believed that those who participated in the nationalist movement should not simply be political agitators against the British but should actively be engaged in social reform work or, as he put it, in "constructive work." When nationalists were not engaged in large-scale political agitation they were encouraged to engage in rural constructive activities. Gandhi thus made the nationalist movement a durable movement rather than an episodic activity.

*Its "machine" character.* This last, and some might say its most important, quality today is largely a post-independence development. As we shall see in greater detail later, the active party membership increasingly viewed Congress as a means of obtaining jobs for friends and relatives and of gaining access to the many services and material benefits which government at all levels can bestow. The party had already begun to function in this fashion when after 1937 it took control of many provincial governments and a vast number of district local boards and municipal bodies. Once Congress took office there was no incompatibility between the efforts of its membership to utilize the governmental machinery to further their own interests and the efforts of the movement to expel the British. After independence Congress increasingly took on the qualities of a political machine.

*From Nationalist Movement to Political Party*

The first few years of Indian independence were as traumatic as the infancy of any new nation. The years 1947 through 1951 were filled with

violence and uncertainty. Millions of refugees crossed the Indo-Pakistan borders, and countless Hindus and Muslims were slaughtered in the two new nations. In these four years Gandhi was assassinated, the Communists launched an insurrectionary movement in south India, military outbreaks occurred between India and Pakistan over the control of Kashmir, and force was used by the Indian government to bring about the accession of Hyderabad state. It looked too as though the Congress party were going to fragment into many pieces. The Socialists withdrew to form their own opposition party, and splintering took place on a large scale in several states, especially in Madras and West Bengal.

Although violence and disintegration seemed to characterize these early years, this was also a time in which an institutional ordering process was taking place. The administrative services and the military were reorganized. The princely states were integrated into the Indian Union. The Constituent Assembly agreed upon a new constitution, which legitimized India's parliamentary and federal structures. Despite internal differences the Congress government remained united, wrestled with the immediate post-partition crises, and established a machinery for economic planning. And in late 1951 and early 1952 India's adult population went to the polls to participate in the first elections based upon universal adult suffrage ever held in India.

Congress emerged from the elections as the country's dominant political party and has retained its dominance to this day. At the time of independence it was not clear as to what would emerge out of the nationalist movement — a social service society, an ideological party, an electorally oriented party, a patronage-minded political machine, or something else. In some new nations nationalist leaders have sought to maintain the revolutionary zeal of the nationalist movement, often by continued assaults against the former colonial rulers for retaining portions of their territory or for maintaining economic "imperialism." In other instances the goal of national freedom has been expanded into a Pan-African or Pan-Asian movement for a larger political unit.

The pre-independence Congress had some of the potentialities for becoming an ideologically oriented political party. As a nationalist movement it had many of the psychological qualities of such a party — it deprecated the present, it emphasized the spirit of personal sacrifice, it defied governmental authority, and many of its members identified with a collective whole. Some of its leaders, particularly Subash Chandra Bose, a Bengali who was elected president of the Congress party in 1939, had a revolutionary bent. But the controlling leadership of Congress before in-

dependence was essentially conservative. Jawaharlal Nehru, Pattabhi Sitaramayya, Govinda Ballabh Pant, Maulana Azad, Rajendra Prasad, and, above all, Sardar Vallabhbhai Patel (who was to become India's first home minister) were men who believed that the new order had to be built upon the old one and not, as some of the revolutionaries in the movement believed, upon revolution and chaos.

On the eve of independence Sardar Patel set out to "tame" the nationalist movement into a conservative modernizing force. After the war the nationalist leadership rejected the socialist proposal to prepare the country for an armed struggle and began to conduct negotiations with the British for Indian independence. The nationalist leadership was not sympathetic to a mutiny which occurred within the navy or to the Indian National Army, a revolutionary group created by Subhas Bose during the war with Japanese assistance for the purpose of violently expelling the British. And when independence came, Sardar Patel, as home minister, took steps to protect the members of the Indian Civil Service (despite nationalist criticism that the Indian bureaucrats had been collaborators). Patel guaranteed the salaries, retirement funds, and prerogatives of both bureaucrats and military and sought to create a cordial working environment. Even in dealing with the princes whose domains he appropriated, Patel moved with moderation. They were to lose their estates but not their lives, and they were allowed to retain limited privy purses.

Patel believed that a political party was essential for the creation and maintenance of an orderly stable elective government. But at the same time he felt that steps had to be taken to redirect public attention from the activities of the party to the activities of the government. Most of the nationalist leaders had moved into government positions, and took steps to prevent the party from commanding too much public attention. What would be more fitting than to offer the presidency of the party to the party secretary, a man whose only work for at least a decade was running the party machinery? In 1946 Acharya Kripalani was thus chosen to become party president, replacing Rajendra Prasad, the popular national leader who was to become a minister in the central government and, shortly thereafter, India's first president.

Patel's efforts to tame the nationalist movement were made easier by the very violence of partition. To those nationalists who urged that a clean sweep be made of the bureaucracy, Patel forcefully argued that the bureaucracy was essential for dealing with communal violence. To those

who wanted a purge of the armed forces, Patel pointed to the considerable role played by the army in keeping the country united, forcing the princely states to merge with India, and preventing Pakistani forces from overrunning Kashmir. And finally, to those who wanted a more militant Hindu community as a counter-force to Muslim fanaticism, Patel pointed to the fact that a Hindu fanatic, not a Muslim, had assassinated Gandhi. On many of these issues Patel's own views were changed after partition. He was, for example, known to be sympathetic to some of the views of Hindu communal leaders, but with the assassination of Gandhi he became even more acutely aware of the dangers of Hindu communalism.

Reasoning does not tame a mass movement, and it is doubtful that Patel could have been so successful if it were not for a series of fortuitous circumstances. One, as we have noted, was partition itself, which made a substantial part of the country relish order. The revolutionaries could inflame hope and hold out the promise of a golden future after a period of agitation and violence, but their voices were drowned amidst the violence which to so many seemed pointless. In less violent surroundings Patel's argument for pursuing policies which would maximize order would probably have been less appealing to the country's lower echelon political leaders.

The tragic death of Subhas Bose in an air crash during the war also proved to be an asset to those who wanted to tame the nationalist movement. Bose had been the leader of the militant section of Congress which rejected Gandhi's strategy of non-violence. He dramatically fled from India during the war to form with Japanese support, as we have seen, a military unit of Indians in Southeast Asia. In the late thirties Bose had emerged as a mass leader who commanded devotion and loyalty from his supporters. In 1939 he had the support of a majority of the AICC members, and it was only the opposition of the Congress Working Committee which led him to resign as Congress president. Had he survived the war and returned to India to lead the revolutionary forces — as Ben Bella did in similar circumstances in Algeria — the history of the Congress party and of India after 1947 might have been quite different.

The fact that the British lived up to their promises to grant India independence was another asset to the leadership in its efforts to avoid violence. The Socialists, the Communists, and the supporters of Subhas Bose believed that the British would not withdraw, and pressed for a militant struggle. Patel, Nehru, and Gandhi were convinced that the British would voluntarily relinquish power. Had the British fought to remain, as the Dutch did in Indonesia, voices of moderation would not have been

heard and the nationalist movement might have followed a different course.

The death of Bose, the assassination of Gandhi by an orthodox Hindu, the integrity of the British, and the violence of partition — all contributed to strengthening Patel's efforts to institutionalize and pacify the national movement and to maintain order. Without these factors it is difficult to say whether even a man of Patel's talents could have succeeded. But Patel himself was an extraordinary man. Though he was deeply involved in the nationalist struggle from the time of his youth and was a major leader in the movement, he was never a passionate orator or possessed with charisma. But he did have a firm grasp of the meaning of power and understood the importance of organization and the uses of coercion as well as persuasion. At the time of independence he understood the important role which the army and the bureaucracy must play if India was to be united, order maintained, and development pursued. He did not hesitate to send armed forces into Hyderabad, Kashmir, and the small princely state of Junagadh and to threaten other princes if they failed to accede. As home minister and minister of information and broadcasting, and as one of the most effective organizational leaders that Congress has produced, he held, in certain respects, more power than even Prime Minister Nehru.

Though Nehru is generally thought of as the dominant figure in post-independence India, it was Patel who largely created the institutional framework under which Nehru functioned. Unlike Patel, Nehru had been a strong critic of both the bureaucracy and the army. Nehru's strength was that he was a far more popular leader in the country than was Patel. But it was Patel who was entrusted with the task of unifying the country in the critical months after independence, and Patel who set out to turn Congress away from general objectives to concrete actions. Not until after Patel's death in 1951 did Nehru assume leadership of the Congress party, and by then it was no longer the mass movement it had been before independence. The party retained mass support, and its leaders continued to speak of sacrifice for a great cause — that of national development — but in fact the party now attracted many men who were concerned primarily with furthering their careers. Although from time to time an effort was made to recapture the spirit of the pre-independence days, Nehru was unable to do so because the party workers were no longer moved by a grandiose vision but rather by the more immediately rewarding advantages of power.

## Organizational Challenges

The day before he was assassinated in 1948, Gandhi prepared a brief memo outlining his proposals for the future course of Congress. He was assassinated before he had an opportunity to present it formally, but shortly after his death the Working Committee — often called the High Command — met to discuss what turned out to be Gandhi's last will and testament. In his memo Gandhi said that Congress "as a propaganda vehicle and parliamentary machine has outlived its use" and that "it must be kept out of unhealthy competition with political parties." He proposed that Congress not put up candidates for public office, but should instead become a non-political, non-governmental social service society concerned with rural development. He believed that those who wished to engage in political and parliamentary work should leave Congress to create their own political party. The High Command rejected Gandhi's proposal, since its acceptance would have left the country without a single political party capable of running the government. The effect of Gandhi's proposal, however, was to clarify the issue: the Congress leadership had clearly decided that they wanted the organization to be a political party.

The Congress leadership quickly turned its attention to a large number of organizational problems. Should Congress tolerate the continued existence of organized parties within its own organization? What should the relationship be between the parliamentary and "constructive" work wings of Congress, and what should their respective activities be? Should there be new rules for membership to prevent "undesirable elements" from joining the party? What should be the smallest operating party unit? Should the governing Working Committee be reorganized and made more representative? What should the role of Congress be in organizing trade unions, students, women, and untouchables? These and related organizational questions have continually occupied much of the attention of national and state party leaders. Memos have been prepared and committees appointed. Amendments to the party constitution have been drafted, debated, and in many instances approved. In some cases deliberate choices were made, in others these problems have continued to perplex the party leadership. An examination of some of the problems which Congress has faced over the years will illustrate for us the complexities of party building in a new nation and throw light on the problems confronted by the district party organizations — problems to which we shall turn in our case-study chapters.

*Movement versus party.* One of the earliest organizational questions

faced by the national leadership was that of the future of the organized political groups which had functioned for so many years within Congress. So long as Congress was a movement which united all those who subscribed to the goal of independence, the leadership tolerated a wide variety of ideological and policy differences. These outlooks were often quite organized. Until 1945 the Communist party had been organized as a unit within Congress. It was expelled that year for having supported the British war effort in opposition to the official Congress party resolution demanding that the British quit India. The Hindu Mahasabha had been an organized group within Congress until its expulsion in the mid-thirties as a "communal" body. Only the Congress Socialist party and a few smaller groups remained within Congress, and the issue here was not whether they subscribed to the party program but whether they should be allowed to continue at all as separate political bodies. Once it became clear that Congress would now contest elections against many of these groups, it was evident that Congress could no longer tolerate a situation in which there were organized parties within itself. In 1948 an amendment to the Congress constitution was passed which forbade any party member to belong to "any other political party, communal or other, which has a separate membership, constitution and programme." With the passage of this amendment, the Congress Socialist party members withdrew from Congress.

*The organizational unit: electoral or administrative?* Before independence, Congress was organized in effect as a parallel government. Its local organizational units — the district and taluka Congress committees — coincided with local administrative units. After independence, some Congressmen suggested that the party be reorganized so that its basic units coincide, not with these administrative boundaries, but with parliamentary and assembly constituencies. After some discussion it was decided to maintain the existing structure, since a large part of the work of the party cadres, members of state legislative assemblies (MLAs) and even members of parliament (MPs) involves presenting local problems to taluka and district administration. Moreover, the creation of new local government units — panchayat samitis (coinciding with taluka boundaries) and zilla parishads (for the districts) — provided an additional governmental unit with which the taluka and district Congress committees could be associated. Of major importance is the fact that the Congress party is one of the few parties in the world whose present local units do not fit the boundaries of state or national constituencies, but instead match local government and administration. This fact calls our attention to the close

INDIAN NATIONAL CONGRESS

*Structural Chart*

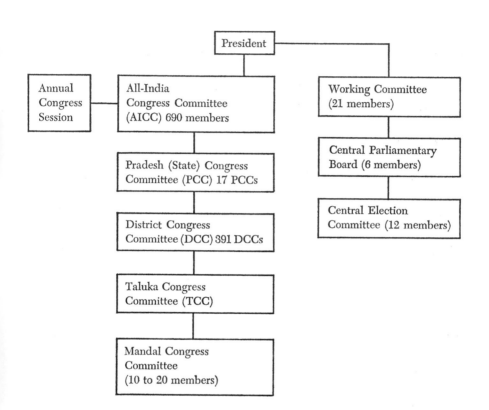

relationship which exists between the local Congress party units and local government and administration.

The relationship between organizational structure and function is particularly uncertain at the level of the smallest party unit—the mandal committee. The smallest unit before independence was the village panchayat Congress, but Congressmen felt that the village was too small for the maintenance of an effective local party apparatus. They also felt that the talukas were too large and that a unit of intermediary size ought to be created. There was thus established a mandal committee to cover a population of approximately twenty thousand persons. The mandal was assigned a long list of party activities, though it is widely agreed that in practice the mandals perform few of these activities and are active only

at the time of elections to party offices if at all. Local Congressmen compete for elections to mandal committees, since it is through the mandals that they can become elected to taluka and district committees. Individual mandal committee members may be active party workers, but as a unit the mandal committees rarely function effectively. The reason perhaps is that they coincide neither with an administrative nor with an electoral unit and therefore cannot effectively link the voter to the local administration, to members of the legislative assembly, or to parliament.

*Organizational versus ministerial wings.* The relationship of one "section" of the Congress party to another has been a constant problem. At any given level of the party — the district, state, or national organizations — there are at least three different "sections": (a) organizational units — that is, the mandal, taluka, district, state, and national committees; (b) legislative and ministerial units — that is, the village panchayats, samitis, zilla parishads, state assembly, or parliament; and (c) the voluntary associations related to Congress — such as the trade unions, cooperatives, youth wing, women's associations, and Gandhian organizations. Though some individuals may be active in all three "sections," individual Congressmen more typically are active in and identified with only one. Problems in the relationship of Congressmen in one "section" to those in another may arise at any level of the organization — in the district, the state, or New Delhi.

The conflict between the organizational and ministerial wings of Congress has presented perhaps the most serious organizational problem. With independence, many Congress leaders took posts in the state and national governments, while others remained in the party organization. Difficulties arose as party leaders complained that they were not being adequately consulted by the governmental leadership. Congressmen who had not received parliamentary or assembly tickets fought for control over the Congress party organization. By gaining control of the party machinery, particularly the important pradesh election committees which nominate candidates, dissident elements attempted to displace the government leadership. When a dissident faction gained control of a state party organization, it would solicit support from members of the state legislative assembly. In several states dissidents won enough support to overthrow the existing Congress party government.

The problem arose even at the national level. So long as Patel was alive, one man exercised control over the party organization while holding a high position in the central government. Upon his death, tension developed between members of the cabinet and the Congress party president.

These difficulties came to a head in 1951 when Nehru resigned from the Working Committee and from the AICC in opposition to the then Congress president, P. D. Tandon. Tandon resigned, and Nehru was elected president of Congress while remaining prime minister. By holding both positions he was able to prevent any conflict between the two wings of the party at the national level. When in 1954 Nehru stepped down as party president he selected his own candidate, and thereafter no one became Congress party president without Nehru's approval.

In the states it has been the practice to prohibit chief ministers from simultaneously being presidents of the state party organizations. In practice the chief ministers have been able to retain control over their party organizations and select both the party president and secretary. Where the ministers have failed to do so, their positions have been threatened. It is important to note that when conflicts occur between the organizational and ministerial wings of Congress, they are rarely reflections of ideological or policy differences but are simply the institutional frames for factional conflicts. The faction of the party which has failed to gain control over the government attempts to wrest control first by establishing a hold within the party organization. The important point is that the party machine is sufficiently powerful — after all, it does determine who will be nominated for public office — for dissident factions to see it as a vehicle for winning state power. There have been various proposals for bringing together the organizational and ministerial wings, generally by establishing joint committees. But, in practice, struggles for control have been avoided only when one faction controlled both the government and the party machinery. In effect this has meant that the group which controls the government has prevented other factions from dominating the party organization. This general pattern of governmental control over the organizational wing seemed, however, to be changing in 1963, but it is still too early to be sure of any sharp reversal. In that year the chief minister and Congress leader of Madras, K. Kamaraj, persuaded Prime Minister Nehru to remove a number of important chief ministers and cabinet members from their posts. One cabinet member, S. K. Patil, returned to the Bombay city party organization and began to devote his energies to organizational work. Kamaraj himself resigned as chief minister of Madras and was subsequently elected national president of Congress. In the state of West Bengal the Congress party boss, Atulya Ghosh, had already emerged as the king maker when he exercised a decisive hand in selecting the new chief minister in 1962. These three men, all party leaders without offices in the state or national government, played

key roles in the selection of Lal Bahadur Shastri as Nehru's successor. Moreover, Shastri let it be known publicly that on major political matters, including the composition of his cabinet, he would turn to the party president, Kamaraj, for guidance. And when Shastri died, it was Kamaraj who again played the role of king maker in selecting Indira Gandhi as prime minister. In several states too it appeared that the Congress party leaders were emerging as powerful men independent of the chief minister. In the 1967 elections, however, three Congress leaders — K. Kamaraj, Atulya Ghosh, and S. K. Patel — lost their parliamentary seats, but many Congress chief ministers and cabinet members were defeated as well. Whether party leaders will exercise great power without holding executive office still remains unclear.

*Congress and its auxiliaries.* Another major intra-organizational conflict — between the voluntary organizations and the Congress party and Congress governments — has been less dramatic but of no less importance. A number of voluntary associations are closely allied to and in some instances affiliated with the local Congress organizations. There are the Youth Congress, the Mahila (Women's) Congress, the Seva Dal (a social service youth corps), and — of great importance — the trade union section. After the war the trade unionists in Congress withdrew from the Communist dominated All India Trade Union Congress (AITUC) and organized a new national federation known as the Indian National Trade Union Congress (INTUC). INTUC supports Congress and government efforts to minimize strikes and in general to exercise restraint on the labor force. However, some local INTUC unions have sought greater government support in their conflicts with management than the government has been willing to provide. State INTUC groups have often pressed, usually without success, for the appointment of one of their members as minister of labor. Moreover, conflicts have also arisen over the selection of party candidates for assembly and parliament, since INTUC unions frequently feel that they are not adequately represented. In Madurai and in Calcutta, both of which contain large trade union organizations, there has been constant tension between Congress trade unionists and other Congressmen.

There has also been some tension between the Gandhians and the regular Congress party workers. Under Gandhi's leadership a large number of "constructive" associations were created which were closely allied to the Indian National Congress. These associations were highly specialized, and each was concerned with a specific problem, such as the improvement of untouchables, the development of village industries, the

production of handspun, handloomed cloth (known as khadi), the incul-
cation of "basic education" into villages, and the care and protection of
cows. After Gandhi's death a new organization of Gandhian constructive
workers was formed to support the work of Vinoba Bhave, a disciple of
Gandhi who toured the country calling for the voluntary redistribution
of land and the voluntary establishment of village collective farms. Many
of the Gandhian activities — particularly the encouragement of village industries and the production of khadi — now receive large-scale government support. Congress workers have often found jobs in government
agencies created to support these activities. Many of the Gandhian workers, however, are critical of what they call "government" work as distinct from working with the "people," and are particularly critical of those
Congressmen who spend their time dealing with government officers. The
Gandhians also feel that Congress cadres tend to work closely with peasant proprietors who are most ready to avail themselves of the new development facilities provided by the government, and give less attention
to the needs of those sections of society who are less prosperous. While
party workers deal most frequently with those members of the community who are politically alert and who command control over large numbers of votes, the Gandhians place greater emphasis on working with the
more backward, less politically active sections of the community. Though
many Gandhians continue as active party workers, others have become
aloof from the party organization and now devote their energies exclusively to one or more of the Gandhian organizations.

*State versus central organizations.* Important changes have also occurred in the relationship between one level of the party organization
and another. We have already noted that Congress is federal in structure
and contains state units as well as a national party organization. Before
independence the central party organization had more power than it
does today. A handful of men — Gandhi, the Congress president, and
members of the Working Committee — determined over-all Congress policy. If one takes an overview of the period from 1920 to independence,
one is struck by the extent to which Gandhi and his associates were able
to exercise control. Even after Congress took office in many states after
the 1937 elections, the Congress high command was able to exercise
authority over state governments. The question of whether a state organization should form a coalition government with other parties when
they did not have a clear majority was an issue that was decided by the
high command. The question of who was to become the Congress chief
minister in each state was also a decision of the Congress high com-

mand, and on at least one occasion the national leadership dismissed a state chief minister. Finally, the Congress high command occasionally exercised its ultimate sanction of suspending or expelling individuals and units from the party. Members of Hindu communal organizations were expelled in the 1930's, Communists in 1945, and in the early 1940's the Bengal Pradesh Congress Committee for violating national policy. I am not trying to suggest that before independence the Indian National Congress was a monolithic organization with power totally concentrated in a small oligarchy in the central office. The movement was in fact torn by many internal conflicts, and the national organization tended to be permissive of a wide variety of viewpoints. Moreover, the high command did not consist of disembodied national leaders cut off from their state and local organizations. Their national position was often based upon views powerfully supported in their own states. Vallabhbhai Patel was a leader in Gujarat, Rajendra Prasad in Bihar, Govinda Pant in Uttar Pradesh, and Pattabhi Sitaramayya in Andhra.

Nonetheless, it is important to note that a new class of state political leaders has risen since independence – the state chief ministers and party leaders. The state party organizations are now financially autonomous. The state leaders have access to patronage for their membership, and their influence over state and local administration makes it possible for them to "service" the voters. According to the party constitution, the Central Election Committee under the Working Committee determines who will receive both parliamentary and state assembly seats; in practice the Election Committee accepts the recommendations of the state party organization unless the state organization is divided (see chart on page 41). Otherwise the national organization does not overrule the state organization; to do so would be to repudiate the state party and to create a conflict between the central party and the state which the central organization would not welcome and might not even win.

This is not the place to discuss either the growing power of the state chief ministers in relation to the center or, more generally, the changing relationship of state and national governments in India. The important point here is that the state chief ministers, when they effectively control their own party organization, can make political decisions at the state level without turning to the center for advice. Moreover, the state leaders can now exercise considerable influence at the national level. It is unlikely, for example, that a prime minister would be selected without the approval of the chief ministers dominating powerful party organizations in the larger states. In fact, it is now customary for the Congress Working

Committee to invite to its deliberations those important chief ministers who are not members of the Working Committee when any questions of national importance are discussed. Thus, when the Working Committee met to discuss the question of Nehru's succession, all the chief ministers were invited.

The emergence of powerful state chief ministers does place limitations on the exercise of central government authority. Those who feel that India's development is dependent upon the existence of a cohesive and powerful leadership at the national level view with some concern the emergence of strong state chief ministers. The chief ministers are, however, an important force for the maintenance of the parliamentary as well as of the federal system. Though the state leaders may be reluctant to select as prime minister a man with a desire to create a powerful central government, they are eager to find a prime minister on whom they can all agree — most of the chief ministers are thoroughly aware of the destructive consequences for the party and for their own state organizations of a failure to agree upon a national leader.

The growing independent power of the state organizations has led some Congressmen to propose a reorganization of the Working Committee so that it consists of elected representatives from the states. A Congress Reorganization Committee appointed in 1959 looked into this and other proposals. The committee rejected the proposal, declaring:

> We feel, on closer consideration, that the Working Committee today is the one stable and stabilising factor in the Congress organization. If we are seeing more and more clearly the inconveniences of elections in the Congress organization it seems to us that it would be the right thing to do if that part of it which, from its vagaries, is allowed to retain this freedom [sic]. The Congress President still occupies a unique position in the Congress organization. He should have a committee of his choice. He strives to see that most of the States, the minorities, the youth, women etc. are represented and together they form a harmonious and effective team. In view of these considerations we are loath to recommend any change in the composition of the Working Committee."[1]

[1] *Report of the Reorganization Committee* (Bangalore: Indian National Congress, 1960), p. 6.

Nonetheless, a compromise was reached, and now one-third of the Working Committee is elected — but by the AICC, not by the state organizations.

*State versus district organizations.* While the state party organizations have grown in importance and power in relationship to the center, the district Congress committees have also become more important — and for similar reasons. Before Congress took control over local and state governments in an independent India, the national leadership could exercise relatively clear, undivided authority. The struggle against the British required a concentration of authority and a measure of obedience — qualities characteristic of all organizations confronted by an enemy with coercive powers. Today both district and state party leaders are freed from the ideological cry for unity and have considerable independent powers. The district organizations frequently raise their own funds for party work and for elections. The president of the DCC has direct access to the district administration, panchayat samitis, and zilla parishads, to members of the state legislative assembly, to parliament, and to the state and sometimes national governmental leadership. Moreover, when the president of the DCC has a relatively unified district organization under his command, he is able to exert strong influence over the state party organization in the selection of district candidates to the state assembly and to parliament. In the most effective state party organizations in India there is a close working relationship between the president of the Pradesh Congress Committee and the presidents of the DCC.

This changing distribution of power within Congress toward greater autonomy of smaller units has created new problems in the selection of candidates for public office. Each unit wishes to exercise control over the selection of candidates for offices elected within the territory under its jurisdiction. Thus the taluka committees wish to determine who shall run for panchayat samitis and who shall receive assembly tickets. Similarly, the district organizations want to determine who shall run for the parliamentary seats, assembly seats, and district and taluka governments. In principle, the national and state organizations agree that the views of local units should be taken into account in nominating candidates, since the local party unit is best able to decide who is most likely to win an election within the locality. But if local units actually had the power to allocate seats, then the state and national organizations would not exercise control over members of state assemblies and parliament. Party discipline within elected bodies — which has generally been maintained since independence — would crumble. Moreover, ethnic minori-

ties who are so scattered that they do not predominate in any one constituency would have few opportunities to get elected to public office if the local party units had complete power to allocate tickets. For these and other reasons the state elections committees have often overruled the recommendations of district and taluka units.

*States' reorganization and Congress.* Conflicts within the larger society have been an important source of tension within Congress. Most of these conflicts are of a local nature, and the Congress party leadership at the local level has shown an extraordinary capacity to accommodate different factions, castes, and economic interests within the party. The fact that Congress is a political organization whose leadership is concerned with providing material and status satisfactions to its members, rather than an ideological party faced with the problems of reconciling diverse intellectual positions, is a key to the accommodating character of Congress.

Moreover, since most of the disputes have been local, they have not threatened the party as a whole throughout the country. There was, however, one important exception when Congress unity was threatened by its inability to reconcile conflicting sentiments on a matter of public policy affecting a large part of the Congress membership and leadership – the controversy concerning states' reorganization.

Shortly after independence, sentiment grew throughout India for the creation of unitary linguistic states, particularly in Bombay and in the multi-lingual states of South India. Such sentiment had existed before independence but was overshadowed by the independence struggle. After 1947, loyalties to language (and in a few areas to tribe and religion) excited men in the same way that nationalist loyalties had during earlier years. Many pointed out that democracy and administration would function better in unilingual states and that this would simplify the educational systems, recruitment of personnel into state administrative services, and so on. But the national leadership was distressed by the primordial quality of the movement – by the deprecation of other ethnic groups which so often accompanied the deep-seated passionate emotional attachments to language, regional history, and ethnic community. As linguistic sentiments rose within majority groups in each region, the insecurity of minorities increased. So long as political discussions centered on such issues as what language would be used in the schools, to what extent particular groups should have positions reserved for them in administration, and how much attention to economic development an area should receive, then loyalties were sufficiently concrete to be managed – which is to say that the demands were bargain-

able. But when the issue became more generally the creation of separate linguistic states, then passions became inflamed. Congress units in multilingual states took opposing positions. This was the only important issue since independence on which pradesh party organizations were bitterly opposed to one another. The national party and government leaders hoped that by postponing the question of linguistic reorganization for an indefinite period passions would subside. They tried to press this position on the state party organizations. In several instances the state organizations, contrary to local sentiments, subscribed to the national party position, but when they did, the effect was often a defeat for the Congress party in state and local elections. In some areas, as in Maharashtra, large-scale defections from Congress took place, again resulting in electoral defeats for the party. The decision was ultimately made by the national government to reorganize the states more or less along linguistic lines in 1956. This decision may have created many new national problems, but it did result in a settling of passions within each of the states and within the state party organizations. The linguistic movement largely disappeared and linguistic sentiments were reduced in importance once the new states were formed. Conflicts over language have generally settled down to concrete issues. Moreover, once the linguistic demands were satisfied, defectors from Congress soon returned to the party organization.

*Congress and the bureaucracy.* After independence it was necessary for Congress to establish a new relationship with the bureaucracy. When the Congress party took office it was confronted with an existing administrative framework recruited by civil service commissions. While political parties in the United States developed *before* a large-scale merit bureaucracy was established, in India the administrative framework preceded the establishment of partisan politics. During the British colonial era the power to make decisions and to implement them was largely in the hands of the bureaucracy. Independence meant not only that power would be transferred to Indians but also that the functions of policy making and policy implementation would be more sharply divided.

The local, district, and state party organizations have become increasingly concerned with the administration of government policies. The recent expansion of development activities at the local level has led agriculturalists and merchants to approach local and state administration for loans, fertilizers, wells, roads, and schools. The party is increasingly called upon to serve as a liaison with local administration. Moreover, local party workers recognize that grievances against the local adminis-

tration may injure the political position of the party. Party workers are also attracted by the patronage in the hands of local administration. Then too, any decision by a local bureaucrat affecting the wealth or status of someone in the community is of interest to the local party. There is thus a tendency for the party to be increasingly concerned with gaining access to or even control over local administration.

There has been a considerable mutual adjustment of politicians and bureaucrats which in the main has permitted politicians to use the administrative framework to provide rewards for their supporters without jeopardizing administrative efficiency. The lower one goes in the administrative echelon, however, the more the interests of the politicians are served and the less those of the bureaucracy.

Politicians and bureaucrats have in general learned to use each other to achieve their own ends. Politicans seek to influence the bureaucracy; but as the powers of the politicians grow, it becomes more necessary for local bureaucrats to turn to elected politicians for the things they want. A school teacher, for example, dissatisfied with the village to which he has been assigned, may request a transfer from the Congress president of the zilla parishad. A local bureaucrat wants a good word said for him to the minister so that he may be promoted or transferred to a better position. The community development officer will turn to local Congress workers for help in achieving some of the goals established for him by his ministry.

The line between party "influence" and "interference" in the actions of local administration is a very thin one. Crossing the line not only imperils the performance of local administration but may lead to a great deal of local resentment that may backfire against the party. Most state Congress leaders encourage their party workers to present grievances to local administrators but to avoid making threats, requesting transfer of administrators, or employing bribes. In Madras, for example, bureaucrats speak proudly of their freedom from political control while at the same time they indicate a willingness to "cooperate" with "popular" (that is, elected) bodies. On the other hand, the Congress government in the Punjab has been criticized for encouraging the party to interfere in administration, and administrators have been transferred for political considerations.

Paul Brass, in his study of the Congress party in Uttar Pradesh, argues that "inter-penetration has sometimes been carried to a degree which threatens the continued existence of a neutral bureaucracy." It is certainly no easy task to balance the need for administrative independence

with the need of the party for incentives for its members and supporters. The balance established between the local party organization and the local administration varies considerably from one district and one state to another, but continues to constitute an important unsettled problem for the Congress party.

*Congress and local government.* Closely related to the issue of the local party and local administration is the relationship of the party to local government. The central issue here is how partisan should local politics be. National Congress leaders, supported by Gandhians throughout the country, have been eager to prevent panchayat, samiti, and zilla parishad elections from being partisan, on the grounds that local government should be primarily concerned with non-partisan development problems. Moreover, the national leadership feels that the intervention of party politics in the village will intensify caste, religious, and factional conflicts. Congressmen who participate in district and local politics view the principle of non-partisan local politics as being a lofty ideal, but argue that it is impractical. They point out that control over local bodies is essential if the party is to win assembly and parliamentary seats. The party must seek to maintain good relations with men of status and power within the village and wherever possible to persuade such men to become members of the local party.

Conflicts within the village, however, have constantly presented problems for local party leaders. If the party becomes too closely associated with any one faction, the party is in danger of losing a substantial portion of the village in assembly and parliamentary elections. It has been in the interests of the party, therefore, to reduce factional conflicts in the village, to stress village harmony, and to urge all groups in the village, irrespective of their attitudes toward each other, to join together in support of Congress assembly and parliamentary candidates. But where opposition parties have been active, it has been difficult for Congress to build its program on village harmony. If one faction becomes associated with an opposition party, Congress has had no choice but to identify itself with an opposition village faction. Moreover, the pressure on the local Congress organization to support a faction, even in village panchayat elections, has been intensified since panchayati raj was created.

Under panchayati raj in most states the panchayat samitis and zilla parishads — that is, the block and district councils — are elected indirectly by village panchayat presidents. Control over the samitis and parishads is politically essential to the local Congress party organization, since these two bodies have power over development within the district and have

access to patronage. Congress, therefore, must attempt to win the support of village panchayat presidents. Other parties attempt to do so as well. Where village elections are contested by candidates who do not belong to political parties, then, upon the election of the village panchayat president, Congress and other parties will try to get the president to join their party. But local Congress leaders will often informally give support to one candidate because he is more likely to join Congress upon election or because he is a known Congressman. If one candidate is known to be associated with an opposition party, the local Congress party organization will invariably try to get a Congressman to stand against him.

Apart from the role played by village panchayats in selecting samitis and parishads, the village panchayats are themselves of great political importance. Panchayat presidents have considerable influence within their village; although they cannot always swing the village to one party's assembly or parliamentary candidate, they do considerably influence the election. The panchayat president does, after all, have sources of patronage — he can obtain aid for his village from the samiti or parishad, and he can approach government officers for direct assistance to his village. Within the village he is a man of substantial local power who can affect the political attitudes of many villagers.

The national Congress party leadership has, as we have seen, opposed party participation in village panchayat elections. An AICC meeting in Delhi in June, 1962, passed a resolution stating that the party would not participate in panchayat elections and asking that other parties pursue a similar policy. This resolution, interestingly enough, was passed unanimously with only a handful of critical speeches, even though the bulk of the local party workers who attended the AICC meeting privately rejected such a policy as politically unworkable. The national leadership, as we have noted, feels that party conflicts within the village would further intensify rural conflicts. But astute local Congressmen retort that conflicts in the village are already present, that these conflicts are often along caste or factional lines, and that party conflicts would at least inject some issues into village politics, thus cutting somewhat into caste politics. They add that control over the village panchayat by a non-Congressman would endanger the party's prospects in the general elections and would, given the system of indirect elections to samitis and parishads, involve loss of control of these bodies as well. They conclude that there is nothing to prevent a villager from being associated with a political party, and, because of the importance of the village panchayat president,

other parties will woo him if Congress does not. Thus, it would be impractical for Congress to show no interest in the outcome of local elections.

The conflict between the views of many local party workers and those of the national party leadership thus quietly continues. In practice the local party organizations informally participate in panchayat elections even while the national party continues to pass resolutions unanimously calling for non-party panchayat elections. The effects on the performance of the local party organization as a result of these conflicting views is another theme we shall pursue in our case studies.

In this chapter we have suggested that the Congress party was confronted with many formidable organizational difficulties as it was transformed from a nationalist movement concerned with winning independence to a political party concerned with winning elections, exercising power, and pressing for the country's development. We have also noted in the preceding chapter that the character and functioning of the local party organizations have been affected by the policies pursued by Congress governments.

Now we shall take a look at the actual performance of the local party organization — at the way in which it recruits and trains its membership, deals with internal conflict, and wins public support. In the chapters which follow we shall try to suggest how the local Congress party performs these tasks as it interacts in a wide variety of local social systems, cultural patterns, economic relationships, and power structures. We shall thus view the Congress party as an intermediary institution between government on the one hand and society on the other — always affected by both. Once we proceed to this level of analysis it is necessary that we turn from general theory to concrete description, and from a macro-view of the national scene to a micro-view of the local party organization.

TABLE 3

CONGRESS PARTY PARLIAMENTARY ELECTION RESULTS, 1952–62

| State | 1952 | | | 1957 | | | 1962 | | |
|---|---|---|---|---|---|---|---|---|---|
| | % of Vote | Seats Won | Total Seats | % of Vote | Seats Won | Total Seats | % of Vote | Seats Won | Total Seats |
| Andhra Pradesh. . | 31.7 | 13 | 40 | 51.5 | 37 | 43 | 48.0 | 34 | 43 |
| Assam . . . . . . | 53.2 | 11 | 12 | 51.7 | 9 | 12 | 45.2 | 9 | 12 |
| Bihar . . . . . . | 45.8 | 45 | 55 | 44.5 | 41 | 53 | 43.9 | 39 | 53 |
| Delhi . . . . . | 49.4 | 3 | 4 | 54.3 | 5 | 5 | 50.7 | 5 | 5 |
| Gujarat . . . . . | 46.4 | 16 | 22 | 54.4 | 17 | 22 | 52.6 | 16 | 22 |
| Himachal Pradesh. | 39.0 | 2 | 3 | 47.3 | 4 | 4 | 68.7 | 4 | 4 |
| Kerala. . . . . . | 29.9 | 7 | 18 | 34.8 | 6 | 18 | 34.3 | 6 | 18 |
| Madhya Pradesh . | 49.0 | 34 | 38 | 52.1 | 35 | 36 | 39.6 | 24 | 36 |
| Madras . . . . . | 42.5 | 25 | 41 | 46.5 | 31 | 41 | 45.3 | 31 | 41 |
| Maharashtra . . . | 52.6 | 35 | 40 | 46.4 | 21 | 44 | 52.9 | 41 | 44 |
| Manipur . . . . . | 23.8 | 1 | 2 | 28.0 | 1 | 2 | 30.9 | 1 | 2 |
| Mysore. . . . . . | 54.9 | 25 | 27 | 55.5 | 23 | 26 | 52.7 | 25 | 26 |
| Orissa . . . . . . | 42.5 | 11 | 20 | 40.0 | 7 | 20 | 55.5 | 14 | 20 |
| Punjab. . . . . . | 40.6 | 18 | 23 | 51.3 | 21 | 22 | 41.3 | 14 | 22 |
| Rajasthan . . . . | 41.8 | 11 | 22 | 53.6 | 19 | 22 | 37.6 | 14 | 22 |
| Tripura . . . . . | 25.6 | 0 | 2 | 46.0 | 1 | 2 | 42.8 | 0 | 2 |
| Uttar Pradesh. . . | 53.0 | 81 | 86 | 46.3 | 70 | 86 | 38.2 | 62 | 86 |
| West Bengalᵃ . . . | 42.1 | 24 | 34 | 48.2 | 23 | 36 | 46.8 | 22 | 36 |
| India total . . . | 45.0 | 362 | 489 | 47.8 | 371 | 494 | 44.7 | 361 | 494 |

Note: All election results were computed by state according to the 1962 boundaries. Between the 1952 and 1957 elections the states of Andhra Pradesh, Bombay (later divided between Gujarat and Maharashtra), Kerala, Madhya Pradesh, Madras, Mysore, Punjab, and Rajasthan were either created or reorganized, resulting often in states of the same name but with vastly different territory. Consequently, 1952 figures for Madras, for example, refer to the present state of Madras not to the state which in 1952 was called Madras.

ᵃWest Bengal MP and MLA figures for 1952 do not include data from Purulia district, which was then a part of Bihar, and subsequently was joined to West Bengal. In 1952 this area voted largely for the Lok Sangh party.

TABLE 4

CONGRESS PARTY LEGISLATIVE ASSEMBLY ELECTION RESULTS, 1952–62

| State | 1952 | | | 1957 | | | 1962 | | |
|---|---|---|---|---|---|---|---|---|---|
| | % of Vote | Seats Won | Total Seats | % of Vote | Seats Won | Total Seats | % of Vote | Seats Won | Total Seats |
| Andhra Pradesh. . | 29.7 | 58 | 206 | 41.3ᵃ | 187 | 301 | 47.3 | 177 | 300 |
| Assam . . . . . . | 43.8 | 76 | 105 | 52.4 | 71 | 108 | 48.3 | 79 | 105 |
| Bihar . . . . . . | 41.4 | 240 | 330 | 41.9 | 210 | 318 | 41.4 | 185 | 318 |
| Gujarat . . . . . | 54.9 | 164 | 190 | 48.7 | 97 | 132 | 50.8 | 113 | 154 |
| Keralaᵇ . . . . . | 34.3 | 45 | 137 | 37.8 | 43 | 126 | 34.1ᶜ | 63 | 126 |
| Madhya Pradesh . | 48.1 | 261 | 337 | 49.8 | 232 | 288 | 38.6 | 142 | 288 |
| Madras. . . . . . | 40.0 | 109 | 216 | 45.3 | 151 | 205 | 46.1 | 139 | 206 |
| Maharashtra . . . | 45.2 | 138 | 168 | 48.7 | 137 | 264 | 51.2 | 215 | 264 |
| Mysore. . . . . . | 51.5 | 176 | 209 | 52.1 | 151 | 208 | 50.2 | 138 | 208 |
| Orissa . . . . . . | 38.8 | 67 | 140 | 38.2 | 56 | 140 | 43.3ᵈ | 82 | 140 |
| Punjab. . . . . . | 34.8 | 121 | 186 | 47.5 | 120 | 154 | 43.7 | 90 | 154 |
| Rajasthan . . . . | 39.7 | 95 | 190 | 45.2 | 119 | 173 | 40.0 | 88 | 176 |
| Uttar Pradesh. . . | 47.9 | 390 | 430 | 42.4 | 286 | 430 | 36.3 | 249 | 430 |
| West Bengalᵉ . . . | 38.9 | 150 | 238 | 46.1 | 152 | 252 | 47.3 | 157 | 252 |
| India totalᶠ . . | 42.2 | 2,248 | 3,283 | 45.5 | 1,893 | 2,906 | 44.4 | 1,772 | 2,855 |

ᵃA composite figure made up of the results from the mid-term election in Andhra in 1955 and in Telengana in 1957.

ᵇBy-elections were held in the old state of Travancore-Cochin in 1954 in which Congress won 45.3 percent of the vote and 45 out of 117 seats.

ᶜThis figure is for by-elections held in 1960. In by-elections held in early 1965 Congress won 32.5 percent of the vote and 36 out of 133 seats. A splinter Congress group, the Kerala Congress, won 23 seats with 12.4 percent of the vote.

ᵈThis figure is for by-elections held in June 1960.

ᵉThe 1952 figure excludes Purulia district, which was then part of Bihar.

ᶠThis figure is for the actual results of the three general elections. It is not adjusted for by-elections as are the state figures.

## TABLE 5
### CONGRESS PARTY MEMBERSHIP, 1955–59, BY STATES

| | 1955 | | 1957 | | 1959 | |
|---|---|---|---|---|---|---|
| | Primary | Active | Primary | Active | Primary | Active |
| Andhra . . . | 488,950 | 5,463 | 152,000 | 2,800 | 163,000 | 5,100 |
| Assam. . . . | 172,356 | 2,825 | 121,000 | 2,500 | 268,000 | 5,000 |
| Bihar . . . . | 708,018 | 11,643 | 632,000 | 7,200 | 334,000 | 9,800 |
| Bombay. . . | 201,402 | 1,575 | 87,000 | 1,200 | 66,000 | 2,000 |
| Delhi . . . . | 117,651 | 1,023 | 139,000 | 1,100 | 148,000 | 2,100 |
| Gujarat . . . | 229,220 | 4,529 | 226,000 | 4,200 | 210,000 | 4,400 |
| Himachal . . | 14,175 | 126 | 16,000 | 521 | 7,000 | 41 |
| Kerala. . . . | 193,296 | 1,926 | 174,000 | 2,000 | 156,000 | 1,400 |
| Maharashtra. | 408,904 | 4,430 | 319,000 | 6,417 | . . . | . . . |
| Madhya Pradesh . . | 228,688 | 3,976 | 283,000 | 4,900 | 212,000 | 5,100 |
| Mysore . . | 195,934 | 2,615 | 328,000 | 4,600 | 200,000 | 4,400 |
| Punjab . . . | 521,531 | 6,245 | 331,000 | 4,600 | 201,000 | 4,700 |
| Rajasthan . . | 438,122 | 7,402 | 503,000 | 9,140 | 225,000 | 4,000 |
| Tamilnad . . | 227,135 | 3,336 | 16,000[a] | . . . | 10,000[a] | 848[a] |
| Utkal. . . . | 232,188 | 2,596 | 156,000 | 1,600 | 33,000[a] | 550[a] |
| Uttar Pradesh | 1,194,968 | 8,816 | 643,000 | 9,200 | 162,000 | 4,200 |
| W. Bengal . . | 452,761 | 7,296 | 383,000 | 5,900 | 159,000 | 4,100 |
| Total . . . | 6,191,198 | 76,403 | 4,510,000 | 68,000 | 2,554,000 | 57,739 |

(note incomplete figures for some states)

[a] Apparently incomplete.

SOURCES:
1955 membership figures adapted from Susanne Hoeber Rudolph, *The Action Arm of the Indian National Congress: The Pradesh Congress Committee* (working paper), Center for International Studies, M.I.T., March 21, 1955. Original source given as M. P. Bhargava, Permanent Secretary to the AICC office in letter to the author, February 25, 1955.

1957 figures copied by the author from Congress membership figures in the AICC office in November 1962.

1959 figures adapted from *Indian National Congress: Report of the General Secretaries*, January, December 1960.

## TABLE 6
### CONGRESS PARTY MEMBERSHIP, 1960–62, BY STATES

| | 1960 | | 1961 | | 1962 | |
|---|---|---|---|---|---|---|
| | Primary | Active | Primary | Active | Primary | Active |
| Andhra . . . | 667,872 | 11,167 | 1,094,713 | 17,618 | 223,017 | 8,904 |
| Assam. . . . | 196,114 | 3,285 | 312,765 | 5,782 | 137,261 | 3,158 |
| Bihar . . . . | 381,460 | 2,038 | 1,092,306 | 15,382 | 118,733 | 4,087 |
| Bombay. . . | 86,600 | 2,296 | 181,700 | 1,669 | 22,855 | 1,499 |
| Delhi . . . . | 67,500 | 1,283 | 252,489 | 2,520 | 30,118 | 1,141 |
| Gujarat . . . | 149,884 | 2,878 | 352,605 | 6,012 | 104,713 | 2,853 |
| Himachal . . | 5,982 | 74 | 10,372 | 184 | 11,540 | 225 |
| Kerala. . . . | 408,862 | 6,103 | 260,180 | 3,504 | 493,664 | 6,847 |
| Madhya Pradesh . . | 280,232 | 5,974 | 728,667 | 12,090 | 84,823 | 2,987[a] |
| Maharashtra. | 737,039 | 10,883 | 597,304 | 11,425 | 410,340 | 7,825 |
| Manipur. . . | . . . | . . . | . . . | . . . | 19,308 | 210 |
| Mysore . . . | 292,894 | 5,522 | 478,545 | 8,896 | 176,748 | 4,167 |
| Pondicherry . | . . . | . . . | 10,320 | | 10,320 | . . . |
| Punjab . . . | 421,176 | 7,760 | 842,908 | 12,937 | 130,549 | 4,072 |
| Rajasthan . . | 151,556 | 3,635 | 547,542 | 8,447 | . . . | . . . |
| Tamilnad . . | 57,300 | 2,960 | 369,727 | 4,432 | 2,800 | 750 |
| Utkal . . . . | 30,769 | 640 | 195,954 | 2,069 | 44,216 | 955 |
| Uttar Pradesh | 516,757 | 10,006 | 1,700,925 | 19,111 | 131,448 | 4,100 |
| West Bengal . | 229,779 | 4,775 | 428,983 | 6,440 | 222,669 | 3,422 |
| Total . . . | 4,644,436 | 74,436 | 9,458,005 | 138,518 | 4,291,459 | 44,168 |

[a] Incomplete.
SOURCE: G. B. Patki, Permanent Secretary to the AICC, in a letter to the author, September 4, 1965.

## TABLE 7
### Congress Party Membership, 1963–64, by States

| | 1963 | | 1964 | |
|---|---|---|---|---|
| | Primary | Active | Primary | Active |
| Andaman. . . . . | 3,000 | 200 | . . . . | . . . . |
| Andhra. . . . . . | 142,785 | 5,583 | . . . . | . . . . |
| Assam . . . . . . | 156,866 | 3,599 | 323,659 | 5,423 |
| Bihar. . . . . . . | 98,211 | 4,788 | 296,345 | 4,611 |
| Bombay . . . . . | 37,749 | 2,499 | 142,737 | 2,436 |
| Delhi. . . . . . . | 76,995 | 2,877 | 95,804 | 1,055 |
| Goa . . . . . . . | 31,740 | 543 | . . . . | . . . . |
| Gujarat. . . . . . | 143,051 | 3,182[a] | 189,316 | 2,261 |
| Himachal. . . . . | 10,636 | 291 | 37,586 | 720[a] |
| Kerala . . . . . . | 255,889 | 4,051 | . . . . | . . . . |
| Madhya Pradesh. . | 78,744 | 3,931 | 313,863 | 4,919 |
| Maharashtra . . . | 425,255 | 8,511 | 750,000 | 11,500 |
| Manipur . . . . . | 17,239 | 275 | 38,324 | 525 |
| Mysore. . . . . . | 160,000 | 3,650 | 190,563 | 3,929[a] |
| Punjab. . . . . . | 300,904 | 6,134 | 545,197 | 8,393 |
| Rajasthan . . . . | 102,017 | 2,265 | 83,149 | 1,461 |
| Tamilnad. . . . . | 191,500 | 4,400 | . . . . | . . . . |
| Tripura. . . . . . | 16,125 | 67 | 69,775 | 1,239 |
| Utkal . . . . . . | 29,370 | 858 | 98,559 | 1,005 |
| Uttar Pradesh. . . | 144,005 | 5,972 | 1,181,186 | 11,663 |
| West Bengal . . . | 253,402 | 3,912 | 281,145 | 4,354 |
| Total. . . . . . | 2,023,664 | 52,238 | 4,637,208 | 65,494 |

Source: G. B. Patki, Permanent Secretary to the AICC, in a letter to the author, September 4, 1965

[a] Incomplete.


## TABLE 8
### National Congress Party Membership, 1955–64

| | Primary | Active |
|---|---|---|
| 1955 . . . . . . . . . . . . . | 6,191,198 | 76,403 |
| 1957 . . . . . . . . . . . . . | 4,510,000 | 68,000 |
| 1959 . . . . . . . . . . . . . | 2,554,000 | 57,739 |
| 1960 . . . . . . . . . . . . . | 4,644,436 | 74,436 |
| 1961 . . . . . . . . . . . . . | 9,458,005 | 138,518 |
| 1962 . . . . . . . . . . . . . | 4,291,459 | 44,168 |
| 1963 . . . . . . . . . . . . . | 2,023,664 | 52,238 |
| 1964 . . . . . . . . . . . . . | 4,637,208 | 65,494 |

Note: The variations in *primary* membership reflect partly the aggressiveness with which the party signed up millions of members during the year and partly intra-party disputes which led to the wholesale fabrication of membership figures by factions seeking to increase their votes for party offices. The variations in *active* membership are more apparent than real. Putting 1961 aside — an election year — the range is small. It is even smaller when we make adjustments for the unreported states and for states whose data is incomplete. If we make these adjustments, the annual membership figure ranges from a low of approximately 50,000 in 1962 to a high of around 75,000 in 1955, 1960, and 1964.

# BIBLIOGRAPHY: THE CONGRESS PARTY

This study is based upon three sources: (1) interviews, (2) unpublished local records, (3) published reports by government, the Congress party, and scholars. I have tried to avoid burdening the text with excessive footnoting and have instead prepared extensive bibliographies for each of the parts. Each describes the number and kinds of persons interviewed and the published and unpublished sources utilized.

Since I have been primarily concerned with studying how Congress functions at the district level, most of the interviews were conducted within the districts and the documents selected were those providing data either on the local Congress party or on the economic, cultural, and social environment in the district within which the party operated. Approximately 240 interviews of an intensive nature were conducted within five districts between July, 1961, and December, 1962. Though these were largely with Congressmen — from members of parliament to party cadres — some of the interviews were with members of the bureaucracy, opposition politicians, and journalists. In the bibliography at the end of each part I have indicated how many persons were interviewed in each district and who they were. In addition to these intensive district interviews, there were also brief encounters and discussions with hundreds of other local persons — villagers, party workers, petty bureaucrats — who are not referred to in the text but who provided me with an invaluable "feel" for local politics.

In the bibliographies I have also indicated the kinds of local documents which I have found most useful for the study of the districts. These vary of course from district to district. The most valuable have

been the membership records made available to me by the District Congress Committees in Belgaum and Kaira. Four of the DCCs — Calcutta was the exception — generously permitted me to look at their files which included correspondence and reports of the activities of auxiliary bodies. A third local source has been election data. While the over-all results for each parliamentary and assembly constituency is published by the Election Commission in New Delhi, the results for each polling station is available only in the files of the government returning officers within the districts. Though these results are public information, they are deposited in different government files throughout the district and are difficult to trace. Many of the reports are, however, in the district collector's office, and it is common for candidates to maintain a complete list of the results in each polling station within their own constituency. This village voting data can be matched with demographic data available in the census. In this study such data were available for Kaira, Belgaum, and parts of Guntur and Madurai. Similar data was available for municipal elections in Calcutta and Madurai. For this study I have made limited use of these data, since a thorough analysis would require a substantial volume in itself and would lead us into the complex and larger area of Indian voting behavior.

I have also found useful the reports of election tribunals established to inquire into election disputes, reports of local government bodies — especially panchayat samitis, zilla parishads, and municipal corporations — and that invaluable literature published by caste associations, candidates for public office, political parties, philanthropic bodies, and religious sects classified by librarians as ephemera.

### The Nationalist Movement

There is no standard account of the history of the nationalist movement before 1947 covering all important aspects of the movement. There is an official history of the party written by Pattabhi Sitaramayya, *The History of the Indian National Congress* (Bombay: Padma Publications, 1946–47), dealing with the party at the national level. There is also a well-known account by Nehru, *Discovery of India* (New York: Doubleday, 1959). Several state governments have appointed freedom committees which are preparing official histories of the nationalist movements in each of the states. There is also a large number of official reports on the movement, the most interesting and famous of which is the *Sedition Commit-*

*tee Report* of 1918, which describes the movement in its terrorist phase and gives considerable information on personnel.

There are many biographies of Congress leaders; for a listing of these and other historical accounts, one might turn to *South Asia: An Introductory Bibliography*, edited by Maureen L. P. Patterson and Ronald B. Inden (Chicago: University of Chicago Press, 1962), especially Section D2 on political development from 1861 to 1949. There is a vast literature on and by Gandhi. The important items are cited in the Patterson-Inden bibliography and in Joan Bondurant's *Conquest of Violence: The Gandhian Philosophy of Conflict* (Princeton: Princeton University Press, 1958). On Gandhi's disciple Vinoba, see *Vinoba and Bhoodan: Bibliography* (New Delhi: Jagdish Saran Sharma, 1956).

The most comprehensive bibliography ever published on the Congress party before independence is Jagdish Saran Sharma, *Indian National Congress: A Descriptive Bibliography of India's Struggle for Freedom* (Delhi: S. Chand, 1959). Another useful bibliography is Patrick Wilson, *Government and Politics of India and Pakistan,* 1885–1955 (Berkeley and Los Angeles: University of California Press, 1956), especially pages 110–23; this bibliography has a particularly useful list of Indian National Congress documents.

Among the most useful scholarly accounts are the following: Bruce Tiebout McCully, *English Education and the Origins of Indian Nationalism* (New York: Columbia University Press, 1940), which covers the development of nationalist organizations to the founding of the Indian National Congress in 1885; Robert I. Crane, "The Leadership of the Congress Party," in *Leadership and Political Institutions in India,* edited by Richard L. Park and Irene Tinker (Princeton: Princeton University Press, 1959), which deals with the movement from its terrorist phase at the turn of the century through to the 1930's; and P. C. Ghosh, *The Development of the Indian National Congress, 1892–1909* (Calcutta: Firma K. L. Mukhopadhyay, 1960); and Gopal Krishna, "The Development of the Indian National Congress as a Mass Organization, 1918–1923," *The Journal of Asian Studies* 25 (May, 1966): 413–30. A general account of the movement from the viewpoint of intellectual history is Stephen Northrup Hay's "Modern India and Pakistan," in William T. de Bary, editor, *Sources of Indian Tradition* (New York: Columbia University Press, 1958).

Source materials for the study of the pre-independence national movement are available in the National Archives in New Delhi and in the various record offices in Madras, Bombay, and Calcutta. There are also special collections available in smaller libraries, such as those of the All

India Congress Committee, the Indian Council of World Affairs, and the Diwan Chand Political Information Bureau (now under the council) in New Delhi; the Gokhale Institute of Politics and Economics and the Kesari Library in Poona; and the Sarat Bose Academy and of course the national library in Calcutta.

In England, materials can be found at the British Museum, the Colonial Office and Commonwealth Relations Office Joint Library, and the Library of the School of Oriental and African Studies.

## The Congress Party: Post-Independence

It is surprising how little has been written on the Congress party since independence, particularly in view of its great importance in the country's political life. Several studies of organizational units of the Congress party were prepared in 1955 by Susanne Rudolph for the Center for International Studies at Massachusetts Institute of Technology. These include: *The Action Arm of the Indian National Congress: The Pradesh Congress Committee*; *The All-India Congress Committee and the Annual Congress Session*; and *The Working Committee of the Indian Congress Party: Its Forms, Organization, and Personnel*.

In addition, there are three studies by students of mine at the University of Chicago: Marcus Franda, "The Organizational Development of India's Congress Party," *Pacific Affairs* 35 (Fall, 1962): 248–60; Baldev Raj Nayar, *Minority Politics in the Punjab: Diversity and Political Order* (Princeton: Princeton University Press, 1966); and Paul R. Brass, *Factional Politics in an Indian State: The Congress Party in Uttar Pradesh* (Berkeley and Los Angeles: University of California Press, 1965). Other studies include: Susanne Rudolph, *Some Aspects of Congress Land Reform Policy* (Cambridge: Center for International Studies, Massachusetts Institute of Technology, 1957); Myron Weiner, "Prospects of India's Congress Party," *Far Eastern Survey* 23 (1954): 182–88; Rajni Kothari, "The Congress System in India," *Asian Survey*, 4 (Dec., 1964): 116–173; and Gopal Krishna, "One Party Dominance — Development and Trends," *Perspectives, Supplement to the Indian Journal of Public Administration* 12 (January–March, 1966): 1–65. Shortly before the 1967 elections, there appeared a number of articles and doctoral dissertations dealing with some aspects of the Congress party. For a list of some of the more useful of these studies, see W. H. Morris-Jones, "The Indian Congress Party: A Dilemma of Dominance," *Modern Asian Studies* 1 (1967), 109–32. There

are also many studies of the three Indian elections which contain analyses of the Congress party. For a list of these, see the bibliography in Myron Weiner and Rajni Kothari, eds., *Indian Voting Behavior* (Calcutta: Firma K. L. Mukhopadhyay, 1965). For the Congress point of view of elections, see *Congress and the Second General Elections* (New Delhi: INC, 1957); Sadiq Ali, *The General Elections, 1957, A Survey* (New Delhi: AICC, 1959); and *The Pilgrimage and After: The Story of How the Congress Fought and Won the General Elections* (New Delhi: AICC, 1952).

*Primary Sources: Periodicals and Reports*

There are a number of regular publications of the All India Congress Committee in New Delhi through which one can trace any aspect of Congress party development since independence. These include: *AICC Economic Review*, a fortnightly journal, and the *Congress Bulletin*, which contains minutes of the Working Committee meetings, official party resolutions, circulars issued by the AICC to Pradesh Congress Committees and other subordinate bodies, and other internal party communications. The *Bulletin* is published irregularly, three or four times a year. A useful index to the circulars printed in the *Congress Bulletin* is Jagdish Saran Sharma, *AICC Circulars: A Descriptive Bibliography* (New Delhi: INC, 1956).

Perhaps the most valuable party documents are the *Reports of the General Secretary*. These reports have been published annually since independence and contain descriptions of almost all of the important developments in the national party organization, accounts of the elections, occasional reports on membership statistics, descriptions of the sections of the AICC, and, accounts of Congress party activities in each of the states.

Finally, the Congress party publishes the speech of the president to the annual Congress party session. These speeches generally focus on the state of India but will sometimes contain comments on the country's political developments as seen by the Congress party presidents. In addition, there is generally published a volume on each of the annual sessions of the INC which contains articles on Congress policies and organization by both national and regional leaders. See, for example, *66th Session Indian National Congress, Souvenir*, Ramlal Parikh, editor (Bhavnagar:

Reception Committee, 1961); and *Indian National Congress, Souvenir of the 65th Session* (Bangalore: Reception Committee, 1960).

A number of other journals regularly contain reports on the Congress party. Of these, two are of special interest: the *Congress Forum,* published by a left group within the Congress party, and the *Indian Recorder and Digest,* published by the Diwan Chand Institute of National Affairs and containing reports on activities within Congress and other political parties.

## Party Organization

There have been a number of Congress party documents concerned with the internal organization of the party. A number of these were published around the time of independence when the party was in the throes of reorganization, but many of the questions raised then have persisted and are discussed in party publications. These include: S. K. Patil, *The Indian National Congress: A Case for Its Reorganization* (Bombay: Padma Publications, 1945); Acharya J. B. Kripalani, *The Indian National Congress* (Bombay: Vora and Co., 1946); Acharya J. B. Kripalani, *The Future of the Congress* (Bombay: Hind Kitabs, 1948); N. V. Rajkumar, *Development of the Congress Constitution* (New Delhi: AICC, 1959); P. P. Lakshman, *Congress and Labour Movement in India* (Allahabad: AICC, 1947); M. K. Gandhi, *Congress and Its Future,* compiled by R. K. Prabhu (Navajivan Publishing House, Ahmedabad, 1960).

Others are: *Report of the Reorganization Committee* (Bangalore: INC, 1960); K. Hanumanthaiya, *Report on Congress Constitution* (Bangalore: INC, 1959); M. V. Ramana Rao, *Development of the Congress Constitution* (New Delhi: AICC, 1958); *Indian National Congress, Proceedings of the Meetings of the Presidents and Secretaries of the Pradesh Congress Committees* (New Delhi, 1955); *All India Congress Committee, Report of the Constructive Workers' Conference, Amritsar, February 7, 1956* (New Delhi: AICC, 1956).

See also: Shriman Narayan Agarwal, *Constructive Programme for Congressmen* (New Delhi: AICC, 1953); *Congress Party in Parliament of India, Secretary General's Address at Indore* (New Delhi, 1952); *Constitution of the Indian National Congress* (as amended at the Bhavnagar Session of the Indian National Congress in January, 1961) (New Delhi: AICC, 1961); *Handbook for Congressmen* (Bangalore: Central Publicity Board, INC, 1951); *Indian National Congress Rules* (New Delhi: AICC,

1960); *Padayatra; A Report* (New Delhi: AICC 1959), *Programme for Constructive Work* (New Delhi: AICC, n.d.); Surindar Suri, "Problems of Congress Organization," *Indian Affairs Record* 6 (June, 1960); *Training and Education Scheme for Congress Workers* (1960); Whips Conference at Indore, Congress Party in Parliament of India, (New Delhi, 1952).

## Party Ideology and Public Policy

Many publications reflect the Congress party position on public policy questions. These are expressed in official AICC resolutions, the many pamphlets published by the Congress party in parliament, the special reports of subcommittees appointed by the AICC, and various election tracts. Among these are: *Background of India's Foreign Policy, Resolutions* (Bangalore: INC, 1952); Congress Planning Sub-Committee, *Report of the Ooty Seminar* (May 30–June 5, 1959) (New Delhi: AICC, 1959); *Congress and the Problem of Minorities, Resolutions Adopted by the Congress, the Working Committee and the AICC since 1885 and Connected Matters* (Allahabad, 1947); *Congress and the Second General Elections* (New Delhi: AICC, 1957); *Election Manifesto, 1957* (Delhi: AICC, 1957); *Election Manifesto, 1962* (New Delhi: AICC, 1962); *Our Immediate Programme,* (New Delhi: AICC, 1950); *Parliament Supervision over State Undertakings, Report of the Sub-Committee of the Congress Party in Parliament* (New Delhi: Congress Party in Parliament, 1959); *Report of the Congress Agrarian Reforms Committee* (New Delhi: AICC, 1949); *Report of the Congress Village Panchayat Committee* (New Delhi: AICC, 1954); *Report of the Congress Planning Sub-Committee* (New Delhi: AICC, 1959); *Report of the National Integration Committee* (New Delhi: AICC, 1959); *Resolutions on Economic Policy and Programme, 1924–54* (New Delhi: INC, 1954; *Resolutions in Economic Policy and Programme 1955–56,* (New Delhi: INC, 1956; *Resolutions on Foreign Policy, 1947–57*(New Delhi: AICC, 1957); *Resolutions on Goa* (New Delhi: AICC, 1956); *Resolutions* (New Delhi: AICC, 1953, 1954, 1955, 1956); *Resolutions, INC, 56th session, 1950, 57th session, 1951, 58th session, 1953, 59th session, 1954, 60th session, 1955; Indian National Congress, Resolutions, Sadashivanagar (Bangalore),* (New Delhi: AICC, 1960); *Indian National Congress, Resolutions, Sardar Nagar (Bhavnagar)* (New Delhi: AICC, 1961); *What Congress Fights For: Election Manifesto of the Indian National Congress, 1945–46* (Bombay: INC, Central Election Board, 1945); *What Congress Stands for: Election Manifesto,* (New Delhi: AICC, 1951); *The Socialist Pattern, in Terms of the Con-*

*gress Resolutions* (revised and enlarged) (Bombay: INC, 1945); *Resolutions on States Reorganization, 1920–1956* (New Delhi: AICC, n.d.); *Congress Planning Sub-Committee, Ooty Seminar, Papers Discussed* (May 30–June 5, 1959 (New Delhi: AICC, 1959).

There is still another group of publications written by Congressmen on policy or ideological matters but which do not necessarily reflect the official party position. Among the most important of these are: Humayun Kabir, *Congress Ideology* (New Delhi: AICC, 1951); Sadiq Ali, *The Congress Ideology and Programme* (New Delhi: AICC, 1958); U. N. Dhebar, *Towards Constructive Revolution* (New Delhi: INC. 1956); U. N. Dhebar, *Towards a Socialist Co-Operative Commonwealth* (New Delhi: INC, 1957); Shriman Narayan, *Towards a Socialist Economy* (New Delhi: INC, 1956); Jawaharlal Nehru, *Towards a Socialistic Order* (New Delhi: AICC, 1956); and Sadiq Ali, *Towards Socialist Thinking in Congress* (New Delhi: AICC, 1961).

See also H. D. Malaviya, *Concept of Socialist India as Conceived by the Indian National Congress,* mimeo; *The Congress President and the Laski Institute* (full text of the correspondence between Shri Reddy, Shri Nehru, Shri Mavalankar and others) (Ahmedabad: Harold Laski Institute of Political Science, 1961); Shankarrao Deo, *The New Congress* (New Delhi: AICC, 1949); U. N. Dhebar, *The Role of Panchayats in New India,* (New Delhi: INC, 1957); *Is India a Party State?* (based on a correspondence between Nehru and the Institute of Political and Social Studies) (Calcutta, 1961); Humayun Kabir, "Essentials of the Ideology," *Souvenir, 66th Indian National Congress* (Bhavnagar, 1961); Keep the Flame Alive (thesis by a group of Congress workers) (1957); G. V. Mavalankar, *A Great Experiment* (New Delhi: AICC, 1951); *Nehru-Jayaprakash Talks* (Bombay: Praja Socialist Party, 1953); *Jawaharlal Nehru and Academician Yudin, on the Basic Approach* (being the full text of Nehru's note, "The Basic Approach," in *AICC Economic Review* [August 15, 1958], and Yudin's reply, "Can We Accept Nehru's Basic Approach?" in *World Marxist Review* [December, 1958] (New Delhi: Communist Party, 1958); Jawaharlal Nehru, *Letters to the PCC Presidents* (New Delhi: NC, 1955); Congress Socialist Forum, *Nehru Must Give the Lead* (New Delhi: Kitab Mahal, 1960); Shriman Narayan, *A Plea for Ideological Clarity* (New Delhi: INC, 1957); Gulzari Lal Nanda, *Progress of Land Reforms in India* (New Delhi: INC, 1957); T. N. Singh, *Public Sector: Its Need and Justification* (New Delhi: AICC, 1961); Shriman Narayan, *Socialistic Pattern of Society* (revised and enlarged) (New Delhi: INC, 1955).

*Auxiliary Bodies*

There is a substantial literature published by the auxiliary bodies of the Congress party. These bodies include the Youth Congress, the INTUC, the Congress Seva Dal, the Women's Wing. The INTUC publishes an annual report describing its activities and containing its resolutions. In addition, there is an annual report of the general secretary of the INTUC, the annual presidential address, and a fortnightly magazine called the *Trade Union Record.*

The Youth Congress publishes a monthly magazine called the *Youth Congress.* In addition, the following reports have been published by the AICC dealing with YC affairs: *The Fourth All India Convention of the Youth Congress Outline and Programme, Jaipur (Rajasthan) December 24–27, 1960* (New Delhi: AICC); *Fourth All India Convention of the Youth Congress Annual Report, Jaipur (December 24, 1960); Reports of the All India Youth Camp* (New Delhi: Youth Department, AICC, 1959); *Vision of Young India, Baroda* (New Delhi: Youth Department, AICC, 1958); *Youth Camps: Information for Congressmen* (New Delhi: AICC, 1955); *Youth Congress – A Handbook* (New Delhi: AICC, 1956); *Youth Congress: Model Constitution, Structure, Activities* (New Delhi: AICC, n.d.); *Youth Congress – Structure, Objects, Programme,* (New Delhi, AICC, 1958); U. N. Dhebar, *Youth and National Reconstruction* (New Delhi: INC, 1956); *Youth and Nation-Building, Report of the AICC Youth Training Camp* (New Delhi: AICC, 1955).

The following publications deal with the activities of the Congress Seva Dal: *Congress Seva Dal: Constitution and Rules, Manual 1* (New Delhi: AICC, 1959); *Congress Seval Dal: Demonstrations, Manual IX* (New Delhi: Navin Press, 1960); *Congress Seval Dal: The Organization, Manual 2,* revised fifth edition (New Delhi: AICC, 1961); *Technique and Methods of Training in Congress Seva Dal* (New Delhi: AICC, n.d.).

On the Women's Wing, see *Constructive Programme for Women: A Handbook* (New Delhi: INC, 1958); and *Women's Wing of the Congress* (New Delhi: Women's Department, AICC, 1958).

# PART II. SEGMENTATION AND POLITICAL PARTICIPATION: KAIRA DISTRICT

# 4. THE CONGRESS PARTY OF KAIRA

> What we are witnessing is the passing of power not from
> a few to the many but from an enlightened few to a slightly
> larger class uninhibited by those constraints on thought and
> behavior that come from a liberal, rational, humanistic edu-
> cation. If that is democracy, India has it.[1]

Our first case describes the Congress party organization in a predominantly rural district located midway between the cities of Baroda and
Ahmedabad in the state of Gujarat in northwestern India. In one respect
it is the least typical of the five cases, since it is the only one in which the
Congress party suffered an overwhelming electoral defeat while the research was being conducted. We shall take advantage of the fact that
this is a deviant case: by examining the circumstances of the party's defeat, we may better understand why the party wins elsewhere.

I selected the Congress party in Kaira as, ironically, an example of a
well-organized, highly successful party unit in one of the more prosperous
rural areas of the country. Other Congress units in the state often pointed
to the Kaira Congress unit as a model district organization with dedicated party workers, comparatively little internal dissension, and considerable popularity. In the 1957 elections Congress won eight of the district's thirteen assembly seats and one of the two parliamentary seats,
with 50 per cent of the total vote, several percentage points above the
national average. Earlier, in the 1952 elections, Congress did even better,

[1] Flibbertigibbet (the pseudonym of a Bengali journalist), "The Euthanasia of
English," *Economic Weekly* (May 18, 1963), p. 807.

winning both parliamentary seats and all thirteen assembly seats, with a total vote of 62 per cent for parliament and 53 per cent for the state assembly.

However, during my stay in the district it became apparent that Congress was losing its hold upon a large section of the local populace, that it could very well lose the forthcoming elections, and that these developments were related to some important changes occurring in the social system within Kaira district. The capacity of the party to gain new recruits, to win support, and to cope with internal party conflicts were all related to the ways in which the party leadership coped with — or, more precisely, failed to cope with — these social changes.

In Kaira two social groups — one of which felt that its political power was not commensurate with its status, and the other seeking to raise its social status through politics — joined together to defeat the Congress party and the social groups which dominated it. Why these groups organized, why the Congress party was unable to adapt itself readily to this new situation, and what the consequences were for the state and party as a whole became the central problems of my field research.

To understand why the party failed to absorb new political aspirants, we found it necessary to see who controlled the party and what their notions were of how to run the party and for what purposes and, second, to see who the new aspirants were, how they organized, and what they wanted.

TABLE 9
ELECTION RESULTS IN KAIRA DISTRICT

| | SEATS WON | | | NUMBER OF VOTES | | | PERCENTAGE OF VOTES | | |
|---|---|---|---|---|---|---|---|---|---|
| | 1952 | 1957 | 1962 | 1952 | 1957 | 1962 | 1952 | 1957 | 1962 |
| Legislative Assembly | | | | | | | | | |
| Congress. . | 13 | 8 | 5 | 274,118 | 310,725 | 232,217 | 52.6 | 50.0 | 43.8 |
| Swatantra . | . . | . . | 10 | . . . | . . . | 264,818 | . . . | . . . | 50.0 |
| Kisan Mazdoor Praja party | . . | . . | . . | 158,764 | . . . | . . . | 30.5 | . . . | . . . |
| Independents | . . | 5 | . . | 47,532 | 310,806 | 23,150 | 9.1 | 50.0 | 4.4 |
| Other parties | . . | . . | . . | 40,392 | . . . | 9,921 | 7.8 | . . . | 1.3 |
| Total . . | 13 | 13 | 15 | 520,806 | 621,531 | 530,106 | 100.0 | 100.0 | 100.0 |
| Parliament | | | | | | | | | |
| Congress. . | 2 | 1 | 0 | 283,033 | 267,351 | 267,876 | 62.1 | 50.6 | 45.6 |
| Swatantra . | . . | . . | 2 | . . . | . . . | 303,228 | . . . | . . . | 51.7 |
| Kisan Mazdoor Praja party | . . | . . | . . | 77,514 | . . . | . . . | 16.7 | . . . | . . . |
| Independents | . . | 1 | . . | 102,652 | 261,156 | 15,765 | 22.2 | 49.4 | 2.7 |
| Total . . | 2 | 2 | 2 | 463,199 | 538,507 | 587,869 | 100.0 | 100.0 | 100.0 |

Two themes, which we shall develop at greater length, emerged from this inquiry. One is that the social relationship between the several politically aspiring castes changed as they entered politics. As we know from studies of politics elsewhere, social mobility is an important element in the quest for political power; here we were able to see how political mobility served in turn to modify the system of social stratification. In particular, caste politics was itself transformed when it became interwoven with competitive party politics. In this case study, therefore, we shall have as much to say about the way in which political parties affect the social system as we will about the way in which the social system affects the Congress party.

The second theme which emerged from this inquiry is that the peculiarly segmented character of the Indian social system reduced the danger to the Congress party in the state when the district party organization failed to adapt itself to the demands of new participants. As we shall explain in more detail later, the Congress defeat in Kaira did not seriously weaken the party organization in neighboring districts, since the segmented character of the Indian social system tends to quarantine local political breakdowns. The result, as we shall see, is that even within the district itself the party has a high recuperative capacity and there is good reason to expect Congress to do better in subsequent elections in Kaira.

## The Setting

Kaira is a densely populated district with nearly two million persons in approximately 2,600 square miles. It is in the state of Gujarat, which was formed in May, 1960, out of the old state of Bombay. The new state has 72,000 square miles and a population of about sixteen million. In 1962, when my investigations took place, Gujarat was having its first statewide elections. Of course Gujarat had previously participated in the state and national elections as part of Bombay state. In 1952 the Gujarat region of Bombay elected a solid Congress party majority to the state legislative assembly and to the national parliament. In 1957, when there was agitation in the Gujarat region for the partition of Bombay, Congress did not do so well as in 1952, though even then Congress carried the Gujarat region easily. In 1962 Congress had the same success as in 1957, so it was with some surprise that Congress did badly in Kaira district.

Gujarati Congressmen are well known throughout India, and it is not uncommon for many Indians to say that the country has been governed largely by leaders from Gujarat and Uttar Pradesh, birthplaces of Nehru,

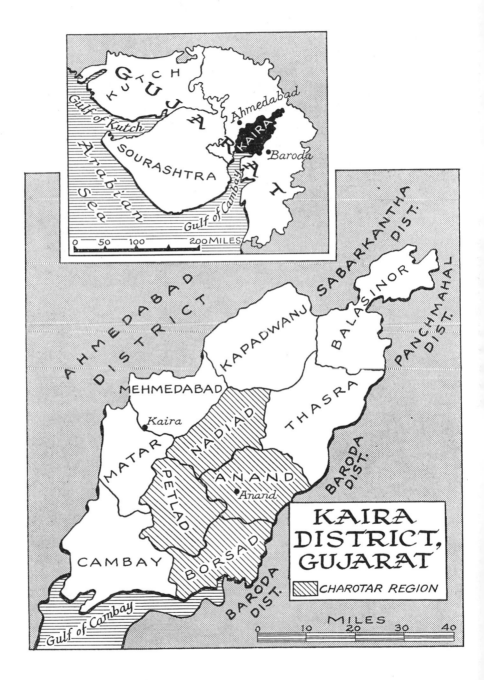

Shastri, and Indira Gandhi. Sardar Vallabhbhai Patel, the first home minister of India and a powerful Congress party leader whose influence in the development of Congress in the early post-independence years we have discussed in a preceding chapter, is a native of Kaira district. Morarji Desai, former finance minister who has often been described as the leader of the conservative element in Congress, is a Gujarati. U. N. Dhebar, the Congressman who succeeded Nehru as Congress president, is from Saurashtra, a region which is now incorporated into Gujarat. Other members of the cabinet, the Congress Working Committee, and several past presidents of Congress come from Gujarat. Certainly the most famous Gujarati Congressman is Mahatma Gandhi.

Gujarat became prominent in national politics at the end of the First World War when Gandhi became the leader of the nationalist movement. Gandhi's advocacy of non-violent civil disobedience won support throughout the country, but it was especially in Gujarat that the idea was most appealing. The Vaishnavite and Jain religious traditions, from which Gandhi drew many of his notions about non-violence, are traditions which have historic roots and great appeal in the entire Gujarat region. It is therefore no surprise that so many in this region found Gandhi's ideas compatible with both their religious and political sentiments. Gandhi's constructive work program, for example, was enthusiastically adopted by Gujaratis. In the early twenties young villagers and townsmen, generally from more prosperous and educated families, flocked to the Gandhian banner and began to organize peasants, students, and factory workers. The Congress organization in Gujarat became one of the best organized, most effective nationalist units in the country. Gujarati leaders, increasingly known for their nationalist fervor, their devotion to Gandhi, and — of great importance — their organizational skill, played an important role in building the Congress organization elsewhere in the country.

Kaira was a prototypical unit in the Congress party of Gujarat.[2] It had a large number of four-anna primary members and a smaller number of effective active workers who pursued the twin programs of civil disobedience and village constructive work. The nationalist movement in Kaira was not episodic but continuous, and its continuity rested upon a superbly managed organization.

[2] One of the earliest civil disobedience movements under nationalist leadership was organized in Kaira in 1918 to demand that the government postpone the collection of land revenue as a result of widespread crop failures. The agitation and the relationship established between Sardar Patel and Gandhi, both of whom participated in the movement, are described by Narhari D. Parikh in *Sardar Vallabhbhai Patel* (Ahmedabad: Navajivan Publishing House, 1953), pp. 48–89.

*Social Organization and Congress*

In the 1962 elections in Kaira district Congress was badly defeated by the newly formed Swatantra party. In Kaira the Swatantra party, nationally known as a pro-business, free enterprise, conservative party, drew its strength from an organization known as the Kshatriya Sabha. This organization is made up of a number of castes which classified themselves under the classical rubric of "Kshatriya" ("warrior"). The Congress party in turn drew its strength predominantly from those castes which are generally described as the dominant castes (in power, not numbers) in the district: the Banias, the Brahmins, and — most important of all — the Patidars. Congress and Swatantra leaders frankly describe the 1962 elections as a clash between the Patidars and the Kshatriyas, and although that is not completely accurate it is important that the political participants saw the struggle in these terms.

Before 1947 the Kshatriyas played no important role in district politics. There is some disagreement locally as to how important they were in the 1957 elections, but, in any event, in that year the Kshatriya Sabha worked with the Congress party. Yet by 1962, when the Swatantra party won ten of the Kaira seats in the Gujarat legislative assembly against only five for the Congress party, there could be no doubt that it had become an independent, powerful force in the district. The Swatantra victory was all the more surprising in view of the impressive organization which Congress had created in the district and of what appeared to be the impressive hold of the dominant castes on the other castes. To understand the political factors in the district, we must first turn to an examination of the social organization and the economic context within which political conflicts occurred. In the next chapter we shall attempt to show how political institutions and processes affected social organization and social relationships in the district. Here we shall focus on how society affected politics rather than how politics affected society.

Visitors to Kaira district are first struck with the extraordinary modernity of the area. "If the rest of agricultural India looks like Kaira district within the next ten or even twenty years, there will have been an agricultural revolution in this country," one visitor remarked. One sees in the villages of Kaira more brick homes than one commonly sees elsewhere in the country. Nearly every large village in Kaira district has electricity. Almost every village has a primary school, and most larger villages have high schools as well. Clock towers, libraries, large panchayat halls, dispensaries, and maternity homes are common features of many of the villages in the district. Main roads are well developed, considering that

this is, after all, a part of rural India. One sees Jeeps and trucks on the road and even tractors in the fields. Villagers have invested heavily in irrigation pumps and wells, and there are many smaller factories processing the tobacco which grows in the fields of Kaira.

For those who argue that high population density in agricultural areas may prove to be a barrier to agricultural development, Kaira district stands as a marked exception. Though there are 629 persons per square mile, the highest population concentration of all Gujarat, the land in the district is well developed and agricultural production is high. Every piece of land in the district that can be used for agricultural purposes appears to be in use, and there is great diversification of crops. There is a heavy investment in cash crops, such as cotton and tobacco, and relatively little in cereals — contrary to what one finds elsewhere in the countryside of India. As Kusum Nayar has pointed out,[3] the prosperity of Kaira is not due to the natural resources of the area but to the energy and enterprise of its agricultural population. The Patidars are a large, prosperous landholding and cultivating community who engage not only in the production of agricultural commodities but also in trade, commerce, and in the processing of their agricultural produce. The profit of the land remains in the villages, since farmers own the ginning mills, process the tobacco, produce the finished products like bidis (local cigarettes), and market their own crops as well. A half-century ago a British officer writing in the local district gazetteer described the Patidars as "the best farmers in the district, sober, quiet, industrious, and except on such special occasions as marriages, thrifty."[4]

At the turn of the century many Patidar families migrated to East and South Africa as a result of a famine in Kaira district. Many of the schools and clock towers found in the villages of Kaira were financed by the money sent home by Patidars in Africa. The readiness of Patidars to move outside their district and indeed outside the country in order to maximize their prosperity is a mark of their extraordinary mobility and enterprise. For reasons which, incidentally, have never been studied, the Patidar community is characterized by the "Protestant spirit," so often described as one of the conditions necessary for entrepreneurship.

The energies of the Patidars have been directed not only at economic enterprise but at political organization as well. They were the organizers, leaders, and followers of the nationalist movement in Kaira district. And

[3] *Blossoms in the Dust: The Human Element in Indian Development* (London: Gerald Duckworth and Co., Ltd., 1961), pp. 170–78.

[4] *Gazetteer of the Bombay Presidency,* Vol. III (Bombay: 1879) Kaira and Panch Mahals.

as we shall see shortly, they were the organizers of a network of political and economic institutions throughout the region. Before turning to the political role of the Patidars, however, let us first briefly examine their social organization.

The Patidars constitute approximately 20 per cent of the population in Kaira district, and are most numerous in talukas in the center of Kaira known as the Charotar region. The Patidars are divided into several social groups, the most important of which is the Leva Patidar group, a landholding agricultural caste living in the Charotar region. By general agreement these Patidars in Charotar are the most prestigious in the Patidar community. Hypergamy — the practice of marrying into a higher social group — is commonly practiced among the Patidars. "We take daughters from them, but we do not give," say the people of Charotar speaking of other Patidars in the surrounding areas, and their claim is recognized by others who are proud to give their daughters to the Patidars of Charotar. A Patidar within any one of the castes that make up the Patidar community may increase his social status first by increasing his personal wealth. Once he has wealth he may then begin to act as a "good man" (*saro manas*). D. F. Pocock, an English anthropologist who has studied the Patidars and from whose writings this description is largely taken, has described at length the qualities of a good man among the Patidar community.[5] A good man avoids extravagance and ostentation. Though he may have the wealth to do otherwise, he will travel to conduct his business to Baroda and Bombay city by second-class trains or even in the crowded and less comfortable third-class carriages. A good man builds a large house for his son and for his entire family. A good man will display his hospitality by feasting as large a group as he can possibly afford on the occasion of a death in the family, a marriage, or on some holy day. A good man will establish high schools in his village and support or establish welfare institutions. If the Patidar does not live in the Charotar region of Kaira or if he is not one of the Leva Patidars, he may then seek to marry his daughter into a preferred social group. For such hypergamous marriages, a Patidar will have to pay a very high dowry (paithan), and the rule is that the higher he goes the more he must pay. Hypergamy does serve the important function of facilitating a change in traditional ritual status. Since individuals can raise their status by increasing their wealth, behaving in a fashion appropriate to men of wealth, and marrying their daughters to those of higher ritual status, we thus have here a

[5] David F. Pocock, "The Hypergamy of the Patidars," *in* K. M. Kapadia, editor, *Professor Ghurye Felicitation Volume* (Bombay: Popular Book Depot, 1954), pp. 195–204.

status system which is partly ascribed and partly achieved. Moreover, here is a traditional status system which provides mobility based in the first instance upon an increase in wealth. It is for this reason perhaps that the Patidars are so enterprising in efforts to increase their wealth and will seize upon economic opportunities elsewhere in India and in the world to do so.

Two other social groups are of political and economic importance in Kaira district and have been active in the Congress party: the Banias, and the Brahmins. The Banias constitute about 4 or 5 per cent of the Hindu population, and they are themselves divided into numerous subdivisions, some seventeen in all according to the gazetteer. Some of the Banias are engaged in buying and selling cloth, grain, molasses, oil, and, in recent years, tobacco. The wealthiest are money lenders, making advances to petty village usurers, traders, merchants and the wealthy agriculturalists, and many are industrialists, government servants, and professionals. The Brahmins are reported to be about 6 per cent of the Hindu population. Most are landowners, money lenders, traders, and, especially, local government servants, doctors, lawyers, and teachers. Though elsewhere in India other social classes emulate the behavior of the Brahmins, in Kaira district the Patidars claim the status of vaisya, traditionally thought of as the mercantile class. According to local genealogists, however, the Patidars once claimed to be Kshatriyas; according to two anthropologists who have studied the Patidars, the higher esteem now given to business activities led the Patidars to change their varna.[6] Today the Patidars are proud of their vaisya status, proud of their occupation and industry, and reject the claims of both Kshatriyas and Brahmins of belonging to a higher social order. For reasons we shall explore later, the Patidars' definition of their own social status has not led them into any major clashes with the Brahmin community, though it has resulted in differences with the Rajputs.

The Congress party in Kaira district has been a vehicle for the politically minded Banias and the Brahmins. But in the main it has been the Patidars who have provided the leadership in Kaira district. As we have already indicated, Vallabhbhai Patel, a Patidar, was a major organizer of the party in the district, and the leadership of the party has remained in the hands of Patidars. During the time this study was undertaken the leading political figure in the Congress party of the district, Tribhuvandas Patel, was a Patidar, three of the Congress MLAs belonged

[6] See A. M. Shah and R. G. Shroff, "The Vahivanca Barots of Gujarat: A Caste of Genealogists and Mythographers," *in* Milton Singer, editor, *Traditional India: Structure and Change* (Philadelphia: American Folklore Society, 1959), pp. 62–63.

to the Patidar community,[7] and 45 per cent of the party cadres were Patidars.

## Congress Activities

Two ideals which characterize the Patidars — community service, and the concern for finding methods for improving one's economic well-being — fit well with the Congress party program and activities. It was the Congress party workers — mostly Patidars — who took the leadership in the early 1950's in the formation of Amul Dairy, a cooperative venture well known throughout India. Kaira has a small but substantial dairy industry as a result of the presence of a substantial number of milk-producing buffalo owned by many peasants. Congress party workers, led by Tribhuvandas Patel, organized Amul Dairy, a cooperative organization now made up of some two hundred local village dairy cooperatives. Each local unit collects the milk brought to it by the owners of buffalo. The milk is weighed and tested for fat content and then picked up by truck and sent to the large dairy near the town of Anand. There the milk is pasteurized and sent by train to Bombay city. Some of the milk is also turned into dairy products such as cheeses. The close relationship between the prominent Congressmen who built the dairy in the early 1950's and the national government made it possible for the dairy to receive assistance in the form of credit and machinery from the central government. Today Amul is one of the largest and most modern dairies in the country, with an annual income of approximately thirty-five million rupees ($7,350,000), of which one million is profit. The dairy has a fine guest house, and most ministers of the central government and of the state government have at one time or another been guests of the dairy. There is a fine technically skilled professional staff of Indian engineers, many of whom have been trained abroad. The general manager is himself a graduate of Michigan State University. Though every effort is made to separate the political aspects of the dairy from its technical performance and the technical personnel are free from political interference, politics is not far afield from the dairy.

The dairy now has some fifty thousand members in its 220 local village units. Each village cooperative employs about four persons, including a full-time secretary, a man who collects the milk and keeps the records,

[7] In the 1962 elections all of the seven Congress Patidar candidates were defeated. Of the five Congress MLAs elected, one was a Muslim, one a Harijan woman, one a Bania, and the other two Kshatriyas.

a milk tester, and a laborer to move the cans. The chairman and the secretary of each village cooperative are invariably Congressmen. The chairman of the dairy is Tribhuvandas Patel, the Congress boss of Kaira district. Though much of the expansion of the dairy comes from its own
funds, it has had to borrow from time to time from the Kaira district
cooperative bank. The director of the bank is therefore automatically a
member of the governing board of the cooperative. The bank director
is a Congressman who ran for the legislative assembly in the 1962 elections. It is the Congress workers who have organized each of the village
cooperatives and who tour areas to form new cooperative units. Local
persons view the cooperative as an institution created by the Congress
party leadership. Though the bulk of the profits from the dairy go to the
members of the village cooperatives, some of the funds are kept by the
local village cooperative; with these funds the cooperative may build a
meeting house or an office of its own or sponsor some community project.
Whenever the local village unit undertakes a new venture, Congress
leaders from the dairy elsewhere in the district are sure to give their
support to the new activity. It is clear that Amul Dairy has performed
an important economic service to the district as a whole and to its many
thousands of members. But it is also clear that the Congress party has,
understandably, reaped political rewards for its activities in the dairy.
There is of course some patronage associated with the dairy, since, as we
have noted, the village units employ hundreds of individuals locally. But,
more importantly, the fifty thousand individuals who belong to the dairy
and who profit from its activities view the Congress party as the institution responsible for the dairy's success.

The power of the Congress party in Kaira district also rests on its
control of many governmental and quasi-governmental institutions in the
district. The district local board has been under Congress control since
1925. The board controls the construction and maintenance of roads, wells,
many public buildings, dispensaries, and — above all — the school board
in Kaira district. In the early 1930's Congress also gained control over
several municipal governments in Kaira district, and today many of the
towns are run by Congressmen or by Congress supporters.

Finally, the taluka rural development boards which have the responsibility for development programs are under Congress control.

Since independence a large number of quasi-governmental institutions
have been established in Kaira district as in other districts throughout
the country. There is now a district cooperative bank, a district industrial
cooperative society, a khadi and village industries association, and a dis-

trict cooperative purchase and sales union. These are without exception controlled by individuals who belong to and generally hold positions of power in the Congress party of Kaira district.

Some mention should be made of private institutions in Kaira district and in the nearby city of Ahmedabad with which the Congress party is directly or indirectly associated. All these are Gandhian in origin and orientation and reflect Gandhi's enormous influence in Gujarat. In the capital city of Ahmedabad there are four major institutions under the auspices of the Congress party of Gujarat.

There is, first of all, Sabramati Ashram, which was started by Gandhi as a center for constructive work throughout the state. It now contains a school for Harijan children, conducts research and training programs, and maintains a handicraft program. A number of Kaira party cadres work at the Sabramati Ashram, and a number of Harijan school children from the district also attend classes there.

A second major institution under Congress auspices is the Gujarat Vidyapith, created by Gandhian supporters as a national college different from the British pattern and committed to the Gandhian ideology and work program. The Vidyapith continues in that tradition although it has gradually adopted the curriculum of the British-created colleges in India. Many of the prominent Congress leaders of Kaira district, including Tribhuvandas Patel and the daughter of Vallabhbhai Patel, Manibahen Patel, are graduates of the Vidyapith. In the past the Vidyapith has been a training center for party workers, but in recent years graduates have been going into government service as social workers in trade unions, as officers in the community development program, and as school teachers. Thus not only are a number of party workers in Kaira district graduates of the Vidyapith, but a number of local government bureaucrats have also been imbued with its Gandhian ideology and social service orientation.

A third major Congress institution in Ahmedabad is Navajivan Press, the largest Gandhian printing press in India. It publishes the entire Gandhian literature: the writings of Nehru, Patel, and other national leaders, and literature on the constructive work program of Gandhi. Over the years the press has become an important meeting place for Congress party workers, and most of its employees are Congressmen.

The Ahmedabad textile union is in some respects the most important of the Congress institutions in the city. Under Gandhi's personal leadership the workers in the textile industry were organized in a union dedicated to carrying on its operations in accordance with Gandhian ideology.

The Ahmedabad textile union has established close relations with the business community in Ahmedabad and is one of the few strong trade unions in the country capable of engaging in collective bargaining. The union devotes a large part of its activities to non-economic matters as well, sponsoring social welfare work, providing maternity care, and conducting adult education programs. It is thus very much concerned with easing the urbanization problems of the work force in the textile industry. Much of the strength of the union lies not so much in its Gandhian ideology or perhaps even in its ability to care for the economic demands of the workers — although these are both important — as in its performance of social welfare functions for the membership.

The union, the press, the college, and the Ashram all serve important functions for the party. They provide jobs for party workers, they are party training centers, and they are important instruments of propaganda. But apart from their functions they all signify the extraordinary capacity of the Congress party workers in Gujarat for establishing and maintaining complex organizations.

We have referred to these larger and well-known institutions in Ahmedabad because they are centers in which party cadres from Kaira district participate. But there are also important institutions within Kaira district itself. Of these the largest, as we have seen, is Amul Dairy. Another important institution is the Charutar Vidyamandal, a social service organization started primarily by the leading Patidars of the district. This organization sponsors Sardar Vallabhbhai Vidyapith, a rural university built on local finances and local land contributions to serve the sons of peasants and townspeople throughout the district. The Vidyamandal also sponsors a number of small-scale industries which provide jobs for people of the district and particularly for the students at the university. Though this organization is in no direct way affiliated with or controlled by the Congress party — indeed, its most prominent founder has for a long time been an opponent of the Congress party and is now a Swatantra leader — many of those associated with it are Congress supporters. The vice chancellor of Vallabhbhai Vidyapith is a leading Congressman in the district and was at one time a member of the Bombay state cabinet.

We have seen that Congress workers are engaged in activities in the Vidyamandal, in Amul Dairy, in the Congress institutions in Ahmedabad, in local governmental institutions in the district, and in a large number of smaller, lesser-known voluntary associations in the fields of education and social work. The Congress party in Kaira district has profited enormously from the social welfare inclinations and organizational skills of

the Patidar community, just as the economy of the district has profited enormously from Patidar entrepreneurship and thrift.

How do these many institutions serve the Congress party in the district? More broadly, what work is performed by the Congress party in the district in its effort to win electoral support?

First of all, since Kaira is a rural area, Congress party workers there are concerned with helping agriculturalists solve their problems, particularly those problems which can be dealt with through government action. Party workers help them obtain such commodities as fertilizers, seeds, and cement. They may deal with a government department in an effort to obtain for a village a grant for building a school, road, well, warehouse, or dispensary. They may negotiate for the peasant proprietor with the district cooperative bank for credit. They may handle a dispute over tobacco taxes between a peasant and the excise department. Party workers are particularly active in negotiating with officials of the revenue department and of the community development ministry, since both these engage in activities of special interest to agriculturalists. A villager may discuss his problem with a Congress party worker, who then deals with the agency concerned. Villagers could go directly to the relevant government department, but it is widely known that Congress party workers are effective intermediaries who can speed the making of decisions by local officials. If the villager is himself a prominent person, he may go directly to the officer of the district cooperative bank or the district cooperative industrial society. Since the officers of these institutions are often Congressmen, it is difficult to separate the political and governmental roles which these individuals serve.

In the main, relations between local government officers and Congress workers are good. Many of the local party workers are college graduates, and therefore have a measure of social status which makes it possible for them to deal with government officers. Moreover, government officers are willing to work closely with Congressmen, since the very success of their own activities often depends upon the collaboration of the local Congress party. After all, Congressmen control the district local board, taluka boards, cooperatives, banks, and many of the voluntary associations in Kaira with which officials must deal.

A second related task of Congress workers in Kaira is to find jobs for the unemployed. Since Kaira invests heavily in primary and secondary schools, it produces a large number of educated young men who, as elsewhere in India, prefer non-agricultural employment. The establishment of the Vallabhbhai Vidyapith was a deliberate effort to bring modern knowl-

edge into the rural areas so that young men would remain in the district. Nonetheless, graduates often prefer other kinds of work, and, in any event, agricultural occupations are not always available to those who seek them. High school and college graduates of middle-class families will often visit prominent Congressmen to seek their help in finding employment. Since the Congressmen of Kaira have excellent contacts in the business houses as well as in the various Congress institutions in Ahmedabad and Baroda, they can often find employment for educated young men. A number find jobs in Congress-controlled cooperatives. Those who need help in obtaining admission into neighboring colleges, finding accommodations in college hostels, or obtaining employment in the district or state administration will find Congress officials in the district most helpful. While the numbers who find jobs through local Congressmen is probably not very large, this Congress activity is important since these individuals often come from prominent families.

Third, Congress workers are also engaged in "constructive work." [8] As we have noted, the Amul Dairy is not an explicit instrument of Congress control, but the fact that local units are controlled by Congressmen means that Congress gets credit for the success of the dairy. Congressmen are also engaged in a number of philanthropic activities, particularly in local educational institutions. Moreover, if there is a famine in any portion of the district, party workers may collect funds to help impoverished villagers or may assist villagers in obtaining government help. If there is a fire, local Congress workers may approach a government officer or a wealthy businessman to provide help for the villagers. A local tuberculosis clinic which provides free treatment for the poor is supported by the Amul Dairy and operated by several local Congress workers.

Congressmen say frankly that it is the service and example of their works (as distinct from ideology and program) that create electoral support. It is not necessary for the secretary of the village cooperative dairy or the officer of the local educational institution to refer constantly to his Congress affiliations, but his service to the community is clearly an advantage to the party during the election campaign.

Congress members of the legislative assembly (MLA) are particularly active in serving their constituents. I asked one Congress MLA, a deputy minister in the state government and one of the few women MLAs, to explain what her relationship is with the people in her constituency. She

---

[8] The term "constructive work" is generally used by Congressmen to refer to nongovernmental activities on behalf of the peasantry.

explained that just recently the MLAs listened to a talk by the Indian ambassador to the United States on this theme.

> He said it was our job to listen to all the legislation pro-posed, to study it, to present our views before the party and try to persuade the party if we disagreed. Then we should go to our constituency and explain what the legislation means.
>
> It's not like that at all! Most of my work involves handling complaints. Sometimes some widows who have lost their land to tenants under the land reform legislation come to me for help. I try to help them get other sources of income. For example, if a young widow comes I will suggest that she go to some institution to get training as a nurse or as a teacher. Every day some seven to ten people come to see me in the early morning or late at night at my home to discuss their problems. Sometimes they come to talk for ten or fifteen minutes even though there isn't much I can do for them. It is important to listen to people even when it is not possible to solve their problems.

Congress party workers are also engaged in dispute settlement through-out the district. It is common for individuals engaged in disputes to turn to some prominent local person for conciliation or arbitration, and in most instances the prominent persons belong to the Congress party. One leading Congressman — a sixty-year-old Patidar who joined Congress when he was in high school and who has devoted his life to party or-ganization work — spends the largest part of his time settling factional disputes within villages. In an interview he explained what this entails.

> There are many factional conflicts in the villages here. In fact there are few villages without factional struggles. Some-times they are between Patidars and Bariyas, the two largest castes. But often they are between factions within the same caste. Bariyas on one side and Bariyas on the other, or Patidars on one side and Patidars on the other. This morn-ing, for example, I went to one village where there was a factional struggle between two Patidar groups over the building of a primary school. They had put up the money for constructing a school and had only completed the first floor

when they ran out of money. One faction said that the other faction had not made their payment, and so the struggle began. The difficulty is that each side wants to preserve or strengthen its prestige. In this case, one faction is becoming a little more prosperous and wants to improve its position, so they are deliberately opposing the other faction. Since I am known to this particular village, I went there to try to settle the factional dispute, but occasionally the worker himself may be the member of a faction. In this village we have two active party workers, but each belongs to a different faction. That's why I was called in to help.

Apart from the perennial factional disputes, there has been an increase in litigation in the district during the past few years as a consequence of the passage of the Tenancy Act. Landlords have often sought to remove tenants and assume direct cultivation of the land themselves in order to prevent provisions of the Tenancy Act from going into effect; this has resulted in substantial conflict between tenants and landlords. These disputes can often become violent, and Congress party workers during the past few years have spent much time trying to settle such disputes outside the courts. The president and secretary of the district Congress party, the major officers of the taluka committees, and a few prominent workers are heavily engaged in all kinds of dispute settlement. The leader of the Congress party in Kaira reported that typically there will be four or five persons in each taluka and as many as a dozen in the most active Congress party talukas who are engaged in such activities.

The roles which we have seen Congress workers perform in Kaira district — founding and maintaining cooperatives and other voluntary associations, serving as intermediaries between villagers and local bureaucrats, finding employment for local youths, managing local government bodies, conducting social welfare activities, serving as mediators in village disputes, organizing election campaigns — are performed by Congress party workers all over India. What is most striking in Kaira district, however, is the extent to which the party leaders are aware of the importance of organization in carrying out these roles. Throughout the district one encounters a sense of pride among local active party workers. They are proud of the services performed by their party and particularly of the work carried out by government to aid the poor. They are proud of their

ability to run district local boards, municipal corporations, and the co-operatives.

While in other districts party workers emphasize the importance of sacrifice and motivation in the performance of party work, in Kaira district party workers are constantly judging actions in terms of effectiveness. There is here an almost non-Indian concern for the consequences of one's action which reminds us again of the extraordinary variations in cultural values that exist throughout the Indian subcontinent. Here are workers who have successfully created institutions to serve the entire community and who are not only concerned with being effective but who have also developed the skills to be effective. Any visitor to the Congress party organization in Kaira is immediately struck with the general tone of rationality and modernity that characterizes the party.

Congress workers occasionally refer to the ideology of the party — to socialism and especially to the Gandhian ideology — but the great strength of the party grows out of its functioning as a political machine. While in the pre-independence days the party in Kaira might be viewed as a movement, today it would be more appropriate to view the party as a political organization. It provides jobs, opens contacts to government, engages in social welfare activities, and settles local disputes. Local Congressmen would resent the statement that the party builds itself upon patronage, but they speak with pride of the role played by the party in providing services to the local population. The terminology is not important so long as we understand what it is that the party members actually do. In short, the party is united by what its members do rather than what they believe.

*Party Cohesion and Conflict*

A political party, like the society within which it operates, has many internal conflicts. In each election since the first general election in 1952 there has been increased competition within the party for winning tickets for the legislative assembly and for parliament. This competition has at times become so intense that there has been considerable defection from the Congress party organization. We shall now try to explain some of the reasons for this increase in internal conflict.

There is, first of all, the presence of conflict within each village. Many of these conflicts are of an ad hoc nature between individual landlords or between landlords and those who work for them. But in the main these

conflicts are of a more durable nature, and anthropologists have generally termed the groups around which these conflicts have been organized as "factions." In our chapters on Guntur we shall deal with factionalism at some length, but suffice it to say here that factions cut across caste lines. Thus in any given village the two major factions are invariably made up of individuals who belong to the Patidar community. And each faction may rally to support individuals of various castes within the village. It is not necessary to explore the dynamics of village factionalism, for that is a complex story in and of itself. What is important here is to see the extent to which village factionalism has affected the Congress organization.

Though individual factions may not be old, factionalism itself is, as far as we can determine, an ancient practice in the villages. What has changed over the years is the institutional context within which factionalism occurs. When the British created new law courts in the nineteenth century, village factional groups used the institution of the courts not to settle but to further disputes. When new statutory panchayats were created and powers were gradually turned over to the village councils or panchayats, factional conflict within the village councils grew. As the power of the Congress party has increased since independence (particularly as a result of its increased influence within government administration), the party itself has become a vehicle for village factional disputes. Thus the party can no more eliminate factionalism than can the panchayats or the courts. As new institutions were created — cooperative societies, purchase and sales unions, and village industries associations — factional conflicts took place within these new institutions. As villagers and local factional leaders became aware of the important powers of the members of the legislative assembly and of the members of parliament, conflicts intensified for the control over these offices too.

A second factor in the increased competition for parliamentary and assembly tickets has been the democratization of the process by which party candidates are selected. The Congress party is in theory a highly centralized organization. As we noted earlier, the Congress Election Committee in New Delhi, a subcommittee of the Working Committee, has the final authority for selecting Congress candidates not only to parliament but to all the state legislative assemblies. Recommendations for parliamentary and assembly tickets are made on the state level by the pradesh election committee of the Pradesh Congress Committee. In practice, unless there is a major disagreement within the PCC, the Congress Central Election Committee in New Delhi accepts the PCC's recommen-

dations. In recent years the Election Committee and the PCCs have encouraged the local units of Congress, particularly the mandal and taluka committees, to make recommendations for assembly candidates. Encouragement for decentralizing the selection of candidates has come from the national party office, but the PCCs have not been particularly enthusiastic about this decentralization. The power of selection has not, it should be noted, been delegated to local units, but the mandal units have been encouraged to make recommendations. In many cases the recommendations of the mandal and taluka units to the District Congress Committee or to the PCC have been overruled. Frequently the PCC has wanted to allocate an assembly seat to a woman, a Muslim, or a representative of some other minority; this practice has meant giving the ticket to someone who would not otherwise be selected by the mandal or taluka unit of the party.

Shortly before the 1962 elections there was great bitterness in one taluka Congress committee toward the state party organization for not having selected their choice for the legislative assembly. Their candidate, a sitting member by the name of Madhavlal Shah, had the support of nearly all the party workers in the taluka. I interviewed one of his supporters who was the chairman of the district local board and one of the most influential Congressmen in the district. He has been with Congress since he was fourteen years old and has been a full-time public worker since 1948.

> The PCC selected a Muslim gentleman, my personal and good friend, but he is not a Congress worker. In fact, he is only a big zamindar, a landlord. So people in my constituency are not going to accept that man. One deputation went to see the president of the PCC, but he replied to them in an arrogant manner and so when they came back from Ahmedabad they all resigned from their offices. There was the president and secretary of the taluka committee and the Presidents of the mandals. They resigned from their offices but they are not leaving Congress. There are only two of us who did not resign, Madhavlal and myself. But none of us will accept a candidate who is not one of us. Madhavlal is a popular man. He is loved and liked by us all. If he had received the nomination he would have been returned with the greatest majority in the constituency ever.

I asked him if he would support the Muslim candidate.

> Madhavlal and I will support the candidate, whoever he
> is, but I can't say how the other party workers will be-
> have.[9] We have always been loyal to people in this country —
> to the Rajas, to the landlords. The difficulty is that we don't
> feel loyalty to institutions or to society. Our workers are
> loyal to Shah and it is difficult to make them realize that
> it is important to work for the party even if Madhavlal
> doesn't get the seat. But I feel too that we must be con-
> sulted and must be persuaded. Before independence we
> were soldiers — well, almost like soldiers though we fought
> nonviolently. Then we had to blindly follow our leaders,
> such great men as Vallabhbhai Patel and Gandhi. But now
> we are free and this is a democracy. We must learn to make
> this democracy work. We cannot blindly follow our leaders.
> The state leadership cannot tell us what to do. There must
> be discussion and consultation.

A third source of intra-party conflict results from land reform legislation passed by the Gujarat state government. The national and state
Congress Party governments have pressed for state land reform legislation to achieve social justice for tenants and agricultural laborers. In
Gujarat the land reform legislation was bitterly opposed by many Patidar
landlords, who said frankly that it was they who had fought for independence, not the tenants and agricultural laborers, whose role in the pre-
independence struggle was negligible. "Why should these people be given
land that belongs to the Patidars?" they asked. Many Patidar Congressmen — including a number with substantial land holdings — supported
the legislation for ideological reasons, but they had considerable difficulty
justifying the legislation to many Patidar landlords.

Ironically, the legislation did not result in support from all the tenants
in Kaira district. Some Patidars, through their control over land record
keepers (talatis), were able to manipulate land titles or to use provisions
of the act to take rights away from the tenants and make them agricultural laborers. Though the state government justified the legislation
on the grounds of social justice, the government has also been concerned
with protecting property rights and avoiding measures which would decrease agricultural production. Provisions were therefore made to repay

[9] The Congress candidate won, by a narrow vote of 20,183 to 20,150.

landlords for land taken from them and to give them the option of re-suming cultivation of certain lands which had been cultivated by tenants. The effect of this latter provision was to permit many landlords to evict tenants and to make these tenants agricultural laborers. A landlord could thus claim that he was no longer an absentee landlord but cultivated his land with the assistance of agricultural laborers.

A fourth source of conflict within the Congress party of Kaira district stemmed from conflicts within the state party organization. When the Gujarat region was part of the larger state of Bombay, there was consid-erable conflict within the Gujarat Congress party organization over whether to press for a bifurcation of the state or to support the con-tinuation of Bombay as a multi-lingual unit made up of Marathi- and Gujarati-speaking peoples. The Gujarat PCC supported the maintenance of a multi-lingual state, but sections of the party advocated bifurcation. Some defection took place to the opposition party, the Mahagujarat Parishad, during the 1957 elections. However, the party sustained these defections well, and although Congress lost a majority of seats in the Marathi-speaking districts of Bombay State, the Congress party in Gujarat retained a substantial majority in the Gujarati region. In Kaira district too, where there was considerable agitation for the creation of a separate Gujarati-speaking state, the Congress party won a solid majority of seats in the 1957 elections.

When the new state of Gujarat was formed — a decision of the national government which grew out of pressure from the Marathi-speaking area — an older conflict within the Gujarati region came to the surface. The new state of Gujarat was in itself an amalgamation of at least two major regions: Saurashtra, and Gujarat. Before independence Saurashtra had consisted of a number of princely states which subsequently had been merged into the state of Bombay and was now a part of the new state of Gujarat. The Saurashtra group had always been a significant ele-ment in the Gujarat PCC, and the Congressmen from the Gujarati re-gion generally felt under-represented.[10] In 1961, shortly before the can-didates were selected for the 1962 elections, the national Congress party president suggested that there be a ten-year limit on office holding in the state and central governments. He proposed that those who had been

[10] The conflicts within the state Congress are more complicated than I have sug-gested here. Though the Congress opponents of Chief Minister Jivraj Mehta (who comes from Saurashtra) were led by a spokesman from the Gujarat region, the chief minister also had opponents within Saurashtra. To some extent, then, the factional struggle cut across regional lines. The main point for us, however, is that Kaira Con-gressmen supported the dissident faction against the Jivraj ministry and saw the ten-year rule as a way of unseating it.

in office for ten years resign and return to work in the party organization and in district political life. The proposal was quietly opposed by most of India's national leadership, for its implementation would clearly have disrupted state and central governments. Most states ignored or opposed the proposal and no official action was taken. However, the Gujarat PCC officially endorsed the proposal. Congressmen from the Gujarati region saw the proposal as an opportunity to reduce the Saurashtra element in the government and thereby increase their own representation. With the passage of the resolution by the PCC the Gujarati group in the state legislative assembly and in the state ministry announced that those individuals who had been in the assembly for a ten-year period would not stand in the forthcoming 1962 elections. The Saurashtra group refused to follow such a policy and used as their justification the decision of the central party organization that such a policy should not be imposed. Therefore, for a period of several months in late 1961 there was considerable confusion within the party organization. Several Kaira district MLAs who had been in office for ten years announced that they would not stand for reelection; by the time they realized that their self-denying ordinance was not being carried out by Congressmen in the Saurashtra region, it was often too late to offer their names for reelection. To say the least, by early 1962 there was considerable resentment in the local units of the Congress party organization in Kaira district when several very prominent Congressmen who had been in office for ten years or longer did not receive tickets for reelection.

In conclusion, therefore, we may note that though many of the conflicts within the Congress party organization in Kaira district were primarily expressions of personal ambition; as in parties elsewhere in the world, many were expressions of broader social and economic divisions within Gujarati society. As the party organization successfully penetrated into the village, the factionalism characteristic of village political life permeated the party organization. Economic conflicts within Kaira district affected the party organization when many landlords defected from the party over the passage of land reform legislation. And, finally, conflicts between the Saurashtra and Gujarati regions of the state affected political relations within the Congress party. No one of these conflicts in itself would have resulted in the enormous defeat experienced by the party in the 1962 elections; it was the relationship between the Congress party and the Kshatriyas of the district which proved to be a turning point for the party.

## 5. THE PARTICIPATION CRISIS

What were the changes taking place in Kaira that led to the surprising Congress defeat of 1962? In the 1950's two social groups whose statuses were changing came into increasing conflict with the Congress party. One of these, the upper-caste Rajputs, were resentful of their lack of power in district and state affairs. The other, a group of numerically large lower castes, were upwardly mobile. It was the coalescing of these two very different elements — one was high caste and the other low, one predominantly landowning and the other predominantly tenant — into an organization known as the Kshatriyas Sabha. Today some 40 per cent of the population claims Kshatriya status. In one sense the Kshatriyas constitute a new social group. Those who call themselves Kshatriyas today are in fact somewhat different from those who called themselves Kshatriyas centuries ago. To understand how this new group was formed or how an older group changed its composition, we must briefly examine the social organization of those groups that make up what is now known as the Kshatriya community.

The term "Kshatriya" refers to one of the four social classes or varnas found in the Vedas — Brahmin, Kshatriya, Vaisya, and Sudra — and should not be confused (though it often is) with caste or jati. The word "caste" is not Indian at all, but comes from a Portuguese word meaning "race." Today "caste" is confusingly used to refer both to varna and to jati, the countless endogamous social groups (sometimes called subcastes) which make up Hindu society. In this study we shall use the word "caste" to mean jati.

Those who now call themselves Kshatriyas actually belong to a num-

ber of endogamous castes. Of these, the highest in status are the Rajputs. In the pre-British era the Rajputs were the rulers of large parts of Gujarat, the region known as Rajputana, and other parts of northern India.[1] During the British era many of the Rajputs remained in power as maharajas. The Rajputs are divided into various clans, each of which is known by its surname. Each surname is indicative of a ruling group in some part of northern India. In much of Gujarat the former ruling dynasty of the Rajput caste belonged to the Solanki clan.

While in many parts of northern India the Rajputs were the dominant caste, in recent times in Kaira district, as we have already indicated, Patidars were the dominant caste. Nonetheless, there are individual villages and portions of Kaira district in which the Rajputs are the dominant element. According to the district gazetteer report of 1879,[2] there were some fifty-one estate holders (thakurs or talukdars) in Kaira district, most of whom were Rajputs. Though the Rajputs of Kaira are neither numerous nor powerful, they have often been rivals of the Patidars. The British officers in the district were generally much more sympathetic to the industrious Patidars than to the Rajputs. The district gazetteer described the Rajput landed gentry as "careless and improvident" men who were "heavily burdened with debt" and whose estates had been "deeply mortgaged," in contrast to the "sober, quiet, industrious . . . and thrifty" Patidars.

According to the classic vedic texts, the Kshatriya is by tradition a warrior. It is believed by many anthropologists and historians of ancient India that invaders into India and tribes within India adopted the Hindu faith and then proceeded to adapt themselves to Hindu social organization by assuming a varna classification. A rising social group, therefore, may seek to improve its status by adopting a high varna classification. According to this theory, the Rajputs and other warrior groups called themselves Kshatriyas when they became part of Hindu social organization. Other castes or tribes have sought to *raise* their status by becoming Kshatriyas or Brahmins. A caste or tribe might adopt new surnames, emulate the ritual of another high caste, or adopt a high varna classification, all as a means of establishing a higher place in the social hierarchy. Hindu social organization is not so static as popular belief would make it appear, for social groups have from time to time changed their

[1] For a careful analysis of the precise position of the Rajputs and their political relationships to both Kolis and Patidars in the pre-British period, see A. M. Shah, "Political System in Eighteenth Century Gujarat," *Enquiry* 1 (Spring, 1964): 83–95.

[2] *Gazetteer of the Bombay Presidency*, p. 113.

social position. There is, however, an appearance of stability, since rising social groups have often legitimized a change in social position by adopting a new ritual classification.

It is in this context that we must understand the changing position of a number of castes in Kaira district which now choose to call themselves Kshatriyas. Among these are a group of castes popularly known locally as the Kolis.

The Kolis made it difficult for the British to preserve law and order throughout a good part of the early nineteenth century. The Kaira district gazetteer of 1879 has this to say about the Kolis:

> The Koli element forms the largest tribe or caste with a total strength of 35.9% of the entire population. As a class their position has improved most under British rule. Idle and turbulent in the early part of the present century, they are now as a body quiet and hardworking. Even in the most settled times of Gujarat history, the Kolis were only partially brought under order, and during the disturbances and misrule of the 18th century they threw off every restraint and for the most part in 1812, though they had begun to forsake their former habits, they are described as a lawless race, conspicuous as the perpetrators of gang robberies and other atrocities. In 1825 they were still one of the most turbulent predatory tribes in India. Regular troops, even European cavalry, had continually to be called out against them. In no other part of India were the roads so insecure; in none were gang robberies and organized plundering excursions more frequent, or a greater proportion of the gentry and landed proprietors addicted to acts of violence and bloodshed. . . .[3]

The Kolis are divided into two groups — Talpadas and Patanwadiyas — which neither intermarry or interdine. These two endogamous groups are divided into exogamous lineage groups. In Kaira district it is reported that the Talpadas are the larger of the two groups. The Talpadas are often referred to as Dharala (armed), but the term is considered derogatory. It does, however, indicate the popular belief concerning the militancy of this community. The Talpadas are divided into various lineages

[3] *Ibid.*, pp. 32–33.

among which the Bariyas are considered to have the highest status, so much so that the Talpadas have adopted Bariya as their caste name.[4]

The Bariyas (a term which now includes all Talpada Kolis) like to think of themselves as Rajputs. They point out that they too belong to a martial tradition. On the one hand they resent the British policy of treating them as criminals, while on the other they are proud of their militant past. Moreover, the daughters of some Bariyas have married into Rajput families. The Rajputs, like the Patidars, practice hypergamy, and have taken wives from Bariya chiefs and their kinsmen. Since some of the Bariya chiefs are large estate holders (talukdars or thakurs) like the Rajputs and have Rajputized their way of life, Rajputs are willing to accept Bariya daughters. As Shah writes, "Rajput hypergamy has thus provided a rope by which Kolis can pull themselves up." [5]

The Bariyas can also upgrade themselves by the myth that they were once Rapjuts. Some Bariyas claim that they were originally Rajputs who "lost" caste because they took water and food from lower-caste Bariyas. Others claim that they were the younger sons of Rajput families who, because of the Rajput system of inheritance, were not given land by their families and were thus degraded into menial petty landholders. Since the Bariyas are now an aspiring caste, there is much myth creating and adopting of new genealogies and Rajput clan surnames. Thus many Bariyas call themselves Solanki or Mahida, after two Rajput clans which were once politically powerful in parts of Gujarat. This process has gone so far that it is now difficult for an outsider and even for many persons in the locality to know whether a particular estate holder is truly a Rajput or is a Bariya who has assumed a Rajput surname. In my examination of the Kshatriya movement in Kaira, it has not always been possible to find out precisely to which caste an individual leader belongs, but in most instances I have indicated local opinion.

## The Organization and Leadership of the Kshatriyas

The defeat of the Congress party in the elections of 1962 is a consequence of two developments: the growth of an organization known as the Kshatriya Sabha, and its defection from the Congress party. Like many

[4] For this description of the social organization of the Bariyas, I have relied heavily on A. M. Shah and R. G. Shroff, "The Vahivanca Barots of Gujarat: A Caste of Genealogists and Mythographers," pp. 58–61.

[5] *Ibid.*, p. 60.

political organizations in India, the Kshatriya Sabha was at first a social reform movement. Its founder and first president was Narendra Singh Mahida, now a member of parliament. Mahida describes himself as a Rajput, though many "real" Rajputs do not recognize his claim. He is a tall, middle-aged man, a forceful and popular local leader. In parliament he wears the tightly buttoned jacket which has become the Indian national dress, but in addition proudly wears a saffron turban as a mark of his Rajput association. I interviewed him in his small bungalow in Baroda in September, 1961. Above his chair on the veranda was a large Indian flag, and opposite him was a large mirror in which he could see the flag. He is sensitive to the accusation that he is "communal" and during the interview said that he often looks at the Indian flag in the mirror, "and that reminds me that I should be true to the national ideals." A shrewd politician who can effectively calculate how to build his political strength, he is also a man with a passion for social reform.

> When I was in England — my father sent me for study — I met Gandhi, who told me that the princely order would collapse. Gandhi said that if I wanted to help India I should go back to the villages. But what shall I do in the villages, I asked him, and he told me to see one of the great religious leaders of Gujarat. I met with this man and in 1945 went with him to address some crowds. This gave me my first opportunity to come in closer contact with the villagers of Gujarat.
>
> I marched on foot from village to village to persuade the members of the Kshatriya community to adopt prohibition and to reject the custom of death feasts. The Rajputs have all been boozers and I know many young men who died in their twenties and thirties because they drank so much and their minds became fuzzy. I wanted to do social work of this sort, but I also wanted to arouse the martial feeling of the people of my community.
>
> Many people ask me who was a Rajput. *I told them that a Rajput was one who was willing to serve and die for his country.* [Italics added.]

Here we see clearly Mahida's efforts to find a new way of defining Rajput so that other communities could identify themselves with the Raj-

puts. However, members of the Rajput caste were split over Mahida's efforts to incorporate the Bariyas and other low castes into a new association with the Rajputs. At first Mahida tried to bring the Bariyas into one of the Rajput educational associations, "but many Rajputs were opposed and felt that we had no place bringing these other communities into our association." Other Rajputs saw this as an opportunity to widen the political appeal of the Rajputs. One of these men, Natvar Singh Solanki, became one of the most dynamic organizers of the new organization. In 1947 he and Mahida persuaded many Rajputs in the former princely states of Kutch and Saurashtra to join with the other Kshatriya communities to form the Kutch-Gujarat Kathiawad Kshatriya Sabha.

Solanki is a large landowner and once the talukdar of an unusually poor village in Kaira. He is a somewhat portly man of forty-six, who at seventeen took active control of his father's property. He is extraordinarily energetic, and like his father (who had been entangled in a murder case) he is often described locally as a "hotheaded man." While some Congressmen will describe Mahida as a good but misguided man, few Congressmen respect Solanki. He is described as a powerful landlord concerned with exploiting the poor and using "communal appeals" to win political support from tenants and agricultural laborers who would not otherwise support him. Like many Rajputs, Solanki is aware of the political power once wielded by his community. "I come from the Solanki dynasty which ruled Gujarat before the Muslim invasions," he explained to me. "The Rajputs ruled almost all of Gujarat, Kutch, and Sourashtra before the Moghuls came."

His father — like many other Rajputs — was active in social reform activities within the Rajput community. Solanki was active in one of the social reform organizations which had been created by his father, and then became active in efforts to improve education among the Rajputs. "Then I felt why should I work only for the Rajputs. Why should I not work for all members of the Kshatriya class. *The Kshatriyas are a class, not a caste.* [Italics added.] The Rajputs are only one part of this class but they consider themselves above other members of the class. The Solanki dynasty would consider itself of high blood and they would not want their children to marry the children of Bariyas."

According to Solanki, he was moved by a passion for social reform when he first began to work among the lower castes. He met Narendra Singh Mahida, who was similarly moved, and together the two began to tour Gujarati villages on foot.

We covered some 7,000 miles trying to get people within
the community to eliminate various evils. We marched with
a group of twenty-two supporters. Twenty-two was to sym-
bolize the fight of the ruler of Mewar at Udaipur against
the Muslim rulers. This Rajput ruler is very famous for
winning his struggle. He fought with twenty-two thousand
men and therefore the number twenty-two symbolized our
fight against evil. First of all there was drinking, which is
a great evil in the Kshatriya community. Then we opposed
the dowry system. We opposed the death feast known as
barma. That is a feast held on the twelfth day for all the
relatives and friends of the deceased. It is very expensive.
Whenever we heard that a barma was going to be held, we
sent out workers to the village to prevent the holding of
such a feast. Our worker would often go there and threaten
to go into a fast unless the ceremony was cancelled.

The organization's first conference demonstrated the success of the appeals being made to the Kshatriya community, according to Mahida.

In 1948 we decided to hold a conference of the Kshatriya
Sabha. It was attended by some 30,000 people. I was myself surprised to see that many people here. We had already
begun a program of training the Bariya community to march
in step and to take military exercises, but I was surprised
to see so many people marching in step at this conference.

One of the first attempts to convert numbers and enthusiasm into political power was a move by the Kshatriya Sabha leaders to get the entire
community listed as a backward class by the Gujarat government on the
grounds that the community was predominantly illiterate and poor. Solanki went to see the chief minister of the state, Morarji Desai, who
turned down the request on the grounds that the costs would have been
prohibitive for including such a large section of the population on the
list as backward. Children who are classified as belonging to the backward classes are given free college educations, free lodging and boarding
in hostels, free books, special scholarships for going abroad, and priority
in government employment. Though the Kshatriya Sabha failed to persuade the government to place the Kshatriya castes on the backward

class list, they continued to urge the state government to take steps to improve their educational opportunities.

In 1949 a crisis took place within the Kutch-Gujarat Kathiawad Kshatriya Sabha over relations between the Rajputs and the lower castes. The issue was not caste — for by this time many Rajputs were aware of the political advantages in working with lower-caste communities who for social reasons wanted to be associated with Rajputs — but clashing economic interests. In 1949 the Saurashtra government — a separate government which was later merged into Bombay State — passed legislation taking land away from Rajput landowners. The Rajput landlords in Saurashtra launched a campaign against the government and asked the lower-caste Kshatriyas of Gujarat for support. Solanki was sympathetic to their plea, since he himself was a large landowner. But since most of the Kshatriyas in Gujarat were tenants, he saw that he could not persuade his tenant supporters to support the anti–land-reform agitation of the Rajput landowners. As a result the Rajputs from Saurashtra and Kutch left the Kshatriya Sabha in 1950, and the organization's name was changed to the Gujarat Kshatriya Sabha and functioned only in the Gujarat region of the state.

Rajputs in the Gujarat region remained in the organization. In terms of occupational composition, the organization now consisted of Rajput landowners, several Koli ex-chieftains who were also large landowners, and a vast majority of non-Rajput small peasant proprietors, tenants, and agricultural laborers. Although there existed a wide range of economic interests within the Kshatriya Sabha, sociologically there was much to bind the membership together. The willingness of Rajputs in Kaira to accept as Rajputs the Bariyas and other low castes was a strong incentive for these castes to join the Kshatriya Sabha. This political alliance with the Rajputs thus served an important social function. As Mahida put it,

> We have taken all the backward peoples who are martial by nature and called them Kshatriyas. Bhils, Ahirs, Bariyas, and Dharalas are all Kshatriyas. Congress has taken up the Harijans, so we have taken up these people. Those people who have intense nationalism, they are Kshatriyas. *It is not a question of blood but of spirit and action.* [Italics added.] Kshatriyas have upper and lower classes. We say that if the Bhils [a large group of tribes living next to Kaira district] are brave enough we will call them Kshatriyas. . . . Any-

one can call himself Kshatriya if he wants to. Dharalas don't like that name to be used. I tell them they can use any name they want. What is it if a man uses a Rajput name? There are Rajput clan names like Solanki and Chauhan. Anyone can use them. And if people want to intermarry that is all right too, but that is a personal matter.

In assessing the successful appeal made by Rajput leaders to the Bariyas, one must consider at least three elements: the growing status aspirations of the Bariyas, the growing politicization of the Bariyas, and the services the Kshatriya Sabha is beginning to perform for the Bariyas.

The status element was perhaps the central issue. I asked one Bariya whether in fact the Bariyas were treated as equals within the Kshatriya Sabha. This young man was a relatively well-to-do Bariya, a college graduate in law and a relative of a wealthy landlord family. He was elected to the legislative assembly in 1957 on a Congress ticket and was one of the few Bariyas who remained in Congress in 1962. He therefore spoke as an opponent of the Kshatriya Sabha.

The Bariyas want to feel that they are Rajputs. They feel that by joining the Kshatriya Sabha they could sit next to Rajputs on an equal level. Ordinarily when a Rajput sits on a charpoy [a rope bed often pulled out into the street for sitting purposes], members of these other low caste communities have to sit on the floor in order to be beneath him. But in the Kshatriya Sabha the Rajputs sit on an equal level with people from these communities and take food with them. . . . Mahida is a fine person, very gentle and not at all selfish. He had the brilliant idea of making members of the community wear a common uniform. This included a saffron turban, a cummerbund and a sword. Mahida and his followers would go from village to village and would be joined by Bariyas and other low class communities who want to get some status by association with these Rajputs.

But other changes — apart from status issues — took place in the 1950's to stimulate the Bariyas to enter this new kind of politics. The efforts of the state government to aid the Bariyas and other low-caste groups through tenancy reform, debtor's legislation, and the establishment of

new educational facilities all served to make the Bariyas aware of their own backward position.

The Kshatriya Sabha has successfully tapped this sense of backwardness by stressing the importance of education. One Kshatriya leader — a member of parliament — reported that the organization has opened five boarding schools and is now providing a limited number of scholarships to students with high grades. The association now publishes a fortnightly magazine with a circulation of eight hundred copies, campaigns for education, and, like Congress, tries to find jobs for Kshatriya boys. But while the Congress party workers are concerned primarily with the agricultural needs of local persons, the Kshatriya Sabha workers give greater attention to questions of social reform and education within the Kshatriya community.

It is not surprising that the Bariyas should seek to raise their material and social status by joining an organization dominated largely by Rajputs, but why should the Rajputs seek support from non-Rajput castes and be willing to permit other castes to call themselves Rapjuts? To answer this question, we must first take a look at the political culture of the Rajputs and then examine the relationship between the Rajputs and Patidars on the one hand and that between the Bariyas and Patidars on the other.

## The Political Culture of the Rajputs

Rajputs believe they have the right to govern. As one Rajput officer of the Kshatriya Sabha, whose father had been little more than a clerk in a princely state, put it, "We were once the rulers of this country." Rajputs commonly believe that they are part of a ruling culture even though as individuals neither they nor members of their families ever exercised governmental authority.

Rajputs have memories of being part of a ruling class, for their maharajas once governed princely states in Rajasthan, Madhya Pradesh, and Gujarat. These historic memories of being rulers, or being part of a ruling class, are reinforced by a tradition which sanctifies a martial outlook and justifies their wielding of power. In a study of the personality structure of a Rajput in a Gujarat village, the anthropologist Gitel P. Steed describes the traditional source of authority claimed by the Rajputs.

> Power, allegiance, sacrifice, and bravery were interchangeable and related ideals of a dominant Rajput theme. These same ideals were tangibly rooted in the long history of po-

litical, economic, and military power of the Vaghela Rajputs. Their Rajput heritage was felt and understood by
Kasandra's village rulers. It was symbolized for them in a
simple origin myth which they quoted frequently out of
their subcaste history . . . : "Brahma created the universe.
The Universe, surfeited with non-religious persons, went to
Brahma. At Brahma's wish a Kshatriya, or brave man, was
created with ornaments, dress, and weapons. Brahmaji ordered the Kshatriya to destroy the non-religious persons in
the universe, and then as a reward gave the Kshatriya a
kingdom." [6]

The Rajputs believe that they not only have the right to exercise authority but the capacity to do so. As a result of their high status and their
landed wealth, they have the prestige to deal with governmental authority. Moreover, authority, the Rajputs believe, can best be exercised by
force and manipulation. As Steed explains,

He could apply coercive "control" (*dab*) or manipulate
legal rights; he could employ guilt and shame-producing
mechanisms (*saram*) resembling Chinese "face," impelling
others to respond appropriately through their own efforts to
save face; he could manipulate village-wide aspirations for
prestige (*ijat*); he could demonstrate the personal skills noted
above, as well as the generally esteemed skills of foresight,
judgment, and capacity for self-control; and, last but not
least, he could achieve some of the requirements for authority by manipulating alliances among rulers and allegiances of subjects to rulers in the overlord system. [7]

Social groups within India's hierarchical social system are characteristically concerned with preserving their status. "I care for my reputation
twenty-four hours a day," Gitel Steed quotes one Rajput landlord as
having said. [8] In this respect the Rajputs are no different from most of India's
other social groups. What is particularly characteristic of the Rajputs,
however, and of a few other social groups in India, is an inclination to

[6] Gitel P. Steed, "Notes on an Approach to a Study of Personality Formation in a
Hindu Village in Gujarat," in McKim Marriott, editor, *Village India* (Chicago: University of Chicago Press, 1955), pp. 114–15.
[7] *Ibid.*
[8] *Ibid.*, p. 118.

use power and authority to maintain their status. Before the British arrived in India, the Rajputs were an expanding political force, slowly taking over northern India by military means. The establishment of British power in the eighteenth and nineteenth centuries, however, meant containment for the Rajputs, despite the fact that the British allowed them to govern quasi-independent princely states and to retain control of many large estates. With the withdrawal of British power from the subcontinent in 1947 the power of the Rajputs was further limited. The princely states were absorbed into the rest of India and the maharajas, often Rajputs, were pensioned. In the early 1950's most state governments passed land reform legislation which took land away from the very large landholders — from, in effect, the Rajputs in Uttar Pradesh, Rajasthan, Madhya Pradesh, Gujarat, and Saurashtra.

Since for obvious reasons most Rajput princes and landlords collaborated with the British, there were few Rajputs in positions of influence in the nationalist movement. The newly formed state governments in northern India in 1947 consisted largely of Brahmins, Kayasthas, (a scribe caste), and Banias. From the Rajput point of view, therefore, the castes which took power in the north Indian states after independence lacked the capacity to exercise authority. In short, the Rajputs — even those who had never personally exercised authority — looked down upon the castes which had taken power. Thus the tradition of the Rajputs that says that power and authority are necessary for establishing and maintaining status, the impact of government legislation which deprived the Rajputs of what little wealth and power they had after the British left India, and the condescension Rajputs felt toward social groups which had now taken power — all combined to project the Rajputs into state and national political life.

Since the Rajputs do not like to share power, they could not easily adapt themselves to the new democratic system. A few Rajputs, mainly former princes, stood for parliamentary seats in the 1951 elections, but in general the Rajputs proved to be a feeble political force. It soon became clear to many Rajputs that they could not win popular support simply because they had a martial spirit. Those who lived on Rajput estates might continue to support the Rajputs out of a sense of allegiance, but it would not be long before Congress party workers would divide the Rajput rulers from their former subjects or tenants. From the Rajput point of view, land reform legislation would be particularly devastating, for the Rajputs would not only lose their land but would also lose the economic power on which local allegiances rested. The Rajputs who organ-

ized the Kshatriya Sabha declared that they welcomed into the organization all those who shared the martial outlook of the Kshatriyas and that the other castes could become Rajputs if they so chose. Thus, the Rajputs were prepared to increase their numbers to become politically effective. The Rajputs in the Kshatriya Sabha declared, as we have noted, that an individual becomes a Kshatriya not by birth or blood but by his martial spirit of sacrifice. The Kshatriya Sabha thus represents an attempt by the Rajputs to democratize and modernize their political culture without giving up their central values. Here we see illustrated an important general principle: not only do social organizations affect political life, as political sociologists have argued, but political structures and processes can also have an important impact on the system of social stratification.

The Rajput spirit — and the willingness of many Rajput leaders to incorporate into their community others who accept that spirit — is eloquently described by Mahida.

> We say if Bhils are brave enough, we shall call them Kshatriyas. Yogi, Sati, Kshatriya — they all die for others. It is wrong for someone to force a woman to commit sati. There was a woman some time ago who wanted to commit sati but people would not let her. She said that her life purpose was with her husband. She believed in transmigration and wanted to go with her husband. So she refused to take food and after six months she died.
>
> That is the spirit of sacrifice.
>
> We have a Puja (a ceremony) for husband and wife. They dress as bride and groom and appear before Lord Siva at Somnath and cut off their own heads and then give it to him.
>
> That is the spirit of sacrifice.
>
> I remember some years ago when our people were parading and some military officer was there. Our men were dressed in their uniforms and wearing saffron turbans. I told the officer that I would show him their spirit. We were standing by a cliff near the water. I stood before them and told them all — there must have been a hundred men — to jump into the water. I leaped first, then I looked up behind me and none were there. They had all jumped into the water. And some of the men could not even swim!
>
> That is the spirit of sacrifice.

## Congress and the Kshatriya Sabha

As the popular following of the Kshatriya Sabha increased between 1952 and 1962, its relationship with the Congress party deteriorated. In 1952 the Kshatriya Sabha wholeheartedly supported the Congress party, and several Kshatriya Sabha leaders were given Congress party tickets to the legislative assembly. By 1957, however, relations among the two groups were already strained; though the Kshatriya Sabha formally supported the Congress party, several of its leaders privately supported candidates who opposed the Congress party. In 1960 the Kshatriya Sabha completely broke from the Congress party, and in 1961 the Kshatriya Sabha switched its allegiance to the newly formed Swatantra party. Solanki, the secretary and dynamic organizer of the Kshatriya Sabha, became the organizing secretary of the Swatantra party in Gujarat; Mahida, the president of the Kshatriya Sabha, stood for parliament on a Swatantra party platform. One can point to many areas of tension and conflict during the years in which the Kshatriya Sabha worked with the Congress party, particularly centering on the extent to which the Congress party would offer assembly or parliamentary tickets to members of the Kshatriya Sabha. But neither Kshatriyas nor Congressmen explain the deterioration in relations simply in terms of conflicts over specific questions. The differences were far more complex, far more subtle, far more intangible. The outside observer who sees politics in terms of compromise and conciliation could find many ways in which the differences between the Kshatriya Sabha and the Congress party could have been reconciled, but such a perspective would be quite irrelevant. The common underlying framework which makes it possible for individuals or groups to compromise was clearly absent. For Congressmen, and particularly the Patidars who dominate the Congress organization, differ fundamentally from the Kshatriyas in how they see themselves, each other, and politics itself. It is to these differences that we now turn in order to understand why Congress and the Kshatriya Sabha or, more specifically, the Patidars and the Kshatriyas were unable to work together.

The very clarity with which Congress workers saw their role proved to be a liability in their relationship with the Kshatriyas. We have seen that Congressmen see their tasks as dealing with government on behalf of agriculturalists and businessmen, as establishing and managing cooperatives, conducting social service, settling disputes, and organizing to win elections. Congressmen were willing to give positions of leadership to those cadres who carried on these tasks well, but saw no reason to reward

Bariyas and Rajputs in the party with positions when they lacked these skills.

Congressmen had mixed feelings when the Kshatriya Sabha gave them support during the 1952 and 1957 elections. The national and state Congress leaders were prepared to accept the support of princes, talukdars, and other landlords and to give them tickets to the state assembly or to parliament as part of a national attempt to absorb and integrate rather than annihilate those who had once collaborated with the British. On the other hand, local Congress workers were unhappy to see the party give tickets to those who had not supported the nationalist movement. They were unhappy to see rewards given to men who lacked the efficiency, the devotion, and the sense of organization which they admired. They were unhappy with the growing ties between Rajputs and Bariyas, since Congressmen felt that the Rajputs were exploiting the Bariyas. One Congressman described the Kshatriya Sabha leadership as "Rajas, talukdars, and big landlords. They are top ranking persons of classes, but not men of the masses."

Congressmen were particularly unhappy with the "communal" overtones of the Kshatriya Sabha; though Congress is predominantly Patidar — and the Rajputs attack it as a Patidar organization — Congressmen describe themselves as secular and relatively indifferent to caste in politics. This point will become clearer as we turn to an interview with the president of the state Congress party organization in Gujarat. He spoke at some length on the relationship between caste associations and the Congress party organization.

> Various communities in the state are pressing hard to get their candidates selected by the Congress party. For example, the Bhangis (the lowest of the scheduled castes in Gujarat) have been pressing for seats. They have demanded that half the scheduled caste seats in the states be given to their community. In general local feelings are growing in Gujarat and local people want their own candidates to be selected. As soon as people become a little more conscious politically they become more caste-conscious.

Why did the break occur between the Congress party and the Kshatriya Sabha?

> The main reason is that the Kshatriya Sabha leaders didn't get the seats that they wanted for the legislative assembly.

It was not only that they wanted more seats, but they wanted to make their own selections for the legislative assembly. They wanted the Congress party to automatically accept the candidates that they had selected. It would be a sad day for Congress if we give up our right to select our candidates. It will mean the end of discipline. The difficulty with the Kshatriya Sabha is that they tried not only to get more seats, but more importantly they tried to get control of the Congress organization. They tried to recruit as many Kshatriyas as possible so that they could get control of the mandal committees. And then they would try to get control of the taluka and district committees and then the entire party organization. Because they do constitute such a large part of the population of Gujarat it might have become possible for them to get control of the Congress party organization.

The hostility of the president of the Gujarat Pradesh Congress Committee to the Kshatriya Sabha was no small element in the eventual defection of the Kshatriya organization from the Congress party. Not only did he refuse to give Kshatriya Sabha members seats for the legislative assembly, but in public speeches he denounced the organization as "communal." In his mind there was a substantial difference between allocating seats to particular castes as part of a calculated ethnic arithmetic and a policy of permitting a caste association actually to control a given number of Congress tickets. To accept the proposal of the Kshatriya Sabha would in fact be to destroy the organizational integrity of the Congress party. Moreover, it is one thing to recognize caste as an important part of local politics but quite another to legitimize and formally institutionalize caste within the Congress party organization.

The Congress president's views were shared by many prominent Congressmen. There were others who went a step further in their reluctance to see the Kshatriyas hold any positions of importance within the Congress. Some Congressmen in principle were disinclined to accept the notion of ethnic arithmetic. From their point of view, assembly and parliamentary tickets should be given only to those who had proved their effectiveness as party workers. It was important that a man be skillful in conducting "government business," and it would be foolish from this point of view to give a seat to an inexperienced, ineffectual individual simply because he happened to represent a numerically substantial ethnic group. Moreover, many Congressmen were convinced that even if Bariyas were

not offered seats in the legislative assembly or important posts in the party, they would still cast their votes for Congress rather than for Rajput leadership. They pointed out that many of the Rajput leaders were landlords with whom the Bariyas had little in common, that the state government had passed legislation which had helped the Bariya community, and that the cooperatives, schools, and other voluntary associations which the Congress party had created were all providing services to the Bariya community. These Congress workers felt that the economic rewards and services provided by the Congress government would prove more effective than the "communal" appeal of the Kshatriya Sabha. Congressmen viewed the Kshatriya Sabha as a communal organization, not simply because of its composition, but because it stood for and claimed to represent a particular ethnic group. The fact that the Congress party was heavily dominated by Patidars did not, in the eyes of Congressmen, make the Congress party a Patidar organization. Congressmen argue — with considerable justification — that the secular quality of the organization is determined not by the social groups which make up the party but by the principles on which the party stands. The fact that Congress is and has always been predominantly Hindu does not make it a Hindu party any more than Catholic predominance in a French socialist party makes that party Catholic. Ideas, not social composition, are what matter. To the Congressmen the fact that the Kshatriya Sabha accused the Congress party of being a Patidar organization was simply further indication of the communal-minded character of the Kshatriya Sabha.

Congressmen were caught in a dilemma. Even without granting the right of the Kshatriya Sabha directly to nominate candidates for Congress tickets, Congress could offer individual Bariyas seats in the legislative assembly. But only three of the fifteen candidates selected by the party for assembly elections in 1962 were Bariyas.[9] If Congress had selected many more Bariyas and given members of that community important posts in the Congress party, the Congressmen would no doubt have alienated a large number of the Patidars within Congress. They might have risked this had they been fully aware of the growing political consciousness and increasing participation in electoral politics of the Bariyas. But, as we have already noted, Congressmen were convinced that Bariyas would be swayed more by the services the party could perform than by any ethnic appeals from the Rajputs. The Congressmen simply were unaware of the growing status aspirations of the Bariyas.

If, on the other hand, Congress failed to assign a large number of seats

[9] Two of these were among the five Congressmen elected.

to the Bariya community, they risked losing the votes of a substantial part of the population. There are more Bariyas than Patidars, and if the Congress party failed to woo the Bariyas another party existed which might win their support.

No matter what the Congress party leadership in Kaira district did, the risks were great. To woo the Bariyas might alienate Patidar Congress party workers. To ignore them might be to court political defeat. Much depended upon the Congress assessment of the magnitude of the threat and of the aspirations of the Bariyas. In one sense the Patidar Congressmen had become so development-oriented that they had lost their sense of politics — that is, their appreciation of what must be done to retain political power. Congressmen prided themselves on their close connections with the "masses" but failed to realize that "new" masses had come into politics with new and not just economic needs which a developmentally minded cadre could not satisfy.

Patidar efforts to win Bariya support would in any event have been difficult. Land reform legislation had uneven effects on Bariya-Patidar relations; as we have seen, many Bariyas were shifted by their landlords from positions as tenants to agricultural labor. Moreover, Bariyas were aware that many Patidars viewed them as an indolent people unworthy of higher status within the community until they achieved a higher educational level, became better agriculturalists and harder workers, and were ready to share in the work of the development bodies in the district — in short, until they were, in attitudes and behavior, more like the Patidars.[10]

In contrast with Congress, the Swatantra party in Gujarat was far more skillful and in a far better position to cope with the needs and demands of the Kshatriya Sabha. When the Kshatriya Sabha broke from Congress in late 1960, it sought an alternative party within which it could achieve its objectives. The Kshatriya leaders were frankly shopping around. Though they were drawn to the martial outlook and religious

[10] Many Patidars within Congress, as members of the dominant caste, continued to look down upon the Bariyas and other lower castes and expected to govern through traditional patterns of social control. This older attitude was clearly expressed by Vallabhbhai Patel in a public address in 1921 explaining why Bardoli taluka — another area of Gujarat with a large number of Patidars — should be selected for a civil disobedience movement. According to Patel, "75% of the Patidars are whole-heartedly in favour of the struggle and are prepared to make whatever sacrifices they are called upon to make. No attempt has yet been made to win over the Dubla and Raniparaj [lower castes, usually landless agricultural workers], but their relationship with Patidars is such that they will do whatever the latter ask them to do." Quoted in Narhari D. Parikh, *Sardar Vallabhbhai Patel* (Ahmedabad: Navajivan Publishing House, 1953), p. 156.

overtones of the Hindu communal Jan Sangh party, they decided not to join it precisely because of its communal overtones. The newly formed pro-business Swatantra party offered a haven for the Kshatriya Sabha. The state-wide leader of the Swatantra party — a Patidar, incidentally — approached the Kshatriya Sabha leaders and urged them to participate actively in this newly formed party. He wisely foresaw that with the participation of the Kshatriya Sabha this new party could emerge as the most powerful opposition party in the state legislature. He freely offered the Kshatriya Sabha control over important positions in the party organization and as many assembly and parliamentary seats as they wanted. Some of the wealthier members of the Kshatriya Sabha were personally sympathetic to the pro-business outlook of the Swatantra party, but in any event the program of the party was never a serious item for discussion. The major concern of the Kshatriya Sabha leaders was that they be given a dominant place in the party organization; when this was assured, they heartily agreed to join the Swatantra party.

One Kshatriya leader contrasted the attitude of the Swatantra party to that of a Congress leader who was obviously fearful of any efforts to establish a power base within Congress.

> Congressmen say that they are not a party which can consider community, but I tell you that they are really controlled by the Patidars. The truth is that they want other communities to be submissive to them. I said to Tribhuvandas, [the Congress president] that I wanted to do some work for Congress. Do not give me any power, I said, for I know that you do not want to give me any. Just give me some constructive work. Ask me to do something that other Congressmen will not do, such as prohibition work. But Tribhuvandas remained silent. Then there was a vacancy in the DCC and I asked Tribhuvandas if he would make me secretary, but Tribhuvandas refused to appoint me. Kshatriya Sabha workers throughout the state complained that they weren't getting their share in the Congress organization and so on March 5 — it was the birthday of the Lord Ram, the day on which three years earlier we had joined Congress — we decided to break away.

# 6. THE SOCIAL SYSTEM AND THE PARTY

From our study of Kaira district three central questions emerge around the theme of how a dominant political party is affected by the efforts of social groups to participate in party politics: (1) How does a participation crisis arise? (2) How does the dominant political elite respond to participation demands? (3) What are the likely consequences for the political system as a whole for a given response to this crisis? Let us turn now to an assessment of the origins, the response, and the consequences of a participatory crisis in Kaira district.

It is an oversimplification to say that the participatory crisis arose because a new social group sought to enter politics. The Bariyas and other low-caste groups which made up the Kshatriya Sabha — especially the Rajputs — had after all never been outside politics. Before the late 1950's, politics for the Rajputs was based primarily upon loyalties — upon kinship and clan ties and upon the fealty that the Rajput landlords commanded from subordinate social groups according to religious tradition and economic realities. Moreover, what was also distinctly traditional about this form of politics was the parochial political framework within which it took place. The power of the Rajputs and the few wealthy Bariyas who were village chieftains was limited to a handful of villages. Nor were Bariyas in general outside politics. Within the confines of the village they engaged in conflicts with one another and even on occasion with their superiors.

But these social groups had to contend with a different kind of politics in the latter part of the 1950's. With the establishment of universal adult suffrage in 1952, the Bariyas and Rajputs participated in the general

elections for state assemblies and national parliament, but participation in the larger parliamentary framework was still on a limited basis. There is no evidence that there was any substantial increase in Kshatriya voting in the 1957 or 1962 election. Neither the Bariyas nor the Rajputs — with few exceptions — had participated in nationalist organizations. Relatively few joined the Congress party or, for that matter, any party in the early 1950's. Still fewer stood for state or even district elective office.

The establishment of an elective system based upon adult suffrage and the increased involvement of government at all levels in the private lives of citizens were important factors in the shift, both by Rajputs and by Bariyas, from traditional local politics into the politics of representation. Government efforts to aid the Bariyas served also to make them aware of their backward position. The Rajputs stimulated the lower castes which made up the Kshatriya Sabha to enter party politics. We have already noted that the Rajputs were able to take advantage of the status aspirations of other communities which considered themselves Kshatriyas. Moreover, some Rajputs had themselves begun to identify with the entire Kshatriya movement and had accepted in toto the myths concerning the historic relationship between upper-caste and lower-caste Kshatriyas.

The Congress party proved unable to accommodate itself to the growing aspirations of the Bariyas or the ambitions of the Rajputs. We have noted that this lack of accommodation was related in part to the poor assessment by Congress of the magnitude of the threat and in part to organizational and cultural considerations. But while in one sense the Congress party failed — after all, Congress was badly defeated in Kaira district in 1962 — the political system as a whole was able to respond to the crisis.

It is important to note, first of all, that the Kshatriyas accepted the parliamentary system and even looked upon it as a vehicle for raising their status as well as for bringing about greater government measures for helping their community. One low-caste Kshatriya was elected to parliament in 1962. Mahida, now the secretary of the Swatantra group in parliament, spoke eloquently about the role of his colleague in parliament.

> He does not speak English but he is proud of his power, his position in parliament. He once earned only forty rupees a month but now he gets four hundred. He has brought his wife and his relatives here. They see and get in touch with this world. And he sees parliament and he sees the inside

of the president's house. He will speak of these things to his people when he returns home. Gandhi said "I have not won independence just for the educated classes. I have won it for four hundred million people." So I say let there be uneducated people here too. Democracy is not just for the educated people.

A majority of the party's candidates for the legislative assembly from Kaira district came from the non-Rajput communities in the 1962 elections. And in village panchayat elections, the numerically dominant but politically subordinate Bariyas began to fight the dominant Patidars for control. For the lower Kshatriya castes, the Kshatriya Sabha has become an important instrument for bringing them into the larger parliamentary framework. In this context caste identification has been a liberating force. It has facilitated social reform and, in particular, encouraged education within the lower castes. It has led the lower castes to engage more actively in elections. In some villages it has led the lower castes to become concerned with village government.[1] Moreover, though caste identification is often disintegrative in politics — by drawing sharp lines between one community and another — it may also be integrative. We have already noted that the Kshatriya Sabha is made up of a large number of disparate social groups. We are not dealing here with a traditional social group simply exercising its traditional cohesion in the parliamentary arena. Caste politics should not be confused with traditional politics.[2]

While tension and communal rivalry have emerged in a district where little or none existed before, it should be noted that they have emerged within the confines of the parliamentary system. If an opposition party had failed to elicit Kshatriya support or if the Kshatriyas had not seen the parliamentary and election arena as an arena for carrying out their purposes, we can only speculate as to what other forms this movement might have taken. Thus, while the Congress party failed to cope with this particular participation crisis, the party system did adapt itself.

After its defeat in the general elections Congress expanded its efforts to attract members of the Kshatriya community. One Bariya elected to the assembly on a Congress ticket was made deputy minister in the Gujarat government. Under his leadership Congress has organized a new

[1] This development is well documented in a number of masters' theses on village politics done at the University of Baroda. For citations, see the bibliography at the end of this chapter.

[2] It should be noted that in this context "caste" no longer refers to jati but to new kinds of self-conscious social groupings which had hitherto not existed.

Kshatriya organization concerned with providing the community with educational opportunities. A boarding hostel was started in the town of Anand to provide free accommodations to members of the Kshatriya community. Congressmen are now somewhat more sensitive to the status aspirations of low-caste Kshatriyas and are willing to give them opportunities within the party. It appears likely that Congress will make a greater effort to give seats to members of the Kshatriya community in the 1967 general elections. The new strategy of Congress is to seek support from Bariya and other low-caste Kshatriya groups while ignoring the Rajputs. In turn the Swatantra party is now increasing its efforts to win support from Patidars who resent the government's land reform program and the system of "permit raj." This is not to suggest that there will be no tension between Patidars and Kshatriyas or no violent clashes between the two communities. But the more successful the two parties are in broadening their social base, the more likely it is that both parties will be eager to avoid clashes since their own party workers would be affected. Their efforts to build popular support to win state-wide elections would be diminished by any sharp ethnic division in a society in which no single ethnic group by itself could win a state-wide election.

## Social System Models and Participation Crises

Let us turn now to the larger theoretical issue of the relationship between different kinds of social systems and a participation crisis. It is not uncommon for politically subordinate groups to try to gain greater power within a political system. Nor is it uncommon for the dominant political group to hesitate, particularly in the early stages, to share its power with an aspiring political force.[3]

There are at least two models of social systems in which participation crises may arise. These two models suggest that the character of the social system may be an important factor in determining the *effects* of the failure of leadership to cope with a participation crisis.

In one model, we have a vertically stratified social system in which ethnic groups are territorially confined. The country as a whole is made up of ethnic groups — tribes, races, linguistic or religious groups — living adjacent to one another. In such a vertically stratified system the most pressing problem invariably is how to achieve a measure of national in-

[3] Later in this book I shall draw from this and the other case studies to suggest some of the conditions under which a dominant group within the party is willing to share its power.

tegration. If the national leadership cannot satisfy the demands of one or more of the ethnic groups for greater participation in the political system, for a greater share of goods and services, or for higher social status, then the country is in danger of a civil insurrection. A crisis in such a vertically stratified social system may result in the fragmentation and disintegration of the nation-state.

In a second kind of social system, stratification is predominantly horizontal. There is a hierarchy of classes or social groups spread more or less throughout the entire territory. The hierarchy may be based simply on social class and economic disparities, though classes may have an ethnic overlay. Thus the group on the very top of the hierarchy may be not only the richest in the country but also ethnically identifiable and different from the rest of the population. The important point, however, is that the horizontally stratified social system more or less encompasses the entire territory of the nation-state. In this kind of social system a participation crisis may result in a revolutionary situation in which one social group aims to destroy the political power, status, and economic position of another. While in the first model the nation-state may be threatened by a participation crisis, in the second model it is the social system which is under attack.

There are few countries which are purely one type or the other. In a general way one might say that a large number of the countries of Africa closely approximate the first model, while France and several other European countries of the nineteenth century more closely approximated the second model. India does not fit either case, and suggests that a third model is required. India, to somewhat oversimplify, has a series of hierarchical social systems, each of which is more or less territorially confined. Each linguistic region is made up of a series of hierarchically arranged castes who typically do not intermarry or have close social relations with castes in other linguistic regions. In any one region a given social group may seek to displace another in the status hierarchy. Politics is one arena in which this struggle takes place. It is difficult for an aspiring caste to reach out to a neighboring state or in many instances even to a neighboring district to establish a political coalition. There is almost no reason to do so, because each aspiring caste may have a different enemy; the dominant caste itself is often limited to one or two districts, if that, and at the very most spreads throughout a single state. A few castes cut across state boundaries or large regions of the country, but we need not be concerned here with these few exceptions to our general argument. The main point is that the political struggles which occur in one district

may have relatively little impact on political relationships in a neighboring district. While the limitations in communication may also be a factor, the most significant element is the segmented character of the social system.

There is thus a built-in quarantine effect of crises in the Indian political system. A clash between two ethnic groups or two castes may be seriously disruptive in a given locality. There may be massive violence; the dominant party may be soundly defeated. But what happens in district A may have little or no effect on neighboring districts B and C. While Congress was defeated in Kaira district, for example, the party as a whole did well in the rest of the state. Congress easily won state-wide elections in 1962. The party thus has an opportunity to learn from its limited defeat while it continues to control the state government and the state administration. The local cooperatives, banks, district local boards, and taluka boards are still under Congress control. Five years elapse between general elections, and during this period the Congress party has an opportunity to try to regain the support of those people who defected from the party. With a little more sensitivity to the demands of the Kshatriya community, the Congress party may do better in the 1967 elections.[4] In the meantime a conflict among other social groups may occur in other districts of the state, and elsewhere the Congress may suffer a major defeat. Thus there may be a series of brush fires, each unconnected to the other. As one brush fire is put out, another begins, and fire fighters are transferred from one part of the forest to another. We have spoken thus far as if this were a hypothetical situation, when in fact much of Indian politics can be understood in these terms. Since India achieved independence the Congress party has encountered one state crisis after another. Congress has been defeated in some states even while remaining powerful in others. But the states in which Congress was defeated in 1952 were often the states in which Congress did well in 1957, and states in which the Congress did well in one election were often faced with crises five years later. In 1952, for example, Madras was a crisis state, torn by the demands of the Telugus against the Tamils and of non-Brahmins against Brahmins. But in 1957 and again in 1962 the Congress party emerged as a strong force, and Madras proved in subsequent elections to be among the most stable states in the country. In Rajasthan the

---

[4] Since this was written, the 1967 elections have been held. Narendra Singh Mahida resigned from the Swatantra party and was reelected to Parliament on a Congress ticket. Congress regained its majority in the district by winning 9 of 16 seats (compared with 5 in 1962) with 48.6 per cent of the popular vote as against 7 seats and 45.1 per cent of the vote for Swatantra.

Congress party barely achieved victory in 1952, did extraordinarily well in the 1957 elections, but again won narrowly in the 1962 elections. No national opposition leadership has been able to find a formula which could bring together all the dissident elements in all the states simultaneously. A federal system also serves to quarantine state crises; unlike a highly centralized political system, a central government in a federal system can be relatively unaffected by political crises which occur in any of the constituent parts of the federal union. In India the federal system is an institutional frame for her segmented social system.

For the past twenty years India has appeared to be constantly on the verge of social revolution or internal disintegration. Castes have opposed one another. Religious groups have been engaged in violent combat. Linguistic and tribal groups have demanded special state representation. The Congress party has been torn by factional disputes. But it is because each social conflict and each social group is confined to a limited geographical area that the Indian political system as a whole can show remarkable stability even while its constituent parts may be torn with internal conflict.

# APPENDIX
# CONGRESS PARTY CADRES IN KAIRA

In 1959 the number of active members of the Congress party in Kaira District stood at 741. By consulting party registers, I obtained information concerning age, residence, and occupation for nearly all these members. Although caste affiliation of the cadres was not recorded, it was possible with the help of the secretary of the Congress party organization to identify the caste of about 75 per cent of the party activists. Using these four variables — age, occupation, residence, and caste — I made all possible first-order cross tabulations. The significant relationships are reported below.

### Active Party Membership

*Organization.* The Congress party in Kaira is organized into seventy-one mandal committees and ten taluka committees. Each taluka committee has approximately the same proportion of activist members as its size would prescribe if the party were strictly representative of the population.

*Growth of party membership.* In the seven years from 1953 to 1959 both primary and active Congress membership in Kaira and in Gujarat as a whole have grown sporadically, as Table 10 indicates.

TABLE 10
KAIRA AND GUJARAT CONGRESS PARTY MEMBERSHIP, 1953–59

| | KAIRA | | GUJARAT | |
|---|---|---|---|---|
| | Primary | Active | Primary | Active |
| 1953 . . . . . . . . | 37,964 | 485 | . . . . | . . . . |
| 1954 . . . . . . . . | 27,198 | 410 | 229,220 | 3,722 |
| 1955 . . . . . . . . | 34,205 | 465 | 146,109 | 3,474 |
| 1956 . . . . . . . . | 33,905 | 507 | 309,754 | 5,154 |
| 1957 . . . . . . . . | 21,521 | 365 | 283,817 | 5,200 |
| 1958 . . . . . . . . | 56,671 | 811 | 226,066 | 4,222 |
| 1959 . . . . . . . . | 47,674 | 741 | 407,214 | 6,310 |

SOURCE: From Congress Patrika, November 28, 1959, No. 28, p. 527.

## Urban and Rural Party Cadres

*Rural penetration.* Throughout India the Congress party has done well in rural areas; prosperous, agricultural Kaira has been a district in which it has been particularly strong. Kaira as a whole is heavily rural. 69.5 per cent of the population lives in villages of less than five thousand inhabitants. Slightly fewer Congress party activists (only 57.7 per cent) live in villages of less than five thousand. While there is at least one Congress party worker in every town in the district, there are workers in only 24 per cent of the villages. These villages, however, happen to be the larger ones of the district, so half the actual district population lives in a town or village where Congress is represented.

*Urban-rural comparisons.* Urban and rural (living in villages of less than five thousand) cadres differ significantly along several dimensions. The typical rural Congress party activist is a Patidar agriculturalist. Interviews suggest that these Patidars are landholders rather than tenants. Although Patidars are numerically most likely to be from rural areas (202 of 332), Kshatriyas (Rajputs and Bariyas) are proportionately more often found in rural areas (39 of 54). Banias are the most urban caste (36 of 61), followed by the Brahmins (27 of 53). There is a slight tendency for rural cadres to be younger than urban ones, but the relationship is far from being statistically significant.

## Congress Cadre's Caste Affiliation

The caste distribution within the party membership well reflects the conflicts within the district. Before the departure of the Kshatriya Sabha from Congress in 1959, the proportion of Kshatriyas (Rajputs and Bariyas)

within the party was considerably greater than at present. Census reports no longer include caste distribution, so that it is impossible to estimate how representative the party is. Party leaders, however, estimate that about 40 per cent of the population of Kaira are Bariyas, 20 per cent Patidars, 7 per cent Harijans and the rest, Banias and others. The census report of 1879 claimed that 5 per cent were Banias, 6 per cent Brahmins, and 36 per cent Kolis (another term for Bariyas). Table 11 shows that the number of Patidars in Congress is much greater proportionately than would be expected in a purely representative party.

TABLE 11
CASTE DISTRIBUTION OF PARTY WORKERS IN KAIRA

| Caste | Number | % of Total |
|---|---|---|
| Patidars. . . . . . . . . . . | 332 | 44.8 |
| Banias . . . . . . . . . . | 61 | 8.1 |
| Rajputs-Bariyas . . . . . . | 54 | 7.3 |
| Brahmins . . . . . . . . . | 53 | 7.1 |
| Muslims. . . . . . . . . . | 21 | 2.8 |
| Artisan castes . . . . . . . | 8 | 1.1 |
| Others. . . . . . . . . . | 17 | 2.3 |
| Not identified, but non-Patidars . . . . . | 196 | 26.5 |

## Occupations

*Agriculture.* The Congress party in Kaira is composed primarily of peasant proprietors and businessmen who together account for 75.1 per cent of the cadres. Owners of land, whether cultivators or rent receivers, comprise 52.4 per cent of the population, while 55.7 per cent (413) of the cadres list their occupation as "agriculture." Since most of these latter are probably landowners, it seems fair to conclude that they are representative of the district as a whole, though if all agricultural classes in Kaira are considered, including tenants, the proportion of the population engaged in agriculture rises to 71.1 per cent. It seems, therefore, that Congress party activists are representatives of the upper strata of agriculturalists but not of the landless tenants and farm laborers who comprise 24.7 per cent of the population.

*Non-agricultural occupations.* Of the population as a whole, 15.2 per cent are engaged in business, while 19.4 (144) of the party workers list business as their primary occupation. Full-time political workers make up 5.7 per cent (42) of the cadres, while 12.4 per cent (92) hold white-collar or professional jobs as against 12.7 per cent in the population as a

whole. The full-time party workers are often lawyers or small business-men dealing in grains. Many of the full-time workers own land and are supported by their families. Typically, they receive income also from holding some appointed or elective office. Several Congressmen have salaried positions in the local cooperative unions, and a few earn income as members of the state legislative assembly. The proportion of those employed as political workers increases constantly as the size of village or town of residence increases. Political workers are also the oldest cadres. Businessmen come from the middle-age groups, agriculturalists from all age groups in almost equal proportions. White-collar workers are the youngest, professionals the oldest. Caste and occupation are also significantly related. Brahmins are proportionately more often full-time political workers than any other caste; Patidars, with fifteen political workers, are the most numerous. Banias, as elsewhere, are most likely to be business-men. The Rajputs and Bariyas are the most agricultural caste (81.5 per cent), followed by the Patidars. Brahmins are more likely to be white collar workers than other castes, and Banias are more often professionals.

## Age of Party Cadres

As in most areas in which the population growth rate is high, the population of Kaira district is relatively young. Congress cadres are considerably older than the population at large, the average age being in the early forties. Age and caste were not significantly related, though there was a slight tendency for Brahmins to be the oldest, Banias the youngest. The relationship between age and occupation has been given above.

Table 12 shows the age distribution of Congress party cadres.

The concentration of party activists in the middle-age group suggests

TABLE 12
AGE DISTRIBUTION OF CONGRESS WORKERS IN KAIRA

| Age | Number | Per Cent |
|---|---|---|
| 21–25 . . . . . . . . . . . . . | 26 | 3.7 |
| 26–30 . . . . . . . . . . . . . | 62 | 8.8 |
| 31–35 . . . . . . . . . . . . . | 118 | 16.7 |
| 36–40 . . . . . . . . . . . . . | 136 | 19.3 |
| 41–45 . . . . . . . . . . . . . | 138 | 19.5 |
| 46–50 . . . . . . . . . . . . . | 93 | 13.2 |
| 51–55 . . . . . . . . . . . . . | 75 | 10.6 |
| 56–60 . . . . . . . . . . . . . | 37 | 5.2 |
| 61 and over . . . . . . . . . | 21 | 3.0 |
| Total . . . . . . . . . . . | 706 | 100.0 |

that in the latter phases of the pre-independence nationalist movement cadres were frequently recruited among the young age groups, whereas now the party finds new recruits in all age brackets.

### Congress Party Officials and Elected Representatives

More detailed information was obtained for twenty-seven MLAs, MPs, and district party officials from Kaira.* Some differences between this group and the party cadres as a whole are apparent. They are better educated, twenty-one of twenty-seven having at least a college education. Interviews suggest, however, that taluka leaders are equally well educated, most of them having attended colleges in Gujarat. Some have even done post-graduate work, while others are graduates of Gujarat Vidyapith, the nationalist college in Ahmedabad. The MLAs, MPs, and Kaira district party officials are more active in social and political affairs. In contrast to the cadres, among the elected Congressmen the younger are somewhat more urban than the older. Non-agricultural occupations predominate. The number of organized interest activities participated in by MLAs and MPs is quite high, with an average of four activities per Congressman. Local civics, cooperatives, social reform, and general political activities were mentioned most frequently. In general, this group, in comparison to the cadres, is older, more educated, more involved in politics, more professional, and more urban.

*Data on MPs were taken from the Parliamentary *Who's Who* for 1952 and 1957 and for the state assembly from the *Bombay Legislature Directory* (Bombay: Legislature Congress Party, 1953); and *Bombay Legislature — Congress Party Directory* (Bombay: Legislature Congress Party, 1958).

# BIBLIOGRAPHY: KAIRA DISTRICT

Materials for this chapter were from the following sources: (1) interviews; (2) documents and reports by the Congress party in Kaira and Gujarat, as well as reports of the state and local government and administration; (3) secondary studies of the economy, social organization, and political behavior in the district and state.

## Interviews

The description of the Congress party in Kaira is based largely on extensive interviews with thirty-six politicians and government officials in Kaira district. These included the president and secretary of the DCC, secretaries of several taluka and mandal committees, and officers of the Amul Dairy, the District School Board, the District Local Board, the District Cooperative Bank, the District Sales and Purchase Union, the District Magistrate, and a number of other administrative officers in the Community Development Program. I also interviewed the Congress member of parliament and several Congress MLAs.

Outside Kaira district I interviewed Congress leaders in the Pradesh Congress office in Ahmedabad, including the present and former secretary of the Gujarat Pradesh Congress Committee, as well as several party officers. There were also interviews with the president and secretary of the Congress party in Baroda, the city closest to Kaira district.

In addition to these thirty-six interviews — some of which were many hours long and were in two or even three sessions — I had brief inter-

views with a large number of Congress activists, workers in the Kshatriya Sabha, and local administrative officers. Finally, my general knowledge of the area was illuminated by T. N. Sheth and A. M. Shah, both then in the department of sociology at the University of Baroda, and Rajni Kothari, then in the department of political science at the University of Baroda.

### Documents and Reports

*Congress reports and documents.* On the Congress party itself there are few published documents and source materials. The DCC in Kaira kindly opened its records to me; these contained data on party membership, reports on workings of various auxiliary bodies, and extensive correspondence. Since Sardar Vallabhbhai Patel comes from Kaira district, his biographies contain some description of politics in Kaira before independence. See Mahadev Haribhai Desai, *The Story of Bardoli: Being a History of the Bardoli Satyagraha of 1928 and Its Sequel* (Ahmedabad: Navajivan, 1929); Balkrishna Govind Gokhale, "Sardar Vallabhbhai Patel: the Party Organizer as Political Leader," *in* Richard L. Park and Irene Tinker, eds., *Leadership and Political Institutions in India* (Princeton: Princeton University Press, 1959); Abdul Majid Khan, *Life and Speeches of Sardar Patel: A Study of the Career and Character of Sardar Patel, as Well as His Ideas and Ideals, including All His Important Speeches until His Death* (New Delhi: Indian Printing Works, 1951); and Narhari D. Parikh, *Sardar Vallabhbhai Patel*, Vols. 1 and 2 (Ahmedabad: Navajivan, 1953). On the history of the nationalist movement in Gujarat, see *Source Material for a History of the Freedom Movement in India*, Vol. 1, (1818–1885), Vol. 2 (1885–1920) (Bombay: Government of Bombay, 1957).

A most interesting report on the functioning of the party organization in Gujarat as a whole is *Report of the Sub-Committee of the Gujarat Pradesh Congress Committee to Enquire into the Working of the Congress Organization in Gujarat* (New Delhi: AICC, 1957). On the position of the Gujarat Congress toward states reorganization, see *Memorandum Presented by the Gujarat Pradesh Congress Committee to the States Reorganization Commission, December 6, 1954* (Ahmedabad: Gujarat Pradesh Congress Committee, 1954).

*Government reports and documents.* The gazetteers are valuable sources of information on the social organization, agrarian system, history, ad-

ministration, and geography of the district. The census reports contain basic demographic data for the district and the state. Of special value is the district census handbook, which contains demographic data by village. I have used the following: *Bombay Gazetteer, Kaira and Panchmahals*, 1879; *Bombay Gazetteer Rewa Kantha, Nayuka, Cambay and Surat States*, 1880; *Census of India, 1951*, Vol. IV, *Bombay, Saurashtra, and Kutch* (Part IIa and b) (Bombay: Government Central Press, 1953); *Kaira District Census Handbook* (Bombay: Government of Bombay, 1953); *Handbook of Basic Statistics of Gujarat State, 1960* (Bombay: Bureau of Economics and Statistics, Government of Bombay, 1960).

Four pieces of legislation affecting agricultural relations in Kaira District are important for an understanding of the Kshatriya-Patidar dispute: "Amendment to the Bombay Tenancy and Agricultural Lands Act of 1948," *The Gujarat Government Gazette*, 15 December 1960; *The Bombay Money-Lenders Act of 1946, as Modified up to the 15 February 1961* (Ahmedabad: Government of Gujarat, Legal Department, Government Printing, Gujarat State, 1961); *The Bombay Land Tenures Abolition (Amendment) Act of 1953, as modified to 15 September 1959* (Bombay: Government of Bombay, Legal Department, Government Printing, Bombay State, 1960); *The Bombay Taluqdari Tenure Abolition Act of 1949, as Modified up to 1 September 1957* (Bombay: Government of Bombay, Legal Department, Government Central Press, 1957).

Two other state documents are important for district politics: *Report of the Democratic Decentralization Committee, Part 1*, (Rural Development Department of the Government of Gujarat, 1960), which provided the basis for the reorganization of local rural government in the state; and the *Second Five Year Plan, Bombay State, Kaira District (1956–7 to 1960–61)* (Bombay: Directorate of Publicity, Government of Bombay, 1959).

Of special value for my study of the politics of the Kshatriya community was a judicial report of an election tribunal which looked into a complaint of unfair practices in an MLA constituency during the 1957 elections. I have not been able to find this document in published form, but a typescript was made available to me by a Congress MLA. Another government report of a judicial character that has proved useful is *Report of the Commission of Inquiry on Police Firings at Dohad, District Panchmahals, on the 12th July 1960* (Baroda: Government of Gujarat, 1961).

*Secondary Sources*

*Social organization.* One of the earliest descriptions of the Bariyas — then known as the Kolis — can be found in the writings of N. Bernier, a French physician who toured North India in the seventeenth century. See M. S. Commissariat, *History of Gujarat* (Bombay: 1938). For an ethnographic description of the Bariyas and their social organization, see the following works: A. M. Shah, "Caste, Economy and Territory in the Central Panchmahals," *Journal of the Maharaja Sayajirao* (University of Baroda) IV (March 1959): 65–91; A. M. Shah, "A Dispersed Hamlet in the Panchmahals," *Economic Weekly*, (26 January 1955); A. M. Shah and R. G. Shroff, "The Vahivanca Barots of Gujarat: A Caste of Genealogists and Mythographers," *in* Milton Singer, ed., *Traditional India: Structure and Change* (Philadelphia: American Folklore Society, 1959).

Historians describe Kolis as wild tribesmen, noted for piracy at sea and pillage on land, at least into the eleventh century, when they are known to have fought against the Solanki king. In the sixteenth century they are known to have plundered the towns of Cambay, Ahmedabad, and Baroda as well as the villages of northern Gujarat. In the British period the bulk of the Kolis became petty landholders and agricultural laborers, but a few became rulers of small principalities and independent states.

On the Patidar community the following studies by the British social anthropologist David F. Pocock have been most helpful: "The Bases of Faction in Gujarat," *British Journal of Sociology* 8 (1957): 296–306; "The Hypergamy of the Patidars," *in* K. M. Kapadia, ed., *Professor Ghurye Felicitation Volume* (Bombay: Popular Book Depot) pp. 195–204; and "Inclusion and Exclusion: A Process in the Caste System of Gujarat," *Southwestern Journal of Anthropology* 13 (1956): 19–31. See also T. B. Naik, "Social Status in Gujarat," *Eastern Anthropologist* 10 (1957): 173–81.

There is an extensive literature on the Rajputs. See: John T. Hitchcock, "The Idea of the Martial Rajput," *in* Milton B. Singer, ed., *Traditional India: Structure and Change* (Philadelphia: American Folklore Society, 1959); J. T. Hitchcock, "Surat Singh, Head Judge," *in* Joseph B. Casagrande, ed., *In the Company of Man* (New York: Harper, 1960); Gitel P. Steed, "Notes on an Approach to a Study of Personality Formation in a Hindu Village in Gujarat," *in* McKim Marriott, ed., *Village India* (Chicago: University of Chicago Press, 1955), pp. 102–44; Daniel Thorner,

"Feudalism in India," *in* Ruston Coulborn, ed., *Feudalism in History* (Princeton: Princeton University Press, 1956); James Tod, *Annals and Antiquities of Rajasthan* (first published 1829–32) (London: Oxford University Press, 1950); Morris Carstairs, *The Twice-Born: A Study of a Community of High-Caste Hindus* (London: Hogarth Press, 1957).

Other studies of social organization in Gujarat include: N. C. Desai, *Report on the Joint Family System* (Baroda: Baroda State Press, 1936); Irawate Karve, "Kinship Terminology and Kinship Usages in Gujarat and Kathiawad," *Deccan College Post-Graduate and Research Institute Bulletin* 4 (1943): 203–26; T. B. Naik, "Religion of the Anavils of Surat," *in* Milton B. Singer, ed., *Traditional India: Structure and Change* (Philadelphia: American Folklore Society, 1959), pp. 389–96; Papatlal Govindlal Shah, *The Dublas of Gujarat* (Delhi: Bharatiya Adimjati Sevak Sangh, 1958); Harshad R. Trivedi, *The Mers of Saurashtra* (Baroda: M. S. University of Baroda, 1961); and Y. V. S. Nath, *Bhils of Ratanmak* (Baroda: M. S. University of Baroda, 1960). A number of other studies deal with villages of Gujarat, including studies of the economy and social structure: R. G. Gordon, "Some Notes on the Village System of the Bombay Presidency," *Anthropological Society of Bombay Journal* 12: 92–101; *Bhadkod — Social and Economic Survey of a Village, a Comparative Study 1915 and 1955.* (Bombay: The Indian Society of Agricultural Economics: 1957); Gatoolal Chhaganlal Mukhtyar, *Life and Labour in a South Gujarat Village* (Calcutta: Longmans, 1930); Hasmukhlal Dhirajlal Sankalia, *Studies in the Historical and Cultural Geography and Ethnography of Gujarat* (Poona Deccan College Post-Graduate and Research Institute, 1949); Vimal Shah, *Bhuvel: Socio-Economic Survey of a Village* (Bombay: Vora, 1949); Jadavrai Ghavanishankar Shukla, *Life and Labour in a Gujarat Taluka* (Bombay: Longmans, 1937); Kantilal C. Avidha Vyas, "A Narration of Changing Life in a Gujarat Village," *Sociological Bulletin*, 2 (1953): 18–34.

Other works on the political, social, and economic history of the district are: Edward Clive Bayley, *The Local Muhammadan Dynasties: Gujarat* (London: W. H. Allen, 1886); Rustam Dinshaw Choksey, *Economic History of the Bombay Deccan and Karnatak (1818–1868)* (Poona, 1945); *Forty-second Session Indian Service Congress, Baroda, 1955* (Baroda: M. S. University of Baroda, 1955), especially Y. Y. S. Nath, "People of Gujarat," pp. 58–69, and B. Subbaroo, "Archeology of Gujarat," pp. 44–57; K. M. Munshi, *Glory That Was Gujarat Desa* (Bombay, 1955); K. M. Munshi, *Gujarat and Its Literature* (Bombay, 1935); Stanley Pitcairn

Rice, *Life of Sayaji Rao III, Maharaja of Baroda* (London: Oxford University Press, 1931); B. A. Saletore, *Main Currents in the Ancient History of Gujarat* (Baroda: M. S. University of Baroda, 1960); Lawrence Frederic Rushbrook Williams, *The Black Hills: Kutch in History and Legend* (London: Weidenfeld and Nicolson, 1958); A. M. Shah, "Political System in Eighteenth Century Gujarat," *Enquiry*, 1 (Spring 1964): 83–95.

Economic and administrative studies include: M. B. Desai, *Report on the Administrative Survey of the Surat District*, Research Programmes Committee Planning Commission; M. B. Desai, *Report on an Enquiry into the Working of the Bombay Tenancy and Agricultural Lands Act, 1948 (as Amended up to 1953) in Gujarat (Excluding Baroda District)* (Bombay: The Indian Society of Agricultural Economics, 1958); M. B. Desai, *Rural Economy of Gujarat* (Bombay: 1948); *Economic and Social Survey of Mehsana District* (India Society of Agricultural Economics, 1954); V. Y. Kolhatkar and S. B. Mahabal, *An Inquiry into the Effects of the Working of the Tenancy Legislation in the Baroda District of Bombay State* (Baroda: M. S. University of Baroda, 1958); H. C. Malkani, *A Socio-Economic Survey of Baroda City* (Baroda: Sadhana Press, 1958); J. M. Mehta, *A Study of the Rural Economy of Gujarat Containing Possibilities of Reconstruction* (Baroda: Baroda State Press, 1930); D. P. Pandit, "Creative Response in Indian Economy — A Regional Analysis," *Economic Weekly* (23 February and 2 March, 1957).

*Political studies.* Under the guidance of A. H. Somjee, chairman of the department of political science at Baroda, a number of MA theses were done on villages near Baroda city. These reports are among the few detailed empirical studies of village politics. Somjee himself has done a study of voting patterns in one village in the 1957 general elections: *Voting Behaviour in an Indian Village* (Baroda: M. S. University of Baroda, 1959). The MA theses are: H. M. Amin, "The Role of Patidars in the Politics of Bhati"; Miss Amarjit Chawla, "Panchayat and Leadership in Village Manjalpur"; H. L. Pathak, "Politics of Dominant Social Groups in Gutri"; S. N. Parikh, "Panchayat and Politics of Harni"; Ghanshyam S. Shah, "The Role of Patidars in the Public Life of Kalali"; Ramesh G. Shah, "Panchayat and Politics of Village Gorwa"; Miss Kalpana N. Mehta, "Problems of Panchayat Leadership in Atladra." Rajni Kothari and Rushikesh Maru have written a brief account of the Kshatriya Sabha in their article, "Caste and Secularism in India," *Journal of Asian Studies* 25 (November, 1965): 33–50. Other relevant political studies on Gujarat

include K. S. Desai, *Problems of Administration in Two Indian Villages* (Baroda: M. S. University of Baroda, Department of Political Science, 1961); Rajni Kothari and Tarun Sheth, "Extent and Limits of Community Voting: The Case of Baroda East," *in* Myron Weiner, ed., *Indian Voting Behaviour — the 1962 General Elections* (Calcutta: K. L. Mukhopadhyay, 1965).

# PART III. PANCHAYATS AND FACTIONS: GUNTUR DISTRICT

## 7. THE PROBLEM AND ITS SETTING IN GUNTUR

I selected Guntur district in Andhra for a case study in order to explore the impact of newly established (and enlarged) institutions of local government on the Congress party. The assumption of such a study was that major changes in local government in a rural area were bound to affect the performance of the party — whom it recruited, how it dealt with internal conflict, how it won support and from whom. It seemed appropriate, therefore, to begin by exploring in some detail the character of the social system and the patterns of politics into which these institutions were introduced. It seemed especially important to understand the conflicts within the district and within the party which were being affected by institutional changes. I soon moved into the intricacies of local politics where caste, kinship, and factional loyalties intertwine with personal ambitions for status, office, and profit. It was apparent that I had to explain what people were fighting about and how they grouped together before I assessed the role played by local government institutions in these conflicts.

The question of what it is that people are fighting over and how they are grouped together is not so easily answered as one might expect. On first appearance one might conclude that party politics and panchayat politics in Andhra are essentially the politics of caste. One student of Andhra politics concluded that the struggle between the Communists and Congress was primarily a reflection of ancient conflicts between the Reddi

and Kamma castes, the two major peasant proprietor landholding castes in Andhra.[1] Politicians will attribute caste loyalties to others as the primary (and primordial) force in the state. It is a plausible hypothesis, but, as we shall see, there is strong evidence to suggest that political alignments are only partially affected by caste affiliations.

An alternative hypothesis to explain the behavior of Andhra politicians is that they have ties to their kinsmen, their caste, their village, their friends, and that they pick and choose their loyalties as it suits their personal quest for office. This is a much more plausible hypothesis which would help explain some of the seeming instabilities of political affiliations in Andhra, the readiness with which men appear to shift from one party to another, and the instability of village voting patterns.

We shall suggest as a third hypothesis that politicians have affiliations to factional group, which are in fact multi-caste, and that these affiliations are durable rather than transitory. We shall suggest that factions are the units of political action both within parties and within villages, and that the relationship between party faction and village faction is the single most important variable affecting the outcome of many (but not all) elections. We shall also suggest that it is the intricate relationship among factions which affects the stability of the Andhra government, determines who becomes state chief minister, and affects the relative electoral standing of Congress as against opposition parties in the state. To support this hypothesis, in Chapter 8 we shall analyze factionalism within the Congress party in Guntur as it relates to factional conflicts in political parties throughout the state, and then turn to an analysis of village factionalism in the 1962 elections as it relates to the Congress party. In effect, we shall show how traditional forms of political groupings affect the patterns of conflict and cohesion within Congress and how, paradoxically, intra-party conflicts increase the capacity of the party to win popular support.

In Chapter 9 we shall look at the effects of the new local government bodies on Congress recruitment and on the use of patronage by Congress, then turn to the role of socialist ideology within Congress in legitimizing both panchayati raj and patronage politics. Finally, in Chapter 10 we shall consider more generally the impact of this structural change on the forms and level of political participation in Guntur.

[1] Selig S. Harrison, "Caste and the Andhra Communists," *American Political Science Review* 50 (June, 1956): 378–404.

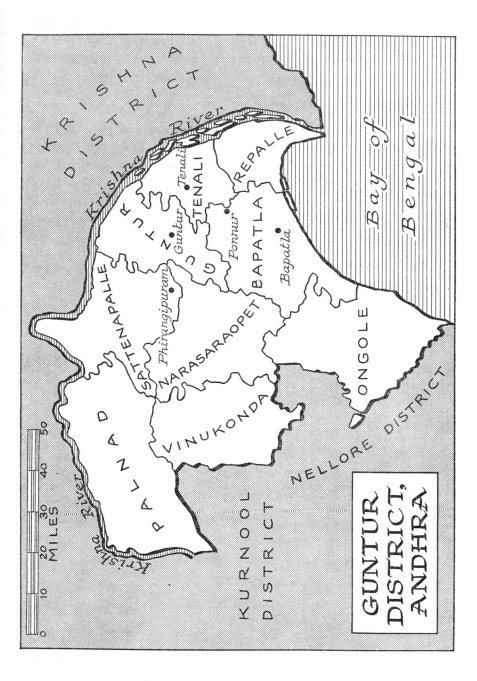

KRISHNA DISTRICT

Krishna River

Bay of Bengal

GUNTUR

Guntur

Tenali

TENALI

REPALLE

Ponnur

BAPATLA

Bapatla

SATTENAPALLE

Phirangipuram

NARASARAOPET

PALNAD

Krishna River

VINUKONDA

ONGOLE

KURNOOL DISTRICT

NELLORE DISTRICT

MILES

0  10  20  30  40  50

GUNTUR
DISTRICT, ANDHRA

## *Guntur District: The Setting*

Guntur district is an area of 5,795 square miles located in the delta of the Krishna River on the eastern shoreline of Andhra. The state itself was first created in 1953 when the Telugu-speaking districts of Madras, including Guntur, were separated to form the independent state of Andhra. Three years later, in 1956, the state was expanded to include the nine Telugu-speaking districts of Hyderabad state known as Telengana.

Guntur is the most populated district in the entire state and one of the most populated districts in all India. In 1961 Guntur had 3,009,997 people, or a density of 613 people per square mile, in a predominantly rural region. About 20 per cent of the population (630,000) live in towns, and the rest live in rural areas. In all there are twenty towns in the district, but only two have populations exceeding fifty thousand: Guntur, the district capital, with a population of 187,068, and Tenali with 78,490.

The chief crop of the district is paddy, and, like other districts in the deltaic region, Guntur is a paddy-surplus area. Chillies, groundnuts, tobacco, and cashews are the chief commercial crops, and these are exported not only to other parts of India but also to England, China, the United States, and the Soviet Union. There is thus in many parts of the district a political sophistication and experience in dealing with government that one commonly finds only in urban centers or in other rural areas which have cash crops.

Politically, socially, and economically, the most important castes in Guntur have been the Brahmins, the Kammas, and the Reddis, the latter two being the traditional agricultural castes of the district. The last detailed census breakdown by caste was conducted in 1921. At that time the total population of the district was 1.8 million. Brahmins numbered 100,000; Kammas, by far the numerically dominant caste, numbered 316,000; and the Reddis were under 150,000. Another caste, the Telagas, also an important agricultural community, totaled slightly under 150,000. The Malas and Madigas, the two largest untouchable castes, together numbered 190,000; but there were another 153,000 Indian Christians, who are generally low in status and income, and 125,000 Muslims.

The district has a reputation throughout the South as a center of leadership for all political parties. The Congress chief minister of the state (as of 1965) comes from Guntur; so does the minister of state for defense in the central government, the head of the Swatantra party of Andhra, and several state-wide leaders of the now defunct Praja Socialist party, including its president. The Communist party of Andhra, one of

the few units of the party in India with a predominantly rural leadership base, derives much of its support and leadership from Guntur. And in the pre-independence era, many of the leaders of the once powerful anti-Brahmin, pro-British Justice party which at one time governed Madras state had Guntur as a major political center.

Several factors probably account for Guntur's importance as a center for political activity by all parties. The district has a substantially large landowning class with a high rate of literacy and a comparatively high income. It is a class which engages in the production of commercial cash crops, is closely associated with commercial and educational activities

TABLE 13

LAND TENURES IN GUNTUR, ANDHRA, AND INDIA
(Per Cent)

|  | Owner-Cultivators | Owner-Lessors | Tenants | Laborers |
|---|---|---|---|---|
| India . . . . . . | 67.2 | 2.1 | 12.7 | 18.0 |
| Andhra . . . . . | 58.0 | 3.4 | 10.3 | 28.3 |
| Guntur. . . . . . | 59.6 | 2.9 | 5.8 | 31.7 |

SOURCE: *Report of the Land Reforms Committee*, (Kurnool: Andhra Government, 1955), p. 5. The committee reports that probably about 15 per cent of the total cultivated land in Andhra is tilled by tenants (p. 9).

in the two major towns in the district, and has a long tradition of involvement with local administration.

The proportion of owner-cultivators employing agricultural laborers is higher in Guntur than is typical for Andhra or for India as a whole.

It is also of some importance that the value of land in Guntur is high, an important factor in the rise of a prosperous landowning class willing to engage in politics and having income and — particularly given the extended family — the time to do so. There has been a gradual rise in the value of land since 1932 as a result of a rapid growth in population, the rising price of crops, increased irrigation, and therefore increased productivity.[2]

Rice yield per acre in Guntur is 1,359 pounds, the highest in Andhra and one of the highest in India. Guntur also leads in per acre yields for jowar, wheat, and gram, and is well ahead of other districts in many other crops. In some parts of Guntur land sells for about five thousand rupees (one thousand dollars) an acre. An acre of land under paddy can bring in three hundred rupees (sixty dollars) profit, so that a landowner with fifty

[2] About 500,000 acres (of 3,693,000) are irrigated mainly by government canals. This will increase when the Nagarjunasagar Project to control the waters of the Krishna is completed. Much of the upland dry land will then be converted into wet-crop paddy land.

acres can earn three thousand dollars a year — an extraordinarily high income in a country where the average per capita yearly income is only about sixty-five dollars. Only a small number own such large holdings, but a substantial number of farmers — unfortunately no reliable data are available to tell us precisely how many — own five or ten acres. It is these men who constitute the rural gentry class of Guntur and from whom the political activists are recruited.

The presence of a relatively prosperous agricultural community is an important factor in the high literacy of the district. It was 27.4 per cent in 1961, about the same as that of other districts in the delta, but nearly twice that of the Telengana region of Andhra to the west. Male literacy was particularly high — 35 per cent — again nearly twice that of the non-delta districts of Andhra.

Many of the landowning families have close educational and commercial connections to the two major towns in Guntur: Guntur and Tenali. Both towns are important trading centers for the rural hinterlands of the district. A large part of the commercial crop of the district is marketed through these two towns. In Guntur town alone, there are over five hundred commercial establishments and about five thousand persons engaged in commercial activities; one hundred employers are engaged there in wholesale trade. Both towns are railway centers, and Guntur is also the major center for money lending and banking in the district. Finally, the two towns are social and educational centers for the district. Guntur houses several colleges, and Tenali one plus an Oriental college for the study of Sanskrit. The sons of the wealthier members of the peasant proprietor class are generally educated in the two towns.

The landholding families in Guntur are usually extended families. Since among the upper castes cross-cousin marriages are preferred, families' relations are unusually intimate. In a single household it is customary for some members of the family to engage in the supervision of agricultural labors (rarely in direct cultivation). As we have seen, there is one agricultural laborer for two owner cultivators, compared with a ratio of nearly four to one in the rest of the country. Moreover, there are far fewer tenants in Guntur than elsewhere in India. Among the more prosperous landowning families in Guntur it is therefore common for the land to be directly managed by one or two members of the family, for the cultivation to be done by hired labor, and for one or more members of the family to be educated members of the professions, participating in commercial or political activities at the village, district, or state level.

# 8. PATTERNS OF POLITICAL BEHAVIOR

In order to separate caste, kinship, family, and occupational interests in the politics of Guntur, it is first essential that we describe how politicians behave. We shall begin with an account of the development of party politics in Guntur, then turn to an analysis of the role of factions in politics, and finally to the ways in which Congress maintains a measure of cohesion in the midst of conflict.

## Party Politics in Guntur

Among the earliest political associations in Guntur was a group known as the Young Men's Literary Association of Guntur, founded around 1910. Like many of the earliest political movements in India and other developing countries, this association was an expression of regional sentiment. It called for the creation of a separate Andhra province out of the Telugu-speaking districts (of which Guntur is one) of the state of Madras and pressed for the establishment of an independent University of Andhra. A few years later a new and more active regional association was formed, known as the Andhra Mahasabha, which successfully persuaded the Indian National Congress to pass a resolution calling for the division of India into linguistic provinces. In the early 1920's, after Congress reorganized itself into linguistic units so that there was a separate unit for Andhra, the active members of the Andhra Mahasabha devoted their attention to supporting the nationalist movement for independence.

In the early twenties, however, neither the Andhra Mahasabha nor Con-

139

gress was as politically influential as a group known as the Justice party. This powerful and increasingly popular organization had the support of the major non-Brahmin agricultural castes in Guntur: the Kammas, the Reddis, and the Telagas. It existed not only in Andhra but also throughout South India and was known everywhere as an anti-Brahmin, pro-British organization strongly opposed to the Indian National Congress. To appreciate fully the hostility of the Justice party to the nationalist movement, one must understand the role played by Brahmins in Congress. For many years it was the Brahmins who dominated the Indian National Congress, not only in Guntur and in Andhra, but in most of the South. As the most educated, professional middle classes, the Brahmins were — as we have come to expect from middle classes elsewhere — among the first to become active in nationalist politics. Brahmins built the Congress organization in most of the South, and throughout the 1930's they held the most important party positions. The non-Brahmins, especially those who were upper-caste landholders, resented the powerful position of Brahmins in the state bureaucracy and saw in the rise of electoral politics an opportunity to unseat the Brahmins. They opposed independence for India until they could be certain that the non-Brahmin leadership could garner enough votes to defeat the Brahmins.

By the mid-1930's, however, many non-Brahmins, especially the sons of Justice party members, became critical of the pro-British, anti-national position of the Justice party, and — surprisingly — the Brahmins were not opposed to this development. First of all, Brahmin nationalists genuinely hoped to build a mass movement against the British, and recognized that support from the Kammas and Reddis was essential if such a mass base was to be built. Second, Brahmins were themselves split, and each faction within Congress hoped to improve its position by allying itself with the incoming Kammas and Reddis or with factions in each of these castes.

In the 1930's the Congress party increasingly nominated members of the Reddi and Kamma castes for elective office in order to win mass support. In the western part of Andhra the Reddis are numerous, but in Guntur it was the Kammas who soon became active within Congress. In Guntur two Kamma politicians — N. G. Ranga and K. Chandramouli — actively fought for a dominant place within the Congress party. These men come from families which have for a long time feuded with one another, and their disagreements reflected these family differences rather than any significant issues of public policy. Ranga allied himself with one of the leading Brahmin politicians in the state, T. Prakasam, a popular leader in the nationalist movement who had spent many years in jail

and had fought in so many civil disobedience movements against the British that he was often called the Lion of Andhra. Chandramouli thereupon allied himself with another familiar Congress leader, P. Sitaramayya, well known as the official historian of the Indian National Congress, also a Brahmin, and the leader of an opposing faction within Congress.

The Ranga-Prakasam factions gained control of Congress in the mid-forties. In 1946 Ranga was elected president of the Andhra Pradesh Congress Committee (APCC) and the following year Prakasam was elected chief minister of composite Madras state.

The coalition failed to hold power for long. Within a year the Prakasam ministry was overthrown on a no-confidence motion. Almost immediately the anti-Ranga faction in Guntur took steps to displace Ranga as president of the APCC. They supported Sanjiva Reddi, a powerful member of the Reddi caste in western Andhra, for the office of Congress president. Reddi had the support of Prakasam's Brahmin opponent, P. Sitaramayya. The anti-Ranga group gained control of the Guntur District Congress Committee and, through complicated legal maneuvers, successfully prevented some twenty-five supporters of Ranga in Guntur from participating in the APCC elections. Ranga lost by a handful of votes, and almost immediately he, Prakasam, and their factional supporters withdrew from Congress. It was the first major split in the Congress party of Andhra after independence, and for a while it looked like the beginning of large-scale disintegration.[1]

Congress also appeared to be threatened by a growing Communist movement throughout the delta. In the 1930's, while some Kammas and Reddis joined Congress, many of the sons of Kamma landowners in the delta flocked into the Communist party. Selig Harrison suggests[2] that geographic accident led the Kammas into the Communist party and the Reddis into Congress once their united front inside the Justice party came to an end with the decline of Brahmin power in Andhra. The Reddis, he points out, predominate in Rayalaseema, as the western districts of Andhra are called, and the Kammas in the delta. Harrison provides persuasive evidence for the thesis that the Communist movement in the delta was predominantly Kamma. In the 1946 elections, for example, nine of the eleven Communist candidates for the state assembly in the delta dis-

[1] Once Prakasam and Ranga were out of power their coalition fell apart. Prakasam formed the Kisan Mazdoor Praja party (KMPP) which became affiliated to a national party of former Congressmen, and Ranga created the Krishak Lok party, which was confined to the Andhra region.

[2] Selig Harrison, *India: The Most Dangerous Decades* (Princeton: Princeton University Press, 1960), p. 212.

tricts were Kammas, and almost every Communist leader in Guntur was a Kamma.

However, a close examination of the Congress party in Guntur suggests that it too was predominantly a Kamma organization. Ranga, popularly called the Archbishop of the Kammas, was a Congressman; his faction, though allied to a Brahmin, was predominantly Kamma. An examination of the caste background of presidents of the DCC in Guntur from 1935 to 1962 shows that seven of the ten presidents were Kammas and that they held office for eighteen of the twenty-seven years. While elsewhere in Andhra the Reddis were growing in importance — and a Reddi ultimately became chief minister — in Guntur no Reddi has ever been president of the DCC.

It is important to point out these caste affiliations to dispel the notion that the struggle between the Communists and the Congress in the 1952 elections and thereafter was simply a conflict between Reddis and Kammas. It is relevant to note that in the 1952 elections and again in 1955 the largest single caste designation of the candidates of *all* major parties for legislative assembly seats — the Communists, Congress, and Ranga's Krishak Lok Party — was Kamma. But it is also relevant to note that while the Communist party and the Ranga group in the delta were almost exclusively a Kamma party insofar as their leadership was concerned, the Congress party in the delta did have a somewhat more diversified leadesrhip.

It was the linguistic state issue which proved to be destructive of the Congress position in Guntur and in the Telugu districts of Madras. Early in 1951 the movement for the creation of a separate Andhra state became particularly active. In August, 1951, a prominent leader of the Andhra Mahasabha, Swami Sitaram, started a fast unto death at Guntur to force the Indian government to accede to the request of the Andhras. After the swami had fasted for thirty-eight days, Vinoba Bhave, the well-known disciple of Gandhi, persuaded the swami to give up his fast on the assurance that Vinoba would mediate with Nehru in finding a solution to the demand for creating an Andhra province. During the elections Nehru toured the Telugu districts and visited Guntur, but would not commit himself on the Andhra issue. Nehru was reluctant to accede to the request; it would have clearly opened the doors for states' reorganization generally, and Nehru was unsympathetic to the movement. Moreover, if the Telugu districts of Madras were permitted to form an Andhra state, the movement for taking the Telugu districts out of Hyderabad — thereby disintegrating the only state apart from Kashmir in which Muslim interests

were strongly involved — would grow. Most of the Congressmen in the Telugu districts favored creating an Andhra state, but they were handicapped in the elections since it was a Congress government in New Delhi which stood in the way of creating such a state. On the other hand, the Communists had no such inhibitions and actively supported the demand. When the election returns were in, Congressmen were startled to discover that they had been badly defeated throughout the Telugu districts of Madras, having secured only about forty of a total of 140 seats.

After the elections, agitation for the creation of an Andhra province increased. A leader of the Andhra Mahasabha launched another dramatic fast unto death on October 19, 1952, in the city of Madras. After his death from fasting for fifty-eight days, law and order began to collapse in many parts of Madras. Within a few days Nehru announced that the government would agree to the creation of an Andhra state. Six months later, legislation was introduced in parliament, and in October, 1953, the new state of Andhra was formed. Since Prakasam had been the most prominent non-Communist politician favoring the creation of an Andhra state and it was apparent that Congress did not have enough strength in the new assembly to form a government on its own, the Congress party agreed to support Prakasam as chief minister but on the condition that he resign from his party. A coalition government was formed, consisting of Congress and Prakasam's Praja Socialist party, but bitter struggles continued within the ministry and within Congress over where the high court should be located. Only thirteen months after the state was formed, the Prakasam ministry collapsed on a vote of no confidence, president's rule was established, and Andhra was placed under the direct administration of the central government. Elections were scheduled for early 1955. It is interesting to note, as we keep in mind the relationship of factions to one another, that though Ranga had once been allied with Prakasam he did not support the Prakasam ministry.

As the elections drew near, the Ranga group, the Prakasam group, and sections of the Congress party feared that the Communists might take control of Andhra in the first elections held since the new state was formed. An electoral understanding took place involving Congress, the Krishak Lok party of Ranga, and the Praja party of Prakasam's followers, and the United Congress party was formed. In most constituencies a straight fight took place between the United Congress party and the Communists with the result that the Communists were routed.

The provincial issue again upset the relationship among factions within Congress and among the parties in Andhra. Immediately after the 1955

elections Ranga and his followers rejoined Congress and threw their support behind a Reddi from western Andhra, Gopala Reddi, for chief minister of Andhra. Gopala Reddi was elected, and Ranga's followers were given posts in the new cabinet. But in November, 1956, the factional balance was completely upset. In that month Andhra Pradesh was enlarged to include the Telugu-speaking region of Hyderabad known as Telengana following a decision earlier in the year by the government of India that Hyderabad state be dissolved. Sanjiva Reddi, deputy chief minister of Andhra and, as we have seen, an opponent of Ranga when Ranga attempted to be reelected as APCC president, had the support of about forty of the fifty MLAs from the Telengana region; with their support he was able to overthrow Gopala Reddi and become the new chief minister of the enlarged Andhra state.

Sanjiva Reddi brought a new style of politics into the Andhra government. While Gopala Reddi had made an effort to maintain the support of many factions within Congress, Sanjiva Reddi as chief minister was primarily concerned with giving power to members of his own faction, both in the government and in the party organization. Ranga was bitterly opposed to the Sanjiva Reddi government, and in late 1959 he found an issue on which to resign from Congress. Ranga declared his opposition to a recent Congress party decision in favor of establishing cooperative farming throughout India, and with other opponents of Congress in other parts of the country he helped to create the conservative Swatantra party.

The withdrawal of Ranga did not mean an end to internecine factional warfare within Congress. With few exceptions the Kamma politicians within Congress continued to oppose Sanjiva Reddi, for they felt that he was paying particular attention to aiding the Reddi caste and that few members of their own community were given posts in the cabinet or had any positions of power within the government.

In early 1960 Prime Minister Nehru asked Sanjiva Reddi to step down as chief minister of Andhra to assume the presidency of the Indian National Congress. Sanjiva Reddi did so, but apparently with much reluctance. He retained his membership in the Andhra legislative assembly, thereby symbolically staking his claim to return in the near future, and sought to nominate as the next chief minister one of his close associates, a Reddi from Guntur district. The delicate power balance within Congress was now disrupted with the withdrawal of Sanjiva Reddi to Delhi, and all his opponents, including most of the important Kamma politicians, rallied behind a member of the Raju caste. When a deadlock occurred, Sanjiva Reddi offered to break it by permitting his opponents to nomi-

nate a compromise figure, Sanjivaiah, a Harijan leader in the cabinet. An agreement was reached, and Sanjivaiah became the first Harijan chief minister of an Indian state.

It is of great interest that factional struggles within Congress provided a Harijan with the opportunity to assume power in the state. Actually the Kamma group which dominated the Guntur DCC would have preferred to have one of their own people as chief minister; but since they were prepared to accept almost anyone who was not a Reddi or a part of Sanjiva Reddi's faction, they gladly welcomed the selection of Sanjivaiah. Thus both dominant castes, unable to accept a member of each other's community, could agree upon a Harijan. One immediate and important consequence was that the complexion of the political support for Congress began to change. Harijans — most of whom are agricultural laborers — provided the hard core of the Communist vote in Andhra; with a Harijan as chief minister, Congress was able to draw many members of that community back into the fold. Sanjivaiah, as one might expect, paid special attention to his own community, pressed for appointments of Harijans into government service, increased their opportunities for higher education, granted government loans for housing sites and housing, and — above all — gave his community a sense of pride at having one of their members as chief minister.

Sanjiva Reddi was, however, eager to relinquish his post as president of the Congress party to return to what he viewed as the more important post of chief minister of Andhra. Shortly before the 1962 general elections Sanjiva Reddi announced that he intended to return to Andhra, with the result that the selection of candidates for the state legislative assembly became deeply embroiled in the issue of who would be the next chief minister. Nominations from each of the DCCs were forwarded to the Pradesh Congress Committee in Hyderabad, but it soon became apparent that there would be a battle over each nomination. A three-man committee was appointed to make the selections; though after much haggling they agreed on a majority of the nominations, a substantial number could not be settled. The Congress constitution provides that the final nominations are to be made by the Congress Parliamentary Board in New Delhi. Since there were similar controversies in many states where there were also struggles over the office of chief minister, decisions on disputed seats had to be delegated to one-, two-, or three-man committees appointed by the Congress Parliamentary Board. Sanjiva Reddi persuaded the board that stability in Andhra could be restored only if he returned to the state

as chief minister; moreover, as president of the Congress party, he had the prerogative of deciding who would decide how state disputes would be settled. Thereupon, Sanjiva Reddi took the responsibility of settling the disputed seats for the Andhra legislative assembly, and as a result a solid majority of the Congress assembly tickets were given to his own supporters.

Sanjiva Reddi could not be sure which Congress nominee would support him, and so for advice and guidance he turned to his most powerful supporters in each district. In Guntur he turned to a local supporter, Brahmananda Reddi; it was generally understood that in effect Brahmananda Reddi made the recommendations as to which local Congressman would support their group in the assembly. Thus, though the Guntur District Congress Committee was controlled by the supporters of Sanjivaiah, the majority of the twenty-five seats were given to supporters of Sanjiva Reddi.

The 1962 election thus became a struggle between two groups within the Congress party rather than a struggle between Congress and the opposition. The very strength of the opposition parties throughout the state was viewed as an asset to each faction within the party, since each faction could thereby ally itself with an opposition candidate if the local Congress candidate belonged to an opposing faction. It was widely thought, therefore, that Congress would lose many seats in the legislative assembly; some Congressmen feared a return to the 1952 situation, when Congress failed to win a majority of seats in the Andhra region. These fears proved groundless. Though Congress did lose a number of seats, its position in the state legislative assembly proved to be secure, Sanjiva Reddi easily won with a solid majority within his own party, and — of considerable interest — the vote for the Congress party was actually an increase over previous elections.

The number of seats won by the Congress party in all elections since 1952 is not a good indication of the local popularity of the party, since internal schisms and external coalitions have often determined precisely how many seats Congress and other parties won. An examination of the total votes won by Congress is somewhat more indicative of the party's position in Guntur.

The figures in Table 14 show that while Congress won only twelve seats in the 1962 elections compared to sixteen in 1955, its percentage of votes increased slightly, from 39.3 per cent to 41.5 per cent; though the Communists increased their seats from two to nine, the 1962 elections proved to be a severe blow in terms of votes, since the party dropped

TABLE 14
ASSEMBLY ELECTION RESULTS IN GUNTUR

| | 1952 | | 1955 | | 1962 | |
|---|---|---|---|---|---|---|
| | Assembly Votes | | | | | |
| | Number of Votes | % of Votes | Number of Votes | % of Votes | Number of Votes | % of Votes |
| Congress. . . | 225,691 | 25.2 | 443,084 | 39.3 | 500,178 | 41.5 |
| Communists . | 289,691 | 32.3 | 460,243 | 40.8 | 314,865 | 26.1 |
| Other parties and Inde- pendents. . | 379,284 | 42.5 | 223,390 | 19.9 | 391,059 | 32.4 |
| Total valid votes . . . | 894,666 | 100.0 | 1,126,717 | 100.0 | 1,206,102 | 100.0 |
| | Assembly Seats | | | | | |
| | Seats Won | Seats Contested | Seats Won | Seats Contested | Seats Won | Seats Contested |
| Congress. . . | 3 | 18 | 16 | 17 | 12 | 25 |
| Communists . | 10 | 14 | 2 | 25 | 9 | 18 |
| Other parties. | 3[a] | . . . | 7[b] | . . . | 0 | . . . |
| Independents. | 2 | . . . | 0 | . . . | 4 | . . . |
| Totals. . . | 18 | . . . | 25 | . . . | 25 | . . . |

[a]Praja Socialist party.

[b]Krishikar Lok party.

from 40.8 per cent to 26.1 per cent. Only part of the difference can be explained by the reduction in the number of Communist candidates standing in 1962, since the Communists had put up more candidates than in 1952, when their vote was higher. Other factors were clearly at work in the decline of the Communist vote, and, as we have seen, there is reason to believe that this results in part from the defection of many Harijan landless laborers away from the Communists.

## Castes and Factions

Caste appears to be the overriding source of political conflict within the district. Kammas and Reddis, the two dominant agricultural castes in the region, have long records of conflict. Each has been known to burn crops in the fields of the other. Fights over land rights and cattle are common, and there are frequent struggles for control of village panchayats where the two castes are numerically balanced.

Other castes have also been engaged in conflicts. The Malas and Madigas, the two major downtrodden Harijan castes in the area, have a long

history of opposition to one another.[3] These two low castes have long fought for social ascendancy, and have continued to fight even when members of both castes converted to Christianity.

Caste opposition to the Brahmin community has already been referred to. Brahmins served in the pre-British Moghul administration and continued nearly to monopolize public offices under the British in Madras presidency. Largely because of their literary traditions and the position they already held under the Moghuls, the Brahmins turned readily to British education and sought to solidify their position in the higher ranks of administration. As Kammas, Reddis, and other high castes sought to increase their own influence on government, they clashed with the Brahmin community. The Congress-Justice party conflict of the 1920's and 1930's was an expression of these social and political differences.

The changing relationship of castes to one another is certainly an important feature of political life in Guntur and throughout India, and to some extent these conflicts can be understood in the context of traditional social relationships. While there is generally no disagreement on the social ranking of the major castes (i.e., the relationship between, say, Brahmins and Kammas, or Kammas and Madigas), the castes that are relatively close to one another in the ranking system are frequently in dispute over their relative ranking. Moreover, ranking is not and has never been fixed; changes in educational patterns and in occupation and changes in the relationship of a particular caste to the land or to those who have political authority are all factors in the ranking system. Politics has often played a role in changing the social status position of particular castes. Historically, entire castes have changed their position in the social hierarchy by their success in gaining political power. Petty chieftains taking to the sword have often led their followers into positions of local political and military power; when they have held power for any lengthy period, they have been able to redefine their social position. Similarly, the defeat of local chieftains has often been followed by a decline in the social position of the entire caste to which the chieftain belonged. Many castes in Andhra and elsewhere can trace themselves to some important king or local chieftain. These changes in ranking are often legitimized by a rewriting of the caste history, a change in its name, and changes in some of the community's cultural patterns, such as its attitude and practices

[3] A. T. Fishman, an American Baptist missionary in the Telugu region, describes the conflicts between these two groups of converts in his study of the Madiga caste, *Culture Change and the Underprivileged* (Madras: Christian Literature Society for India, 1941; originally a doctoral thesis at Yale University). See especially pages 148–49.

with respect to meat eating, widow remarriage, marriage customs, or religious rituals. Caste is thus not so immobile as tradition prescribes, for it has been possible to redefine the tradition in order to legitimize changes in the positions of particular castes. Because we observe changes in the contemporary relationships of castes, we often mistakenly assume that the system is breaking down when in fact the system provides for a considerable amount of change within its own framework.

Changes in political institutions in the nineteenth and twentieth centuries often simply provided new arenas within which conflicts among castes could take place. In the latter part of the nineteenth century, when the census was created, castes viewed the census commissioner as an object of political pressure because the label the commissioner gave to a caste in the census enumeration was an important factor in that caste's efforts to effect change in its social position.[4] Similarly, with the establishment of local government bodies by the British and later by the Congress governments in 1937, the struggle for control of these bodies was often part of the long-term efforts of particular castes to improve their social positions. Thus, even from a traditional point of view, caste leaders deem it of social relevance to participate in political struggles.

As we have seen, however, it is quite impossible to explain the conflicts within the Congress party and between political parties simply on the basis of the caste affiliation of politicians. Though the struggle for social change in the relationship between castes has long been a subject of inquiry and discussion, less has been said of the intense factional struggles within castes for social ascendancy. The struggle between prominent landholding families of the same caste within a village or municipality has frequently been the single most important factor in political conflict within the village.

Some have argued that beneath these status conflicts are always important material considerations. Two families, of the same or of opposing castes, may be concerned with controlling the land, having influence with local administration with respect to land, taxes, or the performance of local services such as the construction of roads and wells, or in the granting of agricultural loans (taccavi). It is of course true that some landowning families have achieved their position at the expense of other landowning families and have been able to do so through their political position, but it would probably be difficult to trace more than a handful of family feuds to concrete economic conflicts. One might argue, though,

---

[4] Lloyd and Susanne Rudolph, "The Political Role of India's Caste Association," *Pacific Affairs* 33 (1960): 1–22.

that the increasing role of local government and administration in development activities has lent a strong material overcast to traditional status struggles of rival families, but the rivalries themselves are often long-standing. Many of the current disputes in Guntur date back many generations.[5]

Associated with each family engaged in a political struggle is a host of other families, some of the same caste, but mostly of other castes, related to the patron family by a network of economic relationships. The patron family settles conflicts within its faction, protects members of the faction in litigious disputes with members of other factions, represents members in criminal cases, helps younger men find employment within or — increasingly — outside the village, and in general is a go-between for the villager in dealing with governmental administration, the judiciary, and police authorities.

It is relatively easy to describe the social composition of factions; it is more difficult to explain what gives them cohesion. The faction is first of all a political unit. Its members do not share rules of pollution, marriage customs, religious rites, or ritual status. Members characteristically belong to different castes, practice different occupations, and have wide differentials in income. Typically, each faction (there are usually two in a village, but there may be more) has as its leaders prominent members of the dominant caste in the village. The leaders of each faction generally have the support of their own kin group, but there are instances when brothers are the leaders of contending factions. Patron-client relations are important in bringing artisans, tenants, and agricultural laborers into the faction led by a large landowner. Kinship ties, personal friendships, financial obligations, and status aspirations may all be elements in leading individuals to associate with a particular faction. A skillful factional leader must provide a wide variety of rewards for his followers.

The faction is typically engaged in standing up for its members when they are involved in disputes with members of contending village factions. A dispute between two landlords or two peasant proprietors over stray cattle or land and water rights may involve the major village factions. Factions are also likely to fight for control over village panchayats, village school boards, and village cooperatives. Since taluka and district

[5] A study of the relationship between agrarian interests and the British administration in Guntur district in the nineteenth century shows that conflicts between castes, multi-caste factions, villages, and families are deeply rooted and pre-date modern developments in administration and in local government. See Robert Eric Frykenberg, *The Administration of Guntur District, 1788–1848* (London: Oxford University Press, 1965).

local boards have been established, and villagers have been given the right to vote for assembly and parliamentary elections, village factions have sought to win village votes for these outside bodies.

When we speak of factions, we are referring to parts of a whole. Only a part of a village belongs to a faction. Those who are wealthy and of high caste are most likely to join factions, but there are many men of high status who choose not to participate. Individuals who are low in caste, landless, and poor are less likely to be factional supporters, but they also are found in factions. There are many disputes in the village which involve only the factions; but, with the establishment of adult suffrage for district local boards and assembly and parliamentary elections, each faction must seek support from villagers who do not belong to factions. Moreover, a faction cannot always be certain of the allegiance of all its supporters. Factions are not permanent groups, though many have endured for long periods with only small changes in their composition. It is not common, but individuals do occasionally leave one faction for another.

An energetic factional leader must function like a political party boss — hustling from one corner of the village to another to satisfy the needs of his supporters, constantly endeavoring to win the support of the uncommitted, and harassing the opposing faction. If the style appears to be modern, one must remember that we are describing a pattern of political activity in the village which pre-dates the development of party organization and which in any event also operates outside political parties. Some fifty years before political parties were organized, the district collector of another Telugu district wrote: "Though there are factions in every village of the district, and these are by no means confined to the Kapus [Reddis], yet in the black cotton country where this caste largely predominates they are developed to a very high degree of animosity and are a fruitful source of crime, as they not infrequently result in regular blood feuds. The highest ambition of a wealthy Kapu . . . is to become the leader of a power faction."[6] Frykenberg, a historian studying Guntur district in the early part of the nineteenth century, confirms the observation for other landowning castes as well.

It is the arena which has now changed. While in the past village factions used their power to exercise influence within administration, now the politics of administration has been partially replaced by the politics of party. This is not because factions see public policy rather than administration as subject to their influence or even as relevant to their lives. They continue to see administration at the local level as significant,

[6] C. F. Brackenbury, *Madras District Gazetteers* (Cuddapah, 1915): 66–67.

but they recognize that influence within the party and over assembly and, to a lesser extent, parliamentary candidates is relevant to exercising that influence.

Precisely how factions are intertwined with caste, kinship, ideology, and party can be demonstrated by an examination of two Guntur constituencies in the 1962 general elections. It is necessary first to note that there were few constituencies in which the opposing candidates came from antagonistic castes. When candidates were from different castes, they typically sought the support of their fellow caste members in much the same way that American candidates often seek the support of the ethnic group to which they belong. There was, however, only one constituency in the 1962 elections in which caste conflict was pointed to by local politicians as a determinant of both party and voting behavior. Since this case is an exception to my hypothesis that durable multi-caste, multi-occupational factions are the primary units of political action, it is useful to examine this constituency.

The contest in Phirangipuram constituency was between a Congressman, Brahmananda Reddi, a member of the Reddi caste and deputy chief minister of Andhra, and his Swatantra opponent, a Kamma and leader of the Swatantra party in the state. Each candidate appealed to his own caste for support. But two facts in this caste conflict demonstrate that even here kinship and faction are intertwined with caste. First of all, the two candidates were engaged in a long-time family rivalry. The two men came from landowning families that had fought against one another for political power in the constituency for many years. Both families once owned thousands of acres which by the mid-1930's had been divided among many sons, and both had been powerful influences within the district administration. In the 1937 elections Reddi's elder brother successfully ran as a Congress candidate for the assembly against a leader of the Justice party. The defeated man's son, a Swatantra party candidate, was elected to the assembly in 1955 in another constituency but decided to change his constituency in 1962 in order to oppose his old family rival. It is interesting to note that local persons were quite aware of the traditional family rivalry and of the earlier conflict between members of their respective families.

A second important point is that while the Kammas predominate in the constituency, Brahmananda Reddi won the elections. The Kammas do not constitute a majority of the constituency, so that while each candidate appealed to his own castemen, both candidates had to seek support from others in the constituency. In each village the Reddi or Kamma

supporters of each candidate had influence among other castes in their village. Where the Congress or Swatantra village supporter controlled the village panchayat, he tended to win the support of a majority of the village. The constituency contains two panchayat samitis, one of which was controlled by the brother of Brahmananda Reddi, and the other was not functioning as a result of internal conflict. In the area of the constituency under the jurisdiction of the panchayat samiti controlled by his brother, Reddi won by a margin of 2,883 votes and lost the remainder of the constituency by 2,380 votes. Reddi thus won by 27,494 to 26,991, a margin of only five hundred votes. It is clear that even in this case where the two contending candidates were from antagonistic castes, kinship competition, control over the panchayat, and appeals beyond caste were elements in the outcome.

In Ponnur constituency, a predominantly rural constituency on the banks of the Krishna River in Guntur district, we have a more typical example of the role of factions. Here we can see how intra-Congress party factions relate to village factions in determining the outcome of an election. In this election, both the Swatantra and Congress assembly candidates were Kammas; of the three candidates for parliament, the Communist and the Swatantra candidates were Kammas, the Congressman a Brahmin. In this constituency a majority of villagers elected a Congressman to the state assembly but then proceeded to elect, by a solid plurality, a Communist to parliament. A village-by-village analysis of voting patterns shows that neither caste nor occupational division is as useful a predictive guide to voting patterns as is the association of village factions to the factions within each of the political parties.[7] The Kamma Congress candidate for the assembly in Ponnur exchanged support with the Communist candidate for parliament. He did so because the Kamma Congress candidate of an opposing faction in a neighboring constituency tried to undercut him by supporting the Swatantra assembly candidate. Both Congressmen belonged to opposing factions within the state Congress party. Both Congressmen — the one standing in the constituency, and the other supporting his opponent — bid for the support of village factions. Village factions readily joined in the party factional struggle, for they saw the elections as an opportunity to gain assistance for their village or, more precisely, for their own faction within the village. In this constituency multi-caste, occupationally diversified village factions were the basic working units for each candidate in his quest for votes, and the factions —

[7] For a detailed analysis of Ponnur, giving village voting data and an analysis of the factional composition of a number of villages, see Appendix I at the end of chapter 10, below.

not caste — shaped the outcome of the elections. As a result of the influence of factional leaders, split voting was so common that Congress carried these assembly seats while the Communists carried the parliamentary seat. It is of some interest that in the state as a whole, as a consequence of Communist alliances with factions within Congress which were reflected in the voting patterns of village factions, the parliamentary vote for the Communists was nearly double their state-wide assembly vote.

The point is that party politicians are typically loyal to their faction, not to their caste (and often not to their party), and that factions typically cut across caste.[8] When candidates of antagonistic castes oppose one another in an election, they readily make electoral appeals to caste since caste constitutes a potential voting bank. When one faction is manifestly multi-caste in leadership and the other is predominantly from one caste, the first group will typically denounce the second on the basis of "casteism" in order to reduce its appeal to other castes. When, as in Ponnur, candidates are from the same caste, neither is likely to make caste an issue at all; both will bargain intensively for the support of multi-caste village factions.

### Cohesion and Conflict in Congress

Given the extraordinary amount of factional in-fighting in Congress, we may well wonder how it is that the Congress party in Guntur continues to gain recruits and continues to win elections. It is first important to note that factionalism within the Guntur Congress is, paradoxically, the result in part of the political success of Congress. As the Congress party spread its organization into the rural areas in the 1930's and established a mass base, it was quickly affected by the social tensions and conflicts present in the countryside. If other parties suffer less from these tensions, it is because no other party so successfully encompasses such divergent elements and spreads its net over so wide a geographic and social base.

Indeed, social groups and families often use the Congress party for their goals. Families which supported the pro-British Justice party joined the Congress party after independence. Many landlord families, eager to protect themselves against the proposed land reform legislation, joined Congress and, in some instances, entered the legislative assembly to play

[8] We have already noted that in the late 1940's the major factional leaders within Congress belonged to the same caste. Two Brahmins — Sitarammayya and Prakasam — led contending factions in the state, and within Guntur each had the support of two opposing Kamma factions, one led by Ranga and the other by Chandramouli. Moreover, each of the factions had members from other castes.

an influential role in shaping the character of the legislation. In any event, their influence on the enforcement and interpretation of the legislation by local officials has been enhanced by their participation in the local Congress party and in local government bodies. The leaders of many middle and low castes saw participation in Congress party politics as an opportunity to enhance their positions within their own communities. Many recognized, too, that the party which controlled the government could and did help its caste fellows get roads, wells, and housing sites, admission to schools and colleges, posts in administration, and other beneficial services.

The point is that while Congress as a nationalist movement housed many social groups — castes, families, and factions — each with its own aspirations, the party became even more diversified after it took power, first in 1937, then again in 1946. The basic internal problem for Congress, therefore, has been not how to prevent these conflicts but how to reconcile them or at least subdue them within the framework of the party organization.

At first appearance it would seem that the Congress party in Andhra in general and in Guntur in particular has been quite unsuccessful at coping with these internal conflicts. Ranga and Prakasam both left the party before the 1952 elections and took with them many of their followers. And no sooner had the state of Andhra been created than the party was torn by internal conflicts of such magnitude that the state ultimately had to be taken over by the central government. The elections of 1955 at first appeared to be little more than a reprieve for the party; as we have noted, though the Communists were defeated by the Congress, that was largely because the non-Communist parties had banded together in a coalition to prevent a Communist victory. Disputes over who would be the chief minister have continued to tear the party, and from 1955 to 1962 there were three changes and four Congress chief ministers. The 1962 elections seemed to foreshadow further disintegration within the party and possibly a narrow victory.

Nonetheless, the party emerged in 1962 in firm control in Guntur district and throughout Andhra [9] and in general it appears that the party has continually increased its popular following even when sections of

[9] Popular vote in Andhra Assembly elections (or areas subsequently joined to form the present Andhra Pradesh) was as follows:

| | 1952 | | 1955 (and 1957) | | 1962 | |
|---|---|---|---|---|---|---|
| | seats | % of votes | seats | % of votes | seats | % of votes |
| Congress | 58 | 29.7 | 187 | 41.3 | 177 | 47.4 |
| Communists | 41 | 22.8 | 37 | 29.2 | 51 | 19.5 |

the party have withdrawn and internal conflict has been magnified. One must turn then to how the party has maintained its cohesion in spite of these apparent conflicts; without understanding the cohesive factors at work within the party, it is not possible to understand why the party has thus far succeeded to the extent it has, both in the district and in the state as a whole.

Counterbalancing defections from the Congress party have been defections from other political groups to the Congress. The most notable of these took place in 1953 when Prakasam, who had left the Congress party earlier, resigned from the Praja party — which he had created — and rejoined Congress. Since the Praja party had earlier merged with the Socialist party, his defection resulted in the total disintegration of the Socialist movement in Andhra. Gradually his old supporters returned with him to Congress, accompanied by many of the Socialists who had left the Congress shortly after independence. By the 1962 elections, the Praja Socialist party was non-existent in Andhra, and its members were part of one or more factions within the Congress party. The absorption of the old Praja party and the Socialist party by Congress constituted a substantial accretion of strength.[10]

There were five political parties of importance in the Andhra area in the 1952 elections: the Indian National Congress, the Socialist party, the Kisan Mazdoor Praja party, the Krishikar Lok party, and the Communist party of India. In contrast, ten years later there were only three parties of importance: Congress, Communist, and Swatantra (formerly the Krishikar Lok party). In the process of absorption and merging which took place during this ten-year period, Congress benefited, for most members of the two groups which disappeared turned to Congress.

The absorption of other political groups into Congress contributed to the factional character of the Congress party. Both before and after independence, factions have struggled for control of the party organization or for control of the Congress Legislative party. Though at first glance it would seem that these factional struggles have weakened the party organization, in some respects they have been an important factor in the party's popular strength.

It is clear, for example, that intense competition for control of the District Congress Committee or the Pradesh Congress Committee has led to an increase in party enrollment. Primary members elect mandal com-

[10] In the 1955 elections the PSP won 5.6 percent of the vote, but this did not include the Telengana area which was subsequently added to Andhra. When elections were held in Telengana in 1957, the PSP had already merged with the Congress party.

TABLE 15
ELECTION RESULTS IN GUNTUR DISTRICT, ANDHRA

| | SEATS WON | | | NUMBER OF VOTES | | | PERCENTAGE OF VOTES | | |
|---|---|---|---|---|---|---|---|---|---|
| | 1952 | 1955 | 1962 | 1952 | 1955 | 1962 | 1952 | 1955 | 1962 |
| Legislative Assembly | | | | | | | | | |
| Congress. . | 3 | 16 | 12 | 225,691 | 443,084 | 500,178 | 25.2 | 39.3 | 41.5 |
| Communist. | 10 | 2 | 9 | 289,691 | 460,243 | 314,865 | 32.3 | 40.8 | 26.1 |
| Swatantra . | .. | .. | .. | . . . . | . . . . | 222,603 | . . . | . . . | 18.4 |
| Kisan Mazdoor Praja party | 3 | .. | .. | 115,319 | . . . . | . . . . | 12.9 | . . . | .. |
| Krishak Lok party . . | .. | 7 | .. | 114,046 | 177,292 | . . . . | 16.1 | 15.7 | . . . |
| Independents and other parties. . | .. | .. | .. | 120,218 | 46,098 | 168,456 | 13.4 | 4.1 | 14.0 |
| Total . . | 18 | 25 | 25 | 894,666 | 1,126,717 | 1,206,102 | 100.0 | 100.0 | 100.0 |
| Parliament | | | | | | | | | |
| Congress. . | 1 | 3 | 1 | 162,222 | 444,553 | 448,779 | 31.6 | 56.5 | 43.5 |
| Communist. | .. | .. | 2 | 101,738 | 111,963 | 270,516 | 19.8 | 14.2 | 26.2 |
| Swatantra . | .. | .. | .. | . . . . | . . . . | 161,094 | . . . | . . . | 15.6 |
| Kisan Mazdoor Praja party | .. | .. | .. | 53,858 | . . . . | . . . . | 10.5 | . . . | .. |
| Krishak Lok party . . | .. | .. | .. | 116,742 | . . . . | . . . . | 22.7 | . . . | .. |
| Independents and other parties. . | 1 | .. | .. | 79,300 | 230,813 | 151,031 | 15.4 | 29.3 | 14.7 |
| Total . . | 2 | 3 | 3 | 514,222 | 787,329 | 1,031,420 | 100.0 | 100.0 | 100.0 |

mittees, and these committees in turn elect representatives to higher bodies within the party, up to the Pradesh Congress Committee. Competing factions therefore try to increase their votes in party elections by recruiting primary members. In 1962 there were about a hundred thousand primary members of the Congress party in Guntur District; in 1946–47, when there was an intense struggle for control of the Andhra Pradesh Congress Committee, it is reported that membership passed the four hundred thousand mark.[11]

A substantial part of the increase consists of bogus membership. Membership fees are only four annas (about five cents) per year, and wealthy members of opposing factions often contribute the money to add to the membership of the party. Names are often copied from voter lists, signatures forged, and countless primary membership forms sent to the district

[11] These are estimates given by the District Congress Committee. Precise figures were not available.

and state office. But even when the additions consist of bogus names, the competition in intra-party elections increases the activity of the active members, improves the financial position of the party through the membership fees, and may even result in a certain amount of legitimate increase in primary membership.[12]

The bitterness of factional conflict obscures the fact that from time to time — though admittedly only periodically — there has been accommodation among the various factions. The government formed by Prakasam in 1953 represented an amalgamation of a number of factions within the party. And though a member of the Reddi caste — Gopala Reddi — formed a government in 1955, it too represented a balance of forces within the party. When Sanjiva Reddi took control of the party the following year, factional conflict within the party was intensified and Kamma defection increased. The struggle between the various factions surrounding Sanjivaiah and those around Sanjiva Reddi in 1961 and 1962 were perhaps the most bitter conflicts since Ranga left the party in 1949. Sanjiva Reddi as chief minister has probably been the least accommodating of the various Congress chief ministers, but even then the dissident factions have found a place within the party. The dissident elements were able to win a substantial portion of the assembly seats. Sanjivaiah himself was brought to New Delhi in 1962 to become the new Congress president to replace Sanjiva Reddi, and there was considerable satisfaction within the dissident sections in Andhra that their leader had thus been elevated even though he had been taken out of Andhra politics. Moreover, the dominant group, even if it does not share its power with the minority group in the state government, has not liquidated minority members from positions of power in the districts or in the party organization. At least one leading opponent of the chief minister is a minister in the central government. Many others are in parliament and in the state assembly. Still others hold important positions in local government and in the district Congress party.

The readiness of factions to support opposition party candidates is often pointed to as the most destructive consequence of party groupism, for the party often loses seats because of such sabotage.[13] However,

[12] Bogus membership, not only in Andhra but elsewhere in the country, has often reached such proportions that many leaders of Congress advocate the abolishment of the four-anna primary member. The party has, however, understandably refused to abolish this class of membership since it constitutes a significant link between the party and the masses, even if membership is only a nominal affair.

[13] Hugh Gray, in an unpublished manuscript on politics in Andhra, notes that landowning families protect themselves by having one son in local politics, one as a member of the legislative assembly, another in a profession, and a fourth as manager

this crossing of party lines works both ways; while Congress often supports opposition candidates, opposition parties also often support Congress candidates. In Ponnur constituency the pro-Sanjivaiah group supported the Communist candidate for parliament, but in turn the Communists supported the Congress assembly candidate against Swatantra. In another assembly constituency the pro-Sanjiva Reddi forces supported a Swatantra assembly candidate in a neighboring constituency in return for Swatantra support in their own assembly constituency. Each Congress assembly candidate knows that he can depend upon support only from members of his own faction, not from all members of the Congress party. As a result he often strikes alliances with opposition party candidates in neighboring assembly constituencies or with opposition candidates for the parliamentary seat in his own constituency. But factionalism is far from a total electoral loss for the party; when one faction sabotages the candidates of another Congress faction by supporting an opposition candidate, it almost always solicits opposition support for their own candidate. Sabotage almost always involves a *quid pro quo*.[14]

Factionalism in the party is closely related in both a sociological and political sense to factionalism in the villages. We have noted earlier that conflicts within the village are often reflected in the local party, since each faction within the local Congress party associates itself with a village faction. There is constant factional tension within almost every village in the delta, and for election purposes each political party is forced to ally itself with at least one faction in each village. If Congress were united, the opposition parties would invariably get the support of one of the two factions in each village. But when Congress is itself divided, then Congressmen can frequently ally with both village factions, where one Congress faction works with one village faction while another Congress faction works with the other village faction. Were party factionalism unrelated to factionalism in the social system, the local Congress party might long since have totally fallen apart, as political parties have in many other underdeveloped countries. It is this close interrelationship between factionalism in the village and factionalism within the party that has made

of the land. It is also common for family sons to be in several different parties. The family thus seeks to protect itself by having sons in a variety of occupations and in contending parties. Therefore, what from one point of view can be seen as party "sabotage," from another can be seen as a consistent effort on the part of an extended family and faction to protect its interests and its social status.

[14] These alliances across party lines are always done without official party support and are always vigorously denied publicly by those who engage in them. They rarely involve ideological considerations, but are generally marriages of political convenience.

it possible for the party to sustain popular support in the midst of intense intra-party conflict.[15] Factionalism has also been, as we shall see, an important factor in the adaptation of the Congress party to the new patterns of local government known as panchayati raj.

[15] For a discussion of the integrative functions of factions in another state Congress party, see Paul R. Brass, "Factionalism and the Congress Party in Uttar Pradesh," *Asian Survey* (Sept., 1964): 1037–47.

# 9. CONGRESS AND PANCHAYATI RAJ

In 1959 legislation was passed creating new local government bodies in Andhra and expanding the powers of existing governments. Local bodies were given new legal powers, new sources of revenue, larger budgets, and larger administrative staffs. Here we shall explore the impact of these changes on the functioning of the Congress party organization in Guntur. In interpreting the data provided here, two cautions are particularly necessary. First, the new pattern of local government — generally referred to by Indians as panchayati raj — was adopted to further, not the powers of Congress or the central government, but the goal of rural, especially agricultural, development.[1] Here we shall not examine the impact of panchayati raj on India's economic development, for the proclaimed mobilization features of panchayati raj deserve a separate study and are quite apart from our interest in their effect on Congress.

Second, panchayati raj was first established in Andhra in 1959, and while there are important antecedents to the program which make the new institutions less original than they might at first appear, we are nonetheless looking at institutions which are only a few years old. The conclusions we draw must therefore be unusually tentative.

## The Legislation

Andhra was the first of two states (Rajasthan was the other) to pass panchayati raj legislation. The movement toward expanding the powers

[1] In this respect these institutions differ from local government bodies in Pakistan. In Pakistan the system of "basic democracies," as local government units are called, was established partly to further rural development, partly to provide popular political participation *in the absence* of political parties.

of local government bodies and creating new local government institutions received its impetus from a central government commission appointed to examine the functioning of the Community Development Program and the National Extension Service, two programs concerned with India's rural development. The study team had been empowered by the government to investigate its major programs for raising agricultural productivity, improving rural living conditions, and evoking popular initiative. In a lengthy report[2] the committee recommended that a new system of local government be established to take control of the government's development program. Popular control over these rural development programs, the committee reasoned, would, by making the people feel more personally involved, ultimately accelerate development efforts.

Less than two years after the committee's report, Rajasthan and Andhra launched the new program now called panchayati raj.[3] Under this program a three-tiered system of local government was established. At the base is the village panchayat which coincides with the village or, in areas where villages are small, with several villages. At a second level is the panchayat samiti, a new unit of local government established to coincide with the administrative area under the jurisdiction of the Community Development Program and National Extension Scheme. The samiti consists of the heads of the village panchayats and covers an area containing between sixty thousand and one hundred thousand persons. At a third level is the zilla parishad, which consists of all the panchayat samiti presidents, members of the legislative assembly, MPs, and important government officers within the district. The district generally contains about a million persons.

Panchayati raj differs from pre-existing local government institutions in several respects. First, the panchayat samiti as an intermediate body between the village panchayat and the district level zilla parishad is a new institution of local government. Second, local government bodies are given far greater powers with respect to rural development activities than they had previously.[4] Third, the three tiers of local government are or-

[2] *Report of the Team for the Study of Community Projects and National Extension Service* (New Delhi: Committee on Plan Projects, 1957), three volumes. The report is popularly known as the *Report of the Balvantray Mehta Committee*, after its chairman.

[3] The committee spoke of "democratic decentralisation," but upon the advice of the prime minister the term "panchayati raj" was introduced in subsequent discussions.

[4] "The main objective of enactment of the Andhra Pradesh Panchayat Samitis and Zilla Parishads Act, 1959, is to develop community spirit among the people and local leadership at Village, Block and District levels so that they can plan for rural development and execute their programmes with the active help of the people, voluntary organisations and departmental assistance." *Panchayat Raj in Andhra Pradesh*

ganically linked through a system of indirect elections. Panchayat presidents are members of the samitis, and samiti presidents are automatically members of the zilla parishads.

In Andhra, as in most other states in India, the new legislation was built upon an existing body of legislation dating to the latter part of the nineteenth century when the British viceroys, especially Lord Ripon, took steps to develop local government bodies throughout India. Moreover, an important piece of legislation affecting village panchayats in the Telugu area of Madras state now in Andhra was passed shortly after independence (the Madras Village Panchayats Act, 1950). The panchayat samitis have their antecedents in the old taluk boards, which covered an area about three or four times larger than the samitis. And finally, the zilla parishads have their antecedents in the old district boards, which had considerable authority to maintain district roads, hospitals, and many other local services.

The new institutions were thus not entirely new, and the developments which flowed from them were simply accelerations of changes which had already begun to take place. But perhaps the most important political consequence of panchayati raj is that it has given political parties direct control over development activities. Although panchayati raj refers to a three-tiered structure, the major innovation in the system was the middle tier — the panchayat samiti. The samiti is in effect the vehicle for the government's rural development program. The powers given to the samiti were essentially those belonging to the CD or NES programs. In effect, therefore, the creation of the samiti meant that the government's program would be transferred from the state-directed administration to an indirectly elected public body.

This meant that the samiti was given control over such matters as where roads would be laid, wells constructed, and dispensaries established. In addition, some of the powers of the old district boards were transferred to the samitis, including control over primary education within the samiti region. The construction of primary schools and the control of teachers (including their transfers) were now matters in the hands of the samitis. All funds hitherto allocated by the state and central governments to the Community Development Program were now funneled through the panchayat samitis.

Since the primary purpose of the system of panchayat raj was to remedy the lack of enthusiasm and participation by rural people in the develop-

(Planning and Local Administration Department, Government of Andhra Pradesh, 1959), p. 1.

ment program, it is understandable that the samiti would become the kingpin of the new local government structure. Indeed, whatever changes were made in the functions of the village panchayats and the district boards (now renamed zilla parishads) were due to the creation of these new development-oriented units of local government, the panchayat samitis. In Andhra no changes were made in the legislation with respect to village panchayats, but it was now understood that by making the presidents of the panchayats members of the samitis there would be a closer link between the village panchayat and the development program. Presumably the panchayat presidents would take a keener interest in this work if they were represented on a body primarily responsible for development. Legislation did abolish the old district boards and create zilla parishads, but the changes were again related to the creation of the panchayat samiti. The zilla parishads were to be made up of the presidents of the samitis, as well as MLAs, MLCs, and MPs from the district. Moreover, the zilla parishad was given responsibility for "supervising and advising" the samitis. They were also to have responsibility for controlling secondary schools and maintaining district roads and other district-wide services, but in the main these were also the responsibility of the old district boards.

To understand the significance of this transfer of powers from the developmental administration of the government to elected bodies, one must first appreciate the extraordinary powers in the hands of the district bureaucracy. Under British rule, districts in Andhra, as elsewhere in India, were governed by an administrative structure headed by the collector. Magisterial, police, revenue, and administrative powers were in the hands of a single man, invariably a member of the famed Indian Civil Service (ICS).

This concentration of authority in the hands of a single man was not an attempt to impose British traditions on Indian conditions. To the contrary, the new administrative structure was a conscious rejection of the Anglo-Saxon tradition with its emphasis on popular local government. But when the British spread their power in the subcontinent in the eighteenth century, they sought simultaneously to establish military control, enforce law and order in the district, and provide revenue for the East India Company. Britishers argued that the unsettled conditions of the time required the concentration of powers in the hands of a single local authority. When later in the nineteenth century powers were delegated to other officials — as in the creation of the office of superintendent of police — the new officers were subordinate to and responsible to the collector.

Thus there developed an administrative framework much more akin to the administrative system found on the continent of Europe, in which local administration was concentrated in the hands of a prefect, than to the Anglo-Saxon tradition of popular local government. This tradition of weak local governments and strong local bureaucracies in the districts was the prevailing pattern in India throughout the period of British rule. Since the latter part of the nineteenth century efforts have been made to expand the powers of local government, but local government remained subordinate to the collectorate.

As departments of the state government were created or expanded, they continued in one way or another to be under the control or supervision of the collector and his subordinate, the tahsildar, who had primary responsibility for governing the district. With the establishment of the Community Development Program, however, responsibility for some of the new developmental functions was shifted to other sections of the bureaucracy. Community Development was placed under the direct control of the Planning and Local Administration Department of the Andhra Pradesh government, and at the block level (an area including between sixty thousand and one hundred thousand persons), it was the block development officer (the BDO), rather than the tahsildar under the collector's authority, who had extraordinary powers. The financial and developmental powers of the district agricultural officer, the engineer of the public works department, the district educational officer, and other district officials of the state administration all increased. For fertilizers, seeds, implements, and credit, the cultivator had to deal with a department officer within the district. Thus, while the omnipotence of the collector as a kind of pro-consul within the district was reduced, the over-all powers of bureaucracy at the district level grew after independence.

The pre-independence pattern of local politics, in which men of status sought to influence local administration for their own benefit and for the benefit of kinsmen, castemen, and members of their factions, persisted after independence. The system of paying local officials for performance of services, legal and otherwise, continued, and what was once viewed as simply traditional mamools (the tradition of payment in kind for services rendered) was now seen as massive corruption. Although revenue, police, and public works departments continued to be the most corruptible departments at the district level, the ministries concerned with development were not free from corruption. With the expansion of governmental departments and the withdrawal of British officers from the state public

service commissions, nepotism in appointments also became more common. At the level of both the state public service commissions and the district departments, ascriptive criteria have become increasingly important in administrative appointments.

Efforts by the citizenry to influence administrative appointments and to affect administrative decisions became commonplace after independence. Individuals approached local administrators to obtain seeds, fertilizers, credit, jobs for their sons, licenses to purchase cement or sheet metal, permits to open shops, aid in gaining entrance for their sons into local colleges, and so on. Because the Congress party had gained control of the state government after independence, efforts to influence administration increasingly took place through the local Congress party organization. Men of local influence who had hitherto remained outside party politics joined the Congress party in order to maintain or strengthen their influence on local administration. Those who had once participated in the now defunct Justice party also joined Congress.

In short, with the expansion of government after independence and, in particular, with the growing role of government in developmental activities, local administration had extraordinary patronage powers to which local citizens sought access. First, there were patronage powers with respect to personnel, involving appointments to administration, seats in colleges, and transfers of administrative personnel (such as school teachers). Second, there was patronage associated directly with developmental functions, involving the needs of individuals for credit, seeds, and fertilizers, and the needs of villages for roads, wells, and panchayat halls. Third, there was patronage associated with the regulatory character of government — for example, in obtaining permits for raw materials or opening a shop. Fourth, there was the traditional patronage associated with the office of *tahsildar*, involving land titles and land revenue.[5] This form of patronage or influence became particularly important when the state government passed land reform legislation which threatened the interests of larger landowners.[6] Fifth, there was contract patronage involving the dispensing of contracts (generally by the public works department) for the construction of roads, buildings, and wells.

[5] An official of the Andhra government, after reading this manuscript, demurred, saying: "Regarding panchayati raj and the bureaucracy I agree with most of your conclusions, though I would not castigate every tahsildar as being corrupt. I don't think that more than 25% of the revenue department is corrupt."

[6] *The Report of the Andhra State Government Corruption Inquiry Committee* admits that the influence of landowners on tahsildars has weakened the effectiveness of land reform legislation.

*Political Parties and Panchayats*

Panchayati raj meant in effect that some of these patronage powers which had developed within local administration would be transferred into political hands. The Congress party, ideologically sympathetic to democratic decentralization, found the argument for transferring these powers to elected bodies politically most attractive. At the national level, however, members of the cabinet, including the prime minister, expressed the hope that political parties would not struggle for control of the village panchayats or even the panchayat samitis and zilla parishads. They often viewed these bodies as developmental bodies, free from political conflict, devoted in an harmonious fashion to the development of the rural areas. Though this utopianism was repeated frequently by state politicians, at the local level politicians recognized that they could not abstain from participating in local government politics without committing political suicide.

For one thing, the tiered structure of panchayati raj almost forces local units of political parties to seek control of village panchayats. The samitis are made up of the presidents of the village panchayats, and the zilla parishad contains the presidents of the samitis. Since both the samitis and parishads have considerable financial powers and control over so much of the government's local development activities, they are naturally an object of party interest. Parties, therefore, want to control the samatis and parishads and since these bodies are elected by the panchayats, it follows that political parties must attempt to exercise influence within the panchayats.

Thus, the establishment of panchayati raj forced the Congress party and other parties as well to increase their efforts to gain control of village panchayats. A few years before the panchayati raj legislation was passed in 1959 in Andhra, legislation was passed increasing the powers of the village panchayats. The very reasons, therefore, that made parties interested in gaining control of samitis and parishads led them to enter the panchayats. So long as the panchayats had little power, there was little reason for political parties to have much interest in them; but once their powers were increased, parties were drawn to them. Those who argued, as many Gandhians did, that local bodies should be given more power but that there should be no politics in the local bodies — whether involving political parties or castes or factions — were taking a contradictory position. Wherever there is power there must be politics — a law as fundamental in political science as supply and demand is in economics.

In India, as in other democratic countries, political parties have built

themselves upon a local government base. Long before the Labour party in Great Britain assumed national power it had won power in many municipalities. In India too the work of Subhas Bose and C. R. Das in strengthening the nationalist movement in Calcutta by gaining control of the municipal corporation is well known. Similarly, the Justice party established itself by winning control of district local boards, and in recent years both the D.M.K. and Jan Sangh have tried to gain control of local bodies — both of municipalities and of village panchayats — in their quest for state and national power.

Local politicians in Andhra are well aware of the importance of these local bodies. The president of the panchayat has considerable influence in the village, even with respect to how a substantial part of the village will vote in assembly and parliamentary elections. It does of course happen that a village panchayat president is of one party and the village votes for another party in the general elections, but more often the panchayat president can sway a substantial part of the village. In Ponnur constituency, for example, we found that almost every village that the Swatantra assembly candidate carried or that gave the Swatantra candidate a large vote in the 1962 elections had a Swatantra panchayat president. Thus even if local politicians choose to deny themselves the patronage available to those who control village panchayats, they must try to win the support of those who control these bodies in the general elections. They may try to win the support of the panchayat president for their party's assembly or parliamentary candidate, but it is far safer to help elect, as president of the panchayat, a man who is already known to be a party supporter.

Throughout Guntur, village leaders have found it advantageous to be associated with a political party. As we have noted earlier, most of the villages in the delta are divided; where a village is divided, both groups ally themselves with a political party or with a faction of a political party within the district. The village group may lend its support to a party in the general elections, for the party candidate may in return give them money to help them organize and strengthen their village faction. Moreover, the village faction may also feel that if their man is elected to the assembly, villagers who belong to neither faction are more likely to give them support. Then too the assembly or parliamentary candidate they have supported may be of some help to them in panchayat elections: he may give them money, or his open support may in and of itself be an asset.

It is thus a mistake to think that villagers are constantly being exploited by political parties, for it is no less true that political parties are ex-

ploited by village factions seeking to maximize their own interests by associating themselves with district political organizations. At the local level, there is often much bargaining between the village factions and the party candidates for the assembly. The village faction may press for a well, a road, a school, a telegraph office, or electric power connections. The individual villager may seek the help of the party or the MLA in obtaining permits and licenses from a local bureaucrat. The villager is often prepared to give his political support to some party or candidate in return for having some influence; once a connection is established between the villager and the local MLA, it can hardly be severed for the purposes of village panchayat elections.

Officially, village panchayat elections are non-party elections. In practice, however, the competition for control of village panchayats by political parties in Guntur — and elsewhere in Andhra — has been most intense. Enormous sums of money are spent, and MLAs, MPs, and local Congress leaders actively lend their support to one side or another in panchayat elections. Since the government takes no official notice of the role played by parties in these elections, it is impossible to report in any statistical way on the relative position of political parties in the panchayats of Guntur district. The party affiliation of samiti chairmen is, however, an indication of the respective position of various political parties in the village panchayats, since the panchayat presidents elect samiti chairmen. Of the thirty-five samiti chairmen in Guntur, twenty-nine belonged to the Congress party. The Communists control a few samitis in the district [7] and a number of the village panchayats in Congress-dominated samitis. But in the main Communist success in winning some legislative assembly and parliament seats for Guntur is not reflected in the Communist position in local government bodies. In 1962 the Communists won nine of twenty-five assembly seats and 26 per cent of the votes in Guntur district, compared with twelve seats and 41 per cent for Congress.

One reason for the weakness of the Communists in local government bodies is that, in the smaller villages throughout the district, elections were until recently by a show of hands rather than through a secret ballot.

[7] The Communists controlled three samitis in 1962 shortly before the general elections. All three elected Communist MLAs or Communist-supported independents. In Sattenapalle the seat was contested by the Congress president of the zilla parishad, but a Communist-supported independent was reelected. A number of factors were involved in the Congress defeat, but local people reported that the Congress zilla parishad president was unable to utilize his position by virtue of the fact that Congress did not control the local samiti. In other areas Congress control of the samiti proved to be an important and, in a few instances, a decisive factor in the outcome of the general elections.

Since a substantial part of the Communist strength comes from agricultural laborers, leather workers, and sweepers — all members of underprivileged communities who depend upon the patronage of the wealthier classes for their livelihood — these classes cannot afford to vote Communist in open elections.

Throughout the district, Congressmen report that the effect of panchayati raj has been to strengthen the position of the Congress party. The patronage available to the party is one source of strength. Still another is that, in the words of one Congressman, "our workers have something to do." Congressmen are deeply involved in the work of the panchayati raj bodies, particularly the panchayat samitis. Some of the samiti presidents and many of the members are only nominally members of the Congress party, but a number are old party workers and supporters. Moreover, local Congressmen who are not in the samitis are often engaged in activities associated with the samitis. A simple list of the functions of the samitis indicates the amount of work available to party workers and also the enormous political power the party can derive from such work. Under the Andhra Pradesh Panchayat Samitis Act, all the activities of the Community Development Program are taken over by the samitis. This includes work in the fields of agriculture, animal husbandry, health and sanitation, elementary education, cottage industries, and social welfare. More concretely, the samiti has primary responsibility for the multiplication, storage, and distribution to the cultivators of improved seeds, for sanctioning loans to hire and purchase agricultural implements, for all taccavi loans (short-term agricultural loans), and for granting permits to individual farmers to purchase fertilizers from the local co-operative societies. The management of elementary schools, adult literacy centers, primary health centers, and school hostels is in the hands of the samitis. The samitis can also construct community halls and supply radio sets to scheduled castes from funds supplied to them by the state social welfare department.

The central point is that the roles performed by local Congress party members were profoundly affected by the transfer of developmental functions from the district bureaucracy to popularly elected bodies controlled by political parties. The Congress party — or, for that matter, whatever party gains control of the panchayati raj institutions — receives credit or blame for the performance of these local government bodies. Moreover, the local party directs its energies at running local government bodies and at utilizing its patronage powers to maximize its political position. This does not necessarily mean that the party crudely rewards its

friends and punishes its enemies; frequently the party may woo voters who in the past supported the opposition. Agricultural laborers, for example, have been strong supporters of the Communist party in Guntur district and elsewhere in the Andhra delta. Congressmen in control of the panchayat samitis have often been particularly active in providing services for the scheduled castes that constitute a large proportion of the agricultural laborers. Since the legislation empowers the samitis to acquire housing sites and provide loans for housing to members of scheduled castes, the assistance rendered to Harijans by Congressmen in the samitis can be an important instrument for winning political support for the party.

We have already suggested that in the 1962 elections the substantial decline in popular vote for the Communists in Guntur district and elsewhere in Andhra may in large part have been due to defections by members of the scheduled castes. The fact that Andhra had a Harijan chief minister was no doubt a factor in the support many Harijans gave to the Congress party. But local political leaders also note that the panchayat samitis, the vast majority of which are controlled by Congress, have been increasing their services to the Harijans; though there has been no substantial improvement in the income or, therefore, in the living conditions of most Harijans, the growing availability of primary schools, hostels, housing sites, and administration jobs has given them a sense that the government in general and the Congress party in particular have taken steps to improve their conditions. It should be noted, however, that funds for Harijan welfare come from the state government and are not locally raised and that there have been frequent complaints from Harijan leaders that local bodies are not giving them adequate attention. Further, it should be noted that the budget of the social welfare department (which provides welfare aid to the Harijans) has been steadily rising, with rather substantial increases several months before general elections.

This is not to suggest that the Harijans have become an independent force within Congress as a consequence of adult suffrage or of panchayati raj. In the past the lower castes have not actively participated in village politics or in the politics of administration, and do not therefore readily adjust themselves to the new roles suggested by democratic party politics. Typically, only castes that have participated in village politics find it possible to step into the larger arena. However, the main point here is that adult suffrage has made the political acts of the Harijans of interest to those groups which do compete in the arena of party politics; pan-

chayati raj institutions have provided factions with greater resources for winning Harijan support.

The development of local government institutions has also had an effect on the pattern of recruitment into the Congress party and, of great importance, on the structure of power within Congress at the district level. The president of the District Local Board was always an important figure in the party organization; today the president of the zilla parishad is also an influential figure. But, in addition, panchayat samiti presidents have become increasingly important within the party — some say even more important than members of the legislative assembly. Samiti presidents do in fact have more access to patronage than do members of the legislative assembly; though in the 1962 elections none of the samiti presidents were candidates for the assembly, they played an important role in the selection and election of candidates.

Not all the samiti presidents who are members of the Congress party were members of the party before their election. The samiti president is after all simply one of the village panchayat presidents elected by other presidents to this position; though he may already be a member of Congress or some other party, he may not belong to any political party. The district Congress leadership assiduously woos the panchayat samiti presidents, since it is in the party interests for the samiti president to be a Congressman. A number of local Congressmen therefore enter the party *after* — not before — they have established their political hold in a portion of the district.

In Guntur, as in other districts of rural India, Congress attracts individuals who are already in positions of local power.[8] Office bearing in the party is not simply a means of obtaining power — though it is that too sometimes — but also a way of affirming an individual's local power. One can postulate the hypothesis that in rural areas election to the District Congress Committee is an affirmation of one's status, while in the urban areas of India it is more often an expression of efforts to achieve status.

In the past, men who have sought state-wide office in the legislative assembly have first held power at the local level in their villages, in the taluka and district councils, in cooperatives and school boards. The old pattern is likely to continue; though no samiti presidents stood in the 1962 elections, we may expect the office to be a stepping stone to state politics. Insofar as this occurs, we may also expect that much of the in-

[8] For a statistical analysis of leadership patterns within the Congress party of Guntur and descriptions of the social backgrounds and career patterns of its major leaders, see Appendix 2 following chapter 10, below.

tense factional conflict now taking place over party nominations for the state assembly will also occur at the samiti and zilla parishad level, and that party factions will become even more concerned with controlling panchayati raj institutions than they are now. If over the coming years it becomes clear that samiti presidents are readily elected to the assembly or that support by samiti presidents is essential to election—and there is already some evidence to support this view—then it is likely that the influence of these men on the affairs of the party will grow and that the intra-party factional struggle for control over these offices will be intense. The importance of control over village panchayats (the samiti is, of course, made up of village panchayat presidents) is already indicated by the fact that the village voting turnout for panchayat elections now generally exceeds the turnout for the general elections for assembly and parliamentary seats.

The shift from administrative to party politics has thus been accelerated by the establishment of panchayati raj. Men who once sought to exercise influence in the traditional way—by working within the local taluka and district bureaucracy—now find it essential to join political parties and run for public office, and are naturally more concerned with how government administers what it does than with the policies and ideologies which underlie governmental action. But these new party members enter an organization which does have policies and an ideological orientation. How local Congressmen adapt ideology to suit their interests and how they relate the activities of the panchayati raj institutions to the party ideology were themes of many of our interviews.

## Patronage and Ideology

In revolutionary political parties, ideology often determines the party forms and functions. In the case of the Congress party—as in many other democratic political parties—the structure and functions of the party have shaped the party's ideology and program, not vice versa. We have already noted that the internal conflicts of the party are not related to ideological disputes or, for that matter, to disputes over major questions of public policy. Caste and kinship ties and, above all, factional affiliations related to the need for status and prestige or to the desire for material rewards have been crucial factors in intra-party conflict. Withdrawal from the party has often been justified on the basis of ideological or policy considerations; but, for that matter, the Socialist party of Andhra which

claimed it had ideological differences with Congress was absorbed into the Congress organization.

The Congress party at the national, state, and district levels is committed to "socialism." The term must be put in quotes, for what socialism means in European literature is of little relevance to what Congressmen mean. The Congress party has adapted the European concept of socialism to the particular needs of the party organization. Socialism as understood by most Congressmen does not mean class conflict or the expropriation of privately owned means of production. European socialist writers are not read by Congressmen, and the notion of the dialectic is alien to Indian socialist thought — at least within the Congress party. In the course of my field work in Guntur I asked Congressmen what socialism meant, and below are some of the typical replies.

One high official of the Congress party said:

> We stand for socialism. It means that the have nots should have economic, political, and social benefits. We don't want capitalism, because some businessmen exploit others for profit. . . . The difficulty is that agricultural laborers and others want immediate help. We urge our workers to keep in constant touch with the people, not only to solve their problems, but also to educate them. It is more important to educate them. They must understand and appreciate your approach, even when you fail. Take them into your confidence. Tell them the difficulties in solving the problems so when you fail they will not leave you so easily. That's what our workers must do. . . . The purpose of this organization [Congress] is to win elections. Then with power we can do things.

One prominent Guntur Congressman who holds a high ministerial position in the Andhra government explained that the Congress party stands for democratic socialism. "What do you mean by socialism?" "Greater equality," he replied. "Does that mean that you favor land reform legislation in Andhra?"

> In my district in Guntur property is generally evenly distributed. There is little scope for cutting down land ceilings. Except perhaps for a dozen landlords in the district, very few have much land. In my own village, everyone is within the ceiling. Yes, family members redistribute their land to

evade ceilings. There is some of that, but we passed the land reform act to prevent further large holdings. . . . The main needs of the district are more water, power, and fertilizers. And these must be provided by government. . . . The first five year plan had many big projects, but their benefits were not immediately felt. In the second plan, more attention was given to building schools, dispensaries, roads, and hospitals, so people felt the improvements. Now people want fertilizers, electricity, drinking water, and more roads. People see some benefit. Panchayati raj has helped. Patronage used to be with the administration, and now patronage is with the local bodies.

"What do you mean by patronage?" "Laying of roads, giving wells, loans and so on. . . . There is a need for more credit. Now taccavi [loans] is given by tahsildars [revenue officers], but we are thinking to give it to the samitis. They should have the patronage. This is a democracy." "But isn't there the danger that loans will be given for non-productive purposes?" "Perhaps, but there will be rules about giving loans. As for efficiency, I am not more efficient than my secretary [i.e., the secretary of his ministry], but this is a democracy."

"Does socialism mean cooperative farming?" I asked another local Congressman. "Yes, I speak of that in my election speeches. But we mean service cooperatives, nothing more. Yes, I support ceilings, since it will prevent further concentrations." "What needs to be done in the next five years?" "We need to extend irrigation, develop small-scale and cottage industries to provide employment, and establish minimum wages for agricultural laborers. In my speeches I tell people of the Congress accomplishments and what Congress is doing to raise standards of poor people."

"How has socialism affected the work of the party workers?" I asked one MLA, an important party organizer. "Our workers used to engage in constructive work. But now government has taken over work with khadi, soap making, tanning, and other parts of the constructive work program. So Congressmen have had to take to this other work — working with the government."

The deep involvement of party workers in the affairs of a "socialist" government was commented on by another MLA.

Between elections the taluka committees do very little work. Congress people are presidents of panchayats and samitis,

and they function in these capacities not as officials of taluka or mandal committees. But if meetings have to be held, then the Congress committees do function. They arrange meetings with visiting ministers. They celebrate Gandhi's birthday and independence day. They are expected to sponsor small savings schemes, but they don't do much of this kind of work since the panchayat presidents do some of this. The official machinery is there, so they work through that.

One important local Congressman who had left the Socialist party to join Congress spoke bitterly of this tendency to identify the party organization with the government.

> My belief is that there is no Congress party organization in India. Congress has identified itself completely with the government machinery. When the government is lost, then Congress will disappear. I have tried in Guntur to see my Congress friends in a group. I have yet to see a meeting of the Congress workers. They only meet when some minister comes. Otherwise they do not meet to pass resolutions or carry on any party business.

Congressmen in Guntur welcome the expansion of governmental activities. They believe that government ought to play an increasingly active role in sponsoring development, which is viewed largely as greater financial allocations by government for rural amenities — electricity, schools, and drinking water, as well as fertilizers, agricultural credit, irrigation, and seeds. Investing for future growth and providing for the greater distribution of goods and services are seen as the primary functions of government. One does meet Congressmen with a particular concern for investment, but to a large extent Congressmen in Guntur are concerned with the distributive measures pursued by government. "The have nots should have benefits." Socialism means "greater equality." Congress is raising "standards of poor people." Socialism is thus equated with measures to ensure a more equitable distribution of wealth.

To local party leaders panchayati raj means a shift in patronage from the local bureaucracy to local elected officials who in the main belong to the Congress party. Thus the party instinctively welcomes all efforts to expand investment in schools, dispensaries, roads, wells, and other local services. Moreover, the state government's attempts to provide greater

amenities for the poorer classes are particularly welcomed by the local Congress organization, since the underprivileged groups, are still attracted to the Communist party.

Local Congressmen are not particularly enthusiastic about ceilings on landholdings. In any event, ceiling legislation permits so many legal loopholes that only the very large landowners are affected. Few of the important Congressmen in the district are themselves cultivators of land, but almost all are landowners. Some Congressmen say that they or members of their family "supervise" cultivation, and they look upon this as a legitimate form of economic activity. These Congressmen accepted the ceiling legislation but did not view it as an attempt to provide land for the landless. One Congress MLA explained:

> One purpose of the legislation was to encourage landlords, mostly Reddis and Kammas, to return to cultivation. Most of the land in the delta is cultivated by one or two members of the family while other members of the family live as absentee landlords in the small towns. The ceiling forced families to redistribute their holdings to members of their own family. This might encourage members of the family to cease to be absentee landlords. Then another purpose of the legislation was to discourage landlords from enlarging their existing holdings. We hope that landlords would invest their surplus wealth in business rather than in enlarging their land holdings.

The land in Guntur was raiyatwari land—that is, land for which the British government settled the revenue relationship with the cultivator directly rather than with some intermediary landowner as in zamindari, jagidari, and inamdari areas. But this difference is not so great in practice as in theory. Some of the raiyats are, in fact, substantial landowners with many tenant cultivators working for them. The ceiling legislation in Andhra was aimed at eliminating the gross inequalities, just as in other states the legislation to abolish zamindars and inamdars was in fact aimed at reducing gross inequalities. Still, it is possible for an individual in the delta to control several hundred acres of land, though rarely any more. The vast majority of the agriculturalists in Guntur are small landowners, some of whom themselves do the cultivating, many of whom rent part of their land to tenants, and a very substantial number of whom hire agricultural laborers on daily wages to assist them in cultivation.

These small landowning peasants — whether they cultivate the land themselves or have hired labor — are deeply interested in the government's development activities, since their access to fertilizers, seeds, irrigation, and credit directly affects their financial well-being. It is this class which is so deeply involved in the credit cooperatives, the panchayat samitis, the village panchayats, and in party politics throughout the district. The government's program to assist agricultural laborers, mostly Harijans, by helping them to get housing sites and to send their children to schools and by giving them jobs in the lower levels of administration is accepted by the small landowning peasants, for these efforts by government to "uplift" the poor in no way infringe upon the rights of those who own land.

"Socialism," then, with its emphasis on government assistance for development and government efforts to aid the poor, constitutes no threat to the small proprietors. In the 1962 elections the Swatantra party attacked the Congress party on the grounds that Congress' commitment to cooperative farming was a threat to small proprietors. Swatantra charged that cooperative farming meant joint farming in which each man would lose title to his land — in effect, a system of collectivization — and local Congressmen went to great lengths to explain that by cooperative farming they only meant service cooperatives — that is, farmers banding together to share farm implements, purchase seeds, store their goods in warehouses, and market their goods.

Congress supporters of socialism do not look upon private ownership as contrary to what they define as socialist principles. A few — but only a few — of the younger workers in the party speak of the need to redistribute land to the poor and to impose lower ceilings on land holdings. But most Congressmen who call themselves socialists equate socialism with measures that assist the poor without infringing upon the rights or threatening the well-being of the prosperous peasantry. Whatever the origin of socialist ideology in the Congress party — a question whose implication go beyond the scope of this study — socialism as local party workers define it amiably suits the purposes and organization of the local party.

# 10. FROM BUREAUCRATIC TO PARTY POLITICS

We have analyzed the impact of panchayati raj on the Congress party in the context of local social and economic conflict and have shown that the struggle of various social groups to maximize their interests — interests involving prestige and status, as befits a hierarchical social system, and interests involving more material rewards — predates modern politics. While before 1900 the struggles had taken place largely within the powerful local bureaucracy, the trend since 1920 — the year provincial government was established — has been to extend the struggle into the open arena. The Kammas and the Reddis, as the major landowning groups in the district, and local village factions which cut across caste lines have, with adult suffrage, expansion of government functions, and the recent transfer of powers to elected units of local government, become increasingly interested in party politics. Panchayati raj, therefore, simply accelerated the shift of politics from a bureaucratic framework to an open arena — that is, the arena of party politics.

As the most powerful party in the district, the Congress party has borne the brunt of this shift. It is understandable that bureaucrats feel uncomfortable in the loss of their authority and, more particularly, in having to take orders from men of less education and less governmental experience. Some block development officers and many of the technical personnel assigned to the Community Development Program and now responsible to the elected members of the panchayat samiti find it difficult to accept the new authority, and for some years to come we can expect considerable tension between bureaucrats and politicians at the local level as they establish a new relationship.

Powers once in the hands of bureaucrats are now in the hands of Congress members, with the result that patronage has now increased — a patronage utilized primarily by the Congress party but which has become so much a part of the local political scene that any party in control of a unit of local government recognizes the value of patronage for political purposes. Neither the need nor the ability to utilize effectively a given government allocation is as important a factor in many local government decisions as various political considerations. One consequence is not widespread public withdrawal from politics (although some of the more educated are considerably disillusioned) but rather an intensified political participation by the leaders of village factions who have become aware of the potential gains to their faction and their village from particular political alliances.

The conflicts between the Kammas and the Reddis, the growing importance of the Telegas and, to a lesser extent, the Malas and Madigas and other castes of less education and income in the district, and the struggles between multi-caste factions at the village level — all are part of the social scene to which political parties must adapt. We have suggested that these traditional social conflicts — now often fought out in the open arena of party politics — affect not only the struggles between Congress and other parties but the intra-party struggles as well. As a consequence of its mass character and, to a greater extent than other parties, its representative character, Congress suffers more from the internal dissensions related to social conflict within the society than do other political parties. In part, the party mirrors the conflicts found within the social system.

But party politics is not simply a reflection of social conflicts; the political conflicts have a certain dynamic of their own which affects social relationships. Political necessity has drawn together castes which once had little contact with one another. In recent years the leading Kamma politicians in the Congress party of Guntur district eagerly supported the Harijan chief minister and sought to rally the support of the Harijan community to the party in order to prevent a member of the Reddi caste from becoming chief minister of Andhra. Moreover, the establishment of panchayati raj and of adult suffrage has made the poor but populous communities more important; while these communities have a long way to go before they achieve political influence commensurate with their size, the state government and the Congress party have been particularly active in serving the needs of many of the scheduled castes.

The new local government bodies are not always well run by Congress. Sometimes one faction of the party controls the office of panchayat presi-

dent, while other factions control the various standing committees which have much of the authority; as a consequence internal conflicts reach such a magnitude that there is paralysis of governmental functions. At least one panchayat samiti in the district has been superseded by the state government. Favoritism and corruption are not uncommon, and the complaints one commonly hears from citizens throughout the world with respect to their local governments are frequently heard in the bazaars and fields of Guntur. Moreover, since officially the Congress party neither takes part in village panchayat elections nor attempts to win control of the panchayat samitis, it has no official program for the functioning of local government bodies. Nor does the party attempt to impose any discipline on its membership in these local bodies. Though, in practice, the ideological commitment of the national leadership to bring about a withdrawal of party politics in the villages and samitis, if not in the zilla parishads, is ignored by local leaders for reasons we have discussed earlier, the local party still takes no official notice of the political role it is actually playing. There is, thus, a political engagement by the party but no assumption of responsibility.

It is beyond the scope of this study to explore the impact of the party on panchayati raj (as distinct from the impact of panchayati raj on the party). It is relevant, however, to note that the party does encourage a kind of responsiveness to the demands of groups which had hitherto been neglected. Political considerations sometimes make upper-caste men who have no special sympathy for the plight of the poor willing to assist lower castes and economic groups. The responsiveness of the local party to local needs also makes the party — and the local government bodies — more concerned with distributive measures than with measures to increase production. Thus the panchayat samitis and the village panchayats are particularly active in the construction of roads, schools, children's nurseries, panchayat halls, and the like, while they make little effort to induce farmers to experiment with new methods. The village level workers — the officers of the old Community Development blocks responsible for teaching new agricultural methods and for performing the many other functions of the development program at the village level — are now reduced to minor officers of the panchayat samiti and given an increasingly heavy administrative load. In Guntur district at least — and there is no evidence to show that the situation is different elsewhere — panchayati raj has increased local participation in those areas of the Community Development Program which involve the distribution of goods and services (that is,

amenities) to the village, but has had little direct impact so far on efforts to increase agricultural production.

From another point of view the most significant effect of panchayati raj has been to strengthen the links between village politics and party politics. In recent social science literature much attention has been given to the effects of literacy, urbanization, new patterns of communication (such as radio and newspapers), and new transportation links (the building of roads, railways) upon political participation. This study calls attention to the impact of institutions on the political behavior of individuals. When administrative functions were turned over to elected local government bodies, the traditional struggle for administrative influence moved into the arena of open electoral politics at the village level. It is far too early to predict that the village power structure will become more open, but it is now increasingly common for factions within the village elite to seek support from lower castes — a policy which in the past in India and elsewhere has ultimately ended in changing the composition of the elite itself.

# APPENDIX 1

## VILLAGE AND PARTY FACTIONALISM IN AN ASSEMBLY ELECTION, 1962*

Many of the points made in this chapter concerning the interrelationship between factionalism within Congress and factionalism within villages can be illustrated by an examination of voting patterns in a single constituency. Here we shall show how factional relationships, rather than simply caste or class conflict, shape the outcome of an election.

Ponnur constituency, on the delta of the Krishna River in Bapatla and Tenali talukas has an erratic voting record. It was carried by a Communist in the 1952 assembly elections, by a member of the Krishikar Lok party in 1955, and by a Congressman in 1962. In the parliamentary election we have been able to isolate the vote of this constituency for two elections. In 1957 a Congressman won, and in 1962 a Communist. The constituency has thus not only been erratic, but there is apparently a substantial amount of split voting.

The results for the various elections are shown in Table 16.

As we can see in the 1962 elections, Congress won the assembly seat in a straight fight with Swatantra while the Communists won handsomely in a three-way contest for the parliamentary seat. It first appears as if the Congress assembly vote went to the Communist parliamentary candidate, and perhaps even part of the Swatantra assembly vote switched to the Communist MP candidate. Or, alternatively, we might conclude that

*An earlier version appeared as an article in *The Economic Weekly* (Bombay) Sept. 22, 1962, as "Village and Party Factionalism in Andhra: Ponnur Constituency."

the Communists simply maintained their 1957 parliamentary vote and, since they had not offered an assembly candidate in 1962, asked their voters to support a Congress rather than the Swatantra candidate. As we shall see, neither explanation is satisfactory.

An examination of the relationship between occupation and voting does not reveal any clear relationships. We were able to isolate the voting patterns of agricultural laborers. According to the 1951 census, agricultural laborers and their dependents constitute 26 per cent of the population of Ponnur constituency. Cultivators who own land wholly or in part and their dependents comprise 52 per cent.

TABLE 16
PONNUR ELECTION RESULTS
(Percentage of Vote)

| Party | 1952 | 1955 | 1957 | 1962 |
|---|---|---|---|---|
| | | Legislative Assembly | | |
| Congress . . . . . | 15 | Endorsed KLP | | 60 |
| Communist. . . . | 37 | 35 | | No Candidate |
| KLP-Swatantra. . | 21 | 65 | No Election | 40 |
| KMPP. . . . . . | 17 | . . | | . . |
| Independents . . . | 10 | . . | | . . |
| | | Parliament | | |
| Congress . . . . . | | | 57 | 23 |
| KLP-Swatantra . . | Not Available | No Election | Endorsed Congress | 32 |
| Communist. . . . | | | 43 | 44 |

If we rank villages by the size of their agricultural labor force, we find there is no relationship to the Communist parliamentary vote.

Five of these villages gave the Communist candidate a percentage substantially less than the 44 per cent he won in the entire constituency. Moreover, other villages with a smaller proportion of agricultural laborers gave the Communist a higher than average vote.

An attempt to correlate the Swatantra MLA vote to the number of cultivating landowners yields no positive results either. According to the 1951 census, eight villages have a higher than taluka average of cultivating landowners. Only one of these voted for Swatantra; in a second, Swatantra lost by only a handful of votes. A third voted for the Congress MLA but voted for the Swatantra MP candidate. The remaining villages voted overwhelmingly for the Congress MLA candidate by a vote of about two to one.

Swatantra carried a majority (or near majority) in only five of the thirty-

one villages in the constituency, and did reasonably well in another five villages. Only three of these villages have a high proportion of owner-cultivators. There is thus no evidence that this class voted for the Swatantra party in any larger numbers than for the Congress party. Moreover, since the Swatantra vote in many of these villages exceeds the number of voting owner-cultivators, clearly Swatantra must also have received support from tenants if not from some agricultural laborers.

An analysis of the Communist parliamentary vote also fails to show any clear class voting. The Communists carried thirty-three of fifty polling stations (for which data were available), and these cover all types of vil-

TABLE 17

COMMUNISTS AND THE AGRICULTURAL LABOR VOTE
IN THE PONNUR PARLIAMENTARY ELECTIONS
(Percentage of Vote)

| Village[a] | Agricultural Labor | Communist |
|---|---|---|
| Edlapalle . . . . . . . . . | 46 | 42 |
| Manchalla . . . . . . . . . | 30 | 42 |
| Brahmanakodur . . . . . . | 29 | 57 |
| Voliveru . . . . . . . . . . | 29 | 39 |
| Munipalli . . . . . . . . . | 28 | 39 |
| Patchalatadiparru . . . . . | 28 | 69 |
| Dandamudi . . . . . . . . | 28 | 32 |
| Chundur . . . . . . . . . . | 24 | 36 |
| Chebrole . . . . . . . . . . | 21 | 37 |

[a]Four other villages have a high proportion of agricultural laborers, but polling station statistics for the parliamentary seat were not available.

lages. The seventeen polling stations lost by the Communists were in six villages, three of which voted for Swatantra and three for Congress. And in only two of these villages did the proportion of owner-cultivators exceed the average for the two talukas. Again, we must conclude that the vote for — or, for that matter, against — the Communists is not based on occupation.

This is not to say that the Communists failed to secure a heavy vote among the agricultural laborers, for there is some evidence that they did; but clearly the Communist victory for the parliamentary seat was based on a much wider appeal. Nor can we conclude that Swatantra failed to get the vote of owner-cultivators, but clearly owner-cultivators voted heavily for the Congress as well; and for the parliamentary seat, many voted Communist.

To understand the dynamics of voting in this constituency, we must move from a statistical analysis to a descriptive examination of the factions in each village as these were related to each of the candidates.

*The Candidates and Congress Factionalism*

N. Venkatarao, the victorious Congress candidate for the assembly, spent most of his political career in the Congress Socialist party and the Praja Socialist party. At one time he was the president of the Praja Socialist party in Andhra. In 1958 he and other members of the Praja Socialist party returned to Congress. Along with other prominent former Praja Socialists, Venkatarao opposed Sanjiva Reddi and was a supporter of Sanjivaiah. The Socialists felt that Sanjiva Reddi was intolerant of those outside his own political group and was generally more helpful to his own caste, the Reddis, than to other communities. They felt that he was particularly hostile to the Kamma community, to which most of the former Socialists belonged.

Much of the hostility to Sanjiva Reddi was derived from political conflicts within Guntur district. In the nearby town of Tenali a powerful local Congress party boss, Mr. Alapati Venkatramaiah, chairman of the municipality and president of the powerful District Cooperative Bank, which distributes agricultural loans throughout the district, was for many years a bitter opponent of the socialists. Though a Kamma himself, he is a strong ally of Brahmananda Reddi, the finance minister and right-hand man of Sanjiva Reddi. Brahmananda Reddi's constituency and main political base are in Guntur district. Politics had united these two men from opposing castes — an illustration, incidentally, of the way in which the urge for power often overrides caste loyalties. These two men had emerged as two of the most powerful politicians in the district. Indeed, their position was further strengthened when both won assembly seats in the 1962 elections and both became ministers in Sanjiva Reddi's new government.

Venkatarao tried unsuccessfully to obtain the Congress ticket from Tenali constituency — his home; it was given instead to Venkatramaiah. Venkatarao was given a ticket in nearby Ponnur constituency, although he is not a resident of that area. He thus suffered from two handicaps. He was not a local man, and it was clear that Venkatramaiah would try to defeat him. Venkatarao thus could not depend upon those sections of the local Congress organization which belonged to Venkatramaiah's group. He did, however, have the support of three important local politicians: the boss of the Congress party organization in that portion of his constituency which fell in Bapatla taluka, one of the vice presidents of the District Congress Committee whose home and political base is in the constituency, and an energetic Congress member of the Rajya Sabha who had been one of the prominent Socialist politicians in the district and state.

P. Buchinaidu Chowdary, the Swatantra candidate, had never run for an assembly seat before. He was a large landowner in the constituency and, like the Congress candidate, he was a Kamma. He was a close friend and political associate of Ranga, the state Swatantra leader, and in fact came from the same village.

It was widely reported that Venkatramaiah had instructed his workers to support the Swatantra candidate for the legislative assembly. In turn, Venkatarao and his followers were reported to be supporting the Communist candidate opposing Venkatramaiah. (On the basis of the election returns, both reports appear to be correct.) They had apparently decided to support the Communist over the Swatantra candidate for two reasons. First, since the Communist candidate had won 40 per cent of the vote in 1955 against Venkatramaiah, he clearly had a better chance of winning. Second, some of the former Socialists reasoned that Swatantra represented more of a threat to Congress than the Communists did: if Swatantra did well, there might be substantial defections from Congress; but if the Communists did well, the anti-Communist forces would unite within Congress (this had occurred in the 1955 elections).

This reasoning was also applied by Venkatarao's followers to the parliamentary election. There were three candidates for parliament. The incumbent was Ranga, the Swatantra leader, a member of the Kamma community, a good organizer, and a popular leader throughout the district. He was opposed by a Communist, Kolla Venkaiah, also a Kamma, and a well-known party worker and peasant organizer. The Congress put up Narasimharao, a veteran Congressman who ironically had once been a close personal and political associate of Ranga. Narasimharao had, however, two disadvantages: he was a Brahmin, which meant that he lacked a base in any numerically large community, and he did not come from the constituency but from the nearby town of Guntur.

The Congress MLA candidate in Ponnur reasoned that since the Communists did not have an assembly candidate in this constituency they might be prepared to back him if in turn he supported the Communist parliamentary candidate. No advantage was to be gained by supporting the Congress parliamentary candidate, since he had nothing to offer whereas the Communists did. Moreover, the Congress parliamentary candidate was not a supporter of the Sanjivaiah group.

There were rumors that Venkatramaiah was not only supporting the Swatantra assembly candidate in Ponnur but was also giving support to Ranga for the parliamentary seat in return for Swatantra support for his effort to win the assembly seat in Tenali. Since Swatantra had its own assembly can-

didate in Tenali, this rumor first seemed unlikely, but Venkatramaiah's opponents have noted since the election that several villages which he is known to have controlled cast a majority for Swatantra, both for the assembly and for parliament. However, the evidence is by no means clear. It is clear that neither faction of the party was particularly interested in helping the Congress parliamentary candidate. Venkatarao was primarily interested in attracting Communist votes, and Venkatramaiah was eager to get Swatantra votes. How people voted for parliament was of secondary consideration; and since both factions considered the Congress candidate to be weaker than the Congress assembly candidates, nothing was to be gained by either faction in working closely with him.

## The Candidates and Village Factionalism

The struggle by factions within the Congress party in Andhra was thus the most important factor in the strategic considerations of candidates in all parties. This struggle was closely related to factional struggles taking place within the villages in the constituency, and it was the relationship between these two levels of factionalism which often determined how a village would vote.

It is exceedingly important to recognize that the villages were not simply passive agents in the struggle within and between parties. Conflicts existed within each village, and each village faction looked upon party struggles as an opportunity to further its own interests within the village.

There are few villages in the constituency and elsewhere in the delta that are not torn by factional conflicts. Since Kammas are the powerful landowning class here they dominate most factions, but in some instances the Reddis (also a large landowning community in this area) organize factions of their own. The local cooperative society, village officers like the munsif (the village judge) and the karnam (who maintains land records), and a powerful faction in control of the panchayat are in a position to protect and extend their own economic interests and to use their power to weaken others. In the past, conflicts centered in land rights, stray cattle, the use of water facilities, and the like. In recent years the increased powers given to panchayats and the access which the village now has to goods and services distributed by government agencies have added new elements over which struggles can occur. Landowners want wells, cement and sheet metal for construction purposes, seeds, fertilizers, and storage facilities. The faction in control of the panchayat often has better access to these com-

modities and facilities than have those not in power. Moreover, the demand for permits and licenses and loans and credit far exceeds the available supply; then too, power, not need and capacity to utilize, is often a primary consideration in their allocation.

The village faction may endorse a candidate because by supporting him they are better able to solidify their own popular following in the village. After all, the factions include numerically only a small part of the village, and supporting a candidate who can win in the village is one way of improving their own position within the village. The party, caste, and personality of the candidate are important considerations.

TABLE 18
ASSEMBLY ELECTIONS IN THREE "STABLE" VILLAGES IN PONNUR
(Number of Votes)

| VILLAGE | 1955 | | 1962 | |
|---|---|---|---|---|
| | Congress | CPI | Congress | Swatantra |
| Sangamjagarlamudi | 1,109 | 805 | 1,048 | 873 |
| Chebrole . . . . . | 2,452 | 1,680 | 2,659 | 1,934 |
| Aremanda . . . . | 678 | 345 | 761 | 319 |

Second, the faction is interested in the candidate's ability and willingness to do things for the village, which in turn of course will benefit the faction. Harijans want to know if the candidate is willing to look into their request for permits for housing sites. Another group wants to know if he can provide fertilizers, help them obtain irrigation, tanks, drinking water facilities, grain storage facilities, or more loans. While generally the Congress candidate has an advantage, opposition candidates may also have some power in the panchayat samiti, the zilla parishad, the district cooperative bank, or have influence in the tahsildar or collector's office, or with the superintendent of public instruction, or with the district Public Works Department. Moreover, as in this instance, the Congress leader with whom a village faction is associated may ask the faction to vote against the official Congress candidate; their doing so will of course in no way reduce the faction's access to those in the district who wield power.

A faction may therefore support Congress in one election and an opposition party in the next. The fact that Congress may get the same vote in a village in more than one election is quite misleading, since factions may be switching sides. Villages in Ponnur illustrate this point in Table 18.

Upon first examination one might conclude that the Congress vote in these villages has been stable. Actually, the 1962 Swatantra vote mainly went to Congress in 1955, while most of the 1955 Communist vote went

to Congress in 1962. It is thus quite likely that the hard core Congress vote in Sangamjagarlamudi was only 236 (1955 Congress minus 1962 Swatantra) while in the other two villages only 518 and 359.

Let us turn now to specific villages to see how party and village factions are related to one another.

*Edlapalle.* This large village of 6,200 (according to the 1951 census) voted overwhelmingly for Congress in 1955 with a vote of 1,925 against 998 for the Communist candidate. According to the 1951 census, there are 2,900 agricultural laborers and their dependents in the village, but local people estimate the figure as somewhat higher. As in other villages, however, control over the panchayat has rested in the hands of owner-cultivators, most of whom belong to the Kamma caste. There are two factions in the village, both led by Kammas — A. Suryanarayan, and M. Satyanarayan. Suryanarayan, age thirty-five, is a local Kamma landowner with considerable popularity among agricultural laborers, whom he is reported to have assisted. He has always been a Congressman, and in this election was supporting the official Congress candidate. He is supported by C. B. Reddi, a small landowner who is a member of the Communist party but who supports Suryanarayan in village disputes. Reddi has some influence on agricultural laborers and on the weavers (padmashalis) in the village. Since the weavers in Andhra are generally with Congress this is unusual, but it was explained that a now deceased local Communist leader, a small Kamma landowner, had paid special attention to this community. He too had been in Suryanarayan's village faction. Since the Suryanarayan group included the local Communists, it was generally understood that they would support the Communist candidate for parliament.

The opposing faction, led by M. Satyanarayan, is in control of the village panchayat. In the past this leader has also supported Congress candidates since he was a close friend of Vankatramaiah, the Tenali assembly candidate. Swatantra leaders appealed for support to Satyanarayan, himself a substantial local landlord and a Kamma. Venkatramaiah, anxious to see the local Congress candidate defeated, was reported to have given his blessings. This faction could thus vote for Swatantra without in any way jeopardizing its relations with the powerful Tenali Congressman.

Thus, in a village which had voted overwhelmingly for Congress in 1955, the Swatantra assembly candidate won 1,338, and the parliamentary candidate, 1,354. The Congress assembly candidate carried the village with 1,531, and the Communist parliamentary candidate came in second with 1,250. Since neither faction supported the Congress parliamentary candidate, he received only 373 votes.

*Sangamjagaralamudi.* In 1955 this village of 4,300 cast 1,109 votes for Congress and 805 for the Communist candidate for the assembly. It is said that the two main factions in the village both supported the Congress candidate in 1955, but parts of each faction supported the Communists. Furthermore, as in other villages, the factions do not command support from all the voters.

In 1962 the president of the panchayat, the leader of one of the two factions, decided to support the Swatantra candidate for the assembly. One reason he did so is that the leader of the opposing faction, a Kamma landowner, was known to be a close personal friend of the Congress assembly candidate. It would not be in the interest of the panchayat president or of his faction to have as an MLA a friend of the leader of the opposing village faction.

A second factor — of very great importance — is that in this village the factions are more or less (though not completely) divided along caste lines, one (led by the panchayat president) associated with the Reddi community, the other with the Kammas. At one time two or three Kamma families owned one-third of the total land in this village; while I was told that this was no longer the situation, the Kamma community still owns most of the land. (The deputy defense minister comes from one of the larger Kamma landowning families in this village.) The Reddis own some land, but generally they are small landowners, tenants, and agricultural laborers. They are numerically the largest community, followed by the Kammas. The third largest community is the Harijan, consisting of Malas and Madigas. The Muslims and other communities are small.

The Reddi panchayat president was associated with Venkatramaiah, the Congress party boss who himself is a Kamma but who, as we have noted earlier, is supporting the Reddi group in Congress. Venkatramaiah was thus able to persuade the Reddis to cast their vote for the Swatantra assembly candidate, not as an expression of support for Swatantra, but as a means of preventing the Kamma group in Congress from strengthening their position. Furthermore, since the village Kammas were supporting Congress, the Reddis naturally turned to Swatantra even though the Swatantra candidate too was a Kamma. The Reddis would not, however, vote for Ranga, the Swatantra parliamentary candidate, since he has been so closely associated with the interests of the Kamma community for his entire political career. The Swatantra assembly candidate therefore received 873 votes, but the parliamentary candidate only 397 votes. It is not clear whether the other five hundred votes went to the Communist or Congress parliamentary candidate, though on the basis of the final returns it appears

more likely that the Reddis voted for the Congress parliamentary candidate.

The Congress assembly candidate not only attracted the Kamma vote in this village, but he received support from the Harijan community. In the past the Harijans, most of whom are agricultural laborers, supported the Communists, but in this election the Communists had urged them to support the Congress assembly candidate. Furthermore, the Congress candidate was known to be a supporter of Sanjivaiah, the Harijan chief minister. And finally, Harijans in Andhra had begun to swing to the Congress party, partly because the chief minister is a Harijan and partly because the government had recently paid special attention to the Harijans, providing them with sites for houses, schools for their villages and hamlets, and more jobs in administration. The Harijans could thus express their new political loyalty without giving up their older political attachment by voting for the Congress MLA and the Communist MP.

There were also reasons why many Kammas, who supported the Congress assembly candidate, might transfer their parliamentary vote to the Communist. The Communist candidate was, after all, a Kamma, while the Congress candidate was a Brahmin. Moreover, the Brahmin Congressman was associated with the anti-Kamma faction of the local Congress party, and his election would therefore be a blow to the Kamma community. The election of a Communist presented no such threat.

Thus, in a village, which gave the Congress assembly candidate a clear majority (1,048 to 873 for Swatantra) and which had voted heavily for Congress in 1955, only 541 votes were cast for the Congress parliamentary candidate compared to 1,033 for the Communist candidate. And it is very likely that a substantial part of the Congress parliamentary vote came from the Reddi community, which had voted for the Swatantra assembly candidate.

*Chebrole.* This settlement of fourteen thousand gave 2,452 votes to Congress and 1,680 to the Communists in 1955. According to the 1951 census, there were nearly four thousand agricultural laborers and their dependents in this large village. Chebrole also has many textile establishments and other small industries employing nearly two thousand, including dependents. Another thousand are supported by commercial activities, mostly small shops catering to the village and the surrounding rural areas. Only 3,300 persons including dependents, or less than one-fourth of the population, are owner-cultivators. Nonetheless, political leadership still rests with the Kamma landowning community.

In the pre-independence era a substantial number of Kamma landlords

supported the anti-Brahmin, pro-British Justice party. The leader of the Justice party in the village was the village munsif, who then had considerable control over a large section of the village. A section of the Kamma community had opposed the munsif, supported the national struggle, and today continues to support the Congress party. The munsif no longer holds his village office, but he remains a substantial landowner and recently became the president of the village panchayat. Though after independence he became a Congressman, he continued to oppose the older pro-Congress group within the village. Recently the panchayat president joined the Swatantra party. It was said that he had joined Swatantra because that party's assembly candidate had agreed to help him build up his own electoral machinery in the village by providing him with money. The leader of the pro-Congress faction explained to me that the two factions were frankly more concerned with the forthcoming panchayat elections in June than with the general elections, and that they both looked upon the general elections as an opportunity to build their strength within the village.

The pro-Swatantra panchayat president was on good terms with the Tenali Congress boss. The faction could thus support the Swatantra candidates without in any way endangering their relationship with the district Congress party machinery. With the support of this faction, the Swatantra assembly candidate won 1,934 votes and the parliamentary candidate 1,512. It was reported locally that while the Kamma community was split, probably the larger part voted for Swatantra.

Though the pro-Congress group was also led by a Kamma, it had the support of the numerically large Harijan landless laborers and the large weaving community. A substantial part of the Congress assembly vote was therefore given to the Communist MP as part of the arrangement discussed earlier. Thus, the Congress MLA carried the constituency with 2,659, but the Congress parliamentary candidate came in third with only 1,473. The Communist parliamentary candidate led with 1,776 votes.

*Brahmanakoduru.* This village is as close to being a Communist stronghold as any village in the constituency. In the 1955 elections nearly half of its voters supported the Communist assembly candidate — 729 against 815 for Congress. Although the 1951 census reports that only 962 villagers (including dependents) of 3,231 were agricultural laborers, local people estimated that more than half the population consists of laborers. A young Communist worker had been active in the village since 1954. Under his leadership a village Communist cell was created which had been doing some constructive work among the agricultural laborers (including drafting a drainage scheme and conducting a night school for adults). The cell

met every two weeks and had about twenty effective members, mostly laborers and small peasants but including three or four landlords. A few years ago, however, the young Communist left the village to take a job in a company in Tenali; since then the unit has not been functioning well. He had, however, returned to the village for the duration of the election campaign.

There are two factions in the village, both led by Kammas and both with some hold on the agricultural laborers as far as village politics is

TABLE 19
BRAHMANAKODURA VILLAGE POLLING STATIONS
(Number of Votes)

| POLLING STATION | ASSEMBLY | | PARLIAMENT | | |
|---|---|---|---|---|---|
| | Congress | Swatantra | Congress | Swatantra | Communist |
| Predominantly agricultural laborers . . . . . . . | 590 | 94 | 98 | 90 | 531 |
| Predominantly owner-cultivators . . . . . . | 531 | 323 | 155 | 349 | 367 |

concerned. Since the village had been (though I was told this was changed) what is legally known as a minor panchayat in which elections are based on a show of hands, agricultural laborers have been reluctant to vote against the wishes of their Kamma landlords, so that Communists, in spite of their efforts, have made no dent into the village panchayat thus far. But in the secret ballot general elections the laborers have generally voted Communist. In the 1962 election the Communist leader urged his followers to give their assembly vote to Congress.

One of the two Kamma factions decided to vote Swatantra for both the parliamentary and the assembly seat. The other, under the guidance of the Congress assembly candidate, gave its parliamentary vote to the Communists.

This village is of particular interest since its two polling stations were so divided that agricultural laborers, who live in one section of the village, tended to vote in one station, while Kammas and other communities voted in the other station.

*Upparapalem.* This village polling station also served a nearby hamlet of Muslim and Harijan agricultural laborers. According to local reports, Swatantra won a majority in Upparapalem but lost the hamlet to Congress. The total vote recorded in the combined polling stations gave Congress 875 and Swatantra 708 for the assembly seats. In the 1955 elections

the Communists won 786 votes compared with 706 for Congress; it was reported locally that the bulk of the Communist votes came from the hamlet.

I visited the village and the hamlet with the Congress assembly candidate accompanied by the vice-president of the District Congress Committee, a man of some local importance. The following extract from my field notes on the visit is revealing for the light it throws on the way the Congress worker appealed to the villagers and the ways in which the villagers dealt with the candidate.

> As soon as we drove into Upparapalem, we proceeded to the panchayat office, about the only visible brick building in this otherwise poor village. As we went to the village, Prasada Rao [the vice-president of the District Congress Committee] explained to me that the panchayat president was with Congress so they expected to get a good vote. He said that there were many agricultural laborers in the village, most of whom were from the Telaga caste. A group of fifteen or twenty villagers met us at the panchayat office. We all crowded into a small room. It was a blazing hot sunny afternoon. Prasada Rao asked them how the village was going to vote. They said that some of the prominent persons in the village had decided to go to Swatantra. He asked them what they were going to do. They said that they hadn't decided. Prasada Rao grew visibly angry, raised his voice, and waved his hands emotionally. He said that these big men never suffer no matter how they vote, but they [the people in the room] would. He said that the Congress MLA would naturally help those people who were with him and that if they should go to him or to some ministers with their problems, they shouldn't expect any help. He grew even more angry and told them that he didn't care what they did but that he was only telling them what the situation was. Then he walked out of the panchayat office, accompanied by the Congress candidate (who had remained silent) to the car, and we drove off. When we reached the outskirts of the village, he asked one person in the car, a local Harijan leader who had once been an MLA, to return to the village to see what effect his remarks had had. The man returned later (at another village) and said that they still seemed to be with Swatantra. Prasada Rao then

sent for one of the prominent men in the village and said that
he would still try to persuade them.

We then went to the nearby hamlet of Itemkampadu, which
shares the same polling station as Upparapalem. The village
contains mostly Muslims and Harijans. The president of the
panchayat is a Muslim, and the vice president a Harijan.
Both men, along with other villagers, met us under a
large shady tree at the edge of the village. The panchayat
president told Prasada Rao that they would vote for Congress
but that they didn't know the Congress assembly candidate
personally. He said that he wanted an assurance from Prasada Rao that if they had any problems or needs they could go
to him, since they knew him, rather than to the MLA. They
wanted to know if Prasada Rao would take care of their problems. On that assurance he said they would vote for Congress.
Prasada Rao then said a few words about what Congress had already done for them, then said that he personally
would see to it that their problems were taken care of. Venkatarao [the MLA candidate] did not speak much. Prasada
Rao seemed to be intimately acquainted with a number of the
villagers here.

These two villages were thus opposite sides of the same coin, for in
Upparapalem the Congress party worker was using his influence over development activities as a bait and even a threat, while in Itemkampadu
the villagers were using their votes as a bait to elicit promises from the Congress party. I was told later that in spite of Prasada Rao's threats Upparapalem gave a majority of its votes to Swatantra. The hamlet remained uncertain for some time. Both Congress and Swatantra are reported to have
provided the villagers with a considerable amount of liquor, so that for
several days before the elections many of the men in the village were drunk.
But the hamlet finally voted for Congress.

*Nidubrolu.* This is the second largest settlement in Ponnur, with a population of 8,225. Its importance lies in the fact that both Swatantra candidates, Ranga and Bachinaidu, come from this village. So does Prasada Rao,
the vice-president of the District Congress Committee.

The village has few agricultural laborers (less than a thousand, including their dependents). It has a substantial number of owner-cultivators
(three thousand including dependents), and many handloom shops and
small industrial establishments employ about six hundred persons (includ-

ing dependents). In 1955 Congress overwhelmed the Communists by a vote of 2,658 to 989. In 1962 the Communist MP candidate defeated Ranga by a narrow margin, while the Swatantra assembly candidate narrowly defeated Congress (by a vote of 2,449 to 2,198).

The party conflict in this village was particularly bitter, since the factional conflicts within the village were directly related to the struggle among the political parties. Two Kamma-led factions in the village had opposed one another for many years. One faction was led by supporters and relatives of Ranga, another by the family of Prasada Rao. The brother of Prasada Rao defeated the Ranga group for control of the village panchayat in the previous election. Prasada Rao himself, a young man of about thirty-three coming from a landowning family of considerable means, joined Congress about four or five years ago. Two years ago the president of the District Congress Committee asked him to serve as vice president, explaining that they particularly wanted someone energetic in Ranga's home territory who could oppose him. Prasada Rao tried to get the Congress ticket for parliament so that he could oppose Ranga, but he was turned down. He was particularly bitter because the party had failed to nominate either an assembly or parliamentary candidate who lived within the constituency. But, as a bitter personal opponent of Ranga, he was prepared to do whatever was necessary to defeat him for parliament and his supporter for the assembly. With great fervor, therefore, he supported the Congress assembly candidate but stumped for the Communist parliamentary candidate, who he thought was more likely to defeat Ranga. It was due to his efforts and to those of his brother, the panchayat president, that the Communist parliamentary candidate carried a village which the Communists had hitherto lost by an overwhelming vote.

## Panchayats and the Elections

It is also important to note the importance played by village panchayats in the election outcome. Although much is said by India's national politicians about the importance of keeping village panchayats free from party politics, local politicians recognize that control over the panchayat is often a critical factor in their ability to carry the village in assembly and parliamentary elections. Although the parties in Guntur have no formal procedure for contesting panchayat elections, in practice they work for a party victory in these elections. Where the victorious candidate for panchayat president is not affiliated to any party, Congress and Swatantra will both

TABLE 20
VOTING IN PONNUR VILLAGES WITH SWATANTRA PANCHAYAT PRESIDENTS
(Number of Votes)

| VILLAGE | ASSEMBLY | | PARLIAMENT | | |
|---|---|---|---|---|---|
| | Congress | Swatantra | Congress | Swatantra | Communist |
| Chebrole. . . . . . . . | 2,659 | 1,934 | 1,473 | 1,512 | 1,776 |
| Doppalapudi . . . . . . | 679 | 675 | 117 | 665 | 616 |
| Vallabharaopalem. . . . | 68 | 601 | n.a. | n.a. | n.a. |
| Upparapalem[a] . . . . . | 875 | 708 | n.a. | n.a. | n.a. |
| Dandamudi[b] . . . . . . | 447 | 409 | 391 | 206 | 286 |
| Munipalli[c] . . . . . . . | 948 | 675 | 369 | 642 | 662 |

[a]Polling station includes a hamlet which had a Congress panchayat president.

[b]This village has a large Reddi community, which supported the Swatantra assembly candidate, but because of its anti-Kamma sentiment voted against Professor Ranga. This would explain why the Swatantra parliamentary vote was nearly half the MLA vote.

[c]Had a Congress panchayat president, but is included here because a nearby hamlet included in this polling station is controlled by Swatantra.

try to win his support. Until the Swatantra party was formed panchayat presidents invariably joined Congress, but they were generally associated with particular factional leaders within the party. With the creation of Swatantra, several panchayat presidents resigned from Congress to continue their association with Congressmen like Ranga who were now in Swatantra. At the time of the general elections, therefore, a half dozen village panchayat presidents in Ponnur constituency had joined Swatantra. These villages and their 1962 voting are shown in Table 20.

The association of the village faction in control of the panchayat with a political party thus proved to be one of the most important factors in determining the way in which a substantial portion, if not the majority, of the village would vote. It might have been the decisive factor were it not for the fact that many agricultural laborers are not influenced by the village factions in the general elections but are influenced by the Communist party, which supported the Congress assembly candidate.

In other villages which gave Swatantra a large vote, the panchayat president was invariably associated with Venkatramaiah's faction within Congress. Here again, control over the panchayat proved to be an important consideration. Indeed, there were only two villages in the entire constituency which gave a large vote to Swatantra but which did not have panchayat presidents who were supporters either of Swatantra or of Venkatramaiah. One was Nidubrolu, which we discussed earlier, and from which both Swatantra candidates come. The other is Vellalur, whose panchayat president supported the Congress assembly candidate. However, Vellalur has a large Reddi community, which voted against the Congress assembly candidate (458 Communist, 293 Swatantra, 224 Congress).

## Conclusions

Factional loyalties within Congress proved to be greater than party loyalties. The Congress candidates in Ponnur and in the neighboring constituency in Tenali were prepared to support opposition candidates when it would further their own election or lessen the chances of victory for the Congress candidate in an opposing faction of the party.

Multi-caste village factions were the basic working units for each of the assembly candidates. Kinship ties, personal acquaintance, and caste affinities were factors which often determined which party became associated with each faction.

Village factions were not passive agents. They often saw the general election as an opportunity to solidify their own followers and to receive outside financial support which might help them in subsequent panchayat elections. Some panchayat leaders hoped that by maintaining or establishing close relations with a party candidate or Congress party boss they might obtain more wells, roads, fertilizers, seeds, loans, and other amenities from the government.

The party affiliation of the panchayat president or his association with the leader of a Congress faction in the district was an important factor in how a large part of a village voted. However, the panchayat president cannot influence the entire village; he is a factional not village leader, so that his influence on the opposing faction within the village is a negative one. Moreover, there are sections of the village which are not under the influence of either faction.

Some castes had affinities or antagonisms toward factions within the Congress party because of the caste overtones of these factions. The Reddis have been opposed to the dominant landowning Kamma community in the district. Because the Congress assembly candidate in Ponnur was associated with what was widely described as the Kamma group in his party, the Reddis opposed him but then generally returned to the Congress for the parliamentary seat.

Kammas were torn because both parties had nominated Kammas. The personal contact or family connections between the Kamma community in a village and each of the candidates or his associates was often a critical factor in the way they voted. But many of those who supported the Kamma faction of the Congress party refused to vote for a Brahmin Congress candidate who was known to be an opponent of this group, and therefore they frequently cast their vote for the Communist parliamentary candidate.

Harijans, who once formed the backbone of the Communist party, have

been increasingly attracted to the Congress party throughout the district and state. The general decline in the Communist party throughout Andhra is probably due more to their losses among the Harijans than to any other single factor. In this particular constituency, however, the alliance between the Communists and Congress meant that the Harijans did not have to choose but could vote for the Congress assembly candidate and the Communist parliamentary candidate with the blessing of both parties.

Bargaining by the Congress assembly candidates in Tenali and in Ponnur with parliamentary candidates of opposing parties and opposition assembly candidates in each other's constituencies was the major reason for split voting. Village factions thus knew that no matter how they voted there would be at least one faction of the Congress party which would support them. Threats by politicians to deprive the faction or the village of government benefits could play no effective part in the election. Both factions of Congress bargained for votes with other parties; their goal was to improve their own power position within the party organization. Factions within the villages bargained with party candidates and even split their vote from the assembly to parliamentary candidates; their goal was to improve their own power position within the village while at the same time maintaining access to sources of power outside the village. Clearly, the party politicians and village factions play the game of politics in much the same way.

# APPENDIX 2
# CONGRESS PARTY LEADERS IN GUNTUR

Detailed statistical data on Congress Party cadres in Guntur were not available. However, limited data were available on the party's active leadership: past and present DCC (District Congress Committee) presidents, the membership of the executive committee of the DCC, and Congress candidates for assembly elections in 1962. We report this below and then turn to a more detailed description of the social backgrounds and career patterns of selected district party leaders.

Caste information was available for the most important Congressmen in the district. From 1935 to 1962 there have been ten presidents of the District Congress Committee. Seven of these were Kammas, one a Muslim, one a Raju, and the last was of unknown caste. Among the present seventeen-man executive committee of the DCC (the DCC itself contains 192 members), there are six Kammas, three Reddis, three Naidus (a subcaste of the Kammas), one Brahmin, one Muslim, one Vaisya, one Padmashali, and one Harijan. This pattern is repeated among the twenty-five Congressmen who ran for assembly seats in Guntur in the 1962 elections. There were eleven Kammas, five Reddis, two Telegas, two Harijans, and five scattered among as many castes: a Raju, a Brahmin, a Vaisya, a Gowda, and a Padmashali. It is interesting to note the factional affiliation of these twenty-five candidates. Sixteen were known to belong to the pro-Sanjiva Reddi group including, as one might expect, all the Reddis but also including five of the Kammas.

The above data clearly demonstrate that it would be incorrect to de-

scribe Congress in the delta as a Reddi party; it is, if anything, predominantly Kamma, but even the Kammas constitute less than half the members of the DCC executive committee and less than half of those nominated for assembly seats. (The Kammas did proportionately better in getting elected; six Kammas were elected to assembly seats in 1962 as against three Reddis, two scheduled castes, and none for other communities).

Geographically, Congressmen are well distributed throughout the district. There are 125 mandal committees in almost as many villages, each with about six or seven members. These are organized into nine taluka committees. There are approximately two thousand effective members in the district. The number of primary members has varied considerably from one year to another, often passing the quarter-of-a-million mark, but these figures are often fabricated as a result of the efforts of each faction to maximize their votes within the organization. Unfortunately, party records on age, occupation, and residence of the effective members were not available in Guntur as they were in some of the other districts in which research was conducted, so I shall instead provide here brief descriptions of ten of the most important leaders of the organization — men frequently cited by other Congressmen, MLAs, opposition leaders, and government officers as among the most important Congressmen in the district.

*The president of the District Congress Committee.* Here is a good example of a Congressman whose family has long been engaged in politics. His father, a landowner and businessman who produced and sold turmeric, was an active supporter of the pro-British Justice party and a member of the District Local Board. The DCC president was born in 1918, took part in the civil disobedience movement of 1942, and was in jail for three years. He is a member of the Kamma caste and, like his father and most of his relatives, he also is a small landowner in the turmeric business. A close cousin is also a member of the District Congress Committee, and a more distant cousin is the deputy defense minister in the central government and a parliamentary representative from Guntur. It should be noted here that among members of the Kamma caste, cross-cousin marriages are the preferred marital pattern. Ties among cousins is thus doubly close, and in Telugu one speaks of one's cousin-brother in affectionate terms. It should also be noted that all the DCC president's relatives mentioned here belong to the same faction within Congress.

*The president of the Indian Chamber of Commerce in Guntur.* The most active business supporter of Congress in the district, he is also treas-

urer of the Andhra Pradesh Congress Committee. He was born in 1906 and entered nationalist politics as a young boy. Like his father, he is a prominent merchant and mill owner in Guntur and has been the managing director of several local industrial concerns, banks, and insurance companies. The chamber of commerce has four hundred members and twelve affiliated associations, including the local Tobacco Merchants Association. There are, in all, 266 tobacco establishments in the district (the largest, the Indian Leaf Tobacco Development Company, employs five thousand workers), 101 rice mills, forty-nine oil mills, a jute mill, and a cement factory. There is also a substantial handloom industry and a number of bidi (indigenous cigarettes) manufacturing centers. The Guntur chamber, like other business groups in India, takes no overt part in party politics, but the president is an active Congressman, and the vice president is the vice chairman of the Guntur Town Congress Committee. Both men are Vaisyas and, like most members of their community, are primarily in business not land. The bulk of the members of the chamber are involved in trade and are therefore particularly concerned with obtaining permits and export-import licenses. However, it should be pointed out that many Kammas and Reddis are businessmen as well as landlords. The line between business and land in Guntur is a thin one. Many landlords own rice mills for the pounding of their own rice and that of others in the surrounding region. Producers of turmeric are in the turmeric export business. A number of landlords who grow tobacco also own tobacco-processing mills and are concerned with the sale of tobacco. The larger businessmen in the district — such as the president of the Guntur Chamber of Commerce — have more influence on members of the state secretariat and the Andhra cabinet than they do on the district and state party organization.

A *lawyer.* While the position of the business community within Congress has improved, the influence once wielded by lawyers and other professionals has considerably diminished. One of the few remaining survivors of the old guard politicians in Guntur, a lawyer and, typically, a Brahmin, is the defeated parliamentary candidate. He is an elderly man, in his seventies, who helped build Congress in Guntur in the early 1920's. Though he was once one of the most powerful men in the district, his influence there and within the party is now slight. He was a close associate of Prakasam, another Brahmin, the first chief minister of Andhra state; when Prakasam resigned from Congress, so did he. Though he is now back in the party, like the few Brahmins remaining in the party, he is a bitter critic. "The Congress party in Andhra," he remarked bitterly, "has

a program to redistribute the land, but the Kammas and Reddis as land-lords oppose this program. They have joined Congress to block the government's land program."

*A central government minister.* The leading Kamma politician in the Congress party in Guntur is a member of parliament from Guntur constituency and minister of state for defense in the central government. For some years he was known to Krishna Menon, who first brought him into the government as the deputy defense minister in charge of the navy and of the ordnance factories. But in spite of his national role, his reputation within the district has been built largely on his role as chairman of a central government commission to look into the problems of exporting tobacco. Excise taxes for tobacco are also under the control of the central government, and as a member of parliament he looks into any excise problems raised by his constituents. "My work on tobacco means more to the people here than my work as a deputy minister." He is himself a substantial landlord and a member of an old and prominent Kamma family long engaged in public affairs. As one of the few nationally known leaders in the district, he has become a rallying point for many of the district leaders who oppose the Sanjiva Reddi faction controlling the state government.

*President of the zilla parishad.* While the businessman, the lawyer, and the MP we have just described are all college graduates, the zilla parishad president did not even complete high school, having left in the early 1930's to join the nationalist movement. He is a member of the Telega community, a caste of small cultivators and tenants which in recent years has taken a more active interest in party politics. He comes from a small landowning family and has devoted his life almost exclusively to political work as a profession. In the mid 1930's he was elected secretary of the Guntur District Congress Committee; in 1947 he was elected to the legislative assembly and reelected continuously thereafter until his defeat in 1962. Known locally as an effective expediter in dealing with government departments, he is generally described as a calculating politician and accused by many of having used his position as zilla parishad president to enhance his private wealth. Many claimed that he allied himself with the Sanjiva Reddi group to further his ambitions in state politics. Moreover, in the 1962 elections he requested and received permission from the party to change his assembly seat in order that a friend, a local tobacco merchant, could run in his constituency; it was also widely be-

lieved locally that the candidate to whom he gave his seat agreed to finance his election on a generous scale. In the 1962 elections, however, he was defeated by a Communist-supported independent.

*A state government minister.* The leader of the pro-Sanjiva Reddi group in Guntur district was Brahmananda Reddi, minister of finance and deputy chief minister in the Andhra government. In 1964, when Sanjiva Reddi moved to the central government to become a minister in the cabinet, Brahmananda Reddi became chief minister of Andhra. He is a tough, politically sensitive, and politically shrewd politician, a member of another prominent political family in Guntur. His elder brother was a leading Congressman in the district who successfully defeated the leader of the Justice party in the 1937 elections. He is one of the last of the older politicians — he was born in 1909 — to have studied law. His political career followed conventional patterns: he was a member of the taluka and district boards from 1932 on, was elected president of the district local board in 1946, and in the next year was elected to the legislative assembly. He was for some years a close associate of Sanjiva Reddi, and rose to a position of prominence in state politics along with the rise of his political colleague. Though the pro-Sanjivaiah faction is strong in the DCC, the strength of the Sanjiva Reddi group at the state level made it possible for Brahmananda Reddi to have the single most influential role in selecting candidates for the legislative assembly for Guntur seats in the 1962 elections.

*A municipal leader.* The number two man in the pro-Sanjiva Reddi group in Guntur district is the MLA from the town of Tenali. He is a good example of two features of Congress party leadership: though he is a Kamma he is a leading member of a faction which is predominantly Reddi; and second, his power in the party rests upon his control over or influence in a large network of quasi-governmental bodies in the district. He is the president of the Guntur District Cooperative Bank and chairman of the Tenali municipality, thereby holding a powerful urban and a rural institution under his control simultaneously. As a bank president he has direct access to the men of power and influence in villages not only in his own but also in surrounding constituencies, and he is thereby able to build his own influence throughout the district. Though he was a prime target of the Communists in the 1962 elections and though the anti-Reddi group of Congressmen in his constituency supported his Communist opponent, he won easily with 60 per cent of the two-party vote.

He is an excellent example of an expeditor. He has represented his con-

stituency in the assembly since 1952 and, like most Congress legislators, looks upon his position less as a legislator concerned with issues of public policy than as a go-between representing the needs of his constituents to the government. He has actively worked for getting schools, hospitals, fertilizers, electricity, and irrigation facilities for villages in his constituency; though he says, "I work particularly on those problems which affect the village as a whole," he is also active in serving the needs of individual cultivators and businessmen. It is widely said that he will not provide aid to factions who oppose him and that, as one opponent put it, "He can distribute any amount of favors."

He is a small landowner with about eighty acres — by local standards, therefore, a man of some means. He is in his mid-forties and has been in Congress since 1939, when he was nineteen. Like many of the other successful MLAs, he is well versed on the caste and religious composition of his constituency and has considerable detailed knowledge of the economic problems of particular social groups and individuals within each village as well as an incisive knowledge of the power structure of each of the villages within his constituency. He has acute political antennae and, though he is not a well-educated man (he did not go to college and does not speak English), he was readily taken into the Andhra Pradesh cabinet by Sanjiva Reddi after the 1962 elections as minister for municipal administration. Among his first responsibilities as a minister was to use his political skill to aid Congress in the municipal elections in the town of Vijayawada, the second largest city in Andhra. Until the elections in September, 1962, the municipal government was controlled by the Communist party. Since Vijayawada has been the center of Communist activity throughout the delta, his efforts to break the Communists in the city would have substantial repercussions elsewhere in the region. After a bitter election Congress emerged with nineteen seats against sixteen for the Communists and their supporters. The Tenali Congressman had demonstrated his skill as a campaign manager outside his own constituency, and for the first time in twelve years Congress gained control of the municipal corporation.

*A nationalist leader.* While the number two man in the Sanjiva Reddi group is a Kamma, the number one man in the anti-Reddi group is a member of the Raju caste. This political leader was born in 1905 and joined the nationalist movement in 1919. Like many other young nationalist enthusiasts, he left school to take an active part in politics and, like his opponent in Tenali, has devoted his entire life to full-time poli-

tics. He has, like his opponent, been active in many local institutions and was for many years director of the District Cooperative Bank. He rose through the party ranks in Guntur to become president of the DCC, then later became secretary of the Pradesh Congress Committee. Like many of the older nationalist workers, he was once active in social reform; he was a popular advocate of widow remarriage, worked for the removal of untouchability, and made efforts to eliminate animosity among Hindus and Muslims. But like many of the older Congress, in recent years he has devoted less effort to social reform and more to development projects for his constituents. He has been active in getting government grants for school buildings, maternity hospitals, and water supply schemes, and has been particularly active in organizing and establishing political control over cooperatives in the district.

It should be noted that the expansion of the cooperative movement in the state has been a major concern of Congressmen. In this one constituency there are forty cooperatives, all controlled by Congress. It is also interesting to note that of the thirty-seven village panchayats in his constituency, thirty are controlled by Congressmen; the panchayat samiti is also controlled by a Congressman. Here, as elsewhere in the district, Congressmen are keenly interested in winning panchayat elections and in gaining control of cooperative societies.

*A Socialist intellectual.* One of the members of the Rajya Sabha from Guntur district is the recognized leader of the old Socialist party group within the local Congress. He is a tall, thin man, about forty years old, and the son of a local Kamma landowner. He is one of the more intellectually energetic members of Congress in Guntur and among the rare ideologically-oriented party members. The history of the Socialist party in Andhra which he once led need not concern us here. It is sufficient to note that after a number of reorganizations, alliances, and internal schisms the Andhra Socialist group joined Congress in an effort to influence the ideological content of the party. Once inside Congress, however, the Socialist group lost its cohesion. It now exercises almost no intellectual influence on Congress but remains a strong critic in favor of equalitarian measures in party and government policy. Most of the Socialists supported the Sanjivaiah group within Congress.

*The vice-president of the DCC.* Our last example of a leading Congressman returns us to a typical case: a young man in his thirties of a Kamma landlord family which has for generations been engaged in village politics as the leaders of one of two major village factions. Like so

many other Congressmen we have described, he views himself as an expeditor who deals with government on behalf of his constituency. He is not a man with great sympathy for agricultural laborers — in this respect quite different from the Socialist Congressmen. He feels, indeed as most Congressmen do, that the party must derive its strength in Guntur from what he calls the middle classes — that is, to use his own words, "those who earn between five hundred and five thousand rupees per year and own some land from which they derive income." He thus views the peasant proprietor — whether he cultivates the land he owns or employs labor is of secondary importance — as the hard core of popular support for the Congress party. He believes that the way the party can keep the support of this group is to bring their needs before government. Again, to quote him, "We have to look after getting the ryots (peasant proprietors) proper manures, canal waters, and so on. We take their needs to the government. Where there is a local problem we must bring it to the government, and government has to solve these problems for the people. That is what government is for."

## Summary

While there may be some differences among local people as to whether the ten men described here are the most influential figures in Congress, every one of these names would surely appear on almost every list of the top twenty. They are, as we have noted, members of the state and national cabinets, the president and vice-president of the DCC, and men of state-wide prominence.

One is struck first of all by the wide range of ages, castes, occupations, educational backgrounds, and even outlooks. But there are many similarities. They are all men of property. They are all members of upper castes (five Kammas, one Brahmin, two Reddis, one Vaisya, one Telega). They are almost all men who have spent their lives in politics and whose families have been deeply involved in politics. They are all members of factions, and they are almost all concerned with relating their village influence to the party — that is, using their party influence to strengthen their village ties and using their village ties to strengthen their party influence. For all, except perhaps the Socialist, ideology is of secondary importance compared to electoral victory — or, to put it another way, ideology supports but does not determine their political actions. They want to win and they bargain with each other and with village factions.

Since these men are concerned with their political success, they readily turn to the instruments at their command: patronage when available, and threats to withdraw assistance when credible. They may appeal to castes for support when it suits them and condemn casteism when it does not. They speak different messages and make different promises to the landless laborers and to the peasant proprietors. They are, in short, acutely sensitive to the political market place.

# BIBLIOGRAPHY: GUNTUR DISTRICT

*Interviews*

This study is based largely on intensive interviews with forty-four party leaders, officers of panchayati raj institutions, and government administrators. Among those interviewed were many MLAs, MPs, the president, vice-presidents, and secretary of the DCC in Guntur, the Zilla Parishad president, several presidents of panchayat samitis, and district administrative officers responsible to panchayati raj bodies. In addition to those intensive interviews, there were countless brief encounters with local party workers, village panchayat presidents, and prominent villagers.

Apart from my work in the two main towns in the district, Guntur and Tenali, I went on four separate extensive tours of the district. One was with the deputy collector, who was also the secretary to the Zilla Parishad in Guntur. Through him I met and was able to interview many of the Block Development officers. I went on a second tour with Mr. Raghuramaiah, a member of parliament running for reelection and at that time India's deputy defense minister.

I also went on an extended tour of Ponnur constituency in Guntur through the cooperation of Mr. Chakradhar, a member of parliament from the Rajya Sabha, and Mr. N. Venketarao, the Congress MLA candidate in Ponnur. Finally, I made a fourth tour of portions of the district with a revenue divisional officer engaged in organizing the elections.

As elsewhere, I also interviewed leaders of the opposition parties — both Swatantra and the Communists — as well as the working journalists in Guntur.

Since the Congress party in Guntur is divided into a number of factions, I made a special effort to interview members of all the factions in the district. I also spent some time meeting Congress officials in the PCC office in Hyderabad.

### Descriptions of Andhra and Guntur

Until 1955 Andhra was part of Madras; during the British period it was within the presidency of Madras. Accounts of these portions of Andhra during the British era will therefore be found in reports and studies of Madras. Andhra was, however, an independent kingdom during the first millennium. The history of Andhra is described in Nilakanta Sastri, *The History of South India*, 2d ed. (London: Oxford University Press, 1958), and a more detailed account may be found in K. Gopalachari, *Early History of the Andhra County* (Madras: University of Madras, 1941). In 1955 Hyderabad state was dissolved and its Telugu districts added to Andhra. For earlier materials on the areas known as Telengana, one must therefore turn to the extensive literature on Hyderabad. "Historic" memories of great kingdoms and controversies play an important role in the discourse of contemporary Andhra politics; these are described by Selig S. Harrison in *India: The Most Dangerous Decades* (Princeton: Princeton University Press, 1960), pp. 27–37.

Historical accounts of particular districts in Andhra, including Guntur, can be found in the various district gazetteers published by the Madras presidency. See especially G. MacKenzie, *Manual of Kistna District* (Madras: Government Press, 1883) (Guntur and Kistna districts were once united). Similarly, demographic data can be found in the various censuses of Madras through 1951. Before independence the Madras government published two detailed statistical reports on Guntur district: *The Madras District Gazetteers* and *Statistical Appendix for Guntur District* (Madras: Government Press, 1929, 1933). Of special value to me has been Robert Eric Frykenberg, *The Administration of Guntur District 1788–1848* (London: Oxford University Press, 1965).

For this chapter I have made great use of the *1951 Census Handbook, Guntur District* (Madras: Government Press, 1953). In 1958, three years after the new state of Andhra was formed, a *Statistical Abstract of Andhra Pradesh* was published by the Bureau of Economics and Statistics, Government of Andhra Pradesh in Hyderabad. For the 1961 census, see A.

Chandra Sekhar, *A Picture of Population of Andhra Pradesh 1961, According to Provisional Figures of 1961 Census.*

## Social Organization

There are no anthropological studies focusing specifically on Guntur district, but some of the studies on social organization in other parts of Andhra or in the surrounding areas are relevant. An American missionary, Alvin T. Fishman, who until his retirement in 1962 worked in Guntur, has written two accounts of Baptist missionary work among the Madiga community: *Culture Change and the Underprivileged: A Study of Madigas in South India under Christian Guidance* (Madras: Christian Literature Society for India (United Society for Christian Literature), 1941); *For This Purpose*, Guntur: 1958. Other studies of lower castes include: Sydney Nicholson, "Social Organization of the Malas — An Outcaste Indian People," *Royal Anthropological Institute of Great Britain and Ireland Journal* 56 (1926): 91–103; N. Subha Reddi, "Community Conflict among the Depressed Castes of Andhra," *Man in India* 30:1–12.

The eminent Indian anthropologist S. C. Dube has done a number of studies on Andhra: "A Deccan Village," *Economic Weekly, India's Villages*, M. N. Srinivas, ed., (Calcutta: Development Department, West Bengal, 1955); *Indian Village* (Ithaca: Cornell University Press, 1955); "Ranking of Castes in Telengana Villages," *Eastern Anthropologist* 8:182–90. Christoph Furer-Haimendorf, the distinguished British anthropologist, has written extensively on tribes in Hyderabad, some of which are now in Andhra: "The Chenchus," in *The Aboriginal Tribes of Hyderabad* (London: Macmillan, 1943), Vol. 1; "The Raj Gonds of Adilabad," *The Aboriginal Tribes of Hyderabad* (London: Macmillan, 1948), Vol. 1; "The Reddis of the Bison Hills: A Study in Acculturation," *The Aboriginal Tribes of Hyderabad* (London: Macmillan, 1945), Vol. 1.

A lively account of relations between the Kamma and Reddi castes can be found in Selig Harrison's book cited above, pp. 204–13. For accounts of specific castes in Andhra, see the standard work, Edgar Thurston, *Castes and Tribes of Southern India* (Cambridge: University Press, 1909), 7 volumes. For an account of a Reddi-dominated village, see Richard Bachenheimer, "Elements of Leadership in an Andhra Village," *in Seminar on Leadership and Political Institutions in India*, Richard L. Park and Irene Tinker, eds. (Princeton: Princeton University Press, 1959).

## Economic Studies

In recent years two major studies of the economy of Andhra have appeared: Venkata Vemur Ramanadham, *The Economy of Andhra Pradesh* (New York: Asia Publishing House, 1959); and A. V. Raman Rao, *Economic Development of Andhra Pradesh 1766–1957* (Bombay: Popular Book Depot., 1958). In addition, there are the usual state government reports on the five-year plans. For material on Andhra during the first-year plan, see the publications of Madras state. For the second and third plans, see *Second Five-Year Plan Programme for 1960–61* (Hyderabad: Planning and Local Administration Department, Government of Andhra Pradesh); *Second Five-Year Plan, Andhra Pradesh: Review of Progress 1959–60* (Hyderabad: Bureau of Economics and Statistics, Government of Andhra Pradesh, Government Press, 1960); *Third Five-Year Plan*, Hyderabad: Planning and Local Administration Department, Government of Andhra Pradesh, 1960). There is also a special report on Guntur district, *Guntur District Five-Year Plans, 1956–61* (Planning and Development Department, Government of Andhra Pradesh); see also K. V. Rao, "Planning in Andhra State," *Indian Affairs Record* 2 (September, 1956): 1–5.

For a description of the land tenure systems in Andhra and proposals for its reorganization, some of which have been put into effect, see *Report of the Land Reforms Committee*, Hyderabad: Government of Andhra Pradesh. N. G. Ranga has written extensively on the peasant movement in Andhra, of which he was the primary organizer; see his *Outlines of National Revolutionary Path* (Bombay: Hind Kitabs, 1945).

## Government and Politics

*Administration.* After the new state was formed, a number of government committees were appointed to look into land revenue, the system of village affairs, the state's administrative structure, the organization of local education, and to investigate administrative corruption. Out of these various committees came: *Andhra Pradesh State Administration Report, 1959–60* (two volumes), (General Administration Department); *Report of the Administrative Reforms Committee, 1960* (Hyderabad: Andhra Pradesh Government, 1960); *Report of the Anti-Corruption Enquiry Commission* (Hyderabad: Government of Hyderabad, Home Department, Government Press, 1954); *Report of the Land Revenue Reforms Committee, 1958–59* (Part I, Vols. 1, 2; Part II, Vols. 3, 4, 5) (Hyderabad: Land Revenue Department, Government of Andhra Pradesh, Government

Stamps Press, 1959); *Report of the Special Committee for Basic Education, Andhra Pradesh, 1961* (Hyderabad: Education Department, Andhra Pradesh, 1961); *Report of the Village Officers Enquiry Committee* (K. N. Anantaraman, Chairman) (Hyderabad: Stamps Press, 1958).

*Politics.* Guntur and the delta area generally were major centers for nationalist activity before independence and were also major centers of the movement for the creation of a Telugu-speaking state out of Madras. The agitation for the creation of an Andhra state and the subsequent political development are described by Selig Harrison, cited above, pp. 204–45. See also "Andhra and Telengana states," *Economic Weekly* 7 (1955): 1283–84; "Vishalandhra," Economic Weekly 7 (1955): 1311–12.

On the Communist movement in Andhra, see: G. S. Bhargava, *A Study of the Communist Movement in Andhra* (Delhi: Siddhartha Publications, 1955); Ajoy Ghosh, "The Andhra Election and the Communist Party," *New Age* (March 11, 1955); Selig S. Harrison, "Caste and the Andhra Communists," *The American Political Science Review* L (June, 1956): 378–404; P. Sundarayya, *For Victory in Andhra* (New Delhi: Communist Party Publications, 1955).

On elections in Andhra, see, in addition to the election commission reports on the 1952 and 1957 elections, India (Republic) Election Commission, *Report on the General Election to the Andhra Legislative Assembly, 1955* (Delhi: Manager of Publications, 1956). There are two analyses of the 1955 elections, the first held after the creation of the new state. See G. N. S. Raghavan, "Reprieve in Andhra," Encounter, July 155; and Marshall Louis Windmiller, "Andhra Election," *Far Eastern Survey* 24 (1955): 57–64. On the 1962 elections, see Hugh Gray, "The 1962 Indian General Election in a Communist Stronghold of Andhra Pradesh," *Journal of Commonwealth Political Studies* (May, 1963): 296–311; Hugh Gray, "The 1962 General Election in Musheerabad, Andhra Pradesh," *Journal of Local Administration Overseas* (1962): 195–203; Hugh Gray, "The 1962 General Election in a Rural District of Andhra," *Asian Survey* (September, 1962): 25–35; and Myron Weiner, "Village and Party Factionalism in Andhra: Ponnur Constituency," *The Economic Weekly* (September 22, 1962). For a study of panchayat elections, see K. Sheshadri, Fasihuddin Ahmed, Afzal Mohammed, "A Study of Voting in the Panchayat Elections in Hayathnagar, Andra Pradesh, 1964" (unpublished manuscript).

For other accounts and documents on party politics in Andhra, primarily dealing with the Congress party, see "Andhra Ministerial Episode," *Economic Weekly* 12 (May 28, 1960): 797–98; *Constitution of the Andhra*

*Pradesh Congress Committee* (Hyderabad, 1957); Selig S. Harrison, *Some Notes on the Study of State Politics: The Andhra Case* (Chicago: Committee on State Politics in India of the Association for Asian Studies, 1961); M. Ramachandra Rao, "Political Piracy in Andhra," *Janata* 14 (January 17, 1960): 9–10; "Rift within Andhra Congress; Top Leadership Must Act," *Economic Weekly* 12 (October 8, 1960): 1497–98; "Third Plan for Andhra Pradesh: Necessary Political Stability Lacking," *Economic Weekly* 12 (September 3, 1960): 1339. When the AICC session was held in Hyderabad, the capital of Andhra, in October 1958, the Andhra Pradesh Congress Committee published a souvenir volume, *Andhra Pradesh Congress Committee Souvenir, AICC Session, October 1958* (Hyderabad: Gandhi Bhavan, 1958). This 528-page volume contains many articles on the history, politics, and economy of Andhra by politicians and officials of the Andhra government. Of special interest are the following articles: "Activities of the Andhra Pradesh Congress Committee," by N. Ramachandra Reddi, p. 46; "Evolution of the Congress as People's Party," by Alluri Satyanarayana Raja, p. 49; "Andhra through the Ages," by Dr. M. Rama Rao, p. 59; "Andhra and Visalandhra States," by A. Kaleswara Rao, p. 65; "Story of Andhra Pradesh," p. 71.

## Panchayati Raj

As each state adopts panchayati raj legislation, the number of documents and studies has increased. I have listed below the major studies and reports of the national government and of the Congress party and a few of the more important state studies, and then turned to an enumeration of materials from Andhra. *Bibliography of Community Development,* NICD Bibliographical Series No. 1, Mussoorie (UP): Clearing House, National Institute of Community Development, 1962; S. K. Dey, *Panchayati Raj: A Synthesis*: (Bombay: Asia Publishing House, 1962); U. N. Dhebar, *The Role of Panchayats in New India* (New Delhi: Indian National Congress, 1957; M. K. Gandhi, *Panchayati Raj,* compiled by R. K. Prabhu (Ahmedabad: Navajivan Publishing House, 1959); H. D. Malaviya, *Village Panchayats in India* (New Delhi: All India Congress Committee, 1956); "Panchayati Raj in the Punjab," *Public Opinion Survey* (Indian Institute of Public Opinion) VI (May and June, 1961); *The Pattern of Rural Government: Report of a Seminar (February 1958),* New Delhi: Indian Institute of Public Administration; *Report of the Congress Village Panchayat Committee* (New Delhi: All India Congress Committee,

1954); *Report of the Study Team on Community Development* (Bal-wantry Mehta Committee) (New Delhi: Committee on Plan Projects, 1957), 3 vols.; *Report of the Working Group on Panchayats*, Ministry of Community Development and Co-operation (Department of Community Development) (New Delhi: Government of India, 1959); *A Report on the Panchayat Elections in Rajasthan 1960.* Evaluation Organisation (Cabinet Secretariat) (Jaipur: Government of Rajasthan, 1961); *Some Successful Panchayats — Case Studies* (Programme Evaluation Organization Plan-ning Commission Government of India, 1960); *A Study of Panchayats* (Chapter IV of the Fifth Evaluation Report) (Delhi: Programme Eval-uation Organisation Planning Commission, 1958); *Study Team's Report on Panchayati Raj in Rajasthan* (New Delhi: Congress Party in Parlia-ment, 1960).

A special issue of *The India Journal of Public Administration* VIII (October–December, 1962) was devoted to panchayati raj. See especially Myron Weiner, "Political Parties and Panchayati Raj," p. 623.

There are two first-hand descriptions of panchayati raj in Andhra. One is by the Association of Voluntary Agencies for Rural Development, *Re-port of a Study Team on Panchayati Raj in Andhra Pradesh* (New Delhi, 1961). The other is an unpublished report by Jean Joyce, a representa-tive of the Ford Foundation, who prepared a report on a brief tour of several samitis in Andhra. See also "Andhra Pradesh Panchayat, Samitis and Zilla Parishads Act, 1959," *Andhra Pradesh Gazette* (September 18, 1959), pp. 163–206; *Community Development Program — Andhra Pra-desh, 1959–60 Report*, Planning and Local Administration Department, Hyderabad: Government of Andhra Pradesh; *First Intra-State Seminar on Community Development at Hyderabad: Main Recommendations and Conclusions* (Andhra Pradesh: Planning and Development Department, 1957; *Panchayat Raj in Andhra: A Brief Outline* Government of Andhra Pradesh, Planning and Local Administration Department; "Panchayat Raj in Andhra Pradesh," *Economic Weekly* 12 (November 19, 1960): 1681–82; *Panchayati Raj State Sammelan at Tirupathi* (Planning and Local Ad-ministration Department, Andhra Pradesh, 1961); *Thoughts on Pancha-yats*, (Hyderabad: Department of Information and Public Relations on Behalf of Planning and Development Department, Government of Andhra Pradesh, Government Press, 1960).

Under the auspices of the zilla parishad of Guntur District, a district-wide conference of samiti presidents, MLAs, MPs, and government of-ficers was held in March, 1961. For their report, see *Panchayat Raj — The*

*First District Level Sammelan,* (Guntur: Zilla Parishad Office, 1961). Minutes of the zilla parishad meetings and of the panchayat samiti are maintained, and in 1961 annual reports were published. For this study, I have made use (in translation) of the reports in Telugu of the following samitis: *Mangalagiri Samiti, Maddipadu,* and *Rajupalen.*

*PART IV. THE POLITICS OF DIVERSITY:*
*BELGAUM DISTRICT*

# 11. LANGUAGE, CASTE, AND LAND IN BELGAUM

The political organization of diverse ethnic communities is one of the most challenging tasks facing the new nations of Africa and Asia. The role an effective central authority plays is of course essential for providing a framework within which diverse peoples can learn to live together, but so is the role played by local political institutions.

Historically, political parties have played both integrative and disintegrative roles. They have at times so intensified conflict between linguistic or religious groups that civil wars and disintegration of national states have resulted. On the other hand, political parties also have brought together those who are divided by language, religion, caste, or tribe but who have in common a desire to share power. In India the local Congress party organization has played an important role in this integrative process. For the purposes of this book we are of course concerned primarily with how the party functions in an environment of diversity — how it recruits and trains personnel, wins electoral support, and reconciles internal party conflict — but insofar as a political party is able to cope with diversity, it is in fact an integrative agent. In this case study we shall try to show how the party has dealt with diversity in Belgaum.

I have selected Belgaum district for analysis because it is one of the more diverse areas in the subcontinent, for it contains a variety of conflicting castes, former princely states, and, above all, two conflicting linguistic groups: a Marathi-speaking minority and a Kannada-speaking majority.

This is in no sense a history of unqualified success. To the contrary, for Congress has been a party to, rather than a mediator in, the bitter linguistic controversy which has torn the district. But while Congress has been unsuccessful in bringing these two communities together, it has been successful in dealing with other kinds of local diversity. Side by side with, and often inseparable from, linguistic conflict are caste conflicts which have been handled in the main within the Congress party organization. Tension between the Brahmin and the Lingayat communities within the party in the mid 1930's has in general quieted down and resulted in the party's being considerably more representative in caste and occupation today than in the past. Furthermore, the district has within it a number of former princely states or portions of princely states, and it has been Congress' task to integrate these localized power structures into the larger power structures of the district and of the state. To make the task more difficult, these localized power structures were based upon their own landowning systems, so that the local power structures varied considerably from one portion of the district to another.

In short, while the party did not adapt itself well to linguistic controversy, it did well in adapting itself to other features of the social system, at least within the Kannada-speaking area. In the following chapters we shall explore in some detail one feature of this adaptation: the way in which the party has utilized traditional political roles to carry out the tasks required by the party. The roles party workers perform and the relationship of those roles to traditional political roles performed in the district comprise one of the major themes in this case study, for it is a theme which throws considerable light on many of the factors which determine whether or not Congress succeeds.

Belgaum district, with its incredible diversity in language, caste, political organization, and economic structure, is a kind of microcosm for studying the larger problem of diversity in the nation state. By exploring the way in which the local Congress party has adapted itself to an environment of diversity, we begin to understand the role played by a political party in the creation of a political community, the *sine qua non* for a party's functioning.

### The District

Belgaum district, bordering the state of Maharashtra on the northwest and the centrally administered territory of Goa on the southwest, is in

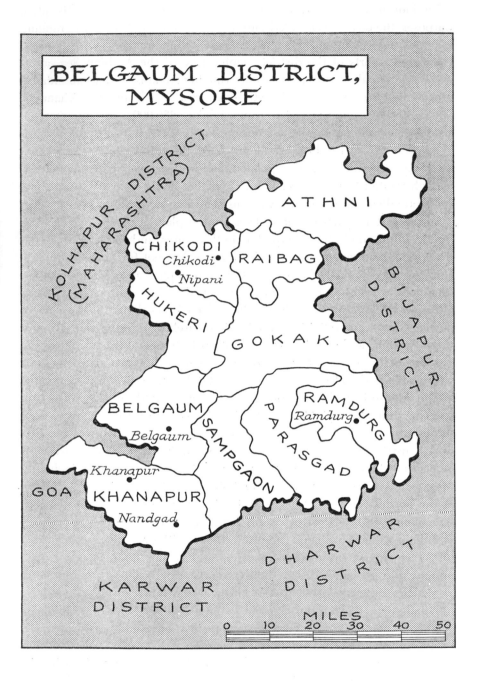

BELGAUM DISTRICT, MYSORE

KOLHAPUR DISTRICT (MAHARASHTRA)

ATHNI

CHIKODI
Chikodi •
• Nipani

RAIBAG

BIJAPUR DISTRICT

HUKERI

GOKAK

BELGAUM

Belgaum •

PARASGAD

RAMDURG
Ramdurg •

SAMPGAON

Khanapur •

GOA

KHANAPUR

Nandgad •

KARWAR DISTRICT

DHARWAR DISTRICT

MILES
0    10    20    30    40    50

the northwestern portion of Mysore state. It had a population of about 1.7 million in 1951 and an area of 5,553 square miles. For administrative purposes, the district is divided into ten units (known as talukas) ranging in population from ninety thousand to more than a quarter of a million. In the western parts of the district, sloping toward the Arabian Sea, are a succession of valleys and rugged hills, running streams, and an abundance of trees and brushwood. In this attractive area, which includes Khanapur taluka (99,000) and parts of Belgaum taluka (280,000), are innumerable small villages containing from a dozen to a hundred huts, often far apart. While the tops of the hills are almost bare, the lower slopes and valleys are fairly well wooded and populated, and in these wet lowlands there is enough rainfall to grow rice. For a good part of the year the weather is cool and villagers wear coarse woolens as well as cotton.

In the eastern parts of the district are the plains drained by the Malprabha in the south, the Ghatprabha in the center, and the Krishna in the north. The land generally is too dry for rice, but not for maize, turmeric, chillies, and millets. In the summer the western portions of the district are often steamy and hot, but the heat is checked by intermittent heavy rainfall until the monsoon finally breaks and cools the land; in the eastern portions there is no relief from the blazing, parching summer sun. At night there is often neither a breeze nor a drop in temperature to relieve the burdens of the day. And when the rains come, they are sparse or pass with such speed that some of the eastern talukas are stricken with famine.

The Marathi-speaking population is concentrated in the west, and stretches from the neighboring district of Karwar on the Arabian coast, through the southwestern part of Belgaum, up to the northwestern part of the district. Khanapur taluka on the western fringe of the district is 54 per cent Marathi and 34 per cent Kannada; Belgaum taluka, including the town, is 49 per cent Marathi and 35 per cent Kannada, and Chikodi in the northwest is 42 per cent Marathi and 49 per cent Kannada. The remaining portions of the district are almost completely Kannada-speaking.

Although the Maratha and Kannada communities are the dominant cultural elements in the district, other cultural groups have played an important role. Belgaum district borders on Goa, which was for four hundred years, until late 1961, part of Portugal's far-flung, dispersed, and, by imperialist standards, tiny colonial empire. Though Goa was militarily contained by the British, there was considerable contact between the people of Goa and the neighboring peoples of Belgaum. The Konkani-speaking people of Goa established commercial and cultural ties with the neighboring Marathi-speaking people, and it was not uncommon for Sara-

swat Brahmin girls of Konkani families to marry Saraswat Brahmin boys of Maharashtra.

Partly because of the proximity of Goa, the British maintained a military unit in the cantonment of Belgaum town. Here, in what the British referred to as the "lugubrious climate" of Belgaum, was stationed the famous Maratha regiment. The sleepy town of Belgaum, with only seven thousand inhabitants in the latter part of the nineteenth century, grew and grew until by 1951 it had a population of a hundred thousand. It became an important British military post, a gateway to Goa, a meeting place for Marathi- and Konkani-speaking people, and a bridge between Bombay state and Mysore state.

Until 1956 Belgaum district was part of multi-lingual Bombay state. This large state contained three major linguistic communities: Gujaratis in the north, Maharashtrians in the center, and Kannadas in the south. When the central government reorganized India's states in 1956, the area known as the Southern Karnatic region of Bombay state was transferred to Mysore. This region consisted of four districts, including Belgaum, which had Kannada-speaking majorities, Kannada being the language of Mysore state. Though there were obviously many practical reasons for the Kannadas' desire to be transferred to Mysore state and the Marathas' desire to remain in Bombay, the conflict between these two communities was intensified by the fact that each could recall separate political traditions of its own.

The Kannada-speaking people pointed to the fact that all of Belgaum district was once part of the historic Kannada kingdoms of medieval India, but the Marathi-speaking people noted that immediately before the British invasion most of the area was under Maratha rule. In the seventeenth century the area was conquered by the great warrior-ruler of Maharashtra, Shivaji, and after his death the area fell under the control of a number of different Maratha rulers. In fact, when the British established their power in and around Belgaum district, they permitted a number of these Marathi-speaking rulers to maintain their princely states. Before 1947 these areas were interlaced in the British-administered areas of Belgaum district. The state of Ramdurg, ruled by a Marathi-speaking Brahmin, was southeast of the district. A portion of Kolhapur state, ruled by a descendent of Shivaji, was within Belgaum district. Before independence the political behavior of the Marathi-speaking population within Belgaum district was greatly influenced by politics within the Maratha state of Kolhapur. Other small tracts of the princely states, including patches of Jath, Jamkhandi, Sangli, and Kurundvad, were also within the district. After

independence all or parts of these former princely areas were merged into Belgaum, enlarging the district from 4,600 to 5,553 square miles. The integration of these states — particularly Ramdurg and the portion of Kolhapur which was merged into the district — into the political life of the district was a special problem for the district Congress party organization.

Caste constitutes still another factor that affects politics within the district. Of the many castes within the district, the Marathas, Lingayats, Kurubas, Brahmins, Jains, Berads (a distinct tribe), and scheduled castes (particularly Holiyas) are the largest. There is also a substantial Muslim population. The post-independence census gives no statistical breakdown on the size of these ethnic groups, but earlier census reports suggest their relative sizes. The ethnic composition of the entire district appears to be relatively stable. According to the 1881 census, 64.4 per cent of the population spoke Kanarese, and 26 per cent Marathi. The 1951 proportion is 63 per cent to 26 per cent. The 1881 census reports that 91 per cent of the population was Hindu and 7.6 per cent Muslim, while the 1951 census reports that the proportions are 86 per cent to 8.4 per cent. It is not unreasonable to assume therefore that the Hindu caste composition has not drastically changed.

The largest single ethnic group is Lingayat, so called because its members wear a lingam, the emblem of the god Shiva. To be exact, the Lingayats are not a caste but a group of castes whom many consider to be a separate, non-Hindu religious community. The Lingayats are Kannada-speaking and are to be found throughout Mysore state, where they form the largest single ethnic group. In some areas of Belgaum district they constitute a majority of the Kannada population. They practice many occupations: trade, oil pressing, goldsmithing, weaving, pottery, agricultural labor, and agriculture. Many are now in government service. In recent years the political power of the Lingayats has grown, and the politically dominant group in the Mysore government is predominantly Lingayat.

The group of castes known as the Marathas is the largest ethnic group within the Marathi-speaking community and the second largest single ethnic group in the district. The Lingayats constituted about 30 per cent of the Hindu population at the turn of the century; the Marathas were about 15 per cent. The 1881 census refers to the Lingayats as "even tempered, orderly and kindly" and to the Marathas as "hardworking, strong, hardy and hospitable, but hot tempered." Both the Lingayats and the Marathas would probably subscribe to this British description. The Marathas consider themselves to be a martial community and boast of their historic political supremacy in western and central India when their

leader, Shivaji, conquered most of the Deccan and founded a great kingdom. Just as the Lingayats are the politically dominant community in Mysore, so the Marathas are the politically dominant community in the state of Maharashtra. In the forefront of the conflict between Kannada- and Marathi-speaking people in Belgaum district have been these two numerically large and politically important groups of castes.[1]

The Brahmins, though small in number, constitute another important community within the district. Like the Lingayats and Marathas, the Brahmins are made up of a number of subdivisions. In 1881 they totaled less than 4 per cent of the Hindu population. There are Marathi-, Kannada-, and Konkani-speaking Brahmins within the district. Professions like law, medicine, and journalism include large numbers of Brahmins. Many are landowners or administrators. In both the Maratha and Kannada portions of the district, the Brahmin community once held considerable secular and religious power. At the village level, Brahmins were in powerful positions, often as landlords and nearly always as kulkarnis (village land record keepers). These hereditary officials kept the village accounts, wrote up landholder receipt books, prepared the findings of village juries, and were paid partly in land and partly in cash. Almost all village kulkarnis are Brahmins. The village headman, called patil in Marathi and gauda in Kannada was usually in charge of collecting revenue and performing police functions. His position too was hereditary, and his source of profit was generally an allotment by the government of rent-free land. Since most of these village headmen could not write, they tended to be under the influence of the village kulkarnis. Most headmen in the Kannada area were Lingayats; in the Marathi areas, Marathas. Village and district conflicts between Marathas and Lingayats on the one hand and Brahmins on the other constituted, as we shall see, still another source of intense political conflict.

Most of the Belgaum district falls in the area in which the British established a raiyatwari land system — that is, a system in which the state taxes the landowning cultivator directly. However, even in raiyatwari areas a separate class of absentee landowners arose. According to the 1951 census for Belgaum district, 450,000 persons were reported as agricultural laborers or tenants, 794,000 as owner-cultivators, and 55,000 (in-

[1] The States Reorganization Commission estimated in 1955 that in the newly-created state of Mysore the Lingayats totaled 20 per cent, Harijans about 17 or 18 per cent, and Vakkaligas 13 or 14 per cent. They estimated, moreover, that in the Kannada-speaking areas outside the old princely state of Mysore, the percentage of Lingayats is as high as 35 or 40 per cent. It has been variously estimated that the Marathas total about 25 per cent of the entire Marathi-speaking community.

cluding dependents) as non-cultivating landowners. Moreover, a portion of the land was under the inamdari system, in which whole villages are privately owned. According to the 1881 Gazetteer, 239 of 1133 villages were entirely inams or privately owned villages. The inamdar collected rent from his villages and then paid tax to the government. Some of the inams were gifts made by local rulers and by the British to reward military or political service. Still others, the largest number, were watani — that is, lands given to hereditary village officers. Kulkarnis, but sometimes patils and gaudas, were watandars. The Brahmin kulkarnis were thus the most important landowners in the district, but many of the non-cultivating landowners, particularly the smaller ones, were Lingayats and Marathas. The actual cultivators also came from the Lingayat and Maratha castes, as well as from others, but only rarely from the Brahmin community. This interweaving of landownership and ethnic community played an important role in both the linguistic and caste conflicts within the district (see Chapter 12).

The continued concentration of landownership within the district constitutes another factor of great political importance. According to a report of the Mysore government (see Tables 21, 22, and 23), there are 267,000 individual or family landholding units for the nearly two and a half million acres of land in the district. More than one and a half million of these acres are in units of less than thirty acres owned by a quarter of a million peasants. The remaining acreage (over eight hundred thousand) is in holdings of above thirty acres and is owned by 13,695 landowners. Only a small part of the total acreage in the district is officially leased to tenants (15.49 per cent). The proportion leased naturally rises among the large landholders. Half of the three-hundred-acre-sized holdings are given out to tenants. Thus, a small class of landowners, constituting about 5 per cent of those who own land, have holdings exceeding thirty acres. This economic fact assumes great political importance, since almost all the political leaders in the district are recruited from this small class of landowners.

TABLE 21

DISTRIBUTION OF LAND IN BELGAUM DISTRICT

| Size of Holding (Acres) | Number of Holdings | Area (Acres) |
|---|---|---|
| 5 or less. | 143,795 | 320,900 |
| 5–10 | 56,216 | 398,534 |
| 10–15. | 25,159 | 318,043 |
| 15–30. | 28,685 | 602,946 |
| 30–45. | 7,978 | 289,572 |
| 45–60. | 2,906 | 148,896 |
| 60–75. | 1,173 | 78,163 |
| 75–100 | 827 | 72,190 |
| 100–150. | 512 | 60,846 |
| 150–200. | 162 | 28,233 |
| 200–300. | 97 | 23,863 |
| 300–500. | 42 | 15,661 |
| 500–1,000 | 39 | 37,567 |
| More than 1,000 | 19 | 67,743 |
| Total | 267,610 | 2,462,977 |

SOURCE: Report of the Mysore Tenancy Agricultural Land Laws Committee, Bangalore, Government of Mysore, 1957, pp. 130–32.

TABLE 22

PROPORTION OF LEASED-OUT LAND IN BELGAUM DISTRICT

| Size of Holding (Acres) | Acres Owned | Acres Leased Out |
|---|---|---|
| 5 or less. | 320,900 | 45,243 |
| 5–10 | 398,534 | 39,833[a] |
| 10–15. | 318,043 | 39,364 |
| 15–30. | 602,946 | 84,997 |
| 30–45. | 289,572 | 41,419 |
| 45–60. | 148,896 | 21,819 |
| 60–75. | 78,163 | 12,756 |
| 75–100 | 72,190 | 13,899 |
| 100–150. | 60,846 | 11,879 |
| 150–200. | 28,233 | 7,963 |
| 200–300. | 23,683 | 3,807 |
| 300–500. | 15,661 | 7,101 |
| 500–1,000 | 37,567 | 19,690 |
| More than 1,000 | 67,743 | 33,136 |
| Total | 2,426,977 | 381,409[b] |

[a]Source gives 398,336, apparently erroneous by a factor of ten.

[b]Percentage of leased-out land: 15.49 (land owned = 100 per cent).

SOURCE: Report of the Mysore Tenancy Agricultural Land Laws Committee, Bangalore, Government of Mysore, 1957, pp. 133–39.

TABLE 23

POPULATION ACCORDING TO OCCUPATION IN BELGAUM DISTRICT
(1951 Census)

| | Number | % of Total |
|---|---|---|
| Owner-cultivators. . . . . . | 754,636 | 45.8 |
| Tenant-cultivators . . . . . | 227,845 | 13.8 |
| Agricultural laborers . . . . | 192,391 | 11.7 |
| Non-cultivating owners . . . | 54,567 | 3.3 |
| Total Agricultural . . . . | 1,229,439 | 74.6 |
| Non-agricultural . . . . . | 416,956 | 25.4 |
| Grand total . . . . . . | 1,646,395 | 100.0 |

SOURCE: Report of the Mysore Tenancy Agricultural Land Laws Committee, Bangalore, Government of Mysore, 1957, p. 136.

# 12. THE DEVELOPMENT OF CONGRESS IN BELGAUM

## The National Movement

Although Belgaum district is predominantly Kannada-speaking, the early nationalist influences came from the Marathi-speaking areas in the north. It was in Maharashtra, first under the leadership of Gokhale, then under Tilak, that the nationalist movement first developed in western India. The national movement in Belgaum district is reported to have had its origin in 1906 when Tilak visited the town. A movement for boycotting British cloth began in the town, and a small terrorist movement was started under Marathi leadership. The nationalist movement developed on a larger scale after Gandhi's visit in 1920.

In the beginning the Congress movement was led largely by Brahmins: in Maharashtra there were Gokhale and Tilak; in Belgaum the most prominent popular leader was Gangadharrao Deshpande, a Brahmin; the leading lawyers, doctors, and journalists in Belgaum town were Brahmins, and it was from this professional class that the movement drew its support.

Generally, non-Brahmin leaders within the district stayed aloof from the nationalist movement until the mid 1930's. In both the Marathi- and the Kannada-speaking regions, strong anti-Brahmin, anti-privilege, pro-British movements developed. A non-Brahmin party was created in the district in 1921. Its initial support came from leaders of the Maratha community, but by the mid 1920's it also had strong Lingayat support. Elections were held in 1921 and again in 1924 for the Bombay Legislative Assembly and for the Central Assembly in New Delhi. A. B. Latthe, who was a Jain, a

prominent leader of the anti-Brahmin movement, and minister (diwan) of the princely state of Kolhapur, was elected to the Delhi assembly. In the 1924 elections a Maratha and a Lingayat won.

Because it was boycotting all legislative bodies, Congress refused as a matter of principle to take part in these elections (although some Congressmen did contest in the name of the Swaraj party). Not until the 1937 elections did the Congress party put up candidates. Meanwhile the non-Brahmin party controlled, until 1937, the District Local Board, the most important local government body in the district. As we shall see, the only reason Congress was able to win the assembly seats and the control of the District Local Board after 1937 was that the leaders of the non-Brahmin movement joined Congress and took it over.

But before we turn to the internal changes within Congress, we shall explore the nature of the non-Brahmin versus Brahmin conflict within the district. As we noted earlier, the Brahmins' power derived less from their religious role than from their control over administration. The village kulkarnis and the district collectors were Brahmins. The strongest opposition to the Brahmin community came from the Maharaja of Kolhapur. This elderly, rotund man who, as a staunch supporter of the British sent his sons to England and shot tigers with his British resident, took steps to educate non-Brahmins in his princely state and to deny power to the local Brahmins. As a direct lineal descendant of Shivaji, who is virtually the patron saint of the Maratha community, the maharaja could legitimately claim leadership of the Marathas. Since the local Congress was both anti-British and Brahminical in leadership, the maharaja discouraged his followers from supporting the movement.

Among his earlier efforts to improve the position of the non-Brahmins was the Coronation Patils' School, opened in Kolhapur in 1913. Explaining the purposes of the school in an official proclamation, the maharaja said: "This is a special school opened in 1913 to impart instruction to the sons of hereditary village officers in accordance with the provisions of the Vatan Act. The principal object of this institution is to fit the *Patil* for the efficient discharge of his duties and to make him independent of the *kulkarni*, who always takes advantage of his illiteracy and uses him as a tool in his hands."[1] In 1918 the maharaja went a step further to relieve the hereditary kulkarni of his powers, at least within the state of Kolhapur, by appointing new officers. His official biographer wrote that the abolition of the kulkarni system was "necessary as a preliminary to the introduction

---

[1] A. B. Latthe, *Memoirs of His Highness Shri Shabu Chhatrapati, Maharaja of Kolhapur*, Vol. II (Bombay: Times Press, 1924).

of the village panchayats in the state. The *watandar kulkarni* is an obstacle in the way. . . . If the panchayat is introduced with a *watandar kulkarni* in the village all power will pass into the hands of the said *kulkarni* and a few people of his caste, and the interests of the larger agricultural population will suffer. The *watandar patil* being one of the agriculturalists is not likely to endanger the work of the panchayat." [2]

The maharaja's activities within Kolhapur state had repercussions in nearby Belgaum. He created Rajaram College in Kolhapur as a center for non-Brahmin higher education throughout the Deccan. In 1913 he started the Satya Shadhak School in Kolhapur to teach non-Brahmins throughout the region "all the religious formalities which the Hindus wish to observe in their religious performances and which the non-Brahmins were hitherto declared to be unfit to learn." [3] These institutions in Kolhapur attracted young men from Belgaum.

The maharaja also supported British rule as "a blessing which gives equal justice to all and which recognizes the duty of Government to educate its subjects." [4] He pressed the British for a system of government nomination of non-Brahmins to the newly created legislative councils rather than for an election system, on the grounds that nominations "could be much better in the interests of the Marathas, Jains, Lingayats and Mahars who form the backbone of the country than the reservation [of seats]. . . . A good canvasser would go to a village, join hands with five monsters of the village such as the *Kulkarni*, Brahmin Sawakers and Joshis [priests], etc. and would get votes willingly or unwillingly for a particular Brahminised Maratha." [5]

The old maharaja died in 1922, but his son continued to support the non-Brahmin movement. He too opened schools for non-Brahmins and opposed the nationalist movement. In other Marathi-speaking areas of Bombay state, the non-Brahmins began to enter the nationalist movement in the early 1930's. Prominent Maratha leaders in Poona joined Congress and brought with them a large part of the Maratha community.[6] Lingayats too began to enter the nationalist fold in the early 1930's. By the 1936–37 elections the non-Brahmins throughout Bombay had become staunch supporters of Congress and helped Congress win a resounding victory. In the Kannada-speaking areas too the non-Brahmins, particularly the Linga-

[2] *Ibid.*, p. 508.
[3] *Ibid.*, p. 380.
[4] *Ibid.*, p. 463.
[5] *Ibid.*, p. 582.
[6] See Maureen Patterson, "Caste and Political Leadership in Maharashtra," *Economic Weekly* (Sept. 25, 1954).

yats, entered the movement in large numbers. In Belgaum, A. B. Latthe, a Marathi-speaking Jain, resigned as diwan of Kolhapur, stood as a successful Congress candidate, and later became finance minister of Bombay state. Diwan Bahadur Angadi, a prominent Kannada-speaking Lingayat who with Latthe had won an assembly seat earlier on a non-Brahmin ticket, joined the Congress party and became deputy speaker in the Bombay legislative assembly. It was the large-scale entrance of the non-Brahmin castes, particularly the Lingayats, that made it possible for Congress to gain control of the District Local Board, win the 1937 elections, and become a mass movement in Belgaum district.

By the mid-1930's a shift in power had taken place within the Congress party organization. Table 24, enumerating the presidents of the Belgaum District Congress Committee, illustrates the changes which took place.

TABLE 24
DISTRICT CONGRESS COMMITTEE PRESIDENTS IN BELGAUM

|  | Date | Language | Caste | Occupation |
|---|---|---|---|---|
| Gangadharrao Deshpande . . . | 1920's | Kannada | Brahmin | Pleader |
| D. Belavi. . . . . | early 1930's | Kannada | Brahmin | Pleader |
| Narayan Rao Joshi. | early 1930's | Kannada | Brahmin | Pleader |
| Venkareddi Hooli . | 1936 | Kannada | Reddi | Agriculture |
| K. S. Patil . . . . | 1937–40 | Kannada | Lingayat | Pleader |
| K. Sheikh. . . . . | 1940–46 | Kannada | Muslim | Agriculture |
| Veerappa Sutagath. | 1947–51 | Kannada | Lingayat | Agriculture |
| Sivanagouda Patil . | 1951–58 | Kannada | Lingayat | Agriculture |
| Basappanna Aragavi | 1958–60 | Kannada | Lingayat | Agriculture |
| Venkareddi Hooli . | 1961– | Kannada | Reddi | Agriculture |

In the mid 1930's several important changes took place in the power structure of the Congress party. With the election of a member of the Reddi caste as president of the District Congress Committee, control of the party shifted away from the Brahmin community. Though Gangadharrao Deshpande continued as the single most prominent leader in the district and as a powerful force throughout the Karnatak region (he was popularly called the Lion of Karnatak), the non-Brahmin castes which had already won power within the district now began to dominate the local Congress party organization. Congress candidates for the Bombay legislative assembly and for the District Local Board were with few exceptions non-Brahmins. It was not that Congress had taken control of the district, but that those who had control of the district had taken over Congress.

The new leaders of Congress had much stronger roots in the rural areas

of the district than the older Congress leaders. Though the Brahmin DCC presidents were all substantial landowners (Gangadharrao Deshpande was in fact one of the largest inamdars in the district), they lived in Belgaum town and practiced the urban profession of law. The new non-Brahmin leaders were with a few exceptions men of less wealth and less education, with roots in the taluka towns and in the countryside, and without professional skills. They were not generally known outside the district, and even within the district their influence was often confined to one or two talukas. The pleaders continued to wield influence because their work kept them in touch with landowners involved in law suits throughout the district, but those who lived in the taluka towns and villages had a much more intimate knowledge of local conditions and, for reasons that will become clear, greater opportunities to build up pockets of local power.

Although the Brahmins were increasingly losing power within Congress, as nationalists they welcomed the massive entrance of the non-Brahmins, for they recognized that without non-Brahmin support the movement could not prosper. Once the national leadership of the Congress party decided to participate in the 1937 elections for the new provincial governments, the district parties had no choice but to try to broaden their base. Since the suffrage was based upon landownership, upon payment of property taxes, and upon education, the district party leaders had to woo the locally powerful smaller landowners who constituted a large proportion of the electorate. Gangadharrao Deshpande and the other Brahmin Congress leaders in the district thus encouraged men like Latthe, Angade, and other prominent non-Brahmin leaders to join the party and stand for the Bombay legislative assembly on Congress tickets. Thus, the decision to participate in the elections for the provincial assemblies helped bring about an important change in the power structure of the district Congress party.

But while the Lingayats and other non-Brahmins in the Kannada-speaking population were entering the Congress party, the Maratha community continued to remain aloof. There were of course a number of Marathas who did enter the Congress but, compared with other communities, their participation was small. The pro-British, anti-Brahminical influence of the Maharaja of Kolhapur on the Maratha community continued. It is interesting to note that other Marathi-speaking groups did join Congress; there were many Marathi Brahmins in the Congress, and Latthe, though a Jain, was a Marathi speaker. Marathas did take part in the anti-British Quit India movement, but they did so outside Congress. The non-Brahmin party, to which many Marathas continued to belong, gradually lost

its hold throughout the district except for the few predominantly Marathi-speaking areas. Their candidates unsuccessfully contested several seats in the 1937 elections, and in the 1946 elections did not put up any candidate against Congress. In 1948, a year after independence, the non-Brahmin party reorganized itself into the Workers and Peasants party, whose appeal continued to be exclusively in the Marathi-speaking areas, particularly among members of the Maratha community.

In the Marathi-speaking areas of the district, the Congress party continued to remain in the hands of the Brahmins. Although these Brahmins also urged the Marathas to join Congress, the Maratha leadership was discouraged by the fact that it had little hope of establishing its power in the district Congress organization. Though elsewhere in the Maratha districts of western India the Maratha community had gained local power, in Belgaum district they were perpetually doomed to be a minority in a Kannada-dominated organization. As politically rising castes, the Lingayats and the Marathas were not disposed to share power. Moreover, the Kannada-speaking politicians were not eager to bring large numbers of Marathi speakers into the party, for without Maratha support they could still get control of all district-wide organizations and win the two parliamentary seats and all but a handful of the assembly seats. Furthermore, the Kannada leaders felt that there were certain dangers in bringing the Marathi-speaking population into the party.

The tensions between the Marathi and Kannada speakers had their political origins in 1920. At that time the national leadership of the Indian National Congress decided to reorganize the party organization into a series of Pradesh Congress Committees (PCCs). These PCCs were to coincide with the country's linguistic boundaries rather than with existing state boundaries. Each unit would thus have the advantage of being able to function in a single language; moreover, the organization of units on linguistic lines was an expression of the Congress policy eventually to reorganize India into a series of unilingual states once the country had become independent.

It was further decided that the District Congress Committee (the DCC) would be the basic unit of the PCCs. The four predominantly Kannada-speaking districts of Bombay state were therefore joined with other Kannada-speaking districts in the neighboring states into the newly created Karnatak Pradesh Congress Committee (KPCC). Since the district was to be the basic unit, there was no question of bifurcating a district along linguistic lines, and Belgaum district with its overwhelming Kannada majority was placed under the jurisdiction of the KPCC.

In 1929 an open controversy arose between the Marathi and Kannada elements in Belgaum town. Political and literary leaders in Maharashtra proposed that a literary conference be held in Belgaum. There was considerable objection from local Kannada leaders who, in the words of one of them, "feared that this was the thin end of the wedge which the Marathis were using to gain control of the city." At this time, the Kannada leaders were insistent that eventually the district be merged into a larger Kannada-speaking state. Gangadharrao Deshpande as a spokesman for the Kannada group met with the sponsors of the conference, who then agreed to pass a resolution noting that Belgaum district was an integral part of Karnatak and that they were only pressing for due recognition for the Marathi language within the district.

The 1929 literary conference left the Kannada leaders with a considerable amount of discomfort. Moreover, the complaints made by the Kannada leadership about the Bombay government had of necessity anti-Maratha overtones. One prominent Kannada-speaking Congressman, recalling the problems which they had when the district was in Bombay state, had the following to say.

> When we were in Bombay state, Belgaum had no proper educational facilities. Most of us had to go to Poona or to Bombay to attend college. The first major college here, Lingayat College, was started in 1933, and R. P. College was not started until the 1940's. We had to go therefore to colleges where everyone spoke Marathi. Because we went to Poona and Bombay, we saw the best of the Marathi-speaking area. Since we come from a border area and our Kannada is not very good, they saw the worst of the Kannada-speaking people. We developed some kind of inferiority complex with respect to the Marathis.
>
> We were surrounded by Marathi-speaking princely states in those days. We tried to get Kannada schools introduced in the Marathi states but with little success. So many of our children had to study in Marathi-speaking schools. The director of instruction in the district was not a Kannada man but was Marathi-speaking. All of the officers in the district before 1956 were Marathis,[7] and they had all been working for the Marathi-speaking people. Only the minor clerks were

[7] This is not true, but many Kannada leaders now assert it. Several of the district collectors and many important district officials were Kannada-speaking. Both Kannada and Marathi were the official languages within the district.

Kannada speakers. When they were in power they did everything against the Kannada people. Now it is our turn.

Although there were a number of Marathi-speaking persons within
the Congress and particularly in Belgaum town, the position of the District
Congress Committee with respect to the ultimate disposition of the district was well known. Indeed, when the central-government–appointed
States Reorganization Commission held hearings, the District Congress
Committee testified on behalf of the Kannada community and argued
that the entire district, including the Marathi-speaking portions, should
be transferred to the new state of Mysore. On the other hand, prominent Maratha leaders pressed for the partition of the district on the basis
of language and for transferring to Mysore state only those villages in
which a majority of the population spoke Kannarase and which were contiguous to Mysore state.

The District Congress Committee was therefore a party to the dispute
between Kannada and Maratha leaders. While the party was thus capable of absorbing the non-Brahmin Kannada-speaking elements in the district, it was neither able nor willing to attract the non-Brahmin Marathi
speakers.

The problem of language did not arise in the princely areas in and
around Belgaum district. There are two substantial former princely areas
in Belgaum district. About thirty-six villages of Kolhapur state formed an
isolated pocket within the district. And on the eastern side of the district
was the small princely state of Ramdurg with about thirty-three villages.
These two areas were eventually merged into Ramdurg taluka and added
to Belgaum district. Both these areas had Marathi-speaking rulers, although almost the entire populations are Kannada-speaking. The system
of watan kulkarni formally operated in the villages, which were a part of
Kolhapur, but the system was abolished in 1918 as part of the maharaja's
anti-Brahmin move and also as a means of increasing the maharaja's revenue from the area. The chief official of the area, appointed by the maharaja, was the mahalkari, a Marathi-speaking official.

Ramdurg was under the direct control of a Marathi-speaking Brahmin
maharaja. The Maharaja of Ramdurg, like the ruler of Kolhapur, was pro-
British, but unlike him, the Ramdurg ruler was also pro-Brahmin. Reportedly, he recruited only Marathi Brahmins into the senior positions in
his government, so that strong anti-Brahmin and anti-maharaja sentiment
developed in Ramdurg. While initially there was no political movement
in the villages which were part of Kolhapur, a movement against the Ma-

haraja of Ramdurg developed in the late 1930's. A local pleader who led the movement was arrested in 1939. When local demonstrators marched on the jail, the maharaja called out the police. In the ensuing struggle, the jail was burned, seventeen policemen were killed, and a number of demonstrators were killed or injured. Thereafter, since many of its leaders had been arrested, the movement remained dormant, but many persons remained sympathetic to the nationalist movement. Because prominent local men were excluded from the administration of the state, this class formed the core of the anti-maharaja group. It included a few of the larger non-Brahmin landowners, a number of local merchants (most of whom were Lingayats), and some of the professional men in Ramdurg town. The movement in Ramdurg thus attracted much the same kind of person who was attracted to the nationalist movement in the British-administered areas.

By the late 1930's and early 1940's the Indian National Congress in Belgaum district had the basic organizational structure and membership which was to persist through the 1950's and 1960's. In the princely areas which were later to be merged in the district and in the British-administered areas the nationalist movement won support from the socially, economically and politically powerful — men whose power, and this was extremely important, did not rest on the British or the maharajas but on their own independent control of land, their position in local business, their influence on local administration, and their popularity within their own communities. As these elements, almost always non-Brahmin Kannada speakers, grew in political importance in the district, they entered and took control of the Congress party. Since their own power was highly localized, the District Congress Committee increasingly became the meeting place for those who already had power.

In contrast, the Maratha community generally stayed outside the Indian National Congress, at first because of the anti-Brahmin attitude of the Maharaja of Kolhapur, but then because of growing Kannada-Marathi conflict. The result was that in the Marathi-speaking areas of Khanapur, Belgaum, and Chikodi talukas the position of the party was not strong at the time of independence.

## Post-Independence Developments: The Language Controversy

Immediately after independence the princely areas which were within the confines of Belgaum district were merged into the district. A few months later agitation broke out in Ramdurg to secure the release of

those persons who were convicted in the 1939 riots. Administration broke down, and at the maharaja's request Ramdurg was immediately transferred to the administration of Bombay state. A few months later the rulers of the Deccan states met in Bombay, and the terms of integration were agreed upon. In early 1949 Kolhapur was made a separate district in Bombay state, but a small portion was merged with Belgaum.

The question of whether Belgaum district would remain in a multilingual state of Bombay or be merged into a new Kannada-speaking state continued to agitate persons on both sides of the linguistic border. Throughout the Kannada-speaking areas of South India a strong movement had developed for creating a new Karnataka state. A number of literary associations had been formed in the Kannada region in the latter part of the nineteenth century. An all-Karnataka literary body was formed in Bangalore in 1915. In 1961 an organization known as the Karnataka Sabha was started in the town of Dharwar with the political goal of a united Karnataka province. In 1920, delegates from the Kannada-speaking area to the annual Congress session in Nagpur pressed for a separate Kannada Congress organization. That year Congress agreed to create twenty-one linguistic Congress units, including the Karnataka Pradesh Congress Committee. In 1924 the annual session of the Congress party was held in Belgaum town, and the same year the first Karnatak Unification Conference was held there under the auspices of the newly formed Karnataka Ekikarana Sangh. This organization pressed its claim within the Congress party and before British government commissions. After independence Karnatak organizations, including the KPCC, continued to press their claim before the Indian government for the creation of a new state.[8] In 1955 the government of India appointed the States Reorganization Commission to make recommendations with respect to linguistic demands. On behalf of a united Karnataka state, the KPCC presented a memorandum to the commission. The District Congress Committee of Belgaum presented a detailed memorandum pressing the claims of the district to be included in a united Karnataka.[9] Testimony supporting these claims was also presented by the Belgaum City Congress Committee, the District Local Board, the District School Board, the District Central Co-operative Bank, and a number of associations representing particular

[8] This brief account of the history of the Karnatak unification movement is taken from *Glimpses of Karnataka* (pp. 111–15), by M. V. Krishna Rao, *et. al.* (Bangalore: Reception Committee of the Mysore Pradesh Congress Committee, 1960). A more detailed account of the movement has been written in Kannada by R. R. Diwakar.

[9] *Memorandum Submitted to the States Reorganization Commission under the Joint Auspices of the District Congress Committee and the Karnatak Karya Samiti* (Belgaum, 1955).

castes, religious groups, journalists, and merchants. Gangadharrao Desh-pande and Dattopant Belvi, two prominent Congress leaders — both were Kannada leaders who had been former presidents of the District Congress Committee — also proposed that the entire district be transferred to a Karnataka state.

The Maratha claim that the Marathi-speaking areas contiguous to the Maratha region should be included in the proposed new state of Maharashtra was presented by an organization known as the Maharashtra Ekikaran Samiti (MES).[10] The Samiti was organized in Belgaum district in 1946 in anticipation of the struggle over the reorganization of the state boundaries. The MES consisted mainly of the members and leaders of the Peasants and Workers party (the former non-Brahmin party), a number of independents, and a few Marathi Congessmen who differed with the District Congress Committee on the language issue. Though the strongest support for the MES came from the Maratha community, other Marathi-speaking castes lent their support. In fact the president and later elected MLA from Belgaum town is a Marathi-speaking Brahmin. The language controversy thus brought together both Maratha and Brahmin elements who in the past had bitterly opposed one another.

The Samiti welcomed the appointment of the States Reorganization Commission and endorsed the principle that new states should be formed on linguistic lines. It thus supported the creation of new Marathi- and Kannada-speaking states, but took the position that Belgaum district should be partitioned and that contiguous villages and towns with Marathi- or Kannada-speaking majorities should be transferred to Maharashtra and Mysore respectively.

The States Reorganization Commission proposed that a new Karnataka-speaking state be formed, made up of old Mysore state, Coorg, the predominantly Kannada-speaking districts in Madras, Andhra, Hyderabad, and Bombay. Belgaum district was to be included in the new state except for one small taluka, Chandgad, which was to remain in Bombay state.[11] As expected, the Maharashtra Ekikaran Samiti, representing the Marathi-speaking sections of the district, issued a strong note of protest.[12] Nonetheless a States Reorganization Act was passed by the central government, and in November, 1956, a new Karnataka state retaining the old

[10] *Belgaum City — Integral Part of Maharashtra. Memorandum Submitted to the State Reorganization Commission by the Maharashtra Ekikaran Samiti* (Belgaum, 1955).

[11] Government of India, *Report of the States Reorganization Commission*, 1955, pp. 90–100.

[12] *Belgaum: An Appeal Against the S.R.C.'s Findings* (Belgaum: Maharashtra Ekikaran Samiti, n.d.).

name of Mysore was inaugurated which included the controversial district of Belgaum.

The conflict between the Ekikaran Samiti and the Mysore government became increasingly bitter. A civil disobedience movement began, and from time to time outbreaks of violence occurred in the district occasionally accompanied by police firings. The Samiti battled the District Congress party for control of all local bodies within the Marathi-speaking portions of the district and also fought in the 1957 and 1962 elections for parliament and for the Mysore legislative assembly. In 1961 the governments of Mysore and Maharashtra appointed a joint commission to look into this and other outstanding border disputes, but no agreement was reached. It was generally agreed that the controversy would have to be settled by the Home Ministry of the central government, which in mid-1962 expressed renewed interest in the matter.

The controversy raises many questions about the relationship between loyalties to language and material interests and — most important from our point of view — about the effect of such a conflict on the behavior of the Congress party organization within the district.

Before turning to the effects of the conflict on the Congress party, I must say a word or two about the attitudes of the respective governments of Mysore and Maharashtra. Since the claims of each linguistic group had popular support within their respective states, neither government could afford not to support its linguistic side. From the point of view of principle too, each side had its own claim to make. But also significant was the fact that both states had special material interests in Belgaum district. Belgaum town, with a population of over a hundred thousand, is a substantial trading center, and therefore constitutes a source of tax revenue to whichever state it is in.

Moreover, the controversial portions of Belgaum district and the neighboring district of Karwar border on the centrally administered territory of Goa. It was widely assumed in India after independence that unless Goa in due course was merged with India and the Portuguese left freely, as the British and French had done, coercion might ultimately be necessary. When Goa became part of the Indian Union, it would presumably be merged with either of the larger political units with which it shared a common border: Mysore or Bombay. One determinant would be the linguistic factor, although there is some dispute as to whether the Konkani language is more akin to Marathi or to Kannada. There are linguistic similarities between Konkani and Marathi, for both belong to the Indo-Aryan language group, while Kannada is a Dravidian tongue. To strengthen

their argument Maharashtrians point to the fact that many people of Goa speak Marathi, have intermarried with Maharashtrians, and have close commercial and cultural ties with Bombay, but few with Mysore. But more crucial than the linguistic issue to either Bombay or Mysore is the realization that Goa's natural resources and particularly her fine harbor at Panjim — reputed to be second only to Bombay on India's western coast — would be a fine economic asset. Mysore state has a long coastline but no adequate natural harbor and is therefore particularly eager to have Goa. The disposition of Belgaum district ties in closely with the Goa issue. If all of Belgaum and Karwar districts remain in Mysore, Mysore retains a common border with Goa on the south and east, so that her claim to Goa has some credence. If the disputed Marathi-speaking tracts of Belgaum and Karwar are transferred to Maharashtra, Mysore would have no common border with Goa, thereby making Maharashtra's claim unassailable. Goa would either remain a separate political unit or merge with Maharashtra. There would be no third choice.

These considerations obviously could not be placed before the States Reorganization Commission. The commission therefore had to listen to the arguments of those who lived in the district, and it is to these arguments that we now turn.

### The Kannada Case

The heart of the Kannada argument was a historical one. The entire area had been under the rule of various Kannada dynasties until the fall of the Vijayanagar empire when Muslims conquered the region. The Peshwas (Marathi speakers) conquered the area in 1754 and remained in control until the area passed into British hands in 1830. The Kannada political leaders claim that the Harijans and Berads form the indigenous population of the western tract, and they speak Kannada. Konkani-speaking people fled from Portuguese proselytisation into Belgaum district where, under the influence of Maratha rulers, they adopted Marathi. "We can clearly see from these facts that it is merely due to historical accidents that Marathi entered into these parts. The Maharashtrians cannot, therefore, claim this part as their own on linguistic grounds." [13]

The Belgaum District Congress Committee noted that Belgaum town was the crux of the problem. They argued that urban areas are generally cosmopolitan and so their linguistic distribution should not be a factor in

[13] *Belgaum D.C.C. Memo to S.R.C.*, p. 15.

deciding what should be done with the surrounding area. Moreover, the report went on to say, in 1880 only 7,650 persons lived in Belgaum compared with 29,000 in 1921, 58,000 in 1941, and 103,000 in 1951. "Thus the population which is fast swelling consists mostly of immigrants. It is the indigenous population that can claim the city and not the immigrants" (p. 17). The report then went on to show that the original population was predominantly Kannada-speaking and that "the Marathi-speaking population is mostly immigrant and not indigenous" (p. 19). Streets have Kannada names, there are Karnatak temples in the city, and "all the hereditary village officers of this city . . . are Kannad" (p. 20). "Even granting that the Marathi people form a majority in the Belgaum city," the report continued, "that fact alone cannot support their claim" (p. 25).

The District Congress Committee further argued that the disputed towns of Belgaum and Nippani are commercially tied to the surrounding Kannada areas and that if they were joined to Maharashtra their trade would suffer. Moreover, Belgaum town as the district seat would decline in importance if it were not an administrative capital, and in turn Belgaum district would lack an administrative center.

Several years later the Kannada leaders continued to speak with fervor of their struggle for a Karnataka state and for the inclusion of all of Belgaum in it. In an interview the chief minister of Mysore, who had been a leader of the Karnataka movement, defended the decision to keep all of Belgaum in Mysore.

> We feel that a few villages on each side of the border might be transferred, but the real issue is Belgaum town. The Ekikaran Samiti and the Maharashtra Congress have made it a political issue and an emotional matter. We don't want to give up the town. *It has always been with us.* [Italics added.] Even N. C. Kelkar [a famous Maratha leader] agreed that the entire district should be in Karnataka. They wanted to hold a Maharashtra literary conference in Belgaum, and the Kannada people objected; but then Kelkar and others said that they wanted to have the conference there for the sake of convenience, but agreed that Belgaum was in Karnataka. But still we are willing to shift a few villages with 60 per cent or more of one linguistic group. But we won't give up Belgaum. We have spent crores of rupees on the colleges here. They have only one college there.
> I don't believe the 1951 census is accurate. It was con-

ducted by Marathis and they created mischief. I understand
that they are not a majority in the present census. This time
there were two enumerators, one Kannada and one Marathi. . . . We are willing to allow Marathi schools. We are
printing forms in Marathi. If they want other things, we are
willing to help them.[14]

In Belgaum district, a local Kannada leader spoke with greater fervor.

There are Kannada-speaking areas in Andhra and Madras.
We won't consider Belgaum on a village basis until the entire issue is opened elsewhere. But on historic grounds Belgaum belongs to Karnataka. We don't kick up a row as the
Marathis do. It creates bitterness. They are fanatics. We
are prepared to give them their language for schools or
even publish laws in Marathi. What is that? *This area has
always been part and parcel of Karnataka.* [Italics added.]
Time alone will kill these feuds. It is a question of time.
The vigor is already dying down. The opposition won eleven
and we got seven in 1957, but in 1962 we got twelve
and they got six. The Samiti won about seven or eight seats
last time, now only four or five. They fight on that issue, but
we don't fight the elections on those lines. We don't recognize that it is an issue.

Another prominent Congress worker in Belgaum district who joined
the party in 1929 and who has been a staunch advocate of including the
entire district in Mysore state discussed the history of the dispute with
some frankness. It was noted that the memorandum presented by the District Congress Committee not only proposed that all of Belgaum be transferred to Mysore, but also argued that if a new Marathi-speaking state
were formed the city of Bombay should be excluded on the grounds of
its multilingual character. Why, the question was asked, did the District
Congress Committee concern itself with the future of Bombay city?

I tell you frankly. It was to checkmate Maharashtra to prevent them from getting Belgaum. We wanted to get the support of the Gujaratis for getting all of Belgaum into Mysore
state, in return for our supporting Gujarati efforts to keep

[14] Interview in Mysore with Mr. Nijalingappa, April 17, 1962.

Bombay City out of Maharashtra. . . . I tell you frankly that all of the good political leaders from the Gujarati and Karnatak side privately told the members of the States Reorganization Committee they wanted an independent Bombay city, since the clannish Marathis would try to control the city. The Gujaratis actually wanted a multi-lingual state to prevent the Maharashtras from getting control of Bombay city. Those people are clannish. People all over India know that. Even now that the Maharashtrians are in control of the city, things aren't particularly good for many of the Gujarati and other businessmen in the city.

A Kannada officer in the Mysore administration — a high official I might add — argued that the dispute should not be settled on linguistic grounds alone, that in effect the criteria for a decision should be historical.

Urban areas should be excluded in making a decision, since people from all over come to the urban areas. The language of the rural people would indicate the historic situation, and on that basis the area is Kannada. . . . It is true that business in Belgaum is in Marathi hands, and generally they look toward Bombay rather than Bangalore or Mysore. Upper-class Marathas settled in the town when it was surrounded by small Maratha states. Then it became a fashion for everyone to speak Marathi. But before the Maratha invasions, the area was a Kannada one.

## The Marathi Case

In presenting its case to the States Reorganization Commission, the Samiti tried to counter the historical arguments of the Kannadas as well as the administrative and economic arguments which were presented. But while the Samiti insisted that for any of these considerations the Marathi-speaking portions of the district ought to be transferred to Maharashtra, the Samiti's main argument was linguistic. The MES argued that some general principles ought to guide the reorganization of states and proposed the following: (1) linguistic majority; (2) contiguity; (3) village as a unit; and (4) wishes of the people. On the basis of these principles, the Samiti claimed the towns of Belgaum and Nipani, all of Changdgad taluka, most of Khanapur, Belgaum and Chikodi talukas, and a number

of Marathi-speaking villages in Hukeri, Athni, and Raibag tulakas. In all, 578 of 1306 villages and towns with a total population of 784,000 were claimed as predominantly Maratha.

Although the border controversy seemed to rest heavily on historical or linguistic considerations, much of the controversy also concerned the more practical and material consideration of schools and jobs. In their report to the States Reorganization Commission, the Samiti bitterly complained that the District Local School Board is "the most powerful instrument in the hands of the Kannadigas and it is being relentlessly directed against Maratha education in the District." [15] They complained that the school board started so few Marathi-speaking schools that Marathi speakers had to create their own private schools in the district. They noted that of the 608 Maratha primary schools (containing a total of 49,000 children) in the district in 1953–54, more than half, or 306, were privately run. By comparison, 620 of the 1,050 Kannada schools (containing nearly 100,000 children) were run by the District Local School Board. In the same year, there were 620 Kannada schools run by the District Local School Board in the district's 720 Kannada villages compared with 302 Maratha schools in 578 Maratha villages. Moreover, Marathi speakers complained that Kannada schools had a larger number of trained teachers than the Maratha schools, that a number of Maratha schools were converted into Kannada schools, and that the board spent less money for the repair of Maratha schools than for Kannada schools.

As for job discrimination, the Marathas claimed that Kannada speakers had gained complete control over the district's administrative machinery, that recruitment into government offices was largely from among Kannada speakers who were then assigned to Maratha areas, that the recruitment of talathis (local revenue officers) was made mostly from Kannadigas, and that consequently Maratha village records were being changed into Kannada, which was gradually being made the language of the district.

When the district, including the Maratha areas, was transferred to Mysore, these complaints grew in intensity. Before we turn to these developments, I shall briefly report the decision made by the central government's States Reorganization Commission.

## The States Reorganization Commission's Recommendations

The States Reorganization Commission recommended that Belgaum dis-

[15] *M.E.S. Memo to S.R.C.,* p. 68.

trict, with the exception of one taluka, be transferred in its entirety to Mysore. Its recommendations and its reasoning were as follows:

> The Chandgad taluka of Belgaum district is predominantly Marathi-speaking, and it has been established as a result of the re-sorting of census slips that the Marathi majority in the taluka is as high as 92.4 per cent. It can conveniently be administered by the State of Bombay and Karnataka should have no objection to this proposal.
>
> As regards the remaining ten taluks of Belgaum District, it has been claimed that two of them, Khanapur and Belgaum (including Belgaum town), as well as portions of Chikodi taluka have closer affiliations with the Marathi-speaking districts of Bombay than with the adjoining areas in the proposed Karnatak State. The Marathi majorities in Khanapur and Belgaum taluks are slight, being 53.9 and 51.4 per cent respectively. Six out of the remaining seven taluks are predominantly Kannada-speaking, and in the seventh, namely, Chikodi, the Kannadigas constitute the largest single language group. All the taluks of Belgaum district have economic relations with both the Marathi as well as the Kannada speaking areas. The Belgaum town is the centre of the transit trade in this area, which is chiefly in cotton and oil seeds. Neither the Belgaum town nor the other disputed areas, however, have any particularly marked economic affiliations with the Marathi-speaking districts of Bombay. There is no case, therefore, for detaching either Khanapur or Belgaum or portions of Chikodi from the rest of the Belgaum district.
>
> It has been argued that Belgaum town has an absolute Marathi majority and that due consideration should be given to this factor. Separate mother tongue figures for this town were not compiled during the last census. In the past, it has, however, for a variety of reasons, attracted a steady stream of immigrants from many areas. Even if it is admitted that this town has now a Marathi majority, in view of the very slight Marathi majority in the taluk of Belgaum and the fact that economic relations are not particularly marked with any linguistic area, the future both of the taluk as well as of the town should, more properly, be decided on administrative

grounds. If as many as nine out of the eleven taluks go to Karnataka (Chandgad going to Bombay and Belgaum being disputed) then, on administrative grounds, the Belgaum town, which is the district headquarters, along with the Belgaum taluk, should also go to Karnataka. We have recommended earlier that the Bellary town, along with the Bellary taluk, should go to Andhra, although the town, according to Shri Justice Misra's report did not have a predominantly Andhra complexion; our recommendation in respect of the Belgaum town follows the same principle.[16]

Earlier in the report, the commission said: "The retention of the Kolar district in the Karnatak state and the addition of the major part of the Belgaum district to it, will, in our opinion be more advantageous to the new state than the continuance in it of the eastern portion of the Bellary district."

In effect, the commission rejected the *historical* argument of the Kannadigas and the *linguistic* argument of the Marathi speakers. Although the commission reports that Belgaum is a trading center (though not, as the report erroneously states, in cotton and oil seeds), it notes that "economic relations are not particularly marked with any linguistic area." Economic considerations too are therefore rejected. The report bases its decision on two considerations: (a) administrative, and (b) political. On the administrative side, the report argues that since Belgaum town is an administrative center, it would be particularly convenient if it remained the headquarters of the district. On the political side, the report hints that Belgaum town and the disputed areas are being given to Mysore in return for giving the predominantly Kannada-speaking portions of Bellary district and Bellary town to Andhra state. Since the administrative argument is not a strong one — after all, several other towns in the Kannada-speaking areas of Belgaum could be developed into a district town, and Belgaum could become the center for a newly organized district in Maharashtra — one is forced to conclude that the political considerations were paramount in the recommendations made by the Commission.

The Maratha reaction to the report was, as might be expected, bitter and hostile. The Samiti issued an appeal against the commission's recommendations. It noted that economically Nipani and Belgaum are more closely associated with Maharashtra than with the Kannada areas; it argued that the town of Ghataprabha in the Kannada area could be con-

[16] *States Reorganization Commission Report*, pp. 97–98.

verted into a district headquarters and that meanwhile Belgaum could continue to serve as the headquarters for a new Kannada district; it complained that the report failed to examine the case of the Marathi-speaking people in Hukeri and Athni talukas and in the disputed parts of Karwar district. The appeal concluded that Belgaum was being used for "recompensating the loss of the Bellary areas to the new Karnatak state." [17]

It is not necessary here to recount in any detail the agitations launched by the Ekikaran Samiti to press for a change in decision. In a by-election held in a Marathi-speaking area in Belgaum taluka in November, 1955, the Samiti defeated a Marathi-speaking Congress candidate on the border issue. A civil disobedience movement was launched in early 1956, and on November 1, 1956, when the new state was formed, the Samiti organized a silent procession in Belgaum town. The Samiti, as we shall see, won the assembly seats in the Marathi-speaking areas in the 1957 elections and again in 1962. In November, 1958, two years after the transfer the samiti again launched a civil disobedience movement followed by a no-tax campaign in the form of non-payment of land revenues. Several months later the Samiti terminated the agitation. In early 1961 the two states appointed a joint committee to look into the border issue.

As earlier, the conflict centered heavily on the question of language in the school system. Parents and children often resent having to study a "foreign" language. Moreover, linguistic minorities are particularly resentful because they are handicapped in the competition for admission into colleges and into administration. In Mysore, for example, as in most other Indian states, knowledge of the regional language along with English is a prerequisite for a post in the higher levels of administration; even where the regional language requirement is waived, it is invariably a precondition for promotions. Moreover, in this particular dispute the linguistic minority, unlike minorities in most other states, are unable to reconcile themselves to a minority position because they live contiguous to a Marathi-speaking state and in their own localities are far from a minority. They are, as it were, a minority by virtue of the artificial drawing of boundaries, and could be reconverted into a majority by shifting those boundaries. Therefore, since they do not accept their minority status, the Marathi speakers do not feel that the recommendation made by the central government commission is a satisfactory solution. A local medical doctor of Konkani descent said:

[17] *Belgaum: An Appeal Against the S.R.C.'s Findings*, p. 2.

The major difficulty in the present arrangement is that it has a terrible effect upon the children. Only a few years ago the Mysore government introduced Kannada into the schools and now requires it for all school children. Jetti [then the Chief Minister] said that it is not compulsory for primary schools to introduce Kannada as a first or second language. But recently I talked to the Jesuit father who is the principal of a local school, and he said that he had nothing in writing but he was in effect told by the educational inspector that they had to introduce Kannada into the school. If they failed to introduce Kannada, then the government would find some other excuse for failing to renew the grant to the primary school. Our children are returning from school complaining bitterly about having to take classes in Kannada. If our children could study the languages which they want to study and have adequate opportunities to get admitted into the technical schools, then we wouldn't have this urge to be in Maharashtra.

A sense that they have been discriminated against, not only by the Mysore government, but also by the central government pervades the Marathi-speaking community. The States Reorganization Commission had recommended that the border districts of Bellary and Hospet, though containing Kannada-speaking majorities, be transferred to the new state of Andhra since the Tungabhadra Dam in Hospet would benefit primarily the people of Andhra. But when the report came out, a satyagraha (civil disobedience) movement took place in Hospet and the people in that area threatened to keep the waters from Andhra. As a result the central government decided that Hospet and Bellary should be turned over to Mysore state. Since the reasoning was essentially the same behind the SRC's decision to grant Belgaum town to Mysore and to grant Bellary and Hospet to Andhra, the reversal of the latter decision, argued the Marathi leaders, should be accompanied by a reversal of the former decision. They feel that the government's not having done so indicates discrimination against the Marathi people. An angry Marathi-speaking lawyer in Belgaum who left the Congress party on the border controversy noted:

In England the proposal to nationalize steel was given up when people demanded it. Here, though we have won the election, the government has done nothing. We are dis-

gusted. These people work with prejudiced minds. When there is a peaceful agitation the police are given full powers to do anything. The S. P. [Superintendent of Police] recently said that the government has given him full powers. . . . If the government brought about reorganization, it should have been done in the right way. You are trying to hold down a martial people. It would have been better that there had been no reorganization unless the government did it the right way. . . . The foreigners studied these matters before deciding anything, but the SRC did not.

The joint commission of Mysore and Maharashtra toured the disputed areas. The four-member commission ultimately agreed to split, with the two members of each state touring separately and issuing separate reports to their own governments. When the Maharashtrian members of the commission toured Belgaum, the Ekikaran Samiti submitted at length a re-statement of their case. The Samiti concluded their case:

It is often said that unity of the nation is the first concern, and agitation for the transfer of area from one state to an-other is detrimental to it. There can be no argument more fallacious than this. The whole story of reorganization of states is itself one of transfer of areas and reconstitution of of states. Had this area been included in Bombay initially, the point of danger to the national unity would not have arisen at all. But that the mistake has somehow been committed and the rectification of that mistake is a reasoning which passes our comprehension. It is the duty of a democratic government to do whatever they do as perfectly as possible. Having formed two linguistic states side by side, it lies on the government to adjust the border in such a way as to leave the least number of people of a different language in any state.[18]

## The Continuing Struggle for Belgaum Town

The acrimony and invective arising from the quarrel of the Kannada and Marathi speakers over Belgaum town recall the controversy over Trieste.

[18] *Memorandum Submitted to the Maharashtra-Mysore Border Committee* (Belgaum: Maharashtra Ekikaran Samiti, 1961; mimeographed), pp. 39–40.

Language, culture, and even national pride are at issue; even though the town will after all remain in India whether it is in Maharashtra or Mysore, the two communities often sound as if they were struggling over an international border. The leadership of the two communities recognizes of course that they are not. Indeed, both sides are fond of arguing that their position is on the side of national unity. The Kannadas declare that the issue is settled, or at least ought to be considered settled, and that both sides should devote their energies to the more important tasks of national development. The Marathas declare that national unity can be strengthened only when "artificially created minorities" are allowed to live at peace in the linguistic state to which they rightfully belong.

The most bitter dispute is over Belgaum town. Mysore has indicated its willingness to transfer a few of the disputed villages to Maharashtra, but is adamant with respect to the town. Many of the villages in the disputed area are so overwhelmingly Marathi-speaking that their transfer would hardly inconvenience any Kannada speakers. But Belgaum town has only a bare majority of native Marathi speakers, and at least a quarter of the population is Kannada-speaking (the remaining population is Hindi-, Urdi-, or Konkani-speaking). Both groups stake their claims in passionate and often irrational and irrelevant terms. At times these claims appear comic — but only to the outsider. References are made to the linguistic composition of the city of the mid-nineteenth century; claims are based on the language of inscription at local archaeological sites; street names are pointed to as evidence of historical antiquity of a particular community; the use of its language in official records is cited by each side; statistics on octroi taxes are quoted to prove that there are trade connections between the city and one of the linguistic regions; even the number of books in each language in the Belgaum General Library is made part of the argument.

But what is the fight all about? We have already noted the obvious inconveniences experienced by the Maratha population throughout the district who have to live in a Kannada-speaking state: conflicts over the language in the local schools; inconveniences with respect to the language of government legislation and even government application forms; and, most importantly from the Maratha point of view, little opportunity for educated Marathas to obtain jobs in government administration. These same inconveniences, now experienced by slightly over half the population of Belgaum town, would fall to the one quarter who speak Kannada if the town were transferred to Maharashtra.

From a political point of view, the Kannada-speaking Congressmen —

who are the leaders of the movement to retain Belgaum in Mysore —
would be seriously weakened by a transfer. While the Congress party
does not control the taluka board in Belgaum or the municipal corporation, and while the local member of the legislative assembly is the president of the Maharashtra Ekikaran Samiti, the Kannada politicians in Belgaum town are not without power for they control the Belgaum town
Congress Committee. At present there are few Marathi-speaking Congressmen in Belgaum town. Many Marathi-speaking politicians not now
in the Congress frankly state that they will join the Congress party once
the disputed areas, including the town, are transferred to Maharashtra.
The Congress party in Belgaum town would undoubtedly be strengthened,
and those who now control local bodies as non-Congressmen would soon
control them as Congressmen. But as a consequence the Kannada leaders
of the Congress party in Belgaum town would find that their sources of
power — their links to the government and administration of Mysore —
would come to an end as would their control of the town Congress Committee.

The Ekikaran Samiti has firm control over the municipality. Over the
years the municipality has passed many resolutions criticizing the Mysore
government and calling for the transfer of the town to Maharashtra. The
Mysore government attempted in 1959 to supersede the municipality (that
is, to abolish the elected council and place the town under the direct
control of the state government), but the municipality successfully challenged the state government on the grounds that it had no legal right to
dissolve the municipality unless it could demonstrate that the municipality had failed to perform the duties imposed on it by the Municipal
Act or any other law. The state government was forced to withdraw its
show-cause notice, but in 1961 returned with a new proposal to supersede, this time on the grounds that the municipality had failed to comply
with the Municipal Act. A host of detailed charges were presented — the
failure to complete a government-sanctioned water supply scheme, to levy
certain taxes, to recover municipal dues, to provide adequate sanitary arrangements for the town, to provide residential quarters for scavenging
staff, and so forth. The municipality replied point by point, and as of mid-
1962 no effort had been made by the state government to carry through its
threat of supersession. Maratha leaders in the town felt that if the government were to supersede it would appoint a Kannada-speaking executive officer who would discharge members of the Marathi-speaking staff,
introduce Kannada into the municipal administration, perhaps even make

changes in the school system, and in general do what is possible to make Belgaum a Kannada city.[19]

Neither the Mysore nor the Maharashtra governments can concede Belgaum town. While politically the Mysore government can afford to surrender some of the villages with few Kannada speakers, Belgaum town has such a substantial number of Kannadas, including many men of political importance, that it would be politically difficult for Mysore to make any surrender. There is little likelihood that any opposition party could overthrow the state government, but factional conflicts within the state Congress party are sufficiently great so that a politically unpopular decision of this magnitude might result in major shifts within the party. Marathi leaders within the town are convinced that the Mysore government will never voluntarily give up the town. Their agitation against the Mysore government has therefore been primarily directed at keeping the issue alive and public, so that the central government may feel called upon to resolve the dispute. The Marathi leaders are confident that central intervention would result in the transfer of the town; for the same reason, many of the Kannada leaders in Belgaum are reluctant to see the central government intervene. Nonetheless, the more responsible state governments have cooperated with the home minister of the central government by providing detailed reports stating their case. Perhaps they have little choice, since the central government has the legal power to adjust the boundaries of states.

[19] According to the 1951 census, the population of Belgaum town was 101,038. The Marathi-speaking population was 53.4 per cent, the Kannada-speaking population 24.9 per cent. The Ekikaran Samiti candidate for the assembly carried Belgaum town in 1957 with 58.2 per cent of the vote, and was reelected in 1962 with a whopping 67 per cent of the vote, suggesting that more than half of the population which speaks neither Marathi nor Kannada (21 per cent) supported the Samiti candidate. The Samiti also controls the Belgaum Taluka Board (twelve of nineteen seats), and thirty-four of the forty-four elected councilors in the municipality are Marathi speakers.

# 13. THE CONGRESS PARTY ORGANIZATION AND HOW IT WORKS

While the language controversy has been the most dramatic challenge confronting the Congress party in Belgaum district, there have been other, perhaps less dramatic, but equally difficult challenges.

## Political Roles

During the nationalist era, party workers were engaged in agitational activities — organizing and participating in street processions, launching boycotts and civil disobedience movements, fighting with the police, and going to jail — and in constructive or reform activities — encouraging peasants to produce handloom cloth, give up alcohol, end discrimination against untouchables, and so on. Of these two important roles performed by workers in the nationalist movement in Belgaum and elsewhere before independence — agitational and constructive — the first role has disappeared and the other is of reduced importance. The transformation of the Congress from a mass nationalist movement concerned with winning power from the British into a political party and its adjustment to the various changes which have taken place within the district have meant, in the final analysis, a transformation in the roles performed by the party membership.

These old roles were clearly inappropriate to the requirements of the Congress party after independence. The transfer of authority from the British to the Indians and from the maharajas to the elected representa-

tives meant in effect a transfer of power of the party vis-à-vis local district administration. Furthermore, the new national and state governments imposed a series of changes to which the local Congress party had to adapt. For one thing, the government announced the establishment of universal adult suffrage. By 1952, when the first general elections were held, the local Congress party had to nominate candidates and create a new election apparatus that would reach all potential voters within the district. That same year the national government launched the Community Development Program for the development of the country's rural areas. New administrative machinery for development activities was created, forcing the party to make some major adjustments. Third — and this is by no means a complete list — the state government passed land reform legislation which affected the position of tenants and landlords. Within Belgaum district, as elsewhere in the state, the party had to adjust to deal with the struggles that often took place involving control over land.

In short, the party now had to develop a formal organization for the winning of electoral support, had to adapt to a new relationship with administration, and had still further to refine and develop a machinery for dealing with conflict within the party and within society at large. The party soon created roles for the performance of these functions, and recruited and trained persons for the performance of these roles. We can specify four such roles which developed within the party.

*Party, public, and government: The expeditor.* The decision by India's governmental elite to utilize and expand the governmental machinery for purposes of economic development and social change has been the single most important factor in changing the role requirements of the local party organization. The expansion of government has meant the expansion, in both numbers and functions, of local administration. Local administrative activities are at least of three types: (1) regulatory, (2) extractive, and (3) distributive. The regulatory functions involve placing limits upon what individuals can or cannot do without administrative approval: to open a shop or construct a factory, a businessman must first obtain a permit. In fact, legislation regulates the relationship between landlords and tenants and between peasant proprietors and agricultural laborers. The extractive functions involve the taking of things from individuals: the government has imposed taxes on land, set rates for the use of water provided by the new irrigation schemes, imposed excise taxes on commercial sales, and so on. Land reform legislation permits the state to take land from those whose holdings exceed a legal ceiling and, under various circumstances, to transfer land from landlords to tenants. Finally, a vast amount of government

activity involves the distribution of goods and services to the population. Some, such as road and school construction, electrification, irrigation, and distribution of agricultural credit and fertilizers, is concerned primarily with economic growth. Others, such as the allocation of housing sites for Harijans (untouchables), the establishment of nursery school programs, the granting of college scholarships to the poor, and the reservation of jobs in government to classified backward communities, are primarily concerned with providing social justice and social welfare.

The party has responded to this expansion of administrative activities by creating a class of expeditors who serve as links between administrators and citizens. To say create is, however, quite misleading, for that implies a conscious decision and program of action, and a new role. To the contrary, under British rule there was a class of individuals who had access to local administration and used that access to further their own or their group's interests. But before 1937 — when the Congress won control over the state government and for the first time shared power with the British at the state level — relatively few persons within the Congress party performed this function. When the party took power, those who had performed expediting roles joined the party; and as the activities of government expanded and the party increasingly handled local grievances and used the administrative machinery for patronage purposes, more and more individuals within the party began to assume this role.

The elected representatives to the state legislative assembly from Belgaum district are important expediters. Indeed, as a group they are more concerned with performing their roles as expediters than as legislators. While a few legislators are concerned with public policy problems, most are more interested in serving their constituents and therefore spend much time in the local constituency offices of the chief revenue officer (the mamlatdar) and the chief development officer (the block development officer). In addition to the legislators, many prominent party officials engage in expediting administrative activities for local persons. In fact, a conscious criteria of the party for the selection of candidates to the state and national legislative assemblies is whether the prospective candidate is a skillful expediter.

One example of an effective expeditor in the district Congress is Mr. Panchagavi, the MLA from Gokak. He is more intelligent and better educated than most MLAs in the district (he is a college graduate and holds a law degree) and, by any standards, a modernist. He was first elected to the assembly in 1952, and has been reelected in the two subsequent elec-

tions by an overwhelming vote. He is now the deputy speaker of the Mysore Legislative Assembly.

Panchagavi as a young boy became active in the civil disobedience movement of 1930–31 (he was born in 1913 of a middle-class agriculturalist family in a village in Ramdurg Taluka but has spent most of his life in Gokak where he attended high school). As a young man he was active in a number of social service and cooperative activities within the taluka. He is a Lingayat by community and a small landowner with about fifty acres of land. Though he spends a good part of the year in Bangalore attending the legislative assembly, he maintains a law practice in Gokak. At some length he described his activities on behalf of his constituency.

> I make presentations to government for building roads and schools. I am on the NES [National Extension Scheme, the program for community development] Committee in Gokak. Previously money came from the District Local Board, the *P.W.D.*, Education Department, and Irrigation Department. Even now, money comes from these departments. There is not so much money from the CD [Community Development] Block because of the many restrictions.

Such as?

> Villagers cannot contribute so much money for constructing metalled roads. They want to build a kutcha [dirt] road and need some financial help, but government will not help build kutcha roads.

Why is that?

> The authorities insist on metaled roads or no roads at all. They feel that it is difficult to maintain a kutcha road, whereas metaled roads need very little care for eight or ten years. But our villages are too poor to put up money required for a metaled road.

What are you doing about it?

> I am trying to get the PWD Minister to change this rule.
> Then there are schools. Government used to give 60 per cent, and 40 per cent had to come from the village. Now

government says they will give only Rs 1000 per room, but it costs about Rs 4200 to build a room. It will not suffice. Now it is the very poor villages that have not come forward with the 40 per cent to build schools. So with this new rule, which was passed just this year, the poor villages will find it even more difficult to raise the money to build schools. The more prosperous villages have already come forward.

Why was this new rule passed?

There is so much demand for school buildings the government thought it would spread the money around to build more schools. But now the poor villages cannot come forward for school grants at all.

What do you do in the field of agriculture?

Irrigation is a problem. There is not enough water and the rates are also high as compared to Bombay state. Then some of the rules are bad. A peasant is penalized for leaving part of his land dry if he takes irrigation water for some of his land. That is to prevent him from using the water for his other lands. But the peasant cannot afford to take water for all his land every year, so he leaves some dry. I am trying to get some new rules for irrigation. In this respect some of the rules in old Mysore state are better than those in Bombay, though from an administrative point of view the Bombay rules were better. . . . Then there is the tenancy legislation. There are only a few watandars [landowners] here with a few hundred acres. The ceilings should be lower, but only a few tenants will get some more land from the landowners. In this taluka there are only six watandars with a few hundred acres each. And even then they have been selling their lands to their tenants at a higher price than that set by government. But the tenants here are not strong enough to resist.

Is there much interest in increasing productivity? Do Congress workers encourage such an interest?

It is true that little effort is given to agricultural productivity. Some of the rich cultivators come forth to take advantage of

the new insecticides — but not the small landowners. One problem is that not enough agricultural credit is given, only about 15 per cent of the farmer's normal requirements come from the government and cooperatives. I have organized a land mortgage bank, but we have practically no power to give loans. We only make recommendations to Bangalore so it takes a long time before credit can be given. . . . The government workers [in the Community Development Program] have little practical knowledge of agricultural work. They give lectures to the farmers which is little appreciated.

He spoke of other agricultural difficulties in the constituency, particularly the lack of fertilizers, the prevalence of illiteracy among the peasants, and difficulties with the irrigation facilities. He then spoke about the role of the Congress workers.

Our Congressmen are mostly progressive cultivators. They try best to teach others, but mostly they are rich people. Poor people cannot experiment with new methods. They cannot afford to fail. . . . The cooperative societies do some good work, especially in distributing fertilizers. Our Congressmen are active in the cooperatives. But we need more selfless leaders to make these cooperatives work well.

As the deputy speaker in the Mysore Legislative Assembly, Panchagavi has particularly good access to both district and state leaders and is concerned with legislative policy, but it is striking that his interests also tend to center heavily on questions of administrative policy and its implementation. Many local Congressmen will bring administrative problems to Panchagavi, though many Congress workers will also deal directly with local officials.

It will be relevant to our discussion of the training of Congressmen for their roles to note here that most expediters come from the local agricultural gentry. Expediters in Belgaum are generally not lawyers, professionals, or townsmen unless they have rural gentry backgrounds. The expediters often come from families of large landowners (inamdars and watandars) or from families which held positions of authority within the village. Two such expediter-officers, discussed earlier, were particularly important: the hereditary village land record keeper (the kulkarni) and the village headman (patil or gauda). Both village functionaries, occupy-

ing as they did hereditary offices of profit, often became the largest land-owners in their villages. Through a process of family fragmentation, many of the large landowners no longer hold positions as village officers, but they are almost always related to those who do.

Consequently, inamdars, watandars, kulkarnis, patils, and their descendants abound in the local Congress party. In the past those who held these positions exercised great influence within local administration for themselves, for their families, for their village faction or caste group, or — though less often — for the village as a whole. Though in the past local administration was more concerned with the extractive than with the developmental and distributive functions, it has not been difficult for this class to extend its influence from the revenue to the new developmental departments of local government. It is not simply that these individuals — or their sons who join the Congress party — know how the government administration works, or even that they have access to it by virtue of their past power or their present wealth (though, of course, these factors are at work) but rather that they are psychologically capable of dealing with local and state administration. In a hierarchically stratified social system such as India has, those who are low in the hierarchy find it difficult even to converse with those in positions of high authority let alone to make demands. While there are low-caste persons in the Congress party organization in Belgaum district, they rarely perform expediting roles. In the main, expeditors come from the higher castes and, most often, are the descendants of those who, as landlords and as village officers, were frequently engaged in dealing with local and state administration.

*Party and public: The constructive worker.* Since independence a large amount of social service work which was previously completely voluntary now receives governmental support. Today private schools, cooperatives, Harijan welfare activities, and other social service organizations receive government support and often take on a quasi-governmental character. The production of khadi (handspun, handloomed cotton cloth), which before independence was primarily a non-governmental activity engaging the attention of many nationalist workers, now receives official encouragement by the Khadi and Villages Industries Board, a statutory body. In Belgaum district this board is controlled by a local Congressman, and the chairmen of most of the cooperative banks in the district are also Congressmen. There are also a number of schemes to develop the woolens industry in the district, and these are under the control of government-supported, Congress-controlled cooperatives. The school board is controlled by Congress and the District Local Board, and the Taluka (a unit

of the district) Development Boards are controlled mainly by Congress-men.

Thus many of the men once engaged in constructive work on a volun-tary basis are now engaged, often on salary, in governmental or quasi-governmental bodies. Much of what is still called constructive work in the district is now of this nature. Today the term "constructive worker" refers to the party worker engaged in aiding those who are particularly needy, whether or not the activity is wholly non-governmental. Thus, one prominent constructive worker is secretary of a boarding and lodging hostel for poor students in the district; another is active in organizing the Kurubars, a caste of shepherds and weavers, into cooperatives to further the production of woolen blankets; another is the head of the Congress-sponsored Women's Congress, concerned with educating women and de-veloping children's centers, ladies' clubs, and a milk distribution program.

The emphasis of this role is service — to help those who cannot other-wise help themselves. Though some of this work involves dealing with government administrators and is therefore indistinguishable from the role of expeditor, the conduct of constructive work in the main is related to the tradition of philanthropy found in the district. Indeed, many of those who are described locally as constructive workers are essentially philanthro-pists operating within the framework of the Congress party. A prominent Jain businessman constructed a hostel for Jain students. Several other leading Congressmen, now with some government assistance, are building a hostel for poor college students just outside Belgaum town. One mem-ber of parliament, a prominent local landlord, was for many years (even before he joined Congress) active in building and maintaining a local boys' school. Moreover, the president of the District Congress Committee, (the highest ranking party officer in the district) and the senior member of parliament from the district are active in religious sects and temples in and around Belgaum. Thus, the philanthropic tradition lends itself easily to the constructive work program of the local party.

This is not to say that all those who are engaged in constructive work come from wealthy families who have engaged in philanthropic activi-ties — far from it. A number of the constructive workers come from fami-lies of modest means. A few are younger men who have been assigned constructive work by the party leadership. Some are given salaried jobs as secretaries of cooperatives or student hostels. But the institutions for which they work are often the creations of those whose families have been benefactors to the local temples and leaders of social reform and educa-tional activities within the district, even before the Congress party and

the nationalist movement developed. The existence of a philanthropic tradition within the district thus provides a model for the creation of the constructive work role.

*Dispute settlement: The arbitrator.* The spate of legislation passed by the Bombay government when Belgaum was still part of Bombay state has resulted in considerable conflict between landlords and tenants in many villages in the district. In order to avoid the effects of ceiling legislation, many landlords have sold some of their lands to tenants; others have redistributed titles to members of their families; and still others have evicted tenants, reduced them to the position of agricultural laborers, and claimed the right of personal cultivation.

A large number of the Congress leaders and active members in Belgaum district are small landowners. A few, particularly in Ramdurg but scattered throughout the district, are men of substance who hold several hundred acres or more. In some instances the Congressman supervises cultivation on his land, but in most cases supervision is undertaken by a member of the Congressman's family. A few of the local Congressmen — including those who have income from the land — are nonetheless staunch supporters of the principle of "land to the tiller." But there is little conflict on the issue within the district, for even those who have found ways to evade the law — and many are available — insist they subscribe to the principle. But these same men defend the right of the landlord to resume personal cultivation or, more accurately, to supervise his own land. As one prominent Congressman, a member of the legislative council, frankly explained:

> The New Mysore Land Reform Act is intended to eliminate the landlord and give land directly to the tiller. The aim is to eliminate absentee landlordism. But the tenant won't receive the land in all cases. The landlord can cease being an absentee landlord by resuming cultivation under his personal supervision. A man of ten acres would have to hire agricultural labor. The law says that personal cultivation may be by your own labor or it may be with the assistance of agricultural laborers under your personal supervision. That was the consideration in drafting the new legislation. We feel that a landlord can supervise hundreds of acres.

But doesn't the law impose a ceiling?

Yes, the law doesn't permit a man to have more than twenty-seven standard acres. The reason is that there must be an equitable distribution of land. It is the argument for social justice which led to the system of ceilings. In Belgaum district twenty-seven standard acres may be anything from about fifty to 150 acres of land depending upon the quality of the land.

How do Congressmen here feel about the new legislation?

It was the high command and the planning commission that has wanted this land reform. The state policy comes from the center and we try to make the center's proposals fit the conditions in the state. In Bombay the Congress workers were enthusiastic about land reforms, but not so in Mysore. Fifty per cent of the Congress MLAs come from the landlord class, so they are not enthused about the legislation. [The speaker is himself a substantial landlord.] In Bombay I feel people are progressive, but here in Mysore we are more conservative. I tell you that if Communism comes, it will come to Bombay first. That's why we were afraid to put Bombay city in a Maharashtrian state. We thought that if the Communists got control or some leftist group they would pressure the central government to nationalize business. After all, they have fifty members in parliament. So we didn't give them Bombay. But they demanded, and this is a democracy so we had to give in. And after all, the Bombay people are good fighters.

Until 1962 the new Mysore legislation had not been put into effect, but Belgaum fell under the Bombay Tenancy and Agricultural Lands Act of 1948. Under the act certain classes of tenants were given security of tenure, but under certain conditions the landlord could evict the tenant if he wished to resume the land for personal cultivation. An amendment to the act in 1952 provided that in cases where the landlord's personal holdings exceeded a particular size, he could not resume more than half the area leased to the tenant. A further amendment in 1957 provided that in no case could a landlord take more than half the land leased to a tenant. The act also specified conditions under which the tenant could become the owner of his holding.

After the district was merged with Mysore, an ordinance was issued in 1957 suspending the provisions of the act permitting the landlord to resume land for personal cultivation and the provisions permitting the tenant to become the owner of the land. In 1957 a commission of the Mysore government made recommendations with respect to new tenancy legislation for the entire new state of Mysore.[1]

The passage of land reform legislation has resulted in conflicts between medium and large landowners and their tenants. Many of these disputes arise when landowners attempt to resume the right of personal cultivation either to evict their tenants or to reduce them to wage laborers. The Congress party organization in the district can hardly ignore these conflicts, because tenants constitute a substantial part of the voting population and landlords constitute a substantial part of the political leadership in the party. It is then in the interests of the local party to resolve such disputes without political agitation or court litigation, and several leaders of the party are therefore involved in attempts to arbitrate disputes between landowners and tenants.

Landlord-tenant disputes are not the only areas of conflict within the villages. There are boundary disputes between landowners, fights over stray cattle, and criminal accusations. All of these may be handled by a local Congress politician. One such politician engaged in resolving these conflicts summed up his role as follows.

> We have a saying here that people fight over honnu [gold], henno [women], and mannu [land]. We try to settle these disputes out of court. Sometimes we bring the disputes to the panchayats [elected village councils], but mostly we try to bring the two sides together. It is a matter of giving satisfaction to both sides.[2]

When the party worker hears of a local dispute, he generally visits the opposing parties. Often he is asked to do so. As a local man he invariably knows the local situation — that is, not simply the dispute at hand but the pattern of relationships which surrounds the dispute. But the arbi-

[1] See *Report of the Mysore Tenancy Agricultural Land Laws Committee* (Bangalore: Government of Mysore, 1957).

[2] Note that the object is not to apply some abstract principle of justice, but to give "satisfaction to both sides," a typically Indian attitude toward the resolution of conflict. It is reminiscent of a statement made by Vinoba Bhave to the effect that only God can provide justice while man's task is to provide satisfaction. For a systematic comparison of the traditional Indian and British viewpoints toward the resolution of conflict, see Bernard S. Cohn, "Some Notes on Law and Change in North India," *Economic Development and Cultural Change* (Oct., 1959).

trator is not selected because he is a Congress party worker. In Belgaum a class of persons exists from which those who perform the role of arbitrators are recruited. In most disputes involving members of different castes, it is generally a Lingayat, the socially and politically dominant caste in the region, who mediates or arbitrates the dispute. A large and respected landowner or a local grain merchant, irrespective of his caste, may also be asked to perform this role. What is important to the participants is (1) that the arbitrator not be a party to the dispute; (2) that he be a man of high status; (3) that he understand the whole complex of interrelated conflicts which actually make up the dispute, not simply the issue at hand; and (4) that he be a man of such local power that the disputants would hesitate to ignore his advice for fear of retribution.

In Belgaum district the role of arbitrator is a traditional one. For reasons related to cultural patterns and traditional social organization, contending parties have always sought external intervention for the resolution of conflict. The Lingayats' entry into the nationalist movement in the 1930's meant that the Congress acquired within its ranks the single most important community of individuals capable of settling disputes.

Those who settle disputes, whether within the party or outside it, are not only exercising their power; at the same time they are increasing it. Those who successfully resolve one conflict are respected for their impartiality and called upon to resolve others, and those who benefit from a man's intervention in a dispute feel a sense of obligation to him. During elections to local bodies and to state national assemblies, the arbitrator may return to the village to exercise his influence.

Mr. Aragavi, the vice-president of the District Congress Committee and a Lingayat, is widely thought of as a powerful man within the district, partly because of his capacity to deal with internal party conflict. In late 1960, for example, the secretary of the Pradesh Congress Committee informed the president of the DCC that Aragavi had been requested to tour the district to select candidates for president and vice-president for taluka development boards on a Congress ticket. Aragavi's task was to consult Congress party members in each of the taluka boards, then consult with the Selection Committee of the DCC before selecting the Congress candidate. Aragavi was thus recognized as an effective arbitrator within the party; by giving him the power to make selections, his influence throughout the district was extended.

*Housekeeping: The party organizer.* The performance of the mundane and routine tasks of political organization — the recruitment of membership, the maintenance of party records, the transmission of information

and instructions from one level of the party to another, the raising of finances, and the running of a party office — are all *sine qua non* of a modern political party. When these tasks are not well performed, a party degenerates into a loose association.

The Belgaum District Congress Committee is one of twenty-one district or city Congress committees in Mysore state. Beneath the DCC are ten taluka Congress committees, and beneath these are eighty mandal committees, in theory at least, the basic functioning unit of the party organization.[3]

The Congress party maintains an office in every taluka in the district and a central office in Belgaum town. Few of the mandal committees function at all, except for infrequent meetings to elect representatives to the taluka committees and to participate in the elections to the District Congress Committees. In theory the mandal Congress committee takes responsibility for recruiting primary and active members and carries out the basic work of the party within the villages and towns. In practice, the basic work of the party is done by members of the District Congress Committee and some of the more active members of the taluka committees. It is the DCC which is most active; complaints of local people about local administration are brought directly to members of the DCC, who see the collector and other government officers to resolve these complaints. DCC members are particularly active in handling grievances associated with developmental activities.

Though the executive committees of the DCC and the taluka Congress committees meet several times a year, the larger bodies meet infrequently. Occasionally, there may be a district camp of members of the Youth Congress, but the general body of the party never meets. Nonetheless, contact among members is considerable. The offices of the DCC and the taluka committees are frequent meeting places, in much the same way that the ward offices of American political parties are important informal meeting places. In the afternoon one can almost always find several Congressmen napping in party offices, and in the evening a stream of people walk in and out. The president of the DCC and other important Congressmen living in Belgaum town will sit together for long hours in the

[3] Each mandal committee is supposed to have ten members or more, elected by the primary members of the party. For each mandal committee member there must be at least twenty-five primary members. Each mandal committee therefore represents approximately two hundred fifty primary members. Office bearers of the mandal committees automatically become members of the taluka congress committees. Moreover, the DCC is elected directly by the mandal committees. In Belgaum district, which had eighty thousand primary members in 1960, the mandal committees are larger than the minimum requirement.

evening in the loft of the wooden house in which the DCC is located. Visiting MLAs and other Congress officials in the district will invariably drop in to the party office when in Belgaum. One small room in the DCC office houses the records; another rather large room is used as the office for the permanent secretary; it is also used as a waiting room for petitioners; a third room, in which the telephone is located, houses the president and his associates, who squat on the floor, reclining against the many bolsters scattered around the room.

The taluka offices are smaller but, like the office of the District Congress Committee, they are located in the heart of the town. The taluka offices rarely maintain good records; but though they give the appearance of being sleepy, they are also the meeting places for local Congress workers. Next to the taluka office may be the local sales emporium of the Khadi Board, and a local marketing cooperative may share some of the rooms. Bags of jowar or paddy are often next to a bookcase containing some party records. A distinct agricultural smell fills the air.

None of the offices keeps records efficiently, and the party is often lax in replying to correspondence. The Pradesh Congress Committee complains that reports requested are rarely sent, and even membership lists are not promptly sent; the local office tends to be more efficient about sending membership lists when party elections are due, since the size of the local party determines how much representation it will have at various levels within the party.

Membership recruitment is actively pursued because of internal controversies. Contenders for office — whether in the mandal committee, the taluka, district committees, or the PCC and the AICC — recruit primary members whose votes they would obtain. Inflation of membership is common, and it is therefore difficult to assess the significance of the membership increases which have taken place. But considering that one does meet a number of young people in the party throughout the district, there is some reason to think that not all the membership increases are the results of inflation.

Local party leaders privately estimate that there are between 200 and 250 active party workers throughout the district — not the 1,312 listed in the party rolls. Active members are engaged in work in the local cooperatives, the taluka boards, and the schools. Many recruit members for the party, and nearly all are active in the various local elections and of course the general elections which take place in the district. Except for recruitment and election work, it is difficult to say when a man is working for the party and when he is functioning in an individual private capacity. But

Congress leaders rightfully point out that a man engaged in cooperative work commands considerable support during the elections; the difficulty of course is that if the party worker for one reason or another chooses to support an independent candidate, he is often able to bring his people — that is, those for whom he has performed services — to support him. Much of the local work therefore serves to strengthen personal rather than party loyalties.

Although active members of mandal committees naturally do their party work within the villages covered by the mandal committees, there is no formal allocation of geographical responsibilities to party workers as there is in the precinct organization of American political parties. In practice, the most active party workers are often engaged in work which goes beyond the geographical area of the mandal to which they belong. This is particularly true for those engaged in work in the taluka- or district-wide cooperatives and local government bodies such as the taluka boards of the District Local Board.

During the elections, some villages may be neglected through oversight, though this is less likely now than a decade ago. But even now after several elections most of the local party units in Belgaum have not developed the machinery for conducting elections that one finds not only in American parties but even in some other units of the Congress party in other parts of India.

The party does employ several full-time paid workers.[4] Several party secretaries are on salary. There is a paid district organizer for the Congress youth group, and there are several full-time but unpaid organizers in the women and youth sections of the party. But by any standards such organizational work as there is is not well performed.

While the modern party roles of arbitrating disputes, expediting requests through local administration, and conducting constructive work are variations of traditional roles, the role of party organizer is essentially a new one. Perhaps that is why this role is performed least effectively. Almost no one is experienced in maintaining effective party records, preparing reports on activities for the state office, and — most importantly — assigning responsibilities to workers throughout the district to carry out

[4] The DCC does not earn enough to cover its expenses. The party collects four anna (about five cents) from each primary member, or about twenty thousand rupees a year. One-fourth goes to the DCC, another fourth to the PCC, three-eighths to the mandal committees, and the remainder to the AICC. No portion is given to the taluka committees, which receive a lump sum from the DCC yearly. DCC money is used to finance the few full-time paid workers, an office, a Jeep, and other incidental expenses. To meet its expenses the DCC must make a general collection.

the complex organization necessary for the conduct of elections. For these, after all, are new skills, and traditional experience is of little avail. Moreover, so long as the local Congress party is not presented with any continuous challenge by any strong opposition party, there is little pressure to improve organizational skills or innovate with new organizational techniques.[5] Opposition from the Marathi community constitutes no threat to the party in the bulk of the district where the Marathi community does not live. In fact the effect of the Marathi attack is to strengthen the Congress hold in the Kannada-speaking areas. Ethnic loyalties have thus reduced the need for improving organization.

## Recruitment

Who joins the local Congress party and why? One older pre-independence Congress leader in the district asserts bluntly: "It is natural that everyone comes into Congress, since it is the ruling party and everyone wants power." Still another older leader claimed that 50 per cent of those who have come into the organization are opportunists who seek power. In Ramdurg taluka one local Congressman, speaking to me in the presence of many recent entrants into the party, frankly said that many of the new Congressmen joined Congress to protect their land. Other material considerations — access to permits and licenses, fertilizers, water, and whatever else local administration can dispense — also draw many into the party. There are few reasons why a local businessman or small landowner should not join the party and clearly many reasons why he should.

Partly as a result of these incentives, the party in Belgaum has recruited large numbers of persons since independence. It is striking, however, that the party has attracted not simply older persons but also younger men who had not supported the nationalist movement before independence. In fact, the bulk of the new membership came of age after independence. For example, in 1959 in Khanapur taluka eighteen of the fifty active members were thirty-five or younger; in Ramdurg, forty-four of seventy-six; in Belgaum, twenty-nine of ninety-one; and in Gokak, which has the largest active membership in the district, 112 of 265. About 40 per cent of the active members were barely twenty at the time of independence, and al-

---

[5] The complacency and the reasons for it were well expressed by the secretary of the Taluka Congress in Gokak. When asked what important problems the local Congress organization had, he replied: "There are no special problems here. If we had problems we wouldn't be so strong. We call this the 'Congress taluka.' We are the only party in the taluka so we have no political problems."

most all of these younger men joined the party in recent years. Moreover, the age structure of the party has not changed substantially. Between 1952 and 1959 the average age of party members increased by only two years in Khanapur (where the language controversy nearly eliminated recruitment among Marathi speakers) and by only 0.4 years in Ramdurg. This would indicate that the party continues to recruit young persons and does so on a substantial scale.[6]

Although naturally the bulk of the young men who join the party are agriculturalists (either non-cultivating landowners or cultivators), a surprisingly large number are in non-agricultural occupations. In Ramdurg, for example, twelve of the forty-four young men are in non-agricultural activities, including seven who are businessmen. In Khanapur, eight of the eighteen young men are in business. In Belgaum, there are five young businessmen and several pleaders and doctors, mostly from Belgaum town. In Gokak, again, most of the younger members are in agriculture, but there are also eighteen businessmen, eleven men employed by others, and three pleaders. There are also several men engaged in social work and one full-time Congress worker.

Numbers of active members alone can be somewhat misleading, since the term "active member" refers merely to a party designation obtained largely by paying an annual fee to the party. An examination of the background of the presidents of the mandal committees, the taluka Congress committees, the executive of the District Congress Committee, and the MLAs and MLCs from the district are more revealing (See Table 25).

Though social background in itself is no indication of motivation, it is striking that nearly half the active membership comes from the dominant caste in the district, the Lingayats. And although only seven of the 114 individuals for whom occupational information was available were reported as landlords, actually the bulk of the agriculturalists are men of property,

[6] Membership figures by taluka for 1960 were as follows.

| | Primary members | Active members |
|---|---|---|
| Ramdurg | 4,077 | 70 |
| Khanapur | 3,259 | 46 |
| Chikodi | 8,826 | 157 |
| Parasgad | 8,177 | 133 |
| Hukeri | 4,673 | 91 |
| Sampgaon | 7,715 | 143 |
| Gokak | 14,193 | 255 |
| Peta Raibag | 3,107 | 66 |
| Athni | 12,023 | 191 |
| Belgaum | 14,366 | 160 |
| Total | 80,416* | 1,312 |

*In 1955 primary membership was 35,000.

TABLE 25
SOCIAL BACKGROUND OF BELGAUM PARTY OFFICERS
(1961–62)

| | DCC Executives | Mandal Presidents | Taluka Presidents | MLA's | MLC's | Total |
|---|---|---|---|---|---|---|
| *Occupations* | | | | | | |
| Agriculture. . | 13 | 43 | 5 | 8 | 1 | 72 |
| Business. . . | 2 | 11 | 2 | 1 | 1 | 17 |
| Pleader . . . | 1 | 4 | . . | 3 | 1 | 9 |
| Political worker. . . | 1 | . . | . . | . . | 1 | 2 |
| Landlords . . | . . | 5 | 2 | . . | . . | 7 |
| Others. . . . | 1 | 5 | . . | . . | 1 | 7 |
| Total . . . | . . | . . | . . | . . | . . | 114 |
| *Castes* | | | | | | |
| Lingayats . . | 9 | 36 | 5 | 4 | 2 | 56 |
| Reddis. . . . | 2 | 3 | . . | 3 | 1 | 9 |
| Brahmins . . | 2 | 7 | 1 | . . | 1 | 11 |
| Marathas . . | 2 | 3 | 1 | 1 | 1 | 8 |
| Jain. . . . . | 1 | 10 | 1 | 1 | . . | 13 |
| Kuruba . . . | 1 | 5 | 1 | . . | . . | 7 |
| S. C. . . . . | 1 | 1 | . . | 2 | . . | 4 |
| Others. . . . | . . | 5 | . . | 1 | 1 | 7 |
| Total . . . | . . | . . | . . | . . | . . | 115 |
| *Language* | | | | | | |
| Kannada. . . | 16 | 71 | 8 | 11 | . . | 106 |
| Marathi. . . | 2 | 4 | 1 | 1 | . . | 8 |
| Total . . . | . . | . . | . . | . . | . . | 114 |

NOTE: Since data were not available on all items for all individuals, there is some disparity in the totals. There is also some duplication, since several MLA's and MLC's are also members of the DCC Executive; however, this duplication does not affect the over-all pattern of the table.

most of whom cultivate with the aid of tenants or agricultural laborers. The party does not recruit its active membership from the laboring classes.

None of this information makes the Congress party in Belgaum different from political parties in most other countries; to the contrary, the type of men attracted to the party and their reasons for joining it are not unusual. What is striking, however, is that these developments are considerably at variance with the hopes of the national Congress leadership and even those of some of the older party leaders in Belgaum district.

Within the district there is still much talk of sacrifice, but it has become highly ritualized. The organizer of the Seva Dal says that he tries to create sacrificial personalities. How? "We teach them the history of Congress. Our history is a sacrificial history. Without sacrifice we cannot get anything successful. We have ignorant, illiterate, poor people. We must help them. So we must have people who will sacrifice to give them help." But in practice sacrificial work, as he described it, meant becoming active in the cooperative movement.

Ideological enthusiasm attracts few if any active members. In a general way the more articulate party workers speak of the need to help the poor. One Congress worker, explaining the meaning of socialism, said that it means "greater equality for all, less differences between rich and poor. We don't want to destroy; we want to uplift. We don't want to rob the rich to give to the poor. We want to achieve equality slowly. We must take the people with us. First we must educate the poor and give them some status. Then they will rise." But few workers are able to explain the differences between Congress and other political parties or speak with any clarity on the government's national development program. On the whole, however, workers were familiar with the types of activities going on in their own areas and often revealed a substantial knowledge of local problems.

The Congress party, in the Kannada areas at least, is a primary center of political power within the district. In general the important landowners and businessmen of the district join the party, and one might go so far as to say that in the main they control the party. A few politicians — especially some of the older members — have a strong sense of party loyalty. But for the remainder — perhaps the larger number — the Congress party is simply one object of power, along with the District Local Board, the taluka development boards, and the banking and credit institutions. The desire to maintain control over land, to have access to credit, to influence the local market, and to obtain licenses and permits for oneself and more often for one's relatives and friends constitutes a powerful motive. Nor should we dismiss the desire to maintain one's status within one's community in a society in which access to power, along with caste, wealth, and education, constitutes a source of prestige.

With few exceptions, men do not build their political careers merely by working within the party organization, rising from the ranks into a position of responsibility in the party. More often a man establishes his influence within his village, controls the local cooperative, moves into the taluka development board and the District Local Board, and gets elected to the board of the District Cooperative Bank. Somewhere in the course of his political rise he joins the Congress party and becomes an office bearer of the party. If the party fails to give him recognition — that is, fails to give him a position within the party commensurate with the power he believes he holds outside the party — he may defect from the organization. It is this hypothesis which may help us understand why Congress lost so many seats to independents in the 1957 elections but regained them in 1962. Of the eleven seats Congress lost (of a total of eighteen) in 1957, six were to independents and five to the Maharashtra Ekikaran Samiti. In 1962 Con-

gress regained all of the six seats which independents won earlier. All of the independent candidates elected in 1957 were former Congressmen. By 1962 Congress had made adjustments with the sitting independent MLAs in four constituencies, so that in 1962 it was necessary for Congress to oppose only two of the independent incumbents.[7]

The party leadership in the district is thus faced with the delicate task of balancing the demands of the old, loyal workers in the party and those of the men of power within the district whose loyalty to the party is secondary to their overriding urge for political power within the district. Some of the active workers thus complain bitterly that tickets are given to men who have not served the party but whose claim is that they have influence within a section of the district.

The secretary of the Pradesh Congress Committee in Mysore defended this policy. "In distributing tickets, we must take community representation into account. We can't always give tickets to our most active constructive workers if it means too much representation for some communities and not for others." A Congress leader within Belgaum district, explaining the Congress defeats by independents in 1957, argued that the party had often selected candidates "who were financially poor and did not have enough money to properly contest the election." When asked what the criteria should be for the selection of candidates, he said that there had to be many considerations, among which "the man had to be a person with considerable local influence and he should also be a man who is financially well off so that he can finance his own campaign." Wasn't this unfair to your active workers who didn't have enough money? "That is true, but circumstances are like that. People who oppose the Congress party are not ordinary people. They are often influential men who are generally better off, and therefore the Congress candidate has to have quite a bit of money too."

Outside the Marathi area there is almost no opposition to the Congress party from any other political party. In 1962, for example, opposition to Congress in the twelve seats in the Kannada area came almost exclusively

[7] The 1957 victor in Anthni ran on the Congress ticket (and won) in 1962. The winning independent in Raibag, a double-member constituency, joined Congress and was given the parliamentary ticket, which he won in the 1962 elections. The decision by the Raibag independent to join Congress assured Congress of both assembly seats, since it was with the help of this independent in 1957 that a member of the Scheduled Caste Federation won the reserved seat. In Sadalga, the sitting independent, a Jain, decided not to run against the Congress nominee, also a member of the Jain community. In both Ramdurg and Parasgad, Congress waged a strenuous campaign to defeat the sitting independent MLAs, both former Congressmen who refused to join the party. Congress carried both seats in 1962, but they were the closest Congress victories in the district. In the 1962 elections Congress lost six seats, five to the Samiti and one to a Samiti-supported independent.

from independent candidates. In one seat a Swatantra candidate stood, in three others PSP candidates, and in a fifth a candidate of the Republican party (formerly the Scheduled Caste party). And in only one of these five seats did the opposition candidate succeed in getting more than half as much as the victorious Congress candidate.

The difficulty faced by the local Congress organization is that it cannot give tickets to all the local men of power. It must somehow pacify those who do not receive tickets and build a strong coalition around those who do. The party is thus forced to rotate tickets, and, unlike many other democratic systems, sitting members of the state assembly and parliament cannot be assured of renomination by the party.[8]

The party has many claims to satisfy. It can offer tickets to the legislative assembly (eighteen in all, with a good prospect of carrying the thirteen in predominantly Kannada areas), six elected Taluka Boards, several municipalities, the District Local Board, six seats in the Mysore legislative council, and two for parliament. Since there is no effective opposition in the Kannada-speaking areas, nomination virtually means election except when a strong local candidate who fails to get the nomination decides to stand as an independent. When the party skillfully allocates tickets, as it did in the 1962 elections, almost every seat (in the Kannada area) was a sure victory. (In nine of the twelve assembly seats won by Congress, the winning candidate had more than twice the votes of his closest opponent.)

Apart from political office, the party also can offer jobs. Influence can be used by party leaders for finding employment for young men in the cooperative societies and in the lower echelons of administration. Influential party members can also help a young man find employment in a local college or a local business. Moreover, party leaders can be of great assistance to their villages and their friends by obtaining various kinds of assistance from government.

The party does not use any of these incentives to attract Maratha supporters. While on the one hand the party made a strong effort to win the assembly seats in the Marathi-speaking portions of the district, on the other they have been reluctant to recruit Maratha workers. The Kannada leaders wish to keep the border controversy outside the district party organization and, therefore, will in practice recruit only those Marathi speakers who

[8] Three of the seven sitting Congress MLAs were not given tickets in 1962. Generally from one-third to one-half of the sitting members of parliament and state assemblies in the Congress party are not given tickets. There is thus an extraordinarily high turnover of parliamentarians in India. In some states as many as half of the MLAs are new even though there has been little change in the distribution of seats among the various parties.

support the Kannada position. So long, therefore, as the DCC is a party to the dispute, every effort will be made to maintain its Kannada complexion throughout the district — even in the predominantly Marathi-speaking areas.

## Socialization

There is very little training of workers in any formal sense. Some of the party workers have attended state-wide or national party camps, but these camps are often viewed by the workers as recognition for the work they have done for the party rather than as opportunities for training. Moreover, many members of the party, as we have already suggested and will show in greater detail, seek to achieve their own purposes by being members of the party and have little commitment to the party's program or to the party itself. But the party does have a hard core of loyal supporters, mostly older men but including a number of younger people as well, who in both an emotional and a programmatic sense are attached to the party.

In part, however, socialization to the performance of roles within the party is achieved by experience, not by formal training. Younger men work closely with some of the older party workers. Those who work in the cooperatives, for example, soon learn the rudiments of their job from some of the older, more experienced hands. It is beyond the scope of this study to explore the extent to which those who work with cooperatives, local government bodies, and community development programs are doing a competent job. But in passing we might observe here that many of the local Congress workers are remarkably well informed on the conditions in the areas in which they operate. Indeed, the expertise with respect to local conditions which one used to find among senior government officials in the collector's office in the districts has been rapidly diminishing, while the knowledge of local politicians has been increasing. As developmental work is increasingly being shifted to local bodies and away from administrative agencies, it is only natural that the skills shift as well. One does, however, find that officials of the local revenue department are still better informed about local conditions than are administrators involved in developmental work. This is related to many factors, though one obvious factor may be of greatest importance — that personnel in the developmental administration travel through the villages speedily in Jeeps, while revenue officials are still required to use bicycles to move around the district.

Since the MLAs, MLCs, and the party bosses deal constantly with local

grievances, and because they must depend upon the villagers for votes and local merchants for financial support, they go to great pains to maintain local contact. It was widely said, even by Congressmen, that the Congress MLA elected in Chikodi constitutency in 1957 was defeated by a Samiti-supported independent in 1962 largely because he failed to maintain continuous contact with his voters. In contrast, the independent victor of 1962 (who was the defeated candidate of 1957) had spent the intervening years "servicing" the voters.

The opportunities for MPs to maintain continuous local contact are not great. A good part of their time in office must be spent in New Delhi. Moreover, the services which they can perform for the constituencies are few. There are no large industries or commercial crops in Belgaum district with which the central government is involved. Most of the concerns of voters involve district administration or state administration or policy, almost never the central government. As a result there are no strong forces at work to support the MPs, as there are in support of the MLAs. Congress lost the Chikodi parliamentary seat in 1957 to a candidate of the Scheduled Caste Federation and won the Belgaum seat with only 51.8 per cent of the vote. In 1962 the Chikodi MP decided to stand for the Belgaum seat instead, since his strongest supporter in 1957, an independent MLA, had joined Congress and was now standing for the Chikodi seat. But the Belgaum Congressman again won, this time with 53.6 per cent of the vote.

The Belgaum Congressman, Mr. Datar, is an elderly pre-independence nationalist leader, a pleader by occupation, an intensely religious man, and a Brahmin. In 1957 he became a minister of state for home affairs in the central government. Partly because of his age (seventy years) but also because he is a minister in New Delhi (where he maintains year-long residence), he is unable to devote much of his time to the constituency; local Congressmen were not energetic supporters during the 1962 elections.

Though party workers have learned a great deal about the way in which they should perform their roles within the party, it is important to note that a large part of the work is done by men who would perform these roles whether or not they were party workers. We have suggested that the tradition of men of power arbitrating local disputes is an old one and that many of the landowners who now perform this role as Congressmen did so in the past as non-party local leaders. Similarly, a substantial amount of the constructive work of local Congressmen is essentially philanthropic work, carried on in the past by wealthy local men. Moreover, the expediting role of local Congressmen predates the Congress party. Whether under the rule of the maharajas or the British, local inamdars, watandars, and large land-

owners generally looked after their own interests and those of the general locality in which they lived or the community to which they belonged. Since many of these men were kulkarnis or patils or belonged to such families, they developed considerable experience in local government and in conducting the day-to-day negotiations with higher levels of political authority. We have noted that patils, gaudas, inamdars, watandars, and their descendants are invariably in the local Congress party. They have all the confidence and expertise of men who have influenced local administration in the past, and they are psychologically and politically capable of adapting themselves to any new patterns of administration established by government.

Most of the role requirements of the local Congress party (organizational work excepted) are thus those which in the main can be easily filled by men of property, wealth, and local power, for traditional experience lends itself remarkably easily to the requirements of the local party. Here, then, is clearly a case where traditional experience lends itself well — for the moment at least — to the solution of a modern problem.

# 14. SOURCES OF POWER: TWO CASES

Thus far we have indicated, on a district-wide basis, something of the kinds of people who are being recruited into the party, the roles which they perform, and the ways in which they have been socialized into these roles. We have referred to some of the sources of power of local Congressmen but have not examined these sources in any systematic way. It is to this latter problem that we shall now turn.

Power within Belgaum district is typically localized. A man may wield considerable power in one part of the district but be without influence in another. We have already pointed out that the president of the District Congress Committee was defeated when he stood for an assembly seat in a constituency next to the one in which he lives, but five years later he was able to win in his own constituency. Given this localized power situation, it is necessary that we describe power at a level lower than that of the district organization. We turn to the taluka, not because it is *the* unit of local power, but because it is one of the more important units. The talukas have their own local boards which are responsible for a certain amount of development activity within the area; there are taluka-wide cooperatives of some importance; in some instances, the taluka is also an assembly constituency; and, most critical, the taluka is a revenue and administrative unit of the state government and of the district administration. Both the mamlatdar (the local officer in charge of development activities, generally assigned to the taluka board) and the tahsildar (the local officer responsible for the maintenance of land records and the collections of land revenues) are the two most powerful government officers in the taluka. Finally, the taluka Congress committee is, for all practical purposes, the smallest func-

tioning unit of the party. With few exceptions the smaller mandal units do not function, whereas there is a sense of camaraderie among the taluka workers. Most important, local people regard the taluka as a kind of natural political unit; almost all discussions about local government, the general elections, struggles for control over the District Congress Committee, and the like treat the taluka as a unit, just as discussions at the state level treat the district as a unit.

We have selected two talukas for closer examination. They are among four taluka organizations in Belgaum district studied by the author. One taluka, Khanapur, was selected because it lies in the disputed region containing a large Marathi-speaking population, and an examination of this taluka throws some light on how the Congress party functions and survives in the midst of a linguistic dispute. The second taluka, Ramdurg, is in a Kannada area, and it is selected because it is made up largely of former princely states later merged into the district. An examination of this taluka throws some light on the way in which the area was politically integrated into the district as well as on the important role played by the landowning class in the party organization.

## Khanapur

The struggle for the rolling hills, forests, and paddy lands of the small taluka of Khanapur (population, 99,000; area, 675 square miles) grew with intensity after 1952. In the election of that year, a local Congress leader won the assembly seat with 44.8 per cent of the vote against 41.4 per cent for the candidate of the Peasants and Workers party. In the 1957 elections, with the same candidates, the Peasants and Workers party soundly defeated Congress with a vote of 67.3 per cent to 32.7 per cent. In the 1962 elections the sitting Peasants and Workers candidate was returned with 63.2 per cent against a Congress vote of 36.8 per cent.[1] Since only 34 per cent of the population of the taluka is Kannada-speaking, it appears that the Kannada vote is solidly for Congress while the remaining population (54 per cent Marathi and a scattering of Konkoni and Urdu speakers) supports the Peasants and Workers party demand for joining Maharashtra. This is generally the picture, but there are some interesting variations; an

[1] The Khanapur election results for state assembly are as follows:

|  | 1952* | | 1957 | | 1962 | |
|---|---|---|---|---|---|---|
| Congress | 18,264 | 44.8% | 12,822 | 32.7% | 14,614 | 36.8% |
| Samiti | 16,856 | 41.4% | 26,401 | 67.3% | 24,162 | 63.2% |

*In the 1952 elections, a KMPP candidate won 3,433 votes (8.4 per cent) and a Communist 2,204 votes (5.4 per cent).

examination of these variations provides us with an opportunity to explore the structure of power in the taluka.

In 1959–60 the Khanapur taluka committee reported that there were fifty active members of the Congress party in the taluka, six of whom were in Khanapur town. This compared with forty-five active members in 1952–53, of whom sixteen were in the town. During these seven years there-

TABLE 26

CONGRESS PARTY WORKERS IN KHANAPUR TALUKA

| | 1952–53 | | 1959–60 | |
|---|---|---|---|---|
| | Number of Workers | Percentage | Number of Workers | Percentage |
| *Residence* | | | | |
| Town . . . . . . . | 16 | 35.5 | 6 | 12.0 |
| Rural . . . . . . | 29 | 64.5 | 44 | 88.0 |
| Total. . . . . . | 45ᵃ | . . . | 50ᵇ | . . . |
| *Occupation* | | | | |
| Business . . . . . | 17 | 37.7 | 14 | 28.0 |
| Agriculture . . . . | 23 | 51.0 | 28 | 56.0 |
| Other . . . . . . | 5ᶜ | 11.3 | 8ᵈ | 16.0 |

ᵃAverage age: 37.1.

ᵇAverage age: 39.7.

ᶜFour employed by others and one teacher.

ᵈOne employee, one carpenter, one teacher, one pleader, two persons in village industries, and two who listed themselves simply as "Congress workers."

fore, the active membership shifted almost entirely into the rural areas, and the Marathi-speaking membership of the party withdrew almost completely. Table 26 indicates some of the changes which took place during this period.

Table 26 shows the marked drop in town membership, a small decrease in number of businessmen, and a corresponding increase in the number of agriculturalists and other occupations. Indeed, a closer examination of the occupational background of the rural membership actually shows an increase in number of individuals engaged in businesses in the rural areas. Of the twenty-nine members from rural areas in 1952–53, only four were businessmen, while twenty-two were in agriculture. In 1952 only three of those not in agriculture and business (one teacher, two employees) lived in the rural areas, while in 1959–60 all of those in other occupations were rural-based. A shift in the strength of Congress from urban to rural areas and the growth within the rural areas of occupational diversity are the most notable changes within the taluka; though to some extent these

changes reflect a loss in Maratha support, they have also occurred in other parts of the district where the linguistic conflict is absent.

Most leadership within the district is highly localized or particularized — that is, a man may have influence within a group of villages, a single caste, or perhaps only a faction within a village. But within the district and within the taluka there has also developed a network of administrative agencies associated with developmental activities, and influence upon these bodies is a new and growing source of power. Side by side, therefore, with the more traditional sources of power is a new source, and it is often the interconnection between these two that provides much of the dynamics of politics within the taluka. We shall therefore briefly describe three types of leaders within this single taluka, each based upon a different source of power: power in administration, power as a landowner, and power within a caste.

## Power in Administration

Perhaps the most influential Congressman in the taluka is Mr. Aragavi, who from 1958 to 1960 was president of the District Congress Committee and thereafter the vice-president. He was born in Nandgad village, where he still resides. He has a large family of eleven children, six of whom are sons. ("If I had known anything about family planning in those days, I would not have had such a large family.") He is a dealer in food grains, particularly rice, and is also a contractor for the public works department. ("When my family grew large, I took to being a contractor.") He left secondary school at the age of sixteen to work in his father's business, and almost immediately became active in Congress politics. He participated in the nationalist agitations of 1930, 1941, and 1942 and spent three years in jail as a consequence of his political activity. In 1942 he was elected president of the Belgaum District Local Board. For a brief time as a young boy he, with friends and relations in Nandgad, supported the non-Brahmin movement; but when Gandhi visited Nandgad village in 1921 on one of his tours, Aragavi and many others were attracted to the nationalist cause. The non-Brahmins were then under the influence of the Maharaja of Kolhapur. Mr. Aragavi is a Kannada-speaking Lingayat. Around 1921 the non-Brahmin movement grew in the Marathi area, while many of the Lingayats were already being attracted to the nationalist movement ("A few people wanted leadership and they wanted a platform, so they started this non-Brahmin movement"). The government created the taluka Local Board as the main

agency of local self-government in the late 1920's; from then on, the Lingayats and Marathas alternated in control. In 1961 the Local Board was replaced by an elected taluka Development Board. Today the taluka Development Board is controlled by nine Ekikaran Samiti, who outnumber the six Congressmen. ("Of the six Congressmen, there are two Marathas, one Harijan, and three Lingayats. Of the nine Samiti members, eight are Marathas and one is a Brahmin lady. This shows you that the Samiti is a caste movement of the Marathas.")

Since it is the policy of government to encourage the growth of cooperative societies as part of its development program, there is a cooperative society in nearly every village in Khanapur taluka. Within the district as a whole there were 1,161 cooperatives in 1961, about seventy of which are in this taluka. About sixty of these are credit societies, and four or five are industrial cooperatives. There is also a Khanapur Taluka Agricultural Produce Marketing Society which services the entire taluka. All of the cooperatives in the district are affiliated with the District Central Cooperative Bank in Belgaum, and the industrial cooperatives are in addition affiliated with the District Industrial Cooperative Bank. Mr. Aragavi is chairman of the Khanapur Taluka Agricultural Produce Marketing Society, and since 1950 has been chairman of the District Industrial Cooperative Bank.

The marketing society not only undertakes the marketing of agricultural produce but also provides marketing finance and, of great importance, the wholesale distribution of fertilizers. It also provides several warehouses, built with governmental assistance, for the storage of produce. The District Industrial Cooperative Bank (which has 253 member cooperatives) provides credit for many small-scale and cottage industries in the district. All credit from the reserve bank and from governmental departments is funneled through these and other cooperative societies. Since there is a shortage of low interest credit from the cooperatives, and those who fail to get credit from this source must borrow money from high-interest private money lenders, control over these bodies is of extraordinary local importance. Mr. Aragavi thus has access to, if not control over, important institutions in the fields of agricultural marketing and industrial finance.

His influence also extends into the field of education. While primary schools are run entirely by the government, secondary schools are privately run with government financing. There are three secondary schools in Khanapur taluka, each servicing a different ethnic group. St. Paul's, in the town of Khanapur, services the small Christian community; the Maratha Mandal, also in Khanapur, services the Marathi-speaking community; and the Nandgad Rural Education Society school, in the large village of

Nandgad, services the Kannada speakers. The society was founded by Mr. Aragavi in 1945, and he has remained chairman ever since. "Are your activities largely confined to the Kannada-speaking community?" I asked.

> Not at all. I have more contact with the Marathi people than I have with the Kannada people, and certainly more contact than any of the Samiti people. In the cooperatives I work with both people. The linguistic problem was started by these Samiti people. Actually, the election here was not on the language issue, but people voted for their own caste. In the eastern portions of the taluka, the Marathas speak Kannada and they voted for the Samiti too. Maybe 40 per cent of the people here belong to the Maratha community, 15 or 20 per cent are Muslims, 5 per cent are Christians, and maybe 20 per cent or less are Lingayats. Kannada students speak Marathi, but the Marathi people will not speak Kannada even if they know it.

A local Congress politician interjected, "Everyone knows that the Marathas, the Sikhs, and the Bengalis are the ferocious people in India." Has this controversy affected development work?

> Yes. The CD block was started here in 1958. Mr. Biraje (the Samiti MLA) would not cooperate. But the work has gone on anyway. The cooperatives are all working in spite of the controversy. Actually, the Samiti has no organization. It arises only during the elections.

Are there any disadvantages in having the Samiti control the taluka board?

> Yes. If there is a good chairman, then he approaches the government and he gets more money and more schemes for the taluka. But if he just sits there and signs the papers, then not much is done.

He spoke of the land situation in the taluka:

> Few landlords have lost their land as a result of the tenancy act. There are few landlords here since this was a raiyatwari area. Watandars were there but they were few in

number and didn't have much land. Now they cultivate their land. Yes, landlords did take possession of the land from some tenants, but they had to give some of their land to the tenants. . . . There aren't many landless agricultural laborers here, perhaps only 20 or 25 per cent of the population.

## Power through Control over Land

Mrs. W., the defeated Congress candidate in 1962, is a Marathi-speaking Brahmin and the wife of a prominent landowner in the taluka. The family, along with others who share the same surname, come from a village of that name in Goa. In the middle of the nineteenth century when disturbances took place inside Goa, they left their business and land to migrate to neighboring Khanapur taluka where they became kulkarnis. "In return for being kulkarnis [village accountants] the government gave us watan land. We could earn rent from it, but could not sell it without government permission. We have about 100 acres. Up till recently when the tenancy act was passed, some tenants tilled it. Now we till it ourselves." Do you or members of your family actually work in the fields? "No, we have it tilled by monthly laborers. We give them the bullocks and seeds. We sold some of our land to tenants. We have left our work as kulkarnis, but we retain the watan land as our own land. We had to pay something to the government."

How do you feel about the language issue? Should Khanapur remain in Mysore?

> We want to be loyal to the government. We are Brahmins, and we want to be loyal. We were loyal to the British and received honors. My husband was a Rao Sahib. We will be loyal to Mysore or to Maharashtra. Some people in my family want to be with Maharashtra, so on this issue there are some differences. But we want our minority interests to be protected.

What rights do you want to protect? Do you include your land rights? She answered obliquely: "As compared to Maharashtra, tenancy laws in Mysore are more convenient as far as the rights of landlords are concerned." Who are the other landholders here and how do they feel?

> Mr. Swami. He is a Marathi Brahmin. He is religious and has no political views. Mr. Rao Deshpande. He is a Brahmin,

with Congress. He says he must be at one with the government and the party as we do. He is indifferent on the language
issue, but he supports Congress. Mr. Damle. He supported
the Samiti for a while, but now he is with Swatantra and is
indifferent on this issue. He is also a Brahmin. Mr. Desai. He
is a Maratha landowner. He is with the Samiti. The smaller
Marathi-speaking landowners are with the Samiti.

Were all the landholders here kulkarnis?

Mostly. The system of patils and kulkarnis was abolished.
Now the talatis [the new name for kulkarnis] and the patils
are appointed by the government. Watan land was given to
us by the government after we paid some sum. Rao Deshpande was a big inamdar. He was given land by the British
government for supporting them. The kulkarnis are all Brahmins, and most of the patils are non-Brahmins, Lingayats,
or Marathas.

Was the non-Brahmin movement strong here?

Mr. Hosmani [a Lingayat landowner] and Mr. Desai, [the
Maratha landowner] were their leaders. At one time the Brahmin kulkarnis controlled the villages because of their position
in the government. And they are intelligent. The kulkarni was
the only literate man in the village. Not even the patils were
literate. The non-Brahmin movement came here from Kolhapur. It was here until 1936; then Congress got it. The patils
were the pioneers in this movement. They were led by Aragavi, and before that by H. Naik [a Kannada man] and
Pitre [Marathi]. They were both Brahmins. Aragavi and
Sandikop [both Lingayats] came later — after 1930 I think.
Few Marathas came into Congress here. Mostly they stayed
in the non-Brahmin party. Even now they are in the Peasants
and Workers party.

Would you lose your land if this area became part of Maharashtra? She
again answered obliquely: "The ceiling legislation hasn't affected the rights
of the Kannada landowners here." Why? "There are few landowners who
have more than the ceiling." And if you join Bombay?

The Samiti says that if this area goes to Maharashtra, then the tenants will get the land. So naturally tenants vote for the Samiti. There is no language question here. The Samiti, PSP, and Communists say that the tillers should be owners of the soil. That's not possible. Widows cannot cultivate the land, so she must give it to tenants. We are not big landlords here. No one owns more than a hundred acres. They say that tenants have been paying rent so the land now belongs to them, but how can that be?

*Power in a Caste*

The jump in the vote of the Samiti candidate from 41.4 per cent to 67.3 per cent between 1952 and 1957 was clearly a consequence of the language dispute. Though the Samiti — or more precisely, the Peasants and Workers party, and before that the non-Brahmin party — has been active in Khanapur since the early 1920's, it declined in importance from 1937 to 1952. Once the Lingayats, who constitute such a substantial block of voters even in Khanapur, joined the Congress party, Congress became the dominant force in the taluka. Though Marathas generally stayed outside Congress, other Marathi speakers, Christians, Muslims, and even some Maratha voters gave their support to the Congress movement. In the 1952 elections, before the taluka was transferred to Mysore, Congress was able to win a substantial vote in the Marathi-speaking areas.

Congressmen have argued with some force that the vote is not exclusively along language lines. Mr. Biraje, the Samiti candidate is a Maratha, and his strongest appeal is to members of his own community. "There is a general presumption here," said one Congressman, "that Lingayats are Kannada-speaking and Marathas are Marathi-speaking, but that is not always so. Many Marathas are Kannada-speaking, and they will vote for Biraje. So caste counts here more than language."

Biraje was a primary school teacher in the taluka for twenty years. He resigned as a school teacher to run against the Congress candidate in 1952. He is a small landholder. "Biraje's brother got some waste land from the government," spoke Congressmen caustically. "Biraje approached the government to get it. Then they cut for firewood and earned ten thousand rupees. Then they rented the land to another party to cultivate it. But Biraje tells people not to take help from government. He tells villagers not to pay revenue to government."

Congressmen speak bitterly of Biraje's ability to appeal to caste and language at a time when the Congress is actively pursuing a development program in the taluka. "The Marathi MLAs ask no question in the assembly," said one young Congress leader. "They are not interested in any development work — only the language issue. Our Congressmen go to the officials to get work done for the public. But the Marathi people do not visit the villages. They only approach the masses during the elections. The Marathi people unite during the elections and do not care about what constructive work has been done. Aragavi [the Congress leader] has always worked for the Marathi people; but when he ran for the assembly, communalism worked against him."

A statistical breakdown of voting patterns by language is not available, but the over-all voting figures provide inferential evidence that neither the patronage-service orientation of Congressmen nor, in some instances, their control over land successfully bridges the language gap. Though a few upper-class Marathi landlords — especially those who are Brahmin — are moved more by their economic interests than by their linguistic loyalties, the bulk of the Marathi-speaking population is obviously opposed to Congress. Moreover, as we have already noted, identification with the Maratha caste has grown to such an extent in recent times that only caste identification makes inroads into linguistic identification. Nonetheless, while a few Marathi-speaking landlords support Congress, there is no evidence that these landlords are able to retain the electoral support; after all, the Marathi-speaking Brahmin landlord who was the Congress candidate in the 1962 elections was soundly defeated. Clearly, among the Marathi-speaking tenants and agricultural laborers loyalty to one's community has proved more politically significant than loyalty to a landlord.

But before we conclude that landlords are without influence among lower-class voters, let us turn to an examination of Ramdurg taluka.

## Landlords in Ramdurg

The power wielded by the princes who controlled territory in Ramdurg taluka before independence was completely replaced by the power of local landowners. The taluka was created after independence out of some villages in the British-administered sections of the district, some thirty-six villages of Kolhapur state, and all of the former princely state of Ramdurg (thirty-three villages and Ramdurg town). Administratively, all these areas were merged and placed under direct Indian administration in

1948. Politically, the area was integrated when local nationalists and some local people who had not been in the nationalist movement joined the Congress party in Belgaum district.

In the first election of 1952 a substantial section of the old Ramdurg nationalists who had joined Congress withdrew from the Congress party to support their own assembly candidate when Congress nominated some-one from an area which had been part of British India. Nonetheless, Congress swept the assembly seat with 19,078 votes (65.5 per cent) against the dissident Congressman's 10,049 (34.5 per cent). In 1957, Congress again named an assembly candidate from outside the old princely area and in fact nominated the president of the District Congress Committee who lived outside the constituency. Another dissident Congressman, a Mr. Pattan, a prominent Lingayat merchant with considerable local influence in a substantial group of villages in old Ramdurg, was able to defeat the Congressman by a vote of 17,212 (58.6 per cent) to 12,147 (41.4 per cent). He appealed to local sentiment against an outsider. Moreover, as a Lingayat in an area in which more than a quarter of the population is Lingayat, he was able to appeal to his castemen against the Reddi running on the Congress ticket.

There was much competition within the Congress party for the ticket in 1962. The taluka Congress committee was unable to make a unanimous recommendation and so forwarded a list of names to the District Congress Committee. The DCC, after much discussion, decided to give the ticket to R. S. Patil, a young man in his early thirties, a large landowner, and one of the few educated men in the taluka. His name was approved by the Mysore Pradesh Congress Committee. He fought in one of the more intense elections in the Kannada region of the district and won the seat for Congress by a vote of 19,287 against the incumbent independent MLA, who lost with 16,849 votes. Though like the defeated Congress candidate of 1957 Patil is a Reddi, he was an insider, being a resident of Ramdurg town, the capital of the old princely state.[2]

Both the independent opposition and the Congress party derive their strength from the well-to-do landlord and business community in Ramdurg taluka. The taluka itself is extraordinarily poor. The main crops are jowar, wheat, ground nut, and cotton, but production of none of these items is

[2] The assembly struggles in 1957 and 1962 had a direct effect on the parliamentary vote within Ramdurg. In 1957 the Congress candidate (who carried the parliamentary seat) lost in Ramdurg by a vote of 12,940 against 13,318 for a PSP candidate endorsed by the powerful independent candidate for the assembly. But in 1962 the incumbent Congress candidate won with 19,837 against the independent endorsed candidates of the Republican party (a party of scheduled castes), who won 17,722 votes.

particularly high. Jowar, which is planted on more than half the acreage in the taluka, was harvested at three hundred pounds to the acre according to crop cutting estimates in 1956; this was the lowest productivity in the district (elsewhere in the district jowar varied from four hundred to 1,050 pounds to the acre and averaged about six hundred pounds, or twice that of the Ramdurg average).[3] The taluka suffers from severe drought and has frequently been declared a famine area.

No taluka-wide data are available on landownership, but local people report that a substantial part of the land is held by large landowners. As we have reported elsewhere in this study, 5 per cent of those who own land in the entire district (less than 2½ per cent of the population) own one-third of the land. The proportion is probably higher in Ramdurg. The Congress assembly candidate admits owning four hundred acres of land. Still another local Congressman reported that he too owns four hundred acres. The husband of the Congress MLC owns 120 acres of land and was formerly an inamdar under the Maharaja of Kolhapur. Some local holdings are reported to be as large as one thousand and even two thousand acres.

It is particularly remarkable that even within the local party organization there are men who are openly critical of the landlords. "The tenancy act is not enforced at all here," said the former president of the taluka Congress committee, a local pleader and one of the few important Congressmen who is not a large landowner. "The local landlords here control the tahsildar [the local revenue official], and many of them are prominent Congressmen. They have dispossessed many tenants. There is Mr. P., one of the biggest landlords with 800 acres." How did he get so much land? From the maharaja? "No, he is a Lingayat who had business, and gradually he purchased more and more land. The maharaja sold most of his land and has moved to Bijapur. . . ." He pointed to a man in the room. "Mr. K. there has four hundred acres. He cultivated with hired labor but pays wages on a yearly contract. He provides the workers with implements and seeds. He fixed up the land records. That's why he still has so much land." Why don't the tenants fight back? "The tenants don't put up a battle. Hindus do not want to covet the property of others. It is the effect of our religion. . . . These Congressmen publicly support the legislation. They say they are for socialism, but then they privately look after their own interests."

The local club is a symbol of the concentrated power in Ramdurg. The club was started before independence by the local maharaja. Residents

[3] Unpublished data kindly provided by the district agricultural officer, Belgaum.

may join for fifty rupees a year. The club now includes all the important local doctors, pleaders, and landlords. In the early morning before the rays of the sun are too strong, members play a couple of sets of badminton. At the end of one game we spoke with two of the members, both large land-owners, one of whom was a powerful inamdar, the other a prominent Congressman. They were asked to describe the effects of the tenancy act. The inamdar spoke first.

> The act strains relations between tenants and landlords. Now the tenant goes to court for many little things which we used to settle amiably. I feel that the act is one-sided in favor of the tenant, but I doubt if it really helps him. Some landlords have sold their land to the tenants, but the tenants still cannot pull on without the landlords.

Have landlords taken land from the peasants?

> There is a provision in the act permitting the landlord to take title from the tenant, but there are so many difficulties in doing this. There are also provisions giving tenants rights over the land. Recently section 32 was suspended giving tenants right to take land or landlord to take possession. Before the act was passed there was unity between tenant and landlord, but that relation is now gone away. The landlord used to give some concessions when rent had to be paid or in other ways help the tenant. Now tenants are worried that landlords will take possession, so they do not invest in the land. They won't develop the land, so there is a decrease in production. We have had four years of famine now when the government has given half suspension [that is, a reduction in the collection of land revenue]. In the last twenty years we have had only one good year.

Aren't there irrigation facilities here?

> There is some irrigation here, but people don't know how to use it with the proper drainage. In some places the peasants have just flooded their fields without proper drainage. So the water stagnates and the crops are ruined, or else the salts come up and the produce fails. Our agriculturalists

are ignorant of this work. They do not know how to use the new irrigation. There has been no time to go from dry to irrigated crops.

What about the agricultural officers and the village level workers?

There is only one agricultural officer in the entire taluka and about ten gram sevaks, but they are ignorant of their own work. Some are good and helpful, but they don't know much about agriculture through experience — one or two maybe.

What does the Congress party here do to improve living conditions? The local Congressman spoke of their work in starting cooperatives.

People here still fear government. They feel that if government does something for them, then later the government will take something from them. They don't have much confidence in other people. Our villagers don't go out of their village much. Maybe they visit three or four other villages in their life at the most. They have no occasion to visit the towns or travel much. As a result they are shortsighted, and if help is offered they suspect it."

The inamdar spoke.

In my village I wanted to help them start a kumbul [wool weavers'] society and to put up half the share capital, but they would not trust me. They thought that it would be in my interest — the interest of the inamdar. But just a few years ago they finally started such a society. And now it runs very well. It takes wool from the producer and gives it to the weaver. The weaver then makes his kumbul [blanket] and brings it to the society, where he is paid cash immediately. He doesn't have to go to the bazaar to sell it. The society purchases it, fixes a price, and then sells it in the bazaar. The society hires merchants to sell it. The point is that the weaver gets his cash immediately and doesn't have to sell his work at any price because he desperately needs cash. Now they say that it would have been better if they had formed the society years earlier when I was willing to help.

The Congressman generalized:

> Actually there is more cooperation in this area since some representative form of government was established. The old maharaja did nothing here, so people knew nothing about government affairs. They had no experience, so it takes longer to make schemes work here than in other parts of the district.

Local Congressmen then described the schemes in the taluka. They praised the help government has given to develop the kumbul industry and the rope industry in the villages. Government, they said, has been subsidizing the production of handloom and khadi, and there are also societies to help the potters in the villages. Is the concern of the local party and local people with increasing productivity or with getting more facilities for the village? The Congressman spoke again.

> We need more wells here to irrigate the land. Otherwise how can we produce more? But the main work of the overseer now is to watch over the construction of all the new Block Development buildings going up, so he doesn't have time to watch over the construction of wells. Peasants get taccavi [loans], but they often build wells in the wrong place. They don't get enough technical advice from the officers. The officers don't give so much attention to agricultural development. The officers point to the new buildings and the schemes you can see, but it's hard to point to the fields and say there has been an increase in production.

Local Congressmen do not blame the land system for the low level of productivity within the taluka. Nor does the government Block Development officer, though he too agrees that, with the exception of a few villages, interest in development work is low. The psychological effects of living under the maharaja's rule was frequently referred to. One Congressman noted, "Our people want to remain poor"; and the Block Development officer complained, "We plant trees, but no one takes care of them."

Nonetheless, the two local assembly representatives, the MLAs and MLCs are deeply involved in local developmental activities. Mrs. Nimbalkar, the MLC, is an active woman social worker and the wife of a former inamdar.

"There has been a division of land," she said, "so the tenancy act has had no effect [on us]." A photo of her husband dressed elaborately as an inamdar attending the durbar ceremony of the Maharaja of Kolhapur was prominently displayed in her village home. Her husband is a member of the Agricultural Produce Marketing Committee in Ramdurg which regulates the price of agricultural commodities by supervising local auctions. Mrs. Nimbalkar has been active in local affairs since 1945 or 1946 and was elected to the District School Board in 1952.

The local MLA, though only in his early thirties, is already a member of the District Central Cooperative Bank and the Agricultural Produce Marketing Committee. He has four brothers, who look after the four hundred acres of land owned by the family. "Well, the family was taking care of the lands," he said when asked why he took to politics, "so I had nothing to do and therefore went into politics." That was in 1956–57.

Both the MLA and the MLC, along with several other local Congressmen, have close ties with the Block Development officer. Whenever there are local development needs, the Congressmen raise the matter with the officer or sometimes go directly to the collector's office in Belgaum. Since interest in agriculture is relatively low, both on the part of the peasantry as well as on the part of the Block Development officer, greater attention is paid to the development of small-scale industries of one kind or another. In a tour of Hulkund village, a model village for the BDO, great pride was shown in the new carpentry shop where ambar charkhas (which spin cotton) are repaired, the small shop where about a dozen women spin cotton on the charka, several handlooms, and a sales emporium where khadi is sold. The village also has recently acquired a pre-school nursery, a compound for keeping stray animals, and a new primary school building. The village has a number of local landlords who are active in village and taluka affairs. They are in firm control of the panchayat since there has been no contested election in the village. In the general elections well over 75 per cent of the village votes for the Congress candidate.

Although there has been much recruitment into the taluka Congress organization in Ramdurg, there has been no fundamental change in the power structure. In 1959 there were more businessmen in the party then in 1952, for as elsewhere in the district there has been some influx of rural and small-town merchants into the party. The membership of agriculturalists has increased, but there is no indication that there is much recruitment outside the landowning class. Because of the creation of the kumbul societies a number of members of the weaving caste — the kurubas — have joined

the party.[4] The party in Ramdurg clearly reflects the local distribution of power. The party makes no attempt to change that distribution; but, on the other hand, for the time being there is within the taluka no threat to the prevailing power structure. Though all three general elections in the constituency have been hotly contested, the struggle has been within the land-owning groups. For these landowners, membership in the party is a necessary step for preserving their positions of power against the inroads of state legislation. Paradoxically, the restrictions imposed on merchants have not turned these classes against the government but, to the contrary, have provided a powerful motivation for joining the governing party.

In matters that are of crucial importance to them — control over land — these men exercise overwhelming influence on local officials. They have no objection to the government's development program, for it in no way threatens their positions of power. In fact, they readily share in the work of the Block Development officers; they are ready and willing to form co-operatives; they would welcome the growth of small-scale cottage industries; they press for more wells and irrigation channels; when necessary, they give financial support to help finance village schools, roads, and the panchayat halls. None of these activities threatens their positions of power. Indeed, their positions are strengthened by participating in the work of the government and of the party.

Communication and trade from one village to another and from the villages to the small town of Ramdurg are so limited that villagers are hardly aware of the larger economic and political developments taking place in the district as a whole, much less the state and nation. Although there are five mandal committees in the taluka and in 1962 seventy members who were officially considered active, plus about four thousand primary members, party loyalties are not very deep. Moreover, the low level of participation in community development activities also limits the effectiveness of the party. It is no accident that Congress is strongest in the few

[4] There were forty active members in Ramdurg in 1952 and seventy-six in 1959–1960, as follows.

|  | 1952 | 1959–60 |
| --- | --- | --- |
| rural | 38 | 64 |
| townsmen | 2 | 12 |
| average age | 36.7 | 37.1 |
| *occupations* |  |  |
| agriculture | 34 | 52 |
| business | 2 | 13* |
| doctors | 3 | 2 |
| pleaders | 1 | 2 |
| students | 0 | 2 |
| weavers | 0 | 5 |

*Includes one local contractor

villages where the community development program has had the greatest success. Hulkund village, for example, which we referred to earlier, is not in old Ramdurg but in a village which had been in British-administered territory. Not only had there been substantial nationalist activities in the village before independence, but there are several substantial landowners and merchants who have sent their sons to college and in one instance even to the United States.

Many of the villages in old Ramdurg have still not been affected, psychologically at least, by the new level of paternalistic administrative activities. Powerful local landowners who chose to remain out of the party can elicit much local support; the Congress party is not so well developed that it can always break into this highly localized, highly particularized power structure. If one landlord with nine or ten villages under his control can bring with him some other men of local power — and this in effect took place in the 1957 and 1962 elections — it is possible and has been possible to beat the Congress party candidate, for the Congress party in Ramdurg taluka is itself just such a collection of local men of power. They work within the Congress party and with the government in much the same way that many of them worked with the former princes. A few of the landlords opposed the maharaja, but the leadership of the anti-maharaja movement (which in any event did not begin until 1938 in Ramdurg state and in the Kolhapur area in Ramdurg taluka not until about 1945) was largely in the hands of a few local pleaders. In Ramdurg the party is today a vehicle for the protection of the interests of the local landowners.

Yet one cannot say that the local party in Ramdurg or, for that matter, the landowning and business class is in any way politically threatened. For whatever reason — the subsistence level of the economy, the low literacy rate (12 per cent for the combined rural tracts of Gokak and Ramdurg, compared with 15 per cent for the rural areas of the district as a whole), the absence of much internal trade and therefore contact, the persistence of landholding class with more substantial holdings than one finds elsewhere in the district, or the psychological effects of living under the rule of maharajas — the fact is that the lower castes, the landless laborers, the tenants, and even the small landholders have not seen fit to organize themselves in any concerted way. Should they ever do so, they would have to come to terms with the local Congress organization — either by opposing it or, as others have done in the past, by taking control of it and using it as an instrument of their own.

# 15. CONGRESS AND THE SOCIAL ORDER

The president of the Central Cooperative Bank in Belgaum district is a Congressman. The president of the Belgaum District Industrial Bank is a Congressman. The Khadi and Village Industries Board, the District School Board, the District Local Board, and four of the six elected taluka boards are controlled by Congressmen, along with several hundred cooperatives, village panchayats, municipal bodies, and educational institutions. The two members of parliament from Belgaum belong to the Congress party, and so do twelve of the eighteen MLAs and all six members of the Mysore Legislative Council. Congressmen are thus in firm control of the district. But to what extent does the Congress party have firm control over the Congressmen?

At one extreme, one finds within the party organization men who are completely dedicated and loyal to it and thoroughly committed to its program and ideology. Though in the main these are older, pre-independence Congressmen, a few are younger members of the party. At the other extreme are men who join the party to further their own interests and those of their village, caste, or occupational group. As long as the Congress party dominates the state, such men use the party for their own interests. Though in a general way they support development activities and the creation of cooperatives, these activities in no way conflict with their interests and are often advantageous to them. But when necessary they are prepared to leave the party and stand as independent candidates for elections to local bodies, the state assembly, or parliament. Rivalry for Congress tickets in the general elections is therefore bitter, forcing local aspirants to ally themselves with factional leaders of the Congress party at the state level in the

hope that the influence of the chief minister or the president of the Pradesh Congress Committee will ensure them such tickets. Factional conflicts at the state level thus have important repercussions in the district, because local men who fail to achieve power within the party commensurate with their real or imagined power in the community ally themselves with state leaders.

There are far more local men of power than there are seats available in the legislative assembly or in parliament. One man is powerful within his caste; another, a landlord, commands influence in a handful of villages; another landlord carries on extensive local philanthropic activities; another man exercises influence within the cooperatives and banking institutions. Sources of power are many and, moreover, so localized that men often miscalculate on such an important matter as how many votes they are likely to win in an election. Though from twenty thousand to forty thousand voters take part in the assembly elections, there are many independent candidates who receive only a few thousand votes and in several instances only a few hundred. But they remain hopeful because on occasion men of extensive local power have successfully stood as independents to defeat Congress. Many of these independents defected from the Congress when they failed to receive tickets, and subsequently rejoined it.

The district and even the state Congress party leadership believes there is no point in alienating the men of local power, and would for many reasons like to absorb them into the party and offer them seats in the legislatures. With their support, the party can easily win. Without their support, it cannot.

If electoral victory is the party's aim — and it is — there is in fact little choice other than to welcome such men into the party. In Belgaum district the party functions in a political environment in which the interests of the bulk of the population are thus far not articulated. Nearly half a million persons in the district are agricultural laborers and tenants or their dependents. Their literacy and aspirations are apparently low, as is their capacity to express their interests through political action. Indeed, only the landowners — both small and large — and the mercantile community actively engage in political life. They include the Lingayats, Marathas, Brahmins, Jains, Reddis, and Muslims. Largely as a result of the activities of Congressmen in developing cooperatives, some of the kurubars (shepherds) have begun to enter political life in the district, invariably under the guidance and leadership of Congressmen.[1]

[1] A prominent leader of the Mysore State Wool Weavers' Societies — primarily an association of kurubars — is the vice-president of the Belgaum District Congress Committee and himself a kurubar.

There have been conflicts within the district, but these largely involve individual tenants or laborers and their landlords and, as we have noted earlier, are generally arbitrated by local leaders. There has been no massive discontent — least of all in the areas which have regularly experienced famine. One can find in Belgaum district ample evidence for the hypothesis that there is a level of living beneath which it is difficult to sustain modern political organization. As Eric Hoffer has so vividly put it, the poor are too occupied trying to survive to sustain any hope, to have any aspirations, or to create a vision of a better future.

Congress thus recruits its active members and its leaders from the small merchant community, the professionals, and the 5 per cent of the landowning population with more than thirty acres of land. The urban, professional, Brahmin bias of the leadership has over the years gradually shifted to a rural, agricultural, non-Brahmin base. We have already indicated that these men have an extraordinarily high capacity to create and sustain a modern political organization, because the tasks which the organization must perform can be based upon traditional skills. These men were philanthropists, arbitrators in local disputes, and mediators between the cultivators and the administration long before the creation of the Congress party. Even the modern version of patronage — helping a man to get a license or his son to get a job or admission into a local school or college — has its precedents in earlier district activities. The expansion of governmental activities on the district level and the transfer of much power from appointed officials to elected representatives have caused some change in the channels and a considerable increase in scale, but the roles are still very much the same. What is new, however, is the role of party organizer. Here tradition is no guide, and the notions that meetings ought to be held regularly, that records ought to be properly maintained, that some system is necessary for assigning responsibilities to local party workers, and that an election requires a high degree of organization are ones which few workers or leaders understand. But at the moment there is no strong challenge which requires that the organization be modernized, and no one visualizes any such threat in the near future.

The party is threatened only by the language dispute, but even here the controversy is confined to limited portions of the district. The local party has failed to integrate the two major linguistic groups in the district, but the local Kannada leadership has never even attempted to do so. There is some truth to the argument that if the Marathi-speaking community had entered the local Congress party en masse the district might have been partitioned, but the resultant intra-party struggle would surely

have been as intense as the extra-party struggle is now. From the viewpoint of the Kannada political leaders, the loss of Belgaum town to the Maharashtrians would have constituted a severe political, economic, and cultural loss. From the Kannada viewpoint, there was nothing bargainable and therefore nothing was to be gained by recruiting Marathi speakers into the party. The ties of the Maratha community to the anti-nationalist, anti-Brahmin Maharaja of Kolhapur precluded any massive joining of the Congress party until after independence when the language dispute was well under way and the possibility of winning support or power within the local Congress seemed nil. Had the conflict in the district been one of specific administrative policies — what languages should be used in the schools, how many officers of which linguistic group should be posted in the district, and so on — bargaining and therefore a settlement of sorts might have been agreed upon and the Marathi speakers might have entered the party. But once it became clear that the states would be reorganized primarily along linguistic lines, language sentiments became predominant and bitter passions were aroused.

Subsequently, the Kannada-dominated Congress organization could not adapt itself to the demands of the Marathi speakers. Linguistic sentiments within Congress became so great that no concessions could be made. Psychological harassment was intensified on both sides, and Marathi and Kannada speakers were unwilling to speak the other's language, literally and figuratively.

The modernity of the Congress party in Belgaum is only partial. In practice, recruitment is deliberately limited to Kannada speakers or to Marathi speakers who subscribe to the party's position on the border issue. Whereas in the performance of roles the party is able to adapt traditional experiences to the needs of a modern political organization, in its handling of the language controversy the party is a victim of its own traditionality.

TABLE 27

ELECTION RESULTS IN BELGAUM DISTRICT

| PARTY | SEATS WON | | | NUMBER OF VOTES | | | % OF VOTES | | |
|---|---|---|---|---|---|---|---|---|---|
| | 1952 | 1957 | 1962 | 1952 | 1957 | 1962 | 1952 | 1957 | 1962 |
| Legislative Assembly | | | | | | | | | |
| Congress. . | 12 | 7 | 10 | 310,676 | 282,472 | 283,073 | 54.3 | 47.4 | 54.1 |
| Maharashtra Ekikaran Samiti . . | . . | . . | 5 | . . . . | . . . . | 116,368 | . . . . | . . . . | 22.2 |
| Peasant and Workers party . . | 1 | 2 | . . | 51,790 | 35,462 | . . . . | 9.0 | 5.9 | . . . . |
| Republican party(SCF) | . . | . . | . . | 15,153 | 46,365 | 3,125 | 2.7 | 7.5 | 0.5 |
| PSP (formerly KMPP and Socialist) . | . . | . . | . . | 93,354 | 10,204 | 13,438 | 16.3 | 1.7 | 2.5 |
| Other parties | . . | . . | . . | 2,204 | 6,497 | 18,315 | 0.3 | 1.1 | 4.0 |
| Independents | 2 | 8 | 1 | 99,539 | 218,257 | 88,282 | 17.4 | 36.4 | 16.8 |
| Total . . | 15 | 17 | 16 | 572,716 | 601,257 | 522,601 | 100.0 | 100.0 | 100.0 |
| Parliament | | | | | | | | | |
| Congress. . | 2 | 1 | 1 | 252,697 | 232,034 | 287,697 | 55.6 | 50.3 | 56.7 |
| Forward Bloc | . . | . . . | . . | 70,266 | . . . . | . . . . | 15.4 | . . . . | . . . . |
| Jan Sangh . | . . | . . . | . . | . . . . | 57,505 | . . . . | . . . . | 12.5 | . . . . |
| PSP(formerly KMPP and Socialist) . | . . | . . . | . . | 131,901 | 56,408 | . . . . | 29.0 | 12.2 | . . . . |
| Republican (formerly Scheduled Caste Federation) . | . . | 1 | 1 | . . . . | 115,214 | 218,998 | . . . . | 25.0 | 43.3 |
| Total . . | 2 | 2 | 2 | 454,864 | 461,161 | 506,695 | 100.0 | 100.0 | 100.0 |

# APPENDIX 1
## CONGRESS PARTY CADRES IN BELGAUM

From 1952 to 1959 the number of active Congress party members in five of the ten talukas of Belgaum district for which data were available rose from 224 to 512. Accompanying this numerical increase was a profound alteration in the social and ethnic composition of the party, a change reflecting the bitter linguistic controversy which has torn the district. To study these trends, information concerning age, occupation, language, and place of residence was obtained for almost all of the party cadres in 1952 and in 1959. With these four variables, all possible first-order cross-tabulations were made. The significant relationships are discussed below.

*Active party membership.* In each of the five talukas for which data are available on Congress party cadres there has been an increase in membership from 1952 to 1959, but, like so much else in Belgaum, party growth is affected by the language controversy. The largest proportionate increase in party membership (231 per cent) occurred in the most heavily Kannada-speaking area (Gokak), while the smallest (8.9 per cent) took place in the most heavily Marathi-speaking area (Khanapur) (see Table 28).

*Linguistic cleavages.* In 1956 Belgaum district became a part of Mysore state. Consequently, Kannada-speaking cadres, who had made up 53.8 per cent of the active members in the five talukas in 1952, increased their proportion of party activists to 66.7 per cent of the total by 1959. While in 1952 Kannada-speaking cadres were the youngest and Marathis the oldest, the disparity was even greater by 1959, indicating that more young party workers were being recruited in Kannada area.

TABLE 28
GROWTH IN BELGAUM PARTY MEMBERSHIP
1952–59

| Taluka | 1952 Membership | 1959 Membership | % of Growth |
|---|---|---|---|
| Gokak . . . . . . . | 80 | 265 | 231.0 |
| Belgaum . . . . . . | 43 | 93 | 116.0 |
| Ramdurg . . . . . . | 40 | 76 | 90.0 |
| Chikodi. . . . . . | 16 | 29 | 80.0 |
| Khanapur. . . . . . | 45 | 49 | 8.9 |

for Kannada cadres to come increasingly from urban areas (+4.3 per cent).

*Occupations.* In 1952 occupation and language were strongly related, with Marathas more likely to be businessmen and Kannadas much more likely to be in agriculture – a situation which seems entirely consistent with the residential distribution of the two communities. Surprisingly, therefore, in 1959 there were marked changes in this relationship. Marathis were still numerically the largest group of businessmen, though the proportion of Kannada cadres in business had risen slightly, while at the same time the proportion of Marathi businessmen had dropped 24.3 per cent. Similarly, Kannada cadres were still numerically the largest group of agriculturalists, though their percentage of the total for all occupations had dropped somewhat. And, most notable, the proportion of Marathis engaged in agriculture had risen from 6.4 per cent to 50.0 per cent. In 1959 there were no Marathi white-collar workers, while in 1952 they constituted 16.2 per cent of all Marathi cadres. This percentage was offset by a slight rise in the proportion of Kannada-speaking cadres in white-collar professions. These facts seem to indicate that the Marathi cadres in 1959 were

*Urban and rural party cadres.* Differences in recruitment in urban and rural areas are also related to the language dispute. Cadres from Kannada areas are much more likely to be from towns and villages with a popula-

TABLE 29
AGE DISTRIBUTION OF BELGAUM PARTY WORKERS

| Age[a] | 1952 | 1959 | Increase (Per cent) |
|---|---|---|---|
| 20–25. . . . . . . . | 12 | 38 | 216 |
| 26–30. . . . . . . . | 42 | 69 | 40 |
| 31–35. . . . . . . . | 46 | 97 | 110 |
| 36–40. . . . . . . . | 49 | 86 | 75 |
| 41–45. . . . . . . . | 33 | 83 | 150 |
| 46–50. . . . . . . . | 16 | 77 | 380 |
| 51–55. . . . . . . . | 15 | 33 | 112 |
| 56–60. . . . . . . . | 10 | 17 | 70 |
| 61+ . . . . . . . . | 1 | 14 | . . . |

[a]Average age of workers in 1952 was 38.3; in 1959, 39.8

tion of less than five thousand than are the cadres from predominantly Marathi areas. Since Kannada speakers are also the youngest activists, one also finds the youngest party members from rural areas. It seems, however, from comparing 1952 and 1959 data, that there is a slight tendency new recruits from different social strata and that the Kannada cadres, as they move toward more complete control of the party, were becoming more representative of the entire district.

*Age distribution.* Between 1952 and 1959, recruitment into the party was substantial in all age groups. The greatest increase came in the forty-six- to fifty-year-old group, the next greatest in the twenty- to twenty-five-year-old group. Contrary to popular expectation, Congress is remarkably successful at recruiting middle-aged party workers, and as the party has grown the average age of the cadres has increased slightly.

*Congress party officials and elected representatives.* For seventeen MPs, MLAs, and party officials from Belgaum further information was available concerning education and past political and social work. While it is difficult to generalize on the basis of so few cases, we can tentatively conclude that the younger Congressmen differ in several important ways. They have had slightly less education, have done more general political and "constructive" work than older Congressmen, and are less often professionals (doctors, lawyers, teachers). The most significant change is, however, that many younger Congressmen are originally from rural areas and represent rural constituencies, while the older Congressmen are more likely to have urban backgrounds and to represent urban constituencies.

## APPENDIX 2

## A FACTIONLESS VILLAGE — THE CONGRESS PARTY AND DEVELOPMENT

So many accounts have been published of village politics that it is with some hesitation that I add still another. Many of the recent accounts demonstrate that village India is rife with factionalism and caste conflict and that these conflicts are impeding the kind of development activities being pressed by the national government. This account is of an unusual village — one with almost no internal conflict and a great many development activities and which, on the surface at least, corresponds to the national leadership's ideal village. I shall try to describe why there is so little conflict in the village, what kind of development is taking place, and how development comes about.

Our village is called Itagi, and it is located in Khanapur taluka, Belgaum district, in Mysore state on the border of Maharashtra. According to the 1951 census, Itagi had 3,580 residents, of whom about eight hundred were literate. There were approximately six hundred non-cultivating landlords (and dependents), eighteen hundred landowning cultivators, and nearly a thousand tenants and agricultural laborers. The entire population lived in 676 households — about five persons per household.

In 1963 the village population was up to 4,510 in nearly a thousand houses. The village talati (who maintains the village accounts) reports that half the villagers are landless agricultural laborers or tenants. There are now, he reported to me, about 350 landowning families, some of whom rent out their land but most of whom supervise the work of their laborers.

There is a mandal unit of the Congress party in Itagi, containing the landowners and businessmen in the village. It should be noted that in practice businessmen are also landowners and that their business activities are related to their agricultural work. Itagi village has a good-sized rice mill owned by members of the Sanikop family, one of the larger landowning families in the village. This family belongs to the Sanikop community, a subcaste of the Lingayats. There are some two hundred Sanikops in the village, and they include most of the important landowners and businessmen. One Sanikop has been the chairman of the village panchayat for the past six years; before him another Sanikop held the office for ten years. There has been no contested panchayat election in the village for the past twenty-three years, and the village leaders claim that there are no factions within the village. A little memo prepared by the village panchayat for visitors reported "no litigation in this village . . . all disputes will be solved in the village." The extent to which this community is able to maintain political unity within the village is demonstrated by the polling-station results for the assembly election in 1957 (the 1962 figures were not available). In that election the Congress candidate received 1,511 votes, or 92 per cent, as against 133, or 8 per cent, for the opposition candidate.

Those who control the village are proud of their accomplishments. The village has a post office, a telegraph and telephone office, a cooperative society, and a Kannada school. Under construction or recently completed are a new school building, a medical quarter, a samiti mandir (a panchayat building where the fifteen-member panchayat meets), a gram sevak quarter, a gymnasium, a dispensary, a kindergarten school, a mahila mandal (women's association), a youth club, and a library. A newly built metaled road passes through the village and connects to a main taluka road three miles away. Since the income of the panchayat is only fifteen thousand rupees yearly, most of the developmental work has been done with outside funds.

"What kinds of developmental activities have taken place in this village?" I asked the panchayat president. He enumerated the new buildings constructed or under construction, the telegraph and telephone office that had recently been added, and the new road. Asked about the use of new agricultural methods, he said that a few villagers were using the Japanese method of transplanting paddy, which gives them thirty maunds per acre, instead of the twenty under the old system. He felt that there would be more improvement when electricity comes in a few years and enables them to have lift irrigation and a double crop. And they might also start some rice mills.

The panchayat president spoke with pride of his success in obtaining the new roads and buildings from the government. He spoke of these developments as a tribute to his own skill and that of other village leaders. Several of the village leaders were active in the local Congress party, and this gave them access to government officials.

One younger Congressman, also a Sanikop, was active in the district and state Congress party and had been very helpful to the village. His father was once a prominent Congressman in the district. The young Sanikop is a graduate of a college in Belgaum, one of five graduates in the village (three of whom are Sanikops). His family owns the major rice mill just outside the village. He is the secretary of the Youth Congress in Mysore state and is therefore a constant traveler between Belgaum and the state capital at Bangalore. When the village leaders expressed an interest in having a telegraph and telephone connection for the village, he got in touch with an influential friend in the telegraph department in Bangalore and invited him to the village. "When he came here he said that the village was only three miles from the main line, so it would be easy to connect them. That's how it was done. It is the only village in this area with a telephone and telegraph connection."

The dominant caste within the village is thus able to strengthen its own control within the village and over the village panchayat by establishing close associations with the Congress party and with the district and state administration. The benefits this leadership has been able to obtain for the village have, however, largely benefited the more prosperous sections. The modern facilities are available mainly to the business and landowning agricultural families. The headmaster of the primary school said: "There is compulsory education now for the last five years, but about 40 per cent of the village children are not in school. Mostly they are from agricultural labor families. But," he added to indicate that the legislation would be enforced in the future, "now we go house to house each year to register all children who reach the age of six and bring them to school." But the content of education is not geared to laboring families. "No, we do not teach many practical subjects. Elementary education should be given up to age twelve. Then practical education. We teach some spinning and weaving . . . no, we do not teach any agricultural subjects. That is for a higher standard."

But it would be misleading to argue that the less prosperous sections of the village do not gain any benefits from the politically dominant group. The improved road, the dispensary, and the school affect more and more of the village. When the village leadership is able to use its influence to obtain more grants for building and road construction, work opportunities in-

crease. When the village succeeds in prying from administration more fertilizers and other facilities for the increasing agricultural productivity, the work force benefits.

The village leadership has what is essentially an instrumental view of the political and administrative process. The political power of the village leaders has grown as they have established new ties with the district and state political leadership. The village leadership is concerned not with issues of public policy but with the kinds of access it can develop to various levels of administration. This access is great even though the constituency has elected a Samiti assembly candidate, and even though the taluka development board is controlled by the Samiti. The Congress leadership does, after all, control the state, district, and taluka administration. Congressmen control the district cooperative organizations, including agricultural credit and marketing facilities. The village leadership needs not, and does not, turn to the Samiti MLA but can work directly with such leading Congressmen as Aragavi. There are so many channels to authority that if one is blocked others can be utilized.

The village leadership delivers the vote to the Congress party because the Congress government in turn delivers material aid of importance to the village leadership. The village leadership feels strongly about remaining in Mysore, not simply because of the language sentiment — although this is certainly part of it — but because the village has already effectively established its connection with the Mysore government and administration. If a transfer of the village occurred, the local leadership would have to rebuild its political and administrative connections.

Though several villagers were nationalist supporters before independence, the membership of the party has grown in recent years, as it has throughout the taluka. If one takes into account the decline of the party in the Marathi-speaking areas — so great that the predominantly Marathi-speaking town of Khanapur has only six active members (in 1958–60) compared with sixteen in 1952–53 — then the rise of membership in the Kannada-speaking area is phenomenal. Since Congress is not an elite, but a mass, party, its requirements for active membership are few. Throughout the taluka the party readily attracts those who want to improve their access to administration and government. A former secretary of the District Congress Committee summed up the motivation of many who joined the party: "It is natural that everyone comes into Congress since it is the ruling party and everyone wants power. Also Congress controls the district. All the government officers listen to the party in power."

Access to local administration is essential for any kind of development

within the village, since the budget of the panchayat is nowhere commensurate with the needs of the village. The land revenue of Itagi village is only ten thousand rupees, and the annual income of the panchayat is only fifteen thousand rupees. For the construction of schools, irrigation facilities, metaled roads, water tanks, storage facilities, and such, assistance must come from outside.

The individual needs of a larger agriculturalist also require administrative attention. Seeds, fertilizers, and loans come from government agencies. Businessmen need permits and licenses for almost any kind of activity. In these circumstances the villager is prepared to use any kind of influence available, including bribery of the local administrator, to obtain a prompt decision. The young Sanikop Congressman, asked about the problem of corruption in the district and taluka, said: "There is quite a bit of corruption among the local officials. If a peasant goes to a government office about some matter, he would have to wait for several days. So, rather than pay the cost of lodging in Belgaum or Khanapur, he pays something to the official. If you want a permit or license or anything, you have to pay these local officials." How much? "Anything from five rupees to several thousand. . . . Increasing the salaries of officials wouldn't make any difference. Some of the higher officials in the district are also corrupt and they get good salaries." Are the Congress party people involved? "Some say that, but I don't think so. People go directly to the government officials concerned."

The point is an important one. The village leaders of Itagi, all of whom support the Congress party, have direct access to local administrative officials, to district and, as we have seen, even to state administrative officials, and to elected Congressmen. Congress may even lose control over the assembly seat in Khanapur taluka, as it has in both the 1957 and 1962 elections (to the Ekikaran Samiti, which is pressing for the transfer of Marathi-speaking villages to Maharashtra), but the leadership of Itagi remains with Congress. One obvious reason is that Congress retains control over the state government. Another is that Congress controls the local quasi-governmental, quasi-voluntary cooperatives, and other local institutions in the taluka. The leadership of Itagi thus remains with Congress, not because of party loyalty or support for Congress ideology, but because Congress is the government and because the village leadership — and this is of great importance — has direct access both to the party and to the government even when Congress fails to elect its candidate to the local assembly seat.

To return then to our earlier questions. Itagi remains united because a small landowning community in control of the village is united. Development consists largely of roads, a telegraph and telephone station, a school

building, and other public works constructed by the government. Political unity and an astute alliance by politically skilled village leadership with the Congress party has resulted in a substantial flow of outside governmental assistance into the village. Development is thus not the result of civil action as the national and state leadership anticipates from political unity. In short, villagers work together to obtain assistance from the government, but do not work together to facilitate their own development.

# BIBLIOGRAPHY: BELGAUM DISTRICT

*Interviews*

This study is based largely on intensive interviews with fifty-seven persons. Since Belgaum is torn between Marathi- and Kannada-speaking elements, a special effort was made to gain a balance in interviews. There are a few Marathi-speaking Congressmen in Belgaum whom I interviewed, but most of the Marathi-speaking politicians I spoke with in the district belong to the opposition, the Maharashtra Ekikaran Samiti. As elsewhere, I spoke with Congress MPs, MLAs, and the president and secretary of the Belgaum DCC. I was also able to interview almost all the living former presidents of the DCC.

Among the many active Congress party workers, I interviewed the leaders of the Youth Congress, the Mahila (Women's) Congress, and Seva Dal, and many "constructive" workers. I also interviewed many of the taluka and mandal Congress officers, particularly in Ramdurg, Gokak, Belgaum town, Chikodi, Nipani, and Khanapur.

In Ramdurg I was especially fortunate in meeting almost all the active Congressmen. In Belgaum town, in addition to meeting the officers in the DCC and in the opposition parties, I spent some time meeting elected representatives in the municipal corporation.

Several administrative officers in the district and in Mysore city were particularly helpful, including the collector and deputy collector, the secretary of the Belgaum taluka local board, the district agricultural officer, and the census superintendent. In Mysore I interviewed the president and secretary of the PCC and several of its other officers.

*History*

Belgaum has been a meeting place for Maratha, Karnataka, and Islamic movements. For a general history see Ghulam Yazdani, ed., *A History of the Deccan* (London: Oxford University Press, 1952). There is an extensive literature on the Maratha empire. Some of the standard works are: James Grant Duff, *History of the Mahrattas*, revised and annotated by S. M. Edwards (London: Oxford University Press, 1921), two volumes; Vithal Trimbak Gune, *The Judicial System of the Marathas* (Poona: Deccan College Postgraduate and Research Institute, 1953); Govind Sakharam Sardesai, *The Main Currents of Maratha History* (Bombay: Phoenix Publications, 1959); Govind Sakharam Sardesai, *New History of the Marathas* (Bombay: Phoenix Publications 1946–48), three volumes; Surendra Nath Sen, *Administrative System of the Marathas* (Calcutta: University of Calcutta, 1923); Surendra Nath Sen, *The Military System of the Marathas*, new edition (Bombay: Orient Longmans, 1958); C. K. Srinivasan, *Maratha Rule in the Carnatic*, edited by C. S. Srinivasachari (Annamalainagar: Annamalai University, 1944). For an account of the period of Muslim rule in the area around Belgaum, there is a useful short history in the *Bombay Gazetteer* by E. W. West (Government Central Press, Bombay, 1878), entitled "Historical Sketch of the Southern Maratha Country: Musalma'n Period, 1347–1818" (published separately). For histories of the Karnataka dynasties, including the princely state of Mysore, see: John Faithful Fleet, *Dynasties of the Kanarese Districts* (Bombay: Government Central Press, 1882); George Mark Moraes, *The Kadamba Kula: A History of Ancient and Medieval Karnataka* (Bombay: B. X. Furtado, 1931); Canjeeveram Hayavadana Rao, *History of Mysore, 1399–1799* (Bangalore: Superintendent of the Government Press, 1943–46), three volumes.

There are several source books and "official" histories of the nationalist movements in Bombay state and in Mysore. Belgaum was in Bombay before 1956, but political developments in the Karnataka regions had important consequences for the district, since the district, as we have seen, is predominantly Kannada-speaking. See the following works: Dr. M. V. Krishna Rao, M. Govardhana Rao, and K. Jeevanna Rao, eds., *Glimpses of Karnataka* (Bangalore: Reception Committee, 65th Session Indian National Congress, Sadasivanagar, 1960); M. V. K. Rao and G. S. Halappa, eds., *History of Freedom Movement in Karnataka*, Vol. 1 (Bangalore: Government of Mysore, 1962); *Source Material for a History of the Freedom Movement in India*, Vol. I [1818–1885] and Vol. II [1885–1920] (Bombay: Bombay State

Committee for a History of the Freedom Movement in India, S. K. Patil, chairman, Government of Bombay, 1957).

## Descriptions and Data on Belgaum

As elsewhere, the gazetteers are composite guides to the history, social organization, and economy of the region. There is an eight-volume gazetteer series for Mysore state: C. H. Rao, ed., *The Mysore Gazetteer* (Bangalore: Government Press, 1927–30). Four of these eight volumes provide histories, and one has an extensive description of the Lingayats and other communities in Mysore. These are preceded by a five-volume district gazetteer series published by the Mysore Government Press in 1877, edited by Lewis Rice. Belgaum itself is described in the *Belgaum District Gazetteer*, Gazetteer of the Bombay Presidency, vol. 21, 1884. Statistical data on Belgaum can be found in the Bombay census; for this study I have made use of the *Census of India, 1951*, vol. 4, *Bombay, Saurashtra and Kutch* (Bombay: Government Central Press, 1953), J. B. Bowman, editor. The census data are presented by village in *Belgaum District Census Handbook, 1951* (Bombay: Government of Bombay, 1953).

No new gazetteer for Belgaum has been prepared since 1884, but two gazetteers have been published in recent years for nearby districts with political histories which are helpful for an understanding of political developments in Belgaum. See: *Gazetteer of Bombay State — Dharwar District*, rev. ed. (Bombay: Government Central Press, 1959); and *Maharashtra State Gazetteers — Kolhapur District*, rev. ed. (Bombay: Government Central Press, 1960). It should be noted that there has been much contention over the 1951 census for Belgaum, since each side claims that the linguistic figures for the other side have been exaggerated. The government of Bombay has published under the editorship of J. B. Bowman a village-by-village account of languages spoken in Belgaum district as part of the census series.

Although the research for this study was done in 1962, the Mysore government had not yet released information on the linguistic distribution from the 1961 census. The Mysore government has, however, published the overall census results for 1961 in *Mysore State Census*, Superintendent of Census Operations in Mysore. See also *The Handbook of Mysore* (Bangalore: Department of Information, Government of Mysore, Government Press, 1957); *Mysore, 1951–1961* (Bangalore: Department of Publicity and Information, Bangalore, Government of Mysore). A geographical description of the southern Karnataka region of Bombay, which encompasses Belgaum, can

be found in B. S. Sheshgiri, *The Bombay of Karnataka: A Geographical Survey* (Belgaum: B.S.).

## Social Organization

We are fortunate in having a rich anthropological literature on social organization in Mysore. The distinguished Indian anthropologist M. N. Srinivas has done extensive research in Mysore. So have several American scholars: William C. McCormack, Edward B. Harper, Alan R. Beals, and, on Maharashtra, Maureen L. P. Patterson. Fortunately, several of the following studies, as will be seen from their titles, are concerned with political organization and political leadership: Alan R. Beals, "Change in the Leadership of a Mysore Village," in *India's Villages*, ed. by M. N. Srinivas (Calcutta: Development Department, West Bengal, 1955); Alan R. Beals, "Interplay among Factors of Change in a Mysore Village," in *Village India*, McKim Marriott, ed. (Chicago: University of Chicago Press, 1955); Alan R. Beals, "Leadership in a Mysore Village," and Edward B. Harper, "Political Organization and Leadership in a Karnataka Village," in *Leadership and Political Institutions in India*, Richard L. Park and Irene Tinker, eds. (Princeton: Princeton University Press, 1959); Reginald Edward Enthoven, "Lingayats," in *Encyclopedia of Religion and Ethics*, J. Hastings, ed. (New York: Scribner, 1908–26), vol. 8; Noel P. Gist, "Caste Differentials in South India," *American Sociological Review* 19 (1954): 126–37; Edward B. Harper, "Two Systems of Economic Exchange in Village India," *American Anthropologist* 61 (1959): 760–78; S. M. Hunashal, *The Lingayat Movement: A Social Revolution in Karnatak* (Dharwar: Karnatak Sahitya Mandira, 1947); M. G. Kulkarni, "Family Patterns in Gokak Taluka," *Sociological Bulletin* 9 (1960): 60–81; William Charles McCormack, "Changing Leadership of a Mysore Village," Master's Thesis, University of Chicago, 1956, Department of Anthropology, June, 1956; William Charles McCormack, "Mysore Villagers' View of Change," *Economic Development and Cultural Change* 5 (1953): 257–62; William Charles McCormack, "Sister's Daughter's Marriage in a Mysore Village," *Man in India* 38 (1958): 34–48; William Charles McCormack, "Lingayats as a Sect," *Journal of the Royal Anthropological Institute* 93 (1963): 59–71; Maureen L. Patterson, "Caste and Political Leadership in Maharashtra," *Economic Weekly* 6 (1954): 1065–67; M. N. Srinivas, "The Case of the Potter and Priest," *Man in India* 39 (1959): 190–209; M. N. Srinivas, "A Caste Dispute among Washermen of Mysore," *Eastern Anthropologist* 7

(1954): 149–68; M. N. Srinivas, "The Dominant Caste in Rampura," *American Anthropologist* 61 (1959): 1–16; M. N. Srinivas, *Marriage and Family in Mysore* (Bombay: New Book Co., 1942); M. N. Srinivas, "The Social Structure of a Mysore Village," in *India's Villages*, M. N. Srinivas, ed. (Calcutta: Development Department, West Bengal, 1955), pp. 19–32; M. N. Srinivas, "The Social System of a Mysore Village," in *Village India*, McKim Marriott, ed. (Chicago: University of Chicago Press, 1955), pp. 1–35.

## Politics

Recent political literature on Belgaum deals primarily with the linguistic controversy. The relevant national documents, some of which refer to Belgaum, and all of which are referred to by politicians in Belgaum, include: *Report of Hon'ble Mr. Justice Wanchoo on the Formation of Andhra State* (New Delhi: Manager, Government of India Press, 1953); *Report of the Linguistic Provinces Commission, Constituent Assembly of India, 1948* (New Delhi: Manager, Government of India Press, 1949); *Report of the States Reorganization Commission* (New Delhi: Government of India, 1955); *Resolution of States Reorganization, 1920–56* (New Delhi: Indian National Congress, All India Congress Committee, n.d.)

The basic documents presenting the Marathi case are: *A Case for the Formation of a New Province: "United Maharashtra"* (Poona: Samyukta Maharashtra Parishad, 1949); *Belgaum: An Appeal Against the States Reorganizations Commission's Findings* (Belgaum: Maharashtra Ekikaran Samiti); *Belgaum: A Case for Its Integration with Maharashtra* (Belgaum: Maharashtra Ekikaran Samiti); *Belgaum City: An Integral Part of Maharashtra*, Memorandum submitted to the States Reorganizations Commission by the Maharashtra Ekikaran Samiti, Belgaum; *Reorganization of States in India with Particular Reference to the Formation of Maharashtra* (Bombay: Samyukta Maharashtra Parishad, 1954).

Apart from these documents, there are a number of tracts presenting the Marathi view. These are in English, as are nearly all the documents in the controversy, since the intended audience is the central government and the governments and administration of two separate states. *Atrocities on Satyagrahis by Mysore Police in Belgaum* (Belgaum: Maharashtra Ekikaran Samiti, 1959); *Inhuman Atrocities by Mysore Reserve Police at Garlgunji, Near Belgaum* (Belgaum: Maharashtra Ekikaran Samiti, 1960); *Police Atrocities in Belgaum During Chief Minister Shri B. D. Jatti's Visit*

(Belgaum: Maharashtra Ekikaran Samiti, 1959); R. S. Rege, *Belgaum Pleads for Democracy* (Belgaum: J. Bhosle) Quaerens Veritatem (pseud.), *Justice Shall Prevail: The Struggle for Samyukta Maharashtra* (Poona: J. S. Tilak, 1958); *Why Satyagraha? A Letter to Pt. Jawaharal Nehru* (Belgaum: Maharashtra Ekikaran Samiti).

The Kannada view is stated in the *Memorandum Submitted to the States' Reorganization Commission under the Joint Auspices of the District Congress Committee and the Karnatak Karya Samiti, Belgaum* (Belgaum: K. G. Joshi, 1955).

For scholarly accounts of the states reorganization controversy as they affect Bombay and Mysore, see *Regionalism Versus Provincialism: A Study in Problems of Indian National Unity* (Berkeley: University of California, Indian Press Digests, No. 4, 1958); and Marshall Louis Windmiller, "Politics of States Reorganization in India: The Case of Bombay," *Far Eastern Survey*, Vol. 25 (1956): 129–43.

For other accounts of politics in Mysore, most of which deal with the Congress party and Congress government in the state, see the following: *Constitution of the Mysore Pradesh Congress Committee* (Bangalore, 1957); "Karnataka Is Reborn," *Economic Weekly* 8 (1956): 1315–16; "A Karnataka Viewpoint," *Economic Weekly* 7 (1955): 1255; "Ministerial Tussle in Mysore, from Our Own Correspondent," *Economic Weekly* 10 (1958): 501–2; "Profile of a Southern State — Mysore," *Economic Weekly* 8 (1956): 859–64; T. S. Rao, "Mysore," *Reports on the Indian General Elections, 1951–52*, S. V. Kogekar, ed. (Bombay: Popular Book Depot, 1956), pp. 204–12; *Rules for the Conduct of Elections to Mandala District and Pradesh Congress Committees* (Bangalore: Executive Committee of the Mysore Pradesh Congress Committee, Indian Press, 1957; K. N. Subrahmanya, "Karnataka and Mysore," *Economic Weekly* 7 (1955): 1253–54.

*Government Reports — Economy and Administration*

There is no separately published five-year plan for the district, although there is one document of a quasi-popular nature describing the activities of the Mysore government in Belgaum: *Know Your Country's Plan* (Belgaum: Belgaum District Five Year Plan Celebrations Committee, Vishwa Bharat Co., 1961). On the five-year plans for Mysore, see *The Progress of the First Five Year Plan of Mysore*, Planning and Development Department, Government of Mysore; *Second Five Year Plan for Mysore State (1956–57 to 1960–61)* (Government of Mysore, Planning and De-

velopment Dept., 1957); *Third Five Year Plan for Mysore*: vol. I, *Policy and Programme*; vol. II, *Schematic Programme, Planning, Housing, and Social Welfare Dept.* (Government of Mysore, 1961).

Three important government documents deal with the agrarian system of Mysore: *Mysore (State) Committee for the Revision of the Land Revenue System, Report* (Bangalore: 1950); *Report of the Joint Select Committee on the Mysore Land Reforms Bill, 1958* (Bangalore: Mysore Legislature, Government Press, 1961); *Report of the Mysore Tenancy Agricultural Land Laws Committee* (Bangalore: Director, Government Press, 1956). The 1957 report contains detailed data on land distribution in Belgaum district, which we have used in this study.

At the request of the government of Mysore, A. D. Gorwala, a retired Indian civil service officer, conducted a personal inquiry into the administration of Mysore state. The report is exceedingly well written and one of the frankest accounts to be found of any state's administration: A. D. Gorwala, *The Mysore Administration: Some Observations and Recommendations* (Bangalore: Government Press, 1958).

On local government and community development in Mysore, see Rajendra Prasad, *Panchayati Raj in Mysore* (Bangalore: Department of Publicity and Information, Government of Mysore, 1960); and *Seminar on Agricultural Cooperation and Community Development in Bangalore* (Mysore Pradesh Congress Committee, 1959).

*PART V. THE POLITICS OF PATRONAGE:*
*CALCUTTA*

# 16. THE CONGRESS PARTY OF CALCUTTA

Calcutta has the reputation of being one of the most politically volatile cities in the world. Its Communist party is among the most active and revolutionary. The Communists and the Marxist left parties — remnants of the old Trotsky-Stalin controversies — have been responsible for general strikes which have paralyzed the city's transport system and for countless agitations resulting in destruction of buses and trams, looting of shops, and even attacks upon the police.

The volatile character of the city is a reflection of some basic demographic and economic facts. Though Calcutta is only the twenty-second largest city in the world (but the twelfth largest metropolitan area), it is one of the most densely populated — approximately ninety thousand persons per square mile. It has nearly twice as many men as women (the result of a migratory labor force), an enormous refugee population (the consequence of partition), a vast number of unemployed, a large homeless population, and a degree of poverty which shocks all European and American visitors to the city.

In a city with such a high revolutionary potential it is surprising to find a Congress party which competes — with considerable success — with the Communist and left-wing parties, not through any counter-ideological appeal, but through old-fashioned patronage. Moreover, one cannot attribute Congress strength in the city to the nationalist legacy, for in 1947 the Congress party in Calcutta (and throughout West Bengal) was broken and disorganized. Since then its organization has improved and its popular vote has grown. Its share of votes for parliamentary and state assembly seats in Calcutta has risen in each of the three elections since independence.

Though the Congress party has provided West Bengal with one of the most stable governments to be found anywhere in India — in spite of the frequent violence which rocks Calcutta — it would be hard to attribute Congress success to the quality of the government it provides. The state government, while it has had some success in relocating refugees and providing for rural development in the countryside (though even here its record is mixed), has given little attention to the needs of Calcutta. The municipal government, controlled by a Congress party which has won office through a restricted franchise, is widely viewed as one of the worst in India. Municipal services — from public health to garbage collection — are often described as less adequate than those of Bombay, Madras, and, until recently, Delhi.

In the next two chapters we shall try to understand how the Congress party, which was so disorganized at the time of independence, has successfully built itself into a powerful political force in the city during the past twenty years. But let us first turn to a brief description of the physical, economic, and social environment in which the Congress party of Calcutta operates.

## The City of Calcutta

In a social and political sense, Calcutta can be described as two cities, not the city of the rich and of the poor, but a city of the Bengali and the non-Bengali. Though 39 per cent of the city's population is non-Bengali, there are no non-Bengali representatives from Calcutta in parliament and only one or two in the state legislative assembly. With the exception of the small but powerful Marwari community, a business community originally from the state of Rajasthan, the non-Bengalis play no active part in the Congress party organization or in any other important political party in the city or state. Most of the non-Bengali population comes from Bihar, Uttar Pradesh, and Orissa, but there are substantial communities from the Punjab and Nepal. Approximately 25 per cent of the population is Hindi-speaking.

Calcutta is a city of migrants. About 67 per cent of the city's population, (2,900,000) were born outside Calcutta. Approximately 17 per cent are displaced migrants from East Pakistan who were forced into the city after partition. Roughly seventeen of every twenty migrants who came into the city between 1951 and 1958 came from rural areas.[1] Though the migrants

[1] S. N. Sen, *The City of Calcutta: A Socio-economic Survey* (Calcutta: Bookland Private Limited, 1960), p. 202. The demographic data provided here are from Sen and from the 1951 census for West Bengal.

are frequently married, they come to the city without their families. In 1951 there were 2,600 married men per thousand married women in the city. For the population as a whole, there were 1,754 men per thousand women. A considerable proportion of the city's population lives a single, lonely life. According to the 1951 census there are 606,000 households in the city; of these 56 per cent are single-member households. Calcutta has the distinction of being one of the most male cities in the world.

Calcutta has a large unemployed population. According to a survey done at the University of Calcutta, approximately 10 per cent of the job-seeking population is unemployed.[2] Two aspects of the unemployed population are particularly interesting. The first is that most of the unemployed are young persons. While only 2 per cent of the population above the age of forty-five were seeking jobs in 1954, approximately 21 per cent between the ages of twenty and twenty-four were seeking employment and 41 per cent of those from fifteen and nineteen were unemployed. A second interesting feature of the unemployed is their educational level. Only 15½ per cent of the unemployed were illiterate, while 22 per cent were persons with high school and college educations. Another 37 per cent had attended secondary schools. In other words, approximately 60 per cent of the unemployed had a substantial measure of education. Calcutta's unemployed thus consist largely of educated young persons – a situation quite the reverse of that found in the United States, where unemployment is most common among older persons and those of least education.

Calcutta is a city of inadequate housing accommodations. A substantial portion of the population sleep at night on the pavement. Their exact number is unknown, but estimates range around six hundred thousand. Moreover, more than one-fourth of the population live in slum houses known as bustees. The bustee is a crude house made of wood or mud, generally lacking in lavatory facilities and drinking water. Typically, the slum area is occupied by migrants to the city and is without adequate educational facilities for children. The bustees are not concentrated in a single section of the city, but can be found throughout Calcutta. Bustees can often be found next to palatial homes, and house the servants of those who live in the larger buildings. The rest of the population also live under fairly primitive conditions. A large proportion of households have neither private baths nor adequate drinking facilities, and overcrowding

[2] According to the Government of West Bengal, Survey of Unemployment in West Bengal, State Statistical Bureau, First Interim Report, Vol. 1 (1953), 125,000 matriculates and college graduates were seeking employment in 1953, and the number has been constantly rising.

is typical, with many married couples and families sharing their apartments and houses.

As bad as education, housing, health, and employment conditions are in Calcutta, it is useful to remember that those who move to the city do so because for one reason or another they find life outside the city even less attractive. Calcutta attracts migrants from such far places as Assam, Bombay, Rajasthan, Punjab, and even South India. Landless peasants from Bihar and Orissa clearly find prospects in Calcutta more attractive than those in the countryside. Communal disturbances in East Pakistan have also forced a large number of Hindus to move into the city. The bulk of the migrants to the city are illiterate adult males seeking unskilled manual jobs. For these, opportunities in Calcutta are better than those at home. As we shall see, it is not the migrants who form a revolutionary group.

### The Nationalist Movement In Bengal

Although Bengal was one of the earliest and most lively centers of nationalist activities in pre-independence India, Congress failed to win a single province-wide election in Bengal before India became independent. Before independence the two dominant political groups in Bengal were both Muslim political organizations: the Muslim League, and the Krishak Praja party (peasants' people's party). It should be recalled that pre-partition Bengal was a sprawling province which included all of what is now East Pakistan and West Bengal. Pre-partition Bengal had a Muslim majority, but its Hindu minority was concentrated in Calcutta and the areas which are now in India. Though the Congress party was open to Muslims and had a number of prominent Muslim members, by and large the Muslim population joined Muslim political organizations. Consequently the Congress party which took power in 1947 had not shared power at the provincial level before independence, in marked contrast to the situation in at least half a dozen other provinces where the Congress party won elections in 1939 and subsequently formed provincial governments.

A second important feature of the Indian National Congress in West Bengal in the inter-war period was the fact that its leaders had less influence upon the nationalist leadership as a whole than in the pre-First World War era. From 1885 to the early 1920's Bengalis were among the most prominent of India's national figures. Many of the great Hindu reform movements which were precursors to the development of the na-

tionalist movement had their origins in the province of Bengal. The struggle for increasing the constitutional rights of Indians in relation to Englishmen in India was very much led by Bengalis. If the constitutional side of the nationalist movement was strong in Bengal, so was the terrorist side. Though other provinces had their terrorists, no province was more irritating to the British than Bengal.

With the rise of Gandhi shortly after the First World War, Bengalis held a less dominant position within the nationalist movement as a whole.[3] There were some Bengali nationalists who wholeheartedly supported Gandhi, but others, perhaps the vast majority of the nationalist workers, did not support Gandhi's position although they continued to respect his leadership. The political, personal, and subtle cultural factors which affected relationships between Bengali political leaders and Gandhi and those who surrounded him need not detain us here. It is important to note, however, that the two most important attacks against Gandhi within the nationalist movement during the 1920's and 1930's were led by Bengalis. In the 1920's one of the prominent leaders of the nationalist movement in Bengal, C. R. Das, opposed Gandhi's position that the nationalists should boycott governmental bodies. Das argued that the nationalists all over India should enter the governmental council to demonstrate that the British reforms of the government, known as dyarchy, would be unworkable. To propound this position Das, along with Motilal Nehru, the father of Jawaharlal Nehru, formed the Swarajya party. Gandhi's leadership itself was not personally challenged; but ultimately C. R. Das and the Swarajyists defeated Gandhi, and their proposal became an integral part of Congress policy. In the late 1930's another eminent Bengali, Subhas Chandra Bose, arose to challenge Gandhi. Bose was a young disciple of Das and had been elected president of the Indian National Congress in the late 1930's with Gandhi's blessing. However, on the eve of the Second World War he broke with Gandhi over the issue of Congress militancy. Bose's demand for an immediate movement to force the British out of India was rejected by both Gandhi and Nehru. Bose, and the non-Communist leftists within Congress who rallied behind him, argued that the war should be used as an opportunity to oust the British from India even if it required collaboration with the Germans or Japanese. In a famous resolution the AICC declared that Bose should form his working committee in consultation with Gandhi. When Gandhi made clear that he would not work with Bose, the latter had little choice but to resign

[3] See J. H. Broomfield, "The Vote and the Transfer of Power: A Study of the Bengal General Election, 1912–1913," *The Journal of Asian Studies* XXI (Feb., 1962): 163–82.

as president of the Indian National Congress. Bose was subsequently arrested by the British but escaped from jail. Incognito, he fled across the subcontinent to Berlin, then to Tokyo and finally to Malaya, where he organized a military force to support Japanese invasion troops in a move to free India from British rule.

Bose had been suspended from the Congress party in 1940 because of his opposition to the official resolutions of the movement. But Bose's group, which had been the dominant group in the Bengal Congress, soon formed its own political organization, known as the Forward Bloc. The remaining Congress party of Bengal then fell under the control of what until then had been a minority group. A scramble for control of the organization took place at the time of independence.[4] Since Bengal itself was partitioned, with the larger part going to Pakistan, in effect the Congress party of Bengal was partitioned as well. East Bengali Congressmen who opted for India were in control of the party organization at the time of independence, and it was their nominee who became the first chief minister of West Bengal. During the first year after independence a struggle thus ensued between the East Bengali and West Bengali elements, with the long-run prospects clearly with the West Bengalis. A group of West Bengalis, known as the Hooghly group (named after Hooghly district, in which most of the members lived), led by Atulya Ghosh and P. C. Sen, took control of the Congress organization. Though this West Bengali group won control of the party, their victory was not without internal pangs, since again a substantial section of the party withdrew to form a new political party.

The lack of governmental experience, the defection of the Bose group, the partition of the party, and the post-independence split would have been fatal for the future of the party were it not for the fact that other political groups in West Bengal were in an equally poor position. The Communists were discredited by their opposition to the popular hero Bose and the Quit India movement. The Forward Bloc had led the civil resistance, an underground movement in Bengal during the war, and at the close of the war many of its leaders were popularly admired. But Bose's death during the war in an airplane crash in Taiwan before he had had an opportunity to consolidate his organization put the Forward Bloc in a difficult position at the time of independence. The defection of sev-

[4] For a more detailed account of post-independence political developments in Bengal, see my *Party Politics in India* (Princeton: Princeton University Press, 1957), chapters 4, 6, and 7, and my "Notes on Political Development in West Bengal" in Myron Weiner, *Political Change in South Asia* (Calcutta: Firma K. L. Mukjopadhyay, 1963), pp. 228–56.

eral prominent East Bengali members from Congress was a substantial loss, but on the other hand after partition these party workers had no local organizational roots. Finally, the innumerable left groups which dotted Calcutta and its industrial suburbs failed to create a consolidated party which might have become a major threat to the Congress party position.

## Pre-Independence Congress in Calcutta

Thus far we have spoken of the Congress party in West Bengal as a whole. Now let us take a closer look at the Congress party in Calcutta before independence.

Throughout Bengal the Congress party strength rested largely with the Hindu middle classes who lived in the countryside and who owned or received rent from land which they did not cultivate. In the Muslim majority areas the Hindu middle classes were strong supporters of the Congress movement, but they were never successful at organizing a mass nationalist movement. The nationalist movement was, however, exceedingly active in Calcutta, and the development of the Congress party there is closely bound up with the development of municipal government.

The Bengal Act of 1923, under which the Calcutta municipal corporation functioned until the corporation was suspended in 1948, represented a great victory for the nationalist forces. Until that time the Calcutta corporation (the name given to the municipal body) functioned under the 1899 McKenzie Act, which limited the number of elected councillors. In the early 1920s the British established in Bengal, as elsewhere in India, the system known as dyarchy, under which control of local government, health, and education was placed in the hands of elected Indian ministers while other provincial powers remained in the hands of British officials. Surendra Nath Banerjea, a leading nationalist, was elected by his party to be the minister of local self-government. Banerjea then proceeded to write the act of 1923, which increased the number of elected councillors in Calcutta and made them the supreme authority in administrative and legislative matters. Within a short time the newly constituted corporation became the seat, indeed the only seat, of nationalist power in Bengal, for, as we have already noted, the Congress party was never able to get control of the provincial government before independence. C. R. Das, the leader of the nationalist movement in Bengal in the 1920's, became the first mayor under the new act, and Subhas Chandra Bose, his deputy and ultimately his political successor, became his executive officer.

The municipal corporation soon became more than an institution of local government. It became a forum for the nationalist movement. Nationalist workers were appointed to posts in the municipal administration. Political patronage rather than merit became the criterion for appointments. One councillor explained in an interview:

> Yes, it is true that the old administration was corrupt. The reason was that the political sufferers [a term meaning nationalist workers who had been in jail] were appointed to the corporation. Big businessmen who gave money to support the nationalist movement got contracts from the corporation. The corporation was the only thing we controlled. The corporation maintained the families of political sufferers by giving jobs to sons or brothers. Political sufferers got full salaries while they were under detention. When the new act went into force in 1952, maybe 70 per cent of the corporation were political sufferers. Even now [this interview was conducted in 1962] 40 or 50 per cent are political sufferers. But all of this corruption was for helping the nationalist movement. It was for a good cause. It was not like corruption by one man.

Payrolls padded with the names of nationalist political prisoners, underqualified men appointed to many posts within the municipal administration, and councillors more powerful than the municipal administration became features of municipal government in the pre-independence era. Municipal government in Calcutta has been severely attacked for its poor performance — in terms familiar to those familiar with American urban politics — but the fact is that the Congress movement was strengthened by its control of the municipal corporation.

### The Post-Independence Congress

Independence was a mournful as well as joyous occasion in Bengal. The country and the province were now independent of British rule, but Bengal had been partitioned. The larger part of the province, in both population and size, was turned over to Pakistan. Millions of Hindu refugees from East Pakistan now moved into West Bengal seeking housing, land, and employment. As refugees poured into Calcutta the economic situation in the city deteriorated. Jute mills in the Calcutta region were

unable to purchase raw jute from the hinterlands of East Pakistan. Fish and rice were in short supply. Food prices soared. Almost none of the Congress party leaders who took office in 1947 had had previous experience in the state government. The party organization was torn by factional disputes. In Calcutta it was the Bose group rather than the new Congress party leadership which had a popular following. Within a year after independence the Congress party government collapsed, and another group within Congress, the Hooghly group, took control of the state government. Their nominee, B. C. Roy, a well-known medical practitioner, a nationalist leader active in public life in the 1930's, and an associate of Gandhi, became chief minister of the state. Control of the party organization of the entire state was now in the hands of Atulya Ghosh, an able party leader in Hooghly district who achieved prominence in the struggle to capture control of the party. Ghosh and his associates in Hooghly district now set out to rebuild the party organization in the state.

Since the majority of voters lived in the rural areas, since universal adult suffrage meant that the rural vote would determine who formed the government, and since the left parties and the Forward Bloc had a stronger hold in Calcutta than in the countryside, Atulya Ghosh elected the strategy of organizing the rural areas. Then too, Ghosh and his followers were men of rural background, so that strategic considerations coincided with personal inclinations and political capacity. Moreover, B. C. Roy's close association with the business community in Calcutta provided Ghosh with an easy entrée into the financial resources necessary for building a political organization.

The first test of the Ghosh strategy came in 1952. In that election Congress won 150 seats in the state assembly of a total of 238. Congress had won with 38.9 per cent of the popular vote. In Calcutta, Congress won seventeen of twenty-six seats, with 39.7 per cent of the vote. In the five years between the 1952 and the 1957 elections, Congress strengthened its organization still further in the rural areas; though it lost most of its seats in Calcutta, the party's total position in the state assembly remained more or less the same. In the 1957 elections Congress won 152 of 252 seats in the assembly (the Communists won forty-six, and the Praja Socialist party twenty-one seats). In Calcutta, Congress won only eight of a possible twenty-six seats, but her proportion of the vote rose to 42.6 per cent. Congress had won more seats in 1952 than in 1957 in Calcutta because of the divisions within the opposition parties and the further division of the anti-Congress vote by the large numbers of independents who stood for elections. Only seven of the elected Calcutta

Congressmen in 1952 had received more than 50 per cent of the vote. In the 1957 elections the opposition parties formed alliances to prevent Congress from winning seats by a plurality vote. Thus, though the Congress vote rose to 42.5 per cent, the number of seats won dropped from seventeen to eight. The Communists won ten compared to four in 1952, the Praja Socialists won four seats, and independents won three. It was clearly easier for the opposition elements to unite within the city of Calcutta than in the countryside.

Atulya Ghosh and the Congress party leadership doubted their ability to win elections in Calcutta; while they could not prevent the left from winning assembly and parliamentary seats in the city — where universal adult suffrage had been established by an act of parliament — they had no intention of turning the municipal government over to the leftists. The Calcutta Municipal Act of 1951 therefore did not provide for adult suffrage for the municipal elections. As we have seen, the fears of the state Congress party leadership proved to be well founded. They won a majority of assembly seats in 1952 with a plurality vote; in 1957, when the left was no longer divided, Congress lost the bulk of the assembly seats in the city. Had adult suffrage been established then for the municipal elections, it is very doubtful that Congress could have won. Not until 1965 was adult suffrage established in municipal elections.

The strength of the leftist parties has been primarily within the bustees of Calcutta and among the middle-class Bengalis engaged in services or white-collar jobs in the government and in the commercial houses of the city. The 1951 act gave the vote to rate payers, who constituted less than 10 per cent of the population. House owners, landlords, shopkeepers, and hut owners (that is, those who construct and rent bustees but do not own the land on which they are built) constitute the bulk of the electorate, and naturally their interests predominate in the municipal corporation.

In the first municipal elections under the new act in 1952, the Congress party, which was only then making some effort to rebuild its shattered organization in the city, gave nominations to local ward leaders — men who had been active in the various clubs, social welfare groups, libraries, and neighborhood associations which dot the city in extraordinarily large numbers. Some of the men who received nominations were old nationalist workers. A number were local businessmen or pleaders whose associations with the nationalist struggle were marginal. The leftist parties, banded together to attempt to defeat Congress, formed the United Citizens Council (UCC), but won only twenty-three seats of eighty. In the

1957 municipal elections the left increased its hold to thirty seats against forty-two for Congress; again in 1961 it won thirty-one seats as against thirty-nine for Congress. Finally, in the 1965 elections Congress won forty-nine of a hundred seats as against thirty-five for the left coalition. A number of independents were elected in the earliest elections, and many of these men joined the Congress party in the municipal corporation. Though several independents also joined the opposition, at no point in the past ten years has there been any threat to Congress' control of the corporation, even while the Congress party was losing assembly and parliamentary seats in Calcutta.[5]

## Congress and City Government

Continued Congress control of the Calcutta municipal corporation is based largely upon the access of the elected members of the corporation — the councillors — and therefore of the Congress party to the patronage of the municipality. Obviously it is difficult to get a detailed picture of the way in which the patronage system operated in Calcutta, since it is not a subject on which individuals will freely speak, nor is it a subject on which there are any data available. We have, however, interviewed a large number of municipal councillors, including those who belong to the opposition parties as well as those who are Congressmen. In the section which follows we shall try to describe, on the basis of this information, how the party organization works within the corporation.

It is remarkable that almost all of the councillors we interviewed in 1962 had been in the corporation for ten years. In fact, nearly three-quarters of the present councillors were elected in 1952; while this might not appear unusual in American politics, it is in India, where turnover in elective bodies is generally high. According to estimates of the secretary of the Congress municipal association, six or eight new councillors were added in 1957 and eight or ten in 1962. At the most, therefore, only eighteen of the present eighty elected councillors (in 1962) had been in office for less than three terms. In the national parliament, on the other hand, 40

---

[5] Indeed, in some respects Congress was in a stronger position in the municipal corporation after 1951 than before independence. Congress won a working majority in the municipal corporation in 1934, but in 1939 was able to form a government with the support of only the Muslim League. From 1939 to 1946 the Congress was forced to work with the Muslim League in the municipal corporation. In 1939 and again in 1946 a Muslim League mayor was elected in Calcutta, both times with the support or consent of the Congress party in the assembly. Since 1946 all the mayors and deputy mayors of Calcutta have been Congressmen.

per cent of the present parliament never held parliamentary seats before the 1962 elections. The reason for the low turnover in Calcutta is that both the Congress party and the opposition follow the practice of re-nominating the sitting members, on the grounds that voters support a particular man rather than a party. Moreover, it is assumed that the personal contribution made by the councillor to the rate payer is of greater importance than the position taken by the councillor or by his party on matters of public policy. Thus, for the rate payer it is the personal services performed by the councillor — that is, the administrative and executive performance of the councillor — which is more important than his legislative activities.

Since there are few voters, the councillor can often win elections by providing personal services for his constituents. In the 1961 elections there was a total of 221,000 eligible voters in the entire city of Calcutta for the municipal elections. Constituencies varied in size from a low of 456 eligible voters to a maximum of 5,741. In some of the smaller constituencies there was no election contest, and there are instances where councillors have been elected with less than six hundred votes. And it is a rare councillor who has won a total of two thousand votes. If a councillor provides satisfactory services to about fifteen hundred voters in his constituency, he can generally be reassured of reelection.

Although in principle the act provides for a separation of powers between the executive officer and the municipal councillors, there are in fact many provisions in the act which make it possible for the councillor so to influence the municipal administration that he can easily satisfy the interests of his small voting clientele. The power of filling posts at a salary of 250 rupees or above per month (approximately fifty dollars) is vested in the municipal councillors (with the approval of the Municipal Public Service Commission), not the executive officer (known as the commissioner). The consequence of the prevailing system is to make the senior advisory personnel within the corporation, including the heads of departments in the municipal administration, dependent upon the councillors for their appointments, their promotions, their increments, and even their leaves of absence. Officials are, therefore, frequently more loyal to the councillors than to their executive officer, the commissioner, and there is much private lobbying on the part of the administrative staff with the members of the powerful standing committees. The important standing committees of the corporation through which the municipal councillors work include those for finance, town planning, education, health,

and markets. Under the corporation practices, only Congressmen — that is, the majority party — are represented on these committees.

The councillors, particularly those who are on standing committees, can exert considerable influence over the personnel of the corporation, with an attendant loss in the ability of the commissioner to maintain discipline and enforce standards upon the supervisory personnel with whom he deals. It is true that most of the lower personnel in the corporation — that is, those earning less than 250 rupees — are hired by the commissioner, but, from an administrative point of view, it is clearly of greater importance that the commissioner control the supervisory rather than the subordinate personnel.

In view of the earlier history of the municipal administration, the ability of councillors to interfere in the administration is also enhanced by the fact that nationalist workers were placed on the payroll throughout the 1930's and 1940's. There are now between twenty-five and thirty thousand workers in the corporation, and among these are few who are not close personal friends or relations of one or more members of the municipal council. This net of familial relationships between councillors and administrators improves the capacity of the councillor to influence the administration on behalf of the rate payers. Inspectors making house assessments, engineers responsible for locating street lights, and other technical personnel are readily influenced by the councillors. Indeed, even in the years when the corporation was superseded by the state government — from 1948 to 1952 — local politicians and rate payers were able to exercise influence on administrative personnel. In a society where a tradition of public interest among lower levels of the civil service has not yet replaced traditional ascriptive loyalties, familial connections between elected representatives and the administrators are bound to be a source of corruption. Thus, while the prevailing legal structure of the corporation may contribute to corruption and deprive those in authority of the power to check it, clearly the sources of corruption are built into the social order and transcend the legal framework. One Congress councillor in an interview said frankly that almost every worker in the municipal administration has some patron — either a councillor, the mayor, or some former mayor. He pointed out that, in spite of the demands of the commissioners that their powers over personnel be increased, the previous commissioners themselves have made appointments of lower personnel at the recommendations of councillors. Moreover, the commissioners have rarely brought any cases of indiscipline to the attention of the standing committees in spite of the fact that they have the power to do so. One reason

is that the commissioners are appointed by the state government with the approval of the municipal councillors. Many of the commissioners have been retired civil servants, and their positions often depend upon the good will of the municipal councillors.

There are many other aspects of the formal structure which have contributed to the capacity of councillors to interfere in the day-to-day functioning of the municipal administration. These have been extensively documented in two government reports.[6] The corporation has delegated much of its powers over day-to-day administration to the standing committees. Financial powers, powers over appointments, and — of great importance — the power to call for tenders and settle contracts for purchases and construction are in the hands of standing committees. It takes from three to four months to make decisions for purchases of less than five thousand rupees (one thousand dollars) and as much as eight or ten months for purchases of fifty thousand rupees (ten thousand dollars). In moments of rare self-criticism councillors often recall the words of Sir Alexander McKenzie, who described an earlier municipal corporation as an "armory of talk and an arsenal of delays."

Between 1952 and 1962 the municipal councillors of all parties, including Congress, developed a vested interest in maintaining the legal structure of municipal government. Many councillors personally profited from their powers. Few Congress councillors favored extending the suffrage, since they were clearly the ones who profit most from the system of limited suffrage. Opposition councillors wanted to extend the suffrage, since this would improve their representation and might give them control of the corporation; but even the opposition members have opposed extending the powers of the commissioners or of the West Bengal government at the expense of the elected councillors.

The Congress party organization, led by Atulya Ghosh, was also reluctant to extend the suffrage or diminish the powers of the councillors. A few Congress councillors will frankly admit that a major source of revenue for the Congress party organization has been the contributions made by those who receive contracts from the corporation. It is also clear that Atulya Ghosh has depended heavily upon contributions to the party from Calcutta businessmen for building up the party in the rural areas of the state.

The importance of the corporation to the party is so great that Atulya

[6] *The Report of the Corporation of Calcutta Investigation Commission*, the Government of West Bengal Local Self-Government Department, 1949, generally known as the Biswas Report, and the *Report of the Corporation of Calcutta Enquiry Commission*, Government of West Bengal, 1962, the "Talukdar Committee Report."

Ghosh pays greater attention to exercising party control over the corporation than is characteristic of Congress organizations in many other Indian cities. All Congress councillors belong to the Congress Municipal Association. Atulya Ghosh is president of the association, and there are a deputy leader, a chief whip, and two assistant secretaries. The mayor and deputy mayor of Calcutta are theoretically non-political, but actually they are Congress party men. They do not, however, hold offices in the party organization, and their nomination by the Congress Municipal Association is dependent upon the support of Atulya Ghosh. This prevents the mayor or deputy mayor from becoming independent political forces.

The municipal association meets weekly in, incidentally, the PCC office in downtown Calcutta to discuss policy positions which the party ought to take in the municipal corporation. It was, for example, the municipal association which decided to exclude all opposition parties from the standing committees of the corporation shortly after the 1961 election on the grounds that "Congress ought to have full responsibility for the municipal administration"; but the opposition claimed the decision was directed at giving Congress full patronage powers.

Most of the Congress municipal councillors are presidents of their local Congress mandal committees. Each councillor candidate has to raise money for his own election campaign. It is estimated that each councillor must spend at least fifteen hundred rupees — that is, about three hundred dollars — to conduct his campaign. No salary is paid to the councillors. Most of the councillors are businessmen, lawyers, and doctors.

The chief minister of West Bengal, B. C. Roy, was for many years critical of the Calcutta Municipal Corporation. In 1948, after a period of great turmoil, the corporation was temporarily superseded and Calcutta was governed directly by an officer appointed by the West Bengal government. A new act was passed in 1951 which took away some of the powers the corporation had under the 1923 act. Nonetheless, the bureaucracy and chief minister of West Bengal have continued to be critical of the corporation, and from time to time there has been talk of further limiting its powers and reducing the opportunities for exercising patronage; these proposals have all been successfully opposed by the Congress organization. Not until 1965, when it seemed likely that Congress could win municipal elections based on universal adult suffrage, did the state government pass legislation to extend the suffrage.[7] It is very clear that the party leadership sees control over the municipal corporation as an important

[7] For an account of the 1965 Calcutta Municipal elections, see Robi Chakravorti, "The Personality Factor in Local Politics," *Economic Weekly* (June 26, 1965): 1027–30.

factor in its strategy of combining urban finances with rural votes to give the party control over the state. It is, after all, a strategy which has thus far succeeded.

## Factionalism and Cohesion

Compared to other states in India, West Bengal has enjoyed comparative political stability. Congress has ruled the state uninterruptedly since independence. One chief minister was in office from 1948 until his death in 1962, the longest tenure of any Indian chief minister and a long period of uninterrupted leadership for any elected head of a democratic system. There had been no serious threat to this leadership, and within the state Congress party there have been relatively few squabbles compared to other Congress party organizations in other states. Even compared to other political groups in West Bengal, the Congress party has maintained relatively high cohesion.

The stability of the West Bengal government — which is the direct consequence of the electoral strength and inner cohesion of the Congress party organization — is particularly remarkable in view of the severe economic and social dislocations which the state has experienced. For those who see political stability as an outgrowth of a prosperous and growing economy and instability as the effect of comparative stagnation, the case of West Bengal offers a challenge. In this section we shall look at the factors which account for the inner cohesion of the Congress party organization through 1962, and later shall examine the sources of the party's electoral strength.

From 1947 to 1950 internal factionalism in Congress was so great that it appeared unlikely that the Congress party could hold itself together sufficiently to win the elections of early 1952.

At the time of independence there were at least three important factional groups within the Congress party. One faction, known as the Jugantar group, dominated the Bengal Congress organization. This group was an old and famous terrorist organization that began in 1906. Of course it was no longer a terrorist group, but consisted of rather elderly members of the Congress party who as young men had engaged in terrorist activities. The membership of the Jugantar faction came primarily from East and North Bengal, areas which were absorbed into East Pakistan at the time of partition. A second faction, known as the Gandhians, won the support of the Congress high command in Delhi and soon took control of both the

party organization and the West Bengal government itself. The leader of the Gandhian group became the first chief minister of West Bengal after independence. However, while the Gandhian group had the support of the Congress high command, it did not have the support of the Congress members of the legislative assembly. A third group, the now familiar Hooghly group, had become the single most powerful force within the party organization, particularly among the Congress members of the legislative assembly. In a series of brilliant strategic moves, the Hooghly group took control of the entire party organization, the state government, and the chief ministership. They first joined with the Jugantar group to overthrow the Gandhian group, which then controlled the state government. The Jugantar group was eager to work with the Hooghly group, since they thought this would be one means by which they could regain some of the political strength they had lost as a result of partition. With the support of the Jugantar group, the Hooghly group then proceeded to win over B. C. Roy, a well-known nationalist figure in Bengal who was not a participant in any of the factions contending for power; with the support of the high command, Roy was elected chief minister. Atulya Ghosh then proceeded to reward some of the Jugantar leaders with innocuous posts in the upper house of parliament. Some of the lesser figures were absorbed into the local party organization and into the Hooghly group. A few of the Jugantar leaders and members were dissatisfied; but since they had no local roots in West Bengal, there was no way in which they could actively oppose Atulya Ghosh.

Atulya Ghosh made no effort to pacify the Gandhians. He set out to starve the opposition within his own party, just as later he set out to starve the opposition parties. We need not explore here the details of the struggle between the Gandhians and the dominant Hooghly group, since I have done so elsewhere.[8] Several points are, however, noteworthy. First of all, each of the three factions was relatively cohesive. A simple alliance of two groups against the third made it easy to bring about a change in the government. Second, once in power, the dominant Hooghly group did not try to pacify the losing faction and made little effort to prevent them from leaving Congress. Third, the Gandhian group subsequently left Congress to form their own party, which contested in the 1952 elections. The new party was badly defeated, winning only fifteen seats in the legislative assembly against 151 for Congress. Fourth, the effect of the defeat of the dissidents in the 1952 elections was to strengthen the hold of the Hooghly

[8] Myron Weiner, *Party Politics in India*, pp. 65–97. See also "Political Development in West Bengal," pp. 251–52.

group within the Congress party organization. It was now clear that those Congressmen who disagreed with Atulya Ghosh and who left the party to run as independent candidates would probably be defeated. Atulya Ghosh's strategy for maintaining internal support was simple: he rewarded his supporters with public office, and punished his opponents by denying them public office.

Ghosh gained control of the election committee of the PCC. No Congressman could be nominated for the legislative assembly, parliament, or municipal bodies without the approval of this committee and therefore of Atulya Ghosh. Ghosh recognized that he had two major organizational problems: one was to prevent dissident factions from rising within the party to reduce the power of the Hooghly group, and the other was to maintain the cohesion of the Hooghly group itself. The most serious danger was that B. C. Roy, the chief minister, might support a dissident group within the Congress party organization. Roy himself was not a member of the Hooghly group. He was, as we have noted, a distinguished figure in Bengali public life who had the support of Prime Minister Nehru and the high command in New Delhi. Roy had been unhappy with the state of the municipal corporation, and felt that the West Bengal government ought to have more direct powers over municipal matters. The 1951 act limited the powers of the municipal councillors, but not enough to satisfy Roy. In all likelihood the West Bengal government would have more actively intervened in the municipality, except that the party organization would not have tolerated any further large-scale intervention. Only the bureaucracy of the West Bengal government supported Roy's efforts to diminish the powers of the municipality. Ghosh defended the municipal corporation, and no new legislation could be passed by the Congress members of the legislative assembly without his support. The state government and the municipal government therefore constantly abused and harassed one another. But the Congress party organization itself was remarkably unaffected by this conflict.

Roy had little respect for Atulya Ghosh and the leaders of the party organization. A biographer — a sympathetic one, we might add — referred to a charge in the assembly that, on the basis of an analysis of the government's budget proposals, the chief minister controlled 45 per cent of the state's finances. "I say, Sir, he is entirely wrong," Roy is quoted as having replied, adding, "I control one hundred per cent of the state's finances as the finance minister. Besides, I know about the finances of all other departments." The omnivorous quality of the chief minister as an administrator was further described by his biographer, who pointed out that Roy

had been minister in charge of home, minister of finance, minister of development, minister of cottage and small-scale industries, and minister of cooperation. Other departments of government, like industry and commerce, medical and public health, port and pilotage, printing press, and several miscellaneous departments, had been under his management. These departments, his biographer wrote, constituted nearly three-fourths of the government of West Bengal.[9]

Roy's attitude toward his own administration grew partly out of his autocratic character, but it was also related to the fact that he dared not permit too much power to fall into the hands of the party leadership. From the very beginning, therefore, Roy brought into the cabinet a number of individuals who were not closely associated with the Congress party, particularly with the Hooghly group. But only two of Roy's close associates appeared likely to be a threat to Atulya Ghosh and the Hooghly group. Both were prominent lawyers in Calcutta. Both were "untainted" by factional party politics. Both were widely respected by Calcutta's intellectual and professional population. Through Roy's personal intervention, one was elected to the legislative assembly and brought into the state government as the law minister. The other, Ashoke Sen, also through Roy's efforts, was elected to parliament and subsequently made a member of Prime Minister Nehru's cabinet. Both were Calcutta men, and neither had any substantial success in winning the support of dissident elements within the Congress party organization. The MLA subsequently joined the opposition, but Ashoke Sen continued to work within the Congress party organization. It was widely rumored that Nehru thought Ashoke Sen ought to replace Roy as chief minister when the latter retired.

In 1962 Sen was reelected to parliament from North Calcutta. But Atulya Ghosh had been so successful in combating Sen that the latter had to devote all his efforts simply to get reelected and could do very little to build up any significant opposition to Ghosh within Congress. It is interesting to note the instruments available to the president of the party organization for undercutting opposition within his own party. In the 1962 elections the party organization gave no financial and a minimum of organizational support to Sen. Since he was a member of Nehru's government it would have been impossible for Ghosh to deny him a parliamentary seat, but Ghosh could prevent Congress MLA candidates in Sen's constituency from working for his reelection.

Ghosh also took steps to prevent Sen from establishing any base within

[9] K. P. Thomas, *Dr. B. C. Roy* (Calcutta: West Bengal Pradesh Congress Committee, 1955).

the party organization in North Calcutta. When the mandal committees of North Calcutta had to elect a representative to the AICC, they did not select Sen, their representative in parliament. But since it would have proved embarrassing for Ghosh if Sen, an MP and a member of the cabinet, were not in the AICC, Ghosh had him selected from a district outside Calcutta. It was a district which Sen had not visited and one which could hardly become a stronghold for him. Some of Sen's supporters tried, without success, to get control of the mandal committees in North Calcutta. Sen was returned to parliament in 1962 but, thanks to Atulya Ghosh, he had failed to establish any base within the Congress organization.

Ghosh has had equal success in maintaining a high degree of cohesion within the Hooghly group. Though there have been frequent rumors of a fallout between Ghosh and P. C. Sen, in fact the two have managed to work together remarkably successfully during the last decade. The two men lunch together almost daily. When B. C. Roy died in 1962, it was clear that Ghosh had the power to select a successor. It was Ghosh who proposed the name of P. C. Sen, then the deputy chief minister and it was evident to all, including Sen, that Ghosh was the kingmaker. Ghosh had demonstrated that, as the party leader in Calcutta and in West Bengal as a whole, he has greater power than he has thus far cared to exercise and that he prefers to exercise his power outside the public's range of vision.

### Cadres and Leaders

The composition of the Congress party of Calcutta today is quite different from what it was before independence. As elsewhere in the country, Congress before 1947 was a composite of a wide variety of social and political groups. The Calcutta Congress consisted of many individuals who belonged to organized groups within the Congress party: the Communist party, the Congress Socialist party, the Revolutionary Socialist party of India, and several smaller Marxist political organizations. These all voluntarily withdrew or were expelled from the Congress party organization. Moreover, the bulk of the Congress cadres and leaders from Calcutta were supporters of Subhas Chandra Bose. When he withdrew to form his own party, the Forward Bloc, most Congress party workers supported him. By 1947 the most active party workers and the most prominent politicians in the city were in political groups other than the Congress party. But while Atulya Ghosh and the state party leadership attempted to build

or rebuild the party organization in the rural areas of West Bengal, Calcutta was not completely neglected. As we have seen, the 1951 act which reestablished the Calcutta corporation provided for limited suffrage, thereby making it possible for Congress to retain control of the corporation.

Moreover, there were many Congressmen in Calcutta who actively worked to rebuild the party organization. Few of Calcutta's intellectuals and professionals returned to the Congress party, although these persons had been the mainstay of the party in the pre-independence era. Individuals with a revolutionary bent of mind, concerned with broader ideological questions, turned to the opposition parties. Congress instead won its support primarily from smaller businessmen, contractors, and, in general, individuals who were particularly concerned with the day-to-day activities of government as it affected their own interests. Of the thirteen Congressmen in 1957 who were in parliament or the state assembly or council from Calcutta, five were lawyers and three were businessmen. In the municipal corporation, representation of businessmen was considerably greater.

These changes in the composition of the Congress party in West Bengal are related to changes which occurred in the social system of the state, especially as these affected Calcutta. In the nineteenth century, Bengal's social structure was transformed through the rise of a new class of landowners (zamindars), the growth of an intermediary rural class of noncultivating rent receivers, and the emergence of a non-Bengali factory worker class and non-Bengali commercial class in Calcutta.[10] Until the middle of the nineteenth century, the zamindars were clearly the dominant Indian influence in the politics of Bengal, but thereafter the rural non-cultivating rent receivers grew in importance. This social class turned to the newly created colleges and universities and soon found jobs in government administration and in the British- and Marwari-created commercial establishments. Educated Bengalis flocked into the cities and towns of Bengal, especially to Calcutta, and many found positions in government administration in neighboring states throughout northern India. But by the latter part of the nineteenth century, the educated middle

[10] For descriptions of social change in nineteenth-century Bengal, see S. Gopal, *The Permanent Settlement and its Effect on Bengal* (London: Allen and Unwin, 1949); Mahendra Nath Gupta, *Land System of Bengal* (Calcutta: University of Calcutta, 1940); K. C. Chaudhuri, *The History of Economics of the Land System in Bengal* (Calcutta: The Book Co., 1927); Ram Krishna Mukherjee, *The Dynamics of a Rural Society* (Berlin: Akademie Verlag, 1957); Bruce McCully, *English Education and the Origins of Indian Nationalism* (New York: Columbia University Press, 1940); and N. K. Bose, "Modern Bengal," *Man in India* (Calcutta): 38 (Oct.–Dec., 1958): 229–95.

classes had grown larger than the number of jobs available to them. Young men of rural gentry background, college graduates but unemployed, Westernized men of predominantly high castes (Brahmins, Voidyas, and Kayasthas) — these became the organizers and leaders of Bengal's terrorist movement. In the early part of the nineteenth century the bhadralok or gentlemen, as Bengalis call members of the middle classes, constituted Bengal's active political class in Calcutta, Midnapore, Dacca, Comilla, and Barisal.

After the First World War there was a marked change in the social, economic, and political position of the bhadralok. As the number of educated young men increased in the neighboring states of Orissa, Assam, Bihar, and Uttar Pradesh, the demand for Bengalis in middle-class occupations decreased. Similarly, the development of political leadership in other states, especially in Gujarat, Uttar Pradesh, and Bihar, decreased the national role which Bengali politicians had once played. Bengalis continued in the nationalist movement, but, as we have seen, it was as leaders of dissident elements, not as national spokesmen. Finally, other areas of India were now experiencing the cultural renaissance which had stirred Bengal in the nineteenth century and which had aroused the admiration of Indians of other regions. Bengal no longer held the revered intellectual, cultural, and political position it once had. Thus, developments elsewhere in India decreased the cultural and political standing and employment opportunities of the Bengali middle classes.

This contraction of opportunities, both psychic and material, was of course compounded by partition. As we have seen, middle-class Hindu Bengalis left their homes in East Pakistan to move into Calcutta, now the capital of a small, densely populated, truncated state, larger only than Kerala and tiny Nagaland, and whose economy was severely dislocated. Moreover, tensions grew between the government of West Bengal and the national government over the treatment of Bengali refugees, the issue of Hindi as an official language for India, and the issue of central government allocation of revenue to the states. The middle classes grew more and more hostile not only toward the national government but toward the Congress party of West Bengal, the provincial wing of the national government.

The material well-being of the Bengali middle classes also appears to have substantially declined after independence. According to the census for West Bengal, the cost of living index for Calcutta's middle class jumped from 100 in August, 1939, to 381 in May, 1952. Land reform legislation took rent collecting rights away from an estimated 1.2 million inter-

mediaries. Unemployment among the Bengali middle classes increased and is now proportionately greater than among non-Bengalis and the working classes in general. The neglect of urban services, sanitation, public health facilities, and water supply, along with a deterioration in housing, has been felt more by the Bengali middle classes than by other groups in the city.[11]

Few middle-class Bengalis now actively support the Congress party in Calcutta. Many continue to vote for Congress, but few have remained as active party cadres. Many young middle-class Bengalis have become political non-participants (there is some evidence that voting among the middle classes is slightly less than among other socio-economic groups in the city). Others take part in extremist politics as active supporters of the Communist and Marxist left parties.

It is no accident, therefore, that the most powerful Congressman in the city, Atulya Ghosh, spent most of his political life outside Calcutta. Nor is it an accident that with the declining participation of the middle classes the most prominent party workers should be small entrepreneurs concerned with the day-to-day functioning of the municipal and state administration. This shift from middle-class party cadres to professional politicians and businessmen meant a marked shift in the character of the party, its style, its program, and its outlook. To understand the way in which the Congress organization works in Calcutta and the kind of leadership it now has, let us take a closer look at several party leaders in North Calcutta, then at several Congress members of the municipal corporation, and finally at Atulya Ghosh himself.[12]

*Party secretary.* We have selected the North Calcutta District Congress Committee for examination since this organization typifies some of the changing characteristics of the party organization throughout the city. North Calcutta has a large middle-class Bengali population and was once the center of nationalist activities. Most of the once prominent politicians are now active in the left parties, and most of the legislative assembly seats are in their hands. However, Congress still retains control of the representatives in the Calcutta Municipal Corporation. Party workers are largely small businessmen. The member of parliament, a Congressman (the only Congress MP in the city, incidentally), is an "intellectual," a

[11] I have documented the status and income decline of the Calcutta middle classes in "Political Development in West Bengal," pp. 235–41.

[12] For a statistical analysis of the social composition of the Congress party leadership in West Bengal, see my "Political Leadership in West Bengal," pp. 177–227. This study contains an analysis of 408 political leaders in West Bengal, half of whom were Congressmen.

wealthy lawyer, and a member of the Indian cabinet, but he is disliked and barely tolerated by Congress party workers.

The North Calcutta DCC is one of the four district Congress committees in the city of Calcutta. It consists of twenty-one mandal committees, and covers an area which elects seven representatives to the state assembly. It does not coincide exactly with any single parliamentary constituency, though most of the North West Parliamentary constituency of Ashoke Sen falls in this area. In Calcutta as a whole there are eighty mandal committees, each one coinciding with a municipal corporation ward. Unlike the mandal organizations in the rural areas of India, which do not coincide with any administrative or governmental unit, the mandal committees in Calcutta do fit governmental units. However, as elsewhere in India, it is the DCC rather than the mandal committee which is the most effective unit of the organization.

The area covered by the North Calcutta DCC is a stronghold for left-wing activity. The opposition parties control six of the seven assembly seats. Two are Communist, two are members of the Forward Bloc, which continues to run as an independent party, and two are members of the Praja Socialist party.

The party organization of North Calcutta is run by Suhrid Rudra. Rudra is a tall, middle-aged man, an energetic party worker, who devotes all of his time to political work. He owns a plant which produces printing type, but the business is actually run by his brothers, so that he is able to work full-time for the party. Except for a brief interlude, Rudra has been secretary of the District Congress Committee since 1951. Like other DCC bosses, Rudra is a member of the Hooghly group of Atulya Ghosh.

Rudra runs an active party office. The DCC office is located in a crowded bazaar in a Bengali area, and occupies an entire floor of a rather large office building. The office contains a half dozen rooms and a large meeting hall, all of which are sparsely furnished. There are chairs and tables, a few blackboards, and some large closets containing party literature and record books. One room is used as the office of the Youth Congress, which claims a membership in North Calcutta of fifteen hundred, all between the ages of eighteen and thirty-five. The office contains a small library of school textbooks. A small adjoining room is used for tutoring purposes. Another room is set up as a classroom, and on the days of my visits the blackboards were covered with Hindi script—a party worker teaches classes in reading and writing Hindi. Still another room is reserved for use by the women's section of the party. The DCC also houses the office of the labor department, which consists of Congress party workers in the

Indian National Trade Union Congress. According to Rudra, there are approximately a thousand active members of the North Calcutta DCC and about twenty thousand primary members. Of the active members, only about five hundred actually do any work for the party.

Some of the most active party work, he reported, is done by the Congress municipal councillors. Though Congress has lost most of the MLA seats in North Calcutta, Congress elected fifteen of the twenty-one municipal councillors in this same area. These councillors, according to Rudra,

> look into the tax assessment of houses and complaints of rate payers over things like the supply of filtered water, the clearing of garbage, and so on. These councillors are also on the managing body of the hospitals in their wards, and can recommend a patient to the hospital and look into whether patients are getting proper treatment or not. Then our councillors also look after the primary schools, especially the teachers. If there's a strike of the teachers for salary increments, the councillor meets with them and brings their problem to the Education Standing Committee of the corporation.

Though Congress has not done well in North Calcutta, its position has considerably improved since 1952. According to Rudra, it is difficult for the party to satisfy the demands of urban people as easily as rural people, since people want services which government cannot so readily provide. However, he feels that the growth of the party depends largely upon, as he put it, the "social activities" of the party, by which he meant both social welfare activities and cultural activities. He explained:

> There are so many social work agencies in Calcutta through which the Congress party works. There is the Ram Krishna Institute. All the workers there are Congressmen, so what they do is a help to the Congress party. There is the Sevak Samiti, which provides bustee people with medical aid, free milk, and free clothing. The government cannot help the Congress directly, but the government does give money to these social welfare organizations.

Rudra himself is deeply involved in many of these social work organizations. He is also an active organizer of cultural activities. The Bengali areas of Calcutta — and North Calcutta is predominantly Bengali — con-

tain a large number of social and cultural organizations. There is hardly a street which does not contain one or more clubs — dramatic clubs, social clubs, athletic clubs, and the like. The most active clubs are those engaged in cultural and religious activities, and Rudra is particularly active in these. He was, for example, the organizer of a Tagore festival, of great local interest since Tagore himself had been a resident of North Calcutta.

Rudra is a professional party organizer. He knows every party worker by name. He knows the streets of North Calcutta, the prominent individuals who live on them, the social groups which they contain, and the political predisposition of the residents. He knows the ins and outs of both party organization and the municipal corporation. He is described by fellow Congressmen as a "political animal."

*Trade union organizer.* Another Congressman popularly described as a political animal is Nepal Roy, a trade union leader and the only Congress MLA from North Calcutta. Roy's office, which he shares with the labor department, is housed in the DCC office run by Rudra. It is said of Roy that he is surrounded by "goondas" (a term used to describe professional hoodlums), "but he is a good organizer, particularly among the clubs." Another critic said, "He is in the cement business as an agent, but it is well known that he adulterates cement with mud from the Ganges." He is said to have "no fixed political principles."

But if Roy appears to have many enemies and critics, he also has a vast number of friends and ardent supporters. He is constantly surrounded by young party and trade union workers. He is an energetic politician who exudes self-confidence and who, unlike many Indian politicians who attempt to be self-effacing, is boastful of his accomplishments. He is a calculating politician and proud of it.

Like many professional politicians, Roy entered politics at an early age. He was eighteen years old when he joined Calcutta's Anushilan Samiti, a well-known terrorist organization. He was very active in student politics as an ardent supporter of the Forward Bloc. He ran for the assembly for the first time in 1952 on a Forward Bloc ticket and joined Congress in 1956. At forty-two, he runs a clay factory that employs about sixty workers. He is also an agent and dealer in cement, oil, paint, and other building materials. "I don't have much time for my business these days," he said, "since I must do political work all day long."

Roy claims to have about 250 active party supporters doing political work for him during the elections — most of these, young boys and young men. He explained why he has their enthusiastic support.

I have managed to find employment for thousands of Bengali boys in the government during the last ten years. Many of them are employed as clerks or nurses in the health department. These jobs do not fall under the public service commission but are given simply on the basis of interviews. The head of the health department loves me and my activities very much because of what I have done in the hospitals to eliminate the Communists who were giving much trouble there. The health department is rapidly expanding and so needs many people. Whenever there are openings I send my boys down for interviews.

It was not until 1956, when Roy joined Congress, that he entered trade union work, and the first union he organized was in the Calcutta Medical College and Hospital, located in the constituency of B. C. Roy, the chief minister. "It is the biggest hospital in all of India and it was controlled by the Communists. Only about 10 per cent of the people who work in that hospital voted for B. C. Roy in the last election, and he almost lost the election. I told Roy that these people are government servants, and so we shall organize them to make sure that they are for us. So I decided to do trade union work just to oust the Communists." Today, according to Nepal Roy, the hospital unions are under his control.

Roy also tried to break the Communist hold on the tramway union.

In 1958 I had only seven members in the tramway union and now I have seven thousand members out of a work force of eleven thousand. I built myself up by organizing a strike of the tramway workers. There was even pressure on me from the government to call it off, but in order to keep the leadership of the workers I had to lead the strike. The Communists wanted to settle the dispute without a strike and started to negotiate with the British owners of the company. But we tapped their telephone and found out what they were doing. Before the Communists could announce a settlement I quickly called a meeting of all the tram workers, and at that meeting I asked the workers whether they wanted to strike or not. They all shouted that they did, and then I immediately broke up the meeting. That's how I beat the Communists. I consider myself their first enemy. I am known as a fighter in West Bengal.

*Marwari businessman.* B. P. Poddar, another Congress candidate elected to the legislative assembly in 1962, is quite different from Nepal Roy. While Roy has been deeply involved in terrorist and trade union activities, Poddar has been a participant in more conservative organizations in Calcutta public affairs.

> My family has always been in public life. My grandfather, my father, and my elder brother are all active in public affairs. So that is why I have taken to public life. It is a prestige position for us. I spend four or five hours each day in these things. The Marwari Relief Society takes a good part of my time. It runs hospitals and does so many welfare activities. I am also president of the Bharat Chamber of Commerce. I am a member of the AICC. I am treasurer of the Bharat Sevak Sangh. I am president of several local schools and vice chairman of the Indian Red Cross Society. I am also a trustee of the Calcutta Improvement Trust and spend about six hours a week attending their meetings. I must be a member of at least fifty committees and organizations.

Poddar is one of the few non-Bengalis active in political life in West Bengal and in Calcutta. He belongs to the Marwari community, a mercantile community which migrated from the state of Rajasthan to engage in business activities in Calcutta. Poddar's family has lived in Calcutta for three generations, and, unlike other Marwaris in Calcutta, he speaks Bengali well. Poddar is a very wealthy businessman, and among his other activities he sells automobiles. It is his wealth which makes it possible for him to run his own political organization in his constituency. Only one of the three mandal committees in his constituency is active and can play any role in his election campaign.

> I try to extract some help from these mandal committees, but I don't get much. I tell you frankly that the mandal committees do not always have such good people. They are not generally the respectable people in the locality. There are a few shopkeepers, some schoolteachers, and many people in services. After I received the nomination I contracted the president and secretary of each of the three mandal committees, and they each arranged a meeting with their workers for me. At these meetings I spoke to the workers and asked

them to tell me what problems and complaints they might have.

The difficulty is that every man thinks that an MLA is a ruler who can make decisions in matters of government, so there are many difficulties which the people raise which the MLA cannot actually deal with. You only have access to people that the ordinary man does not have access to. After meeting all these people at the mandal committee meetings I picked out several important people in each of the mandal committees. Then I started door-to-door visits with some of these people. We would walk down each street. I would meet the people that matter in a house—the important people, not everyone. Then after I talked to that person, I would ask him to introduce me to some other people in the house or the locality. But before I enter a locality I pick up some influential person to help me. Then I prepare a list in each locality of the people who are influential and who would help me.

We do hire many boys to work for us during the elections. Some are good, but frankly many are not the right type but simply want to get some money out of the election. But we have to hire some of them to silence them; otherwise these boys may create a nuisance by tearing posters off the wall. We hire about a thousand workers during the campaign. Just recently a man came to me to ask me to hire fifteen of his boys, but I refused, telling him that I just did not have that much money. But then in a day or two the locality was flooded with leaflets by him saying that I was a dishonest man and I made promises now but once I was elected to the legislative assembly I would do nothing for my people.

We talked about the major issues in his locality during the campaign.

Oh, some people say you are from Congress and we are with you, but others say you are with Congress and we have so many complaints. They say that the garbage has not been picked up, or they complain that they cannot get cement or other things. Where it is possible I take down their complaints and see if something can be done to help them. I see if their drainage or garbage collection can be improved.

Sometimes someone legitimately needs a permit, and I try to help; or if someone needs a certificate, then I will help them. Sometimes someone has trouble with a government department, and I try to help them out. There is much difficulty with the police about post mortems. Hindus don't like to have this done to bodies, but sometimes the police require this if there is an unnatural death. I have had to handle many problems like this. I have handled four post mortem examinations in the last four months. In each case I have been able to get the body released from the police. Then sometimes a person comes to me because he is not in a position to buy books — textbooks. Just this morning someone came to my house to ask for medical treatment, and we got them into the hospital without any charge.

It is generally known that the Marwari businessmen in Calcutta are not well liked by the Bengali population. The leftist parties in particular bitterly denounce the Marwari business class as exploiters. Many Marwaris are influential in the West Bengal government, but few take an active part in the entire state; all of these are within the Congress party. The minister of local government in the West Bengal government is a Marwari, as is the treasurer of the Congress party organization. Two or three other MLAs and MLCs in the Congress party belong to the Marwari community.

*Party treasurer.* Another prominent Marwari, Bijoy Singh Nahar, is the treasurer of the Pradesh Congress Committee and is the only Marwari with an important position in the Congress party organization. It is interesting to note, however, that his speech, dress, and manners are so Bengali that many people are unaware of his Marwari origins. In 1962 he was a successful candidate for the legislative assembly. In an interview he spoke eloquently of Congress' weakness in Calcutta compared to the rural areas of the state.

You will not find as much improvement in the towns as you will find in the rural areas. The urban areas have had little improvement in things like water, drainage, and housing, which are big problems. Unemployment is also a very big problem. And the refugees from East Bengal have been another factor in the position of the Congress in the city, although the Congress party does get the refugee votes in the

rural areas. Many of the refugees are unemployed and undernourished and they are carrying on vigorous propaganda against the government. Then too the business people are not satisfied because taxes are high. The ordinary people pay more for food. Education is also a big problem. We have a limited number of seats in the colleges and schools here. A friend of mine just came back from abroad, and he has been having difficulty getting his son into a first-class school.

The third five-year plan pays more attention to the urban areas. There is now a Calcutta metropolitan development scheme, but in the past it was only the rural areas that were cared for. I tell people in my election campaign that we are going to do more for the city. I tell them that we have been working on the rural areas for the last ten years and have been especially concerned with food problems, but now for the first time we shall devote more attention to Calcutta. The development of the rural areas will benefit the towns too. Everyone wants higher status in society. Caste is not so important now, but education is becoming a mark of status. Village boys want more education, and then after they become educated they come to the towns for jobs. We must provide more amenities in the villages so that the educated boys will stay there and find work for themselves there.

In spite of these difficulties, he explained, the Congress party can still win elections in Calcutta. Whether Congress wins depends upon the kind of man nominated. Two factors were always considered, he said.

The first is who is likely to serve the people and then who is likely to win the election. Each of the DCCs listen to the recommendations made by the mandal committees and by individual members, and then the DCC sends a panel of names to the PCC. The PCC makes the final decision. We don't always accept the suggestions made by the base. There is a committee that makes the final decisions, and this committee is chaired by Atulya Ghosh.

We talked about the critical factors which decided whether a Congressman would get elected or not. He stressed the importance of the organization of the candidate.

Mr. Nepal Roy was a very good organizer, and that was one reason he won. But there are some areas that are very difficult for anyone to win, particularly those areas which have many refugees. It all depends on how well you persuade the leaders of the bustees. There are a number of leaders in each bustee, and whoever succeeds in capturing them can win their votes. I was able to win the supporters of the bustees in my constituency because I won the support of the fifteen or twenty leaders in the bustees. The candidate can't really depend upon the local Congress party organization. The mandal committee members can't be depended upon during the elections, and so the candidate must have his own workers. We must pick a man, therefore, who is popular in his locality, who can organize, and collect money to run the elections.

Isn't this somewhat unfair to the good worker who does not have money?

We do sometimes nominate a man who does not have money. In one constituency in South Calcutta we selected a school teacher who was a powerful man in his community. He is a man who has a great deal of local influence, but he does not have money. The PCC raises money for some candidates, but most of the money of the PCC is used for general work such as printing leaflets and posters. I can't say how much money each candidate spends, but a wealthy candidate often has to spend more money than a poor candidate since the public expects that he spend more money.

In fact, the individuals who do receive Congress nominations for the parliament, the assembly, or the municipal corporation are generally men of some financial means. But, as important as their wealth is, what is often more important is that these men are prominent figures in their own localities. Among some of the most important figures of the Congress party in the municipal corporation, one is a regional auditor of Burma Shell, another is a prominent pleader, a third is a businessman, a fourth is the editor of one of the leading Bengali newspapers, a fifth is a multi-millionaire businessman owning many textile mills, and a sixth is an owner of a printing press establishment.

*Party boss.* The most powerful Congressman in Calcutta, and in the

entire state of West Bengal, is Atulya Ghosh, the secretary of the PCC and president of the Congress Municipal Association. He is also the leader of the Hooghly group, which controls the party organization in the state. Though he has many enemies, his control over the party is incontestable.

Ghosh was born in Calcutta in 1905, and at the age of fifteen joined the North Calcutta Congress organization.[13] In 1923 he decided to leave Calcutta to work for the Congress party in nearby Hooghly district, where his ancestral home was. It was in Hooghly that Ghosh acquired many of his organizational skills. He established party units, engaged in flood and famine relief, took part in several non-cooperative movements, edited nationalist newspapers, fought British policemen (he lost his right eye in one such skirmish), and spent a number of years in jail. From 1923 to 1948 Ghosh spent most of his time in Hooghly, and came to acquire not only organizational skills but the reputation of being rural in background, manners, and speech.

Nonetheless, in spite of this reputation, Ghosh has strong connections with Calcutta and urban life. He knows the city well, is articulate and fluent in English, and appears to be well read in Western literature and philosophy. Though he is often described as an uncultured country bumpkin by many Calcutta intellectuals, he is a frequent writer in Bengali and is the author of several books.

While the Bengal Congress movement was being led by two urban leaders, C. R. Das and Subhas Bose, Ghosh and his associates learned to work in the countryside. In 1948 the Hooghly group, which included P. C. Sen, now chief minister of West Bengal, and several of the most important ministers in the present government, took control of the state party organization. Since the Congress party rules forbid any single individual to be chairman of the PCC for more than three consecutive years, Atulya Ghosh has alternated as president and vice-president since 1948. His control over the party organization has never been seriously threatened.

Atulya Ghosh can best be described as a professional politician. He judges all public policies in terms of their political consequences, and frankly views his task as one of maintaining a victorious party machine. Unlike Congressmen in many other parts of India who speak in lofty terms of decentralization, socialism, the cooperative commonwealth, or neutralism, Atulya Ghosh typically speaks only of specific public policies that are likely to affect the position of the party. Thus, in his public and

[13] This brief account of Atulya Ghosh is drawn largely from my interviews with him and his associates and from an excellent paper by Marcus F. Franda, "The Political Idioms of Atulya Ghosh." Atulya Ghosh also wrote to me to correct and comment on an earlier draft.

private conversations he has continually expressed a concern for the problems of relocating refugees and of high food prices, since both of these have serious electoral consequences for Congress.

Ghosh is not a man of great personal wealth. Though he is often accused by opposition leaders of using his position to strengthen the financial position of the party, he is generally thought of as being personally honest. He is a rotund figure, wears dark glasses, and dresses in a dhoti (as do most middle-class Bengalis). In New Delhi he lives in a small house provided for him as a member of parliament (a post he has held since 1952); in Calcutta he lives modestly. Though he is generally disliked by Calcutta's intellectuals, he is enthusiastically supported by party workers.

He has had one major concern: how to build an effective party organization in West Bengal. In an interview he described how the party was rehabilitated.

> Some well-known leaders resigned from the party in 1950 to form an opposition group. This was the condition when we came to Congress. Now all the DCCs are functioning, and some of the mandals are functioning too. All the district boards and all the school boards in the state are in our hands. Out of eighty-three municipalities, we are now running fifty-five. How did we do this? Prior to 1950 Congress was confined to the urban areas, but then we moved to the rural areas around the district towns. Before 1950 it was a paper show. We had representatives from Midnapure and other districts on the PCC, but they stayed here in Calcutta and we did all our recruiting from Calcutta. We were not strong in district towns as we are now, and now we have organizations in the rural parts of the districts too.

What would you say is the difference in the way the PCCs work in Calcutta and the way they work in the rural areas?

> The rural Congressmen are involved in development work — schools, industry, and all kinds of constructive work. If a Congressman says he is working, I ask him how many schools they have, how many roads have they built, and what about canals. That's what constructive work means in the rural areas. In Calcutta you have to have imagination to

see some definite work. The development of steel and coal and the railroads all benefit Calcutta, but people don't see it.

Under the leadership of Subhas Bose, the Congress party in Calcutta commanded the support of the intelligentsia and the urban middle classes, and had strong militant and ideological overtones. In contrast, Congress in Calcutta under Atulya Ghosh has worked largely with the rural migrants, shopkeepers, and businessmen, and relies heavily upon the use of patronage and — when necessary — corruption for the maintenance of its power.

Like machine politicians elsewhere, Atulya Ghosh believes that the strength of the party organization can be built up through the exercise of governmental power. A former mayor and bitter critic of Ghosh gave this intimate view of the way in which Ghosh functions. "I told Atulya Ghosh that if we do some good work for the city then Congress will grow. But Atulya Ghosh said to me, 'You don't know politics.' I told Atulya that if we serve the people we will get their vote, but he believes that the best way to defeat the opposition is to starve the wards which elect non-Congress councillors." Has Atulya's system been working? I asked. "Yes, it has," he said, shaking his head.

## 17. HOW CALCUTTA VOTES

In three consecutive elections the Congress MLA vote in Calcutta has risen from 39.7 to 42.6 to 47.2 per cent. Throughout West Bengal, in the countryside as well as in Calcutta, the Congress vote has improved. In Calcutta, however, there has been a marked polarization between Congress and the left opposition (the Praja Socialist party, the Communist party and the Marxist left parties). While the left opposition in West Bengal increased its rural vote only slightly from 29.3 per cent to 32.1 per cent between 1952 and 1957, during the same period its vote jumped in Calcutta from 34.0 per cent to 43.9 per cent. As a result, though the Congress vote increased in 1957, the leftist parties, who were then united for the first time, captured a majority of assembly seats in Calcutta (fifteen of twenty-six). The Congress increase in 1962 was at the expense of the leftists, the number of Congress seats rising from eight to fourteen of twenty-six.

Data are more readily available for finding out who votes for Congress in the areas outside Calcutta than within the city, since the census reports contain greater details for districts and towns than for individual wards of Calcutta. I have reported the results of an analysis of voting patterns for West Bengal as a whole elsewhere,[1] and shall simply summarize my findings here.

In West Bengal as a whole there is evidence that constituencies with a large Muslim population give a higher vote to Congress than constituencies with a low Muslim population (the correlation coefficient is .516).

[1] "Political Development in West Bengal," pp. 241–44.

20 per cent of West Bengal's population is Muslim; in Calcutta Muslims constitute 12 per cent of the population.

Congress also does well among scheduled castes and tribes. Congress won almost all the reserved seats both for the legislative assembly and for parliament. These communities constitute 23.7 per cent of the state but only 4.8 per cent of the city.

There is mixed statistical evidence that Congress does well among Hindi, Bihari, and other non-Bengali speaking people in the state (the correlation coefficient is .3). In West Bengal as a whole 15.4 per cent are non-Bengali, but in Calcutta the figure is 34.5 per cent. The bulk of the non-Bengalis live in the Calcutta metropolitan area.

Correlations for displaced persons from East Bengal are varied. Refugees who have settled in the countryside appear to vote for Congress, while those who live in the refugee camps in and around Calcutta appear to vote against Congress.

The lowest Congress vote is in constituencies with the largest proportion of Bengali caste Hindus. The correlation coefficient for MP constituencies was —.672 and for MLA constituencies —.465. In fourteen constituencies in which Bengali caste Hindus constituted 50 per cent or more of the population, Congress candidates won less than the state-wide party average of 40 per cent; in ten of the twelve constituencies in which Bengali caste Hindus made up less than half of the population, Congress won more than the state-wide average.

An analysis of state-wide voting patterns therefore shows that Congress strength lies primarily with minority social groups: Hindi, Bihari and other non-Bengalis, Muslims, and the scheduled castes and tribes.

So far we have spoken of the state as a whole. Let us now take a closer look at how Calcutta votes. As we have noted, Congress has shown a continuous increase in the city. In the 1962 elections this increase was spread almost evenly throughout the city. The Congress vote increased in twenty of twenty-six assembly constituencies. In 1962 Congress won more than a majority of the popular vote in ten constituencies and a fraction less than a clear majority in an eleventh. While only two of these constituencies could be described as safe for Congress (that is, Congress candidates had won in all three elections with ease), Congress had done better in these eleven constituencies in at least two of three elections than in other constituencies of the city.

There are seven constituencies in the city where Congress has consistently done badly, with no more than about 46 per cent of the vote and in most instances below 40 per cent. These are shown in Table 31.

TABLE 30
PRO-CONGRESS CONSTITUENCIES IN CALCUTTA
(Percentage of Vote)

|  | 1952 | 1957 | 1962 |
|---|---|---|---|
| Jorabagan. . . . . . | . . . .ᵃ | 46.7 | 58.3 |
| Jorasanko. . . . . | 31.3 | 59.8 | 58.0 |
| Bara Bazaar. . . . . | 71.5 | 74.8 | 74.5 |
| Bow Bazaar. . . . . | 58.7 | 50.1 | 58.9 |
| Chowringhee. . . . . | 60.4 | 69.8 | 72.0 |
| Ekbalpore. . . . . . | . . . .ᵃ | 48.4 | 49.5 |
| Kalighat . . . . . . | 36.8 | 48.0 | 51.1 |
| Fort . . . . . . . . | 65.6 | 51.5 | 51.8 |
| Sukeas Street . . . . | 35.9 | 43.4 | 51.0 |
| Muchipara . . . . . | . . . .ᵃ | 48.6 | 50.7 |
| Taltola . . . . . . . | . . . .ᵃ | 46.6 | 54.4 |

ᵃ These constituencies in 1952 could not be matched with the constituencies existing in 1957 and 1962.

TABLE 31
ANTI-CONGRESS CONSTITUENCIES IN CALCUTTA
(Percentage of Vote)

|  | 1952ᵃ | 1957 | 1962 |
|---|---|---|---|
| Alipur . . . . . . . | . . . . . . . | 37.0 | 41.5 |
| Tollygunge . . . . . | . . . . . . . | 29.9 | 39.2 |
| Rashbehari . . . . . | . . . . . . . | 39.3 | 36.9 |
| Manicktola . . . . . | . . . . . . . | 30.6 | 24.8 |
| Entally. . . . . . . | . . . . . . . | 37.8 | 41.9 |
| Burtola North. . . . | . . . . . . . | 35.8 | 41.8 |
| Vidyasagar . . . . . | . . . . . . . | 44.7 | 45.7 |

ᵃ None of the anti-Congress constituencies in 1952 could be matched with constituencies in 1957 and 1962.

There are some very significant differences between these seven anti-Congress and eleven pro-Congress constituencies. Before turning to a statistical examination of these constituencies, let us first take a look at three constituencies which Congress carried in 1962. These are in North West Calcutta where Congress won its only parliamentary seat in the 1957 elections.

Jorabagan elected Nepal Roy with 58.3 per cent of the vote, a considerable increase over the 46.7 plurality he won in 1957. In describing his constituency, Roy estimated that approximately 20 per cent of the population is Marwari, and another 32 per cent from Uttar Pradesh and Bihar. Less than half the population is Bengali. The constituency has almost no Muslims, and its working-class population consists largely of non-Bengali Hindi speakers. According to Roy, there are some three hundred or four hundred tramway workers and two hundred or three hundred hospital workers, mostly Bengalis, in unions under his control. Roy's strength has been greatest among the Marwari population and the Hindi-speakers,

but his Bengali party workers successfully made a dent in the Bengali population in the 1962 elections.

Bara Bazar has elected I. D. Jalan, the local government minister in the West Bengal government, three times — in each instance with an overwhelming majority of 70 per cent or more. Bara Bazar is thus the strongest Congress constituency in the city and one of the strongest in the state. According to Jalan, only 20 per cent of the population is Bengali, with the remainder Marwari, working-class migrants from Uttar Pradesh and Bihar (many of whom work as sweepers and guards in the buildings and commercial houses in the area), Gujaratis (mainly businessmen like the Marwaris), and Muslims. The constituency contains government buildings and large commercial establishments. Mr. Jalan described his election campaign: "I see the influential people in each locality and try to arrange meetings in the houses of these influential people." Who are the influential people? "They may be lawyers or businessmen or social workers. Since most of the constituency is non-Bengali, I speak Hindi a good part of the time. We also print some of our leaflets in Gujarati. When I talk to Muslims, I change my Hindi a little bit to use some Persian words. Most of the Muslims here are business people, so I am able to get their support."

Mr. Jalan is himself a Marwari — the only member of his community, incidentally, holding a ministerial post in the West Bengali government. He has been minister of local government since 1952, and before that, from 1947 to 1952, was the speaker of the legislative assembly. He has been in the assembly since 1938.

Jorasanko elected B. P. Poddar with 58 per cent of the vote, slightly less than was won in 1957 by his now-deceased elder brother. His brother had been in the assembly for some twenty years and had established excellent contacts in the constituency. It is a mixed area with a substantial number of East Pakistani refugees, a large non-Bengali migrant population, and one industrial ward. Approximately 15 per cent of the population live in bustees. Poddar explained how he organized his campaign:

> I believe that the average man is not interested in the elections. There is not much point in having too many street corner meetings, since only the party workers attend and the average man will not listen. But we will do it anyway in order to increase the tempo of the elections. My idea is to get one person in each house to be in charge for me. Say there are fifty voters in the house. I tell him that he must get as many of these votes as possible. There are about twenty-

five hundred houses in my locality. If I can get someone in each of one thousand houses that will be good. I am not interested in the houses with only one or two families, but those with fifty people or more.

As a result of the large vote given to the Congress parliamentary candidate in Jorasanko, Bara Bazar, Jorabagan, and one other constituency — Bow Bazar — Congress carried the parliamentary seat in both 1957 and 1962. The North West Calcutta parliamentary constituency consists of seven assembly constituencies. It is estimated by local Congressmen that in the entire area there are approximately two hundred thousand Bengalis and as many as a hundred and fifty thousand non-Bengalis. This is a considerably higher proportion of non-Bengalis than is found in the remainder of the city, and helps to account for the Congress victories here. The campaign manager for Ashoke Sen in the 1962 elections, explaining why Sen lost so heavily in three of the seven assembly constituencies in 1957, put it quite boldly: "The larger the Bengali population is, the lower is the vote for Ashoke Sen." He estimated that in one of the three constituencies (Cossipur) the Bengalis were 60 per cent, in a second (Burtola South) 80 per cent, and in the third (Shampukur) as high as 95 per cent.

## Congress and the Migrants

It has often been argued that the high rate of migration into urban centers in the developing nations is politically unstabilizing. According to this proposition, rural migrants are unsettled by the urbanization experience, since male migrants often move to the city without their families, are quartered in urban slums without civilizing amenities, and are frequently cut off from the social controls of their tribe, caste, kinsmen, or village. As a consequence, it is concluded, migrants to cities are attracted to extremist political organizations and are easily provoked to commit violence.

This widely held view was eloquently propounded by Barbara Ward.

All over the world, often long in advance of effective industrialization, the unskilled poor are streaming away from subsistence agriculture to exchange the squalor of rural poverty for the even deeper miseries of the shanty-towns, favellas, and bidonvilles that, year by year, grow inexorably on the fringes of the developing cities. They are the core of local

despair and disaffection — filling the Jeuness movements of the Congo, swelling the urban mobs of Rio, voting Communist in the ghastly alleys of Calcutta, everywhere undermining the all too frail structure of public order and thus retarding the economic development that can alone help their plight.[2]

Since urban areas are rapidly growing in India, as elsewhere, since the urban areas often have a great deal of political instability and violence, and since the growth of urban areas is primarily the result of rural to urban migration rather than of high fertility rates, it is thus logically assumed that it is the migrants who are responsible for political disturbances and violence.

Moreover, since Calcutta has a high Communist vote and conditions for rural migrants are patently poor, it would at first appear as if Calcutta provides evidence to support the proposition. Our analysis of the voting patterns in Calcutta demonstrate just the reverse — the Congress vote appears to be highest among the most recent migrants to the city and lowest for the most settled urban residents.[3] In the remainder of this chapter we shall try to demonstrate this assertion.

Two-thirds of the population of Calcutta were born outside the city. The migrants fall into two groups with quite different characteristics: refugees who, shortly before or after partition, fled from Pakistan because of communal disturbances; ordinary migrants from other portions of Bengal (East or West) and other Indian states. One study of Calcutta proposes that those who entered the city after 1934 be classified as migrants and that those who have lived in the city longer or were born in the city be classified as original residents.[4] This would divide the population as follows: residents, 57 per cent; refugees 17 per cent; migrants 26 per cent.

*Refugees.* When India was partitioned in 1947 into two successor states — Pakistan and India — the state of Bengal was partitioned also.

[2] "The Uses of Prosperity," *Saturday Review* (Aug. 29, 1964): 191–92.

[3] In addition to analyzing the voting patterns of residents and migrants, it would be useful to examine how particular ethnic groups and occupations voted, but, unfortunately, city-wide breakdowns are not available. Even in the analysis of migrant and resident voting patterns, the data are not completely satisfactory, for, in the absence of survey data which could specify how individuals actually vote, we have had to rely upon the less satisfactory technique of ecological correlation. It is, however, the only type of data now available.

[4] S. N. Sen, *The City of Calcutta: A Socio-economic survey, 1954–55 to 1957–58* (Calcutta: Bookland Private Limited, 1960). Other demographic data used here are from *Census of India*, Vol. VI, Part III, *Census of India — 1961 Final Population Totals*, and *Corporation of Calcutta Year Book, 1961–62*.

The larger portion, predominantly Muslim, went to Pakistan; the smaller portion, predominantly Hindu, and including Calcutta, went to India. Hindu minorities in Pakistan soon flocked to India, many of them to Calcutta, while Muslim minorities fled to Pakistan.

The refugees came with their families (there is an almost even ratio of men to women) and, unlike ordinary migrants to urban centers, were completely cut off from their original homes. As one might expect, the refugees were resentful of a government which could neither return them to their homes nor adequately (in a material or psychic sense) compensate them. Voting data suggest that in three consecutive elections—in 1952, 1957, and 1962—the majority of refugees of Calcutta voted against the Congress party. In the city as a whole the Congress MLA vote in the three elections was 39.7 per cent, 42.6 per cent, and 47.2 per cent. In the six constituencies which Congress lost in 1952 with less than 30 per cent of the vote, the refugee population ranged from 12 per cent to 41 per cent. Of the seven constituencies in which Congress won a majority, five had refugee populations of less than 10 per cent and the other two only slightly more. The rank order correlation for the Congress vote and the refugee population in the 1952 elections is −.87. This indicates that where the Congress vote was high there were few refugees and that where refugees were numerous the Congress vote was low.

Similarly, in the 1957 and 1962 elections the areas won by Congress had few refugees (12 per cent or less, except for three constituencies with slightly higher refugee populations, which Congress barely won). On the other hand, the areas with a low Congress vote had larger refugee concentrations, ranging from 16 per cent to 39 per cent. In only one constituency with a refugee population of more than 15 per cent (slightly less than the average for the city) has Congress ever won a majority of votes.

It is important to note that the refugees did not move to Calcutta because they were attracted by the city's employment possibilities or urban amenities. They left their homes because they were forced to do so by communal disturbances. Compared to other migrants, they are better educated, more often come from other urban areas of East Pakistan, and have stronger preferences for white-collar jobs.[5] Unemployment among them is three times that of ordinary migrants (12.2 per cent in 1957 as against 4.8 per cent for migrants and 8.5 per cent among residents), but unlike migrants, they cannot return home.[6]

*Migrants.* Let us now turn to the more typical migrants to the city. Ex-

[5] Sen, *The City of Calcutta*, p. 227.
[6] *Ibid.*, p. 228.

TABLE 32
CONGRESS AND THE REFUGEE VOTE IN CALCUTTA

| | PERCENTAGE OF REFUGEES | CONGRESS VOTE (% OF TOTAL) |
|---|---|---|
| **1952 Legislative Assembly Election[a]** | | |
| *High Congress* | | |
| Bara Bazar . . . . . . . . | 2.8 | 71.5 |
| Coolootola . . . . . . . . | 8.5 | 70.6 |
| Watgunge . . . . . . . . . | 7.5 | 65.6 |
| Fort . . . . . . . . . . | 8.0 | 65.6 |
| Taltola . . . . . . . . . | 10.8 | 60.4 |
| Bow Bazar. . . . . . . . | 6.4 | 58.7 |
| Alipur. . . . . . . . . | 13.3 | 55.8 |
| *Low Congress* | | |
| Burtola . . . . . . . . | 17.3 | 29.6 |
| Kumartali. . . . . . . . | 18.1 | 27.3 |
| Vidyasagar. . . . . . . . | 12.0 | 27.1 |
| Shampukur . . . . . . . | 14.7 | 26.1 |
| Belgachia . . . . . . . . | 27.8 | 24.9 |
| Municktola . . . . . . . | 41.3 | 24.4 |

| | PERCENTAGE OF REFUGEES | [1957] | [1962] |
|---|---|---|---|
| **1957 and 1962 Legislative Assembly Elections** | | | |
| *High Congress* | | | |
| Jorabagan . . . . . . . . | 12 | 46.7 | 58.3 |
| Jorasanko . . . . . . . . | 8 | 59.8 | 58.0 |
| Bara Bazar . . . . . . . | 5 | 74.8 | 74.5 |
| Bow Bazar. . . . . . . . | 8 | 50.1 | 58.9 |
| Chowringhee. . . . . . . | 10 | 69.8 | 72.0 |
| Ekbalpore . . . . . . . . | 9 | 48.4 | 49.5 |
| Kalighat. . . . . . . . . | 15 | 48.0 | 51.1 |
| Fort. . . . . . . . . . | 7 | 51.5 | 51.8 |
| Sukeas Street. . . . . . . | 15 | 43.3 | 51.0 |
| Muchipara. . . . . . . . | 20 | 48.6 | 50.7 |
| Taltola . . . . . . . . . | 11 | 46.6 | 54.4 |
| *Low Congress* | | | |
| Alipur. . . . . . . . . . | 21 | 37.0 | 41.5 |
| Tollygunge. . . . . . . . | n.a.[b] | 29.9 | 39.2 |
| Rashbehari Ave. . . . . . . | 20 | 39.3 | 36.9 |
| Manicktola. . . . . . . . | 39 | 30.6 | 24.8 |
| Entally . . . . . . . . . | n.a.[c] | 37.8 | 41.9 |
| Burtola North . . . . . . . | 16 | 35.8 | 41.8 |
| Vidyasagar. . . . . . . . | 18 | 44.7 | 45.7 |

[a] $r -$ −0.87.     [b] High.     [c] Medium.

cluding the refugees, approximately one-fourth (26 per cent) of Calcutta's population came to the city after 1934. More than one-third come from other portions of the state of West Bengal and speak Bengali. Two-fifths are Hindi speakers from the nearby states of Bihar and Uttar Pradesh. A small number are Oriya speakers from the state of Orissa, just south of Calcutta; another small group are Muslims (all of whom speak Urdu) from other portions of Bengal or neighboring states.

The census reports unfortunately do not tell us how migrants are dis-

TABLE 33
LANGUAGE OF MIGRANTS AND RESIDENTS IN CALCUTTA
(Percentage of Population)

| Language Group | Original Residents | Migrants | Total Population |
|---|---|---|---|
| Bengali | 66.1 | 38.3 | 61.0 |
| Hindi | 20.6 | 42.3 | 25.1 |
| Urdu | 7.4 | 6.6 | 6.4 |
| Oriya | 0.9 | 5.3 | 2.2 |
| English | 1.4 | 0.6 | 0.9 |
| Nepali | 0.8 | 1.8 | 1.04 |
| Gujarati | 0.68 | 0.6 | 0.6 |
| South Indian languages | 0.38 | 1.3 | 0.65 |
| Punjabi | 0.76 | 1.4 | 0.93 |

SOURCE: S. N. Sen, *City of Calcutta*, p. 23. Data for 1957–58.

tributed throughout the city. We do, however, know from the census the number of males and females in each ward of the city, and we have matched these wards to assembly constituencies. The resulting ratios of males to females serve to indicate the proportion of migrants on the one hand and refugees and residents on the other in each constituency since the sex ratios for these two groups are vastly different. Among residents there are 1,480 males per thousand females, and among the refugees 1,220 males per thousand females. Among migrants the sex ratio varies, depending upon where the migrants are from, from 1,900 to 18,500 males per thousand females.[7]

Since we know both the sex ratio and the voting patterns for each constituency of Calcutta, and since sex ratio correlates with the category migrants as well as to that of refugees and residents (who have similar sex ratios), we are able to estimate, albeit indirectly, the voting patterns of these groups.[8] We find, for example, that in the eleven constituencies in which Congress won a majority in 1962 and did well in previous elections there is a sex ratio of two to five — that is, there are 2,500 males per thousand females — a ratio which indicates the presence of a very large

[7] The figures, taken from Sen, are from the 1952 census. The 1962 census figures are almost identical.

[8] The difficulties inherent in ecological correlations of this sort are discussed by W. S. Robinson, "Ecological Correlations and the Behavior of Individuals," *American Sociological Review* 15 (June, 1950). The data cannot "prove" that refugees voted against Congress or that rural migrants voted for Congress; only direct survey data could provide us with evidence as to how individuals voted. However, the correlations are extraordinarily high and consistent, the results plausible, and no other variable fits the voting data as well. It is not unreasonable to consider the conclusion true. For a defense of the use of ecological correlations, see Hanan C. Selvin, "Durkheim's *Suicide*: Further Thoughts on a Methodological Classic," *in* Robert A. Nisbet, ed., *Emile Durkheim*, (Englewood Cliffs, New Jersey: Prentice Hall, 1965), pp. 113–36.

TABLE 34

RATIO OF MALES TO FEMALES IN CALCUTTA LANGUAGE GROUPS
(Males per 1,000 Females)

| Language Group | All Persons | Resident Population | Ordinary Migrants | Refugees |
|---|---|---|---|---|
| Bengali. . . . . . | 1,348 | 1,208 | 2,257 | 1,220 |
| Hindi . . . . . . | 3,952 | 2,268 | 8,850 | . . . . |
| Urdu. . . . . . | 3,571 | 2,732 | 9,260 | . . . . |
| Oriya . . . . . . | 10,204 | 4,166 | 18,537 | . . . . |
| Punjabi . . . . . | 1,349 | 1,136 | 1,938 | . . . . |
| Marwari-Rajasthani | 1,306 | 1,136 | 3,450 | . . . . |
| Nepali . . . . . | 1,897 | 1,350 | 2,688 | . . . . |

SOURCE: S. N. Sen, *City of Calcutta*, p. 16. Data for 1957–58.

migrant population. In the seven constituencies which gave Congress its lowest vote, the sex ratio is one to forty-five, suggesting that these constituencies are populated by Bengalis and East Pakistani refugees. No other variable matches voting patterns in the city as accurately as the sex ratio. In fact, there is not a single constituency in Calcutta with a ratio of two to one (that is, twice as many men as women) which failed to elect a Congressman in the 1962 elections. Constituencies lost by Congress typically have a sex ratio of one to two or one to three, with one case of one to nine.

Knowing that the sex ratio among migrants, who make up 25 per cent of Calcutta's population, is not less than two to three for any large group of migrants and often much higher, and that the ratio for residents and East Pakistani refugees is much lower, we can conclude that in those constituencies where we find a high sex ratio it is due to the large number of migrants from areas other than East Pakistan. In these constituencies Congress consistently wins elections, whereas in constituencies made up of residents and/or East Pakistani refugees Congress does poorly. Since the sex ratio for the city as a whole is one to seventy-five, we can estimate that in a constituency with this ratio approximately 25 per cent are migrants. The anti-Congress constituencies, therefore, with a sex ratio of one to forty-five, clearly have few migrants; the pro-Congress constituencies, with a ratio of two to forty-five, must have large numbers of migrants.

If constituencies are rank ordered on the basis of sex ratio, they range from 3.05 males per female to 1.20 males per female. The rank order correlation between sex ratio and Congress MLA vote in all twenty-seven constituencies in 1957 was $r=+.791$, and in 1962, $r=+.794$.

The data do not demonstrate conclusively that migrants, rather than the more restricted category of non-Bengalis, are the best supporters of Congress. In the absence of survey data we cannot be certain that migrant

Bengalis from other portions of West Bengal (as distinct from East Bengali refugees) cast their votes for Congress as do migrant groups from the states of Bihar, Uttar Pradesh, and Orissa. This would appear to be so, however, since the Bengali migrants constitute 38 per cent of all the ordinary migrants. Were such a large group voting predominantly against Congress, our correlation of sex ratio with voting would not be so extraordinarily high.

Before we speculate on the question of why migrants to the city vote for the governing party rather than for the leftist parties, it is interesting to note some characteristics of the migrants. A larger number of migrants live in single-member households than do original residents. Migrants are less educated than residents. A larger proportion are engaged in unskilled manual work. A larger proportion of migrant earners (77 per cent) earn less than a hundred rupees (twenty dollars) a month than original residents (64 per cent), and correspondingly fewer migrants are in the upper income levels than original residents. Migrants appear to be less adequately housed than the residents, and a substantial number of migrant workers live on the city's pavements. In almost all respects, therefore, migrants are worse off than the residents.

The Calcutta data thus suggest — as the widely held proposition declares — that migrants to the city are materially deprived; but the data also suggest — contrary to the proposition — that it is this group which sustains stable government. Conversely, the group which is materially better off — the residents — are more likely to vote against Congress and for the Communist or Marxist left parties. This pattern is supported by what is known of other aspects of their political behavior. According to the police commissioner of Calcutta, those persons arrested for political crimes and rowdy activities are primarily resident Bengalis rather than migrants. In short, it is the resident rather than the migrant who is most dissatisfied with his lot.

Lacking survey data, we can only speculate as to the reasons for this behavior. Migrants journey to the city to improve their circumstances, and those who fail to do so presumably return home. It is interesting to note in this connection that the unemployment rate among migrants is lower than for residents (5.0 per cent as compared to 8.5 per cent). This suggests that the dissatisfied migrant need not vote against the government, since he has the option of returning home. A second related factor is that the migrant has lower expectations than the resident. His demands in the way of urban services — good housing, adequate water supply, educational facilities — are less than those of residents. Since deprivation is

a comparative matter, we must remember that the migrant in any event is likely to find many urban services, as bad as they are, an improvement over what he has had in the countryside. And so long as his reference group is that of his family and friends in his native village, as is so often the case for married migrants whose families remain in the village, then his standards may continue for some time to be those of a villager. In short, to feel a sense of deprivation the migrant needs to be socialized into urban life. Third, since typically he has come without his family, his needs for adequate amenities (such as education for children) are less than those of the resident urban dweller. Finally, the migrant often comes from the rural areas, where he has had more contact with Congress party workers than with those of the opposition parties. Insofar as he voted Congress at home he is likely to continue to do so in the city.

It would be quite misleading to conclude from these findings that an increase in the migration rate would not unstabilize political life. It may do so for at least two reasons: the influx of migrants typically results in a deterioration of services and a decrease in job opportunities for the residents; and while migration may be increasing, the absolute number of residents is similarly increasing as migrants settle into the city, bring their families, or marry local residents.

## Conclusion: The Transformation in Congress Support

In view of the poverty of Calcutta, the activity of the Communists and Marxist left parties, the alienation of the intellectuals and middle classes, and the poor performance of the municipal government, it is quite remarkable that Congress does about as well winning votes in Calcutta as it does in the rest of India. In the parliamentary elections in 1962, for example, Congress won 46 per cent of the vote in Calcutta as against 45 per cent in the country as a whole.

The sources of Congress support in Calcutta today are quite different from what they were prior to independence. In fact, the very groups which supported the nationalist movement in Bengal most actively — the intellectuals and middle classes of Calcutta and the Hindus (now refugees) of East Bengal — are now among the most ardent critics of Congress. In contrast, the groups which before independence were either relatively passive or anti-Congress are now among its strongest supporters. Today Congress strength is greatest among the working-class migrants, the well-to-do Marwari and Gujarati businessmen, Muslims, and members of

scheduled castes. Together these groups constitute approximately half of the Calcutta population.

Numerically, the two largest groups of supporters are the migrants and the Muslims. The Muslims apparently view the governing Congress party as a greater source of protection than the left wing parties who so actively seek their support. And the migrants, though they live in slums or on the pavements and are in many respects not fully urbanized, are apparently less dissatisfied than the settled urban residents.

So long as Congress depends heavily upon migrants, Muslims, and scheduled castes, there is an upper limit to the Congress vote. We have seen the Congress MLA vote in Calcutta rise from 39.7 per cent to 42.6 per cent, then to 47.2 per cent in three consecutive elections. But there is no evidence yet that Congress has made a strong dent in the refugees and in the Bengali middle classes. Unless Congress is able to do so or unless the migration rate rises rapidly, the Congress vote in Calcutta is likely to reach a plateau.

Calcutta pays a considerable price for a patronage type party. The state government, under Congress control, is unable to reform municipal government, and the Calcutta Corporation continues to remain one of the least effectual local governments in India. Moreover, since the Congress city organization is in effect controlled by the state organization, the rural interests of the state predominate, with the result that rural taxes remain low and government policy and planning have a heavy rural bias. In the 1964–65 budget 25 per cent of the total state budget expenditures were for agricultural development. Industrial development schemes are almost all for rural districts of the state, and even funds for the rehabilitation of refugees have been for establishing new refugee townships and

TABLE 35
CALCUTTA MUNICIPAL CORPORATION ELECTIONS
(Seats Won)

| | 1952 | 1957 | 1961 | 1965[a] |
|---|---|---|---|---|
| Congress . . . . . | 54 | 42 | 39 | 49 |
| UCC[b] . . . . . . | 23 | 30 | 31 | 35 |
| CWB[c] . . . . . . | . . | . . | 3 | 8 |
| Independent . . . | 3 | 8 | 7[d] | 8[e] |
| Total. . . . . . | 80 | 80 | 80 | 100 |

[a] The first municipal election based on universal adult suffrage.

[b] A coalition of the Communists and several Marxist Left parties.

[c] A coalition of the Praja Socialist party and independents.

[d] Three independents joined Congress after the elections, thereby providing Congress with a majority of 42.

[e] Includes one Jan Sangh candidate.

setting up refugee camps outside Calcutta. With the assistance of the Ford Foundation, the Calcutta Metropolitan Planning Organization was established in 1961 under the office of the chief minister but thus far little attention has been given to Calcutta's development by the state government.

It is also useful to note that though the non-Congress vote in the 1962 elections — 53 per cent — was no greater than in other states, the size of the figure is no indication of intensity of feeling. Opposition to Congress in Calcutta is militant and often violent. Mass demonstrations, strikes, processions, and boycotts occur almost daily. The result is that more coercion is exercised by the police in Calcutta than is common elsewhere in India. The use of the Preventive Detention Act and Section 144 of the Code of Criminal Procedure (which prohibits public meetings) is commonplace. The result is a mutually reinforcing relationship of repression and alienation. The ordinary processes of government are thus not exercised by the bulk of the politically active middle classes, and the effort to establish a popular sense of legitimacy and efficacy toward govern-

TABLE 36
ELECTION RESULTS IN CALCUTTA

| PARTY | SEATS WON | | | NUMBER OF VOTES | | | PERCENTAGE OF VOTES | | |
|---|---|---|---|---|---|---|---|---|---|
| | 1952 | 1957 | 1962 | 1952 | 1957 | 1962 | 1952 | 1957 | 1962 |
| Legislative Assembly | | | | | | | | | |
| Congress[a] | 17 | 8 | 14 | 221,840 | 350,961 | 478,544 | 39.7 | 42.6 | 47.2 |
| Communist. | 4 | 10 | 8 | 67,448 | 221,840 | 331,586 | 12.1 | 26.8 | 32.8 |
| Socialist (PSP, KM-PP, Soc.). | .. | 4 | .. | 36,838 | 95,074 | 20,828 | 6.6 | 11.5 | 2.1 |
| Independents | 2 | 3 | 3 | 121,458 | 104,539 | 104,298 | 21.8 | 12.7 | 10.3 |
| Marxist Left | 3 | 1 | 1 | 85,453 | 46,500 | 51,379 | 15.3 | 5.6 | 5.1 |
| Other . . . | .. | .. | .. | 25,202 | 6,136 | 25,162 | 4.5 | .8 | 2.5 |
| Total . . | 26 | 26 | 26 | 558,239 | 824,446 | 1,001,797 | 100.0 | 100.0 | 100.0 |
| Parliament | | | | | | | | | |
| Congress[b] | 1 | 1 | 1 | 205,026 | 334,751 | 523,967 | 36.8 | 40.3 | 46.3 |
| Communist. | 1 | 2 | 3 | 104,138 | 278,658 | 588,706 | 18.7 | 33.5 | 52.0 |
| Jan Sangh . | 1 | .. | .. | 65,026 | . . . . | . . . . | 11.7 | . . . | . . . |
| Revolutionary Socialist party . . | 1 | .. | .. | 74,124 | 6,307 | . . . . | 13.3 | 0.8 | . . . |
| Independents | .. | 1 | .. | 80,256 | 211,684 | 10,636 | 14.4 | 25.4 | 0.9 |
| Total . . | 4 | 4 | 4 | 557,103 | 831,400 | 1,132,776 | 100.0 | 100.0 | 100.0 |

[a] In the state as a whole Congress won, respectively, in the three elections 150, 152, and 157 seats as against 28, 46, and 50 for the Communists.

[b] In the state as a whole Congress won, respectively, in the three elections 24, 23, and 23 seats as against 5, 6, and 8 for the Communists.

ment, which has been so successful in much of India, has been less successful among the middle classes of Calcutta.

Nonetheless, the patronage orientation of the Congress party in Calcutta has gone a long way toward building the party in the city. It has sustained party workers and made it possible to create an effective election apparatus. The party leadership has successfully utilized its patronage powers as an instrument for maintaining internal cohesion. Those who support the leadership are given access to government powers, while those who threaten the party's leadership are denied support of any kind. Congressmen in Calcutta have their differences; but next to the Communists, who are so badly split over the Sino-Soviet and Sino-Indian disputes, and the badly fragmented Marxist left parties, Congress stands as a pillar of unity. The attention given by the party to ethnic minorities — to Muslims, to rural migrants from outside Bengal, and to scheduled castes — has provided some small measure of security to these communities. But most importantly, from the point of view of the party leadership itself, the city organization has won business support and the finances necessary to build the party in the countryside. And in the city itself Congress has improved its vote in three consecutive elections and increased its assembly seating from a low of eight in 1957 to fourteen (of twenty-six) in 1962. The Congress leadership in Calcutta has demonstrated that a party machine, concerned with the day-to-day problems of soliciting and maintaining political support, can, for some time at least, meet the electoral challenge of the ideologically minded Communist party and its left allies.

# BIBLIOGRAPHY: CALCUTTA

Probably more has been written on Bengal in both English and Bengali than on any other region in India. Bengal was the earliest and most important area to be occupied by the British and was, until after the First World War, capital of British India. There is, therefore, a large volume of British government documents on Bengal as well as a substantial scholarly literature by British civil servants. Moreover, Bengal experienced a great cultural renaissance in the nineteenth century which produced numerous Bengali scholars who have analyzed their own economic, political, and social history. The literature on Bengal is thus too vast to enumerate in a brief bibliography; so I have confined the list below to items dealing specifically with Calcutta, except for a few studies, biographies, and autobiographies essential to an understanding of politics in the city. For a longer bibliography on Bengal, see my "Notes on Political Development in Bengal," *in Political Change in South Asia* (Calcutta: K. L. Mukhopadhyay, 1963), and several extensive bibliographies prepared in mimeographed form by the South Asia librarian at the University of Chicago.

## Interviews

I conducted thirty-six intensive interviews in Calcutta, primarily with Congressmen, in 1962. Apart from interviews with the Congress president, the mayor, and the municipal commissioner, most of these interviews were with Congress politicians in North Calcutta. These latter included the secretary and president of the North Calcutta District Con-

gress Committee, the MP and his campaign manager, most of the MLAs, and several councillors in the municipal corporation. I also interviewed journalists of *Jugantar, Amrita Bazar Patrika,* and the *Statesman,* Calcutta's leading newspapers. In addition to these intensive interviews, I have had briefer meetings with countless party workers in the offices of the Pradesh Congress Committee and the North Calcutta DCC. I have also made extensive use of my interview notes from two earlier trips to Calcutta in 1953–55 and 1957–58. Those two trips resulted in the publication of several studies containing much material on Bengal and Calcutta. See my *Party Politics in India* (Princeton: Princeton University Press, 1957), especially chapters 4, 6, and 7, and *Politics of Scarcity* (Chicago: University of Chicago Press, 1962).

I am particularly grateful to several members of the Ford Foundation team, to the Calcutta Metropolitan Planning Organization, and to several Indian staff members of the CMPO who made available to me the unpublished reports and statistical studies of the city and who spoke to me freely of their work.

## Nationalist Movement

Since the nationalist movement was first organized in Bengal many histories of that period contain large sections on Bengal. See especially Reginald Coupland, *The Indian Problem* (London: Oxford University Press, 1943), a standard work by an English constitutional lawyer describing British parliamentary innovations and the Indian response. The last part of this volume contains a series of chapters on the operations of the state governments which took power in 1937, including a chapter on the non-Congress ministry formed in Bengal under Muslim leadership. Bruce McCully, *English Education and the Origins of Indian Nationalism* (New York, 1940), now out of print, contains one of the best descriptions of the impact of English education on the development of the national movement, with a heavy emphasis on the development of the movement in Bengal. The study is, however, limited to the middle of the nineteenth century and stops with the foundation of the Congress in 1885. *The Sedition Committee Report* (Calcutta: Bengal Secretariat Press, 1918), is a classic report by the British government on the terrorist movement in India, with considerable data on the terrorist movement in Bengal, including a report on the age, occupation, and caste of its participants. The movement is of some contemporary importance, since the Communists, Marxist left, and sections of the Socialist and Congress parties come out

of the old terrorist movement and certain aspects of their political style persist in contemporary life.

There are a number of studies which deal primarily with the development of politics in Bengal: Jogesh Chandra Bagal, *History of the Indian Association* (Calcutta: H. N. Mazumdar, 1953); Jogesh Chandra Bagal, *Peasant Revolution in Bengal* (Calcutta: Bharati Library, n.d.); N. S. Bose, *The Indian Awakening and Bengal* (Calcutta: K. L. Mukhopadhyay, 1960); S. Gopal, *The Permanent Settlement and its Effect on Bengal* (London: Allen and Unwin, 1949); *Indian Revolutionaries in Conference*, J. C. Chatterji, ed. (Calcutta: Mukhopadhyay, 1960), a fascinating report of a "class reunion" of old revolutionaries, including brief descriptions of some of the famous terrorist activities in Bengal; Bimanbehari Majumdar, *History of Political Thought: From Rammohun to Dayananda* (1821–84), Vol. I (Bengal, University of Calcutta, 1934); R. C. Majumdar, *Glimpses of Bengal in the Nineteenth Century* (Calcutta: K. L. Mukhopadhyay, 1960); Balraj Modhok, *Dr. Syama Prasad Mookerjee* (New Delhi: Deepak Parkashan, 1954); Haridas and Uma Mukherjee, *The Origins of the National Education Movement* (Calcutta: Jadavpur University, 1957), a study of the attempt (only partially successful) to break away from British patterns of university education in Bengal before the First World War; Richard Leonard Park, "The Rise of Militant Nationalism in Bengal: A Regional Study of Indian Nationalism," Cambridge, Mass.: Thesis, Harvard University (on film), 1950; Amit Sen, *Notes on the Bengal Renaissance* (Calcutta: National Book Agency, 1957); Haridas and Uma Mukherjee, *India's Fight for Freedom or the Swadeshi Movement, 1905–1906* (Calcutta: K. L. Mukhopadhyay, 1958); *Studies in the Bengal Renaissance* (Calcutta: National Council of Education, Jadavpur, 1958).

Several studies contain information on Muslim politics in Bengal: J. H. Broomfield, "The Vote and the Transfer of Power: A study of the Bengal General Elections, 1912–1913," *Journal of Asian Studies* XXI (February, 1962): 163–82; Ram Gopal, *Indian Muslims: A Political History* (New York: Asia Publishing House, 1959); Humayun Kabir, *Muslim Politics in India*; W. C. Smith, *Modern Islam in India* (London: Victor Gollancz Ltd., 1946).

There are also biographies and autobiographies available of M. N. Roy, Aurobindo Ghosh, and Ashutosh Mookerjee and many other volumes on nineteenth-century political and literary figures. For references to these, see Wm. Theodore de Bary, ed., *Sources of Indian Tradition* (New York: Columbia University Press, 1958).

## Political Leadership

The number of books on and by Bengalis is extremely large. Following are a few of special quality or importance. Surendranath Banerjee, *A Nation in Making* (Calcutta: Oxford, 1925). This is a political autobiography of one of the founders of the Indian National Congress and the minister of local government who prepared the 1923 Municipal Corporation Act, which governed Calcutta until the municipality was superseded in 1948. Subhas Chandra Bose, *The Indian Struggle*, 3 volumes (Calcutta: Thacker, Spink and Co., 1948). N. C. Chaudhury, "Subhas Chandra Bose: His Legacy and Legend," *Pacific Affairs* (December, 1953), is an attempt to explain why the legend of Bose's escape from the plane crash persisted in Bengal among many members of the Calcutta middle class. N. C. Chaudhury, *The Autobiography of an Unknown Indian* (MacMillan, 1951), is one of the most interesting accounts of social life and attitudes among the people of Calcutta. Bipin Chandra Pal, *Memories of My Life and Times*, 2 volumes (Calcutta: Modern Book Agency, 1932–51). P. C. Ray, *Life and Times of C. R. Das* (London: Oxford University Press, 1927); K. P. Thomas, *Dr. B. C. Roy* (Calcutta: West Bengal Pradesh Congress Committee, 1955); Chattar Singh Samara, "Subhas Chandra Bose — An Indian National Hero," *in* Richard L. Park and Irene Tinker, eds., *Leadership and Political Institutions in India* (Princeton: Princeton University Press, 1959).

I have prepared a statistical analysis of the social backgrounds of contemporary political leadership in West Bengal — both Congress and opposition politicians — in "Political Leadership in West Bengal," in *Political Change in South Asia* (Calcutta: K. L. Mukhopadhyay, 1963). This study was based upon an analysis of the *West Bengal Legislative Assembly Who's Who, 1957* (Calcutta: West Bengal Legislative Assembly Secretariat, 1957) and data collected from parties and interest groups in West Bengal. A portion of this study, dealing with the changes that occurred in political leadership over a forty-year period, appeared in "Changing Patterns of Political Leadership in West Bengal," *Pacific Affairs* 32 (September, 1959): 277–87.

## Calcutta

*Reports and documents.* *The Calcutta Municipal Act*, 1951 (as modified up to 1 May, 1961) (Calcutta: Government of West Bengal, Law Department, Legislative, 1961); *Constitution of the West Bengal Pradesh*

*Congress Committee, Adopted October 1953* (Calcutta: West Bengal Pradesh Congress Committee, 1953); *Corporation of Calcutta Yearbook, 1961–62* (Calcutta: Corporation Press, 1961); A. Mitra, ed., *Census of India 1951,* Volume VI, Part Ia, West Bengal, Sikkim and Chandernagore, Part III, Calcutta City, Part IV, The Calcutta Industrial Region, Tables (Delhi: Manager of Publications, 1954); North Calcutta District Congress Committee, *Jubilee Issue,* (mostly in Bengali); North Calcutta District Congress Committee, *Seva Dal,* (mostly in Bengali); North Calcutta District Congress Committee, *Report of Political Congress,* (mostly in Bengali); *Relief and Rehabilitation of Displaced Persons in West Bengal,* Statement Issued by the Government of West Bengal, December, 1957; World Health Organization, *Assignment Report on Water Supply and Sewage Disposal, Greater Calcutta,* January 1960; *Second Five-Year Plan of West Bengal Programme for 1956–57* (Alipore: Government of West Bengal, Development Department, 1956). The official organ of the Corporation of Calcutta is the *Calcutta Municipal Gazette,* published weekly; the corporation also publishes its proceedings.

Two post-independence reports describe the functioning and malfunctioning of the Calcutta Municipal Corporation. They are the *Report of the Corporation of Calcutta Investigation Commission* (Calcutta: Government of West Bengal Local Self-Government Department, 1949). This is generally referred to as the report of the Biswas Commission. See also the *Report of the Corporation of Calcutta Enquiry Commission* (Calcutta: Government of West Bengal, 1962). This is generally referred to as the Talukdar Committee Report.

*Secondary socio-economic studies.* S. K. Bhattacharjya, *Passenger Transport Problem in Calcutta* (Calcutta: Bookland); Nirmal Kumar Bose, *Modern Bengal* (Berkeley: University of California, Institute of International Studies, 1959); Nirmal Kumar Bose, "Social and Cultural Life of Calcutta," reprint from *Geographical Review of India* XX (December, 1958); "Calcutta and the World Bank Mission," *Economic Weekly* 12 (October, 1960): 1469–74; Syamal Chakrabartty, *Housing Conditions in Calcutta* (Calcutta: Bookland, 1958); K. P. Chattopadhyay, P. K. Bose, and A. Chatterji, *Undergraduate Students in Calcutta: How They Live and Work, A Survey* (Calcutta: Calcutta University, 1955); Matindra Mohan Datta, "Urbanization in Bengal," *Geographical Review of India* XVIII (December, 1956); Sudhindranath Datta, "Calcutta," *Encounter* 8 (1957); "Development of Calcutta," *Economic Weekly* 13 (January 14, 1961): 41–42; Benoy Ghose, "The Colonial Beginnings of Calcutta: Urbanisation without Industrialisation," *Economic Weekly* 12 (August 13,

1960): 1255–60; Meera Guha, "The Morphology of Calcutta," *Geographical Review of India* XV (1953): 20–28; *Memorandum on the Unemployment Problem Facing the Middle Class Bengalees* (Calcutta: Bengal Trades Association, 1956); S. B. Mukherjee, *Studies on Fertility Rates in Calcutta* (Calcutta: Bookland); *Preliminary Report on the Enquiry into the General Conditions of the Students in West Bengal 1951–52* (Calcutta: Satyayug, n.d.); S. N. Sen, *The City of Calcutta: A Socio-economic Survey, 1954–55 to 1957–58* (Calcutta: Bookland, 1960); *West Bengal – Land and People,* Foreword by Sri Bimal Chandra Sinha (Calcutta: Publication Section, City College Commerce Department, 1956); *West Bengal Today* (Calcutta: Government of West Bengal, Development Department, 1954).

*Secondary political studies.* D. N. Banerjee, "West Bengal," *in* S. V. Kogckar and Richard L. Park, eds., *Report on the Indian General Elections, 1951–52* (Bombay: Popular Book Depot, 1956); Robert Carstairs, *A Plea for the Better Local Government of Bengal* (London: Macmillan, 1904); Robi Chakravorti, "The Decline of the Left in Calcutta: Muchipara Constituency," *in* Myron Weiner and Rajni Kothari, eds., *Indian Voting Behavior – the 1962 General Elections* (Calcutta: K. L. Mukhopadhyay, 1965); P. Chatterjee, "A Plea for Municipal Self-Government in Calcutta," *Calcutta Review* 147 (May, 1958): 121–26; A. K. Ghosal, "Second General Election in West Bengal; an Analysis," *Modern Review* 103 (May, 1958): 374–80; Ernest Goldsmith, "Municipal Government in Calcutta: the Calcutta Corporation," Master's Thesis, Berkeley, University of California, 1960; S. W. Goode, *Municipal Calcutta: Its Institutions in Their Origin and Growth* (Edinburgh: Corporation of Calcutta, 1916); Richard L. Park, "The Urban Challenge to Local and State Government: West Bengal, With Special Attention to Calcutta," in Roy Turner, ed., *India's Urban Future* (Berkeley and Los Angeles: University of California Press, 1962); Naresh Chandra Roy, *A Critical Study of Some Aspects of Public Administration in Bengal* (Calcutta: University of Calcutta, 1945); S. N. Roy, "The Decline of the Left in a Calcutta Suburb: Behala Constituency," *in* Myron Weiner and Rajni Kothari, eds., *Indian Voting Behavior – The 1962 General Elections* (Calcutta: K. L. Mukhopadhyay, 1965); Hugh Tinker, *The Foundations of Local Self-Government in India, Pakistan and Burma* (London: University of London, 1954); M. Venkatarangaiya, "Bombay and Calcutta," *in* William A. Robson, ed., *Great Cities of the World: Their Government, Politics and Planning* (New York: Macmillan, 1957; Myron Weiner, "Violence and Politics in Calcutta," *Journal of Asian Studies* XX (May, 1961): 275–81.

Three articles dealing with economic and political developments in Calcutta appeared on the editorial pages of the *Statesman* on September 1, 2, and 3, 1962 by Asok Mitra, an official of the World Bank.

The Institute of Public Administration in New York has a research project in Calcutta associated with the Calcutta Metropolitan Planning Organization. They have in preparation a number of studies on the administration of the Calcutta metropolitan region.

*PART VI. VARIATIONS ON RURAL THEMES:*
*MADURAI*

# 18. MADURAI AS A PRE-MODERN CITY

While Calcutta is a relatively modern Indian city whose politics, economics, and even architecture show the effect of colonial rule, the city of Madurai[1] in the southern part of Madras state in South India is an ancient city, more traditional in character, and with a more modest industrial sector. These differences and others which we shall soon describe are important elements in the kind of Congress party each city possesses; while Calcutta has a party organization reminiscent of the party machines of urban America, Madurai's party is far less cohesive, far more marked by traditional loyalties, and far more closely associated with the rural countryside to which by historical tradition and social and economic organization it has been closely linked. In this chapter we shall describe the physical characteristics of the city, then turn to the historic antecedents of contemporary politics.

Though Madurai has several large textile mills, is a major railway center, and has one of the largest automobile and bus repair workshops in India, the city is physically dominated by the imposing Meenakshi temple. The temple occupies an area of 830 by 730 feet in the center of the old city, and on its massive outer walls stand the four towers (gopuram) reaching as high as 150 feet in a city with almost no other tall structures. The temple is a religious and cultural center, not only for Madurai city, but for all of Madras as well. In the evening hours, hundreds and often thousands of persons, natives and pilgrims, visit the temple. The lovely Pottamarai Kulam (Golden Lily Tank), whose waters are supposed to be beneficial to those who bathe in it, is a favorite attraction. The count-

[1] Pre-independence Madura.

less shrines, gopurams, internal gateways, and the tank leave the visitor with no single impression of the temple as a European might have of medieval cathedrals or of the more monumental, single-structured temples in Orissa.

A central hallway is, however, functionally unnecessary since the Hindu temple is not a place for communal worship. Community activities take the form not of worship but of festivals, and of these the most important in Madurai is in the month of Chittrai (April–May) when the marriage of Siva and Meenakshi is celebrated.[2] A temple car constructed for the purpose is dragged through the streets surrounding the temple, and several hundred thousand visitors come to the city to witness and participate in the ceremonies.

The city can be divided into three parts: the administrative-governmental offices on the northern side of the river, the industrial areas in the eastern part around the railroad tracks, and the older central city with the temple and the bazaar areas. The central city is the population heartland. Of the city's municipal wards, only three are across the river, four are east of the railway, and two or three relatively dispersed wards sprawl out to the west of the central city.

In 1961, the census reported that Madurai had a population of 424,000, or about 42,000 per square mile (the area of the city is 8.56 sq. miles). Madurai is thus the most densely populated city in Madras state — far ahead of Madras city, with its 29,000 people per square mile. The population density of Madurai is greatest in the old central city around Meenakshi temple. Nineteen of the city's thirty-three wards are within a radius of three-quarters of a mile from the temple, and within these approximately two square miles reside 275,000 persons.

The central city is constructed around the temple. The temple itself, with its imposing gopuram, forms the skyline of the city, but less than a

[2] Though the temple houses many deities, the most important is Meenakshi, the wife of Siva. According to legend, Meenakshi was the daughter of a Pandhyan king and was, to the consternation of her parents, born with three breasts. A fairy, however, told the king that the third breast would disappear as soon as she met her future husband. It did when she first encountered Siva, and they were wedded accordingly with much pomp. It has been suggested that Meenakshi may have been a local Dravidian goddess whom Brahmin immigrants to Madurai found to be too popular to be ousted by their Aryan deities. Her marriage to Siva was therefore a method adopted to reconcile and unite the old faith and the new. McKim Marriott in *Village India* has described the general process of absorbing and universalizing local deities into the great tradition of Hinduism. If we may use this as an opportunity to generalize, we see here a general pattern in Indian life of absorbing and reconciling traditional beliefs with new ideas. The process of refutation and rejection is an unacceptable one; the process of absorption and reconciliation, no matter how contradictory, is psychologically welcomed.

mile away is the lower skyline of the domed Nayak Palace, the ancient seat of the Pandhyan kings, now used to house the more prosaic high court.

Between the temple and the palace and surrounding both of them are the most ancient parts of the city. The temple itself is surrounded by a series of squares which contain the major bazaars of the city. As is common in Indian cities, shops of one trade are grouped together. Several streets are devoted almost exclusively to textile shops. One street has jewelry shops; another, a cluster of bookshops for school children; another, wholesale supplies of food and household commodities; another, hairdressers; and still another, retail dealers in glassware.

The bazaars extend south and west of the temple. The wards east of Meenakshi are predominantly made up of laborers; the wards to the north, overlooking the river, consist largely of white-collar and professional workers. These four elements — the bazaar merchants, the factory laborers, the white-collar workers, and the professionals — constitute the important political forces in the city. One should add a fifth distinct element: the Sourashtras, a community of weavers whose labor force works largely in homes and small shops but whose leadership consists mainly of merchants involved in buying yarn and selling piecegoods. They live west and southwest of the temple near the palace. The Sourashtra community (we shall have more to say of them later) came originally from Gujarat and settled in Madurai in the fifteenth century. Under their leadership Madurai became an important center for textiles throughout the south. In the nineteenth century a thriving modern textile industry was created in Madurai by Scottish manufacturers. They established both Madura Mills and Pandhyan Mills, which together have nearly half a million spindles. Meenakshi Mills, both a spinning and weaving mill, is the second largest in the area, followed by Shri Mahalakshmi Mills, and S. S. N. Chettiar and Company. The modern textile mills in the area employ about twenty thousand workers.[3] The railway which passes into the eastern part of the city marks the beginning of the largest textile area. The textile mills lie to the east, some even beyond the municipal limits, but most of the textile laborers live in the city near the mills. As is customary in other Indian cities, the work force of a given industry tends to live in the same area. Some of the mills provide residential quarters for their own workers. Near

[3] According to the *Madurai District Gazetteer*, 1960, there are about eighty thoussand persons engaged in handloom weaving or other processes associated with weaving in the entire district; though many communities are involved in this industry, by far the largest number belong to the Saurashtra community in Madurai city. In the city itself there are about twelve thousand four hundred looms (pp. 174–75).

the railway tracks is the colony of railway workers, with housing, a hospital, a high school, and places of worship.

As the railway line cuts into the eastern part of the city, so the Vaigai River cuts into the northern part. Two bridges span the river: one overhead for heavy modern traffic, and one wide footbridge for rickshaws, bicycles, jetkas (horse-drawn carriages), bullocks, and pedestrians. The crowds diminish somewhat as one leaves the bazaars to cross the Vaigai. One of the older British residential areas was built on the northern side of the river, and in recent years it has become the residential section of the wealthier citizens of Madurai. On the northern side are also the major government buildings. The municipal office, the collector's office, the superintendent of police, the industries ministry, and the central post and telegraph, along with several colleges and high schools, are here. And beyond is the old English club used by Indians and Englishmen, and still the meeting place of Englishmen from Madura Mills.

Although Meenakshi temple physically and culturally towers over the city, and Madurai is known throughout India as a cultural and religious center, the origins and development of the city can be traced to its role as a political center. It was a center for the Pandhyan kings,[4] later a feudatory of the Vijayanagar emperor, and from the sixteenth to the eighteenth century the seat of the Nayak dynasty. It was during this latter rule that the temple was built, the major streets of modern Madurai laid out, and an extensive double-walled fortress erected around the city (only small portions of the fortress wall now remain in the city). Under the rule of Viswanatha Nayak in the sixteenth century the area around Madurai was parceled out into a number of feudal units governed by a *poligar*, a local ruler responsible for collecting land revenue and supporting a band of retainers for military duty. By the early part of the seventeenth century the Nayaks had extended their rule to the area now comprised of the districts of Madurai, Ramnad, Tinnevelly, Coimbatore, Salem, and Trichinopoly. The fortress city was the administrative center of the Nayak kings, and the city itself was directly under their control.

The Nayaks continued to rule Madurai and the surrounding country,

[4] The earliest historical account of Madurai attributes the foundation of the town to a Pandhyan king in the sixth century before Christ. King Kulasekara is reported to have built a temple to the Lord Indra, and round the temple grew the town. In the third century B.C., Megasthaneses is known to have referred to "Modoura," and in the early centuries of the Christian era there are known to have been commercial and diplomatic relations between the Pandhyan kingdom and the Roman Empire. Ptolemy (A.D. 140) mentions "Modoura, the Kingdom of the Pandion." For some centuries little is known of the city, until about the thirteenth century when Persian and Chinese travelers chronicled their visits. Marco Polo too has described the city.

though after 1693 Madurai nominally became a feudatory of the Muslim emperor in Delhi. In the 1730's Muslim invaders from nearby Arcot took direct control of Madurai, and by 1736 the rule of the Nayak dynasty had come to an end. From then until 1801, when the East India Company took indirect control of Madurai, the city and the region around it were governed by a series of local potentates, mainly Muslim rulers. Since the fortress of Madurai was of military as well as political importance, it was frequently attacked in the eighteenth century.[5]

Before the British took control of Madurai, therefore, a tiered system of local authority prevailed. At the base were the poligars who collected revenue from subordinate political units down to the village. They ran the civil administration and paid tribute (about one-third of the land revenue) to the Nayak rulers in Madurai. The Nayaks and their successors invariably paid tribute to some larger ruling authority, ultimately by late eighteenth century to the East India Company. One layer of authority was thus eliminated, but the poligars continued as estate holders during much of British rule. Their civil and judicial powers were removed, but their control over much of the land within the district continued. Not until 1948 was a law passed abolishing these and other large estates and transferring the rent-collecting powers of the poligars to the state government.[6]

This description of the land tenure pattern in the district is of great importance for an understanding of the political role of Madurai town. Whether under the rule of the Nayaks, Muslim governors, or the British, Madurai town was the administrative and governmental center for the surrounding country. Apart from maintaining flourishing markets and the temples, the town sustained a substantial bureaucratic-administrative class. Moreover, a substantial number of estate holders settled in Madurai town, particularly in the nineteenth century when the military and civil functions of the poligars had disappeared and British administration was established throughout the district.

The sharp line which separated the mercantile classes and the middle classes of European medieval towns from the local rural aristocracy did not exist in Madurai. Landlords could and did take to mercantile activities, and many merchants purchased land. Moreover, the independent municipality of free men — the hallmark of medieval cities — did not develop in Madurai. The municipality of Madurai is a modern creation of the British, dating from the latter part of the nineteenth century. The

[5] For a description of the fortress walls and the various military efforts to take control of the city in the eighteenth century, see W. Francis, *Madurai District Gazetteer*, pp. 63–67.
[6] See S. Baliga, *Madurai District Gazetteer*, p. 367.

municipal council contained both landlords and merchants; when political conflict later arose, it was not between these two classes, but between those who subscribed to the nationalist creed of the Congress and those who continued to collaborate with the British. As late as 1959 as much as a fifth of the council (six members) described themselves as landlords; one of them, the leader of the Congress opposition, said he was both landlord and banker.

Though the nationalist movement had strong roots in Madurai town after the First World War, it would be a mistake to assume that the movement was confined to the city. The close links between the city and the countryside persisted; indeed, the District Congress Committee, which encompassed both the rural and urban areas, drew much of its leadership from the established rural gentry. The influence of this rural leadership on politics within the town declined substantially after independence and even more so in 1956, when a separate District Congress Committee for the town was established. Moreover, the passage of land reform legislation reduced the political power of the larger landowners within the town, thereby permitting the town merchants to play a larger role in the political affairs of the local Congress party and of the municipal government.

The role, however, is a new one, for there are no Indian equivalents of the stout burghers of the medieval English and German towns. The mercantile classes of medieval Europe were comparatively free from domination by the feudal aristocracy, and their municipal institutions were the hallmark of that freedom. Municipal institutions in India have no such foundation. The civic tradition of medieval Europe — the disposition of private individuals to combine their efforts for the public good — has no counterpart in Madurai town, though one may find innumerable cases of individuals acting on their own on behalf of the common good. But benefaction should not be confused with civic spirit. Moreover, though the mercantile community in Madurai has had guilds and to some extent still has them, the role which the guilds played in creating autonomous cities in Europe has no equivalent for Madurai.[7]

Unlike the medieval city, Madurai was the capital for the landed aristocracy who, until the establishment of British rule, combined control over the land with military power. The establishment of the city as a religious center came relatively late in Madurai's history — the great temple

[7] See Henri Pirenne, *Medieval Cities* (Garden City, N.Y.: Doubleday Anchor Books, 1956), pp. 121–51, for a discussion of the origin and development of municipal institutions in medieval cities. Pirenne notes the role played by the guilds in providing for the needs of the city, particularly street maintenance and the construction of defense works (p. 134).

of Meenakshi was not constructed until the sixteenth century. Viswanatha Nayak laid down the general plan and began construction of the temple in the 1560's, but it was not completed for another 120 years, though it apparently received generous financial support from princes, nobles, and wealthy merchants.[8]

Under the patronage of various dynastic rulers, Madurai was something of a commercial center. I surely could not go so far as to argue, as some English writers have, that Indian towns and cities had such a weak commercial base that they disappeared when they ceased to be capitals of political kingdoms.[9] With respect to Madurai, it is difficult to say what would have happened to the city if it had ceased to be a political center, since little is known of its commercial and industrial character prior to the nineteenth century. Surely the establishment of a handloom weaving industry by the Sourashtra community in the fifteenth century suggests that even then it was something of a commercial center, although it is most likely that this early production of textiles was largely for the benefit of the ruling families. Large-scale commercial and industrial activities in Madurai are of more recent origin, and the growth of the city in the twentieth century is largely a consequence of these economic changes. Madurai's population leaped from 106,000 in 1901 to 425,000 in 1961, a fourfold increase.

Under British rule, Madurai was reduced from the capital of a substantial southern empire to a district seat. But by ceasing to be the capital of a political kingdom, the city became free to develop its own political life. Its first modern phase began in the latter part of the nineteenth century when the British established municipal institutions, though rural landlord interests continued to play an important part in the city's political life. These interests, later organized into what was known as the Justice party, exerted influence on the city through and beyond the First World War. Then the nationalist movement grew in importance, supported wholeheartedly by the Brahmin middle classes and by the numerically large and commercially important Sourashtra community. A third phase began after independence when political parties multiplied within the city and bazaar merchants and others engaged in commerce and industry took a more active part in local politics. It is to the role that various caste and oc-

---

[8] J. P. L. Shenoy, *Madura, the Temple City* (Madras: Associated Printers, 1955), p. 29.

[9] W. H. Sleeman, *Rambles and Recollections of an Indian Official* (Westminster: Archibald Constable and Company, 1893), Vol. II, p. 99: "[Indian] Cities and Towns, formed by Public Establishments, disappear as Sovereigns and Governors change their Abodes."

cupational groups have played in the politics of the city and, more particularly, in the development of the Congress party organization since independence that we now turn.

We shall first examine the political role of the Sourashtra community, then turn to the work force and its trade unions, paying special attention to the political and caste fragmentation of the labor force. The intertwining of caste and occupation loyalties will also be explored in our analysis of white-collar and professional classes and particularly the Brahmin caste. Finally, we shall turn to the business interests in the city, the large industrialists, and especially the bazaar merchants, who have emerged in recent years as the single most active political force in the city, in competition with the once dominant Sourashtra and Brahmin communities.

As we describe tension and conflict within and between communities — almost as a central theme of Madurai urban politics — we are soon drawn to a consideration of how Congress copes with these conflicts in its effort to win elections. The answer for Madurai is simple: it is the intervention of the state party organization which has made it possible for the Madurai Congress to maintain sufficient cohesion to win both parliamentary and assembly elections. It was the state organization which selected the parliamentary candidate when the Madurai organization was divided; it was the state organization which dissolved the District Congress Committee and appointed a convener when the local organization was torn by internal dissension. But, in contrast, the state organization has not been able to help the party in its unsuccessful quest for control over the Madurai municipal government. In subsequent chapters we shall try to show how and why the state organization is able to play an active role in dispute settlement, and why it has been able to play the role well enough to make it possible for Congress to win parliamentary and assembly seats in Madurai but not well enough to win municipal elections.

The Madurai case thus throws light on how cohesion is maintained within the local party organization and on the extent of the state party organization's role as arbitrator. It also throws light on the conditions under which an effective urban patronage machine does or does not develop.

# 19. THE POLITICAL BEHAVIOR OF CASTE AND OCCUPATIONAL GROUPS

As in urban centers elsewhere in the world, political behavior in Madurai is shaped by the socio-economic groups to which individuals belong. In some respects, however, Madurai has less diversity than some of the other major urban centers in India. It is an old settlement with a relatively low rate of in-migration. According to the 1961 census, 70 per cent of the population speak Tamil as a mother tongue, and 87 per cent of the population are Hindu. But the statistics on religion and language disguise differences of great political importance.

Urbanization has by no means eliminated caste identification, and political activity, even when it expresses economic interests, has distinctive caste overtones. For one thing, there are a number of caste associations in the city whose interests, though predominantly social, are also political. For another, there is a close, typically Indian, relationship between caste and occupation. The textile handloom weavers, the factory laborers, the professional and middle classes, the commercial and industrial interests, and the bazaar merchants are all made up of distinctive castes. Any assessment of the factors which affect Congress recruitment and its ability to win support and to cope with conflict must consider the caste and occupational groups to which individuals in Madurai belong.

## The Sourashtras

One of the largest and most important castes in Madurai city is the Sourashtra community. It numbers 66,533 (1961 census) or approximately

15 per cent of Madurai, and are engaged mainly in their traditional occupation of weaving and related textile industry work. The Sourashtras are sometimes known as the Patnulkaran or "silk-thread people" because of their work, but they prefer to be called Sourashtras after the place (Saurashtra) from which they originally emigrated. Moreover, since they market their own products and engage in other forms of commerce, they are locally classed chettiars or tradesmen of the weaving class. A fifth-century inscription found in northwestern India describes the community as being famed for their skill as silk weavers, and there is evidence that they enjoyed the patronage of successive rulers of Saurashtra in the northwest part of India. As a consequence of Muslim penetration into the area, the community is reported to have migrated to Deogiri in the twelfth century,[1] then on to Vijayanagar in the fourteenth century, and thereafter further south to Madurai, Dindigul, and Tanjore. Under the great Vijayanagar kingdom which dominated most of South India, Madurai was ruled by the Nayaks as subordinate chieftains. Whether the community moved as a unit or in successive series of waves is not known, but it is believed that they settled in Madurai at the request of the Nayak rulers, who admired the skill of these master textile weavers.

Other communities which fled from Muslim invaders settled in other parts of northern India where language, religious beliefs and practices, food, and dress were sufficiently similar so that migrants were able to merge into their new surroundings. But the Sourashtras who moved south entered Dravidian country, where language and customs were markedly different from those to which they were accustomed. The Sourashtras thus maintain their own language, religion, social customs, and communal and political organization.

Much has been written about the language of the Sourashtras. The community maintained linguistic forms related to early Sanskrit and Pali and an early form of the Devanagari script. Philologists, linguists, and grammarians have therefore been keenly interested in the language and script for the light it throws on the history and development of North Indian languages. Moreover, since the modern language of the community contains many words from Telugu and, to a lesser extent, from Kannada, a study of its language reveals the migration pattern of the community.[2]

---

[1] According to another version, the community fled in 1024 when Muhammad of Ghazni sacked Somnath in modern Gujarat. The circumstances which led the community to migrate have had some impact on their attitude toward the Muslim community.

[2] The Sourashtra Literary Society at Madurai and Madras published a history of the community in 1891, *A History of the Sourashtras in Southern India*, reprinted in 1948. A critical brief description of the history and language of the community was

Less is known about the political organization of the community. According to the official history published by the community,

> When the Sourashtras settled in the south, they reproduced the institutions of their mother country in the new land; but owing to the influence of the Southern Dravidians some of the institutions became extinct. . . . The people were divided into four heads called Govndas [chiefs], Saulins [elders], Voydoos [physicians], and Bhoutuls [religious men]. Some traces of the division still survive in the now neglected institution of Govndans. . . . The chiefs were the Judges in both civil and criminal affairs. They were aided in deciding cases by a body of nobles called Saulins. The office of Govndo is hereditary in Madura District whereas in other centres it is elective. The office of the Saulins is to make enquiries and try all cases connected with the community and abide by the decision of the chiefs. The Voydoos and Bhoutuls . . . had their honours on all important occasions, and they are placed in the same rank with the Elders.[3]

The history goes on to say that the Govndans are not now exercising any of their powers except in some religious matters.

Today the internal affairs of the Sourashtras are managed by a Sourashtra Sabha which was started in 1895. "The Patnulkaranas [Sourashtras]," writes Francis in the *Madura Gazetteer* of 1914 (p. 111), "have a very strong *esprit de corps* and this has stood them in good stead in their weaving, which is more scientifically carried on, and in a more flourishing condition, than is usual elsewhere." A manifestation of the *esprit* is that the society is able to collect an income tax (magamai) from members of the community which it spends on the maintenance of a high school, a temple, and several other institutions. And though the society does not play an overt role in politics, its leaders have been active participants in the political life of Madurai throughout the twentieth century.

Before discussing the political role of the community, it is relevant to call attention to the question of caste in relation to the Sourashtras. The

written by H. N. Randle, the librarian of the India office of London, called "The Sourashtrans of South India," *Journal of the Royal Asiatic Society* (Oct., 1944). The most detailed scholarly work on the community, from which much of the later writings draw their descriptions, is in Thurston's *Castes and Tribes of South India*, Vol. VI (1909), article entitled "Patnulkaran."

[3] *A History of the Sourashtras in Southern India*, pp. 11–12.

Sourashtras claim to be Brahmins, although their rituals differ somewhat from Brahminical practices both in the north and in the south. In the seventeenth century eighteen members of the community were arrested for performing a Brahminical ceremony. The Nayak Queen Mangammal (1689–1704) convened a council of those learned in the Sastras to investigate the caste claims of the community. They declared in favor of the defendants, and the queen recorded the judgment in the form of a palm-leaf award. The palm leaf is still preserved and was used by the community to argue its claims for Brahminical standing before W. Francis, I.C.S., superintendent of census operations, Madras, in 1901. Members of the community use Brahmin surnames such as Aiyar, Achari, and Bhagavatar.[4]

Many Brahmins continued to resist the claims of the Sourashtra community, and throughout the twentieth century (and even earlier) the Sourashtras have made every effort to reassert their claim. After the First World War the growth of the nationalist movement played no small role in bringing these two communities together. For various reasons both communities were attracted to the nationalist cause. The Brahmins, in Madurai as elsewhere, were educated, engaged in government service and the professions, and therefore the leading figures in the early middle-class revolt which almost everywhere constitutes the first phase of a nationalist movement. Indeed, the Brahmin complexion of the Congress was so strong, in the south especially, that non-Brahmins were often repelled by the movement and many joined the pro-British anti-Brahmin Justice party. One notable exception was the Sourashtra community. Before the First World War the community was in no way attracted to the nationalist movement, but the advent of Gandhi brought about a marked change in their political attitudes. Sourashtras felt a great affinity on geographical and religious grounds with Gandhi, a Gujarati and a Vaisnavite. The devotional, ascetic, pious, non-violent qualities of Gandhi were admired by the Sourashtras. Moreover, Gandhi fervently supported the development of India's traditional handloom industry, partly because of his desire to strengthen industries which provided employment in rural areas, partly because of his nostalgia for pre-industrial technologies and ways of life,

[4] A controversy developed at the turn of the century when the director of public instruction of Madras refused to recognize that such a caste as Sourashtra Brahmins exists and decided that if the school managers reported pupils as belonging to such a community their schools would not be entitled to the grants-in-aid intended for the backward classes. Delegations were sent by the Sourashtra Sabha to the director and to the superintendent of the census to advance their caste claims. Their case is presented in a small volume, *The Caste Questions in the Sourashtra Community*, reprinted by the Sourashtra Sabha, Madura, 1941.

and partly because he saw the strengthening of indigenous handloom industries as a means of reducing dependence upon foreign mill-made cloth. He was also convinced that in the long run the hand production of cotton yarn and cloth would provide greater employment than could the indigenous mills. Gandhi therefore had a special appeal to traditional handloom weavers in Mysore, Andhra, and Madras. The Sourashtras thus had both an economic and a spiritual sense of kinship with Gandhi, and shortly after Gandhi's visit to Madurai, after the First World War, they entered the nationalist movement.

The large-scale entrance of other castes into the Congress party in recent years has been a threat both to the Brahmin community and to the Sourashtras, and neither community holds the overwhelming political position which it held earlier. Nonetheless, the Sourashtras do retain a strong position within the Congress party. A few Sourashtras have been attracted to other political groups, particularly the Jan Sangh, partly because Jan Sangh is anti-Muslim and recalls the circumstances which led the Sourashtras to flee from their home nearly a thousand years ago, and partly because the Jan Sangh appeals to the strongly religious and pious attitude prevalent among the more orthodox elements in the community. Some of the younger members of the community have joined the Rashtriya Swayam Sevak Sangh (RSS), a militant youth body of the Jan Sangh. In the 1962 elections the Jan Sangh candidate, a member of the community and a municipal councillor, was able to win slightly less than five thousand of seventy-six thousand votes in the Madurai East constituency, but almost all of these votes came from the Sourashtras. Though the Dravida Munnetra Kazhagam (DMK), the major opposition to Congress in Madurai state, has considerable popularity among the youth of Madurai, it has almost no attraction to the youth of the Sourashtra community, since the DMK is an anti-northern and anti-Brahmin political party; the Sourashtras therefore can only be a target of attack along with the Brahmins.

In the main the Sourashtras are with the Congress party, and in spite of the large-scale intrusion of other communities into Congress, the Sourashtras still play an important role. One of the two MLAs is from the community, and so is the MP. Until a few years ago, almost all the presidents of the Madurai city District Congress Committee were Sourashtras. But in some ways the Sourashtras remain foreign to Madurai, and they have often been unable to adjust themselves to the changes which have taken place within the city, changes which have had consequences in political life within the municipality and within the Congress party.

The rapid growth in population prior to 1951, the expansion of the textile industry within Madurai, the growth in education, and the introduction of universal adult education — all had important consequences for the political behavior of the laboring classes, shopkeepers, and non-Brahmin castes generally. Finally, as we shall see, the political independence of the Sourashtras has been severely curtailed because the community is unable to compete with modern methods of large-scale textile production and depends, therefore, on government subsidies. On the other hand, the small-scale household character of the handloom textile industry is conducive to a measure of political independence and a degree of leisure which permits the more prosperous members of the community to devote a considerable amount of time to political as well as community matters.

Nonetheless, the Sourashtras do play an important part in the commercial life of the city, and to a large extent they have been rightly credited with what little prosperity Madurai has. British textile manufacturers were in large part attracted to Madurai in the nineteenth century because the presence of the handloom textile industry ensured manufacturers of a local market for their mill-made yarn. In 1892 the Harvey brothers established Madura Mills in Madurai, and these mills soon became among the largest in the world, now employing at least twelve thousand workers. Soon Indian-owned mills (for example, Meenakshi Mills and Rajah Mills) were also established in Madurai.

Moreover, the Sourashtras still continue to play an important though diminishing role in the Congress party organization. An examination of the careers of its two elected Congress leaders throws considerable light on the political role of the community and the factors at work limiting its role.

N. M. R. Subbaraman, the MP from Madurai, is not only the best-known Sourashtra, but is also the most prominent of the older nationalist leaders in Madurai. He was an active participant in the nationalist agitations of 1930, 1932, and 1942, and was in jail for several years for his political work. He is widely known throughout the district as a leading Gandhian. For many years he has been treasurer of the Madurai District Nirmana Uliyar Sangh, the central organization for constructive work in the district, and, like many other Gandhians, he has been deeply involved in work to improve the status of Harijans. He has been the leader of the Harijan Sevak Sangh in the district for many years. After independence he turned all his energies to the "constructive" side of the Gandhian movement and left active politics. Earlier, in 1935, he had been elected chairman of the Madurai Municipal Council, a post he held intermittently until

1942. He was elected to the Madras Legislative Assembly in 1935 and again in 1946. He did not stand for public office in the 1952 or 1957 elections, and stood in 1962 for parliament only after he was requested to do so by the Madras state Congress party leadership.

The Congress movement — which Subbaraman joined actively in 1930 — had its beginnings in 1919–20 in Madurai, when a Brahmin lawyer, Vaidyanath Aiyer, led a movement to boycott foreign cloth, the law courts, the government high schools and colleges, and the toddy shops. The Brahmin middle classes were staunch supporters of the movement, but they were quickly joined by the Sourashtra community. Subbaraman (who was born in 1905) was a young businessman in the community. His family owned a knitting factory, a hosiery firm, and several other businesses. Subbaraman increasingly turned his attention toward political and constructive work, and left the management of the family businesses to other members of the family. It was in the 1930 civil disobedience movement, when he was arrested and sentenced to one year's imprisonment, that he became a prominent local Congress leader. The Sourashtra community then constituted about one-fourth of the population of Madurai. Along with the much smaller Brahmin community, they provided the most active Congress workers in Madurai town. Many, like Subbaraman, came from respectable well-known families, and in fact many of their mothers and sisters also courted imprisonment for the nationalist cause.

As a dedicated Gandhian, Subbaraman left active political life after independence to devote his energies to constructive work. He explains his distaste for politics:

> Before independence we never thought of jobs, so there was no questions of this or that caste gaining something. We also did a great deal of constructive work, such as eliminating untouchability, doing sanitation work, rural uplift, and so on. After independence a sense of power got hold of us. So long as Mahatma was with us, we weren't so much after power. He taught us that power should be utilized for the welfare of the masses. But after Mahatma died, people started to think more of power and more of their caste and group. The Hindu-Muslim division started these difficulties, for that made us think of community. Then communities of Hindus became organized to get themselves elected. People organized their own caste. That's why we see so much casteism and groupism now.

Intense factional struggles took place within the Madurai Congress party, but Subbaraman refused to support any faction. As perhaps the only prominent local leader who refused to participate or take sides in these conflicts — on the grounds that he was not interested in politics — he retained the loyalty and affection of the local leaders. When the District Congress Committee was disbanded by the state Congress party because of internal dissension, Subbaraman was one of the few — if not the only local leader — to whom the party could turn. He was asked by the state party to take responsibility for carrying on the local Congress work in the absence of a DCC and subsequently to take steps to have a new DCC elected and to stand for the parliamentary ticket from Madurai in 1962. The Congress party had lost the parliamentary seat in the 1957 elections to a leading Communist trade unionist, and it was widely felt, by both state and local Congress leaders, that Subbaraman was the only local Congressman who could defeat the Communists. Subbaraman initially expressed his reluctance to return to active politics but, after much persuasion from state and local leaders, agreed to run and to become the convener of the Madurai party.

Though he is revered by people in the Sourashtra community, Subbaraman has successfully avoided the taint of being known as a community leader. As one Sourashtra proudly put it, "He is a national leader, then a leader of Congress, and then only a leader of his community." The attitude was apparently shared by others outside the community, for in the 1962 elections Subbaraman took the parliamentary seat away from the Communists.[5]

While Subbaraman's reputation and influence extend beyond his own community, Mrs. Lakshmikantham, one of the two MLAs from Madurai, is very much a Sourashtrian. Her husband, an energetic Congress worker, a businessman, and a leader within his own community, described his wife's political assets:

> Nehru said that he wanted more lady candidates for the legislative assembly. My wife had studied Hindi in several

[5] In 1962 the election results were as follows (party and caste in parentheses):

| | | |
|---|---|---|
| N. M. R. Subbaraman (Congress, Sourashtra) | 140,574 | 39.6% |
| K. T. K. Thangamani (Communist, Nadar) | 123,386 | 34.8% |
| S. S. Mirisamy (Swatantra, Pillai) | 91,459 | 25.6% |
| The 1957 results were as follows: | | |
| T. K. Rama (Congress, Sourashtra) | 78,286 | 34.5% |
| K. T. K. Thangamani (Communist, Nadar) | 79,374 | 35.0% |
| Sasivarna Thevar (Forward Bloc, Thevar) | 64,765 | 28.6% |
| Venkataramayya (Independent, Brahmin) | 4,249 | 1.9% |

northern universities, and she has frequently spoken on Congress platforms. She had also hoisted the national flag at many meetings. So when Kamaraj [the chief minister of Madras] was looking for a lady candidate, it was only natural that he should think of her. So they put her up for the eastern constituency. Since this constituency is made up largely of people from the Sourashtra community, it was only logical that a member of the community be selected, since no one outside the community could win an election here.

Mrs. Lakshmikantham is said to lead a very pious life. Her home, in the midst of the Sourashtra neighborhood in Madurai, is a center for religious worship. Images of Radha and Krishna are prominently displayed in the living room. Women often assemble there to sing bhajans (devotional songs) or to hear Mrs. Lakshmikantham read and teach the Gita (a great Vaishnavite text). The MLA since 1957, she has devoted her work in the assembly and outside to the aid of her own community. Describing her accomplishments, her supporters note that she has collected donations to buy ten acres of land for the Sourashtra High School for Girls in Madurai (she is the secretary of the school). She has formed a ladies association which spins khadi and employs about two hundred women, mostly from the Sourashtra community. She has also formed a ladies association to give religious teaching and to provide lessons in music and handicrafts, and she has been very active personally in teaching Hindi. "She has also helped people here get into higher education. While our community is advanced in commercial activities, it is not educationally very advanced; so people will approach her, and she will give them letters to important persons to get them admitted into higher education."

Though she defeated the Communist candidate by over four thousand votes in 1957,[6] it was feared that the vote of the Sourashtra community might be split in 1962, since a member of that community was standing on a Jan Sangh platform. The Jan Sangh candidate, an active leader of the local RSS had attracted young men from orthodox families in the Sourashtra community. Moreover, he had some appeal among the orthodox Brahmin elements in the town. The fear proved, however, to be ground-

[6] 1957 results, Madurai East Assembly Election:

| | | |
|---|---|---|
| P. K. R. Lakshmikantham (Congress) | 21,859 | 50.07% |
| N. Sankarayya (Communist) | 17,311 | 39.64% |
| B. K. Rajagopalan (Independent) | 3,421 | 7.83% |
| S. Bagavather (Independent) | 1,068 | 2.46% |

less, since Congress easily carried the constituency, though by a slightly reduced percentage.[7]

The constituency has the bulk of the Sourashtras in Madurai, but it also contains a substantial non-Sourashtra factory work force, in which the Communists predominate. Unlike Subbaraman, who, though a Sourashtra, commands support and engages in activities throughout the district and within many communities, Mrs. Lakshmikantham is primarily a community leader and commands little support from other communities.

In concluding our examination of the political role of the Sourashtra community, we should note that the historic and sentimental attachments of the Sourashtras to Congress are reinforced by the government's policy of giving subsidies to the handloom industry. The economics of the industry has become closely associated with government policy, and many prominent leaders of the community say frankly that their industry would be seriously injured if government support were withdrawn. With government support, handloom weavers have started their own cooperatives to free themselves from the control of the master weavers. Government officials organize the cooperatives, grant loans to the weavers, supply some small machines and materials free of cost, and give the societies a rebate of approximately 10 per cent of the sales price of handloom cloth. There are in the district 283 such weaver cooperative societies, of which about a hundred are in Madurai town. The individual weaver receives a wage from the society as if the society were the master weaver. The member is given materials by way of loan, then repays the loan by giving the society the finished cloth, which the society then sells (receiving a rebate or subsidy from the government). The rebate is financed by a tax on the cloth produced by the textile mills.

The individual cooperatives receive loans from the Sourashtra Cooperative Bank, which in turn receives its money from the Central Cooperative Bank and from local depositors. The Sourashtra Cooperative Bank also makes loans to individual members of the cooperatives for domestic and nonproductive purposes, including loans for buildings as well as for weddings. The president of the Sourashtra Cooperative Bank, age fifty-seven, is an important local Congressman, a member of Congress since 1925, a one-time councillor in the Municipal Corporation, a former member of the

[7] 1962 results, Madurai East Assembly Election:

| | | |
|---|---|---|
| P. K. R. Lakshmikantham (Congress) | 36,679 | 48.1% |
| Sankarayya (Communist) | 27,228 | 35.7% |
| Ramu Servai (Swatantra) | 7,408 | 9.7% |
| Ramaiah Seshachari (Jan Sangh) | 4,922 | 6.5% |

District Congress Committee, and a dress manufacturer by profession. Nearly all the other banks in Madurai — the Madurai City House Cooperative Bank, the Madurai City Middle Class Cooperative Bank, and the District Central Cooperative Bank — as well as the majority of the weaver cooperatives are controlled by Congressmen. The Communists control a few of the weaver societies but none of the banks. Congressmen say frankly that they can get loans for their supporters; one Congressman in control of one such bank reported that he has considerable influence over members of the bank and over the weavers generally. "I have told the Sourashtra weavers," he stated frankly, "that so long as Congress is in power there will be a handloom weaving industry; otherwise the industry will die. We can be sure that a Congress government will support the handloom industry, but we do not know what others will do."

Although the cooperatives were intended to protect the small weavers against the master weavers, the master weavers too are strong supporters of the Congress government. For one thing, only about 50 per cent of the weavers belong to the cooperatives; the remainder work for the master weavers. One Sourashtra businessman explained why. "The co-operatives do not always have materials available when the workers want it. So many work for the private master weavers. They get slightly less wages, but they get guaranteed work." Do the master weavers resent the government-run cooperatives?

> Not at all. In the first place, the master weavers often control many of the cooperative associations. Then too, the master weavers often buy cloth from the cooperative associations and then serve as marketing agents to sell the cloth. That way they get the rebate from the government. Actually, the master weavers can produce their own cloth at a cheaper rate than can the cooperative societies. I think that if the government withdrew their subsidies, the cooperative might fold up; but the private master weavers could probably continue, since they could compete with the mill-made cloth.

## The Work Force and the Trade Unions

As elsewhere in India, the work force in Madurai is fragmented into innumerable trade unions dominated by or affiliated or associated with po-

litical parties. According to the 1961 census, more than one-fourth of the total working population in Madurai worked in factories.[8] Textile mills are the largest single employer group. Madura Mills, a British firm, is internationally known, but other large textile establishments are located in and around Madurai. Transport industries also engage a large number of workers, since Madurai is a central railhead in South India; T. V. Sundaram (TVS), India's largest private bus transport company, has its central office and bus terminal in Madurai.

The Indian National Trade Union Congress, the federation which is closely associated with the Congress party, claims that a majority of the twenty-four thousand workers reported to be union members are in INTUC unions. The bulk of these are in the National Textile Workers Union and in the union of TVS workers. But there is other evidence to suggest that in solidarity, if not in numbers, the Communist trade unions in Madurai are stronger. Both in assembly and in parliamentary elections the Communists do well in the predominantly working class areas of the town; and in the municipal elections in 1959 Congress won only four of the eighteen seats in the working class areas against four for the Communists. The Communists thus constitute a formidable foe for the INTUC and for the local Congress party organization as well.

Though INTUC and the local Congress party share a common enemy, they do not work closely together; there are, in fact, times when the two groups are in opposition to one another. One must ask, therefore, why it is that INTUC has failed to make a greater dent into the Communist position in Madurai and, second, why it is that close relations between INTUC and the Congress party have not been established.

The three or four men who control the INTUC organization in Madurai are not generally influential in the district Congress party organization.

[8] 1961 Census, workers in Madurai town:

| | |
|---|---:|
| Total workers | 130,587 |
| Household industries | 16,295 |
| Manufacturing | 37,752 |
| Construction | 3,966 |
| Trade and Commerce | 27,424 |
| Transport | 10,057 |
| Other services | 33,077 |

According to the *Report on the Working of the Factories Act* (Government of Madras, 1961), there was a total of 532 factories in Madurai district (including rural and urban areas) employing 32,698 workers in 1959. Although there has been an increase in the number of factories, there has been a gradual decline in the size of the factory labor force as a consequence of rationalization of textile mills. In 1961, Madurai taluka (which includes the municipal area and the surrounding region) had twenty-eight factories employing more than a hundred workers each. (Statistics provided by inspector of factories, Madurai.)

Mr. Ramchandaran, president of INTUC in Madurai town, is a full-time trade union worker, and though he has been in the Congress party since 1926, he plays no important role within the town organization. Mr. Vellu, the president of the National Textile Workers Union, which with its claimed membership of about seven thousand is the largest single INTUC union in the town, is a member of the District Congress Committee and for some time had been a member of the Tamil Nad Congress Committee. He serves as a liaison between the INTUC organization in the town and the party organization, but his main concern is with protecting labor interests in the party rather than with participating in the recurring internal political conflicts. Mr. Bommiah and Mr. Guruswamy Iyer, the president and the treasurer, respectively, of the T. V. Sundaram Workers Union, control the second largest INTUC union in Madurai (about four thousand workers); while both have been Congressmen since the 1920's, neither is involved in the internal activities of the party.

The local Congress party organization is in general inhospitable to the trade unions. There is no formal union representation on the neighborhood mandal Congress committees; unless trade union workers join and participate in the working of the mandal committees as active members, they are likely to have little influence in the DCC as well. Since the prominent trade union workers are constantly engaged in work to maintain their own trade unions, they have little time for separate participation in the mandal committees. And without establishing direct power within the mandal committees and the DCC, opportunities for trade unionists to get tickets for the legislative assembly, parliament, or even the municipal corporation are small. Thus, while the Communists have put up trade union leaders for various elective offices in Madurai, the Congress party has not.

The reasons for this are related to the internal power structure of the Congress party. The Madurai trade unionists are not directly involved in the party organization. There are, for example, no Congress party mandal units in the factories. Moreover, the struggles within the local Congress party for tickets and for control over the organization are so intense that no group within the party wants to share its limited power with the INTUC group.

This local inhospitability is reinforced by strained relations between the state Congress party leadership in Madras and the INTUC state leadership. When INTUC was formed in 1947, a conflict developed between the leader of INTUC in Madras state and the state minister of labor. There is considerable dispute and uncertainty as to the nature of

the original difficulty; it is said that the INTUC leaders wanted their federation to be made up exclusively of pro-Congress unions, which would be closely associated with the party and the government. Prominent Congress leaders reportedly favored the establishment of a trade union federation which would be free of party politics and which would contain non-Communist unions affiliated with many political parties or independent of all parties. In 1952, the year of India's first general elections, INTUC failed to win Congress support for their candidates for the Madras state assembly and for the national parliament. In fact, the INTUC president of Madras stood as an independent candidate against Congress.

Although at the national level INTUC is supposedly the spokesman for the Congress party in the trade unions front, in Madras, Congress has its own labor department and conducts its own union organizing campaigns. In Madurai itself one leading member of the Congress party and of the Tamil Nad Congress Committee has organized the Madurai National Labour Union in Madura Mills in an effort, as he put it, "to win over some of the labor vote to the Congress party here."

Again, the readiness of this local Congress leader to organize his own trade unions is related to the internal schisms within the party organization. The organizer himself is one of Madurai's leading businessmen who is deeply involved in some of the party's internal conflicts. It is said that by organizing his own unions and then bringing the workers into mandal committees, this Congressman is able to ensure himself a large vote in the elections to the District Congress Committee and to the Tamil Nad Congress Committee. Moreover, he is able to ensure that many of his supporters will also be elected to these party bodies. But this effort to create separate Congress-controlled trade unions would not be possible were it not for the unofficial support given to these efforts by the Congress party organization at the state level.

It is impossible to understand the fragmentation of the trade union movement or its political role without reference to the caste composition of the work force in Madurai.[9] Since the census excluded tabulations on

[9] Madurai's major unions and their affiliations are as follows:

National Textile Workers Union, INTUC
Madurai Textile Workers Unions, AITUC
T. V. Sundaram Workers Union, INTUC
Madura National Labour Union, Independent but controlled by local Congressman; a small union confined to Madura Mills
Madurai District Mill Workers Union, Hind Mazdoor Sabha (associated with the Praja Socialist party)

In addition to these unions with direct political affiliations, there are several important independent unions. The Madurai Labour Union (textiles) is a large independent

the basis of caste, and since no other official agency records such data, one must rely upon local informants. Trade union leaders in Madurai are remarkably well versed with respect to the caste composition of their work force, and much of the political maneuvering which takes place within the trade union movement and between the unions and the parties is based upon estimates of the behavior of particular castes in the work force. A major justification, for example, given by a local Congressman who had organized his own trade union organization in one of the largest textile mills was that he himself was a member of the Thevar community — a general term which includes several related low castes — and that unless he organized these workers there was a danger that they would drift from the Congress fold.

The Thevars constitute a substantial part of the work force. Some estimate that it may be as high as one-fourth of the textile factory laborers. Though many Thevars are in INTUC unions, more are influenced by the caste leaders, who in the main do not support the Congress party. Muthuram Thevar, the leader of the community, is a member of parliament from a neighboring constituency and a member of the Forward Bloc. In the pre-independence era this community was classified by the British as a "criminal tribe" primarily because of its predatory behavior. A considerable part of the community indulged in burglaries and highway robberies. A caste known as the Kallar constitute the largest part of the Thevar community ("Kallar" means "thieves" in Tamil). Under the medieval Nayak kings they were known to have refused to pay any tribute, arguing that the heavens supplied the necessary rain, their own cattle did the plowing, and they themselves carried out the rest of the cultivation operations, so there was no possible reason why they should be charged anything. During the early days of the British Company, in the middle of the eighteenth century, there were a number of military skirmishes between the Kallar and the Sepoys of the company. Though they were controlled militarily by the British, they engaged in dacoity and theft on a substantial scale. The Kallar were not ashamed of their occupation. Francis reported in the *Madura District Gazetteer* in 1914:

> One of them defended his clan by urging that every other
> class stole — the official by taking bribes, the vakil [lawyer]
> by fostering animosities and so pocketing fees, the mer-
> chant by watering the arrack [country liquor] and sanding

union led by a pro-Congress leader of the large Naidu caste. The union has a large number of Naidus.

the sugar, and so on and so forth—and that the Kallans [sic] differed from these only in the directness of their methods.[10]

The Kallar are found in several districts, but their greatest strength is in Madurai. The caste is divided into several endogamous sections which are territorial in origin. The largest group in Madurai district was traditionally under a kind of monarchical ruler, a hereditary headman who was given authority to settle disputes within the caste. Customs and beliefs are martial in character.[11]

As with other martial communities in India, the Thevars have a distinctive political viewpoint and considerable political cohesion. The leaders of the community gave their support to Subhas Chandra Bose in the nationalist movement of the late 1930's, largely because of Bose's militant outlook toward the British. When Bose visited Madurai in 1939 he received enthusiastic support from this community. Muthuram Thevar, a large landowning member of the community (possessing, it is said, two thousand acres of wet land and fifteen thousand of dry land), led his political followers into Bose's political group within the Congress, known as the Forward Bloc. After independence, when the Forward Bloc became independent of Congress, Muthuram Thevar continued to be the leader of the movement in Madras state. Several members of the Forward Bloc were elected to the Madras legislative assembly and to parliament, and almost all of these were Thevars.

Within Madurai district today the Thevars are one of the largest groups in opposition to the Congress party. The Forward Bloc now works closely with the Swatantra party, and its greatest strength continues to be in and around Madurai district. In the 1957 elections the Forward Bloc put up its own candidate for parliament from Madurai, a Thevar, who won 28.6 per cent of the vote (compared with 34.5 per cent for Congress and 35 per cent for the winning Communist candidate). In the 1962 elections the party gave its support to a candidate (but not a Thevar) of the Swatantra party who, with their assistance, won one-fourth of the vote.

The community in Madurai city is scattered in a number of different trade unions in the textile mills, although INTUC claims that the largest

[10] *Madras District Gazetteers* (Madurai, 1914), pp. 89–90.

[11] "It is said that their maidens used to select as their husbands men who had proved their bravery by rescuing the cloth tied to the horns of the bulls let loose in panic amidst the din of drums and music." *Madras District Gazetteer* (Madurai, 1960), p. 119. The Thevars are said to have derived their martial character from having served in the army of the Pandhya and Chola kings.

part is in their unions. However, INTUC and the Congress party have little influence over the voting behavior of the community, which continues to be guided by its own caste leadership. Loyalty within the community — as in other martial groups — is substantial and in general rigorously hierarchical. Muthuram Thevar, the MP and leader of the party and the community, has a firm political control.[12] It is said that his influence over the community was firmly established because he led a movement to end restrictions which the government had placed upon them.

Though the Thevars are probably the most cohesive political group within the working class, other castes in the factories also maintain their community identifications in their political behavior. The Naidus are another large caste in the labor force, and are particularly numerous in the textile industry. Though they are scattered into a number of different unions, there is one large textile union in the Madura mills which has a Naidu leader and in which the Naidus predominate.

There are few Brahmins working in the factories, but a substantial number of Brahmins work in the offices of the various establishments run by T. V. Sundaram. This firm owns and operates a large private fleet of buses in South India as well as South India's largest auto repair shop and a factory in which trucks are assembled and manufactured. TVS employs seven thousand five hundred workers in all, about seven thousand of whom are in a single union; the remainder are non-unionized temporary workers. The shopworkers are of many communities: the staff is largely Brahmin (as is the manager), and a substantial number of the bus drivers belong to the Naidu community.

From the very beginning of the trade union movement in Madurai, as elsewhere in India, political differences have also been a factor in trade union fragmentation. The Communists were among the earliest to organize unions, and thus established for themselves firm roots among the work force, so much so that no other political group has been able to build comparable union or party loyalty. During the war the Communists took firm control of the All India Trade Union Congress (AITUC), which hitherto had been the central federation of unions in which all political parties had worked. After independence the Congress party and the Congress Socialist party (which was then working within Congress) decided to withdraw their members from the AITUC and to organize their own trade union federations. An attempt to create one all-party but non-Com-

---

[12] The Forward Block MLA from neighboring Ramnad district explained in an interview that whether he would stand again in the 1962 elections depended completely on "our own great leader" and that if his leader wanted him to stand again then of course he would.

munist trade union federation failed, and so the Congress leaders formed the Indian National Trade Union Congress, and the Socialists formed the Hind Mazdoor Sabha. In Madurai few Congressmen entered the factories to organize trade unions until after independence, and they found themselves competing against the Communists and a few independent trade union workers. Madura Mills — the Scottish-owned textile company, the largest textile mill in Madurai — had several trade unions already, and the organization of the INTUC union there simply increased the fragmentation. Though caste and political differences were often at the root of these divisions, the mills occasionally encouraged a multiplicity of trade unions on the grounds that a politically divided work force would be easier to deal with. This proved to be no blessing, however, for as one businessman explained, "Now we have many difficulties, because four or five unions are constantly competing with one another in making demands upon the management. Once management has agreed to the demands of one union, then another union will make even greater demands so they can improve their position."

TVS was not unionized before independence. The Communists tried to get control in 1948 but failed. The energetic manager of TVS broke a Communist strike and then took steps to bring in an INTUC union. He explained:

> It was in 1948 when I was out of the country that the Communists decided to use my absence as an opportunity to call a strike. I immediately came back and set out to break the Communist union. Since the union had called a strike when the issue was before a government conciliation board, the strike was clearly illegal, so we got the government to declare the strike as illegal. We then dismissed some 1,800 workers for their illegal strike, and we got some of our own workers to use lathis [sticks] to beat the Communists down. Fortunately we had great support from the police, who are my friends. I took back 1,600 of the 1,800 workers, but the Communist leader of the strike was arrested and jailed for three years because he was involved in some violent activity. Now the Communists make no effort to break into our shop since they know it is impossible. . . . I took steps to make sure that there would be a union in TVS, so we organized an INTUC union here. Some of the government people and businessmen thought that it was foolish to do so, but I felt

that a union was bound to come anyway and it would be a good thing if it were a sympathetic union. . . . I try to make sure that we can discover what discontent there is among the workers before it ever reached a head. I have a number of hired people who spy for me in the factory and in the union who can let me know what the difficulties are. Once I find out these difficulties, than I can take steps to remedy them. Sometimes my friends and assistants in the shop hesitate to report to me the difficulties. The trouble is that the workers are often too meek, too timid to say anything, or else they are too brave and too forward, too cocksure of themselves. . . . If you want to keep the Communists under control, you have to use strong methods.

The TVS Workers Union is the strongest INTUC union in Madurai. Of the total seven thousand members, about four thousand work for the TVS establishments in Madurai city. Of these, 2,200 are in the workshops and 1,800 are in transport, but they are all together in one union. Union membership is four annas a month (about sixty cents a year), and is collected from the workers on payday. The union performs many services for its members. It recently started a cooperative housing society. It maintains a consumer cooperative store, which sells food and clothing; purchases are deducted from the salary by arrangement with the management. The union also maintains its own building in Madurai, which it uses as a hostel for visiting union members from other cities.

Internal differences which often divide unions appear not to be a factor in the TVS Workers Union. Though elections for the branch units of the union have been contested, there has been no contest for the head offices of the union. All four senior officers of the union have held their positions for the past fifteen years. The president and treasurer of the union are both on the national general council of INTUC, and both are on the Pradesh Congress Committee in Madras. One of these men is on the Madurai District Congress Committee. But the TVS union leaders have no more influence in the district or state party organization than do other INTUC leaders.[13] The inhospitability of the local and state party is one factor, but another is their own reluctance to become too deeply

[13] One of the two TVS trade union workers in the TNCC laughingly explained why he was not important in Congress. "I have been with Congress since 1927. I was a cooperative worker for many years. I wasn't arrested, but if I had been then I would have become a politician." He joined the accounts department of TVS after 1947 and then entered trade union work.

involved in party matters. TVS, like other INTUC unions, is made up largely but not exclusively of pro-Congress workers, who are naturally reluctant to involve the union in party affairs that might divide it. Workers are encouraged to become primary members of the Congress and to become active mandal workers, but no TVS workers control any of the mandal committees and none has received Congress nominations for the municipal corporation elections. Moreover, the union as such does not organize processions during the elections or make any contributions to the Congress party or to any of its candidates.

The Communists are the only party who have put up trade union workers for local offices. The only three trade union workers in the municipal corporation are Communists, and, interestingly enough, not one is from a predominantly labor ward. Though ward 10 has a substantial number of workers, shopkeeping is the largest single occupation. And ward 11, which elected two Communist trade union workers, also has a large number of shopkeepers and white-collar workers as well as factory laborers. The Communist MP from Madurai from 1957 to 1962, Mr. Thangamani, is a trade union organizer and leader. And the Communist candidate for the assembly in Madurai in 1962 was also a trade union worker.[14]

There are ten wards (of thirty-three in Madurai city) which contain working-class majorities and eight additional wards which, with the addition of workers in household industries, have working-class majorities. (See Table 37.) In these eighteen wards, Congress contested all the seats for the 1959 municipal elections but won only four. The Communists contested only four seats and won all of them. Of the remaining seats, seven were won by the Indian National Democratic Congress (a party of Congress dissidents and independents who later changed their name to the Swatantra party), two by independents, and one by a DMK. In the previous municipal election of 1956 Congress won ten of the eighteen seats. In two of these wards — 31 and 32 — Congress won with a plurality in a three-way fight which included the Communists. In 1959 the Commu-

[14] According to Communist sources, there are five thousand Communist members in Madurai district, of whom a thousand are in the city. The party entered the trade union field in 1937 at a time when no political group worked among the factory laborers. Thangamani, the former MP, began active trade union work in 1943, at the time he joined the Communist party. He worked mostly in the textile labor field and, until TVS broke the Communist union, among the transport workers as well. By occupation he is a lawyer. Mr. Sankarayya, the 1962 MLA candidate, age thirty-nine (Thangamani is forty-three), joined the party in 1940 as a student organizer. He is the CPI party secretary in Madurai town and now plays an active role in the labor movement and in the handloom movement. He is a member of the Naidu community, while Thangamani is a Nadar.

TABLE 37
VOTING IN WORKING-CLASS WARDS
IN THE 1959 MADURAI MUNICIPAL ELECTIONS

| Ward | Congress | Independent | CPI | DMK |
|------|----------|-------------|-----|-----|
| *Group One*[a] | | | | |
| 1 . . . . . . . . | 2,332 | . . . . | 5,034 | . . . . |
| 12 . . . . . . . . | 587 | 3,316 | . . . . | . . . . |
| 13 . . . . . . . . | 901 | . . . . | . . . . | 1,199 |
| 14 . . . . . . . . | 730 | 1,692 | . . . . | . . . . |
| 15 . . . . . . . . | 1,132 | 2,320 | . . . . | . . . . |
| 16 . . . . . . . . | 744 | 1,962 | . . . . | . . . . |
| 17 . . . . . . . . | 1,156 | 1,787 | . . . . | . . . . |
| 18 . . . . . . . . | 885 | 1,275 | . . . . | . . . . |
| 25 . . . . . . . . | 853 | 1,452 | . . . . | . . . . |
| 27 . . . . . . . . | 715 | 657 | . . . . | 480 |
| *Group Two*[b] | | | | |
| 2-general . . . . . | 2,932 | 2,580 | . . . . | . . . . |
| 2-reserved. . . . . | 2,565 | . . . . | 2,727 | . . . . |
| 24 . . . . . . . . | 1,388 | . . . . | 3,832 | . . . . |
| 26 . . . . . . . . | 2,613 | 1,282 | . . . . | . . . . |
| 30 . . . . . . . . | 936 | 925 | . . . . | . . . . |
| 31 . . . . . . . . | 1,307 | 2,470 | . . . . | . . . . |
| 32 . . . . . . . . | 1,392 | 2,520 | 3,063 | . . . . |
| 33 . . . . . . . . | 2,133 | . . . . | . . . . | . . . . |

[a] Includes only wards in which a majority of employed population is engaged in manufacturing, other than household industries, construction, transport, storage and communications, based upon 1961 census returns.

[b] Working-class majority based upon the inclusion also of workers in household industries.

nists supported the INDC candidates, who thereby won easily in these wards. It can be said, therefore, that the Communists are strong in six of the eighteen working-class wards (1, 2, 24, 31, 32, and 33). That this strength extends beyond the municipal elections is demonstrated by the fact that the Communists carried all but one of these wards in the assembly elections of 1957. (Ward data for the 1962 general elections are not available).[15] Moreover, there are several white-collar wards with substantial numbers of factory laborers in which the Communists won municipal seats.

## The Middle Classes

In the pre-independence era the middle classes of Madurai played an active role in the nationalist movement, but during the past decade there has been a gradual defection from the Congress party. The term "middle classes" is often loosely employed to refer to two related social groups: white-collar salaried employees, and independent professions such as

[15] City-wide results by party for the municipal elections in 1959 were as follows: Congress, 51,529; CPI, 39,417; INDC, 22,786; DMK, 7,575; Independent, 23,843; invalid, 2,828. Total vote, 132,075.

doctors and lawyers. Both groups were active in the various non-cooperation movements which swept Madurai in the twenties and thirties, but the leadership came mostly from those who were in the professions. The most prominent leader was Vaidyanatha Iyer, a graduate of Madura College, a member of the bar after 1912, and an active Congress worker in Madurai from 1921. Vaidyanatha Iyer was a Brahmin and, like many other nationalists of his caste, was a leader of the movement to permit Harijans to enter orthodox Hindu temples. He led movements in Madurai to picket toddy shops and foreign cloth shops, and was frequently in jail as a result of his work in the civil disobedience movement. Under Iyer's leadership, Harijans were ultimately permitted to enter the temples in Madurai, including the Brahmanical temple of Meenakshi. Liberal, educated, middle-class opinion in Madurai supported Iyer, and several years after his death (in 1955) he is spoken of with great reverence by educated men.

Iyer was a member of the legislative assembly from Madurai from 1946 to 1952. He did not stand in the 1952 elections and the seat was carried by a Communist — a Brahmin, incidentally. In 1957 the son of Iyer, a lawyer by the name of V. Sankaran, applied for and was given the Congress ticket for the legislative assembly. Sankaran regained the seat for Congress by more than a ten thousand lead over his nearest opponent, though his vote against the combined opposition was slightly under a majority. In the 1962 elections he raised his percentage to well over a majority.[16]

The bulk of the middle-class population in Madurai lives in Sankaran's constituency. This area elected a Communist MLA in 1952; in 1959 Communist councillors were elected in a number of wards within this constituency; and in the 1957 elections the Communist parliamentary candidate carried the assembly constituency and in fact thereby won the parliamentary seat. There is thus ample evidence to believe that Congress is not strong in this area and that Sankaran's election represents a personal rather than party triumph.

[16] The 1957 results were as follows:

| | | |
|---|---|---|
| Sankaran (Congress) | 20,305 | 47.1% |
| S. Muthu (Independent) | 9,872 | 22.9% |
| Bahulayan (Praja Socialist) | 7,873 | 18.3% |
| Viswanathan (Independent) | 4,565 | 10.6% |
| Muthu Pillai (Independent) | 523 | 1.2% |

The 1962 results were:

| | | |
|---|---|---|
| Sankaran (Congress) | 32,801 | 54.6% |
| Devasagayam (Forward Bloc) | 15,445 | 25.7% |
| Ayyavoo (Independent) | 8,229 | 13.7% |
| Bahulayan (Praja Socialist) | 3,601 | 6.0% |

In the 1959 municipal elections Congress proved to be even weaker among the white-collar workers than among the factory workers. There are nine wards in Madurai in which "services" constitutes the largest single occupation, and these wards elect eleven municipal councillors. (See Table 38.) Congress won only three of these seats, the Communists

TABLE 38
VOTING IN WHITE-COLLAR WARDS
IN THE 1959 MADURAI MUNICIPAL ELECTIONS

| Ward | Congress | Independent | CPI | DMK |
|------|----------|-------------|-----|-----|
| 3-general. . . . . | 2,039 | 2,595 | . . . . | . . . . |
| 3-reserved. . . . . | 1,904 | . . . . | 2,602 | . . . . |
| 4 . . . . . . . . | 1,070 | . . . . | 1,693 | . . . . |
| 5 . . . . . . . . | 1,629 | 804 | . . . . | . . . . |
| 6 . . . . . . . . | 1,450 | . . . . | 3,222 | . . . . |
| 7 . . . . . . . . | 1,164 | . . . . | 2,329 | . . . . |
| 8 . . . . . . . . | 1,508 | . . . . | . . . . | 1,305 |
| 11-general. . . . . | 2,638 | . . . . | 4,968 | . . . . |
| 11-reserved . . . . | 2,885 | . . . . | 4,729 | . . . . |
| 19 . . . . . . . . | 675 | 1,058 | . . . . | . . . . |
| 20 . . . . . . . . | 1,145 | 1,073 | . . . . | . . . . |

NOTE: Includes only wards in which "services" constitutes the largest single occupation, based upon 1961 census returns.

six, independents two. Thus the white-collar wards proved to be the Communist stronghold in the 1959 elections; even in the 1956 municipal elections, when Congress won an overwhelming seven seats (two Communists and two independents), the Communists viewed these wards as prime targets. In the 1956 elections the Communists contested eight of these seats, compared to only four (of eighteen) in the working-class wards.

Many of these service occupations involve working in the offices of the textile firms and other manufacturers in Madurai, and therefore white-collar workers are subjected to considerable Communist trade union influence. If one adds together the wards in which workers — factory and white-collar — predominate, one finds that the Communists won ten, Congress seven, and other parties and independents twelve.

As the Congress MLA from a predominantly middle-class constituency, Sankaran has emerged as the most prominent spokesman in Madurai for the middle classes. Though Sankaran is a Brahmin and most of the Brahmins in Madurai live in his constituency, he recognizes that Brahmins are a minority in the area and has thus avoided building his political and social contacts upon an exclusive Brahmin base. Unlike the other MLA, Mrs. Lakshmikantham, whose political strength rests so heavily upon her work with her own Sourashtra community, Sankaran has sought to build his political career on a non-community base. As a candidate in the

1962 elections, Sankaran spoke frequently of the many accomplishments of the Madras Congress government, particularly those which affected Madurai town. He spoke of the proposed new dam which would improve the city's water supply, the new bridge across the Vaigai River which divides the town, the new agricultural college, the new house building scheme, and the reduction in sales taxes. Sankaran's posture is thus that of a civic rather than a community leader.

Moreover, as an MLA he is particularly concerned with serving the needs of his middle-class voters. A common request upon the MLA, for example, is for a good conduct certificate. If an individual wants a job in the railroads, wishes to take Public Service Commission examinations for state government employment, or wants admission into a medical or polytechnic college, he must produce a letter of good conduct from a gazetted government officer or an MLA. Since Sankaran's home and law office are in a central area of the city and he is generally more accessible than a high ranking government official, many come to him for such a certificate. Generally he asks the person who comes to him to produce a letter from a municipal councillor or any well-known local person testifying to his character, and then asks him to fill out a printed form which he signs; thousands of such letters have been signed by him, mainly for his middle-class constituents, during the five years he has been in the assembly.[17]

Middle-class voters also approach Sankaran for assistance with problems in the local schools and hospitals. Local citizens ask him to arrange for their admission into a local hospital or tuberculosis ward. Though in Sankaran's judgment such assistance is not necessary, he reports that local citizens feel that a letter from him will speed things up. He also hears complaints from them about the conduct of managers of the local public schools. School managers often pocket money intended for school lunches by providing inadequate meals, or sometimes a manager may illegally try to take a part of the salary from a teacher. When such complaints come to the MLA, he in turn brings them to the attention of the district education officer.

Sankaran's services to his middle-class voters, his distinguished family background, and his caste are all political assets, but his victory, as we have noted, obscures the fact that a large part of his constituency is

[17] Apart from assisting those who belong to the middle classes, he also aids those who aspire to join the middle class. Members of backward communities and Harijans also need a letter certifying that they are members of such communities and therefore entitled to special facilities offered by the government. Jobs in administration and seats in the colleges are reserved for these classes. Sankaran reports that he has printed and signed thousands of such community certificates for people in his constituency.

critical of the Congress party. Brahmins in particular are critical, for they feel that the Congress organization in Madurai and in Madras generally has fallen into the hands of non-Brahmins and even anti-Brahmins; they feel that merit in appointments to administration and seats in colleges has been pushed aside, so that Nadars and other large non-Brahmin castes are given special privileges. The Communist and — more recently — the Swatantra parties have attracted many Brahmin voters. But as far as the assembly election is concerned, most local Brahmins find Sankaran's argument attractive.

> I tell the Brahmins that it is a matter of choosing between two evils. There is some truth to the charge that the government does not always consider merit, and therefore that the Brahmin community is not doing as well as it did earlier. But if Congress didn't win, the DMK might, and they are likely to destroy the Brahmin community as the Germans tried to destroy the Jews.

But more important perhaps in affecting their vote is Sankaran's own behavior in the assembly and his work on behalf of his constituents, for many voters who supported Sankaran for the assembly voted against Congress for both the parliamentary seat and for the municipal councillors. One can find many reasons why Brahmins in particular and middle-class voters in general might turn against Congress in Madurai town. The failure of the municipal and state governments to maintain urban facilities that can keep up with the rapid rise in population hits the middle-class population hardest. Water and power shortages, inadequate hospital facilities, and crowded schools and colleges affect the middle classes directly, while the poorer, often recently urbanized classes are less disturbed by these shortages.

A second factor in the alienation of the middle classes from the Congress party flows from the changes which have taken place in the composition of the local party. The infusion of bazaar merchants and the less educated into the party organization was accompanied by a gradual withdrawal of the more educated from party work. As the local party has increasingly moved toward its present concern for patronage and away from the more rarefied ideals of a nationalist movement or ideological party, educated young men have been alienated from the party. While there are now many young men in the Madurai Congress party, they are more likely to come from the mercantile than professional classes. Local Congressmen

confess that their party has little appeal within the colleges of Madurai, where the DMK has a considerable hold. The DMK is a growing anti-northern, anti-Brahmin, Tamil nationalist organization which has a strong appeal among educated non-Brahmin youth. Thus far the party has not been a strong force among the voters of Madurai, but its hold within the student classes suggests that its influence among voters may increase in the next decade. The Communists also have some influence among young persons, but there is reason to think that in recent years their position has been somewhat weakened by the growth of the DMK.[18]

The educated classes of Madurai have found it difficult to communicate with the non-intellectual elites who have been rising in the Congress party in recent years. Likely to view politics from an ideological perspective, educated men find the outlook, style, and interests of the less educated mercantile classes incompatible with their approach. Thus, the changing composition of the party organization combined with the low level of governmental investment in public amenities in the city are important factors in the growing alienation of the middle classes from the Congress party.

### Commercial and Industrial Interests

The Congress party in Madurai town is largely dominated by business-men. Some of the largest businessmen in Madurai have considerable influence with the state government and state administration, but, with a few exceptions, take little direct interest in the affairs of the district organization. In contrast, the smaller businessmen who run the many household textile industries in Madurai and the many shopkeepers, particularly those in the larger wholesale establishments, take a keen interest in municipal affairs and in the city party organization.

The most important pro-Congress businessman in Madurai, T. S. Krishna, the manager of T. V. Sundaram, plays no part in the affairs of the local Congress party organization. The one exception was in the latter part of 1961, when the All India Congress Committee was to hold its national meeting in Madurai before the national general elections. Since

[18] In many constituencies in Madras state the Communists have sought to work closely with the DMK even while opposing their separatist ideology. There has been considerable conflict within the Madras Communist party over their attitude toward the DMK, one section opposing its separatist tendencies while another, though still opposing separatism, wishes to lend sympathy to the DMK's equalitarian, "socialist" outlook.

the District Congress Committee had been superseded, and, moreover, since it was not a particularly well-organized local party, the state Congress leadership turned to Krishna for assistance in making the necessary local arrangements. Under his guidance sixty thousand dollars were raised to build the meeting hall and generally to organize the entire program. White-collar workers from T. V. Sundaram offices were given responsibility for greeting visitors at the airport, maintaining a reception center at the railway station, providing food for the delegates, maintaining snack canteens, and so on.

This service performed by T. V. Sundaram is not unusual, for it is quite common for prominent businessmen to provide such services to the party. When Nehru attended the AICC session, the party leadership asked Krishna to find accommodations for the prime minister at T. V. Sundaram's guest house. Gestures of support of this sort have been a great asset politically to Krishna. This is not to imply that there is in any formal sense a *quid pro quo.* The good will established makes it possible for T. V. Sundaram to maintain close relationships with the chief minister and other leading ministers in the Madras cabinet.

> I try not to get obligated to Congress ministers. It is more important that they become obligated to me. I am hospitable to them and try to give them assistance whenever I can, but I rarely go to a minister for any assistance. If you go to a minister when a man in the secretariat can do something for you, then the secretary will make it difficult for you later.

Krishna, like many other Indian businessmen, is more concerned with what the government does than with its ideology. Since the bus transport business of T. V. Sundaram is widely recognized as one of the country's best-run transportation services, there is no serious talk of nationalization, though bus companies in many other states have been taken over. Moreover, bus transport constitutes only about 20 per cent of the total business of TVS, the remainder being in building truck bodies, retreading tires, selling cars and spare parts, and repairing cars and trucks. About three-quarters of their four-million-dollar income each year comes from these other services. Although TVS is an expanding concern, it devotes particular attention to selecting, training, and then lending money to young men to establish their own business concerns.[19] "It's more important to enlarge

[19] It is of some interest that T. V. Sundaram is a Brahmin-owned concern and that its manager is particularly interested in providing training opportunities and loans to young Brahmin entrepreneurs. Inasmuch as Brahmins are by tradition nonentrepre-

the size of the capitalist class," Krishna explained, "than to enlarge the wealth of an individual capitalist and his family." TVS therefore uses much of its influence to obtain permits and licenses for other businessmen as well as for itself.

As an organization which extends throughout Madras state, TVS finds it possible to establish its influence directly at the state level without any intervening local organization. Similarly, the large textile mills in Madurai have little association with the local Congress party, for their contacts too are directly with the state government and administration. Though they may occasionally make contributions to the local party and to local candidates, their contributions to the party are generally to the state organization. The state organization, needless to say, prefers it that way, for it strengthens the state against the districts and thereby further strengthens the capacity of the parent body to watch over and supervise what is taking place in the District Congress Committees.

The businessmen involved in the District Congress Committee — and, as we shall see, there are many — are not the industrial magnates of the south. They are more often in local trade and commerce than in industry, and those who are in industry are generally those involved in the household handloom textile industry.

## The Bazaar Merchants

One needs the literary skill of a Durrell to describe the Madurai bazaars. To the visitor to the central city around Meenakshi temple, Madurai is primarily a bazaar city. A few shops with modern glass display fronts and counters could easily be transposed to a Western city, but most of the shops have the wide open wooden fronts that characterize the traditional bazaar shop. Shopkeepers stand in front to beckon the tourist to enter with "Come, come in, what is it you want?" Colorful cotton and silk saris are hung from the top of the entrance, fluttering in the evening breezes which sweep the city. Each shop, even the smallest, has several attendants, almost always family members. One wonders how so many can earn a living from such small shops. Most shops have a single chair for the buyer;

neurial, this development marks a considerable change from traditional practices. The recent willingness of Brahmins to become entrepreneurs has in some measure been facilitated by the fact that the government gives so much preference to non-Brahmins in admissions to administrative positions in government, in the recent past the "traditional" occupation of Brahmins. As a result the community has had to seek employment in other occupations.

still others have straw mats for sitting and cushions for reclining. Space is at a premium, and both shelves and floors are crowded with merchandise.

Around the temple, textile shops predominate. The streets are not diversified. One bazaar street may have only barber shops; in another jewelry predominates; in another, wholesale traders in foodstuffs; and in still another a mixture of retail traders in foods. Only the bidi (native cigarettes) and pan (a popular edible leaf eaten with condiments) shops are ubiquitous.

There is an unforgettable liveliness to the bazaar. The shops are crowded in the evening hours, and the narrow streets contain an unbelievable medley of bicycle rickshaws, jetkas, automobiles, stray bullocks and cows, handcarts, and countless pedestrians. Even those who are neither working nor shopping assemble in the bazaar, particularly in front of the pan and bidi shops, the barbers, and the many sweetmeat shops (there are 217 in Madurai), coffee houses, hotels, and restaurants.

There are a number of trade associations in Madurai representing particular groups of merchants.[20] In 1924 the larger merchants and manufacturers in Madurai created an association known as the Madurai-Ramnad Chamber of Commerce for the primary purpose of establishing closer contact between the business community and governmental authorities. During World War II the chamber was particularly active in advising members on how to deal with the new government regulations. After the war the membership of the chamber dropped. But

> after our country gained independence and particularly after the Central Government launched the Five Year Plans, the contact between the authorities and the business community became more and more necessary and the need to make the Central Government assess properly the needs and requirements of the business community became more and more pronounced. As a result . . . the Chamber has been growing stronger and stronger in membership and in every other respect also including its financial position. The present strength of the members is 635.[21]

[20] These include associations of chemists and druggists, dye and chemical merchants, handloom cloth merchants, yarn merchants, handloom cloth manufacturers, oil producers, foodgrains merchant, and petrol dealers.
[21] *Souvenir Volume of the Fourth Zonal Conference of Chambers of Commerce in South India*, organized by the Madurai-Ramnad Chamber of Commerce, Madurai, November 1960, p. 37.

The increasing flow of governmental regulations has thus increased the interest of businessmen and merchants, especially the larger ones, in the affairs of government. But the interest is not confined to the larger entrepreneurs, for even the smaller bazaar merchants have in recent years taken an interest in politics and government. This can be seen most clearly in the composition of the Madurai Municipality. Of the thirty-six municipal councillors, eleven describe themselves as merchants. One, a Communist, is the owner of a teashop. Many are cloth merchants. They constitute the largest single occupational group in the municipality.

The merchants — large and small — also play an active role in the local Congress party; indeed, one might go so far as to say that they are now the single most important group, replacing the lawyers and professional men who played such a dominant role in the party in the pre-independence era. Many of these men, particularly those who belong to the Sourashtra community, were politically active even before independence. But still others are relatively new; among these one must include the Nadar community, which has a near monopoly on the retail trades in Madurai.[22] The Mudaliars and Chettiers, the latter particularly active in banking and money lending, are also among the more important recent additions to the party.

It has not been difficult for the mercantile communities to replace the Brahmins in the political life of Madurai, particularly in comparison with the bitter struggles which took place elsewhere. As is generally known, the Brahmins hold a powerful position in the economic, religious, and political life of South India. Their literary and intellectual tradition made it possible for the Brahmins, more so than for other communities, to adapt themselves to the requirements of British colonial rule. They entered the British schools and universities and soon found employment in the civil service, law, and other professions. However, though the Brahmin temple of Meenakshi had considerable lands in the district compared to other districts such as Tanjore, the Brahmins were neither so numerous nor so powerful on the land.[23] Moreover, though Madurai town is a well-known

[22] The chief minister of Madras state until 1964, K. Kamaraj is a Nadar and has played an important role in attracting his community to the Congress party. He himself is a pre-independence Congressman.

[23] The relationship between particular communities and the land is tied up with the political and revenue history of the district, a complicated matter which need not concern us here. As we have noted earlier, under the Nayak kings, Madura country was apportioned among seventy-two chieftains (poligars), who paid a fixed tribute to the Nayaks, were in charge of local fortifications, and were responsible for the control of their estates. Some were Telugu leaders; others were local men of diverse communities. Many of these were Kallan. In later times (eighteenth century) Muslim rulers had control of much of the land. Even after the British took control of Madurai at

center of Brahminism, Brahmin influence upon the religious and social life of the area is small. Dravidian (that is, non-Brahminical) deities have a strong following in the district. Most castes do not regard it necessary that their marriages should be performed or their funerals attended by any kind of professional priest; in instances where a priest is required, he himself often belongs to the caste. "Thus the Brahmins have not the opportunities of impressing their beliefs and rites upon the people which are in some districts afforded by the indispensability of their presence at domestic ceremonies." [24]

The non-Brahmins launched a formidable political attack against the Brahmins after the nationalist movement was launched. In 1918 a non-Brahmin conference was held in Madurai for propagating the views of the Justice party, a group formed to oppose the Congress and Home Rule parties. The Justice party won control of the Madurai Municipal Council and held control until the elections of September, 1935, when twenty-one of the thirty-six seats were captured by the Congress.[25] But by this time non-Brahmins had begun to enter the Congress movement on a large scale and the character of the Congress had begun to change.

The close collaboration of a number of non-Brahmin communities and the British began to disappear with the formation of the first Congress government in Madras state in 1937. The desire to collaborate with government, which had been a motive leading to closer relations between some communities and the British before 1937, worked to improve relations between these same communities and the Congress party after 1937. Moreover, the establishment of commercial taxes by the Congress minister in 1939 brought smaller shopkeepers and merchants into closer contact with local administration. A General Sales Tax Act came into force in October 1939. The legislation was subsequently amended to include smaller shops and more commodities. A Commercial Tax Department was organized to administer the new taxes. The general principle that political organization is stimulated by the encroachment of governmental regulations on a community is applicable here: as these regulations increased after the war, the interests of the commercial community in local and state politics and administration increased still further.

Moreover, commercial activities have grown rapidly in Madurai since independence. According to a report of the superintendent of police, the number of big businessmen in Madurai increased from three hundred in

the turn of the nineteenth century, Muslims and poligars retained a powerful position on the land.

[24] W. Francis, *Madura Gazetteer*, 1914, p. 184.
[25] Baliga, *Madurai Gazetteer*, 1960, p. 82.

1945 to six hundred in 1955 and to eight hundred in 1960. The rise was even more phenomenal for the number of petty merchants, which increased from eight hundred in 1945 to eighteen hundred in 1955 and to three thousand in 1960. The report notes that about 16,300 workers were employed in the field of trade and commerce in 1960. The 1961 census puts the number even higher: 27,424 engaged in trade and commerce, second only to the number engaged in manufacturing industries. In view of the fact that the growth in population for the city during this period was hardly above the growth in the state as a whole (17.5 per cent from

TABLE 39
VOTING IN SHOPKEEPER WARDS
IN THE 1959 MADURAI MUNICIPAL ELECTIONS

| Ward | Congress | Independent | CPI | DMK |
|---|---|---|---|---|
| 9 . . . . . . . . | 1,143 | . . . . | . . . . . | 2,689 |
| 10 . . . . . . . . | 2,071 | . . . . | 3,386 | . . . . |
| 21 . . . . . . . . | 1,209 | 1,318 | . . . . | . . . . |
| 22 . . . . . . . . | 2,425 | . . . . | . . . . | 1,902 |
| 23 . . . . . . . . | 1,091 | 1,026 | . . . . | . . . . |
| 28 . . . . . . . . | 1,523 | 1,105 | . . . . | . . . . |
| 29 . . . . . . . . | 1,497 | . . . . | 1,826 | . . . . |
| 30 . . . . . . . . | 936 | 925 | . . . . | . . . . |

NOTE: Includes only wards in which trade and commerce is the largest single occupation, based upon 1961 census returns.

1951 to 1961 in Madurai as against 11.7 per cent for Madras state), and that the number of workers engaged in the textile mills has actually declined during this period, the growth in trade and commerce looms large as a fact of both economic and political importance.

It is the latter which is of greatest concern to us here. In the 1959 municipal elections Congress won four of the eight seats in the wards in which trade and commerce constituted the largest single occupation (See Table 39). One ward was won by a DMK candidate (and in another the DMK was a close second to Congress), indicating that the hold of the anti-Brahmin political movements on the non-Brahmin shopkeepers was still considerable and constituted a continuous threat to the Congress party. The Communists won two seats, but one of them was in a ward where shopkeepers were a bare plurality and where both white-collar workers and factory laborers together constituted a majority. Though Congress lost half the seats in this area, it is notable that Congress did better in these wards than in any others in the city. Moreover, in the previous municipal elections of 1956, Congress won seven of the eight seats in these wards; in both general elections of 1957 and 1962, these wards provided Congress candidates with some of their largest vote.

The bazaar merchants bring with them a different style of politics, one

which the older nationalist leadership, particularly those from the higher castes and from professional occupations, often find distasteful. First, the bazaar merchant is unmoved by ideological considerations; politics, like business, is viewed as a matter of calculations. Second, the bazaar merchant is strongly oriented toward his caste [26] and his occupational association rather than toward a political party. The Nadars belong to the Nadar Mahajana Sangh, an association which runs a Nadar bank and several schools. Nadar businessmen put aside a portion of their income for the work of the association, which also runs a weekly newspaper. The Tamil-nad Foodgrains Merchants Association with 113 members and the Madurai Rice and Oil Mill Owners Association with sixty-six members are largely Nadar organizations; while the Madurai-Ramnad Chamber of Commerce includes all communities, Nadars play an active leadership role. The secretary of the chamber, Gangaram Dorairaj, a leading wholesale food merchant and a Congress member of the municipality (and also its deputy leader), is a Nadar. Occupational and caste affiliations thus overlap.

These occupational and caste associations are of such importance politically that the Nadar bazaar merchants are hardly concerned with building an effective local Congress organization. They seek to control and use the party when necessary but not to build it. "We are very powerful," said the secretary of the Madurai-Ramnad Chamber of Commerce, describing the way in which he and other officials of the chamber could go directly to the government ministers without working through the local Congress party organization. But there are many ways in which the bazaar merchants use the party. It can be a stepping stone into the municipality; job patronage, access to departments which provide local civic amenities, and access to tax departments, as well as the intangible element of local prestige — all are attractions. Shop licenses and permits to build houses are under the jurisdiction of the municipal administration. In power, the merchant can also protect himself and his friends against the enforcement of many municipal and state regulations. Unlike the older Brahmin leaders, who felt a strong loyalty to the nationalist cause, and the Sourashtras, who had emotional ties to Gandhi, the Nadars have a more utilitarian orientation toward the party. Thus, although the Nadar merchants have displaced the Brahmins and Sourashtras at many levels of leadership within the party and within the municipality, they lack the party *esprit* which these other communities had.

[26] Caste loyalties have generally been strengthened by the state government's policy of reserving seats in the colleges and state administration on the basis of caste. The Nadars, for example, have been classified as a "backward community" by the state government, and this classification entitles them to these special facilities.

## 20. PARTY CONFLICTS AND HOW
## THEY ARE RESOLVED

In contrast with Calcutta and many other Indian cities, Madurai has a relatively small proportion of migrants. Only 34 per cent of the city's population was born outside the city, and a third of these came from the countryside in the surrounding district. Moreover, only one-fifth of the city's population (21 per cent) was born in rural India, and few of these are recent migrants to Madurai. During the past decade migration into the city has been unusually small, and the growth of the city is actually slightly less than the population growth for India as a whole.

The socio-economic changes which have occurred in Madurai therefore involve changes in the status of existing groups. In short, the Congress party of Madurai does not have the challenge or the opportunity available to Congress in Calcutta of building its electoral strength upon migrants to the city. It must, instead, establish a working relationship with existing groups in increasing conflict with one another.

The contrasts with Calcutta are still more striking. In Calcutta one leader has, through his control over both the city and state party organization, provided an extraordinary degree of party cohesion; moreover, the party has used its control over the municipality to strengthen itself. Neither of these developments has occurred in Madurai. The Congress organization in Madurai — for reasons we shall soon explain — has not established effective control over the municipal government, nor has a single leader established effective control over the party organization. The party has thus been faced with a greater amount of internal conflict and fewer resources for the handling of such conflict. In the absence of a cohesive city

party machine, the state party organization has played an important role in the arbitration of local politics. In this chapter we shall attempt to explain why the district organization itself has not thus far produced effective leadership capable of providing cohesion, and why and how the state organization has performed this function.

### Congress and the Madurai Municipality

Until 1959 Congress controlled the municipal council, but in that year's elections Congress returned only nine councillors of thirty-six, compared with twenty-two in the previous election of 1955.[1] Congress lost to the Communists and to the Indian National Democratic Congress, a group of dissident Congressmen most of whom subsequently joined the Swatantra party. In the three-way battle which took place as a result of the split in Congress, the Communists picked up many seats with a bare plurality while the non-Communist vote split.

The municipal council of Madurai dates back to the Towns Improvement Act of 1865. Initially, the majority of the members were appointed by the then British government, but by 1885 the system was modified so that the majority were elected by rate payers. Factional conflicts, an ingredient of contemporary municipal politics, became so intense that in 1891 the government had to reverse its earlier decision to permit the council to elect its own chairman. A few years later the power was restored to the council.[2]

The municipality has responsibility for the construction and maintenance of roads within the town, electric power and street light, and elementary and high schools, hospitals and dispensaries, maternity and child welfare centers, public latrines, the regulation of markets, sanitation (scavenging services), and water supply.

Mr. Dorasamy,[3] a Sourashtra, was elected leader of the Congress op-

---

[1] The results of the two elections to the Madurai Municipal Council were as follows:

| 1955 | | | 1959 | |
|------|---|---|------|---|
| Congress | | 22 | Congress | 9 |
| Communists | | 4 | Communists | 12 |
| Independents | | 10 | Indian National Democratic Congress | 10 |
| | total | 36 | Dravida Munnetra Kazhagam | 2 |
| | | | Independents | 3 |
| | | | total | 36 |

[2] See *Madras District Gazetteer*, 1914, pp. 221–22, for an early history of the council.

[3] He is the owner of a local rice mill, a banker, and, like many businessmen, a small landowner with fifteen acres of land in a village near Madurai. Incidentally, he is the brother-in-law of Madurai's lady MLA.

position shortly after the 1959 defeat. Many councillors who had previously been in Congress left the party to join the Indian National Democratic Congress or to stand as independents. The chairman of the municipality, Mr. Devasahayam, was a Congressman until the 1959 elections, when, failing to get a ticket, he stood as a candidate of a local opposition Forward Bloc party. After the elections some independents returned to the Congress party, but Congress still lacked the numbers necessary to overthrow the existing chairman.

Party discipline within the council has been limited. While the Congress party at the state and national level maintains considerable discipline, it has not been able to do so at the municipal level. Individual councillors have crossed the floor while in office, and Congressmen who failed to receive nominations or renominations have often left the party and won either as independents or on the ticket of another party. Most of the seats lost by Congress in the 1959 elections went to men who until recently had been Congressmen; in several of the wards where the Communists won in 1959, it was because independents split the non-Communist vote.

The inability of the party to maintain cohesion at the municipal level is related to the structure of the corporation and the nature of local power. For some years there has been an informal arrangement within the council to allocate a specific sum of money for each ward in the town. Each councillor in effect has the responsibility for deciding how that money is to be spent in his own ward, whether for street lamps, latrines, or some other local services. Moreover, the council has the power to decide where in the ward the new facility shall be located. The councillor, therefore, has a kind of feudal political estate with responsibility for governmental expenditures within that estate. Moreover, the councillor has extraordinary powers or, more accurately, influence in the enforcement of municipal taxation. The municipal council has a statutory tax appeal committee which can make decisions without reference to the general body, the municipal council, or the municipal commissioners. It is common for municipal councillors to negotiate taxes — particularly house assessments — with the tax appeal committee as a representative of the taxpayer. The councillor also helps local businessmen and house owners to get licenses for constructing buildings and for getting electric connections to their houses. And, as we have noted, he services local people in such important household matters as graveling roads, lighting, and sanitation.

The councillors have direct access to officials in the municipal corporation. If the public latrine is dirty, the councillor calls a municipal engineer.

If a light is broken or one is needed, he calls the electrical engineer. If rubbish is to be collected, he calls the sanitary inspector. The councillors are invariably local businessmen who in the course of conducting their business have had to deal with the corporation officials; they find it easy to step into the role of councillors.[4] Moreover, the officials of the corporation readily respond to requests from the councillors, and are pressed to grant housing permits or to overlook violations of various housing regulations as well as to provide services. Members of the council may ask questions about the conduct of the corporation commissioner at the council's open monthly meeting. Moreover, the councillors can take steps to get the commissioner or any of the senior administrative personnel in the corporation transferred. The officials are responsible to the minister for local government, and it is not uncommon for the minister to be asked by the chairman or even members of the municipal corporation to intervene with the commissioner. In the circumstances, commissioners and other officials in the corporation are responsive to pressures, legal or otherwise, from the councillors.

Corruption is not unknown. One Congress councillor explained: "Yes, but everywhere there is some corruption. There is some in the engineering department. They handle public works. There is some corruption among the tax officials." What about the elected councillors? "I hate to say so; there is some, but it is so in all parties. I think there is less among the Congress members of the council than in other parties."

Members of other parties, as one might expect, do not agree. The chairman of the corporation, a former Congressman, explained: "When Congress controlled the corporation, they only favored those who supported them." How? "Oh, they got permits for businessmen, or lorry routes for the truck companies. When Congress controlled the corporation, it was natural that they would help their own people." Now that you are in power, do you help your own people?

[4] Of the nine Congressmen elected to the municipality in 1959, three are cloth merchants; one, the party leader, is a rice mill owner and banker; another is a "landlord and merchant"; two more are merchants in food grains (one is also the secretary of the local chamber of commerce in Madurai); one is an engineering contractor; and the last councillor is a retired municipal bill collector. The independents and councillors representing the Indian National Democratic Congress (the party of Congress defectors) are also generally merchants. On the other hand, the Communist councillors include a larger number of full-time professional party workers. Two are trade union workers; one is listed simply as "Communist worker"; and a fourth as "Communist worker and president of a cooperative society." Two Communists are owners of a printing press; another is the president of a local weavers cooperative; another is an advocate; and, finally, one is a tea shop owner. There seem to be no merchants, landlords, or bankers.

No, the opposition helps the general interest, not the particular interest. We have come to serve the people, and we
will not make the same mistakes that Congress has made.
. . . I left the Congress Party because sincere workers had
no place in Congress. They didn't get their due place. No,
it's impossible to improve the organization. Congress has lost
their mass touch. That's why they lost the municipal elections. They're only in touch with other leaders, so naturally
the people have lost faith in Congress. I was a worker in
Congress, and people liked me, but the organization didn't
want me. So I left and joined the Forward Bloc.

The municipal chairman, like many other Congressmen who left the
party, has so much influence within the corporation on behalf of voters
that he is not subject to the influences of the party organization. Moreover, most councillors believe that they could win and maintain their influence within the corporation as independents; at the state or national
level, it is far more difficult for an independent to maintain such influence.
Furthermore, the area of the ward is small, and it is easier for a local politician to extend his personal influence throughout the ward simply with
the support of a few friends than it is for an individual to extend his influence throughout an entire assembly or parliamentary constituency without the aid of some party machinery.

It is no wonder, therefore, that even Congress members of the municipality are not closely associated with the work of the party. Mr. Dorasamy,
the Congress leader in the municipality, is one of the few councillors who
is closely associated with the work of the party. He is the president of a
mandal committee, and therefore a member (automatically) of the District Congress Committee. But other councillors are far less involved or
interested in party work. The deputy leader of the Congress group in the
municipal corporation is secretary of the Ramnad-Madurai Chamber of
Commerce. This local businessman, a dealer in wholesale foodgrains, explained that the chamber has nine hundred members.

When our members have any difficulty, we can go directly
to the government and to the ministers. I am not so interested in Congress affairs. The chamber is neutral but must
support Congress. We are non-political, so we can criticize
the government and ministers if we have to. No, I don't
run the mandal committee in this ward. It's run by some man

named G——, but he only does some propaganda work. He doesn't do any municipal work. I am automatically a member of the mandal committee, but what do they do? There is no real Congress organization in Madurai. Workers aren't paid. The office isn't properly run. What has to be done we do ourselves. No, the DCC doesn't do anything either.

Many of the Congress councillors share this disdain for the mandal committee and for the local Congress organization. As far as local government is concerned, the councillors not only have in effect independent powers but they have access to patronage which the local party organization does not. A permanent statutory committee of the council takes responsibility for hiring personnel for the corporation. The committee includes the chairman, one elected councillor, and the municipal commissioner. Since local government personnel do not fall under any regular civil service examinations, the two elected officials can in effect control appointments. A second statutory committee is in charge of contracts, and this too includes the chairman, the commissioner, and one elected councillor. This body also has considerable power.

The point is that none of these powers proves to be an asset to the local party organization, since the men who exercise these powers can entrench their local influence so well that they can be free of party control.[5] Moreover, since most of what the councillors want can be satisfied through the municipality, there is little or no need for the councillor to depend upon the state government and therefore the state Congress party organization. This is of course not true for the municipal council as a whole. The council's budget is limited, and it must turn to the state government for the construction of new water schemes, bridges, or power facilities. Nonetheless, the councillors work effectively — from a political viewpoint, that is — in an economy of scarcity, for they control and distribute by themselves what little there is. They have developed a system which gives each man enough power so that he need not depend upon the state government, the municipal council as a whole, or the party organization for the exercise of his power. The power and patronage of the

[5] Many explanations have been given by local politicians for the Congress defeat in the 1959 municipal elections. The most common one is that there had been a sudden rise in food prices combined with an increase in state taxes, which turned many local voters against the government. Another is that the party failed to nominate "influential" local people, the implication of the latter argument being that voters are not affected by party labels, since any influential local man can service the community irrespective of his party affiliation.

municipality therefore in no way strengthen the local party organization but in some fundamental ways lessen it.

### The District Congress Committee of Madurai

It is difficult to find anyone in Madurai town who will voice a good word for Mr. Perumal, the president of the Madurai town District Congress Committee until early in 1962. It was said that he failed to keep accurate accounts for the party, that he freely pocketed party money, that he is uneducated and therefore does not command the respect of the important people in Madurai. Perumal does not speak English. The son of a dhobi (washerman), he joined the national movement in the late 1920's when he was still a very young boy (he was born in 1915). At that time he marched in Congress processions waving the Congress flag. In 1936 he became a full-time party worker and served as a spinning instructor for the party. After being trained at the Congress school in Wardha, he worked in a school teaching spinning. Though he comes originally from a village in Madurai district, he settled in the town. He was arrested in 1942 for recruiting people to join the civil disobedience movement of that year. When he was released at the end of 1943, he became a member of the Tamilnad Congress Committee and from then on, to use the words of a local supporter, "He became a big politician and a leading Congressman in Madurai town." He later became secretary of the District Congress Committee in Madurai, and in 1960 became the president. Some of his income comes from the five acres of land he continues to hold in a village in the district; he earns some money as manager of a private higher elementary school in Madurai town, and some money he receives from "friends."

Until Perumal was elected DCC president, the office was held by more prosperous, more prominent figures in the town. Until 1956 the Madurai town Congress organization was part of a larger District Congress Committee which included the entire district. In that year the town committee was converted into a separate district committee. Until then the leadership of the DCC rested with men from outside the town. Rajaram Naidu, onetime president of the Congress party in Madras and a villager, was president of the DCC from 1939 to 1946. From 1946 to 1950 another village-based leader was president of the DCC. The president from 1950 to 1952 came from a small municipal town about forty miles from Madurai. From 1952 to 1956 the previous president was reelected, and in 1956 the DCC was divided into separate urban and rural committees. T. K. Rama,

a Sourashtra leader and a yarn and dye merchant, was elected as the first president of the new town DCC. He was followed by P. N. K. Subaraman, also a Sourashtra merchant and landowner; and he, by Chidambaram Mudalier, a local landowner who resides in Madurai town and who had been elected chairman of the municipal corporation. Finally, in 1960 Perumal was elevated to the office.

Perumal's support came from the mandal committees and the local Congress workers. Madurai is divided into twenty mandal committees, which are grouped into five circle committees. All the mandal committee presidents are members of the District Congress Committee. The mandal committees are arbitrary units, though some effort is made to make them coincide with the wards of the town. Generally one or two wards fall under the jurisdiction of a mandal committee. There were reported to be from five hundred to a thousand active workers in the Congress party in Madurai town as of 1961.[6]

The most respectable men in the town — the larger businessmen, big merchants, lawyers, and doctors — are not active on the mandal committees nor are they office bearers, although they do support the party. Mandal committee presidents are ordinarily small shopkeepers, or clerks, or owners of small dyeing, weaving, or handloom establishments. It is easy to become a member of a mandal committee. There are no direct elections; individuals announce that they are candidates, and in most instances the returning officer need only announce that they are elected.

Mandal committees recruit primary members for the party. On the national holidays — Independence Day, Republic Day, and Gandhi's Birthday — the mandal committees may hold celebrations in their localities. Some of the active mandal workers also care for some local grievances. These are much the same kind of grievances which go to the members of the legislative assembly or, as we have seen, more often to the coun-

[6] Precise details on membership of the Congress party in Madurai were not available. When the District Congress Committee was suspended, most of the membership figures and all of the registers containing names of the party members were transferred to the Pradesh Congress Committee office in Madras. None of this material was made available to the author. According to the records remaining in the Madurai office, there are twenty mandal committees ranging from memberships of eight to twenty-seven, in all a total of about three hundred forty active members. The District Congress Committee has forty-six members. No figures were available on the number of primary members, but local claims ranged from eight thousand to twenty thousand. Party people also claim that the Youth Congress in Madurai has about three hundred members and the Mahila Congress another three hundred, but again no membership lists or statistical records were available in the district office. Local party workers report that generally there are about fifteen active party workers in each mandal on the average and that sometimes as many as fifty Congress members who can be called upon for some kind of assistance.

cillors in the municipal corporation. If the drains are not properly cleaned, the Congress worker may call the sanitation engineer in the municipal corporation. If there is an infectious disease, a local worker may call an ambulance. Since hospitals in Madurai are overcrowded, a local Congress worker may bring a request to the MLA or some other important Congress official, who in turn will confer with a member of the advisory committee to the hospital which passes on admissions. Admissions into schools and colleges may also be handled by local party workers. The local Congressman may write the note which will be presented by a member of a backward class to the local MLA for the certificate necessary to prove that he is eligible for special government assistance. Nor is it unusual for a local Congress worker to approach a more influential Congressman, who in turn approaches the principal of a local college to make an exception so as to admit a member of a backward or scheduled caste who failed to achieve the minimum marks in his school examinations.

Since independence the most prominent persons in Madurai town have become less interested in both the work of the local Congress organization and the municipal council. Responsibilities for the routine work of the local party organization have been increasingly taken on by less educated local citizens. It is to these men that Perumal made his appeal. As a full-time party worker, then as secretary of the District Congress Committee, he worked closely with the local mandal workers. Perumal proved to be an effective organizer of processions and public meetings on national holidays. He collected food for the poor, put together a small fund to be used for the aid of those who had lost their homes through fires, and was skillful at arranging for the construction of pandals, the hoisting of flags, and other such work associated with national holidays. He worked closely with local workers and earned their respect, for the party workers often felt that the prominent men in the city were disinterested in the kind of local work in which they were engaged. One local mandal Congress worker — a thirty-six-year-old carpenter who is the president of a mandal committee — explained why he supported Perumal as president of the District Congress Committee:

> All of us who do mandal work — we elected Perumal. The opposition came from those who wanted a more educated leader. But the difficulty is that a more educated man won't do this kind of work, but will want to go to the PCC or the AICC. A less educated man like Perumal will do good work.

He is a good organizer. We like him and wanted him as our leader.

One trade union leader supported this view:

> The major difficulty in the Madurai Congress organization is that none of the local officer bearers gets paid, so they all take some money from the party accounts. If a man of wealth takes office, he doesn't do any work; and if a poor man takes office, he works, but he also takes funds and doesn't keep proper accounts. Then the morals suffer, but it's a question of the morals suffering or the work suffering. . . . I had no serious objection to the complaint about Perumal taking party funds. We have told the TNCC [Tamilnad Pradesh Congress Committee in Madras] that their people must be paid, even in the mandal committees. There is enough money for this. In our textile union, we maintain six full-time people, so why shouldn't the mandal committees be able to support one person?[7]

But the willingness to tolerate irregularities in financial accounts is not shared by many party members in Madurai, and no sooner had Perumal taken office than efforts were made to dislodge him. The accusation over the accounts, however, was the focal point, not the cause, of the attack. Most of the Sourashtras were staunch opponents of Perumal. In his effort to win support from the mandal presidents for his election as president of the DCC, it was reported that Perumal argued that a non-Sourashtra man ought to lead the party. Many of the non-Sourashtra party workers resented what appeared to them to be Sourashtra domination of the party in the town, and therefore were attracted to Perumal's appeal. Much opposition to Perumal came from other aspirants for the office, irrespective of community. In the past, competition for control of the DCC has been intense, and much of the opposition to Perumal in 1961 came from those who had hoped to be in his position.

The importance of the office of DCC president throws considerable light on the relationship between status and power in the town. "For everything and anything you must go to the government, and it's best to go to the government through a man with influence," one local politician ex-

[7] I was told that the annual budget of the DCC is about twenty thousand rupees. However, the official income and expenditure account issued by the DCC in 1960 reports only twelve thousand rupees for the year.

plained with great clarity. The MLAs have a great deal of influence, but they are not always available in the constituency. Moreover, they are often so busy in the legislative assembly that they do not always have the time to tend to all the demands made within the constituencies. Then too, the MLAs themselves may be influenced by the president of the District Congress Committee. The DCC president is nearly always available in the town. Moreover, in those matters that require the attention of the collector and other local district officials, he can be extraordinarily influential. The same Congressman explained in some detail:

> If you want some electrical connection in your house, or some government contract, or the construction of a school, hospital, road, or an industrial license or permit, these things are ultimately handled by the state administration. But there must be a recommendation from the district officials. If I want a school in my locality and go to a minister, the minister will then go back to the district educational officer for a recommendation. And that's where the local Congressman has his influence. A decision may be made by the state government to build a post office, but the politician here may persuade the local administration to put it in one ward instead of another. Their recommendation to the state administration is more or less final.

Is there any pressure on the administration from the politician?

> Generally, no direct pressure. Sometimes a man is transferred from one area to another for political reasons — not often. Most of the local administrators want to get on with the ministers, so they have to get along too with the local politicians. It is in their interest to get on well with the local people.[8]

[8] While the research for this study was taking place, the municipal commissioner of Madurai, who had only recently been appointed, was suddenly transferred. Local people insisted that it had been done because a complaint had been lodged against him by a prominent local Congressman, a member of the TNCC. Important administrators in the area deny that transfers are made on political grounds — though they can invariably recall one or two exceptions. But all agree that it is best to get on well with local politicians if they are to do their job well. It should be noted that senior administrative posts are not patronage appointments, as in the United States. No man need fear that he will be dismissed on political grounds. But where he is posted and the speed of his promotions can be affected by the judgment of ministers. Administrators are thus subtly convinced that it is best for their careers to "get on with" local

The president of the DCC has direct access both to government ministers in Madras and to local administrators in Madurai, and it is this combination which makes his influence so great and the office so important. The local administrator is aware of the fact that the DCC president (and a few other prominent local Congress leaders) can exercise influence on his superiors, the ministers, in Madras. When the ministers, including the chief minister, visit Madurai or any other town, it is customary for the president of the DCC to organize a welcome committee and to be host. Other local Congressmen may also share the limelight, but the DCC president is never absent.

Congress leaders in Madras have noted that the struggle for control of the DCC in the towns is even more intense than in the rural areas. One explanation given is that in the rural areas it is generally known who the prominent people are — the head of the cooperative bank, a few big landowners, and the president of the District Local Board. But in the town, leadership is more widely dispersed. The DCC president and perhaps the chairman of the municipal corporation, are the two visible officers of power in the town.

Still another factor is that in the rural areas of Madras, including the areas around Madurai town, Congress leadership is in the hands of respectable and powerful local people; in Madurai town, as in many other towns, power has shifted from the respectable lawyers, professionals, and rich generally to the small shopkeepers. An official of the TNCC in Madras reported:

> When we give out books for enrolling primary members in the rural areas, we give them to the presidents of the district boards, panchayat presidents, landlords, and to other respectable men. The people in the rural areas are the big men, but in the towns enrollment of primary members is by the small shopkeepers. The head of the cooperative society or the landlord collects primary members in the rural areas, so he also gets elected to the local Congress committee. But in the towns it's the less educated shopkeepers who collect primary members. Since whoever collects primary members seems to get elected to the DCC, it means that the shopkeepers predominate on the District Congress Committees in the towns.

politicians. Corruption is not unknown, either. In the municipal corporation especially, officials are susceptible to bribes, and municipal councillors not only make bribes but receive them as well.

This is certainly so in Madurai town. The shopkeepers, the artisans, the small businessmen who in recent years have become so active in the local Congress organization and in the municipal corporation have learned quickly about the uses to which their power can be put. Both status and money are important to them.[9] Though local persons often speak of the material gains of office and of being an important party official—particularly in a situation of great scarcity, where the demand for electricity, water supply, permits, licenses, and the like far exceeds what is available from the local and state administration—men also speak frankly of the status and prestige of being president of the DCC.

In a hierarchical social system the struggle for status is of considerable political importance. In many rural areas where the local landlords are simultaneously the men of high caste and of learning and where there are few men in the modern professions, the spread of education, the development of new occupations, and the diminishing importance of caste ranking all blur the hierarchy. And in the towns it is even more difficult for individuals to rank one another. In a hierarchical social system where the traditional criteria for status are becoming blurred, certain political offices grow in importance as clear marks of status. The struggle for control of rural panchayats—in areas where elder men report that in the past it was not necessary to hold elections, since everyone knew who ought to be their leader—is one manifestation of this development.

The struggle for control of the DCC is not simply between the rising shopkeepers and the higher-caste, better-educated citizens, for the competition for power among the shopkeepers and the poorer classes is generally very intense. If Perumal fails in his struggle to establish control of the DCC, there are other men of low status who are ready to challenge the Brahmins, the Mudaliers, and the Sourashtras—the large businessmen, the pleaders, and the bankers who have in the past controlled the local party organization.

In late 1961 an attempt to replace Perumal through a non-confidence motion was made without much success, for in the main the mandal Congress presidents continued to give Perumal their support. Nonetheless, dissension became so great and so bitter, and so many complaints were lodged with the state party organization, that the TNCC decided to suspend the DCC and to appoint a convener. Perumal had been temporarily defeated, and the entire District Congress Committee and even the mandal committees were more or less ignored during the 1962 general elec-

---

[9] One local journalist in Madurai, discussing the question of why the struggle for control over the DCC in Madurai has been so intense, insightfully remarked: "Those who are well off want status; those who are poor want money."

tions. (Ad hoc election committees functioned in their place.) But even if Perumal fails to return as DCC president, the fact is that the character of the local organization has changed considerably; his election was an indication of those changes.

At the leadership level there is likely, nonetheless, to be continued instability. There is in fact inherent leadership instability in all political organizations in a society where modern political organizations are relatively new and where the roles required of leadership have changed so drastically in recent years. Promotions in a political organization are frequently based upon loyalty and seniority, not upon merit — that is, the capacity to perform the roles required by the party. It is not uncommon in politics, therefore, for men to be placed in positions beyond their capabilities. But the frequency of public and party elections makes it easier for most political organizations (and for that matter, for governments) to absorb the shock of incompetence than for an economic organization to do so.

Moreover, whereas in India the local party organization has recently taken on new roles, there is little experience as to what kinds of skills are necessary for the performance of these roles. The example of previously successful men in the role is not relevant, and in general there is no experience to draw from. Judgments are made on the basis of what the office *previously* involved, rather than its current requirements, and so incompetent men are often selected for the new roles.

Since independence the Congress party in Madurai has not been able to find leaders capable of performing the new roles required by the local organization. As a result the turnover in officers has been considerable, and since a separate urban DCC has been established, there has been a new DCC president almost yearly. Political organization in an urban area requires more skill than in a rural area. Political competition is tougher, demands upon government are greater, the local population has more political knowledge and sophistication, and there is a greater complexity in occupations and caste affiliations. Moreover, organization as such — the regularity with which party workers fulfill tasks assigned by the party — is often a more important factor in an urban area, for in a rural area traditional loyalties may be more easily harnessed for political purposes.

Nonetheless, one would expect that an urban area could produce leadership to fit its political needs, but this has proved to be difficult in Madurai because of the continuance of many features of traditional social organization. In the main, leadership in the Congress party has arisen, not through the party, but through prevailing caste and occupational groupings within

the city. Mrs. Lakshmikantham, the MLA, has built her career through activities within her own community; this is true, with a few exceptions, for many other Sourashtra leaders. The very coherence of the community, among the younger as well as the older generation, had made it difficult for its leaders to be civic as distinct from caste leaders. Subbaraman, the MP, is a notable exception, but his efforts have been largely in the rural areas around the town; in no sense could he be called an urban politician, though he may temporarily be the convener of the urban District Congress Committee.

The deputy leader of the Congress party in the municipal corporation is first and foremost a bazaar merchant and spokesman for the smaller businessmen in Madurai, particularly those who belong to his own Nadar community. The Brahmin MLA comes closest to being a civic leader, but his caste has thus far foreclosed his playing a more positive role within the party organization. His father was indeed an acceptable civic leader for the entire party, but he rose to power at a time when Brahmin influence within the Congress was acceptable.

The skills now required by the party are more likely to be found within the party than outside, and it is no wonder, therefore, that the party workers sought to elect a DCC president from within their own ranks rather than from outside. It is difficult to predict what kind of leadership the party is likely to select in the future, but it is perhaps not too far-fetched to suggest that the selection of a local party worker as president in 1960 may not have been a fortuitous accident but may be the beginning of a new development within the party organization.

## The Resolution of Conflict

In the absence of a unified and powerful leadership within the Madurai Congress party, the capacity of the local party to reconcile its internal conflicts has depended almost entirely upon the readiness of the state Congress leadership to enter the thicket of district politics. It is necessary, then, that we briefly discuss the rise of the present leadership within the state organization before we turn to the role of the state leadership in Madurai politics.

At the time of independence Madras was a sprawling state which included present-day Madras, Andhra, and portions of Mysore and Kerala. The Madras Congress was beset by powerful regional and caste conflicts. The Andhra Pradesh Congress Committee pressed for secession of the Telugu area from Madras. Kannada Congressmen similarly pressed for the

creation of a separate Mysore state. Non-Brahmin castes attacked what they felt to be Brahminical domination of the politics and government of the state. And Communist strength in the industrial areas of Madras and some of the rural areas of the Andhra region was a further unstabilizing element.

Rajagopalachari, India's first Indian governor general in the early days of independence, was summoned by the national party leadership to take over as chief minister of Madras state. But the tenure of this politician-statesman was short-lived. Congress barely won the elections in Madras state in 1952. In 1953 agitation in the Telugu region led the central government to partition the state into Andhra and Madras. The Congress legislative party in Madras replaced Rajagopalachari with Kamaraj Nadar, the head of the organizational wing of the Congress party in the Tamil area of the state. The rise of Kamaraj, for many years the president of the Tamilnad Congress Committee, marked the success of the organizational wing of the party and moreover symbolized the shift of the position of the non-Brahmin forces within the government. Kamaraj is a member of the Nadar caste. Unlike the English-speaking university-educated Rajagopalachari, the new chief minister was less educated and spoke only Tamil. Though he had not been a national leader, he had established his career within the nationalist movement in Tamilnad, and, as the president of the Tamilnad Pradesh Congress Committee, had become a powerful boss within the party organization. Throughout the state his selection was greeted as the victory of a man of the people.

Under Kamaraj's leadership Madras soon developed one of the most stable and well-administered governments in India. Some of the credit is due to the fact that the non-Tamil areas were separated from the state, thereby removing a major source of political tension. Moreover, Madras as a former British presidency was always among the better-administered areas of the country. Nonetheless, without the cohesion established by Kamaraj within the party organization, it is doubtful that Madras could have had such a comparatively effective government.

The skillful management of the organization by Kamaraj was a crucial factor in the recovery made by the party throughout the state. He did not succeed in preventing sections of the Congress party from joining the opposition. Indeed, it now appears that part of the strategy was to encourage the least loyal elements to get out of the party, thereby leaving within the party a more disciplined, loyal, active membership. But the success of Kamaraj has been largely in his ability to cope with conflict within each of the district organizations.

Conflicts within the organization at the state level are invariably reflections of dissension within the districts. Dissident district factions ally themselves with well-known dissident state-wide leaders. The dissident group at the state level is therefore often a coalition of diverse district dissidents who share a common desire to gain control of the party and of the government. Thus a district Congress boss or strong dissident element within the district which feels that it is not getting its share of power from the state government may ally itself with a dissident group within the state leadership. The first target of the dissident elements is always to gain control of the Pradesh Congress Committee, for in the final analysis it is this body, through its subcommittee, the Congress Election Committee, which determines who gets tickets to the state legislative assembly. And of course the state legislative party has the final voice as to who becomes chief minister.

Since Kamaraj rose to power by winning control of the state organization, he was careful as chief minister to keep control of the party organization. Kamaraj thus protected himself against the organizational-government conflict which has been such a key factor in the disintegration of governments in so many other states. Moreover, Kamaraj has paid particular attention to the resolution of conflicts within each of the district organizations, thereby ensuring that no effective state-wide dissident faction could threaten his government and his hold on the party.

As with other district organizations, the Madurai Congress party has had much internal conflict over the years. Until 1956 there was a single DCC for all of Madurai district, including both the city and the rural areas. As we have noted, the DCC was throughout this period dominated by the more numerous rural elements, and during this period there was often conflict between the rural leadership and the leadership in the city. After a separate DCC was established for the city, conflict broke out for control of the new DCC. We have noted that shopkeepers, tradesmen, and smaller businessmen generally took a more active interest in the organization, and the position of the Sourashtras and Brahmins, both of whom had played such an important part in the national movement in Madurai, was no longer secure. Soon men of lower education, lower caste, and lower income obtained important positions within the party and clamored for more influence in the selection of candidates for the state assembly and for the municipal corporation. The result, as we have seen, is that in 1960 one of their leaders, a party worker of a washerman caste, was elected president of the DCC with support from a majority of the mandal committees.

From the viewpoint of the state leadership, who controls the organiza-

tion has been of less concern than the need for maintaining a cohesive organization. The state leadership has sought to identify itself with no one group in the various local struggles, but has attempted, successfully as we shall see, to play a conciliating role. In recent years the state leadership has played this role in two important local conflicts: the selection of candidates in the 1962 elections, and the management of the campaign and the controversy over the control of the District Congress Committee. An exploration of these two regions of conflict throws considerable light on the attitude of the local leadership toward dispute settlement and on the way a state party leadership effectively copes with threats to party cohesion.

## The 1962 Elections

Although the DCC has been politically torn, the selection of candidates for the assembly and parliamentary elections of 1962 was remarkably free from rancor. The two incumbent MLAs were willing to run again, and for various reasons no group within the party felt powerful enough to challenge their position. Mrs. Lakshmikantham was, as we have noted earlier, selected by the state party leadership because they were eager to increase the representation of women in the Madras assembly. Opposition to her candidacy, therefore, would have brought a local group against a policy of the state leadership. The position of the other MLA, Mr. Sankaran, was also secure, partly because of his overwhelming victory in 1957 (his nearest opponent received less than half his vote) in an area which the Congress lost in 1952 and which the parliamentary candidate of 1957 failed to carry. Moreover, in the 1962 elections, the prime target of the Congress party was the parliamentary seat held by a Communist, and the state organization wished to maintain its strong and popular assembly candidates so as to strengthen the party's chances of winning the parliamentary seat. And, finally, Sankaran ran in a constituency with a substantial Brahmin population and which contains within it the Brahminical temple of Meenakshi. He could win Brahmin support (Brahmins in recent years have been turning toward the Swatantra party) without alienating non-Brahmins, since Sankaran was the son of an eminent nationalist leader who had been in the forefront of the movement to permit Harijans to enter the Meenakshi temple.

There was some controversy over the parliamentary seat. Had it not been for the early intervention of the Congress Election Committee of the Pradesh Congress Committee, conflict might have grown, the defeated

group might not have supported the Congress candidate, and the chances that Congress could regain the parliamentary seat would have been considerably lessened.

The procedure for the selection of candidates is more or less determined by the national party organization. Candidates submit their names to the Pradesh Congress Committee. In Madras a twelve-man Congress Election Committee appointed by the president of the Congress party in Madras (in this case with the assistance of the chief minister) makes the initial decisions. The committee itself is divided into four groups, each one in charge of four districts. A three-man committee visited Madurai and three other southern districts to meet with local party workers before making their recommendations to the larger committee. The committee considers the likelihood of success for each possible candidate. Attention is paid also to the potential candidate's financial ability to conduct an election. It is estimated that the assembly candidate must be prepared to spend about five thousand rupees (one thousand dollars) of the minimum ten thousand rupees needed in the campaign; since many elections far exceed their minimum sum, the candidate must be a man of some means or, by virtue of his local influence, have access to local sources. Apparently the Committee is also interested in hearing statements by local party workers about the usefulness that a particular candidate might have for them if he is selected to the assembly. Is he capable of dealing with government administrators? Does he have good relations with the party members who are in touch with the voters, and will he give them assistance if he is elected?

The three-man committee for the southern region was a high-powered one. One member was the home minister in the Madras government, and the second was the treasurer of the PCC and at one time its president. Moreover, the committee worked closely with the chief minister, who maintained a close interest in as many of the constituencies as possible. The committee realized that the candidates who had offered themselves for the parliamentary ticket in Madurai were not strong; not only did they lack the popular appeal of the incumbent Communist MP, but the selection of any one of them would further divide the local party. For this reason the committee quickly turned to Mr. Subbaraman who, as a Gandhian constructive worker since independence, had won much local popularity and had not participated in the struggles for power within the local party organization. Subbaraman had the advantages of being an outsider in the psychological sense without actually being an outsider in the geographical sense. Subbaraman's very reluctance to apply for the seat, his

reported reluctance to return to active politics, proved in fact to be one of his stronger political assets (a phenomenon not unknown elsewhere).

Even after Subbaraman was given the parliamentary ticket and the campaign began, the state party organization established very close links with each of the constituencies. One member of the three-man candidate selection committee was placed in charge of the assembly and parliamentary elections for the four southern districts. A central office was opened in Madurai to supervise fifty-four assembly seats and eleven parliamentary seats. The office took responsibility for the printing and distribution of posters and other election materials. The office also looked after the financial needs of the party's candidates, handled the distribution of jeeps, cars, and other vehicles, and sent speakers to each of the constituencies.[10] But an even more important responsibility of the officer-in-charge was to heal rifts within the party in each of the constituencies. Each morning he sat in the central office to receive calls from the constituencies on the developments of the previous days and on special local problems. When it was reported that local Congressmen were not supporting the official candidate, it was the responsibility of the campaign officer to visit the constituency and resolve the conflict.

The officer therefore had to be a man of stature, whose arbitrational role would be acceptable to all. Mr. Naidu, the treasurer of the Congress party in Madras state who performed this role commanded respect from all sections of the party. He had been in the party for some thirty years, was president of the DCC in Madurai district before the urban and rural areas were separated, and was then president of the Tamilnad Congress Committee before becoming treasurer. Because he was a close associate of Kamaraj, recommendations made by him were likely to win the support of the state party executive.

## The Supersession of the Madurai DCC

In mid-1961, controversy within the Madurai DCC grew so intense that a motion of no confidence in the president was passed. The president of the Tamilnad Congress Committee presided over the meeting. As a result of the resolution, the TNCC recommended that the DCC be dissolved pending new elections. The decision was ultimately ratified (as required

[10] This system of having campaign managers supervise the elections for a group of districts was established for the first time in the 1962 elections at the recommendation of the general secretary of the Congress party, who drew a number of his ideas from American election methods, which he studied in the United States in the presidential campaign of 1960.

by the rules of the Congress party) by the national Congress president. Later in the year, after parliamentary and assembly candidates had been selected, the president of the TNCC appointed Mr. Subbaraman, the Madurai parliamentary candidate, as the convener for the DCC. This meant that in the absence of the DCC responsibility for the local party was in his hands. He appointed an assistant to take charge of the party office and informally consulted local people on the problems associated with the management of party affairs. It was expected that sometime during 1962 new elections for the District Congress Committee would take place and that the new committee would again select a chairman.

In the party's management of the elections and in the conflicts within the District Congress Committee, what is most striking is the extent to which the local participants were willing to accept decisions made by the state party organization. The state organization has only limited means for enforcing its decisions on local units. Legally, the Election Commission of Madras state will not grant a symbol to a candidate unless that candidate has the approval of the state party. A rump group, therefore, cannot use the party label, but it can put up independent candidates. Moreover, insofar as settling a dispute within the local party is concerned, the state organization intervenes only at the request of the local body. There is of course nothing in the rules to prevent the DCC from resolving its own disputes. And while the state organization has control over much patronage, the fact is that the DCC has enough patronage of its own, enough autonomous influence on local government and administration, that it would be very difficult for the TNCC to enforce its will upon a local District Congress Committee. The fact is that it frequently happens, particularly in other states, that the DCC and the state party leadership are at odds with one another.

There are no structural explanations, therefore, for the willingness of the Madurai District Congress Committee to accept the arbitration of the state organization. To understand the reasons for this willingness, one must search more deeply into the attitudes which underlie the behavior.

It is first necessary to note that the various groups within the local party completely accept the arbitrational role of the state organization. Almost everyone welcomed the selection of Subbaraman as the parliamentary candidate, though he did not initially offer himself. There was also no question that Naidu's presence as a kind of over-all election manager was welcome. The decision to dissolve the DCC and appoint a convener was also welcomed by all groups. And finally, there was no dissension when Subbaraman was appointed as a convener.

All of these decisions were patently reasonable ones which were palatable to local people. It was widely agreed that Subbaraman was the only Congressman of sufficient local popularity who had a good chance of defeating the sitting MP. Moreover, since he was an outsider to the disputes within the local party, his appointment as a convener was acceptable. And finally, once a no-confidence motion was passed, it was impossible for the DCC to function any longer.

But throughout the various disputes, all eyes were turned toward Madras. The judgment of the Madras leadership was particularly acceptable because it was a unified judgment. Unlike other states where the central party leadership is divided — and local groups within the party are all associated with state-wide factions — the Madras leadership is not divided and has not been divided since the dissident state-wide elements withdrew from the party in 1957.

The general notion too is widely held that disputes should be settled by an outsider arbitrator rather than through a process of contest and struggle or bargaining. Here, and as we have seen in other areas in India as well, one finds that there is a long tradition of settling disputes through arbitrations. Few of the fathers of the older leaders in Madurai had taken part in modern politics. But many were active as trustees of local temples and as leaders of caste associations. One local politician, describing his father, explained:

> Whenever there was a dispute within our caste [a low-caste community of pot makers] or between our caste and other castes, my father was very active. My father and grandfather were powerful people in this area. In the nineteenth century my grandfather was an agent for the British in the years before there was a railway service here. He handled the postal service for this area. As a result of this work for the British, he acquired much property from the British government. He was an important leader of Rameshwaran temple. My father was also a religious man. He was very good at solving disputes within our community and with other castes.

This local politician — and many others had similar backgrounds — came from a family which had been active in traditional politics in the days before there had been a nationalist movement. Traditional leadership meant essentially the capacity to resolve conflicts. It is thus not difficult

for local politicians in Madurai to perform the role of arbitrator and to accept this as a legitimate role for others. Therefore, what elsewhere in the world might be treated as outside interference is accepted as legitimate, partly because it is a traditionally approved and respected role which members of the party today continue to perform.

The arbitrational role can, however, be satisfactorily performed only when parties to the dispute believe that the arbitrator is impartial. Obviously, if it is felt that the arbitrator has an interest in one side or the other, his role is not acceptable. Thus, the role can be performed well in Madras state because the state leadership is unified, but not so well in other states which are torn by state-wide factions. On the other hand, the energy employed by the Madras leadership for dealing quickly and effectively with each district dispute reduces the chances that there can be a coalition of dissenting groups within the state party. Herein lies the skill of the state leadership.

# 21. CONCLUSION: CONDITIONS FOR MACHINE POLITICS

Congressmen in Madurai are dissatisfied with the state of their local party organization. "There is no real organization here and no real leadership," said one prominent Congressman. Party activists clearly have a higher standard than victory in the general elections, since at the time this study was conducted Congress had lost only one out of its two assembly seats in three elections (and that loss was in 1952) and lost the parliamentary seat only once (in 1957). Workers sense that the party needs more discipline and loyalty and a more effective apparatus to carry out the party's day-to-day work. "There is so little organization here," the Congressman went on to say, "that the chief minister couldn't ask the District Congress Committee to make arrangements for the AICC session."

The most frequent complaint is lack of loyalty by workers to the party.

> Congress could have won the municipal elections, but there were so many dissidents in the party organization that they were not able to work together. Well, for example, the present chairman of the municipal corporation applied for a Congress ticket in the 1959 municipal elections. When he was denied a ticket, he ran as an independent. In fact one group in Congress supported him, and that was why he was able to win the elections. Then for the first time Congress lost control of the municipality.

Internal dissension is related by another Congressman — a member of the TNCC — to the absence of adequate work for the party workers.

TABLE 40
ELECTION RESULTS IN MADURAI

| PARTY | SEATS WON | | | NUMBER OF VOTES | | | PERCENTAGE OF VOTES | | |
|---|---|---|---|---|---|---|---|---|---|
| | 1952 | 1957 | 1962 | 1952 | 1957 | 1962 | 1952 | 1957 | 1962 |
| Legislative Assembly | | | | | | | | | |
| Congress. . | 1 | 2 | 2 | 33,843 | 42,164 | 69,480 | 38.6 | 48.6 | 51.0 |
| Communist. | 1 | . . . | . . | 16,337 | 17,311 | 27,228 | 18.6 | 20.0 | 20.0 |
| Forward Bloc | . . | . . . | . . | . . . . | . . . . | 15,445 | . . . . | . . . . | 11.3 |
| Independents | . . | . . . | . . | 31,641 | 19,440 | 8,229 | 36.0 | 22.4 | 16.0 |
| All others. . | . . | . . . | . . | 6,040 | 7,873 | 15,931 | 6.8 | 9.0 | 11.7 |
| Total . . | 2 | 2 | 2 | 87,911 | 86,788 | 136,313 | 100.0 | 100.0 | 100.0 |
| Parliament | | | | | | | | | |
| Congress. . | 2 | . . . | 1 | 385,707 | 78,286 | 140,574 | 52.6 | 34.5 | 39.6 |
| Communist. | . . | 1 | . . | 96,036 | 79,374 | 123,386 | 13.1 | 35.0 | 34.8 |
| Independents | . . | . . . | . . | 12,933 | 4,249 | . . . . | 1.8 | 1.9 | . . . . |
| All others. . | . . | . . . | . . | 239,086 | 64,765 | 91,459 | 32.5 | 28.6 | 25.6 |
| Total . . | 2 | 1 | 1 | 733,762 | 226,674 | 355,419 | 100.0 | 100.0 | 100.0 |

People in towns live close together, and that leads to more conflict. Furthermore, they are not given full work; and when there is less work and people are close together, there tends to be more fighting. Then in the towns, the Congress president is a big man. He meets the ministers. But in the rural area there are many big men, such as the president of the district local board, the head of the cooperative bank, many big landlords, and so on. The DCC president is a more coveted post in the towns than in the villages, so there is more fighting over it.

The campaign manager for the four southern districts in 1962 elaborated on the theme that there is not adequate leadership.

Yes, it is true there are more disputes here than in the rural areas. The difficulty is that there are no big leaders here as in the rural areas, so everyone thought that he would be the leader. There was Vaidyanath Alyer, who died four or five years ago. He was a good leader. Then N. M. R. Subbaraman, who left politics and just recently came back. We don't have this problem in Coimbatore, which is a separate district. Coimbatore city is overpowered by the rural areas, and leadership comes from the rural areas. The president of the DCC there is a man from the rural areas who was a small

lumber merchant. But in Madras and Madurai there are separate city DCCs, so we have this difficulty. Before 1939, Madurai district was joined with Dindigal district in one DCC. Then a division took place. Then in 1956 the town was separated from the district. Until then all the leaders were from the rural areas. In fact the major leaders in Madras state, even the chief minister, came from the rural areas.

That the workers have no work to do is a recurrent complaint. A former chairman of the municipal corporation, one who has been a Congressman for several decades, explained:

> Before independence there was much work that we had to do, but now we don't have to have any mass contact since the administration does most of the job. I feel that it is necessary to have paid workers who would do much of the work for the party. For example, the paid workers could check the voters lists. Now it is necessary to remunerate the workers. We should have one paid person for each assembly constituency.

The need for paid workers is argued by many Congress leaders. The routine but necessary party work is not being done properly. Party records are badly kept. Voters lists are not maintained. The pre-election work of scrutinizing voters lists to see that new voters were added and deceased voters dropped is not systematically done. Since there are no other incentives for encouraging party workers to do these tasks, many party leaders feel that workers should be paid.

In addition to the lack of discipline and loyalty on the part of party workers, their unwillingness to do routine work without payment, and the absence of strong party leadership, relations between the party and the municipal corporation and between the party and the trade unions are poor.

Since Congress was defeated in the 1959 municipal elections, the party no longer derives any political benefit from the corporation. The vice-chairman of the Madurai DCC explained:

> According to our party constitution, the president and secretary of the party are to attend all meetings of the Congress members of the municipal corporation. In practice, we go only to important meetings. We no longer control patronage. There is an appointment committee of the corporation.

It appoints school teachers, nurses, doctors, clerks, and other officers up to a certain grade. There are several hundred such appointments a year. Generally there is an individual favoritism and nepotism, but appointment is not strictly on party lines. Now a few Communists are getting jobs, while under the Congress government none were appointed. Then there is some discretion with contracts. Under Congress control we gave contracts to the best businesses, not on party lines. But then we got donations from these businessmen. That's how we worked. Now we don't have power, so we can't do that.

We have also described earlier the lack of coordination between the INTUC trade unions and the Congress party, the recent attempt by Congress to create its own trade unions, and the failure of the Congress party to carry a majority of the working-class wards. However, only a handful of local Congressmen expressed concern about these developments, for some argue that it is not possible for Congress to compete effectively with the Communists among the working class. The Communists, they feel, can make irresponsible promises and lead agitations; Congressmen cannot, for the Congress party and government is, after all, committed to a policy of maximizing the country's production and therefore discouraging strikes and disorder of any kind. Many Congressmen therefore conclude that Congress must win elections without any sizeable labor support. "I don't think the trade unions here and in the south generally are strong," explained one pro-Congress businessman. "This is true both of the INTUC and AITUC unions. In fact, their strength has not increased at all during the last few years. Maybe they are weaker. Anyway, I feel that Congress can get most of its votes from the women and the Harijans in Madurai and that the trade union force is not terribly important for it." Not many Congressmen in Madurai would disagree with him.

The Congress party in Madurai is not an ideologically oriented party. Few party workers know or care much about the ideology of socialism. There is a vague commitment to development and to the ideas of equality, but there is much more concern about the day-to-day acts of administration and government and about the specific consequences of new pieces of legislation and taxation. Congressmen are particularly concerned with improving the position of their own castes, their friends, their relations. Status and material considerations, not ideology, are the crucial ingredients in the struggle for power.

Psychologically, the mandal party workers would feel comfortable in the kind of party machine common to many large American cities at the turn of the century or the kind one now finds in Calcutta. Indeed, the election of Perumal, an uneducated low-caste man, a party worker and organizer, and a man concerned with power for its own sake, was an indication of the readiness of the active membership to see such a machine created. But Perumal did not prove to be skillful enough to build such a machine, nor for that matter did he have the power to do so. To build a powerful political machine, there must first of all be some major structures of power which can be controlled. The party machine brings together existing structures of power and in the process creates a new instrument of power. In the United States the urban boss had access to the police; above all, he had control over the municipal government and all the patronage associated with it. Patronage and coercion, the proverbial carrot and stick, were the sources of his power. In Madurai, as in most other cities, it has not proved possible for any political party to establish a network of links with the local police, primarily because police are controlled by the home ministry of the state government, not by the municipality. The municipal corporation of Madurai has far fewer powers than those held by municipal bodies in the United States. Moreover, while there has been a large-scale expansion of governmental activities in the rural areas, this has not occurred in the large towns and cities of India. The cooperative movement, the Community Development program, panchayati raj, and the heavy investment in roads, schools, and dispensaries have been proportionately greater for the rural than urban areas. While the rise in food prices has been of benefit to some agriculturalists, it has led to considerable dissatisfaction among the urban middle classes. Investment in urban housing and other amenities has also been low, and this too reduces the popularity of the government.

The party machine is an instrument for the political distribution of goods and services generated by an active government, and its purpose is the perpetuation in office of those who control the political machine. A precondition, therefore, for the creation of an urban party machine is a high level of government activities over which it has control. The lack of municipal autonomy for Madurai thus diminishes the resources available to the local Congress for creating such a machine. Larger businessmen are not eager to work closely with the local party, because their interests can be satisfied by the state and central governments, not by the municipality. Even in industrial relations and the maintenance of law and order, businessmen must seek assistance in the state capital, not in the

offices of the municipal corporation. Unions also do not have any pressing reason for becoming deeply involved either in the municipal corporation or in the local Congress party.

Even the limited powers of the municipal government are not, as we have noted earlier, an asset to the Congress party organization. Each councillor has considerable influence of his own, which is used to strengthen his political position rather than that of the party. The chairman does have, by virtue of his membership in the contracts committee and appointments committee, important patronage powers, but in the past these have been used by the chairman not on behalf of the party but on his personal behalf. Since as a policy the Congress party organization does not permit those who hold positions in government to hold positions in the party, the party prevents the president of the District Congress Committee from running for the office of chairman of the municipal corporation. Were one man to hold both offices simultaneously, then the party might be able to utilize the powers and patronage of the municipal corporation more successfully to strengthen its own position.

Congress has been able to win elections in Madurai less because of the effectiveness of its organization than because of the independent power and influence of its candidates and because of the continued close association between the party and the Sourashtra community. But even the Sourashtra vote will defect from the party when Congress fails to nominate influential members of the community. The party's failure to do so in several municipal council seats in 1959 was a contributing factor to the party's defeat in the elections of that year. The local population is clearly wedded not so much to a particular party as to particular local men and local institutions. Evidence for this argument can be derived from the common pattern of split voting in the 1957 general elections to parliament, when a Congressman easily carried one assembly constituency while at the same time his voters gave heavy support to the victorious Communist parliamentary candidate. In that election the Congress parliamentary candidate was so closely associated with the Sourashtra community that non-Sourashtras withdrew their support; in the 1962 elections the new Sourashtra candidate had built his career on servicing other communities as well and was viewed by all as a truly civic leader who would serve the whole society.

As one speaks with local politicians in the Congress party, one is struck by the wide variety of loyalties and motivations at work. Some party workers and leaders are strongly attached to their caste, and use the party as a vehicle for maximizing the interests of their groups. Others, particu-

larly the members of the trading and business communities, want more wealth for themselves, their families, and their business friends. Then there are those workers who are driven by a hunger for political recognition, status, or power for its own sake. Like the recent president of the DCC, they are men without money and without high caste or education. One also finds a few men who are genuinely motivated by a desire for service, whose sense of compassion and empathy is so great that they seek their satisfactions in working for the depressed classes. Finally, there are men who are driven by an impassioned loyalty to other men. In the tradition of the chela to the guru, devotion and affection and a desire to do whatever is commanded by the leader are characteristic.

There are thus many incentives to drive men. But party loyalty is rarely one of them. Men are of course loyal to the party, but there is invariably a prior motive at work — communal loyalty, material interest for one's self or family, the urge for personal status, humanitarianism, personal devotion. Congress leaders do in fact recognize that party loyalty is not primary, and therefore they rarely appeal to it to influence behavior of the rank and file.

If we have a single concluding hypothesis in this chapter, it is that the Congress party is essentially the vehicle through which diverse social groups and individuals attempt to maximize their power and social status, and that the party itself lacks the resources to provide continuous rewards and thereby ensure loyalty. The Congress party in Madurai has not generated an ideology which can serve to provide the loyalty which sustained the nationalist movement before independence. Nor has it, to the extent that the party in Calcutta has, been able to substitute patronage and office as alternative incentives for ensuring party loyalty.

The Madurai District Congress Committee is hardly a machine in the modern sense. Nor has the party produced a boss whose advice to state leaders must be heeded because of his ability to control a local party unit and local government bodies. One does find bosses in the Congress party in Madras, but their base is in the rural districts. The sudden expansion of governmental activities in rural areas had made it possible for the rural boss to take power, for power is there to be taken. There are men in Madurai city who would like to be such a boss; but unless a large-scale expansion of governmental activities which can be influenced by the local party takes place within the city, it will be difficult for any DCC president to have enough influence and patronage in his own hands to build a cohesive and loyal organization.

# BIBLIOGRAPHY: MADURAI DISTRICT

## Interviews

Fifty persons were intensively interviewed for this study of the Madurai Congress party, including the MP and MLAs from Madurai, several MLAs in the rural areas of the district, and the president, vice-chairman, and secretary of the DCC. There were also intensive interviews with several former presidents and secretaries of the DCC, the chairman (mayor) of the Madurai Municipal Corporation, and several of the municipal councillors. I had more intensive interviews with Congress party workers in Madurai than in most of my other studies. These included several mandal committee presidents, full-time party workers (many of whom, like the municipal councillors I interviewed, were bazaar merchants), and trade unionists. There were also intensive interviews with several businessmen in Madurai, at T. V. Sundaram and Co., Pandyan Motors, several of the officials in textile mills, and officers of the Madurai-Ramnad Chamber of Commerce. The editor and correspondent for the *Indian Express* in Madurai and the correspondent from the *Hindu*, published in Madras, were very helpful to me, as were the municipal commissioner and the police commissioner.

Finally, several opposition party leaders in the Praja Socialist party, the Communist party, the Swatantra party, the DMK, and the former Justice party were interviewed, as were several officials of the Sourashtra Prachar Sabha, the leading cultural-social organization in the Sourashtra community.

Although I was able to see some records of the Madurai DCC, the

membership files had been sent to the party office in Madras when the Madurai DCC was suspended. I interviewed several PCC officers in Madras on their relationship with the Madurai organization, but was unfortunately unable to see the Madurai membership records.

*History*

Since the literature on Madras is extensive, I have confined this bibliography to those items which relate to Madurai town and the surrounding areas. For a general history of South India and a description of source materials and scholarly works, see Nilakanta Sastri, *A History of South India*, 2d ed. (London: Oxford University Press, 1958). There are two standard works on the Nayak kingdom which ruled Madurai before the advent of British power: Satyanatha Aiyar, *History of the Nayaks of Madura* (London: Oxford University Press, 1924); and K. D. Swaminathan, *The Nayaks of Ikkeri* (Madras: Varadachary, 1957). Apart from the British gazetteers and census reports, there are a number of valuable histories of the Madras presidency during the British period. See R. S. Srinivas, *Memorandum of the Progress of the Madras Presidency during the Last Forty Years of British Administration* (Madras: Superintendent Government Press, 1893). The most famous governor of Madras was Sir Thomas Munro, and the standard biography is John Bradshaw, *Sir Thomas Munro and the British of the Madras Presidency* (Oxford: Clarendon Press, 1894). On changes in land tenure, see Sundaraj Iyengar, *Land Tenures in Madras Presidency* (Madras: Modern Printing Works, 1916). On the development of higher education, see *History of Higher Education in South India*, Volumes I and II, University of Madras, 1857–1957 (Madras, 1957). An interesting account of prominent nineteenth-century Indians in Madras is Govinda Paramesvara Pillai, *Representative Men of Southern India* (Madras: Price Current Press, 1896).

In 1960 the government of Madras published a two-volume collection of essays by B. S. Baliga, the former curator of the Madras Record Office, entitled *Studies in Madras Administration*. These essays deal with such historic governors of Madras as Elihu Yale, the financier and founder of Yale University. They also provide valuable descriptions of changes in the land tenure systems and the development of administration during the British period. Volume I, pages 1–27, contains a note entitled "Nationalism and Independence in Madras" which is of special interest. Baliga is also the author of the *Madras District Gazetteer: Madurai* (Madras: Government of Madras, 1960), which contains (pp. 21–93) a detailed history of

Madurai, its historic kingdoms, Madurai under the British, and the nationalist movement in the district. The volume was published post-humously, and along with Baliga's *Tanjore District Handbook* (Madras: Government of Madras, 1957), represents perhaps the best post-independence gazetteer for any district of India. Baliga's gazetteer replaces two earlier gazetteers for the district, both classic reports. The first is *The Madura Country*, by J. H. Nelson (Madras: 1868), and the second is W. Francis, *Madras District Gazetteers: Madura*, Volume 1 (Madras: Government Press, 1914).

For an account of the terrorist activities in Madras before World War I, see *The Sedition Committee Report* (Calcutta: Bengal Secretariat Press, 1918). For an account of Congress governments in Madurai in the 1930's, see Reginald Coupland, *The Indian Problem* (London: Oxford University Press, 1943).

## Descriptions and Data on Madurai

In addition to the three gazetteers already cited, data on Madurai can be found in the dicennial census reports. See *Census of India 1951*, Volume III, Madras and Coorg, Parts I, II-a, and II-b, by S. Venkateswaran (Madras: Government Press, 1953). There was also published a *1951 Census Handbook for Madurai District*. The census office in Madras now has in preparation a volume dealing exclusively with the city of Madurai, containing both historical and current census data. The director of the census in Madurai was kind enough to make available to me the 1961 data for Madurai city. Mr. S. M. Diaz, the superintendent of police in Madurai, also made available to me his unpublished study, "A Note on Greater Madurai and Its Problems." There are also two useful guides to the city: *Know Madurai*, 4th ed. (Madurai: T. V. Sundram Iyengar and Sons Private Ltd., 1960), and J. P. L. Shenoy, *Madura, the Temple City* (Madras: Associated Printers, 1955).

## Social Organization

The standard encyclopedic work on the social organization of South India is the seven-volume study by Edgar Thurston, *Castes and Tribes of South India* (Cambridge: University Press, 1909). See also Edgar Thurston, *Ethnographic Notes in Southern India* (Madras: Superintendent Government Press, 1906).

The data in this chapter on the Sourashtra community in Madurai, apart from interviews, are drawn from the following documents and studies: *The Caste Question in the Sourashtra Community*, Proceedings of the Director of Public Instruction, No. 2793, March 1, 1892, reprinted by Sourashtra Sabha (Madurai, 1941); *The Correspondence between H. N. Randle and K. V. Padmanabha* (Madurai: Sourashtra Vijayabtham 633, 1945); *A History of the Sourashtras in Southern India*, 3d ed. (Madurai: Sourashtra Brahmana Central Board, 1948); H. N. Randle, "The Sourashtrans of South India," *Journal of the Royal Asiatic Society* (October, 1944); A. J. Saunders, "The Sourashtra Community in Madura, South India," *American Journal of Sociology* 32 (1926): 787–99.

There are a number of studies of communities which can be found in Madurai. Surprisingly, there is no study of the important Nadar caste. On other communities, see the following: J. Fritz Staal, "Notes on Some Brahmin Communities of South India," *Art and Letters* 32 (1958): 1–7; J. S. Ponniah, *An Enquiry into the Economic and Social Problems of the Christian Community of Madura, Ramnad and Tinnevally Districts* (Madurai: Department of Research and Extension, American College, 1938); F. J. Richards, "Cross-Cousin Marriages in South India," *Man in India* 14 (1941): 194–96; Louis Dumont, *Hierarchy and Marriage Alliance in South Indian Kinship* (London: Royal Anthropological Institute of Great Britain and Ireland, 1957); T. J. Kumaraswami, "The Adi-Dravidas of Madras," *Man in India* 3 (1923): 59–64. Kathleen Gough has also prepared a number of studies of kinship and caste in a Tanjore village. See her "Brahman Kinship in a Tamil Village," *American Anthropologist* 58 (1956): 826–53; "Caste in a Tanjore Village," *in* E. R. Leach, ed., *Aspects of Caste in South India, Ceylon and North-West Pakistan* (Cambridge: University Press, 1960), pp. 11–60; "The Social Structure of a Tanjore Village," *in* M. N. Srinivas, ed., *India's Villages* (Calcutta: Development Department, West Bengal, 1955), pp. 82–92; "The Social Structure of a Tanjore Village," *in* McKim Marriott, ed., *Village India* (Chicago: University of Chicago Press, 1955), pp. 36–52.

## Politics

I have already referred to the accounts of the nationalist movement in Madurai and in Madras by B. S. Baliga. For other historical accounts, see Sir A. P. Patro, "The Justice Movement in India," *Asiatic Review* 28: 27–49; Ralph W. Nicholas, "Caste and Politics in Madras, 1920–1952," *Anthro-*

*pology Tomorrow*, Journal of the Anthropology Club of the University of Chicago 6 (April, 1960); Gilbert Slater, *Southern India, Its Political and Economic Problems* (London: G. Allen and Unwin, 1936). For descriptions of the pre-independence members of the Madras Legislative Assembly, see *Directory of the Madras Legislature* (Madras: The Madras Legislature Congress party, 1938 and 1950). For reports and data on post-independence elections in Madras, see *Delimitation of Parliamentary and Assembly Constituencies Order for Madras 1956* (New Delhi: Government of India, 1956); *General Election in Madras State, 1957: Election Data Analysis* (Public [Elections] Department, Government of Madras, 1960); T. Balakrishnan Nayar, "Madras," *in* S. V. Kogekar, ed., *Reports on the Indian General Elections, 1951–1952* (Bombay: Popular Book Depot, 1956); K. R. Rajagopalan, "Pondicherry Assembly Elections: An Analysis," *Economic Weekly* 11 (1959): 1269–70; *Return Showing the Results of the General Elections in Madras State, 1951–52* (Madras: Government Press, 1953). The municipal commissioner in Madurai was kind enough to provide me with the election results for the city's municipal elections.

For accounts of contemporary party politics in Madras, focusing particularly on the Dravida movement for an autonomous Tamil state, see Khasa Subba Rao, "Current and Cross-currents in the Political Life of Madras," *Mahratta* (Feb. 1, 1957); Lloyd Irving Rudolph, "Urban Life and Populist Radicalism; Dravidian Politics in Madras," *Journal of Asian Studies* 20 (1961): 283–97; G. S. Seshadry, "The Dravida Kazhagam in Madras," *Indian Affairs Record* 3 (1957): 3–5; Phillips Talbot, *Notes From a Tamilnad Tour* (New York, 1957) (American Universities Field Staff, India PT-7-'57); Phillips Talbot, *Raising a Cry for Secession* (New York, 1957) (American Universities Field Staff, India PT-57).

On the business and labor communities in Madras, see the following: James J. Berna, *Industrial Entrepreneurship in Madras State* (New York: Asia Publishing House, 1960); *Report on the Workings of the "Factories Act" in the State of Madras for the Year 1959* (Government of Madras, 1961); Bahman Postonji Wadia, *Labour in Madras* (Triplicane: S. Ganesan, 1921). The Madurai-Ramnad Chamber of Commerce in Madurai publishes the annual address of its president and an annual report. See *The 34th Annual Report of the Year 1958–59* and the *Souvenir Volume of the Fourth Zonal Conference of Chambers of Commerce in South India* (Madurai: Madurai-Ramnad Chamber of Commerce, 1960). Several of the large businesses in Madurai publish reports of their history and activities. See especially *TVS — The Largest Body Building Unit in India* (Madurai: T. V. Sundram Iyengar and Sons Private Ltd., n.d.)

*PART VII. CONCLUSION*

# 22. WHY CONGRESS SUCCEEDS

Throughout this study we have dwelt on the specifics of each district party organization in the context of the particular social and economic environment in which it must work. Our approach has been clinical rather than statistical, in an effort to see each situation in its entirety rather than to extract from it only those elements shared with other units throughout the country. We have studied five party units, not five hundred, and have interviewed 240 politicians, not 2,400. In the pages that follow we shall nonetheless generalize about the units we have studied, not with any guilt that we lack statistical tables, but with some confidence that the generalizations are supported by clinical studies of a depth which a broader statistical study could not provide.

Nonetheless, just as we must be cautious about samples, we must be careful in generalizing from clinical cases. In each district I have examined how the party recruits and trains cadres, copes with internal conflict, and wins elections. In some respects, each of the party units we have studied in five sections of India is different from the others. India is an enormously diverse country, a subcontinent with a population nearly double that of Africa, and incorporating more than a dozen major languages and a bewildering variety of ethnic groupings that makes analysts despair of making generalizations. Can one say that the Congress party in Calcutta is like that of Madurai, or that Congress in Kaira district has the same problems as Congress in Belgaum?

Nonetheless, there are some remarkable similarities in all the districts, and it is these which shall concern us here. The fact that there are great similarities in how each of the five organizations in five different and scat-

tered districts handles the three essential requisites for party building gives us some confidence in the reliability of our findings. To each generalization we could of course add qualifications, or we could show the variations from one district organization to another; but I shall leave the qualifying to those readers who have diligently read the preceding chapters. Here we shall be concerned primarily with suggesting those general factors at work which account for the remarkable success of India's Congress party.

Let us again be clear that by success we do not mean any normative judgment about the quality of the government that Congress has provided or the integrity and moral worth of the individuals who make up Congress. By success we only mean that Congress has successfully recruited members, won elections in a competitive environment, and coped with internal disputes so as to prevent widespread fragmentation.

One final — but important — caveat. There is no one hypothesis which explains the success of Congress, just as there can be no single hypothesis which will explain why a bureaucracy functions successfully, or an economy grows, or an army is capable of defending a nation. Congress has succeeded because its leadership has done many things well, and it is these correct actions — correct in terms of facilitating the success of the party — that shall concern us here.

Party building takes place within an institutional framework as well as within a social, economic, and attitudinal milieu. Congress was able to work within an established parliamentary system, legitimized by the 1950 constitution but predating it by several decades. Then too, while the very success of Congress served to maintain order and stability within India, the bureaucracy and military have also maintained order, minimized violence, and coped with actual and potential insurgency movements. And let us remember that Congress works in a society where, compared to most developing areas, an experienced, intelligent, skilled, self-confident leadership exists, a leadership which has made many blunders but which has proved itself reasonably capable of running complex governmental machinery.

The Congress party itself has many experienced party workers and leaders who have spent their careers in party organizational work, first in the nationalist movement before independence and then in Congress as a competitive political party. While many factors impel individuals to vote for a party, join a party, or remain party members, certainly the fact that Congress is the heir of a nationalist movement which brought India to independence is relevant. Also, India was fortunate in having in Nehru

a man who chose to exercise his leadership to support the parliamentary system and who was convinced that the party should be the instrument of government and government be responsible to an elected parliament.

None of these factors alone, or perhaps even in combination, need have led to a successful political party in India. In other countries with established armies and bureaucracies and charismatic leaders the nationalist movement has fallen apart, or national leaders have turned the party into an instrument of authoritative rule. Nehru alone or Patel alone could not have made Congress or the parliamentary system work, but a Sukarno might have done much to destroy both.

### Organization

Of the many factors at work, let us note first that the Congress leadership has been very conscious of organizational problems. The proper relationship between party and government, the procedures for selecting party officers, the machinery for settling intra-party disputes, the relationship between local party units and the parliamentary and assembly constituencies — these and other organizational matters have been much discussed by the party's leadership. Congressmen have been very much concerned with constitutional forms. It is true that the party leadership has modified the party's constitution and its many rules or procedures countless times in the last few decades, but what is striking is that the leadership has taken seriously its own rules and regulations.

There is considerable variation in how much attention is given by each District Congress Committee to organizational matters. Almost all keep some membership records, if only because the voting power of each unit for higher party offices depends upon the number of primary and active members. A few DCCs keep village voting records on elections as a guide to their future candidates, but typically this is not done well or at all. The candidates themselves keep such records, and may or may not transmit them to their successors.

In view of the size of the country and the variety of languages, communication within the party is reasonably well performed. The AICC secretariat in New Delhi publishes several internal house organs, and regularly sends these as well as organizational memos to the Pradesh Congress Committees and to the DCCs. These are all transmitted in English and include directives on party matters as well as speeches by the prime minister and the party president on national affairs. The PCCs in turn send

directives on state government and party matters to the district committees, sometimes in English and sometimes in the regional language. Neither the state nor the national party communicates to units smaller than the DCC. The DCC has primary responsibility for communicating to all subordinate bodies down to the mandal committees, and this is typically done in the regional language either in writing or by word of mouth.

Though the flow of information is predominantly downward, there is some upward movement. DCCs and affiliated Congress bodies, such as the Youth Congress, the Women's Congress, and the trade union organizations, are required to send in quarterly or annual reports to parent bodies. As a rule, these are done haphazardly and infrequently.

Perhaps more important than the flow of printed material is the movement of people. Congress is after all an enormous organization, with hundreds of district organizations, urban committees, mandals, taluka committees, and affiliated bodies. Some units function well, some indifferently, and some exist only on paper. No one body — not even the AICC — knows the condition of each unit. A local unit, for example, may not respond to correspondence at all. Therefore, the only effective way of maintaining communication is for party leaders constantly to visit party units. In the office of the AICC in New Delhi and in the offices of most Pradesh Congress Committees, the general secretaries are responsible for maintaining contact, transmitting information, checking on the workings of lower units, and in general trouble shooting for the party. These party workers are thus constantly on tour, as any research scholar who has tried to conduct political interviewing can testify. Of course much of the touring is political. A cabinet member in the state government may visit party units in order to build up support for a subsequent attempt to become chief minister. An MP may tour to ensure local support for his renomination. Whatever the reason, the constant flow of people across not only district, but even state, lines strengthens the feeling in party cadres of belonging to a state and national organization and not simply to a local political faction.

It is of some importance that the flow of information and personnel out of and into the district organization and that in general a concern for organizational matters appear to be greatest in those portions of the country where subsistence farming has been replaced by a market economy and increased monetization. Although this study in no sense proves this hypothesis, the hypothesis is supported by the high level of politicalization in Guntur and Kaira districts, especially in their more affluent portions. Among those peasants who participate in the market economy political participation is high, competition among political parties is intense, and

political organizations are established sooner than in other regions. Perhaps the explanation lies in the psychological effects of participating in a market economy, especially in the concern individuals have for the consequences of their economic actions. Perhaps it lies in the opportunity to widen one's contacts and to receive more information from greater distances, or perhaps in the increasing contact which the peasant and petty merchant now have with the local bureaucracy. Perhaps the explanation is that in such areas increased income makes it possible to obtain increased education, which in turn speeds the process of political participation. And perhaps, most importantly, it is because areas which are monetized have experienced great social and economic change, which generates discontent and creates political demands.

Whatever the explanation, the fact is that political consciousness, to use the popular Indian expression, does appear to be greatest in market areas. And it is these areas of rural India in which some of the first district Congress organizations were created during the nationalist era and which today continue to provide some of the most active Congressmen in the country as a whole.

### Party and Administration

One hypothesis of this study is that the success of the Congress party, particularly in winning elections and recruiting personnel, is related to the close liaison between the local party organization and local administration. We have already noted that the administrative structure of Congress does not parallel the country's electoral units — as do American and British parties — but parallels the country's administrative structure. Thus the District Congress Committee coincides with the district administration, not with the parliamentary constituency. The taluka Congress committee similarly parallels the taluka administrative framework, not the assembly constituencies. The new system of local government established by the panchayati raj strengthens this pattern, for the new units again coincide with the administrative structure of the state government rather than with the assembly and parliamentary constituencies.

The party's parallel with the state and local administration calls attention to the fact that the primary concern of the local party organization is with influencing local administration. The local party is concerned with influencing the developmental functions of state and local administration. The local Congress party aids its membership and its supporters in

the countryside in their efforts to influence tax enforcement, to get the necessary permits for the purchase of cement, fertilizers, and other commodities, and to influence local administration in its appointments and myriad other activities. The party is concerned also with the coercive powers of local administration. Though the administration of justice is generally apolitical, many individuals feel that influence in the local party will protect them in dealings with local police. Though in the districts studied we have encountered no control by the party organization over the local police, it is often reported in other parts of the country, particularly in the Punjab and in portions of Uttar Pradesh, that the influence of the party on police at the local level is substantial.

But perhaps the most important point here is that the expansion of governmental activities during the last twenty years has strengthened the local Congress party organization. The expansion of the public sector, the increase of governmental control and regulations, and the increasing role of government in the distribution of goods and services throughout the society tend to be assets to political organizations which can influence local administration. In our study of Guntur district we suggested that the establishment of panchayati raj (which transferred developmental activities from the community development administration to locally elected bodies) strengthened the local Congress party organization. The ideology of socialism, with its emphasis on a growing public sector, central and state government activities to facilitate development, equity, and social welfare, is also an asset to a party organization linked to local administration. This may also help us understand why it is that a party with many peasant proprietors and local merchants supports a policy of socialism.

A good case can be presented for saying that the strength and popularity of the Congress party depend in large measure upon a high level of governmental performance rather than upon a high level of performance in the economy. Though economic growth in the countryside and in the cities has been modest during the past decade, the expansion of governmental activities has been enormous. While the first five-year plan expenditure was 2,013 crore of rupees (1 crore = $2 million), the second five-year plan was more than double, at 4,800 crore of rupees, and the third provided for a public sector investment of 7,500 crore of rupees. Economists have been irritated by the Indian penchant for focusing on investment rather than production targets, but the main point here is that the volume of government investment and the increasing size of the government payroll have been important factors in the strength of the local Congress party organization.

Moreover, for the bulk of the Indian population there is a greater concern for the position which each group has in relation to every other group than for India's economic position vis-à-vis other countries. Certainly Indians are concerned with the rate of growth, but at the local level there is a greater concern for equity than for development. Perhaps this is why a low rate of economic growth in any particular area of India seems to have no detrimental political consequences. Indeed, famine areas have often given a larger vote to Congress, for economic distress has often provided Congress and the government with an opportunity to demonstrate its concern and, in most instances, its capacity to provide welfare.

In any event, it is more relevant for purposes of political analysis to look at the economic share which each group receives rather than at the country's economic growth rate. The precise relationship between changing income and changing political attitudes and political behavior is one that requires more careful analysis than has thus far been given in the literature.[1] Here we simply want to note the attention paid to the concept of equity by India's national leadership, a concept which is simultaneously ideologically attractive and politically rewarding for the Congress party.

## Party Roles

Why the expansion of governmental activities has strengthened Congress becomes clearer as we take a closer look at what it is that Congress party workers actually do. In our analysis of the activities of party workers in Belgaum district we have suggested that there are at least three important tasks which engage the cadres. While there are variations on these activities in other districts, in general one can find these activities performed by party workers throughout the country. We have described these as expediting, arbitrational, and constructive work roles.

Expediting work — or "doing service," as many Congressmen say — involves helping citizens, both farmers and merchants, obtain assistance from government and unravel the maze of governmental regulations, and, in general, links individuals to local administration. We have already noted that the extractive, developmental, and coercive activities of tax revenue departments, community and agricultural development ministries, and the police are all of active concern to party workers. The MLA or the president of the DCC may help a local businessman see a bureaucrat in the state capital; a party worker may see a government officer on

[1] For a major effort to fill this gap, see George Rosen, *Democracy and Economic Change in India* (Berkeley and Los Angeles: University of California Press, 1966).

behalf of some colleagues about the conditions of the local irrigation canal, or may seek the support of a government officer for the construction of a village road.

Many party workers spend their time arbitrating and mediating disputes in the community. Conflict between two cultivators over stray cattle or between a tenant and landlord over tenancy rights is likely to result in intervention by local Congressmen. One reason for their involvement is that traditionally powerful men were asked to resolve disputes. Why arbitration and mediation by a third party, rather than bargaining by the contesting parties, are the pattern of dispute settlement in most of India is an interesting question which need not concern us here at any length. Perhaps this pattern is related to the problem of maintaining order in a hierarchical social system in which there is little interpersonal trust and where individuals see conflict as the expression of deeper psychological matters and status relationships. In such circumstances, bargaining, which assumes great personal trust, is difficult; individuals in a dispute can more easily turn to an impartial mediator, who can provide satisfaction. Whatever the reason, the important point here is that the traditional social need for arbitrators and mediators is often satisfied by party workers.

Finally, many party workers are engaged in what they refer to as constructive work activities. These activities are an outgrowth of Gandhi's emphasis on the performance of social work by nationalist workers on behalf of the poor. Today much constructive work is actually handled by governmental agencies — handicraft boards, handloom boards, and government agencies concerned with Harijans. Today the term is used to describe those activities of party workers concerned with aiding untouchables and backward social classes. It is also used to describe activities in the cooperative movement.

In our study of Belgaum district we have shown that many of the party cadres engaged in expediting, arbitrational, and constructive work come from families which have traditionally performed these roles. Village headmen, record keepers, revenue officers, and larger landlords often engaged in expediting work. These same persons, especially those who belonged to the dominant local castes, often served to mediate and to arbitrate disputes. Moreover, several of the prominent organizers of constructive work in the district (not so much those actually engaged in organizing cooperatives or youth hostels as their patrons) come from families long engaged in philanthropy. In Belgaum there appears to be greater continuity in rank and power than in many other districts, but the important point is that these traditional activities of local elites — expediting the

needs of peasants and merchants in relation to local administrators, settling disputes, and engaging in philanthropy — fulfill the role requirements of a modern political organization.

The important point too is that party workers are constantly engaged in performing tasks — not simply at election time — that these tasks serve local needs, and that Congress workers are in the main skillful in performing these tasks.

### Personnel

So far we have said little about who these workers are. They vary of course from district to district. In Kaira they are the Patidars, a high caste consisting primarily of prosperous peasant proprietors and merchants. In Madurai the ancient community of handloom weavers, the Sourashtras, and the Brahmins, mainly professional persons, dominated the party in the past but now must contend with an increase in political activity among the bazaar merchants. In Guntur the once-dominant Brahmins have given way to Reddis and Kammas, two agricultural castes. In Belgaum the linguistic controversy has led many Marathi-speaking workers to leave the party but has increased the number of Kannada-speaking cadres, especially from the Lingayat community. The composition of the Belgaum party is becoming more rural-agriculturalist and less urban-businessman. In Calcutta, Congressmen represent a wide variety of castes and occupations but include many full-time professional politicians with backgrounds in small businesses.

The party composition is changing. While in the pre-independence era university graduates with professional-urban backgrounds held important party posts, increasingly the party has at all levels come under the control of less educated men of rural backgrounds. Prime Minister Nehru, born in the city of Allahabad and educated at Cambridge, was replaced by Lal Bahadur Shastri, born in a village near the city of Benaras and educated in Kashi Vidyapith, a national Gandhian institution. Nehru's father was an educated and prominent barrister; Shastri's father was a minor government official. Kamaraj, the Congress president, comes from a rural background in Madras state, is not university-educated and until recently spoke no English. When he became chief minister of Madras state some years ago, he replaced a university-educated, urban, English-speaking Brahmin.

These changes are most apparent at the local level. District party or-

ganizations are usually run by peasant proprietors. At the village and district levels, the prominent Congress leaders are property owners and typically, though not always, members of the dominant caste within the local community. But this generalization has two important qualifications: one, not all members of the local power structure are members of Congress; and two, the local power structure is in flux.

There is usually so much local factional conflict among those who own property and belong to the dominant castes that it is impossible for Congress to recruit all the local leaders. It thus is not feasible — at least not in a competitive environment — for Congress to have a monopoly on local power. For this reason Congress encounters party competition locally throughout almost all of India and typically receives no more than half of the vote in any single assembly and parliamentary election, though it wins some three-quarters of the seats in state assemblies and in the national parliament.

Conflict within the local village elites makes it both necessary and possible for the pro-Congress group to widen its appeal in the community. Because only rarely will a factional struggle involve an entire village, the factions within the local Congress are non-exclusive in character. The local Congress leadership tries to win support from many factions within the village and, since the establishment of universal adult suffrage, from all sections of the community. Universal adult suffrage thus plays an important role in breaking down ascriptive patterns of political leadership.

In discussing our second qualification, we are obliged to note that the power structure of rural India has been changing, for, more fundamentally, patterns of social stratification in India are in a process of flux. Two features of social change are of particular political significance. One is that though there is some individual mobility in India, it is often large social groups whose positions have changed. Thus, it would be impossible to understand the changes that have occurred within Congress without considering the changing social and economic positions of Brahmins, Kammas, Reddis, Lingayats, and Nadars since the 1930's and, more recently, of Bariyas and Rajputs. Second, social mobility or the desire for it is to a large extent a consequence of government policy. The establishment of universal adult suffrage, the vast expansion of schools and colleges, the passage of land reform legislation, and the growth of government-sponsored economic development activities in rural areas — all have unsettled relatively established patterns of social relations. Thus, though India still remains the deferential society par excellence, at the local level it is no longer as clear as it once was who is to be given deference.

Today the local Congress party organizations are faced with a changing local power structure and considerable local conflict. We have seen the consequences of these developments in the districts — how the Lingayat, Kamma, and Reddi castes displaced the Brahmins in Guntur and Belgaum; how the Nadar caste and other mercantile communities now threaten the position of the Brahmins and Saurashtras in Madurai; and how the Patidars are now threatened by the Rajputs and Bariyas in Kaira. The issue is, however, not simply a matter of one caste or group of castes being replaced by another, but of a growing diversification of the castes and occupations of party cadres. The important point is that while governing parties in new nations tend to become vehicles for those who exercise power, Congress is also a vehicle for those who seek power.

Sometimes it is only after castes or factions gain some local governmental power that they seek to get control of the Congress party organization. Congress district leaders will often approach newly elected panchayat presidents to urge them to join the party; it is common for Congress leaders to explain away a party defeat in municipal or state assembly elections on the grounds that they had failed to nominate the local influentials. In Madurai, for example, we have seen that the Congress defeat in municipal corporation elections was interpreted by local Congress leaders in just that way. Thus, the district party leadership is often torn between two incongruent goals. On the one hand, the party leadership wants to attract to the party men of local power and social groups whose support is necessary to win local, assembly, and parliamentary elections. On the other hand, the party leadership is afraid of losing its position within the party. Thus, in Kaira the Patidar Congress leadership feared that the Rajput and Bariya politicians might take over the party. While the reaction of the party to new groups varies considerably from district to district, as one looks over the development of the party during the last two decades one is struck by the success of aspiring social groups in gaining a share of power within the local Congress party.

## Conditions for an Open Elite System

Why have Congress leaders permitted aspiring social groups to gain a share of power within the party? Elsewhere in the developing world elites have often resisted sharing power, and European history is full of accounts of governmental elites who used repressive means to maintain their monopoly of authority. To explain why Congress has been so successful in

absorbing new political elites, we must ask two questions: why have aspiring elites chosen Congress as their vehicle for seeking political power, and why have existing elites within the party been prepared to share their power?

The first question is easier to answer than the second. Congress is, after all, the government party; Congressmen therefore have great access to policy makers and administrators. They have more influence over the distribution of patronage, the allocation of development funds, and the administration of government regulations than do other political parties. Political aspirants are therefore likely to seek power within Congress first and to join the opposition only if they fail in Congress. Thus, Congress is given the option of first refusal. In Kaira, for example, the Rajput and Bariya castes joined Swatantra only after they failed to win the power they sought within Congress. There are few prominent opposition leaders in India at the national, state, or district level who have not at one time or another been Congressmen. In short, one might say that the capacity of Congress to provide rewards has been a key factor in the willingness of aspiring elites to seek power within Congress first.

It is, however, the response of the elite within Congress which is critical, for in most political systems it is the unwillingness of the established elites to share power which turns aspiring elites to revolutionary channels and alienated politics. We have already referred to one reason for the accommodating character of the Congress leadership: the degree of competition within Congress at the local level. Were the local Congress party not so torn by internal factional disputes, Congressmen would not be as eager as they are to seek additional popular support. One faction may seek support from a minority religious group, an aspiring caste, or another faction, not simply because the Congress faction wants to win an election against the opposition, although this is obviously a consideration, but often because the faction wants to strengthen its position vis-à-vis another faction within Congress. To generalize, we might say that competition within the local governing elite, whether it is within a single party or between parties, is an important factor in the capacity of that elite to accommodate the demands for power by aspiring elites.[2]

A corollary of this proposition is that competition within the aspiring elite also facilitates its admission into the governing party. If the aspiring

[2] For a thoughtful analysis of the integrative as well as disintegrative features of factionalism within Congress, see Paul Brass, "Factionalism and the Congress Party in Uttar Pradesh," *Asian Survey* (Sept., 1964):1037–47. Brass gives considerable attention to the role of factionalism in political recruitment into the Congress organization in Uttar Pradesh.

elite is united, the dominant elite is often fearful that it may be completely displaced; if, on the other hand, the aspiring elite is divided, factions within the dominante elite can each compete for sections of the aspiring elite. That is why, strange as it may seem, the capacity of Negroes in the American South to influence the outcome of elections may be greater if Negroes are divided and all candidates must seek their support than if they vote as a bloc, thereby allowing the candidate who does not receive their support to make no concessions and to appeal to white voters to keep Negroes out of office. Similarly, the Kammas who entered Congress in Guntur in the 1930's were very much divided, and each Kamma faction was able to ally itself with a Brahmin faction in the party. It was precisely because the Kammas were divided that each Brahmin faction was eager to solicit Kamma support. In contrast, Patidar factions within the Congress party of Kaira feared Bariya and Rajput domination, because those castes were united in their own association and were clearly trying to exercise power as a bloc within Congress.

A third factor in the capacity of Congress to absorb new elites is that even if some Congressmen are reluctant to allow new elements into the party, it is difficult to stop new elites from coming in. Party membership is after all open, and once a large number of people join the party they can begin to elect their own members to positions of importance within the party and can influence the selection of candidates for assembly and parliamentary constituencies. Moreover, when suffrage is extended, new participants generally try to enter the most powerful party first if the doors are even remotely open. Again, the American example is illuminating. Even in the South Negroes are trying to enter the Democratic party, despite its racist character, because it controls most state and local governments.

Finally, the fourth and perhaps most important factor in the willingness of Congressmen to share power with aspiring elites is that the amount of power to be shared has been growing. For the past thirty years the amount of power available to Congressmen has grown as a result of the increase in the amount of power within the Indian political system, and this growth has made it possible for existing elites to share their power without fear of being totally displaced. The British India Act of 1935 gave greater powers to provincial governments, and for the first time Congressmen fought for control over these governments, with the result that more offices were available to Congressmen. It was during this period, especially around the time of the 1937 elections, that the elite composition of Congress became so diversified. After independence in 1947 there

was a second wave of expanding power when a Congress government replaced the British and men moved out of party offices and jails into state and national governments. Moreover, the expansion of the functions of national and state governments since independence, the establishment of new district and taluka local governments, the growth in the power of village panchayats, the transfer of community development powers and finances from the state administration to elected local bodies, and the establishment of two house state assemblies and of larger cabinets – all have meant more power in more positions to meet the growing demand.

If power were confined to a weak central government – a typical pattern in most new nations – it would be far more difficult and threatening for an elite to share power. In traditional societies there is often a zero-sum view of the political process – that is, a belief that the expansion of power for some must mean its contraction for others. In contrast, in modern political systems, or at least in modern democratic systems, there is a belief that power, like national income, is expandable and that just as a man can pay higher wages without decreasing his profits, so it is possible for state and local governments to expand their functions without reducing the power of the national government and for new participants to enter the political system without displacing anyone. Thus, the more developed a political system, the greater its capacity to handle the demands of new groups. The increasing supply of governmental power in India at all levels – local, state, and national – is a significant factor in the capacity and therefore in the willingness of local elites within Congress to meet the growing demands of aspiring elites for a share of power.

*Incentives*

It would be a mistake to assume that all who join Congress do so only to further their economic or social interests and that Congress is little more than the instrument of local power elites. There are many reasons why individuals join the local Congress party. Organizations differ of course in the nature and variety of incentives they provide to members and supporters. Machine parties generally emphasize material rewards, and ideological parties generally emphasize purposive goals and psychic rewards. The Congress party differs from both these types in that it uses a wide variety of incentives. Congress provides a place for those who are dedicated to social service and who are moved by an equalitarian spirit. For such party workers the party provides opportunities to work in cooperatives or among Harijans or handloom workers. The spirit of self-sacrifice

and self-abnegation, which has a long honorable tradition in Hinduism and which was reformulated by Gandhi, has a place in the local Congress party.

Congress also provides, as we have seen, a place for those who want status and power within the community or who want to translate their economic and social status into political power. As an officer in the Congress party — particularly a secretary or president of the District Congress Committee — one can be seen publicly with the chief minister of the state, with members of the state or even of the national cabinet, and with high ranking officials of state and district administration. Status is of course more than an individual matter, and an entire faction or caste may seek to use Congress as a vehicle for improving or maintaining a status position. As we have so often seen in the case studies, concern for one's social position or the position of the group to which one belongs is an important motive force in Indian political life.

The rewards of membership in Congress are, however, more than psychic. Congress does provide a place for those who have specific demands and grievances — who want permits from government, admission for their sons into college or into state and local administration, and access to development funds for roads, wells, and agricultural financing. While India's national government and the bureaucracy tend to be developmentally oriented, local politicians are very much concerned with questions of distribution. The ideology of Congress, which conceives of socialism as social and especially as economic equity, makes distribution politics legitimate. While it is customary to distinguish between parties of patronage and parties of ideology,[3] what is striking here is the extent to which ideology — in this instance, the appeal to equity — is used to support patronage.

It is, however, important to note that the local Congress party does not have a monopoly over patronage. Prominent local politicians who are not in the Congress party do have access to the credit institutions, to the cooperatives, and to local and district administration. But Congressmen have greater access, and the district bureaucrats, while not controlled by local Congress politicians, are accommodating. There has been a considerable political penetration of the local bureaucracy — some would say to the extent of destroying the political neutrality of the bureaucracy — but, by the standards of nineteenth-century American or contemporary Philippine politics, the penetration has been modest. The main point is, how-

[3] "Patronage" is generally used to refer to all forms of material benefits distributed to party workers and supporters by politicians. See James Q. Wilson, "The Economy of Patronage," *Journal of Political Economy* LXIX (Aug., 1961).

ever, that some of the typical functions of patronage — to induce party workers to be loyal to the party boss, to get voters to support the party, to establish influence within the bureaucracy — are performed by the Congress machine and facilitate the success of the Congress party.

While some Congressmen and some voters are interested in the material benefits which Congress can bestow, others are attracted by the conviviality which the party offers. In each district there may be eight or ten taluka Congress offices located in the small towns where members may meet and engage in the ancient art of politics. One has only to attend these meetings to appreciate the extraordinary pleasure derived from them by Indian politicians. In addition, the All India Congress Committee and the Pradesh Congress Committees have organized Congress training camps which are ostensibly concerned with the training of party workers, but, from the point of view of the cadres who attend, they are often rewards for work done and provide them with opportunities to see Bangalore, Madras, or Delhi, to get together with other local politicians, and to meet well-known state and national leaders. The local party also sponsors various celebrations — for Independence Day, Republic Day, or the birthday of some national or state leader — and this too provides an opportunity for conviviality mixed with a sense of party, regional, and national pride.

Finally, since Congress stands for national integration, economic development, secularism, and representative government, it attracts some dedicated modernists. While at the turn of the century Congress was primarily concerned with greater self-government (and, later, independence) and social reform, by the 1930's the party had broadened its goals. Land reform and economic planning became nationalist planks, and after independence Congress announced that its goal was a "socialistic pattern of society." The national Congress leadership has consistently refused to draw sharp priorities or to recognize what often appears to others to be logical inconsistencies in some party positions. Thus, national Congress leaders believe that there is room for both public and private sectors, room for both the free market and physical planning, and that it is possible for economic planning to be concerned with both equity and development, agriculture and industry, land reform and property rights, equality of opportunity and special considerations for the backward classes. By adopting such a broad program, Congress has successfully undercut the ideological attraction of the Swatantra party's appeal to businessmen and the appeal of the Communist and Socialist parties to many young people. This is not to say that all modernists (in any event a loosely used term) belong to Congress; the important point is that Congress can and does

attract individuals concerned with national development even while it attracts individuals who seek material advantage.

The wide variety of incentives Congress provides and the many different kinds of individuals thereby attracted to it present the party leadership with a delicate balancing act. At the district and state level, party leaders are often fearful of legislation which might change the local power structure or — more importantly — alienate individuals who hold local power. On the other hand, the Congress leaders at the national level as well as many state and district leaders do not want the demands of the local elites to interfere with the modernization program. Keeping in mind the range of interests that Congress encompasses, we can now perhaps understand why the Congress party at the state level passes land reform legislation but incorporates provisions in the legislation to protect the rights of the numerous and influential medium-sized landowners. We can understand why the state Congress leaders have endorsed the national Congress party proposal for cooperative farming but have prudently moved toward service cooperatives rather than programs of collective ownership and management of the land. We can understand too why in principle the party opposes casteism and communalism but at the local level calculatingly engages in ethnic arithmetic.

One final aspect of the problem of incentives and recruitment is worth consideration: the extent to which Congress continues to recruit young persons into the party. In our five-district study, data on changing age patterns have been available only for Belgaum and Kaira districts, and in both it is clear that the active membership has not grown appreciably older. Over a nine-year period in Belgaum, for example, the average age, of Congress workers changed little — and, moreover, the party recruits from all age groups. If the party is, as we have suggested, a vehicle for those who have already established their political position through local governmental and quasi-governmental bodies, we can see why many recruits enter Congress in their thirties and forties. Nor do the data suggest that a substantial portion of the active membership is in the twenty to thirty age bracket. A modernist ideology, conviviality, opportunities for improving one's social status, material rewards, and the satisfaction of being of service — these constitute the mixed bundle of incentives that attract men of all ages and motives to Congress.

Apart from these incentives, the party provides "disincentives" for leaving the party or breaking party rules. Actually, the "disincentives" are so few that while only a small percentage of cadres leave Congress to join the opposition, many party workers violate party discipline. The most com-

mon violation is to oppose a Congress party candidate for the state assembly or parliament after he has been nominated by the party. It is common for Congress dissidents to support opposition candidates. In some states the Congress Pradesh Committee, in an effort to prevent further indiscipline, has expelled such dissidents or suspended their rights to participate in or be elected to any party organization. Other state organizations have taken a more cautious position, and provided either mild punishment or none at all for fear that the secession by dissidents would only weaken the party further. A few state organizations have sought to pacify dissident factions in the party by providing them with some assembly and parliamentary seats and by appointing members of minority factions to the state cabinet. Finally, several of the most powerful party organizations (including Madras and West Bengal) have adopted a policy of "starving" dissident factions.

### Internal Cohesion and Dispute Settlement

Throughout this study we have noted two types of interrelated conflict: conflict in the social environment in which Congress operates, and conflict within the party itself. The modernization process produces conflict in any social system; in a society consisting of a large number of often competing social groups, the expansion of education, the emergence of new occupations, and the establishment of new government development programs tend to intensify rather than reduce social conflict. But in most modern societies there are also accepted dispute-settling institutions and procedures. Social work agencies, churches and other religious organizations, interracial and interreligious groups, labor-management conciliation bodies, and employee councils, as well as individuals working in judicial and non-judicial capacities — lawyers, judges, and policemen, and social workers, psychiatrists, and party politicians — all are important in dispute settlement. Most transitional societies have few such individuals and institutions to resolve conflicts before they become political issues. Consequently, even disputes of a highly personal nature tend to enter the political arena. A dispute between two neighbors could, for example, create in a village two sharply defined factions which then ally themselves with factions in the local party organization.

Because in rural areas there are few institutions capable of resolving disputes, the Congress party has a very heavy arbitrational load. We have already noted that one source of strength for Congress is its capacity to

reconcile local disputes. Within Congress are men who devote their political energies to dealing with disputes in the countryside and in the cities. The procedures Congressmen use for settling community and party disputes are the same. The local mandal committee will frequently turn to leaders at the taluka or district level to help settle a local dispute. Similarly, the factions within the taluka or district organization may turn to the state organization to settle party disputes. The general secretaries of the national Congress party, the home minister, the president of the Congress party, or even the prime minister may be engaged in the settlement of disputes within the state party organization.

The national Congress party leadership has great respect for those in its ranks who can deal with conflicts in the state party organization, and in the state there is great respect for local party leaders who can deal with district party conflicts. Though one may find mediators holding many offices in the party at all levels, there are certain offices which are especially reserved for those who have these skills. In the national office in New Delhi the general secretaries and in the state and district offices the local secretaries devote much of their time to the management of intra-party conflict.

It would be far more difficult for Congress leaders to settle internal disputes were it not for the fact that the disputes themselves tend to be non-ideological. Most of the disputes within the party involve such questions as who will be allocated tickets for assembly and parliamentary seats in the general elections, who will be given posts in the state cabinet, or who will be elected president of the DCC, and the arbitrator often reconciles a dispute by a judicious allocation of party and governmental posts to the various party factions. It would be far more difficult for the Congress party to cope with ideological division within the party. Were a major ideological conflict to break out in the national party organization, one might see dissident factions within the state and district party ally themselves with a national ideological grouping. In such circumstances it would be exceedingly difficult for the national party leadership to find ways and means of reconciling disputes, not only at the national level, but at the state and local levels as well. The national leadership is therefore particularly eager to avoid any breakdown of unanimity at the national level, and especially to avoid letting any conflict at the national level become one with ideological and major policy overtones. To the foreigner it often appears as if India's leadership had an ideological approach to public policy matters. The insider, however, is struck by the extraordinary flexibility, or, if he is less favorably inclined, the vagueness,

of Congress' ideological position. But the socialist ideology to which the Congress party subscribes has helped Congress maintain a measure of party integration.

Still another factor helping the Congress party to cope with internal conflict is, paradoxically, the multiplicity of factional and parochial groupings in the party, for this multiplicity increases the possibility of coalitions. In India as elsewhere, if there are many groups but none had a clear majority, even the largest group must compromise to win power.

Another factor that discourages dissident groups from leaving the party is the party's control over patronage. One might assume that if the party were to lose successive elections at the district and state levels, it would lose much of its patronage power, with the result that larger defections from Congress would be more common. However, since the Congress party is as a rule in control of zilla parishads, schools boards, panchayat samitis, credit banks, and other local financial institutions, it can continue to provide rewards at the local level even if it has lost some of its assembly and parliamentary seats.

Important as all these factors are in preserving the integration of the Congress party, perhaps the single most important consideration is the existence of a leadership with a vested interest in keeping the party united. There is hardly a member of the Working Committee (which consists mainly of chief ministers and PCC presidents — the dominant elements in each state party organization) whose present power could continue if the Congress party were to disintegrate. The power of the provincial and national leadership does not rest upon caste, wealth, control over land, or even popular followings. The term "charisma" could hardly be applied to Atulya Ghosh, the president of the PCC of West Bengal, to Kamaraj, the Congress president, or even to Nehru's successor, Lal Bahadur Shastri. The source of their power is, clearly, their control over the Congress party organization.

Since their power rests upon the party, it is in their interest to maintain the party organization. The groups which control a state party organization are eager to maintain a unified central party organization, for they know that a divided party at the national level would encourage dissident factions within their own state organization, and most members of the Working Committee want unanimity in the selection of a party president or a prime minister.

If the country were unstable, if the army were to take power, or if a civilian dictatorship were to be established, the local leadership now in Congress could probably make its peace with the new authority. The domi-

nant peasant proprietors, who now control the district Congress party, have a remarkable capacity to adapt themselves to whatever local authority exists. In an earlier era they worked with British administration, and before that with the Moghul administration or whatever provincial administration existed in their area. But while local leadership might survive, the provincial and national leadership probably would not. They are quite aware of their sources of power, and dismiss with equal force proposals for military rule and dictatorship and proposals to abolish party organizations and establish non-party government. State politicians have engaged in bitter conflicts during the last fifteen years, but only rarely, especially since 1951, have any important dissident leaders left the party.

Seen from one viewpoint, Congress is not a single party but a coalition of party organizations. The state party organization can be viewed as a coalition of quasi-independent district organizations, and the national party, as a coalition of state party organizations. It can be asserted that India's national Congress party owes its strength to the viability of state and local party organizations, and that each unit depends upon subordinate units for support and upon the higher units to which it is affiliated for patronage and dispute settlement. The viability of the state and local organizations also depends upon the existence of a unified national leadership. There is, thus, a two-way process at work.

While the existence of a state and national leadership committed to a unified party organization is a crucial factor, the essential reason that the Congress party is cohesive — compared with parties in other developing areas rather than in the West — is not because there is little conflict within it but because there are legitimized and institutionalized roles and procedures for the handling of conflict. To generalize from the Indian case, one might say that the internal viability of a party organization is not a function of the amount, kind, or intensity of internal conflicts, but of whether or not there is a socially accepted mechanism for the resolution of conflict. This is not to imply of course that this mechanism always works in India's Congress party, for in fact there is considerable internal breakdown; but the important point is that such a mechanism does exist and that it does work more satisfactorily to resolve disputes than one commonly finds in other parties in developing areas.

Needless to say, Congress has not successfully coped with all internal conflicts. There have been many defections since independence, not only the well-known ones in Andhra, Madras, and West Bengal before 1952 which led to the creation of an opposition party, but also the countless defections of individuals and small factions throughout the country. More-

over, as non-exclusive as Congress has been, there are many instances in which a local party elite successfully resisted the efforts of other groups to enter the party and thereby lost considerable local support.

As we have noted in our analysis of Kaira district, the segmented character of the Indian social system has made it possible for Congress to lose overwhelmingly in a single district — through party defections or otherwise — without having its position in a neighboring district similarly affected. Discontented castes or factions are often geographically confined, and it is unusual for an opposition party to build a coalition of all the discontented social groups within a state. If politics were organized on a class basis and issues did cut across the entire state, it would be difficult for Congress to confine discontent to small areas. The persistence of the parochial and segmented features of Indian life quarantines discontent and has made it possible for Congress to deal with each problem on a piecemeal basis.

*The Relationship of Success Factors*

We began our analysis of the problems of party building by saying that a wide variety of factors was at work, no one of which alone could account for the success of Congress. It is the relationship among these various factors which shall now concern us.

The success of Congress depends very much on its adaptive qualities. We have seen that the local Congress party would rather adapt to than change the local power structure. We have pointed out that in rural areas the party has sought and won the support of those who own land, have wealth, control village panchayats, manage the local cooperatives, and can lead large numbers of persons. We have also noted that the Congress party adapted political roles of an earlier era — that the party can deal with local administration, cope with local conflicts, and perform social services, because in the past, long before there were political parties, there were individuals who, as individuals, performed these roles. We have noted that there is a long tradition in India of aspiring social groups attempting to work within whatever institutions are available to achieve their aims — in the nineteenth century, the law courts and the new administrative framework, and now in the twentieth, the Congress party and the parliamentary system. The expansion of governmental functions and regulations and the close liaison between the party and local administration have made it necessary for those who want things from an expanding government to

work through the party. We have noted too that the customary pattern of mediation and arbitration by third parties for the resolution of conflict is utilized within Congress, and is an important factor in the capacity of Congress to avoid the fragmentation that has destroyed political parties in other developing nations. Finally, we have suggested that the very fragmentation of the Indian social system permits Congress to make more errors than would be the case if India were a well-integrated social system, where single errors of magnitude could reverberate throughout the entire political system.

We have emphasized throughout this study that, in the context of universal franchise and expanding government, adaptation involves more than just coping with existing structures, for the party leadership must find a way to appeal to new political participants. Congress not only has to adapt itself to the existing local social milieu but also has to contend with the changes that the actions of national and state governments create in that milieu.

The primary concern of the state and local party leadership has been with the maintenance of the organization, rather than with the achievement of national goals, and this concern with organizational maintenance has shaped the attitudes of the leadership toward questions of internal organization, of governmental policy, and of the relationship between the party and the social system. It is doubtful that the party would have succeeded had the leadership acted in any other way.

# 23. ADAPTATION AND INNOVATION

What is functional from one point of view may be quite dysfunctional from another. What has contributed to the successful functioning of Congress may not contribute to the successful functioning of the Indian economy or the Indian polity. It can and has been argued that a party which adapts itself well to a rural, traditional society cannot readily change that society. In short, the question facing us is can an aggregative party such as Congress also propagate. Can a party which is adaptive also be innovative?

Some critics have argued that the more widespread political participation is in a developing society and the more responsible its government is to local demands, the more likely it is that that government will be the victim of parochialism and traditionalism. For, they argue, developing societies typically have only a small number of persons who are committed to modernization and who know what steps need to be taken to bring it about. Logically, any political order that diminishes the power of the modernist sector will be dysfunctional to modernization.

For the past twenty years critics have asserted that the Congress party has lost its elan and that the party is increasingly becoming a vehicle, not for the modernists and the idealists, but for the traditionalists and the self-seeking. While some supporters of Congress point to the eclectic character of the party's program and insist that no single ideology is appropriate for Indian conditions, others see this same eclecticism as an indication of inconsistency, uncertainty, and even hypocrisy. Supporters claim that the party, by bringing together party workers from all corners of the country who are committed to national integration and national develop-

ment, has helped unify India's diverse social groups. But critics argue that the party at the local level has opened the doors of administration and politics to the parochialism of caste, religion, and language, contributed to local administrative corruption through a system of patronage, and thereby eroded the country's national administrative services. Finally, many supporters feel that Congress has provided India with that increasingly rare commodity among new nations: national leadership with personal integrity and with a commitment to social welfare. But critics point to the large number of state and local party leaders who are motivated solely by a desire for material gain and status in office.

Many years ago a prominent opponent of Congress described the party as a dharamsala, a hostel intended for religious pilgrims but often filled with beggars, thieves, and others with non-religious motives. Here, it is said, is a party committed to the country's modernization, but whose activists do not include some of the country's most modern intellectuals and professionals. Here is a party which stands for national integration, but which uses ethnic arithmetic in allocating tickets for public office. Here is a party which stands for land reform, but whose local party members take actions that impede the implementation of land legislation. Here, in short, is a party whose national goals are eroded by the many private purposes and group interests which the party contains.

It is worth dissecting these accusations, not simply for the purpose of passing judgment on the Congress party, but, more fundamentally, for considering whether an adaptive party which seeks support from traditional as well as modern elements is an asset or a liability in a country whose government is committed to modernization. We might therefore appropriately look at the impact of the Congress party on government economic policy and performance and then at the impact of the party on political development.

## Congress and Government Economic Policy and Performance

In considering the impact of Congress on India's economic development, it is useful to distinguish between the role which the party plays in the formulation of economic policies in the state and national governments and the role which party workers play at the local level in accelerating or impeding economic change.

Since India's rate of economic growth during the past decade has been disappointingly low, especially in the agrarian sector, it seems appropriate upon first consideration to place some of the responsibility on Congress

as the country's governing party. The difficulty in making such an assessment is that it is difficult to determine which unsuccessful policies pursued by government are the result of pressures from within the party. If state governments are reluctant to tax the agrarian sector heavily, perhaps this is because the state leadership fears antagonizing the very elements upon which its support rests. But is this because of the composition of the Congress party, or is this an expression of the nearly universal tendency of state and local bodies to hesitate to tax voters? If agricultural development has moved more slowly than many hoped, is this because of any opposition to agricultural development policies within the party or because the national leadership has simply not found ways of solving a nearly intractable problem within their own intellectual and ideological framework? Moreover, many of the unsuccessful or inadequate measures pursued by government have strong support from almost all major political parties in India. There is, in fact, a near consensus among politicians on many of the policies most criticized by economists.

In the area of land reform policy, however, one can more easily point to the ways in which the Congress party has limited what the state governments can do. State governments have been able to pass legislation to break up the large landholdings, but have been less willing to break up smaller estates of several hundred acres. Moreover, the planning commission's hope, with Nehru's enthusiastic support, that land might be ultimately collectivized — voluntarily perhaps, but collectivized nonetheless — was quickly killed by state Congress party leaders. But, then, there is considerable disagreement among economists as to whether either of these policies — placing ceilings on landholdings, or introducing collectivization — would increase the rate of agricultural productivity. Most economists believe they would not.

While the planning commission and the Indian government have pursued a number of economic policies which have failed to accelerate economic growth, one would be hard put to blame these policies on the party itself. As in most democratic systems, the national government has a wide range of policy choices. There are few instances in which the national government chooses its economic policies because it fears reactions within the Congress party. When the national government adopts inappropriate economic measures, it does so, more often than not, because of the beliefs of the national leaders as to what ought to be done rather than because of constraints imposed upon it by the party.

Moreover, while most local Congressmen are, to say the least, unenthusiastic about radical land reform proposals, they are typically enthusi-

astic supporters of the Community Development Program. Congressmen willingly form cooperatives, welcome the establishment of a cottage and small-scale industries program, want more wells and irrigation channels, and welcome the construction of village schools, roads, and panchayat halls. None of these activities threatens their positions of power. On the contrary, their positions are strengthened when they participate in the work of the government.[1] Some critics have argued that the lower classes have not established sufficient power either within Congress or within local government bodies to avail themselves adequately of the goods and services provided by the Community Development ministries and other agencies of the government. This complaint is valid for India (as it is for most countries where the poor lack the knowledge and power to obtain what they want and need), but while there is a fundamental issue of social justice here, there is no reason to think — and, more importantly, no empirical evidence to suggest — that greater participation by the lower classes in politics and government would accelerate the rate of economic growth.[2]

Nonetheless, it has been argued that many Congressmen at the local level have little interest in modernization and that many who are concerned with development have only the vaguest notions of what development means, how it can best be achieved, and what role they personally can play. It is certainly true that in the main Congressmen are more concerned with servicing voters in order to win support than in attempting to change the outlook and behavior of voters. Congressmen are more likely to help villagers obtain government aid for building a well or road than to attempt to persuade villagers to use new agricultural techniques. It is

[1] It can in fact be argued that the continued ability of local party units to provide "patronage" is a critical factor in the continued viability of Congress. While the urban intellectuals and national planners are concerned with increasing the country's gross national product, mandal, ward, taluka, and district Congress politicians see development primarily in terms of roads, wells, schools, dispensaries, and rural electrification. It is these improvements upon which the party's patronage system is based. Indeed, Congress would weather a fairly lengthy period of economic stagnation (so long as it was not accompanied by drastic inflation) if the government's development program continued at a high enough level to maintain the present amount of patronage. We might note here that such governmental activities have both developmental and distributive aspects and that patronage activities need not negatively affect the country's over-all rate of growth. They might if there was a large scale diversion of funds from capital investment or if political considerations resulted in the location of public and private sector investments at excessive economic cost or operational disadvantage.

[2] This is an area — the relationship of local structures of power to the process of economic development — where a priori ideological convictions, rather than empirical studies, guide much of the analysis. The main point here is that we have no evidence that at the local level the Congress party is impeding economic development programs. The explanation for the low agricultural growth rate should be sought elsewhere.

easier for Congressmen to support accretive policies than those which explicitly aim at altering existing attitudes and behavior.

But here the criticism is not of what Congressmen do but of what they fail to do. One can present a strong case for saying that a different kind of Congress party, or another type of party altogether, could hasten India's development. Certainly, if the party were more centralized — if, for example, all candidates for state assemblies and parliament were financed by the national organization, so that tickets were not allocated simply because candidates had money — the party would be able to overcome some of the limitations built into a federal system. A more centralized party could give the central government the authority to provide greater guidance in the critical areas of education and agriculture, both now in the hands of state governments. Agricultural taxation could be increased, land reforms more expeditiously carried out, zonal restrictions on the movement of grains removed, and a more rational price policy in agriculture adopted for the country as a whole. A centralized party might be able to overcome the deficiencies of a decentralized governmental structure.

One can also present a strong case for proposing that the party make more effective use of its cadres in carrying out development activities. Party cadres could be trained to organize rural labor for social overhead projects: road construction, small canal construction, and the like. Party workers could also be trained to play a more active role in the introduction of new agricultural techniques and in the distribution of birth control and public health information. In short, modern ideas could be diffused into the countryside by trained party cadres, rather than exclusively through the bureaucracy.

Realistically, the possibility of a more centralized Congress party — assuming for the moment its desirability — is as remote as the possibility of creating more centralized parties in the United States, and for similar reasons. A federal democratic system inhibits the development of highly centralized parties. Moreover, merely to demonstrate that a change in the party would be good for the country — that is, that it might increase the effectiveness of the central government or improve the performance of the bureaucracy — is not sufficient argument for changing the structure of the party. One must also demonstrate that such proposals would not drastically jeopardize the party's position. Indeed, one can argue that any proposal which is directed at facilitating economic development but which weakens the party would in the long run be injurious to the country as a whole. If, for example, the centralization of the party for the purpose of increasing central government authority resulted in a growing defection

of support from the party at the state level and the emergence of either unstable state governments or state governments hostile to national policy, the results would not in fact be the centralization of national authority but just the reverse.

There are no such objections to proposals aimed at increasing the skills of party cadres and encouraging them to play a greater role in development activities. Most of the party workers are landowners and cultivators and therefore naturally in a better position to demonstrate new agricultural methods than the officers of the Community Development Program. If the concept of a demonstration effect has any validity, it would make sense to teach improved methods to those who, by virtue of both their influence on the community and their commitment to development, can provide such a demonstration effect to other villagers. The present party training camps do not provide information and training in new agricultural methods, and it may very well be that many party workers would respond favorably to training camps where they could learn improved agricultural practices. They are likely to apply new methods if it is clear to them that these are profitable, and their local political position is likely to improve if they assist other farmers in making farming more profitable. The very principle which has worked to make Congress an effective political instrument — the harnessing of personal motives for the service of the party — can also be applied in developing an economic role for the Congress organization.

There can be no doubt that substantial portions of the intelligentsia, of the urban middle classes, and of the bureaucracy are critical of Congress. And it is also true that some of what many persons would describe as the less modern elements of Indian society — the middle peasantry, bazaar merchants, small businessmen, and many self-conscious caste associations and religious minorities — are active supporters of Congress. If one accepts at face value the proposition that it takes modern men to make a modern society and that traditional men necessarily impede modernization, then one ought to view with some alarm the changing composition of the Congress party. But the difficulty in applying this proposition is in defining modern and traditional men. All too often we simply assume that those who wear Western dress, have been educated abroad, speak English, and have secular ideas are modern, while those who are religious, uneducated, and attached to their communities are traditional. What we need to ask is what kind of behavior is more likely to facilitate modernization. Whose behavior is more modern — the high-ranking government

bureaucrat hostile to applying profit considerations even to public sector plants, or the private entrepreneur who may have little concern for the broader public interest and who may be attached to his religion, kinsmen, and caste but whose quest for profit results in the expansion of industry, the rise of production, and the growth of an industrial labor force? Whose behavior is more modern — the junior bureaucrat whose concern for conforming to complicated bureaucratic regulations leads him to place obstacles before cultivators eager to obtain improved seeds, fertilizers, insecticides, cement, and water, or the Congress politician who uses his personal influence to ensure that the villagers in his constituency or the peasants in his political faction are assured the necessary agricultural inputs?

In short, though the Congress party has lost much of the intellectual support it had before independence, and is today very much the party of peasant proprietors in the countryside and of businessmen in the towns and cities, there is nothing inherent in the composition of the party which makes it likely that the party and the government it elects will act in non-modern ways.

The danger to government performance lies less in the composition of the party than in the prospect of intense factional rivalries within the party disrupting the functioning of government. A few of the state Congress governments have sought to maintain party unity in part by allocating ministerial posts to representatives of all important factions within the party. The result is that state cabinets are politically well balanced but incapable of working together. One can point to several states where factional rivalries within the party have prevented coordination among community development, irrigation, and agricultural ministries and to situations where chief ministers have been fearful of taking actions which might destroy a precarious political balance.

Under Nehru's leadership the central government suffered less from factional strife than did the state governments. Even so, during the last few years of Nehru's life the struggle for succession often made members of his cabinet more concerned with their own positions than with the over-all performance of government. Coordination among ministries after the 1962 Chinese invasion was reportedly low, and there has been much criticism of the lack of effective ministerial coordination on India's critical agricultural situation in the mid-sixties. If factional struggles within the Congress party multiply and have a greater effect upon the performance of state or national government, the result would be governmental paralysis.

*Congress and Political Development*

An account of the positive functions which Congress has performed for the Indian political system would sound glowingly naïve to anyone deeply familiar with Indian politics. One could, for example, point to the role Congress has played in bringing together divergent interests and ethnic groups; to its role as a two-way communications system between citizens on the one hand and administration and policy makers on the other; to its role in converting into a political reality the legal procedures whereby prime ministers and chief ministers are selected; to its role in helping to develop a sense of national identity in its cadres and supporters; to its role as a vehicle through which individuals and groups may seek in an orderly way to influence the formulation and conduct of public policy, and to its therefore related role of minimizing internal disorder and in effect undercutting prospective insurgency movements; and, finally, to its role in facilitating popular participation in government-sponsored development activities.

Only the most naïve enthusiasts for Congress would unqualifiedly endorse such a list; yet it does contain a considerable measure of truth. One need only speculate as to what India might have been like had Congress fragmented in 1951 and had been defeated in the 1952 elections by a collection of parties unable to form stable governments in the center or in the states. Would India's parliamentary system have survived, order and stability been maintained, or economic development activities been pursued? Has it been only the coercive power of the Indian government which has discouraged the Communists and other dissidents from launching an insurrectionary movement, or do the Communists implicitly recognize that they could win little sustained support in vast areas of the country where Congress has successfully provided an institutional focus for those who have grievances?

Critics have argued that, by adapting itself to local patterns of social organization, Congress has retarded India's national integration. The very willingness of Congress to accommodate castes, religious groups, and factions, to work with the existing local elite structure and to adapt itself to changes within that structure, and to utilize the traditional relationship of local elites to administration has led many Indian intellectuals and many persons outside India to fear that Congress increasingly represents the traditional rather than the modernizing features of Indian life and that it strengthens parochial rather than national tendencies. Many educated Indians argue that by compromising with "casteism, communalism,

and provincialism" Congress has become the vehicle for patronage, corruption, and parochialism.

One may be aware of these limitations without concluding that Congress is in fact preserving the traditional order. To the contrary, the national Congress leadership has attacked the social order — casteism, factionalism, the rural oligarchical power structures, and many of the attitudes and values of traditional India. The zamindars and princes have lost their power. Land reform legislation has eliminated the large estates. Universal adult suffrage and panchayati raj legislation, both the consequences of Congress policies, have served to open the local power structures, so that social groups which had previously not been active in district and state political life have begun to be so. The Indian leadership has clearly chosen to interact with Indian tradition — to accommodate themselves to some features of that tradition while trying to change others.

Moreover, it is necessary to consider the extent to which membership in the Congress party itself transforms individuals. We know that Congressmen are more likely than most Indians to be national-minded, concerned with development, secular in outlook, activist, and perhaps equalitarian. Is this because individuals who hold these values join Congress, or because Congress inculcates such values into its members? The answer is obviously both. Congressmen are more exposed to both modern and national values than are most other Indians. Local Congress organizations sponsor ceremonies to commemorate national holidays. They transmit information from government to party activists on development activities. And the party does encourage tolerance for religious minorities. This is not to suggest that all Congressmen are modernists and nationalists, or that some opposition parties do not inculcate such values equally well, if not even better in some respects. The point is that Congress does attract and nurture modern and national values.

While this aspect of Congress' influence has been highly significant, Congress has probably had its greatest impact on Indian political development in its response to increased political participation. During the past fifty or so years political participation in India has gradually increased as literacy has spread, mass media expanded, urban centers multiplied, and individuals become part of larger market economies. New social classes — factory workers, journalists, lawyers, white-collar workers, industrial entrepreneurs — have emerged; existing social classes — the tribes, castes, linguistic communities, and religious groups — have also sought a more active role in public life. Political participation has been spurred by the establishment of new institutions at the local level which affect the com-

munity in various ways. Schools and colleges change the social status of communities; credit and banking institutions, marketing cooperatives, and cooperatives providing seeds, fertilizers, and storage facilities affect the economic positions of social groups; and new local government institutions, such as district local boards, taluka development boards, and, more recently, zilla parishads and panchayat samitis, determine how public funds may be spent and on whose behalf.

Because, as individuals sought participation in public life, the local Congress party units opened its doors to individuals with a wide variety of motives and objectives, those who entered politics had an accepted institutional outlet for their ambitions and interests. Of course not all new participants in political life joined Congress, but a great many did. Congress, as a vehicle through which individuals and groups of individuals have come to work, has made the political process and institutions of democratic India acceptable to the new political participants. It is often said that a viable political system must be based upon an appropriate mixture of control and consent — that is, upon the objective and subjective elements of authority. While the Indian army, the Indian Administrative Service, and the entire bureaucratic system have provided India with an institutional framework for authority, the Congress party has been the single most important institution in India for establishing consent — not simply consent for specific policies of government but, more importantly, consent for the parliamentary system and the political processes by which India is governed. Support for the institutional framework may not be as enduring or as widespread as it is in many developed countries, but it is surely greater than is commonly found in most developing areas.[3]

*Conclusion*

In assessing the future of Congress it would be foolhardly simply to project present trends, since there are an enormous number of unforeseeable events which could influence such a large, complex, and important organization. Some old problems will continue to affect the party's workings. Conflicts between the ministerial and organizational wings of the party will go on as dissident groups seek first to win control over the organizational machinery and then to replace the government. At the district level

[3] For a thoughtful analysis of the role played by Congress in establishing a basic consensus within Indian society, especially with regard to the legitimacy of the parliamentary system, see Rajni Kothari, "The Congress 'System' in India," *Asian Survey* (Dec., 1964):1161–73.

and below, tensions between party personnel and the local bureaucracy are likely to be prolonged, as the one seeks to extend its influence and the other to maintain its independence. Within the party itself the urban organizations will continue to face conflict between the trade unions and the business community and between the bazaar merchants and businessmen on the one hand and the intelligentsia and white-collar workers on the other. In the countryside aspiring social groups seeking their share of power will continually challenge party elites.

Many new factors could appear and affect the future of the Congress party: the spread of Chinese power over the entire northern border of India, the establishment of a Communist-led insurrectionist movement, victory or defeat in a new war with Pakistan, personal fallings out among the small group of party leaders who took control of the country upon Nehru's death, a split between Prime Minister Gandhi and prominent Congress party leaders, massive inflation and a sharp deterioration in the country's economy, or a coalition of the country's opposition parties. Any one of these could have important consequences for the Congress party. And what of events beyond our imagination?[4]

But of one thing we can be certain: ultimately, the Congress party will be defeated. In a free society no party can hope to remain in power indefinitely. But while defeat is ultimately inevitable, disintegration is not. The challenge for the Congress leadership will be not simply whether it can continue to win elections indefinitely but whether it can sustain the loyalty of its members even when the party is out of power.

This challenge has become imminent with the elections of February, 1967. The margin of Congress seats in Parliament was then considerably reduced, and the party failed to win a majority of seats in eight legislative assemblies. After the elections, non-Congress governments were formed in Bihar, Kerala, Madras, Orissa, the Punjab, Uttar Pradesh, West Bengal, and the newly formed state of Haryana — states in which two-thirds of the Indian population lives. And in Rajasthan, Congress was able to establish a government only with the support of independents. Only in Andhra,

---

[4] To the obvious risk of being wrong in making predictions, I should also add as a hazard to the predictor that his reader will mistakenly assume that his predictions are an expression of his hopes. Bertrand de Jouvenal in his *The Art of Conjecture* (New York: Basic Books, 1967) reminds us that "men ardently desiring a particular form refuse to consider its vulnerability. And not only that: the champions and advocates of a form treat whomsoever denounces its frailty as an enemy; they refuse to allow that he may have a liking for the form while having some doubts about its vitality. If he has displayed any signs of affection for the form, his estimate of its poor chances of success is treated as betrayal. This is a very big obstacle to the progress of the political sciences in general, and of forecasting in particular." (Pp. 291–92).

Assam, Gujarat, Kashmir, Madhya Pradesh, Maharashtra, and Mysore was Congress easily able to form a majority government after the elections.

Without a careful detailed analysis of the election returns, it is difficult to say who defected from Congress or whether new voters gave more votes to the opposition than before, but several conclusions do seem self-evident. First, there was a general decline in the Congress vote from three to eight percent in almost all the states (with an over-all decline of the national vote for Congress of about 5 per cent), suggesting that there were probably some general factors affecting voters throughout the country. The deteriorating economic situation, particularly the serious food shortages, the growing unemployment in the industrial sector, the steep rise in prices, and the slow-up of the government's development programs — all before the elections — may have been important. Second, the alliances of non-Congress parties proved to be more effective than before. In many places the opposition parties united behind a single candidate. The result was that a small decline in vote for Congress in certain areas (and in one instance, no decline at all) resulted in massive Congress defeats. In Madras, for example, the Congress vote declined from 46.1 per cent to 41.8 per cent, and was thus still ahead of the 40.8 per cent won by the DMK, but the DMK won 138 seats, and Congress only 49. Even more dramatically, the Congress vote increased in Kerala from 34.1 per cent in 1960 and 32.5 per cent in 1965 to a high of 35.4 per cent in 1967, but the party dropped from its majority position of 1960 and its plurality of 1965 to only 6.8 per cent of the seats in 1967.

But what of the future? Will Congress lose control over the central government, and if so who will govern? Will India move in the direction of the French Third and Fourth Republics with a succession of shortlived unstable coalitions? And with what long-term consequences? Immobilist central authority? Civil strife between contending parties? A scramble by left- and right-wing opposition parties for support within Congress as each seeks a majority by pulling out sympathizers from a disintegrating Congress party? A non-party government under the authority of the president of India? A military dictatorship? One can think of many such disquieting possibilities, none of which may occur, but each of which highlights the extraordinary stabilizing role which Congress has played in Indian politics for two decades.

The most immediate challenge to Congress is in the central government and in the states which it still controls. In the past, dissident Congressmen were reluctant to defect, knowing that their chances of returning to power outside of Congress were slim. But now that the margin between

Congress and the opposition parties is small, dissidents within Congress know that by defeating and joining a coalition of opposition parties they may gain cabinet positions. They know that, after the last elections, in the states of Uttar Pradesh, Haryana, and West Bengal non-Congress parties were able to form governments with the aid of Congress defectors.

In the states already lost by Congress the party is faced with the feeling of many Congressmen, especially those motivated more by careerist considerations than by party loyalty, that since the party is declining they ought to leave. Moreover, new aspirants to power may no longer find Congress so attractive and may prefer to join rising political parties. And if the Congress opposition, in an effort to boost its morale and win popular support, launches an agitation against a non-Congress government, returning as it were some of the attacks previously made upon them, they may find that they do not necessarily receive support from a central government that is eager to maintain good relations with non-Congress governments in the interests of center-state harmony.

Eventually, at the center itself, Congress will fail to maintain a majority, and either the opposition parties will form a government, or possibly Congress or defecting elements of the party will join a national coalition government. At present it is hard to see any single national party replacing Congress in the central government and hard, too, to see how, barring some massive electoral shifts, a working coalition of either the left- or right-wing parties could be built without some Congress support. Both the left- and right-wing parties, in need of support from Congressmen to form a national government, will press for the disintegration of Congress as a middle-of-the-road party which tries to straddle all ideologies. It will be difficult for many Congressmen to resist the seductions of the right and the left, not so much because of the ideological affinities, but because coalitions appear to be the route to power. Congressmen, from 1947 to 1967, demonstrated a remarkable ability to keep relatively united in winning elections and running governments. Whether in the future, when Congress is no longer in power, they can keep the party together in an effort to regain office, especially if members of parliament are offered posts in a non-Congress government, remains to be seen.

How can Congress sustain the support of its members in the areas in which it is now out of power? One asset still held by Congress, even in those states in which it has been defeated, is that below the state level, in the panchayats, samitis, cooperatives, banks, and local administrations, Congressmen still retain considerable power. Moreover, many of the non-Congress state governments are coalitions with parties whose interests

and ideologies diverge considerably. It is likely, therefore, that several of the coalition governments will themselves begin to disintegrate. If they do, Congress may again have an opportunity to return to power either alone or in coalition.

While the central leadership of the Congress party is concerned with national goals, the state and district leadership tries to be responsive to local demands. If the state and district leadership were successful all the time, national goals would be neglected. Conversely, if the national leadership were successful all the time, the state and local units would lose their popular support; and ultimately the stability of the central government would be endangered. As a result, for the past twenty years there has been considerable tension within the Congress party between the local and state party units on the one hand and the national — and sometimes the state — government on the other. These tensions have intensified as both the state and national governments have pursued policies that affect education, land tenure, agricultural prices, local government, and the role of governmental administration in rural development; all of these have had an impact on the positions of regional social groups, their relationship to one another, and their attitudes toward government and administration.

How to satisfy the demands and concerns of the local party leadership and its supporters while simultaneously pursuing a program aimed at modernizing the Indian society and economy will continue to remain a challenge for India's national leadership. Ironically, the more successful government is in accelerating economic growth and social change, the more tension it creates within the Indian social and political system. For the political system as a whole, therefore, one of the most important contributions of the Congress party has been its ability to cushion some of the changes innovated or accelerated by the actions of its own government.

Underlying this study has been the assumption that political organization is essential for political development and, more broadly, that organization for common purposes is essential to any kind of modernization. It is difficult to see how modern societies, with their complex organizations running industries, universities, and governments, can be created without concerted effort. We have suggested that, in building a party organization, as in building other modern institutions, it is essential to establish a balanced relationship between the interests and ambitions of individuals and the goals of the institutions to which they belong. William Lockwood stated the issue well when he noted that "The problem [in development] is not to regenerate human nature. . . . It is to surround [people] with

inducements that make it personally advantageous for them to function in ways that build a modern social order — whether they are business tycoons, peasants, party politicians, or army officers." [5]

The Congress party has in effect applied this principle by permitting cadres to further their own ambitions and interests within the party in such a way that what they do at the same time facilitates the electoral triumph of Congress and furthers the Congress government's development programs. The balance of private and party interests is obviously a precarious one, and clearly there have been times when personal interests have become paramount over the interests of the party — and of the country. There will be many judgments as to how well, on balance, the Congress party has performed in governing India, but future evaluations must all be determined by how well or how badly its successors perform.

[5] William Lockwood, "Adam Smith and Asia," *Journal of Asian Studies* XXIII (May, 1964): 353.

# GLOSSARY

India can be a linguistic nightmare to a scholar who is not a linguist. The great linguistic mosaic of the country, the English overlay, the variations between classical and contemporary usages and between written and spoken forms, and the absence of universally followed systems of transliteration are all constant sources of confusion in one's effort simply to understand what a given term means or how it should be transliterated into English. I have tried, perhaps at the expense of consistency, to use those forms which I think will be most familiar to my readers; and in the text (but not in the glossary) I have dispensed with diacritical marks.

There are a number of typical confusions of which the reader should be forewarned. First, different terms are often used in different regions of India to denote the same or similar administrative units and offices. Thus, taluka (sometimes taluk) and tahsil (sometimes tehsil) refer to the same administrative subdivisions of a district, and karnam, kulkarnī, talātī all refer to village accountants in different regions who keep land records. There are also a large number of different terms for landlords with similar but by no means identical meanings. For the purposes of this study, however, I have translated such terms as zamīndār, jādīrdār, watandār, ṭhākur, and ināmdār simply as landlord, although each term is associated with a particular form of land tenure.

Apart from the confusion of having different terms referring to the same thing, there are often situations in which a single term has a different meaning in different regions of India and even within the same state and the same village. Thus, the term panchāyat is generally used to refer to a village council, but it may also refer to a caste council. A related source of

confusion is that titles have often become family names and no longer designate an occupation or rank. Thus, a man may be called thākur without being an estate holder, kulkarnī without being a village accountant, and pātīl without being a village headman.

The word caste (from the Portuguese casta, meaning race) is another source of confusion. Caste is sometimes used to describe jāti (an endogamous social group) and sometimes to describe varṇa (social divisions defined in the classical Vedic texts, each varṇa containing many jātis). Throughout this study I have used caste to mean jāti unless I have indicated otherwise. It should also be noted that although I have described a caste as a peasant caste or a caste of shopkeepers, it would be quite misleading to assume that all members of the caste engaged in the same occupation.

| | |
|---|---|
| All India Trade Union Congress | Communist-led trade union federation |
| ambar charkhā | Improved hand machine for spinning cotton |
| Andhra Mahasabha | An organization originally formed in the Telugu-speaking districts of Madras to press for the creation of a separate Telugu-speaking state |
| anna | A small coin, 1/16 of a rupee, approximately equal to one American cent |
| Baniā (Baniyā) | Merchant caste often engaged in moneylending; sometimes used loosely to refer to any money-lender |
| Bāriya | Peasant caste in Gujarat, often called Kolī |
| Berad (Bedar) | Tribe in southern Maharashtra |
| bhadralok | Bengali for gentlemen — that is, those who belong to the educated classes |
| bhajans | Devotional songs |
| Bharat Sevak Sangh | A national social service organization |
| Bhīl | Tribe inhabiting central and western India |
| bidi (biri) | Local hand-rolled cigarettes |
| Block Development officer | Government official in charge of a community development block which carries on rural development activities; in most states these activities (and the BDO) have been transferred to panchāyat samitis |
| Brāhmin | First of the four classical divisions (varṇa) mentioned in the Vedas; by tradition that social class which served as priests |

| | |
|---|---|
| bustee (bastī) | Slum settlement in Calcutta |
| Charutar Vidyamandal | Social service organization in Kaira district which runs a college and a number of small-scale industries |
| chelā | Disciple, pupil, the follower of a religious leader |
| Cheṭṭiār | Caste of shopkeepers, cloth merchants, and moneylenders in Madras |
| Devanāgarī | Script used for the writing of Sanskrit and most of the Indo-Aryan languages of northern India, including Hindi |
| Dharala | Another term for the Kolī community in Gujarat |
| dhobī | Washerman |
| dhotī | Long loincloth commonly worn by male Hindus |
| Dravida Munnetra Kazhagam | Anti-Brāhmin, anti-northern party in Madras; the largest opposition party in the state |
| gauḍa | Village headman in Mysore, corresponding to the pātīl of Maharashtra; typically a prosperous landowner |
| Gītā | From Bhagavad-Gītā, a popular religious text with Krishna, an incarnation of Vishnu, as hero |
| goonḍā (gunḍā) | Professional hoodlum; a "tough" |
| gopuram | Entrance tower on a South Indian Hindu temple |
| Gowḍa (Gauḍa) | Caste of cultivators and cattlebreeders in Mysore |
| grām sevak | Village level worker; a junior officer working at the village level in the community development program |
| guru | Spiritual teacher or guide; now more generally a leader, an elder, or a parent |
| Harijan | Literally "People of God," a term used by Gandhi for former untouchables or scheduled castes |
| high command | Popular term for the Working Committee, the executive body of the Congress party |
| Hind Mazdoor Sabha | Socialist-led trade union federation |
| Hindu Mahasabha | Right-wing Hindu party, the oldest of the major Hindu political parties |
| ināmdār | Type of landlord; the holder of a rent-free grant of land (inām) |

| | |
|---|---|
| Indian Administrative Service | Nationally recruited senior-most civil service corps, formed after independence to replace the Indian Civil Service |
| Indian Civil Service | Senior-most national civil service, replaced after independence by the Indian Administrative Service |
| Indian National Democratic Congress | Opposition party of former Congressmen in Madras which subsequently merged with the Swatantra party |
| Indian National Trade Union Congress | Congress-led trade union federation |
| jāgīrdār | Type of landlord; technically, the holder of an assignment of revenue |
| Jains | Religious community related to but distinct from Hinduism; followers are frequently merchants and moneylenders |
| Jan Sangh | Conservative pro-Hindu, ultra-nationalist party |
| jāti (jāt) | Endogamous social group; generally translated as caste or subcaste |
| jetka | Horse-drawn carriage |
| jowār (jawār, jowār) | Millet, sorghum |
| Justice party | Pre-independence anti-Brāhmin political party active in Madras, Mysore, and Bombay |
| Kallar (singular: Kallan) | Another term for the Thevar castes in Madras ("thieves" in Tamil) |
| Kamma | One of the two major peasant proprietor castes in Andhra, the other being the Reddi caste |
| Kannāḍā (Kannārā or Canarese) | Language spoken in Mysore state |
| Kāpu | In Andhra, another term for the Reddi caste |
| karnam | Village officer in Andhra who maintains land records |
| Karnātak (Karnātaka) | Region governed by Mysore; another term for Mysore state |
| khādī | Handloomed cloth made of hand-spun cotton yarn; formerly a nationalist symbol of the boycott of foreign goods |
| Kisan Mazdoor Praja party | Party formed by ex-Congressmen in 1950 which subsequently merged with the Praja Socialist party |

Kolī

Peasant caste (formerly a tribe) in Gujarat; now commonly called Bāriya

Konkani

Language spoken in Goa

Krishak Lok party

Literally, Peasants Peoples party, formed by ex-Congressmen in the Telugu-speaking districts of Madras and led by N. G. Ranga

Kshatriya (Kśatriya)

Second of the four classical divisions (varṇa) mentioned in the Vedas; by tradition, the warrior class

Kshatriya Sabha

Organization in Gujarat of castes claiming to belong to the Kshatriya varṇa

kulkarnī

Village officer in Mysore responsible for keeping land records; often a substantial owner of land

Kuruba

Shepherd caste in Mysore; also weavers of coarse woolens

lāthī

Stick, club

Lingāyat

Religious sect in Mysore state, often described as a caste

Mādiga

Formerly untouchable caste in Andhra; typically leather workers but now also agricultural laborers

magamai

Contribution or tithe (in Tamil) levied on merchants and cultivators for a temple, now optionally given

Mahagujarat Parishad

Before 1961 an opposition party in the Gujarati-speaking areas of Bombay which campaigned for the creation of a separate Gujarat state

mahārāja

Nobility, rulers of the princely states of India before independence

Maharashtra Ekikaran Samiti

Political party in Belgaum district advocating the transfer of the Marāthī-speaking areas of the district to Maharashtra

Mahīlā Congress

Women's division of the Congress party

Māla

Former untouchable caste in Andhra

māmlatdār

Chief officer of a taluka in Mysore

mamool (mamūl)

Payment to a government officer for services rendered; a traditional payment now seen as a form of corruption

mandal

Smallest unit of the Congress party, usually

| | |
|---|---|
| | covering an area with a population of approximately twenty thousand |
| Marāthā | Peasant caste in Maharashtra |
| Marāthī | Language spoken in Maharashtra; also one who speaks Marāthī |
| Mārwārī | Community originally from Mārwār, a desert tract of Rajasthan, now engaged in business activities throughout India |
| Mudaliar | Weaving caste in Madras |
| munsif | Village judicial officer; sometimes the headman of the village acting as a judicial officer |
| Nadar | Shopkeeper caste in Madras |
| Padmashali | Weaving caste in Andhra |
| panchāyat | Village council, the head of which is called a sarpanch |
| panchāyat samiti | Unit of rural local government made up of the heads of village panchāyats and responsible for governing an area with a population of five thousand to one hundred thousand |
| panchāyatī rāj | New system of local rural self-government, the units being the panchāyat or village council, the panchāyat samiti or taluka council (although there may be two samitis in some talukas), and the zilla parishad or district council |
| Pāṭidār | Agricultural caste in Gujarat; also called Patel |
| pātīl | Village headman in Maharashtra; sometimes used more loosely as a title of respect |
| Patnūlkāran | Another name for the Saurāshtra community of Madurai; literally, "silk-thread people" |
| permit rāj | Literally, rule by permit; an epithet used by critics of governmental regulation |
| Pillai | Peasant caste in Madras; also called Vellāla |
| poligar | Formerly a local ruler and estate holder in parts of south India responsible for collecting land revenue and supporting a band of retainers for military duty |
| raiyatwārī | Land system in which the peasant (raiyat) pays revenue directly to the state rather than to an intermediary landlord |

| | |
|---|---|
| Rājput | Caste in northern and western India, martial by tradition, now typically landowners |
| Rāju (Rāzu) | Peasant caste in Andhra |
| Ram Rajya Parishad | Right-wing Hindu party, the most orthodox of the major Hindu political parties |
| Rashtriya Swayam Sevak Sangh | Militant Hindu youth organization loosely associated with Jan Sangh |
| Reddi | One of the two major peasant proprietor castes in Andhra, the other being the Kamma |
| Sanikop | Caste within the Lingāyat community in Mysore |
| satī | A widow who immolates herself on the funeral pyre of her husband |
| satyāgraha | Civil disobedience movement |
| Saurāshtra | Region of Gujarat formerly made up of a number of princely states |
| scheduled castes and tribes | Former untouchables and particularly backward tribes, so called because they are listed on a government schedule which entitles them to certain social benefits. |
| Seva Dal | Social service youth corps of the Congress party |
| Sourāshtras | A community in Madurai originally from Saurāshtra |
| Śūdra | Lowest of the four classical divisions (varṇa) mentioned in the Vedas |
| Swatantra party | National conservative party; literally, the Freedom party |
| taccavi (takāvī) | Loans advanced by the government to the cultivator |
| tahsil (tehsil) | Administrative subdivision of a district, containing around 100,000 people; also taluka or taluk |
| tahsildār | Administrative officer in charge of a tahsil or taluka |
| talātī (talāthī) | Village officer in Gujarat who maintains land records |
| taluka (taluk) | Administrative subdivision of a district, typically containing about 100,000 people; also tahsil or tehsil |
| talukdar | Type of landlord; an estate holder |
| Tamil | Language spoken in Madras; also one who speaks Tamil |

| | |
|---|---|
| Tamil Nad Congress Committee | Pradesh Congress Committee for Madras state |
| Telaga | Agricultural caste in Andhra |
| Telengana | Telugu-speaking districts of old Hyderabad state subsequently transferred to Andhra. |
| Telugu | The language spoken in Andhra; also one who speaks Telugu. |
| ṭhākur | Type of landlord, a holder of a large estate; now used more loosely as a term of respect applied to persons of rank and authority |
| Thevar | Group of low castes, formerly a tribe, in Madras state. |
| Vaiśya | Third of the four classical castes (varṇa) mentioned in the Vedas; by tradition the social class engaged in mercantile activities |
| varṇa | Four classical social divisions referred to in the Vedas: Brāhmins, Kshatriyas, Vaiśyas, and Śūdras |
| Vedas | Sacred Hindu texts, dating from 1500 B.C. to 500 B.C. |
| watandār | Type of landowner; more precisely the holder of an hereditary right, property, or office; the holder of a patrimony (watan) |
| Yogī | One who practices ascetic devotion; a religious mendicant |
| zamīndār | Type of landlord |
| zilla parishad (zilā or jilā parishad) | District councils |

# INDEX